AF352564

Linguistic Derivations and Filtering

Advances in Optimality Theory

Editors: Armin Mester, *University of California, Santa Cruz,* and
Vieri Samek-Lodovici, *University College London*

Optimality Theory is an exciting new approach to linguistic analysis that originated in phonology but was soon taken up in syntax, morphology, and other fields of linguistics. Optimality Theory presents a clear vision of the universal properties underlying the vast surface typological variety in the world's languages. Cross-linguistic differences once relegated to idiosyncratic language-specific rules can now be understood as the result of different priority rankings among universal, but violable constraints on grammar.

Advances in Optimality Theory is designed to stimulate and promote research in this provocative new framework. It provides a central outlet for the best new work by both established and younger scholars in this rapidly moving field. The series includes studies with a broad typological focus, studies dedicated to the detailed analysis of individual languages, and studies on the nature of Optimality Theory itself. The series publishes theoretical work in the form of monographs and coherent edited collections as well as pedagogical texts and reference texts that promote the dissemination of Optimality Theory.

Published

Optimality Theory, Phonological Acquisition and Disorders
Edited by Daniel A. Dinnsen and Judith A. Gierut

Modeling Ungrammaticality in Optimality Theory
Edited by Curt Rice

Phonological Argumentation: Essays in Evidence and Motivation
Edited by Steve Parker

Hidden Generalizations: Phonological Opacity in Optimality Theory
John J. McCarthy

Conflicts in Interpretation
Petra Hendriks, Helen de Hoop, Irene Krämer, Henriëtte de Swart and Joost Zwarts

Prosody Matters: Essays in Honor of Elisabeth Selkirk
Edited by Toni Borowsky, Shigeto Kawahara, Takahito Shinya and Mariko Sugahara

The Phonology of Contrast
Anna Łubowicz

Forthcoming

Understanding Allomorphy: Perspectives from Optimality Theory
Edited by Bernard Tranel

Blocking and Complementarity in Phonological Theory
Eric Baković

Faithfulness in Phonological Theory
Marc van Oostendorp

Linguistic Derivations and Filtering

Minimalism and Optimality Theory

Edited by Hans Broekhuis and Ralf Vogel

Published by Equinox Publishing Ltd.

UK: Unit S3, Kelham House, 3 Lancaster Street, Sheffield S3 8AF
USA: ISD, 70 Enterprise Drive, Bristol, CT 06010

www.equinoxpub.com

First published 2013

ISBN   978-1-84553-964-1   (hardback)
ISBN   978-1-84553-965-8   (paperback)

British Library Cataloguing-in-Publication Data

A catalogue record for this book is available from the British Library.

Library of Congress Cataloging-in-Publication Data

Linguistic derivations and filtering : minimalism and optimality theory / edited by Hans
Broekhuis and Ralf Vogel.
       p. cm. -- (Advances in Optimality Theory)
    Includes bibliographical references and index.
    ISBN 978-1-84553-964-1 -- ISBN 978-1-84553-965-8 (pbk.)
  1. Optimality theory (Linguistics) 2. Minimalist theory (Linguistics) 3. Generative
grammar. I. Broekhuis, Hans. II. Vogel, Ralf, 1965-
    P158.42.L56 2012
    410.1'8--dc23
                                    2011023143

Printed and bound in Great Britain by Lightning Source UK Ltd, Milton Keynes

Contents

III   OPTIMAL DESIGN, ECONOMY AND LAST RESORT IN OT

IV   THE ROLE OF THE INTERPRETATIVE COMPONENTS

Contributors

Hans Broekhuis, Meertens Institute, P.O.-box 94264, 1090 GG Amsterdam, The Netherlands. E-mail: hans.broekhuis@meertens.knaw.nl

Gema Chocano, Departamento de Filología Inglesa, Facultad de Filosofía y Letras, Universidad Autónoma de Madrid, Tomás y Valiente, 1, 28049 Madrid. Spain. E-mail: gema.chocano@uam.es

Eva Engels, University of Aarhus, Department of Aesthetics and Communication, Section for English, Jens Chr. Skous Vej 4, DK–8000 Århus C, Denmark. E-mail: eva.engels@hum.au.dk

Jane Grimshaw, Department of Linguistics, Rutgers University, 18 Seminary Place, New Brunswick NJ 08901 USA. E.mail: grimshaw@ruccs.rutgers.edu

Kleanthes K. Grohmann, University of Cyprus, Department of English Studies, 75 Kallipoleos, P.O. Box 20537. 1678 Nicosia, Cyprus. E-mail: kleanthi@ucy.ac.cy

Fabian Heck, Institut für Linguistik, Universität Leipzig, Beethovenstr. 15, D-04107 Leipzig, Germany. E-mail: heck@uni-leipzig.de

Gereon Müller, Institut für Linguistik, Universität Leipzig, Beethovenstr. 15, D-04107 Leipzig, Germany. E-mail: gereon.mueller@uni-leipzig.de

John J. McCarthy, Department of Linguistics, South College, University of Massachusetts, Amherst, MA 01003 USA. E-mail: jmccarthy@linguist.umass.edu

Kathryn Pruitt, Department of Linguistics, South College, University of Massachusetts, Amherst, MA 01003 USA. E-mail: kathryn.pruitt@gmail.com

Michael Putnam, Department of Germanic & Slavic Languages & Literatures, Penn State University, 427 Burrowes Building, University Park, PA 16802 USA. E-mail: mtp12@psu.edu

Martin Salzmann, Institut für Linguistik, Universität Leipzig, Beethovenstr. 15, D-04107 Leipzig, Germany. E-mail: martin.salzmann@uni-leipzig.de

Vieri Samek-Lodovici, Department of Italian/Centre for Human Communication, University College London, Gower Street, London WC1E 6BT. E-mail: ucljvsl@ucl.ac.uk

Sten Vikner, University of Aarhus, Department of Aesthetics and Communication, Section for English, Jens Chr. Skous Vej 4, DK–8000 Århus C, Denmark. E-mail: engsv@hum.au.dk

Ralf Vogel, Universität Bielefeld, Fakultät für Linguistik und Literaturwissenschaft, P.O.-Box 10 01 31, 33501 Bielefeld, Germany. E-mail: rvogel@uni-bielefeld.de

Ellen Woolford, Department of Linguistics, University of Massachusetts, Amherst, MA 01003 USA. E-mail: woolford@linguist.umass.edu

Hedde Zeijlstra, University of Amsterdam, Nederlandse Taalkunde, Spuistraat 134 (lsg NTK), NL-1012 VB Amsterdam, The Netherlands. E.mail: H.H.Zeijlstra@uva.nl

1 Introduction

Hans Broekhuis* and Ralf Vogel**

ABSTRACT This chapter will motivate why it is useful to consider the topic of derivations and filtering in more detail. We will argue against the popular belief that the minimalist program and optimality theory are incompatible theories in that the former places the explanatory burden on the generative device (the computational system C_{HL}) whereas the latter places it on the filtering device (the OT evaluator). Although this belief may be correct in as far as it describes existing *tendencies*, we will argue that minimalist and optimality theoretic approaches normally adopt more or less the same global architecture of grammar: both assume that a generator defines a set S of potentially well-formed expressions that can be generated on the basis of a given input and that there is an evaluator that selects the expressions from S that are actually grammatical in a given language L. For this reason, we believe that it has a high priority to investigate the role of the two components in more detail in the hope that this will provide a better understanding of the differences and similarities between the two approaches. We will conclude this introduction with a brief review of the studies collected in this book.

1. The architecture of grammar

The studies collected in this book all discuss the relation between the generative and the filter component of the grammar. The focus will be on syntax although the collection also contains a contribution by John J. McCarthy and Kathryn Pruitt, which discusses the issue for phonology. The starting point of this book is the popular view that current generative theories differ considerably in where they place the burden of explanation: whereas minimalist approaches generally assume that this is the generative component (the computational system C_{HL}), optimality-theoretic approaches generally focus on the filter component (the OT-evaluator). This difference between the minimalist program (MP) and optimality theory (OT) is also reflected in the claims that are normally made about the output of the generator;

---

* Hans Broekhuis, Meertens Institute, P.O.-box 94264, 1090 GG Amsterdam, The Netherlands. E-mail: hans.broekhuis@meertens.knaw.nl

** Ralf Vogel, Universität Bielefeld, Fakultät für Linguistik und Literaturwissenschaft, P.O.-Box 10 01 31, 33501 Bielefeld, Germany. E-mail: rvogel@uni-bielefeld.de)

minimalist approaches normally presuppose that the output of C_{HL} is small and may in fact be restricted to a single representation in many cases; optimality-theoretic approaches, on the other hand, normally maintain that the generator creates a candidate set that is very large or even infinite. It is important to note, however, that proponents of MP normally accept the idea that the generator may overgenerate and that we must therefore assume additional means to filter out the unwanted structures from the reference set. This means that many proponents of MP and OT do agree that the global architecture of grammar has the form in Figure 1.1, where the Generator and the Evaluator can be held responsible for respectively the universal and language-specific properties of languages. The essential property of this model is that the generator defines a set S of potentially well-formed expressions that can be generated on the basis of a given input, and that the evaluator selects those expressions from S that are actually grammatical in a given language L.

This general idea is, of course, not new and has already been formulated by Chomsky and Lasnik in 'Filters and control' (1977), where it is argued that 'to attain explanatory adequacy it is in general necessary to restrict the class of possible grammars, whereas the pursuit of descriptive adequacy often seems to require elaborating the mechanisms available and thus extending the class of possible grammars'. In order to solve this tension they propose that 'there is a theory of core grammar with highly restricted options, limited expressive power, and a few parameters' next to a more peripheral system of 'added properties of grammar', which 'we may think of as the syntactic analogue of irregular verbs'. Chomsky and Lasnik assume that core grammar consists of the phrase structure and transformational rules (the generator in Figure 1.1), whereas the more peripheral system consists of language-specific surface filters (the evaluator), and claim that the introduction of these filters contributes to the simplification of the transformational rules by bearing 'the burden of accounting for constraints which, in the earlier and far richer theory, were expressed in statements of ordering and obligatoriness, as well as all contextual dependencies that cannot be formulated in the narrower framework of core grammar'.

The ideas about which aspects of grammar should be considered part of core grammar or part of the periphery have, of course, considerably changed over the years; the *that*-trace filter, for example, was originally proposed as a language-specific filter for English, but the Empty Category Principle, which ultimately grew out of it, was assumed to be part of core grammar. Nevertheless, the gist of the proposal has survived in the more recent minimalist incarnations of the theory, where core syntax can be more or less equated with C_{HL}, and the periphery with the interface conditions. The task of reducing core grammar as much as possible has been very successful: the reduction of C_{HL} to its absolute minimum (internal and external merge) much contributes to the explanatory adequacy of the theory in the technical

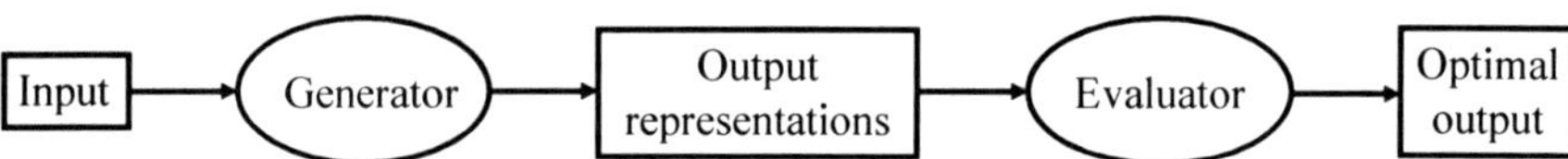

Figure 1.1 The architecture of grammar.

sense that it provides a principled basis, independent of any particular language, for the selection of the descriptively adequate grammar of each language (although it still remains to be shown that the minimalist conception of UG is more successful in core explanatory tasks like modeling language acquisition, explaining the origins of language and so on, than its predecessors). But, as expected, the contribution of core grammar to the descriptive adequacy of the theory has diminished accordingly, so that in this respect we have to rely more and more on the interface conditions.

That the global architecture of grammar has been like that indicated in Figure 1.1 for over three decades now may have been obscured by the fact that earlier phases of the theory assumed a so-called T- or inverse Y-model, according to which the derivation of LF- and PF-representations diverge after a certain point (s-structure or Spell-Out) in order to account for certain mismatches between linear order and semantic interpretation by deriving different input structures for the LF- and PF-component of the grammar. We will see in Section 2.1 that this property of the early *principles-and parameters* (P&P) models has disappeared in the later versions of MP and that, as a result, these later versions fully accord with the linear model in Figure 1.1. Now we have established this, we will briefly discuss the form and the role of the filter component in various stages of the P&P framework, as well as in OT.

2. The filter component

Although Chomky and Lasnik originally assumed that the filter component was not part of core grammar but of a language-specific periphery, it soon became clear that the filter component also had certain universal properties. For this reason, we will replace the notion of core grammar for the derivational component by the notions *generator*, *computational system* and *narrow syntax*. In order to avoid unwanted connotation we will likewise avoid the notion of periphery and use instead the notion of *evaluator* or *filter component*. The generator and the evaluator should both be considered part of core grammar.

2.1 The *principles-and parameters* approach

The introduction of a filter component in 'Filters and control' was motivated by the fact that this made a more restrictive formulation of narrow syntax possible by eliminating ordering statements and language-specific properties from the transformational component of the grammar. By way of demonstration we will consider the derivation of the relative clauses in (1).

(1) (a) the man who I know
     (b) the man that I know
     (c) the man I know
     (d) *the man who that I know

The relative pronoun *who* is base-generated in the regular object position, so that the d-structure of the examples in (1) is as given in (2a). Chomsky and Lasnik further proposed that universal grammar (UG) contains a universal principle 'Move *wh*-phrase' that requires that relative pronouns (and other *wh*-phrases) be placed to the left of the complementizer, as in the s-structure representation in (2b).

> (2) (a) the man [that I know who]   (d-structure)
>   (b) the man [[$_{COMP}$ who that] I know t_{who}]   (s-structure)

The examples in (1) can now be derived by assuming that UG contains a PF-rule Deletion that precedes the filters and freely deletes the relative pronoun *who* or the complementizer *that*; cf. Chomsky and Lasnik (1977: ex. (6)). The resulting PF-representations are given in (3). The desired grammaticality pattern is derived by postulation of the language-specific Doubly Filled COMP Filter, which prohibits the simultaneous realization of the relative pronoun and the complementizer in English. This excludes representation (3d).

> (3) (a) the man [[$_{COMP}$ who ~~that~~] I know t_{who}]
>   (b) the man [[$_{COMP}$ ~~who~~ that] I know t_{who}]
>   (c) the man [[$_{COMP}$ ~~who that~~] I know t_{who}]
>   (d) *the man [[$_{COMP}$ who that] I know t_{who}]

Although the deletion rule is freely applicable, the resulting representation is subject to a recoverability principle, which requires that deleted elements be locally recoverable. This is needed to block deletion of the *wh*-phrase in representations like (4): the recoverability principle in tandem with the Doubly Filled COMP Filter ensures that the representations in (4b–d) are excluded.

> (4) (a) I wonder [who ~~that~~ you met t_{who}]
>   (b) *I wonder [~~who~~ that you met t_{who}]
>   (c) *I wonder [~~who that~~ you met t_{who}]
>   (d) *I wonder [who that you met t_{who}]

By the same means, deletion of a preposed PP in relative clauses like (5) is blocked. Deletion of *about which* would violate the recoverability principle because the preposition *about* cannot be recovered locally.

> (5) (a) the book [about which ~~that~~ he spoke $t_{about\ which}$]
>   (b) *the book [~~about which~~ that he spoke $t_{about\ which}$]
>   (c) *the book [~~about which that~~ he spoke $t_{about\ which}$]
>   (d) *the book [about which that he spoke $t_{about\ which}$]

The virtue of Chomsky and Lasnik's proposal is that by accounting for the language-particular properties of English relative constructions by means of the Doubly Filled COMP Filter, we can keep the transformational rule that derives s-structure (2b) maximally simple (Move *wh*-phrase), which, in turn, makes it possible to attribute this rule to UG.

In the *Government and Binding* (Chomsky 1981) and *Barriers* (Chomsky 1986) period, the attempts to further reduce the transformational component of narrow syntax led to the formulation of the general rule Move α. As far as the filter component was concerned, it turned out that some of the language-specific filters proposed in Chomsky and Lasnik (1977) had a wider application and could be reformulated as more general principles. For example, the so-called *that*-trace filter, which prohibits a trace immediately to the right of the complementizer *that*, was reformulated as/ reduced to the Empty Category Principle (ECP), which requires that a trace be properly governed. Although the ECP was claimed to be universal, that is, to be part of UG, its function is more or less the same as that of the *that*-trace filter: it excludes structures that have been created by narrow syntax. Therefore the formulation of the ECP is not a reason to frown with a skeptical eye on the notion of filter; it rather opened the prospect of obtaining a certain degree of explanatory adequacy in the domain of filters, so that the filter component could also enter the domain of core grammar.

In the *Minimalist Program,* as developed by Chomsky since the mid-1980s, the generator seems to have been reduced to its absolute minimum. The computational system of human language C_{HL}, as it is now called, consists essentially of one merge operation in two guises. External merge combines two independent syntactic objects into a larger syntactic unit, whereas internal merge takes some element from an existing syntactic object, and merges it to the root of this object, thus deriving the effect of movement. Merge is subject to a number of general conditions. For example, it never involves more than two objects at the same time, which results in binary branching phrase structures. Internal Merge obeys certain locality restrictions and is further subject to the Last Resort Condition, which requires that movement be triggered by some unvalued formal feature. As in Chomsky and Lasnik (1977), descriptive adequacy lies mainly outside the computational system: Chomsky (1995: §4.7.3), for example, suggests (rightly or wrongly) that 'rearrangement' phenomena like extraposition, right-node raising, VP-adjunction and scrambling are essentially the result of stylistic rules of the phonological component.

Many of the filters as discussed in Chomsky and Lasnik (1977) have not found an alternative account in MP, but the fact that they are not *discussed* is, of course, no guarantee that they are not *needed.* In this connection it is important to note that Chomsky (1995) explicitly claims that C_{HL} generates a set of converging (= potentially well-formed) derivations satisfying Full Interpretation, the so-called *reference set*, from which the admissible structures are selected by a number of global economy conditions: derivations with a smaller number of derivational steps are preferred (fewest steps), as are derivations with shorter movement chains (shortest steps).

> The language L thus generates three relevant sets of derivations: the set D of derivations, a subset D_C of convergent derivations of D, and a subset D_A of admissible derivations of D. FI determines D_C, and the economy conditions select D_A. ... D_A is a subset of D_C.
>
> (Chomsky 1995: 220)

It is not so clear whether global economy conditions still play a role in the current versions of MP. It seems that very soon they lost independent status by being incorporated into the definition of the movement operation: fewest steps was replaced by Last Resort (Chomsky 1995: 280) and shortest steps by the Phase Impenetrability Condition proposed in Chomsky (2001). As a result, D_C and D_A can be considered identical and we are left with only two sets of derivations: the set of derivations D and the set of converging derivations D_C. Proponents of the so-called crash-proof syntax framework claim that nothing more is needed; more specifically they claim that 'no filters are imposed on the end products of derivations, and no global filters (e.g. comparison of derivations) assign status to derivations as a whole'; see Frampton and Gutmann (2002: 90) and the contributions in Putnam (2010) for extensive discussions of the viability of this claim. Chomsky (1995: ch. 4, 221), however, maintained the more traditional line of thinking by introducing bare output conditions, which are later referred to as interface conditions, which are 'imposed from the outside' by the performance systems that make use of the representations created by C_{HL}: the articulatory-perceptual and the conceptual-intentional system. Chomsky further claims that the interface conditions are involved in the displacement property of language and we will see below that he formulates these conditions in later work in the format of a filter on the output of C_{HL}; cf. Chomsky (2001) and the discussion of (10/20) below.

We already noted that the early P&P models diverge from the linear model in Figure 1.1 in that the derivation of the PF- and LF-representations split at a certain point in the derivation in order to account by means of covert movement for the fact that there can be certain mismatches between linear order and semantic interpretation. Very early in the development of MP, proposals have been put forth to eliminate this property from the grammar. Groat and O'Neil (1996), for example, show that the copy theory of movement makes it possible to account for the discrepancies in PF and LF-representations by assuming that phonology can spell out either the lower or the higher copy in a movement chain; see also Bobaljik (2002). Chomsky (1995: ch. 4) argues that economy considerations can also account for these mismatches when we assume that it is more economical to move a syntactic category without its phonological features; pied piping of the phonological features is possible only when there are independent reasons to do so. The most recent development is the introduction of Agree (feature valuing at a distance) in the *Minimalist Inquiry* framework, which has made movement totally superfluous from a computational point of view. These proposals have in common that they make it possible to assume that the derivation of the LF- and PF-representations proceed in fully parallel fashion. The model of the Minimalist Inquiry framework, for example, is therefore as indicated in Figure 1.2.

Since Agree makes movement superfluous in the sense that it is no longer needed for feature checking, movement must be forced by other factors. More specifically, although movement must still be formally licensed by unvalued formal features, the question whether it actually applies depends on the interface conditions imposed by the conceptual-intentional (LF) or the articulatory-perceptual (PF) component on the output representations of C_{HL}. The intuition underlying this proposal is actu-

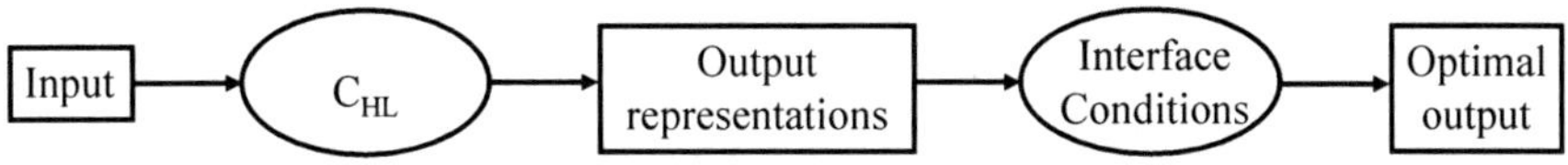

Figure 1.2 The Minimalist Inquiry model (Chomsky 2000 and later).

ally much older than the Minimalist Inquiry framework. For example, it has been argued that the motivation for *wh*-movement is that a *wh*-phrase can only be interpreted if it heads an operator-variable chain; see for example Chomsky (1991: 440) and Rizzi (1996). What is new is that Chomsky (2001) claims that certain types of A-movement are also externally motivated. We will look at this in some detail in the remainder of this subsection.

According to MP, movement of a syntactic object S is subject to last resort: it must be triggered by some unvalued formal feature of a higher functional head H that can be checked or valued by a corresponding feature of S. In the earliest proposal it was assumed that these features of H come in two forms: weak and strong features. A strong feature on H must be checked before the projection of H is merged with some higher head; if checking does not take place, the derivation is canceled. A weak feature on H, on the other hand, cannot be checked before Spell-Out as a result of the economy condition Procrastinate. This proposal led to a very rigid system in which the question whether a certain movement does or does not apply is mechanically determined by the feature constellation of the functional head H. However, it is clear that movement may be sensitive to other factors as well. Consider the case of so-called object shift (OS) in the Icelandic examples in (6).

(6) (a) Jón keypti   ekki   bókina.   *bókina* ⊂ focus
        Jón bought   not   the book
   (b) Jón keypti bókina$_i$ ekki t_i *bókina* ⊂ presupposition

The examples in (6) demonstrate that it is possible in Icelandic to move the direct object to the left, across the negative adverb *ekki*. This movement is not obligatory, however, but depends on the information structure of the clause: OS applies only when the object is part of the presupposition ('old' information) of the clause; it is excluded when it is part of the focus ('new' information) of the clause.

Let us provisionally assume that OS is triggered by the case feature on the light verb *v** (Vikner 1994; Chomsky 2001): if this case feature were strong, we would wrongly expect this movement to be obligatory; if it were weak, we would wrongly predict it to be impossible. In order to account for the apparent optionality of OS, we must therefore introduce additional means. One possibility would be to make the strength of the case feature sensitive to the information structure of the clause: only when the object is part of the presupposition of the clause does *v** have a strong case feature. Apart from being *ad hoc*, this option is not descriptively adequate since OS is never possible in complex tense constructions like (7): OS is excluded irrespective of the information structure of the clause, and (7a) is therefore ambiguous.

(7) (a) Jón hefur   ekki   keypt   bókina.   ambiguous
          Jón has   not   bought   the book
     (b) *Jón hefur bókina ekki keypt t_{bokina} —

Another possibility is to follow Holmberg (1999) in claiming that OS is actually not part of narrow syntax. He proposes that OS is a *phonological* (or, at least, post-spell out) operation that is driven by the interpretation of the object: in the terminology used above, OS is only possible if the object is part of the presupposition of the clause. This is stated in (8a), which paraphrases Chomsky's (2001: (54a)) summary of Holmberg's claim. Holmberg (1999: 22) accounts for the ungrammaticality of (7b) by postulating the additional restriction on the application of OS in (8b): OS is blocked in (7b) because it would move the object across the main verb.

(8) (a) Object shift is a phonological movement that satisfies condition (8b) and is
          driven by the semantic interpretation INT of the shifted object:
          (i)   INT: object is part of the presupposition of the clause.
          (ii) INT': object is part of the focus of the clause.
     (b) Object shift cannot apply across a phonologically visible category
          asymmetrically c-commanding the object position except adjuncts.

Chomsky (2001: 32) argues that Holmberg's proposal is problematic because 'displacement rules interspersed in the phonological component should have little semantic effect' (p. 15), and he therefore develops a proposal according to which OS takes place in narrow syntax. The relevant configuration is given in (9), where Obj is the θ-position of the object, and XP is a specifier position of $v*$ created by OS (note that Chomsky assumes a multiple specifier approach).

(9) ... [$_\alpha$XP [Subject $v*$ [V ... Obj]]]

The representation in (9) is an intermediate stage in the derivation: at some later stage in the derivation the subject is moved into SpecTP and in simple tense constructions the $v*$+V complex is moved to T. Given this, Chomsky (2001: 61) tries to account for the properties of Icelandic OS in (8) by adopting the assumptions in (10), where INT and INT' are again interpreted as in (8a).

(10) (a) $v*$ is assigned an EPP-feature only if that has an effect on outcome.
      (b) The EPP position of $v*$ is assigned INT.
      (c) At the phonological border of $v*$P, XP is assigned INT'.

The EPP-feature mentioned in (10a) has the same function as the strong features in the earlier proposals in the sense that it forces movement of some element into a specifier position of the head that it is assigned to, but it is no longer considered an inherent lexical property of the *lexical* items. Instead, $v*$ can in principle be freely assigned an EPP-feature and it is the function of the clause in (10a), which is claimed to be an invariant principle of grammar, to determine when this leads to an acceptable result; assignment of an EPP-feature to $v*$ is only possible if the resulting movement has some effect on the output representation. According to Chomsky this is only the case when the movement affects the semantic/pragmatic interpretation of the clause, or when it makes A′-movement possible (by placing the object at the phonological edge of the v*P-phase). We will see shortly that this leads to a less rigid system in the sense that movement can be made sensitive to factors other than the feature constellation of the attracting head.

Chomsky claims that (10b) is also an invariant principle: in the terminology employed earlier, this claim expresses that an object occupying the position XP in (9) in the output representation must be construed as being part of the presupposition of the clause; see (8a). It is important to note that (10b) is only concerned with shifted objects, and leaves open the option that non-shifted objects are ambiguously interpreted as being part of either the focus or the presupposition of the clause. This is needed in order to allow the non-shifted objects in Icelandic examples like (7a) to be interpreted as part of the presupposition of the clause, and, of course, also correctly predicts that objects in languages like English, which do not have OS of the Icelandic sort, can be part of either the focus or the presupposition of the clause.

Given that (10b) does not restrict the interpretation of non-shifted objects, we need something in addition to account for the fact that OS is obligatory in examples like (6b). This is where (10c) comes in. Let us first consider the notion of phonological border, which is defined as in (11); since Chomsky does not specify the notion of *phonological material*, we take it to refer to an abstract set of phonological features that will be spelled out in the PF-component.

(11) XP is at the phonological border of v*P, iff:
     (a) XP is a v*P-internal position, and;
     (b) XP is not c-commanded by v*P-internal phonological material.

The main difference between the examples in (6) and (7) is that in the former the main verb has moved out of v*P into T, whereas in (7) it has not and thus occupies a v*P-internal position. Example (7a) is therefore correctly predicted to be ambiguous: since the v*+V complex is v*P-internal and c-commands the object, clause (10c) does not apply and the object can be interpreted either as part of the focus of the clause (INT′) or as part of the presupposition of the clause (INT). Example (7b) is consequently blocked by (10a) because OS has no effect on the outcome as the object can also be assigned the interpretation INT in its base position in (7a). Therefore, in constructions like (7), the EPP-feature can only be assigned to v* if it is needed to enable A′-movement. In (6), on the other hand, there is no v*P-internal phonological material that c-commands the position Obj. Consequently, if the object occupies this position, (10c) states that it must be assigned INT′. Movement of the object into the XP-position in (9) therefore has an effect on the outcome by licensing the interpretation INT, and (10a) consequently allows assignment of an EPP-feature to v*.

It is important to note that statement (10c) clearly functions as a filter in the sense of Chomsky and Lasnik (1977). First, it is clear that it cannot be considered a condition on the derivation: when we would apply it to the intermediate stage in (9), the desired distinction between (6) and (7) could not yet be made locally, because the verb and the subject are moved out of the v*P only at a later stage in the derivation; Chomsky therefore assumes that it applies at the higher phase level (CP). Second, (10c) is a language-specific statement: Icelandic (and the continental Germanic languages) is subject to it, and therefore OS is forced in examples like (6b); the Romance languages, on the other hand, are not subject to it, so that (10a) blocks OS in comparable Romance examples. Thus, statement (10c) has the two characteristic properties of the PF-filters proposed in Chomsky and Lasnik (1977).

This subsection has shown that all grammars proposed during the P&P era have the global architecture of grammar indicated in Figure 1.1, although this was obscured in the early period by the assumption that derivations of the PF- and LF-representation diverge at some point in the derivation. It has been shown that by dropping this assumption Chomsky's recent Minimalist Inquiry framework fully conforms to the architecture in Figure 1.1; the grammar consists of a generative component that creates representations that are subsequently evaluated by a filter component. The filters place both semantic and phonological constraints on the output of C_{HL}, which reflects the fact that the representation(s) that pass these filters are subsequently fed to the articulatory-perceptual and the conceptual-intentional system where they undergo further computation in order to receive, respectively, a phonetic and a semantic interpretation.

2.2   Optimality theory

Optimality theory fits nicely to the global architecture of grammar in Figure 1.1, which is clear from the fact that it can be found in virtually all introductory texts on OT. It therefore also fits in the generative tradition as described in Section 2.1, but crucially differs from the P&P framework in that the evaluator is not taken to consist of universal principles and language-specific filters. The guiding intuition is instead that such principles and filters can be more adequately expressed by means of the ranking of a set of more primitive violable constraints; see Figure 1.3. We refer the reader to Pesetsky (1997; 1998) and Dekkers (1999) for early demonstrations of this.

Furthermore, OT adopts a holistic conception of language in the sense that the grammaticality of an expression E for some language L cannot be established by inspecting E alone, but is determined by comparing it to other expressions produced by the generator. This normally seems to go far beyond what is discussed under the term transderivationality in early minimalism; a derivation that is blocked by an economy constraint yields an ungrammatical expression in minimalism, whereas a loser in one OT-competition may still be the winner of another competition. It must be noted, however, that the latter is also a property of the set of statements in (10), which shows that Chomsky's most recent version of MP converges with this aspect of OT.

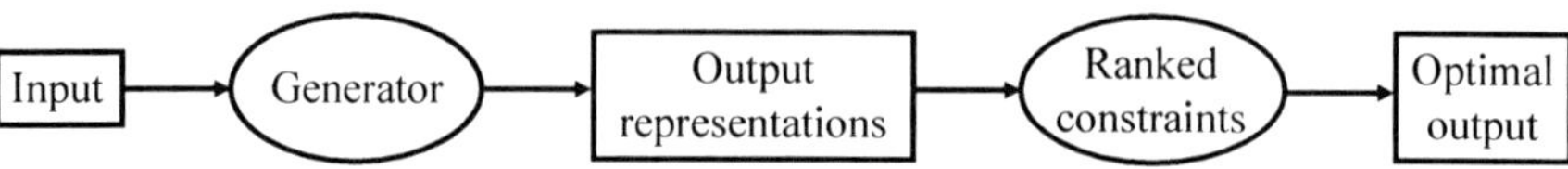

Figure 1.3 Optimality theory.

Like the MP model in Figure 1.2, the OT model in Figure 1.3 entails two notions of well-formedness: one with respect to the generator and one with respect to the evaluator. The usual version of the generator in OT is, however, more liberal and unrestricted than C_{HL}, and allows for a comparatively large candidate set. The OT-evaluator, of course, differs from the one proposed in MP in that it uses ranked constraints instead of interface condition, but they do resemble them in that they often incorporates aspects of the interpretative systems; cf. Vogel (2004; this volume).

An important difference between OT and MP is that the former can also be seen as a meta-theory or a methodological guideline; this is clear from the fact that it may be applied to a wide variety of empirical domains: it can be equally well applied to phonology as to, for example, syntax, and it is certainly conceivable that it can also be successfully applied outside the domain of linguistics. When we restrict ourselves to a certain empirical domain, it may be that the differences between the different OT-approaches are so small that it is actually justified to speak of a more or less coherent theory. This might well be the case for OT-phonology, given that there seems to be considerable agreement among OT-phonologists on the nature of the input, the operations that can be performed by the generator, and the nature of the output. Furthermore, OT-phonologists do not only agree on the basic assumption that the evaluator consists of ranked violable constraints, but they also seem to share the belief that the postulated constraints are of just two types, the so-called faithfulness and markedness constraints. And, finally, there even seems be some consensus about the individual constraints that are needed. Of course, there are also hotly debated issues, such as the question of whether the constraints are part of an innate, universally available set CON, or whether they are acquired on the basis of the primary linguistic data.

The situation in OT-syntax is entirely different: we are clearly not dealing with a generally accepted theory. Although Figure 1.3 is very specific about the nature of the evaluator, which has the defining property of consisting of ranked violable constraints, the nature of the generator is left open entirely; the generator can take the form of virtually any imaginable generative device, and, as a result, the generators of the current OT-approaches to syntax are based on different and often incompatible linguistic theories. Some more or less random examples are given in (12).

(12) (a) Lexical-Functional Grammar: Bresnan (2000); Sells (2001)
      (b) Early Principles-and-Parameters Theory: Grimshaw (1997); Pesetsky (1998)
      (c) Minimalism: Dekkers (1999); Woolford (2007); Broekhuis (2008)
      (d) Others: Müller (2000/2001); Vogel (2006)

Since the generators postulated by the proposals in (12) differ considerably and the generated candidate sets will therefore be constituted by candidates with entirely different properties, the postulated constraints will be quite different as well. As a result, we are dealing with OT-approaches that are as different as (or perhaps even more different than) the theories on which the generator is modeled. We will illustrate this below by comparing the OT-approaches proposed in Grimshaw (1997), Dekkers (1999) and Broekhuis (2008), which are all based on some version of the *principles-and-parameters* theory.

Grimshaw's (1997) proposal was originally written in the early 1990s and is based on the pre-minimalist *principles-and-parameters* framework. Among other things, this is clear from the fact that she tries to capture the directionality parameter, which was still generally assumed at that time, by means of two conflicting constraints HEAD LEFT and HEAD RIGHT (the head is leftmost/rightmost in its projection). In addition, she assumes the constraints SPECIFIER LEFT and SPECIFIER RIGHT (the specifier is leftmost/rightmost in its projection). Given that Grimshaw also assumes that the structures created by the generator conform the general X-bar-schema, the linearization of these structures follows from the language-specific ranking of these four constraints. Broekhuis (2008), which is based on the minimalist machinery proposed in Chomsky (2000) and later work, need not make use of Grimshaw's alignment constraints given that he adopts some version of Kayne's (1994) Linear Correspondence Axiom, according to which linear order is derived from the hierarchical relation between the constituent in the output representation. In his approach, linear order therefore follows from the language-specific ranking of a set of so-called EPP-constraints, which favor movement of a goal into its probe's minimal domain (in the sense of Chomsky 1995: ch. 3), and the economy constraint *MOVE, which disfavors movement. For example, the 'strong' ranking EPP(case) >> *MOVE requires movement of the probed noun phrase into the minimal domain of the unvalued case-features of $v*$ or the inflectional node I, whereas the 'weak' ranking *MOVE >> EPP(case) requires that the probe remain in its original position. Such EPP-constraints, which are used to express the same intuition as Chomsky's Agree-based approach that Agree is normally sufficient for convergence, will find no place in OT-approaches that follow Groat and O'Neil (1996) in assuming that feature checking invariably triggers movement and that the linear order depends on the question whether it is the tail or the head of the resulting chain that is spelled out; such approaches will replace the EPP-constraints, for example, by Dekker's (1999) PARSE-F constraints, which favor pronunciation of moved constituents in the position of their formal features (the head of the chain), and reinterpret *MOVE as a constraint that favors pronunciation of moved elements in their base position (the tail of the chain).

The previous paragraph has shown that properties of the proposed generator are immediately reflected in the nature of the postulated violable constraints of the OT-evaluator. The differences between the three OT-approaches discussed above are still relatively small due to the fact that the proposed generators all find their origin in the Chomskyan generative tradition, but it will be clear that the differences between these OT-approaches and OT-approaches that are based on other (generative) traditions may be much larger. For example, Broekhuis (2008) and Sells (2001) both develop an OT-analysis of Scandinavian object shift, but the two proposals differ at least as much as the minimalist and Lexical-Functional approaches that they are based on: whereas Broekhuis' analysis is built on the restrictions on movement of the clausal constituents, Sells' analysis is based on the restrictions on their phonological alignment.

Let us return to the guiding intuitions that connect all work in OT. The generator is an overgenerating system, which creates the candidate set from which the evaluator selects the optimal candidate(s) for a certain language L. The candidate set is generally assumed to be infinite and to contain many candidates that will never surface because they are harmonically bound by some other candidate (where A is harmonically bound by B if A violates at least one constraint on top of the constraints violated by B). Furthermore, the focus of attention is on the evaluator, which consists of a set of constraints with the properties in (13a–c), which we will more extensively discuss below.

(13) The optimality theoretic evaluator contains constraints that:
    (a) are taken from a universal set of constraints CON;
    (b) are violable; and
    (c) have a language-specific ranking.

The constraints crucially differ from the language-specific filters assumed in the *principles-and-parameters* theories in that they are generally assumed to be universal, that is, to be part of a universal set of constraints CON. These constraints can express language-specific properties by virtue of their properties in (13b) and (13c): languages may differ in the ranking of the universal constraints, and thereby select different candidates as optimal as a result of the fact that violation of a lower ranked constraint is tolerated in order to satisfy a higher ranked constraint. The way the OT-evaluator works can readily be demonstrated by means of Pesetsky's (1997; 1998) analysis of relative clauses. This will also give us the opportunity to show how the OT-evaluator differs from the filters assumed in the *principles-and-parameters* approaches. Consider again the relative clauses in (14) and (15), which were accounted for in *Filters and Control* by an appeal to the Doubly Filled COMP Filter and the recoverability condition on deletion.

(14) (a) the man [[$_{COMP}$ who ~~that~~] I know t_{who}]
    (b) the man [[$_{COMP}$ ~~who~~ that] I know t_{who}]
    (c) the man [[$_{COMP}$ ~~who that~~] I know t_{who}]
    (d) *the man [[$_{COMP}$ who that] I know t_{who}]

(15) (a) the book [about which ~~that~~ he spoke $t_{about\ which}$]
    (b) *the book [~~about which~~ that he spoke $t_{about\ which}$]
    (c) *the book [~~about which that~~ he spoke $t_{about\ which}$]
    (d) *the book [about which that he spoke $t_{about\ which}$]

When we contrast these examples with the French relative clauses in (16) and (17), we see that English and French differ in that the former allows a wider variety of constructions with a bare relative pronoun than the latter. However, when the relative pronoun is embedded in a PP (or an NP), the two languages behave the same.

(16) (a) *l'homme [qui$_i$ ~~que~~ je connais t_i]
    (b) l'homme [~~qui~~$_i$ que je connais t_i]
    (c) *l'homme [~~qui~~$_i$ ~~que~~ je connais t_i]
    (d) *l'homme [qui$_i$ que je connais t_i]

(17)   (a) l'homme [avec qui$_i$ ~~que~~ j'ai dansé t_i]
     (b) *l'homme [~~avec qui~~$_i$ que j'ai dansé t_i]
     (c) *l'homme [~~avec qui~~$_i$ ~~que~~ j'ai dansé t_i]
     (d) *l'homme [avec qui$_i$ que j'ai dansé t_i]

In order to account for the data in (14) to (17), Pesetsky proposed the constraints in (18), which we slightly simplify here for reasons of exposition. Constraint (18a) is simply the recoverability condition on deletion from Chomsky and Lasnik (1977), constraint (18b) is a constraint that expresses that embedded clauses tend to be introduced by a complementizer, and (18c) is a constraint that expresses that function words (like complementizers) tend to be left unpronounced.

(18)   (a) RECOVERABILITY (REC): a syntactic unit with semantic content must be pronounced unless it has a sufficiently local antecedent.
     (b) LEFT EDGE (CP): the first leftmost pronounced word in an embedded CP must be the complementizer.
     (c) TELEGRAPH (TEL): do not pronounce function words.

The ranking of these constraints will determine the optimal output. In order to see this, it is important to note that LE(CP) in (18b) and TEL in (18c) are in conflict with each other: the first wants the complementizer to be pronounced, whereas the latter wants it to be deleted. Such conflicts make it possible to account for variation between languages: when we rank these constraints differently, we get languages with different properties. When we assume that LE(CP) outranks TEL, we get a language in which embedded declarative clauses must be introduced by a complementizer. When we assume that TEL outranks LE(CP), we get a language in which embedded declarative clauses are not introduced by a complementizer. When we assume that the two constraints are in a tie (ranked equally high), we get a language in which embedded declarative clauses are optionally introduced by a complementizer. The evaluations can be made visible by means of tableaux. Tableau T1 gives the evaluation of embedded declarative clauses with and without a pronounced complementizer in a language with the ranking LE(CP) >> TEL.

T1 No complementizer deletion in embedded declarative clauses

		LE(CP)	TEL
… [complementizer …]	☞		*
… [~~complementizer~~ …]		*!	

The two asterisks indicate that the constraint in the header of their column is violated. The first candidate, with a pronounced complementizer, violates TEL but this is tolerated because it enables us to satisfy the higher ranked constraint LE(CP). The second candidate, with a deleted complementizer, violates LE(CP), and this is fatal (which is indicated by an exclamation mark) because the first candidate does not violate this constraint. The first candidate is therefore optimal, which is indicated by means of the pointed finger: ☞. The shading of the cells indicates that these cells do not play a role in the evaluation; this convention is mainly for convenience, because it makes it easier to read the tableaux.

Now consider the evaluation of the same candidates in a language with the ranking TEL >> LE(CP), given in T2. Since TEL is now ranked higher than LE(CP), violation of the former is fatal, so that deletion of the complementizer becomes obligatory.

T2 Obligatory complementizer deletion in embedded declarative clauses

		TEL	LE(CP)
... [complementizer ...]		*!	
... [~~complementizer~~ ...]	☞		*

Tableau T3 gives the evaluation of a language in which the two constraints are in a tie LE(CP) <> TEL, which is indicated in the tableau by means of a dashed line. Under this ranking, the rankings LE(CP) >> TEL and TEL >> LE(CP) are in a sense simultaneously active. Therefore we have to read the tie in both directions: when we read the tie from left to right, the violation of LE(CP) is fatal (which is indicated by >), and the first candidate is optimal; when we read the tableau from right to left, the violation of TEL is fatal (which is indicated by <), and the second candidate is optimal. This predicts that deletion of the complementizer is optional in this case.

T3 Optional complementizer deletion in embedded declarative clauses

		LE(CP)	TEL
... [complementizer ...]	☞		<*
... [~~complementizer~~ ...]	☞	*>	

Let us now return to the difference between English and French with respect the pronunciation of relative clauses. It is clear that English has the tied ranking LE(CP) <> TEL, given that the complementizer is normally optional in embedded declarative clauses. In French, on the other hand, it is clear that LE(CP) outranks TEL given that the complementizer is obligatory in embedded declarative clauses. Pesetsky (1997) has shown that this also accounts for the differences between the English and French examples in (14) and (16), in which a bare relative pronoun is preposed. Assume that in both languages the constraint RECOVERABILITY outranks the constraints TEL and LE(CP); the ranking of the constraints in (18) are then as given in (19).

(19) (a) French: REC >> LE(CP) >> TEL
     (b) English: REC >> LE(CP) <> TEL

The evaluation of the French examples in (16) proceeds as in T4. Since the relative pronoun has a local antecedent it is recoverable after deletion, so that all candidates satisfy REC. The second candidate is the optimal candidate because it is the only one that does not violate LE(CP); the fact that this candidate violates the lower-ranked constraint TEL is tolerated since this in fact enables the satisfaction of the higher-ranked constraint LE(CP).

T4 Relative clauses with preposed relative pronoun

French		REC	LE(CP)	TEL
l'homme [qui~~que~~ je connais t_i]			*!	
l'homme [~~qui~~ que je connais t_i]	☞			*
l'homme [~~qui~~ ~~que~~ je connais t_i]			*!	
l'homme [qui que je connais t_i]			*!	*

The evaluation of the English examples is slightly more complex than that of French due to the fact that LE(CP) and TEL are in a tie: we are therefore dealing with two rankings at the same time: REC >> LE(CP) >> TEL and REC >> TEL >> LE(CP). The first ranking is actually the one we also find in French, and we have seen that this results in selection of the second candidate as optimal. Under the second ranking, violation of TEL is fatal, so that the first and third are selected as optimal. As a result, three out of the four candidates are grammatical in English.

T5 Relative clauses with preposed relative pronoun

English		REC	LE(CP)	TEL
the man [who~~that~~ I know t_i]	☞		*>	
the man [~~who~~ that I know t_i]	☞			<*
the man [~~who~~ ~~that~~ I know t_i]	☞		*>	
the man [who that I know t_i]			*>	<*

Next consider the evaluation of the French examples in (17), in which a PP containing a relative pronoun is preposed. Since the preposition is not locally recoverable, deletion of it leads to a violation of the highest-ranked constraint REC: this excludes the second and the third candidate. Since the two remaining candidates both violate LE(CP), the lowest ranked constraint TEL gets the final say by excluding the fourth candidate. Note that this shows that the ranking LE(CP) >> TEL does not mean that the complementizer is always realized, but that this may depend on other factors; when the complementizer is preceded by some element that must be realized, TEL forces the complementizer to delete.

T6 Relative clauses with preposed PP

French		REC	LE(CP)	TEL
l'homme [avec qui$_i$ ~~que~~ j'ai dansé t_i] ☞			*	
l'homme [~~avec qui~~$_i$ que j'ai dansé t_i]		*!		*
l'homme [~~avec qui~~$_i$ ~~que~~ j'ai dansé t_i]		*!	*	
l'homme [avec qui$_i$ que j'ai dansé t_i]			*	*!

For the English examples in (15) we get the same result as in French: both the second and the third candidate are excluded by REC, and the fourth candidate is excluded because it is harmonically bound by the first candidate: it has a fatal violation of TEL irrespective of the question whether we read the tie from left to right or from right to left.

T7 Relative clauses with preposed PP

English		REC	LE(CP)	TEL
the book [about which$_i$ ~~that~~ he spoke t_i] ☞			*	
the book [~~about which~~$_i$ that he spoke t_i]		*!		*
the book [~~about which~~$_i$ ~~that~~ he spoke t_i]		*!	*	
the book [about which$_i$ that he spoke t_i]			*	*!

2.3 Conclusion

This section has argued that the global architecture of grammar is as given in Figure 1.1, and that the several proposals made within the P&P approach do not differ in this respect from OT. The two frameworks are similar in assuming that we are dealing both with derivations and with evaluations: a generator creates a potentially multi-membered set of expressions S, and an evaluator determines which expressions from S are grammatical in a given language L. The OT view on the evaluator seems to be of a more optimistic nature than that of the P&P approaches. The latter consider the evaluator as a more or less random collection of language-specific filters on the output of narrow syntax. Pesetsky's work has shown, however, that at least some of the filters proposed by Chomsky and Lasnik (1977) can be decomposed into more atomic OT constraints, and Dekkers (1999) has shown this for a number of other constraints/principles like the ECP. Furthermore, since the OT constraints are claimed to be universal, they make precise predictions about the range of language variation that is allowed: Pesetsky, for example, has shown that his proposal is able to account for the differences between English and French relative clause constructions, and Broekhuis and Dekkers (2000) and Dekkers (1999) have shown that his proposal can be readily extended to relative constructions in Dutch.

3.   Where MP and OT do differ: derivations and evaluations

The previous section has shown that MP and OT assume the same global architecture of grammar, but there are, of course, also a number of obvious differences. This subsection will argue, however, that these do not have a principled linguistic motivation, but are the result of a more or less accidental difference in focus of attention between the two approaches: MP is mainly concerned with the universal (derivational) aspects of grammar whereas OT-syntax rather focuses on more language-specific aspects of grammar. This focus of interest is also reflected in the research strategies that the two approaches employ: research in MP tends to attribute to the generator C_{HL} as many properties of languages as possible, whereas Research in OT tends to appeal to the evaluator instead. It is therefore not surprising that the empirical successes of the two approaches also lie in different areas: MP is especially well equipped to account for the universal properties of languages, but there is no generally accepted view on the way we should account for, or even approach, the many ways in which languages may differ from each other; OT, on the other hand, precisely provides such a general theory of language variation, but since there is no generally accepted theory of the generator, current OT-syntax fails to account for the 'truly' universal properties of languages. These differences between MP and OT will be discussed more extensively below.

3.1   Universal properties of language (the generator)

Both MP and OT-syntax hold the generator responsible for the invariant properties of language: the generator determines what representations are contained in the output, and hence can take part in the evaluation. The two frameworks differ, however, with respect to the extent that the generator is developed, or invoked in the analysis of the linguistic data.

The investigation of the generator (C_{HL}) is considered MP's core business. It has resulted in a sophisticated, restrictive theory on the nature of the generator. It is assumed that C_{HL} is constituted by a small set of operations that are subject to inviolable conditions that are relatively well understood. Perhaps C_{HL} can be reduced to a single merge operation, which has two incarnations, external and internal merge. As a result of this, the output of C_{HL} is also highly restricted; although it can be a non-singleton set, the differences between the members of this set are very limited in nature, and perhaps only involve the number of movements that occurred; cf. the discussion of Icelandic OS in section 2.1. It seems that analyses that do not invoke filtering devices are valued higher in MP than those that do, and, as a result, research tends to focus on those phenomena that can be successfully approached by means of a derivational account, with a concomitant reduction of the empirical scope of the theory, as is clear from the fact already mentioned earlier that Chomsky (1995: §4.7.3) suggests that 'rearrangement' phenomena like extraposition, right-node raising, VP-adjunction and scrambling are not part of narrow syntax. It is generally admitted in OT-syntax that the generator is the locus of the 'truly' universal properties of language: Grimshaw

(1997), for example, assumes that the structures formed by the generator conform to some version of X-bar-theory, Pesetsky (1998) and Anderson (2000) adopt some version of generative grammar as the generator, and Bresnan (2000) and Sells (2001) argue in favor of some version of Lexical Functional Grammar. The nature of the generator is, however, not a prominent subject of research; it is rather exceptional for an OT-researcher to account for some phenomenon by taking recourse to the generator given that most research in OT-syntax focuses on the variation that can be found rather than on the universal properties of languages.

Despite the differences in theoretical background (P&P, LFG, etc.), it seems that the view on the generator of many (if not most) OT-syntacticians crucially differs from that of MP-researchers, which becomes especially apparent when we consider the differences in the view on the output of the generator. We have already seen that, although MP allows for non-singleton output sets, MP-researchers generally take it for granted that this set is very small and that differences between the members of this set are limited in type, perhaps confined to differences in movement. In OT, on the other hand, it is generally maintained that the output of the generator can in principle be infinitely large, and that the members of the set may differ in a wide variety of ways. This suggests that the generator is generally taken to contain a larger set of operations in OT than is assumed in MP, and that these operations are probably confined in a less strict manner than the operations assumed in MP.

As a result of this different view on the generator, MP and OT tend to provide entirely different explanations for similar phenomena, the former taking recourse mainly to properties of the generator and the latter to those of the evaluator. This state of affairs seems to strengthen the widely accepted view that we are dealing with two competing and essentially incompatible frameworks. However, it can also be assessed differently, and more positively. Since it is not *a priori* given whether a certain phenomenon should be accounted for by appealing to the generator or the evaluator, it is important to develop alternative analyses that can subsequently be compared and evaluated; the fact that in some domains competing MP- and OT-analyses are available therefore does not mean in itself that we are dealing with competing or conflicting theories.

3.2 Variation (the evaluator)

One of the main concerns of both MP and OT is *cross-linguistic variation*. However, the way they approach this problem is entirely different – at least, at first sight. Let us start with discussing the way MP approaches the issue. Language variation is assumed to arise as a result of additional constraints on the application of the otherwise universal generator (C_{HL}). The generator can basically perform two operations: external and internal merge. Let us provisionally adopt the standard assumption in MP that external merge is indispensable given that it is needed in order to assemble lexical items into semantically interpretable structures, for example, by the saturating the thematic roles of a given lexical head. Despite the fact that internal merge (movement) may have certain semantic implications, it is not essential in the creation of semantically interpretable structures, so that we expect to find language variation in this domain. Note that since MP is mainly concerned with narrow syntax it mainly studies differences between languages that are somehow related to movement: variation in other domains is attributed to other modules (like PF), and is generally not discussed any further.

In early MP, the locus of variation between languages is solely attributed to the lexicon. Differences in the displacement property of languages are due to differences in the 'strength' property of the morpho-syntactic features that trigger movement: strong features trigger overt movement, whereas the weak features allow covert movement (which is favored by Procrastinate). In the more recent Agree-based theories, which reject the idea of covert movement, the core idea is preserved by assuming that movement only takes place if a functional head F contains an EPP-feature, which requires that the specifier of F be present. Under this view, the task of the language learner is to determine whether the functional head F has a weak or strong feature, or, alternatively, whether it has an EPP-feature, and to store this information in the lexicon.

The scope of OT goes much beyond the displacement property of languages: in principle, all (phonological, syntactic, semantic, pragmatic, etc.) properties can be fruitfully investigated, as long as one can plausibly postulate constraints bearing on the phenomenon in question. As we have already seen variation between languages is attributed to the evaluator, more specifically to the differences in ranking of the otherwise universal constraints. Under this view, the task of the language learner is to determine the constraint ranking (as well as the lexicon) of the language.

The discussion above seems to reveal another important difference between MP and OT: in the former, cross-linguistic variation is solely due to differences in lexical specifications, whereas in the latter it is rather due to the ranking of the universal constraints. This is indeed the case when we compare early MP with OT-syntax, but it no longer holds when we compare the most recent Minimalist Inquiry framework and OT-syntax. The early MP thesis that the sole locus of cross-linguistic variation is the lexicon runs into severe problems when we consider *variation within a single language*, because it predicts that languages cannot have 'optional' movement, that is, movements that occur only under well-defined semantic or phonological conditions. One example of this type of movement is Icelandic OS (already discussed in section 2.1), which can only apply when the object is part of the presupposition of the clause (cf. (6)), and when it does not cross the verb (cf. (7)) or other $v*$P-internal material. This kind of optionality cannot arise under the early MP thesis because the postulation of feature strength or an EPP-feature gives rise of to a very rigid system: when a feature is strong/an EPP-feature is present, movement must apply; when a feature is weak/an EPP-feature is not present, movement is blocked by Procrastinate.

We have already seen that this problem has led Chomky (2001) to assume that the EPP-feature, which forces movement, is optionally present. In order to avoid circularity, the choice must be made sensitive to external factors like the semantic and phonological conditions imposed on the pertinent movement, and this is precisely what Chomsky did in his account of OS in Icelandic in (10), repeated below as (20): as we have seen, the language-specific statement in (20c), in tandem with the universal principles in (20a,b), precisely derives the circumstances under which Icelandic OS applies.

(20) (a) $v*$ is assigned an EPP-feature only if that has an effect on outcome.
       (b) The EPP position is assigned INT.
       (c) At the phonological border of $v*P$, XP is assigned INT'.

Chomsky (2001: 36) presents clause (20c) as a parameter that distinguishes OS from non-OS languages. French, for example, has verb movement to I, but nevertheless OS does not apply. This can be accounted for by assuming that (20c) does not hold for French. As a result, the interpretation INT can be assigned to the object when it is at the phonological border of $v*P$; as a result, movement of the object to the EPP-position is not needed and assignment of an EPP-feature to $v*$ is consequently blocked by (20a).

It seems, however, that (20c) is unlike the parameters of the earlier P&P framework in that it is not binary, because it is not the case that languages can be straightforwardly divided between OS and non-OS languages. This will become clear when we consider the Danish examples in (21) and (22), taken from Vikner (1994: 502); The examples in (21) show that Danish differs from Icelandic in that it does not have OS of non-pronominal DPs, whereas the examples in (22) show that it does have OS of weak pronouns.

(21) (a) Hvorfor   læste   studenterne   ikke   artiklen?
             why   read   the students   not   the article
       (b) *Hvorfor læste studentene artiklen$_i$ ikke t_i?

(22) (a) Hvorfor   læste   studenterne   den$_i$ ikke t_i?
             why   read   the students   it   not
       (b) *Hvorfor læste studenterne ikke den?

This can be accounted for by assuming that clause (20c) must be further refined as in (20c'). This clause correctly expresses: (a) that non-pronominal DPs that are part of the presupposition of the clause (= INT) must undergo OS in Icelandic, but not in Danish or the Romance languages; and (b) that definite pronouns (which are assigned INT by definition) must undergo OS in Icelandic and Danish but not in the Romance languages.

(20) (c') At the phonological border of $v*P$, XP is assigned INT'
             (i)   XP = DP   (Icelandic)
             (ii) XP = definite pronoun   (Danish)
             (iii) XP = ∅   (Romance)

What we want to stress here is that the adoption of language specific statements like (20c) or (20c') is a radical breaks with the early MP thesis that the sole locus of cross-linguistic variation is the lexicon. Since these statements essentially function as language-specific filters on the output of C_{HL}, linguistic variation should be attributed to the evaluator in the model in Figure 1.2, and not to the lexicon. In fact, it seems that Chomsky's proposal makes it possible to eliminate the EPP-features entirely: when we assume that movement is subject to Last Resort but applies optionally, we could simply replace clause (20a) by the claim that movement is possible only if it has an effect on the outcome. This would make it possible to attribute cross-linguistic language variation *entirely* to the evaluator, just like in OT. In (23) we attempt to rephrase Chomsky's proposal such that reference to the notion of EPP-feature becomes superfluous.

(23) (a) Movement is possible only if it has an effect on outcome.
      (b) The derived object position is assigned INT.
      (c) At the phonological border of v*P, XP is assigned INT′.
           (i)   XP = DP   (Icelandic)
           (ii) XP = definite pronoun   (Danish)
           (iii) XP = ∅   (Romance)

3.3 Conclusion

Since we have seen that MP and OT assume more or less the same global organization of grammar, we may conclude that the differences in the research strategies of MP and OT are somewhat accidental: as far as we can see, there are no theory-internal reasons for these frameworks to limit their investigation to respectively the generator or the evaluator. The fact that MP and OT occasionally provide alternative analyses for similar data as a result of these differences in research strategy does not follow from insurmountable theoretical differences between the two frameworks either, but simply reflects the fact that it is not *a priori* given whether a certain phenomenon belongs to the computational system or to the filter component of core grammar. Early MP and OT-syntax do seem to adopt conflicting views on the nature of variation between languages: the former adopts the thesis that language variation can be reduced to differences in the feature specifications of the lexical elements (feature strength/EPP-features), whereas the latter assumes that language variation is due to the evaluator, that is, to differences in constraint rankings. In Chomsky's current *Minimalist Inquiry* framework, however, the early MP thesis has been dropped: language variation is (also) attributed to parameters like (23c), which essentially function as language-specific filters on the output of C_{HL}. Current MP and OT therefore both attribute language variation to the evaluator, and the main difference between MP and OT boils down to the question whether the evaluator appeals to output filters or to ranked constraints.

4. Organization of the book

The discussion above has shown that MP and OT-syntax are actually much more alike than is generally assumed or one would think at first sight. The least one can say is that they assume a similar global architecture of the grammar, and thus face a number of similar questions, like:

(24) (a) What are the defining properties of the generator?
    (b) What are the defining properties of the evaluator?
    (c) What is the division of labor between the generator and the evaluator?
    (d) What is the role of the articulatory-perceptual and the conceptual-intentional system?

We therefore have to ask ourselves whether it is still justified to consider MP and OT different, divergent programs, or whether it is possible to combine the best results of these programs into a single theory of grammar. The studies that will follow all discuss these questions from different perspectives and thus provide a collection of possible answers to these questions. Some studies in fact go beyond this and show alternative ways in which the output of the derivational system can be filtered. This introduction will not summarize the individual studies or address their contents in detail; for this we refer to the abstracts and the studies themselves. However, we will conclude this introduction by giving a brief discussion of the organization of the book as a whole and the grouping of the individual studies.

4.1 Part I: combining MP with an OT-evaluation

The first group of studies presents work within the so-called derivation-and-evaluation framework, which explicitly combines MP and OT into a hybrid system: more specifically, it is argued that some version of the computational system of human language C_{HL} from MP functions as a generator that creates a restricted set of potentially well-formed expressions, which are subsequently evaluated in an optimally theoretic fashion by means of limited number of violable constraints. The chapter by Hans Broekhuis introduces this framework and illustrates it by means of a topic that was also extensively discussed in this introduction: Object Shift. He shows that Chomsky's proposal can be readily rephrased in optimality-theoretic terms and that this has a wide range of empirical consequences. The chapter by Gema Chocano and Mike Putnam discusses a number of restrictions on the licensing of parasitic gaps that are problematic in a purely derivational framework like MP but which fall out quite naturally under the hybrid approach by adding a single constraint to the inventory proposed by Broekhuis. Martin Salzmann discusses the dialectal and intra-speaker variation that can be found with dative resumption in relative clauses, that is, the use of a clause internal dative pronoun instead of a trace when the antecedent of the relative clause corresponds to the dative argument of the verb. Salzmann argues that the range of variation shows that locality is an inviolable condition on movement, but that the standard version of MP is nevertheless ill-equipped to handle the attested variation; he therefore concludes that hybrid systems like the derivation-and-evaluation framework are optimal for expressing the correct generalizations.

4.2 Part II: local and global optimization

As we have seen above one of the conspicuous differences between MP and traditional OT is that the former focuses on the derivation (the generator) whereas the latter focuses on the output representations of the generator (the evaluator). The first two studies collected in Part II show that this is by no means a necessary difference between MP and OT and that it is readily possible to formulate derivational versions of OT.

The first example of such a derivational version of OT is *Harmonic Serialism* (HS), which is illustrated by John McCarthy and Kathryn Pruitt on the basis of stress assignment. According to HS, the output of the generator is evaluated in a step-wise fashion by means of a Gen-Eval loop: at each point in the derivation the output of the generator is evaluated by the evaluator, after which the optimal output is sent back to the generator. This results in a process of local optimization that continues until the input and the optimal output representations are identical; this is the point of convergence. McCarthy and Pruitt explicitly compare the derivation of metrical structure in HS to the structure building operations found in MP, and claim that 'both theories seek to explain the derivation of complex structures by deriving them via repeated application of simple operations under the control of an optimizing grammar.'

The chapter by Fabian Heck and Gereon Müller seems to fit seamlessly in this view given that they argue that the application of the structure building operations of MP are constrained by a local optimization in a way that comes very close to HS. They distinguish structure-building features, which trigger Merge, and probe features, which trigger Agree, and assume that the order of saturation of these features is determined in a local, stepwise fashion. Empirical evidence in favor of local optimization is provided by cross-linguistic differences in case assignment to internal and external arguments (that is, the difference between nominative-accusative and ergative-absolutive languages), agreement patterns in German DPs with prenominal dative possessors, the use of the German expletive *es*, and VP-topicalization. Heck and Müller suggest that many analyses that involve larger domains can be rephrased in terms of local optimization, but admit that there may be certain analyses that may require larger optimization domains.

Although the contributions by McCarthy and Pruitt and Heck and Müller show that local optimization has clear advantages when it comes to the application of the operations of the generator, there are cases where global optimization seems more suitable. Heck and Müller, for example, predict a dichotomy between nominative-accusative and ergative-absolutive languages, but Ellen Woolford shows that the distinction is not always clear-cut given that in some languages the expression of ergative case depends on certain contextual properties of the construction as a whole. For example, in Hindi and Nepali ergative case is only used in, respectively, perfective and individual-level contexts; since this information is probably not available or accessible during the derivation it seems less likely that this can be accounted for by means of local optimization.

Another case that requires global optimization involves the order restrictions on Scandinavian object shift constrictions (see Section 3 above). This is again underlined by the discussion of object shift in Scandinavian remnant topicalization constructions by Eva Engels and Sten Vikner, who show that the optimization domain must be at least as large as CP. Their contribution also contains a discussion of the cyclic linearization approach by Fox and Pesetsky (2005), and they show that this approach is less well equipped to account for the set of data they discuss than their OT-approach.

The studies in this section suggest that we may need to postulate both local and global optimization. This need not be frowned upon with suspicion as this actually reflects the current distinction found within MP between local condition on the operations of the computational system C_{HL} and the set of conditions imposed by the articulatory-perceptual and the conceptual-intentional systems on output representations. It simply shows that OT-evaluations may be pervasive in the grammar in the sense that both types of restrictions may be rephrasable in terms of violable OT-constraints.

4.3 Part III: optimal design, economy and last resort in OT

Chomsky has stressed at a number of occasions that the name minimalist program is less felicitous given that minimalist considerations are a defining part of any scientific enterprise; minimalist concerns are therefore expected to play an important role in the development of the more traditional OT-approaches as well. The studies collected in this part of the book are good examples of this.

Vieri Samek-Lodovici argues that when it comes to cross-linguistic variation OT meets the requirement of optimal design better than the traditional versions of MP developed in the 1990s. He shows that under the assumption that no ranking of the universal, potentially conflicting (hence violable) constraints is inherently superior to any other, language variation is a predicted outcome of OT, whereas under the postulation of universal inviolable (hence non-conflicting) conditions language variation requires language-specific stipulations like Chomsky's (1993) postulation of weak/strong features on certain lexical items. Samek-Lodovici further points out that the existence of conflicting constraints is implied by the postulation of bare output conditions: since the sensory-motor and the conceptual-intentional system serve largely independent goals, there is no reason to exclude the possibility of conflicting interface constraints.

One way in which OT and minimalism can coexist and complement each other lies in OT's potential to model the interfaces between syntax, semantics and phonology/ phonetics. A leading idea of minimalism is to reduce syntax to what is ultimately necessary to fulfill the needs of these interfaces. Therefore, the more elaborate the interfaces are constructed, the simpler the syntactic generator might be construable. Ralf Vogel concludes in his chapter that only very few of the specifically minimalist properties of the syntactic generator are necessary for OT's syntax generator, when one exploits OT as interface theory as much as possible. The conception of an OT grammar that he argues for organizes the mapping between semantic, syntactic and phonological/phonetic representations using violable and conflicting mapping constraints. The core concept of OT that is relevant here is faithfulness, formulated in a corresponding theoretic way. Vogel shows that from this perspective the optimal syntactic representations are not necessarily the most economical ones, but rather those that correspond best to semantic and phonological/phonetic representations. He further argues that OT's notion of markedness is more adequate than MP's notion of economy. Unmarked syntactic structures can be seen as part of such maximally isomorphic mappings.

The notion of economy in MP is often linked to the notion of last resort: a certain operation can only be used when it is needed to arrive at a converging derivation. In early MP, for example, movement was claimed to be possible only when it serves to check and eliminate an uninterpretable feature of a certain sort. Jane Grimshaw criticizes this use of the notion given that we could simply remove the 'last resort' concept and state that movement is only possible when a certain feature is present (as is indeed assumed in the later versions of MP that assume optional EPP-features; see our earlier discussion of Chomsky's account of object shift). Grimshaw further claims that the notion of last resort can only receive a coherent interpretation in theories of optimization with constraint interaction. In fact, it is claimed that the notion is in fact entailed by such theories and that the use of *any* grammatical device is the result of last resort: it is the best that can be done in a particular configuration given a certain constraint ranking. This is illustrated by means of the choice between V-to-T/C, *do*-support and free tense (tense not supported by a verb) in a variety of constructions and languages. The discussion shows that, contrary to popular belief, *do*-support is not language-specific but arises in different circumstances in different languages.

4.4 Part IV: the role of the interpretative components

Standard MP assumes that the interpretative components (PF and LF) impose certain conditions on the output of the generator, and we have further seen that such interface conditions can be readily expressed in an OT-fashion by means of ranked, violable constraints. The two studies in this part of the book propose alternative ways in which the interpretative component may affect the output of the generator.

Like Samek-Lodovici, Hedde Zeijlstra argues that the conditions imposed by the sensory-motor and the conceptual-intentional system on the output representations of the generator are necessarily in conflict and therefore (at least partly) violable. This gives rise to a tension that is solved by different languages in different ways, with language variation as a result. Zeijlstra postulates an inviolable principle of Full Legibility, which requires that all elements in the output be legible at the level of LF and PF, but which differs from Chomsky's (1995) Full Interpretation in that it allows legible but uninterpretable elements to be present; as a result, Full Legibility can be satisfied in more than one way. However, given that uninterpretable elements do not facilitate legibility, their number should be reduced as much as possible, and Full Legibility thus invokes simplicity measures that disfavor the presence of such elements. Since the set of legible elements differs for the level of representation (PF or LF) we are dealing with, the simplicity measures imposed on the output of the computational system may be in conflict: reduction of uninterpretable elements at LF may result in an increase of uninterpretable elements at PF, and vice versa. Zeijlstra claims that this may result in more than one 'optimal solution' and that languages may select different solutions as the grammatical option. He claims that the actual choice is determined by the ancestry/acquisition of the language in question: the simplicity measures select the simplest grammar *compatible with the target language* (which may also account for the fact that some languages seem to select a suboptimal solution). Zeijlstra thus agrees with traditional OT that the interpretative components impose conflicting violable constraints on the output representations of the generator without, however, using the OT-formalism of constraint ranking in his account of the selection of the grammatical candidates for a given language L.

Kleanthes Grohmann argues that the PF-component determines how the copies of movement are spelled out. The basic hypothesis is, however, that this is done by means of inviolable, universal conditions on the output representations: he divides the clause in three mutually exclusive domains (in which respectively the thematic, agreement and discourse information is expressed). He further shows that when the moved element and its copy are within the same domain, the latter must be phonetically expressed; in other configurations an 'elsewhere' condition requires deletion of the copy. Earlier work has shown that this proposal may account for a wide range of phenomena, but Grohmann also shows that there is a small range of facts in which the copy is unexpectedly spelled out due to the intervention of other 'independent constraints of the grammar'; cf. his (41b). It seems that such cases may be a good testing ground for some of the proposals discussed in this book.

Acknowledgments

The majority of studies collected in this book were papers presented at the workshops on *Descriptive and Empirical Adequacy* held in Berlin (December 2005) and Leiden (February 2008). We like to thank everyone who made these events possible as well as the contributors to the present book. We especially thank our assistants Ann-Christin Broschinski, Anna Kutscher, and George Moore, who did an amazing job in the final preparations of the manuscripts. Ben Hermans helped us with editing the manuscript by John McCarthy and Kathryn Pruitt.

We hope that this book will encourage people who are currently exclusively working in MP or OT to broaden their vision by also considering the possibilities that the alternative framework offers, and that this will stimulate further fruitful debate among proponents of the two frameworks. The research of Hans Broekhuis for this book was partly funded by a so-called VIDI-grant (2003-8) from the Netherlands Organization of Scientific Research (NWO).

References

Anderson, S. R. (2000) Towards an optimal account of second-position phenomena. In J. Dekkers, F. Van der Leeuw and J. Van de Weijer (eds) *Optimality Theory: Phonology, Syntax and Acquisition*, 302–33. Oxford: Oxford University Press.

Bobaljik, J. D. (2002) A-chains at the PF-interface: Copies and 'covert' movement. *Natural Language & Linguistic Theory* 20: 197–267.

Bresnan, J. (2000) Optimal syntax. In J. Dekkers, F. Van der Leeuw and J. Van de Weijer (eds) *Optimality Theory: Phonology, Syntax and Acquisition*, 334–85. Oxford: Oxford University Press.

Broekhuis, H. (2008) *Derivations and Evaluations: Object Shift in the Germanic Languages*. Berlin/New York: Mouton de Gruyter.

Broekhuis, H. and Dekkers, D. (2000) The minimalist program and optimality theory: Derivations and evaluations. In J. Dekkers, F. Van der Leeuw and J. Van de Weijer (eds) *Optimality Theory: Phonology, Syntax and Acquisition*, 386–422. Oxford/New York: Oxford University Press.

Chomsky, N. (1981) *Lectures on Government and Binding*. Dordrecht: Foris.

Chomsky, N. (1986) *Barriers*. Cambridge, MA: MIT Press.

Chomsky, N. (1991) Some notes on economy of derivation and representation. In R. Freidin (ed.) *Principles and Parameters in Comparative Syntax*, 417–54. Cambridge, MA: MIT Press.

Chomsky, N. (1995) *The Minimalist Program*. Cambridge, MA: MIT Press.

Chomsky, N. (2000) Minimalist inquiries: The framework. In R. Martin, D. Michaels and J. Uriagereka (eds) *Step by Step. Essays on Minimalist Syntax in Honor of Howard Lasnik*, 89–155. Cambridge, MA: MIT Press.

Chomsky, N. (2001) Derivation by phase. In M. Kenstowicz (ed.) *Ken Hale. A Life in Language*, 1–52. Cambridge, MA: MIT Press.

Chomsky, N. and Lasnik, H. (1977) Filters and control. *Linguistic Inquiry* 8: 425–504.

Dekkers, J. (1999) *Derivations & Evaluations. On the Syntax of Subjects and Complementizers*, Doctoral dissertation. University of Amsterdam/HIL.

Fox, D. and Pesetsky, D. (2005) Cyclic linearization of syntactic structure. *Theoretical Linguistics* 31: 1–45.

Frampton, J. and Gutmann, S. (2002) Crash-proof syntax. In S. D. Epstein and T. D.Seely (eds) *Derivations and Explanations in the Minimalist Program*, 90–105. Malden, MA and Oxford: Blackwell Publishing.

Grimshaw, J. (1997) Projection, heads and optimality. *Linguistic Inquiry* 28: 373–422.

Groat, E. and O'Neil, J. (1996) Spell-Out at the LF interface. In W. Abraham, S. D. Epstein and H. Thráinsson (eds) *Minimal Ideas. Syntactic Studies in the Minimalist Framework*, 113–39. Amsterdam and Philadelphia, PA: John Benjamins.

Holmberg, A. (1999) Remarks on Holmberg's generalization. *Studia Linguistica* 53: 1–39.

Kayne, R. (1994) *The Antisymmetry of Syntax*. Cambridge, MA: MIT Press.

Müller, G. (2000) Shape conservation and remnant movement. In A. Hirotani, N. Hall Coetzee and J.-Y. Kim (eds) *Proceedings of NELS 30*, 525–39. Amherst, MA: GLSA.

Müller, G. (2001) Order preservation, parallel movement, and the emergence of the unmarked. In G. Legendre, J. Grimshaw and S. Vikner (eds) *Optimality-theoretic Syntax*, 113–42. Cambridge, MA and London: MIT Press/MITWPL.

Pesetsky, D. (1997) Optimality theory and syntax: Movement and pronunciation. In D. Archangeli and T. Langendoen (eds) *Optimality Theory*, 134–70. Malden, MA and Oxford: Blackwell.

Pesetsky, D. (1998) Some optimality principles of sentence pronunciation. In P. Barbosa, D. Fox, P. Hagstrom, M. McGinnis and D. Pesetsky (eds) *Is the Best Good Enough?*, 337–83. Cambridge, MA and London: MIT Press/MITWPL.

Putnam, M. (2010) *Exploring Crash-proof Grammars*. Amsterdam: John Benjamins.

Rizzi, L. (1996) Residual Verb Second and the Wh criterion. In A. Belletti and L. Rizzi (eds) *Parameters and Functional Heads. Essays in Comparative Syntax*, 63–90. Oxford and New York: Oxford University Press.

Sells, P. (2001) *Structure Alignment and Optimality in Swedish*. Stanford, CA: CSLI Publications.

Vikner, S. (1994) Scandinavian object shift and West Germanic scrambling. In N. Corver and H. van Riemsdijk (eds) *Studies on Scrambling. Movement and Non-movement Approaches to Free Word-Order Phenomena*, 487–517. Berlin and New York: Mouton de Gruyter.

Vogel, R. (2004) Correspondence in OT syntax and minimal link effects. In G. Fanselow, A. Stepanov and R. Vogel (eds) *Minimality Effects in Syntax*, 401–42. Berlin: Mouton de Gruyter.

Vogel, R. (2006) The simple generator. In H. Broekhuis and R. Vogel (eds) *Optimality Theory and Minimalism: A Possible Convergence? Linguistics in Potsdam 25*, 99–136. Potsdam: University of Potsdam: http://www.ling.uni-potsdam.de/lip.

Woolford, E. (2007) Case locality: Pure domains and object shift. *Lingua* 117: 1591–616.

I COMBINING MP WITH AN OT-EVALUATION

2 Derivations and evaluations

Hans Broekhuis[*]

ABSTRACT This chapter departs from the observation that the minimalist framework and optimality theory adopt the same overall architecture of grammar (see also the Introduction): they both assume that a generator defines a set S of potentially well-formed expressions that can be generated on the basis of a given input, and that there is a filter component that selects the expressions from S that are actually grammatical in a given language L. This chapter proposes a hybrid model of grammar which combines the two frameworks: more specifically, it is argued that the computational system of human language C_{HL} from MP functions as the generator that creates the set S of potentially well-formed expressions, and that these are subsequently evaluated in an optimality-theoretic fashion. The properties of this hybrid model will be illustrated by means a discussion of object shift in Icelandic and Danish.

KEYWORDS minimalist program; optimality theory; derivation-and-evaluation model; object shift; verb movement; Icelandic; Danish

1. Introduction

This chapter describes and discusses the derivation-and-evaluation model in Figure 2.1. The central idea underlying this model is that developing an explanatorily and descriptively adequate theory of syntax requires that restrictions be formulated both on syntactic derivations and the resulting syntactic representations. This is obtained by assuming that the framework combines certain aspects of the minimalist program (MP) and optimality theory (OT). More specifically, it is assumed that representations created by some version of the computational system of human language C_{HL} from MP are evaluated in an OT-fashion.

One reason for seriously investigating the properties of the D&E model in Figure 2.1 and for being optimistic about its explanatory and descriptive adequacy lies in the insight that whereas MP has been especially successful in formulating a restrictive theory of narrow syntax, that is, the universal properties of grammar as encoded

---

* Hans Broekhuis, Meertens Institute, P.O.-box 94264, 1090 GG Amsterdam, The Netherlands. E-mail: hans.broekhuis@meertens.knaw.nl

in C_{HL}, OT has been very successful in describing variation between languages and the more peripheral, language-specific properties of languages.

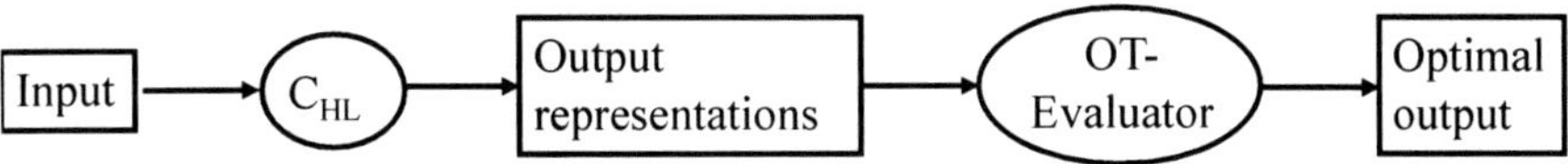

Figure 2.1 The derivation-and-evaluation (D&E) model.

The properties of the D&E model in Figure 2.1 will be illustrated by means of object shift in Icelandic and Danish, and I will therefore start with providing some of the basic facts that will be discussed in this chapter; the Icelandic data are taken from Holmberg (1986), Jónsson (1996) and Thráinsson (2001), and the Danish data come from Vikner (1994, 2006). The examples in (1) show that Icelandic allows object shift both with non-pronominal and pronominal noun phrases. Object shift of non-pronominal DPs depend on the information structure of the clause; it only applies when the object is part of the presupposition of the clause. Object shift of pronominal DPs is normally obligatory. The angled brackets in (1) indicate alternative placements of the object; an asterisk preceding the element(s) within these brackets indicates that that specific placement is not possible.

(1) (a) Jón las   <þessa bók>   ekki<þessa bók>.   [non-pronominal]
          Jón read   this book   not

     (b) Jón las   <hana>   ekki <*hana>.   [pronominal]
          Jón read   it   not

The examples in (2) show that Danish is more restricted than Icelandic in that it does not allow object shift of non-pronominal DPs. As in Icelandic, object shift of pronominal DPs is normally obligatory in Danish. Note that not all Scandinavian languages allow object shift; Finnish-Swedish, for example, does not; cf. Holmberg (1986).

(2) (a) Hvorfor læste studenterne <*artiklen> ikke <artiklen>?   [non-pronominal]
          why   read   the students   the article   not

     (b) Hvorfor læste studenterne <den> ikke <*den>?   [pronominal]
          why   read   the students   it   not

There are also a number of more general restrictions on Scandinavian object shift. The best-known one is probably Holmberg's Generalization, which in its original formulation states that object shift cannot apply across a main verb. The examples in (3) show that in Icelandic object shift of both pronominal and non-pronominal DPs is blocked by the past participle.

(3) (a) Jón hefur   <*bókina>   ekki   keypt <bókina>.   [Icelandic]
          Jón has   the book   not   bought

     (b) Nemendurnir   hafa   <*hana> ekki   lesið <hana>.   [Icelandic]
          the students   have   it   not   read

The examples in (4) show that the same holds for pronominal object shift in
Danish. We find the effect not only in perfect tense constructions like (4a) but also
in embedded clauses with simple tense given that Danish V-to-I is restricted to main
clauses; in embedded clauses the finite verb remains VP-internally.

(4) (a) Hvorfor har Peter <den>   aldrig   læst <*den>?   [Danish]
          why   has Peter it   never   read

     (b) Jeg spurgte   why   Peter <*den>   aldrig   [$_{VP}$ læste <den>].   [Danish]
          I   asked   why   Peter it   never   read

As Holmberg (1999) has pointed out, Holmberg's Generalization must be formulated such that it prohibits object shift across all VP-internal material; this means
that a non-shifted indirect object or a verbal particle will also block object shift of
a direct object. Since this will not be discussed here, I refer the reader to Broekhuis
(2008) for a more complete discussion of object shift within the D&E framework,
which also includes scrambling in languages like German and Dutch.

Chomsky (2001: 32) has argued that the interpretative effect of object shift in
Icelandic examples like (1a) shows that object shift takes place in narrow syntax.
He further assumes that the relevant configuration is as in (5), where *Obj* is the
θ-position of the object, and XP is a specifier position of *v** created by object shift.[1]

(5) ... [$_\alpha$ XP [Subject *v** [V ... Obj]]]

The observed facts above can in principle be accounted for by means of the set of
statements in (6); object shift is only possible when an object is part of the presupposition of the clause (INT) but would be wrongly construed as the focus of the clause
(INT′) in its *v**P-internal position as a result of the language-specific statement in (6c).
Observe that Chomsky's clause in (6a) refers to the output of the derivation and that
we are therefore dealing with an output filter; see Broekhuis (2008) and Broekhuis and
Vogel (this volume) for a more detailed discussion of Chomsky's proposal.

(6) (a) Movement is possible only if it has an effect on outcome.
     (b) The derived object position is assigned INT.
     (c) At the phonological border of *v**P, XP is assigned INT′.
          (i)   XP = DP   (Icelandic)
          (ii) XP = weak definite pronoun   (Danish)
          (iii) XP = ∅   (Swedish-Finnish)

In this chapter, I will provide an account of Scandinavian object shift in terms
of the D&E model in (1). I will assume that unvalued formal features optionally

trigger movement and that the generator will therefore produces a candidate set of representations with and without object shift, with and without verb movement, and so on. The candidate set thus formed will be the input of the evaluator, which will decide in an optimality-theoretic manner which candidate is selected as the optimal one in the given language. I hope to show that this gives rise to an analysis that is far superior to the proposal in (6) in terms of descriptive and explanatory adequacy.

2.   The derivation-and-evaluation model

This section discuss the properties of the D&E model in Figure 2.1 by providing an analysis of the Icelandic and Danish examples introduced in Section 1. The name of the model underlines the claim that the generator and the evaluator are equally important for providing descriptions and explanations of linguistic phenomena. The D&E model differs from the current versions of OT-syntax in that it adopts a version of C_{HL} as its generator, and it differs from MP in claiming that the output of C_{HL} is not evaluated by means of output filters of the sort in (6a) but in an optimality-theoretic fashion. Adopting the D&E model makes it necessary to seriously investigate the *interaction* between the generator and the evaluator: after all, when both the generator and the evaluator are to be taken seriously, they are expected to interact in intricate ways so that properties ascribed to the former may have far-reaching consequences for the design of the latter, and vice versa. Sections 2.1 and 2.2 will therefore discuss the generator and evaluator, respectively, and compare the D&E assumption with those normally adopted in MP and OT-syntax.

2.1   The generator

The derivation-and-evaluation model adopts the standard assumption from MP that the computational system C_{HL} is universal and consists of operations that are conceptually necessary, such as the two incarnations of the merge operation, internal and external merge. Furthermore, D&E adopts the claim that these operations are subject to inviolable conditions: movement, for example, must satisfy the Last Resort Condition, according to which movement of a syntactic object S must be triggered by some unchecked or unvalued formal feature of a higher functional head H that can be valued by a corresponding feature of S.

The main difference between D&E and the 'standard' versions of MP is that the former assumes that C_{HL} is not parameterized: more specifically, it is assumed that there are no strength/EPP-features that may force or block the application of a certain operation, and neither can an operation be blocked by the availability of an inherently more economical option; see Broekhuis and Klooster (2007), who show that there is no general preference for external over internal merge. At any point P in the derivation, C_{HL} may choose at random between applying or not applying the operations that satisfy the Last Resort Condition at P. Consequently, the number of

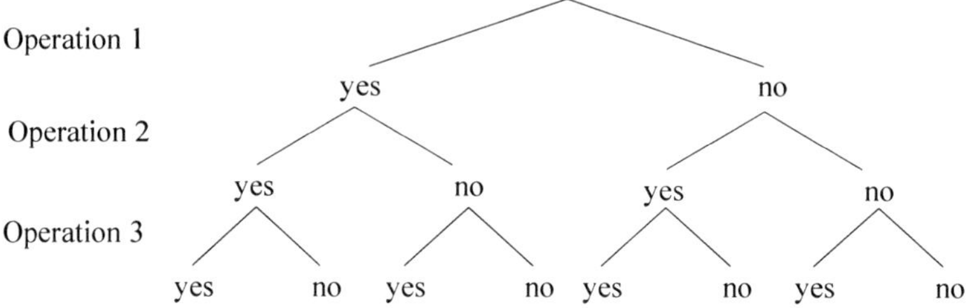

Figure 2.2 The construction of the candidate set.

candidates in the candidate set is at most 2^n, where n is the number of movement operations that satisfy Last Resort: see Figure 2.2.

C_{HL} thus defines a candidate set that contains a limited number of candidates. Of course, the effects of the strength/EPP-features must be mimicked in some way, but Chomsky's (2001) effect-on-output condition in (6a) in effect already determines whether certain movements may or may not apply, so that it makes the EPP-features superfluous. We may therefore conclude that, as far as the generator is concerned, the D&E model in Figure 2.1 comes very close to the more current versions of MP; see Broekhuis (2008) and Broekhuis and Vogel (this volume) for more detailed discussion.

Although the claim that C_{HL} functions as generator in the D&E model is fully in line with the requirement in McCarthy and Prince (1993) that the OT-generator consists of linguistic operations subject to 'very general considerations of structural well-formedness', D&E does not comply with the standard assumption in OT that the OT-generator generates an in principle infinite number of candidates; the claim here that the operations of the generator licensed by the Last Resort Condition can in principle be optionally applied results in candidate sets that are in fact very small.[2] By way of illustration, (7a,b) provide the maximum size of the candidate sets for derivations with respectively 8 and 16 movement operations that satisfy Last Resort. Actually, it is even possible to reduce these numbers much further by adopting some version of phase theory. This is shown in (7a′,b′).

(7) The size of the candidate set:
    (a) 8 operations: $2^8 = 256$
    (a′) 8 operations in 2 phases of 4 operations each: $2 \times 2^4 = 32$
    (b) 16 operations: $2^{16} = 65.536$
    (b′) 16 operations in 4 phases of 4 operations each: $4 \times 2^4 = 64$

I believe that this break with the OT-tradition is also advantageous from the OT point of view. First, of course, C_{HL} can be invoked to provide a non-*ad hoc* account for the truly universal properties of languages, which the OT-evaluator by its very nature is not able to give. Second, since part of the descriptive burden is now placed on the generator, we may hope that this will enable us to considerably reduce *the number of constraints* in the universal constraint set CON. This, in turn, will result in a dramatic decrease of *the number of constraint rankings*, and, consequently, of the number of possible natural languages defined by the model; this may also narrow down the range of predicted typological variation, although it must be kept in mind that different constraint rankings may give rise to typologically identical languages (see the discussion of Table 1 in section 2.3). Third, the fact that C_{HL} does not only limit the candidate set, but also the *types of differences* that can be found among the candidates in this set, which are defined by the application or non-application of the operations of C_{HL}, suggests that it will be possible to also reduce *the number of constraint types*, and, consequently, also the ways in which natural languages can differ from each other. It goes without saying that all these consequences contribute to considerably enhancing the explanatory adequacy of OT-syntax.[3]

2.2   The evaluator

The previous subsection has already mentioned that the D&E model implies that the EPP-features should be eliminated by attributing the intended effects of these features to the evaluator. From the point of view of MP, this step seems quite natural since output filter (6) introduced in Chomsky (2001) actually suffices to determine whether certain movements may or may not apply. A general problem with output filters of this sort is, however, that they tend to take the form of *ad hoc* stipulations that simply reformulate descriptive generalizations or the description of certain states of affairs in a semi-formal language; cf. the language-specific stipulations in (6c). Since it is not obvious that this will lead to any deeper insights, the D&E framework adopts the idea that filters should be subject to further investigation, and be derived from more primitive notions of the theory. It further assumes that this is precisely what OT does: work by Pesetsky (1997; 1998) and Dekkers (1999) has already shown that at least some of the filters from Chomsky and Lasnik (1977) may receive a natural explanation in this way, and this section will show that the language-specific part of Chomsky's output filter in (6c) can also be expressed by means of the interaction of a small set of more primitive constraints; cf. Costa (1998) and Broekhuis (2000).

The previous section has also argued that by adopting C_{HL} as the generator, the OT-evaluator can be considerably simplified: since the inviolable conditions on the operations of the generator carry part of the descriptive burden, we may expect a reduction of the number of constraints that are part of CON, and since the candidates in the candidate set only differ from each other in a small number of well-defined ways, we may also expect the number of constraint types to be rather small.

In order to get some idea about the syntactic constraints and constraint types that we may expect, I will adopt as my point of departure the proposal that the OT-evaluator is a formalization of the interface conditions postulated in MP. If that is indeed so, we expect the syntactic constraints in CON to be somehow related to three components involved: the computational system C_{HL}, which creates the relevant syntactic representations in the candidate set, and the two interpretive systems that interpret them, namely the articulatory-perceptual and the conceptual-intentional component. Let us therefore assume that the syntactic constraints in CON can be divided into the two basic types in (8).

(8) The syntactic constraints in CON are of two basic types:
    (a) C_{HL} constraints
    (b) Interface (PF and LF) constraints

Before I discuss these constraint types, I want to point out that, in my view, it is not only desirable to restrict the number and kind, but also the possible *format* of the constraints. I will therefore adopt Eisner's (1999) proposal that there are basically two formal types of constraints, which should be formulated as positive or negative generic statements. Good examples of positive generic statements are the EPP-constraints in (11) below, which require that all probes attract their goal, and a good example of a negative generic statement is *Move, which bans movement of any kind. Furthermore, I will assume that the formulation of the constraints is simple in the sense that connectives like *and, or, unless,* and so on cannot be used.

2.2.1 C_{HL} constraints

The D&E framework assumes that the application of the operations of the generator is essentially free. Nevertheless, it is clear that most languages exhibit strict restrictions on the application of these operations. A good example of this is object shift: languages like Icelandic have it, whereas Finnish-Swedish does not. Given that the generator is universal and cannot be parameterized, it must be the evaluator that penalizes the application of this movement. Therefore, we must postulate a set of constraints that favor non-application of the operations of C_{HL}, which I will henceforth refer to as *economy constraints*.

A first example of such an economy constraint is STAY, which I prefer to call *MOVE in order to highlight the fact that it is a negative generic statement: *MOVE forbids internal merge, and thus militates against superfluous movement steps in the derivation. Assuming this constraint seems uncontroversial: it is assumed in most work in OT-syntax, and it has its MP counterpart in the claim that movement is a costly operation. In the early MP period, this claim has played a crucial role in the formulation of principles like Procrastinate and Fewest Steps, and it has survived in the later period in the form of the proposal that movement is licit only when an EPP-feature is present.

It has been proposed that the economy constraints on movement may take a more specific form. Grimshaw (1997), for example, proposes the constraint NO LEXICAL MOVEMENT (NOLEXM), which disfavors movement of the lexical (θ-role assigning) verbs.

(9) NOLEXM: don't move lexical (θ-role assigning) verbs.

This constraint is a reformulation of Pollock's (1989) account of the contrast between the English and French examples in (10), which prohibited movement of lexical verbs to weak AGR-phrases: English has a weak AGR, and therefore movement of a lexical (but not an auxiliary or a modal) verb is blocked; French has a strong AGR, and consequently movement of a lexical (as well as an auxiliary or a modal) verb is possible. For a discussion of how NOLEXM may derive contrasts of this sort, I refer the reader to Section 2.3.

(10) (a) John <*kisses>   often   <kisses>   Mary.
    (b) Jean <embrasse>   souvent   <*embrasse>   Marie.

Since economy constraints like *MOVE block the application of the operations of the generator (here: internal merge), we must also introduce means that allow or force the operations of C_{HL} to apply. Therefore, we have to postulate additional constraints that favor movement, so that the relative ranking of these constraints and the economy constraint *MOVE will determine whether a certain movement does or does not take place. Of course, we want to restrict the class of constraints that force movement as much as possible. In order to obtain this let us assume that all probes prefer movement of their goal into their local domain.[4] The assumption that *all* probes prefer to be in a local relationship with their goal means that, in a certain sense, we are generalizing the EPP to all unvalued features. The general form of the EPP constraints is therefore as given in (11), and states that movement of a goal into the local domain of its probe is required. Consequently, if the goal of probe F is an XP, this constraint forces it to move into a specifier of the head that has F as its sublabel, and, if the goal is a head, it will be adjoined to the head that has F as its sublabel. Potential specific instantiations of the 'generalized' EPP constraint, which will play a key role in the analysis of object shift in this study, are given in (11a–c). The constraints EPP(case) and EPP(φ) require movement of a DP into the specifier of a head containing unvalued case or φ-features, and EPP(tense) requires head-movement of the finite verb to T. Note in passing that the number of EPP constraints cannot be larger than the number of unvalued formal features that are postulated in the grammar. The formal features therefore set an outer bound on the set of possible natural languages defined by the D&E framework.[5]

(11) EPP(F): probe F attracts its goal.
    (a) EPP(case): an unvalued case feature attracts its goal.
    (b) EPP(φ): unvalued φ-features attract their goal.
    (c) EPP(tense): an unvalued tense feature attracts its goal.
    (d) etc.

Word order variation between languages is accounted for by assuming that the EPP constraints interact in an optimality-theoretic fashion with the economy constraints. Ranking (12a) expresses that probe F (normally) does not trigger movement due to the fact that the EPP constraint is outranked by the economy constraint *MOVE: this ranking will be called 'weak', since it is more or less equivalent to assuming that probe F is weak or has no EPP-feature associated with it. Ranking (12b), on the other hand, expresses that probe F (normally) does trigger movement due to the fact that that the EPP constraint outranks the economy constraint *MOVE: this ranking will be called 'strong', since it is more or less equivalent to assuming that probe F is strong or has an EPP-feature associated with it. The choice between the weak and the strong ranking of a certain EPP constraint constitutes one of the ways in which languages can be parameterized.

(12) (a) Weak ranking: *MOVE >> EPP(F)
    (b) Strong ranking: EPP(F) >> *MOVE

The contrast in (13) constitutes a concrete example of what one may call a macro-parameter. If we assume that object shift is triggered by the case features on $v*$ (cf. Vikner 1994; Broekhuis 2000; Chomsky 2001; and many others), the two subrankings distinguish between languages with full object shift like Icelandic and languages without object shift like Finnish-Swedish.

(13) (a) *MOVE >> EPP(case): object shift is (normally) blocked.
        (b) EPP(case) >> *MOVE: object shift (normally) applies.

Of course, we have seen that object shift is much more complicated than this, and this is where the interface constraints come in.

2.2.2 The interface (PF and LF) constraints

One of the disadvantages of early MP was that the postulation of feature strength or the association of an EPP-feature with certain formal features gave rise to a very rigid system: if a certain formal feature is assumed to be strong or to be associated with an EPP-feature, it is predicted that it invariably triggers movement; if a certain formal feature is assumed to be weak or not to be associated with an EPP-feature, Procrastinate predicts that the pertinent movement is invariably blocked. As we have seen above, Chomsky (2001) has tried to make the system more flexible by making the selection of the EPP-features dependent on semantic and phonological factors. The three statements in (14), ultimately have the effect that $v*$ is only assigned an EPP-feature (a) when the object is assigned the interpretation INT (= is part of the presupposition of the clause), and (b) when the object is at the phonological border of $v*$P, that is, when object shift does not result in crossing $v*$P-internal material.

(14) (a) $v*$ is assigned an EPP-feature only if that has an effect on outcome.
        (b) The EPP position of $v*$ is assigned INT.
        (c) At the phonological border of $v*$P, XP is assigned INT′.

The clause in (14c) makes the postulation of EPP-features superfluous given that an XP at the phonological border of $v*$P must be moved in order to be assigned the interpretation INT; see Broekhuis (2008) and Broekhuis and Vogel (this volume) for more detailed discussion. This means that we can simply replace (14a) by the assumption that movement is optional in principle but subject to the effect-on-output condition in (15a). Further, Chomsky (2001) claims that the statement in (14c) is a binary parameter: object shift languages have it, whereas non-object shift languages do not. We have seen, however, that the parameter in (14c) does not suffice, since some languages like Danish have limited object shift with weak definite pronouns. This means that (14c) must be further refined as in (15c).

(15) (a) Movement is possible only if it has an effect on outcome.
        (b) The derived object position is assigned INT.
        (c) At the phonological border of $v*$P, XP is assigned INT′.

    (i) XP = DP   (Icelandic)
    (ii) XP = weak definite pronoun   (Danish)
    (iii) XP = ∅   (Romance)

Macro-parameters in the format of (12) introduce the same kind of flexibility as output filters like (15c). Although movement is normally blocked under the weak ranking in (12a), movement can be forced provided that there is some higher ranked constraint A that favors this movement (cf. (16a)); in the terminology of Chomsky (1995: ch.3), one might say that constraint A overrules 'Procrastinate'. Similarly, although movement is normally forced under the strong ranking in (12b), it can be blocked if there is some higher ranked constraint B that disfavors it (cf. (16b)); in other words, constraint B overrules 'Strength'.

   (16) (a) A >> *MOVE >> EPP(F) ⇒ if A favors movement, 'Procrastinate' is overruled.
         (b) B >> EPP(F) >> *MOVE ⇒ if B disfavors movement, 'Strength' is overruled.

The claim that I want to make here is that it is the function of the interface constraints to overrule macro-parameters of the type in (12). The remainder of this section will illustrate this more specifically for the macro-parameter in (13).

The examples in (2), repeated here as (17), show that Danish has object shift of a more limited type than Icelandic: although non-pronominal DPs do not shift, definite pronouns normally do.

   (17) (a) Hvorfor læste studenterne <*artiklen> ikke <artiklen>?   [non-pronominal]
              why   read   the students the article   not

         (b) Hvorfor læste studenterne <den> ikke <*den>?   [pronominal]
              why   read   the students it   not

This can be accounted for by assuming that Danish has the weak ranking *MOVE >> EPP(case) in (13a), but that this weak ranking is overruled by a constraint that requires weak definite pronouns to be *v*P-external. The claim that there is a restriction of this sort on the placement of pronouns is not new: Diesing (1997: 380), for example, claims that definite pronouns are variables that due to their definiteness cannot remain within the nuclear scope of the clause (VP), and Vogel (2006) has argued that weak pronouns must leave the VP for phonological reasons. Let us assume that something of the sort is indeed the case, and postulate the clash constraint D-PRONOUN in (18a), which requires that definite/weak pronouns be *v*P-external. The fact that Danish has object shift with definite pronouns only can now be accounted for by assuming the ranking in (18b).

   (18) (a) D-PRONOUN: *[$_{vP}$ ... pron$_{[+weak/def]}$ ...].

         (b) Danish: D-PRONOUN >> *MOVE >> EPP(case)

This is shown by the evaluations of the examples in (17) in tableaux T1 and T2. T1 shows that object shift gives rise to a fatal violation of *move in case of a non-pronominal DP, and T2 that object shift is required in case of a non-pronominal DP in order to avoid a fatal violation of d-pronoun.

T1 Danish (no object shift of non-pronominal DPs)

	D-PRONOUN	*MOVE	EPP(case)
Hvorfor læste studenterne ikke artiklen? ☞			*
Hvorfor læste studenterne artiklen$_i$ ikke t_i		*!	

T2 Danish (*obligatory* pronoun shift)

	D-PRONOUN	*MOVE	EPP(case)
Hvorfor læste studenterne ikke den	*!		*
Hvorfor læste studenterne den$_i$ ikke t_i ☞		*	

The subranking D-PRONOUN $\gg$ *MOVE can again be seen as a macro-parameter which divides languages without full object shift into languages that do and languages that do not allow pronoun shift. This shows that the constraints we have introduced so far successfully account for the division postulated by the three clauses in (15ci–iii). Observe that the ranking of D-PRONOUN and *MOVE is immaterial for the full object shift languages, since movement of the pronoun is already forced by the strong ranking of EPP(case): see Figure 2.3.

The semantic conditions on the application of object shift in Icelandic can also be taken care of by means of an interface constraint. The examples in (19) make explicit that object shift is normally obligatory in Icelandic, but blocked when the object is part of the focus (new information) of the clause.

(19) (a) Jón keypti   ekki   bókina.   *bókina* $\subset$ focus
          Jón bought   not   the book

      (b) Jón keypti bókina$_i$ ekki t_i *bókina* $\subset$ presupposition

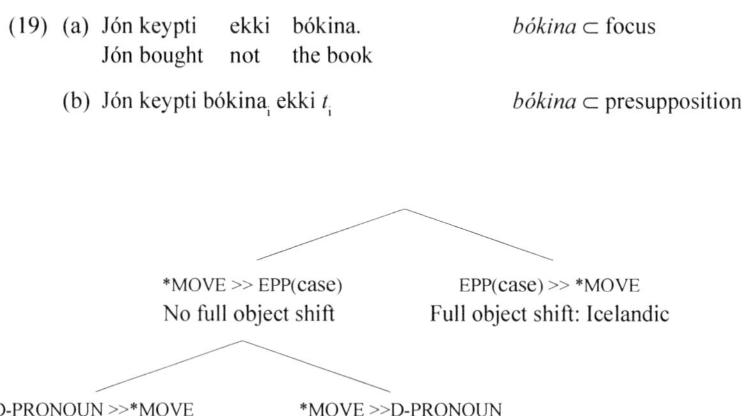

Figure 2.3 Macro-parameterization of languages with respect to object shift.

When we adopt the constraint ALIGNFOCUS in (20a) from Costa (1998) and rank it above EPP(case), we will derive the desired result.[6]

(20) (a) ALIGNFOCUS (AF): the prosodically unmarked focus is the rightmost constituent in its clause.
      (b) Icelandic: ALIGNFOCUS >> EPP(case) >> *MOVE

The ranking in (20b) correctly predicts that all object DPs must undergo object shift, unless they are part of the focus of the clause: object shift of a non-presuppositional object across some other phonetically realized constituent like *ekki* in (19) is excluded. The evaluations of the examples in (19) are given in the tableaux T3 and T4. T3 shows that alignfocus is not relevant when the object is part of the presupposition of the clause, and that object shift is therefore forced by the strong ranking epp(case) >> *move.

T3 Icelandic (object not in focus)

		AF	EPP(case)	*MOVE
Jón keypti ekki bókina			*!	
Jón keypti bókina$_i$ ekki t_i ☞				*

T4, on the other hand, shows that when the object is part of the focus of the clause object shift is blocked in order to avoid a fatal violation of ALIGNFOCUS.

T4 Icelandic (object in focus)

		AF	EPP(case)	*MOVE
Jón keypti ekki bókina ☞			*	
Jón keypti bókina$_i$ ekki t_i		*!		*

The discussion above has shown that we can appeal to the interface constraint D-PRONOUN in (18a) to account for the fact that some languages that do not have full object shift nevertheless exhibit pronoun shift. And by introducing the interface constraint ALIGNFOCUS we are able to account for the fact that object shift is sometimes blocked in languages that normally do have full object shift. By introducing these constraints, we account for almost the same range of data as (15); the only thing that we have not accounted for yet is Holmberg's Generalization, that is, the fact that object shift cannot cross v*P-internal material; cf. the Icelandic and Danish example in (21), repeated in a slightly different form from Section 1.

(21) (a) Jón hefur ekki   keypt   bókina.
           Jón has   not   bought   the book
      (a′) *Jón hefur bókina ekki keypt t_{bokina}

    (b) Hvarfor   har   Peter aldrig   læst   den?
         why   has   Peter never   read   it
         'Why has Peter never read it?'
    (b′) *Hvarfor har Peter den aldrig læst t_{den}?

In order to account for Holmberg's Generalization, I will appeal to a number of PF constraints involving linearization. Since these constraints effectively require that the underlying order of heads and arguments be maintained in the surface realization, I will refer to these as *order preservation constraints*. Two examples of such constraints are given in (22).

(22) **Order preservation (PF) constraints** (do not change the base order):
     (a) Relativized Minimality (RELMIN): X-movement retains the relative order of elements in X-positions, where X = A, A′ or H.
     (b) HEAD-COMPL: a head precedes all terminals originally dominated by its complement.

The constraint RELMIN in (22a) is of course a direct descendant of the most influential 'order preservation' principle from the earlier *principles-and-parameters* period, Rizzi's (1990) Relativized Minimality, and is rephrased here as a constraint on the output of the generator.[7] Although this will not be illustrated here, this constraint plays an important role in prohibiting object shift of a direct object across an indirect object. When we adopt Kayne's (1994) original conjecture that all languages have an underlying head-complement order, the constraint HEAD-COMPL in (22b) can also be construed as an order preservation constraint.[8] It disfavors object shift across the main verb because this results in a surface order that differs from the underlying order. Consequently, by assuming that HEAD-COMPL outranks the constraints that favor object shift, as in (23), object shift will be blocked in the examples in (21).

(23) (a) Icelandic: HEAD-COMPL <> ALIGNFOCUS >> EPP(case) >> *MOVE
     (b) Danish: HEAD-COMPL >> D-PRONOUN >> *MOVE >> EPP(case)

The evaluation of the Icelandic examples in (21a,a′) is given in T5; the use of '<>' in the ranking and the dotted line in the tableau indicate that the relative ranking of head-compl and alignfocus cannot be determined on the basis of the present set of data, since object shift in (21) will be blocked irrespective of whether the object belongs to the focus of the clause or not, that is, whether the star between parentheses is present or not.

T5 Icelandic (no object shift in complex tense constructions)

	HEAD-COMPL	AF	EPP(case)	*MOVE
Jón hefur ekki keypt bókina ☞			*	
Jón hefur bókina$_i$ ekki keypt t_i	*!	(*!)		*

The evaluation of the Danish examples in (21b,b′) is given in T6; violation of D-PRONOUN is allowed since it enables us to satisfy the higher ranked constraint HEAD-COMPL.

T6 Danish (no object shift in complex tense constructions)

	HEAD-COMPL	D-PRONOUN	EPP(case)	*MOVE
Hvarfor har Peter aldrig læst den? ☞		*	*	
Hvarfor har Peter den aldrig læst t_{den}?	*!			*

By introducing the interface constraints D-PRONOUN, ALIGNFOCUS and HEAD-COMPL the present proposal accounts for the same range of facts as the set of claims in (15). There are, however, a number of reasons to prefer the present constraint approach to an approach that appeals to output filters. First, filters tend to take the form of *ad hoc* stipulations that simply reformulate descriptive generalizations or the description of certain states of affairs in a semi-formal language, and it is not obvious that this will lead to any deeper insights. The constraint approach, on the other hand, derives these generalizations from more primitive notions of the theory, and may therefore highlight the linguistic properties that are really at stake. The constraint *MOVE, for example, may be motivated by the wish to make the thematic relations between heads and their arguments visible, whereas the EPP constraints in (11) may instead be motivated by the wish to make the Agree relations visible. Constraint like ALIGNFOCUS and D-PRONOUN can be motivated by the wish to make the information structure of the clause visible, and the order preservation constraints may be motivated by the wish to optimize parsability. In short, it should be possible in principle to ground the simple syntactic constraints proposed in the discussion above, whereas it is much less likely that this is possible with the more complex filters. Second, the constraint (but not the filter) approach makes very precise predictions about what types of natural languages are possible. The postulation of HEAD-COMPL, for example, predicts that there are also languages in which EPP(case) outranks HEAD-COMPL, and which therefore do not obey Holmberg's Generalization but allow object shift across the verb; languages like Dutch and German are of this type. Third, the constraint approach (but not the filter approach) provides us with a general format for approaching other word order phenomena, as well as with the means to express directly that certain movements (or the lack thereof) are motivated by properties of the interpretive (articulatory-perceptual and conceptual-intentional) components of the grammar. And last but not least, the following section will show that the constraint approach leads to new questions which could not arise under the traditional approach.

2.3 The interaction of object shift and verb movement

The high positions of H-COMPL in the rankings in (23) does not only account for the fact that object shift is excluded in complex verb constructions, but also for the contrast between the examples in (24), which show that whereas Icelandic allows object shift in embedded clauses, Danish does not. This contrast is related to a difference in verb movement between Icelandic and Danish. The fact that the finite verb precedes adverbial phrases like *aldrei* 'never' in (24a) shows that the finite verb undergoes V-to-I in embedded clauses in Icelandic; as a result, object shift will satisfy H-COMPL and is thus correctly predicted to be possible. The fact that the finite verb follows adverbials like *aldrig* 'never' in (24b) shows that the finite verb does not undergo V-to-I in embedded clauses in Danish; as a result, object shift will violate H-COMPL and is thus correctly predicted to be impossible.

(24) (a) Éf spurði af hverju Pétur læsi <þessa bók> aldrei t_v <þessa bók>
      I asked why Pétur read this book never   [Icelandic]

   (b) Jeg spurgte hvorfor Peter <*den> aldrig læste <den >
      I asked why Peter it never read   [Danish]

The fact that Danish pronominal object shift can only occur in main clauses, as shown by the contrast between the Danish examples in (21b) and (24b), can therefore be related to the fact that Danish is an asymmetric V2-language.

It is important to note that this conclusion is only sound when V-movement applies in narrow syntax (contra Chomsky (2004), and especially Boeckx and Stjepanovic (2001), who have claimed that head-movement in general is a PF phenomenon). A simple and in my view conclusive argument in favor of syntactic verb movement can be based on the fact discussed earlier that Icelandic object shift is sensitive to the information structure of the clause. Chomsky (2001) concluded from this that object shift must be construed as part of narrow syntax given that 'displacement rules interspersed in the phonological component should have little semantic effect'. Since Scandinavian object shift cannot apply when the main verb remains in v*P-internal position, it follows immediately that V-to-I must also be a rule of narrow syntax; see also Den Dikken (2006, 2007).

In earlier accounts of Holmberg's Generalization, the observation that V-to-I must apply in order to licence object shift was generally the end of the story, whereas in the present approach it can be no more than half of the story given that there are in principle two ways in which H-COMPL could be satisfied: the first way is the one illustrated in (24b), where object shift is *blocked* by the v*P-internal verb; the second way would be a case in which the verb is actually *pushed up* into the I-position by pronominal object shift. A full account of Holmberg's Generalization thus requires an explanation of the fact that Danish does not employ the push-up option in embedded clauses. In order to account for this, we first have to provide an analysis of V-to-I. The constraints that we will use for this are given in (25).

(25) (a) *STRAY FEATURE: formal features of the functional heads are amalgamated with the root they are associated with.
   (b) LEXICALLY FILL TOP F (LFTF): the highest head position in an extended projection is lexically filled.
   (c) NOLEXM: a θ-role assigning head remains in its θ-domain (a main verb does not move).

The constraint *STRAY FEATURE is a generalized version of the EPP-constraints involved in head movement: instead of postulating separate constraints like EPP(tense) or EPP(aspect), we simply require that the formal features in the extended projection of the verb (or other lexical categories) amalgamate with their lexical associate. The relative ranking of *STRAY FEATURE and *MOVE therefore determines whether the verbal root V will move into the higher functional heads (like *v* or I) in its extended projection.

The constraint LEXICALLY FILL TOP F can be held responsible for the asymmetric V2-property of languages like Danish: LFTF >> *MOVE >> *STRAY FEATURE predicts that in the absence of a complementizer the verb must be moved into the highest functional projection in the extended projection of the verb, whereas it will remain in situ otherwise.[9] When we further assume that complementizers must be selected, and can therefore only appear in embedded clauses, it will follow that V2 must apply in main clauses (and in embedded clauses that are complementizer-less for one reason or other).

The third constraint, NOLEXM, is adapted from Grimshaw (1997) and goes back at least to Pollock (1989): its role is to block movement of main verbs, while still allowing movement of auxiliary and modal verbs, and it is used to account for the fact that in English V-to-I is restricted to modal and auxiliary verbs, that is, cannot apply to main verbs; see the discussion of (10) above.

The three constraints in (25) in tandem with the general economy constraint *MOVE suffice to provide a basic typology of V-to-I by defining 24 different languages of six typologically different kinds.

Table 2.1 V-to-I in the Germanic languages.

Ranking	#24	Main clauses	Embedded clauses	Example
1 *MOVE >> {*STRAY FEATURE, LFTF}; ranking NOLEXM not relevant	8	–	–	Japanese
2 LFTF >> *MOVE >> *STRAY FEATURE; LFTF >> NOLEXM	3	+	–	Danish
3 NOLEXM >> LFTF >> *MOVE >> *STRAY FEATURE	1	aux only	–	Proto-Germanic
4 *STRAY FEATURE >> {*MOVE, NOLEXM}; ranking LFTF not relevant	8	+	+	Icelandic
5 NOLEXM >> *STRAY FEATURE >> *MOVE; NOLEXM >> LFTF	3	aux only	aux only	English
6 LFTF >> NOLEXM >> *STRAY FEATURE >> *MOVE	1	+	aux only	Proto-Indo-European

The first type arises when *MOVE outranks the two constraints that favor V-to-I, *STRAY FEATURE and LEXICALLY FILL TOP F, and is characterized by having no V-to-I at all; OV-languages like Japanese may be good examples of this type.

The second and the third types are languages with V2 in main clauses only. The weak ranking of *STRAY FEATURE blocks V-to–I in embedded clauses, whereas the ranking of LFTF above *MOVE forces V-to-I in main clauses. The second and the third type differ in the relative ranking of NOLEXM and LFTF. The third type has the subranking NOLEXM >> LFTF and therefore allows V2 with auxiliary and modal verbs only; reconstructed Proto-Germanic has been claimed to be of this type (cf. Fortson 2004; Dewey 2006). The second type has the subranking LFTF >> NOLEXM, and allows V2 in main clauses with all verbs; Danish and Swedish as well as the Germanic OV-languages are examples of this type.

The fourth type arises when *STRAY FEATURE outranks the constraints that disfavor movement, NOLEXM and *MOVE, and is defined by allowing V-to-I with all finite verbs in all contexts. This type is instantiated by Icelandic.

The fifth and the sixth type arise when we have a strong ranking of *STRAY FEATURE, but NOLEXM outranks *STRAY FEATURE. This results in languages that normally have V-to-I with auxiliary and modal verbs only. The two types differ in the relative ranking of NOLEXM and LEXICALLY FILL TOP F. When the former outranks the latter, V-to-I is restricted to auxiliary and modal verbs in all contexts: English is an example of this type. On the subranking LEXICALLY FILL TOP F >> NOLEXM, V-to-I of main verbs is restricted to main clauses, whereas aux-to-I may apply in all contexts; reconstructed Proto-Indo-European has been claimed to exhibit this behavior (cf. Fortson 2004; Dewey 2006).

Let us now return to the question why Danish has the pattern in (26a) without pronominal object shift and embedded V-to-I, rather than that in (26b) with pronominal object shift and embedded V-to-I.

(26) (a) Jeg spurgte hvorfor Peter aldrig læste den.
          I   asked   why   Peter never   read   it

      (b) Jeg spurgte hvorfor Peter læste   den   aldrig $t_{\mathrm{V}}\, t_{\mathrm{den}}$.
          I   asked   why   Peter read   it   never

This question can now be answered by having a better look at the subrankings independently established so far. We have seen that the subranking in (23b), repeated here as (27a), correctly accounts for the following two facts: Danish only has pronominal object shift and pronominal object shift is blocked in complex verb construction by the non-finite main verb. The discussion of Table 1 has further shown that the subrankings in (27b,c) account for the fact that V-to-I is restricted to main clauses.

(27) (a) H-COMPL >> D-PRONOUN >> *MOVE >> EPP(case)
      (b) LFTF >> *MOVE >> *STRAY FEATURE
      (c) LFTF >> NOLEXM

The question why Danish opts for the blocking of object shift in (26a) instead of push-up of the finite main verbs in (26b) must be answered by appealing to the interaction of the independently motivated constraints in (27). The two obvious candidates that could handle this are D-PRONOUN and NOLEXM, given that the former favors pronominal object shift and the latter disfavors movement of main verbs: the subranking D-PRONOUN >> NOLEXM predicts that pronominal object shift would push up the finite main verb into I, whereas the subranking NOLEXM >> D-PRONOUN predicts that the main verb would block pronominal object shift. From this we may conclude that Danish has the subranking NOLEXM >> D-PRONOUN. When we assume that Danish has the ranking in T7, where the dashed lines indicate that the constraints cannot be ordered yet on the basis of the data discussed so far, we will get the desired result. Note that LEXICALLY FILL TOP F is trivially satisfied in all examples by the phonetically empty, but lexically realized, complementizer of the embedded clause; cf. fn. 9.

T7 V-to-I and pronominal object shift in Danish embedded clauses

	H-COMPL	LFTF	NOLEXM	D-PRONOUN	*MOVE	*STRAYF	EPP(case)
☞ no pronominal OS no V-to-I				*		*	*
pronominal OS no V-to-I	*!				*	*	
no pronominal OS V-to-I			*!	*	*		*
pronominal OS V-to-I			*!		**		

For completeness' sake note that the suggestion in T7 that H-COMPL outranks NOLEXM has not been established yet. In Broekhuis (2008), I argued that next to the type of object shift discussed in this chapter, which I refer to as regular object shift, there is second type of object shift, which I refer to as short object shift and which is triggered by the φ-features on the verbal root V. The latter (which can be identified with the type of object movement identified for English by Johnson (1991) and Lasnik (1999a: ch. 2/8)) does have the property of forcing V-to-*v* in Danish. This can be accounting for by assuming that the constraint EPP(φ), which is responsible for short object shift, is ranked between H-COMPL and NOLEXM. Since I do not have the space here to discuss short object shift, I refer the reader to Broekhuis (2008) for detailed discussion.

2.4 Conclusion

This section has shown that replacing output filters, which have been an (often tacitly assumed but nevertheless) inherent part of the *principles-and-parameters* framework for over the last 30 years, by an optimality-theoretic evaluation results in a grammatical system with entirely different properties. The resulting D&E model is better equipped to capture language variation than the current minimalist approaches and is also readily able to account for apparently optional movements like Scandinavian object shift. Furthermore, I have shown by means of a discussion of the interaction between object shift and verb movement that the postulation of an optimality-theoretic evaluation also leads to new questions due to the fact that constraints proposed for different empirical domains may interact in unexpected ways.

3. Summary

This chapter has provided an updated version of the derivation-and-evaluation (D&E) framework originally proposed in Broekhuis and Dekkers (2000) and Broekhuis (2000). The leading idea of the framework is that, in order to arrive at a descriptively and explanatorily adequate theory, restrictions must be placed both on the syntactic derivation and the resulting syntactic representations. This has been given shape by assuming a framework in which aspects of the minimalist program (MP) and optimality theory (OT) are combined. More specifically, it was claimed that representations created by some version of the computational system of human

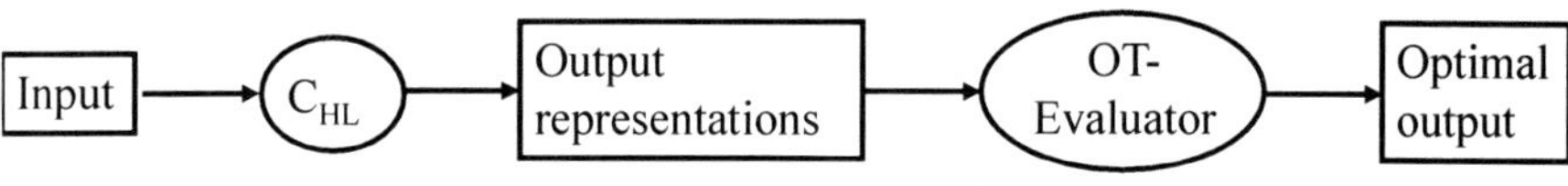

Figure 2.1 The derivation-and-evaluation (D&E) model.

language C_{HL} from MP are evaluated in an optimality theoretic fashion, as indicated in Figure 2.1, repeated below.

In MP and OT-syntax the explanatory burden is normally placed on the generator and the evaluator, respectively. By placing the explanatory burden on both systems, these systems cannot be developed independently in the D&E framework: properties ascribed to the one may have far-reaching effects on the format of the other. Table 2.2 summarizes the central claims of D&E, and compares these to those normally adopted in MP and OT-syntax.

It seems to me that MP and D&E have a descriptive apparatus of more or less the same size, and are facing a similar task in that they both have to identify the features that may trigger movement. The frameworks mainly differ in that they provide different answers to the question what determines whether the movements that are allowed by the Last Resort Condition actually do take place in a given language L. In MP it is commonly assumed that movement is forced by the presence of an EPP-feature, and since certain movements, like Icelandic object shift, only apply under certain well-defined conditions, the question is raised what determines the distribution of the EPP-features. Chomsky (2001) claims that the distribution of these EPP-features is determined by certain 'parameters' that take the form of language-specific output filters. In D&E the answer takes the form of an optimality-theoretic evaluation, as indicated in (12) and (16).

Table 2.2 Comparison of the central claims of D&E with MP and OT-syntax.

Derivation-and-evaluation model	MP	OT
I. The generator is some version of C_{HL}	+	−
(a) all operations of the generator are subject to inviolable conditions	+	?
(b) all operations of the generator are subject to Last Resort	+	−
(c) the generator is autonomous and operations apply at random; there are no EPP-features.	−	+
II. The evaluator consists of a ranked set of syntactic constraints	−	+
(a) the syntactic constraints are taken from a universal set CON	d.n.a.	+
(b) the number of syntactic constraints in CON is small	d.n.a.	−
(c) the number of syntactic constraint types in CON is small	d.n.a.	−

D&E differs from OT-syntax in that the former postulates the computation system C_{HL} from MP as the generator. As a result of this, many imaginable derivations are blocked by the inviolable conditions on the operations of C_{HL}, so that the number of candidates in the candidate set is very small, and the candidates in this set can differ in well-defined ways only. This has led to the conjecture that there are not only a limited number of syntactic constraints, but also a limited number of constraint types. In order to establish these types, I have assumed that the evaluator is actually a hypothesis about the interface conditions postulated in MP, and, consequently, that the constraints fall into two main classes:

(28)   The syntactic constraints in CON are of two basic types:
    (a) C_{HL} constraints
    (b) Interface (PF and LF) constraints

The C_{HL} constraints can be further divided in two families of constraints, viz, economy constraints, which disfavor the operation of C_{HL} to apply, and EPP constraints, which favor their applications. The ranking of these constraints determine whether a certain operation normally does or does not take place. The effects of the weak and strong rankings in (29) can be overruled by the interface (PF and LF) constraints. These constraints seem to be more varied in nature, and it is still an open (empirical) question how many of these constraints there actually are.

(29)   (a) Weak ranking: *MOVE >> EPP(F)
    (b) Strong ranking: EPP(F) >> *MOVE

In a sense, the D&E framework directly descends from Chomsky and Lasnik's (1977) *Filters and Control* in postulating two independent systems for generating and evaluating syntactic structures. Chomsky and Lasnik left open the option that the periphery (the evaluative component) uses 'much richer resources, perhaps resources as rich as contemplated in the earlier theories of TG', but our hope should

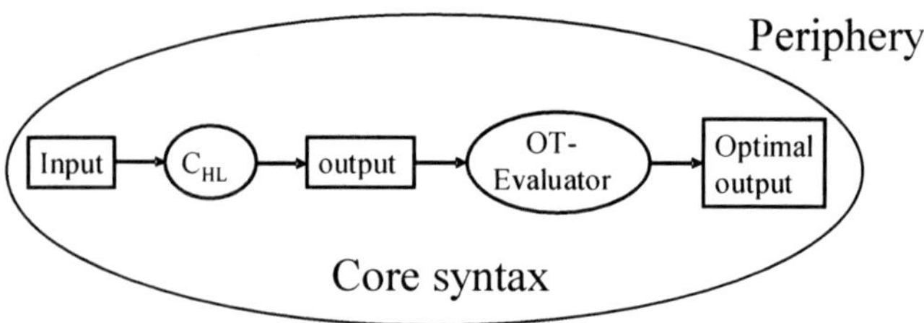

Figure 2.4 Core and periphery in syntax.

be that this will turn out not to be the case, and that also the rules of the periphery will be largely determined by our genetic endowment, that is, by the innate and thus universal constraint set CON. From the D&E perspective, Chomsky and Lasnik's use of the notions 'core' and 'periphery' for respectively the generator and the evaluator is therefore misleading: the generator and the evaluator constitute core grammar together, and the periphery rather lies outside these systems, and should refer to everything that must be learned on an item-to-item or construction-to-construction basis: see Figure 2.4.

Actually, at some places, Chomsky and Lasnik seem to have had something like this in mind as well, given that they 'think of theory of grammar T as consisting of two parts: a universal grammar UG that determines the class of potential grammars and the way they operate, and a system of evaluation that ranks potential grammars in terms of "optionality" or "simplicity"' (Chomsky and Lasnik 1977: 44). This seems a very apt description of the D&E framework, where the generator defines the set of universally available structures and the evaluator determines the subset of these structures that are actually used in a given language L.

Notes

1. Where Chomsky assumes that XP is an outer specifier of v*P, I will assume that XP occupies the specifier position of an extended projection of v* in the sense of, for example, Grimshaw (1997). This alternative has a number of empirical advantages, which are extensively discussed in Broekhuis (2008). One is that clause adverbs can be assumed to be attached to v*P before the application of object shift, which results in crossing of the adverb: first the adjunction structure $[_{vP}$ ADV $[_{vP}$ Subject v* [V ... Obj]]] is created and object shift subsequently results in the extended projection $[_{vP}$ Obj v $[_{vP}$ ADV $[_{vP}$ Subject t_{v*} [V ... t_{Obj}]]]]. This means that clause adverbs can simply be merged in syntax, which is problematic for the multiple specifier structure in (1) as this would result in separation of the inner and outer specifier of v*P: $[_{vP}$ Obj $[_{??}$ ADV $[_{vP}$ Subject t_{v*} [V ... t_{Obj}]]]].
2. What is maintained, however, is that the candidate set for a given input can be assumed to be very similar for all languages: variation may arise but this is mainly the result of differences in the lexicon, such as the availability of certain lexical items or the (non-)affixal status or categorial nature of the lexical elements involved in the derivation. Of course, there may be other ways to eliminate the infiniteness of the candidate sets. The traditional phonological generator, for example, produces an infinite number of candidates because it includes operations like epenthesis that can in principle be repeated infinitely. However, this is simply a specific hypothesis about the generator that might be wrong; see McCarthy and Pruitt (this volume) for a proposal that does not have this feature.

3. The discussion above will make it clear that I strongly disagree with Samek-Lodovici's (this volume) claim that it is an inherent virtue of OT that it is more powerful than MP. Given that the grammar should define the set of possible natural languages, reduction of generative power is desirable when it leads to the exclusion of languages that are likely not to be part of this set.

4. I will use the notion of local domain instead of the notion of checking domain in order to avoid the connotation that movement into the local domain of a head H is required to value the unvalued formal features of H.

5. It is, however, less clear whether the two numbers are equal. Take *wh*-movement. Watanabe (1991) has argued on empirical grounds that *wh*-in situ languages like Japanese actually have overt *wh*-movement of an empty operator: among other things, this accounts for the fact that these languages also exhibit *wh*-island effects. Chomsky (1995: ch. 3) claimed on the basis of Watanabe's findings that *wh*-features are universally strong. When we abandon covert movement in favor of Agree, Watanebe's findings suggest that Agree does not suffice to license *wh*-constructions, but that movement must apply. So the question is: Why? Earlier proposals have maintained that a *wh*-phrase can be interpreted by the conceptual-intentional component only if it heads an operator-variable chain; see, for example, Chomsky (1991: 440) and Rizzi (1996). If so, the obligatoriness of *wh*-movement follows immediately from semantic considerations, since any construction in which *wh*-movement does not apply will either crash as a violation of Full Interpretation or, at least, receive an anomalous interpretation. Consequently, the postulation of a constraint like EPP(wh) has no effect, so that we may safely assume that it does not exist. If movement of the goals of other [+affect] features like [topic], [focus] or [neg] are likewise forced by semantic considerations, we may conclude that they do not fall under the generalized EPP constraint in (2) either. This would eliminate a large set of potential constraints from the grammar, and thus considerably reduce the set of possible grammars.

6. Note that the notion of *prosodically unmarked focus* in (3a) refers to the new information of the clause and stands in opposition to the notion of *presupposition*, and should not be confused with the notion of exhaustive or contrastive focus.

7. For simplicity, I have formulated these constraints in linear terms. Strictly speaking this is not possible given that these constraints are used to evaluate syntactic representations and linear order is only assigned to these representations at a later stage (the PF-component of the grammar). However, since I adopt some version of Kayne's (1994) Linear Correspondence Axiom, it is readily possible to rephrase these constraints in hierarchical terms; cf. Broekhuis (2008); see also Engels and Vikner (2006). Similar constraints/conditions can also be found in Williams (2003), Müller (2000;2001), Fox and Pesetsky (2005) and Koeneman (2006).

8. HEAD-COMPL must not be confused with the alignment constraint HEAD-LEFT that can be found in much OT-work (e.g. Grimshaw 1997), which also requires a head to precedes its complement, but competes with its counterpart HEAD-RIGHT, which does not feature in my proposal. Alignment constraints play a prominent role in OT-syntax, and have generated a lot of new insights. For example, they have been employed by Legendre (2000) to account for the linearization of the clitics in the Bulgarian clitic cluster, by Anderson (2000) to account for verb second and other second position phenomena, and by Sells (2001) for describing Swedish object shift. These alignment constraints differ from HEAD-COMPL in that they do not take recourse to an underlying word order but express certain surface word order generalizations directly.

9. Of course, the notion *lexically filled* in (4b) must be distinguished from the notion 'phonetically realized'; it may be the case that a complementizer that is lexically present is phonetically empty as a result of Pesetsky's (1997; 1998) constraint TELEGRAPH discussed in the introduction to this volume. The constraint LEXICALLY FILL TOP F is similar to the nameless principle independently proposed in Zwart (2001: 38).

References

Anderson, S. R. (2000) Towards an optimal account of second-position phenomena. In J. Dekkers, F. Van der Leeuw and J. Van de Weijer (eds) *Optimality Theory: Phonology, Syntax and Acquisition,* 302–33. Oxford: Oxford University Press.

Boeckx, C. and Stjepanovic, S. (2001) Head-ing toward PF. *Linguistic Inquiry* 32: 345–55.

Broekhuis, H. (2000) Against feature strength: the case of Scandinavian object shift. *Natural Language and Linguistic Theory* 18: 673–721.

Broekhuis, H. (2008) *Derivations and Evaluations: Object Shift in the Germanic Languages.* Berlin/New York: Mouton de Gruyter.

Broekhuis, H. and Dekkers, J. (2000) The minimalist program and optimality theory: derivations and evaluations. In J. Dekkers, F. Van der Leeuw and J. Van de Weijer (eds) *Optimality Theory: Phonology, Syntax and Acquisition,* 386–422. Oxford: Oxford University Press.

Broekhuis, H. and Klooster,W. (2007) Merge and Move as costly operations. *Groninger Arbeiten zur germanistischen Linguistik* 45: 17–37.

Chomsky, N. (1991) Some notes on economy of derivation and representation. In R. Freidin (ed.) *Principles and Parameters in Comparative Syntax,* 417–54. Cambridge, MA: MIT Press.

Chomsky, N. (1995) *The Minimalist Program.* Cambridge, MA: MIT Press.

Chomsky, N. (2001) Derivation by phase. In M. Kenstowicz (ed.) *Ken Hale. A Life in Language,* 1–52. Cambridge, MA: MIT Press.

Chomsky, N. (2004) Beyond explanatory adequacy. In A. Belletti (ed.) *Structures and Beyond,* 104–31. Oxford: Oxford University Press.

Chomsky, N. and Lasnik, H. (1977) Filters and control. *Linguistic Inquiry* 8: 425–504.

Costa, J. (1998) *Word Order Variation. A Constraint-based Approach,* Doctoral dissertation, University of Leiden/LOT.

Dekkers, J. (1999) *Derivations & Evaluations. On the Syntax of Subjects and Complementizers,* Doctoral dissertation, HIL dissertations 21.

Den Dikken, M. (2006) *Relators and Linkers. The Syntax of Predication, Predicate Inversion, and Copulas.* Cambridge, MA and London: MIT Press.

Den Dikken, M. (2007) Phase extension. Contours of a theory of the role of head movement in phrasal extraction. *Theoretical Linguistics* 33: 1–41.

Dewey, T. K. (2006) *The Origins and Development of Germanic V2,* Doctoral dissertation, Berkeley, CA: University of California.

Diesing, M. (1997) Yiddish VP order and the typology of object movement in Germanic. *Natural Language and Linguistic Theory* 17: 369–427.

Eisner, J. (1999) *Doing OT in a Straitjacket.* Los Angeles, CA: UCLA.

Engels, E. and Vikner, S. (2006) An optimality-theoretic analysis of Scandinavian object shift and remnant VP-topicalisation. In H. Broekhuis and R. Vogel (eds) *Optimality Theory and Minimalism: A Possible Lonvergence? Linguistics in Potsdam 25.* Potsdam: http://www.ling.uni-potsdam.de/lip/.

Fortson , B. W. IV. (2004) *Indo-European Language and Culture: An Introduction.* Oxford: Blackwell.

Fox, D. and Pesetsky, D. (2005) Cyclic linearization of syntactic structure. *Theoretical Linguistics* 31: 1–45.

Grimshaw, J. (1997) Projection, heads and optimality. *Linguistic Inquiry* 28: 373–422.

Holmberg, A. (1986) *Word Order and Syntactic Features in the Scandinavian Languages and English,* Doctoral dissertation, University of Stockholm, Department of General Linguistics.

Holmberg, A. (1999) Remarks on Holmberg's generalization. *Studia Linguistica* 53: 1–39.

Johnson, K. (1991) Object positions. *Natural Language and Linguistic Theory* 9: 577–636.

Jónsson, J. G. (1996) *Clausal Architecture and Case in Icelandic,* Doctoral dissertation, GLSA: University of Massachusetts.

Kayne, R. S. (1994) *The Antisymmetry of Syntax.* Cambridge, MA: MIT Press.

Koeneman, O. (2006) Shape conservation, Holmberg's generalization and predication. In J. M. Hartmann and L. Molnárfi (eds) *Comparatieve Studies in Germanic Syntax,* Amsterdam and Philadelphia, PA: John Benjamins.

Lasnik, H. (1999a) *Minimalist Analysis*. Oxford: Blackwell.

Legendre, G. (2000) Morphological and prosodic alignment of Bulgarian clitics. In J. Dekkers, F. Van der Leeuw and J. Van de Weijer (eds) *Optimality Theory, Phonology, Syntax and Acquisition*, 423–62. Oxford: Oxford University Press.

McCarthy, J. J. and Prince, A. (1993) Prosodic morphology: Constraint interaction and satisfaction. Ms. University of Massachusetts, Amherst/Rutgers University, http://roa.rutgers.edu/files/482-1201/482-1201-MCCARTHY-0-1.PDF.

Müller, G. (2000) Shape conservation and remnant movement. In A. Hirotani, N. Hall Coetzee and J.-Y. Kim (eds) *Proceedings of NELS 30*, 525–39. Amherst, MA: GLSA.

Müller, G. (2001) Order preservation, parallel movement, and the emergence of the unmarked. In G. Legendre, J. Grimshaw and S. Vikner (eds) *Optimality-theoretic Syntax*, 113–42. Cambridge, MA and London: MIT Press/MITWPL.

Pesetsky, D. (1997) Optimality theory and syntax: Movement and pronunciation. In D. Archangeli and T. Langendoen (eds) *Optimality Theory*, 134–70. Malden, MA and Oxford: Blackwell.

Pesetsky, D. (1998) Some optimality principles of sentence pronunciation. In P. Barbosa, D. Fox, P. Hagstrom, M. McGinnis and D. Pesetsky (eds) *Is the Best Good Enough?*, 337–83. Cambridge, MA and London: MIT Press/MITWPL.

Pollock, J. (1989) Verb movement, Universal Grammar and the structure of IP. *Linguistic Inquiry* 20 (3): 365–424.

Rizzi, L. (1990) *Relativized Minimality*. Cambridge, MA and London: MIT Press.

Rizzi, L. (1996) Residual Verb Second and the wh Criterion. In A. Belletti and L. Rizzi (eds) *Parameters and Functional Heads. Essays in Comparative Syntax*, 63–90. Oxford and New York: Oxford University Press.

Sells, P. (2001) *Structure Alignment and Optimality in Swedish*. Stanford, CA: CSLI Publications.

Thráinsson, H. (2001) Object shift and scrambling. In M. Baltin and C. Collins (eds) *Contemporary Syntactic Theory*. Malden, MA: Blackwell Publishing.

Vikner, S. (1994) Scandinavian object shift and West Germanic scrambling. In N. Corver and H. van Riemsdijk (eds) *Studies on Scrambling. Movement and Non-movement Approaches to Free Word-order Phenomena*, 487–517. Berlin and New York: Mouton de Gruyter.

Vikner, S. (2006) Object Shift. In M. Everaert and H. van Riemsdijk (eds) *The Blackwell Companion to Syntax*, 392–436. Malden, MA and Oxford: Blackwell Publishing.

Vogel, R. (2006) Weak Function Word Shift. *Linguistics* 44 (9): 1059–93.

Watanabe, A. (1991) *Wh-in situ, Subjacency and Chain-formation*, Doctoral dissertation, MIT.

Williams, E. (2003) *Representation Theory*. Cambridge, MA and London: MIT Press.

Zwart, J. W. (2001) Syntactic and phonological verb movement. *Syntax* 4 (1): 34–62.

3 Filling in the gaps: PF-optimalization in parasitic gap constructions in Dutch and German

Gema Chocano[*] and Michael T. Putnam[**]

ABSTRACT Parasitic gaps (pgs) have proven to offer a significant challenge to purely derivational analyses of natural language syntax. This is primarily due to the observation that the licensing of pgs hinges on well-formedness constraints imposed at S(urface)-Structure. Here we engage in a detailed analysis of pgs in Dutch and German, focusing on two of their most salient characteristics: the licensing of pgs by the scrambling of elements that could not otherwise undergo scrambling (Heck and Müller 2000; Fanselow 2001; among others); and the deviance of structures where the lexical verb of the clause hosting the pg licenser is Verb-second (V2) (Kathol 2000). Adopting a hybrid MP–OT approach to syntactic derivations of the sort in Broekhuis (2008), we account for these salient characteristics of Dutch and German pg structures by resorting to the PARALLELISM REQUIREMENT (PR), a PF-filter.

KEYWORDS Parasitic gaps; Parallelism requirement; Scrambling; Last resort; Webelhuth's Paradox; Derivation-and-evaluation model; Dutch; German; English

1. Introduction

In this chapter we explore two of the most salient characteristics that differentiate Dutch and German pg structures from their English counterparts: (a) the availability of pg licensers that have undergone scrambling (Felix 1983; Bennis and Hoekstra 1984), even if they belong to the class of non-scrambable elements (Fanselow 1995; Heck and Müller 2000); and (b) the requirement that the lexical verb of the matrix clause, which hosts the pg licenser,[1] and the lexical verb of the embedded clause, which hosts the pg, be final (Kathol, 2000). The first property can be seen in (1) for

---

  * Gema Chocano, Departamento de Filología Inglesa, Facultad de Filosofía y Letras, Universidad Autónoma de Madrid, Tomás y Valiente, 1, 28049 Madrid. Spain. E-mail: gema.chocano@uam.es

** Michael Putnam, Department of Germanic and Slavic Languages & Literatures, Penn State University, 427 Burrowes Building, University Park, PA 16802, USA. E-mail: mtp12@psu.edu

German[2] (examples from Heck and Müller 2000) and (2) for Dutch ((2a) from Hans Broekhuis, *p.c.*; (2b) from Neeleman and Reinhart 1998). The second property is illustrated by the German examples in (3) (from Kathol 2000) and their Dutch counterparts in (4) (from Hans Broekhuis, *p.c.*)[3]:

(1) (a) *dass die Maria was$_i$ [ohne   pg$_i$ zu lesen]   dem Fritz   t$_i$*
           that the Maria   something without to read   the Fritz
           züruckgegeben   hat
           back-given   has
           'that Maria gave back something to Fritz without reading (it)'

     (b) *dass die Maria <*was>   dem Fritz   <was>   zurückgeben hat*
           that the Maria   the Fritz   something back-given   has
           'that Maria gave back something to Fritz' Maria'

(2) (a) *dat Marie   iets   [zonder pg$_i$ te lezen] t$_i$ aan Frits heeft teruggegeven.*
           that Marie   something without   to read   to   Frits has   given back
           'that Marie has given back something to Fritz without reading'

     (b) *Heb je   <* iets> vanmorgen <iets>   gegeten?*
           have you   this morning anything   eaten?
           'Have you eaten anything this morning?'

(3) (a) *Hans hat Maria$_i$ [ohne pg   anzusehen] t$_i$ geküsst*
           Hans has Maria   without   at-to-look   kissed
           'Hans kissed Maria without looking at (her)'

     (b) ??/**Hans   küsste   Maria$_i$ [ohne pg$_i$ anzusehen] t$_i$*
           Hans   kissed   Maria   without   to at-to-look
           'Hans kissed Maria without looking at her'

(4) (a) *?dat Hans Maria$_i$ [zonder pg$_i$ aan te kijken] t$_i$ kuste*
           that Hans Maria   without   at-to-look   kissed
           'that Hans kissed Maria without looking at (her)'

     (b) ??/**Hans kuste   Maria [zonder pg$_i$ aan te kijken] t$_i$*
           Hans kissed Maria   without   at-to-look
           'Hans kissed Maria without looking at her'

As far as we know, no previous analysis of pg structures in German and Dutch covers the two sets of facts above. Proposals couched within a purely derivational framework as well as those couched within an Optimality-Theoretic (OT) framework have capitalized on (1)–(2), while remaining silent about (3)–(4). Furthermore, both approaches face some difficulties in their accounts of the sets of data in (1)–(2), for reasons that we will summarize below. The seminal derivational analysis (Bennis and Hoekstra 1985; Felix 1985; Huybregts and van Riemsdijk 1985; Bennis 1986) is nowadays problematic in that it rests on the GB assumption that movement may apply freely (i.e. *Move-α*): in other words, if, as defended in derivational models such as Chomsky's (1993, 1995 and subsequent work), movement operations must be triggered, there is no explanation why the indefinite pronoun must stay in its base-generation position in (1b) and (2b) but not in (1a), (2a). Heck and Müller (2000) solve this problem within a hybrid MP-OT approach by introducing a constraint that disfavors movement without feature checking that may be outranked by a constraint that forces a pg to be A-bar-bound and thus favors movement in pg constructions.

The correctness of Heck and Müller's proposal is crucially dependent on the syntactically vacuous nature of A-bar scrambling in the cases in which it takes place for pg licensing. However, such a syntactically vacuous A-bar nature seems to be at odds with *Webelhuth's Paradox* (Webelhuth 1989, 1992): a scrambled DP may be both a binder and a pg licenser. If, on principled grounds, binding is possible only from A-positions and A-positions are, in turn, the locus for Case- (or phi-feature valuation), scrambling for pg licensing must involve some kind of triggered movement. In other words, scrambling can be neither A-bar nor non-triggered.

The proposal advanced in this chapter basically rejects the view that, curiously enough, the seminal derivational account (Bennis and Hoekstra 1985; Felix 1985; Huybregts and van Riemsdijk 1985; Bennis 1986) shares with Heck and Müller's analysis, namely that there exists such a phenomenon like non-triggered movement. In other words, our proposal will strictly adhere to Chomsky's (1995) *Last Resort Condition*, according to which movement of a syntactic object must be triggered by some unchecked or unvalued formal feature of a higher functional head. Thus, the hypothesis is that examples (1a), (2a) and (1b), (2b) behave alike: in both instances, we are dealing with Case- (or phi-feature) checking (or valuation) between the scrambled DP and the relevant functional head (probably v^*). Note that this would straight-forwardly account for *Webelhuth's Paradox*. On this basis, we contend that what distinguishes the pg grammatical examples (1a), (2a) from the ungrammatical ones (1b), (2b) lies in the violability of a semantic well-formedness condition on scrambling, namely the requirement that it applies only to discourse-given elements (Lenerz 1977; Diesing 1992; Meinunger 1995; Putnam 2007; among many others). To put it differently, non-discourse-given elements may *sometimes* scramble. If this reasoning is on track, our account needs a model of syntactic derivation which allows for both the inviolability of *Last Resort* and the violability of such a semantic well-formed-ness condition. This model is Broekhuis' (2000, 2008) Derivations-and-Evaluations (D&E), which incorporates aspects of the MP and OT into one united framework: the derivation (= GEN in an OT-framework) produces representations that are evaluated (= EVAL) by violable constraints at the PF- and LF-interfaces respectively.[4] The derivation GEN consists of conceptually necessary operations such as *Move*, which is subject to inviolable conditions such as *Last Resort*. Although such a 'marriage' between these two (often assumed) 'competing and contrastive' frameworks might at first glance seem somewhat paradoxical, preliminary explorations in the D&E framework (for example, Broekhuis 2008; Salzmann 2008, this volume) have shown that this model has the ability to improve upon both the conceptual simplicity and range of empirical coverage of 'standard' Minimalism.[5] As discussed by Broekhuis and Vogel (2010) and others, OT-syntax initiated a shift of attention to the representa-tional aspects of grammar, and by doing so provided new means to study empirical domains that were 'outside the scope of, ignored by, or developed in only an impressionistic manner by the mainstream generative research of the last twenty-five years' (263). Most relevant for this study at hand, employing a limited number of finite, well-defined linearization (PF) constraints is necessary to account for the two salient properties of Dutch and German pgs that we discuss in this chapter. In other words, the linearization 'constraints' currently offered in 'standard' Minimalism like the *Phase Impenetrability Condition* from Chomsky (2001) are insufficient.

The violable constraints we adopt from Broekhuis' (2008) treatment of Object Shift (OS) in Germanic languages are Broekhuis' EPP (CASE), *MOVE (STAY), and ALIGN-FOCUS (AF). Although the exact way in which these three violable constraints interact will be shown in detail in sections 2 and 3, we will note here that, in Broekhuis' model, the ungrammaticality of (1b) and (2b) just reduces to the fact that, in German and Dutch, AF, which requires focused (i.e. non-discourse-given) material to appear as the rightmost constituent of the clause, outranks EPP (CASE), which favors movement of the scrambled DP for Case-valuation. The question now is what makes it possible that, in the presence of a pg, Broekhuis' AF may be violated. Our answer draws on the well-known analogy between coordinate and pg constructions in German and Dutch (Bennis 1986; Bennis and Hoekstra 1985; Huybregts and van Riemsdijk 1985): the clause hosting the pg licenser must be identical to that hosting the pg itself, where 'identity', as in the case of coordinate structures, must be understood in terms of the position the common argument (i.e. the pg licenser and the pg itself) occupies relative to its multiple selecting heads. We further contend that such an identity can be rendered in the form of a constraint, the PARALLELISM REQUIREMENT in (5), which crucially outranks Broekhuis' AF. In other words, an otherwise non-scrambable pg licenser scrambles in order to comply with PR.

(5) THE PARALLELISM REQUIREMENT (PR)
     The position of a pg licenser in the matrix clause relative to its selecting head and
     its co-arguments must mimic that of the pg in the embedded clause.

The following two sections are devoted to showing how the adoption of the PR not only solves the problems posed by the structures in (1) and (2), but also provides an insightful clue to a better understanding of the data in (3) and (4). They will also address the issue of how other, less often noticed properties of German and Dutch pg structures may fit our overall proposal. Section 4 concludes this chapter.

2. PF-Optimalization via filters

The present section offers the reader a detailed implementation of the proposal sketched in the previous paragraphs to the sets of data in (1) and (2). In section 2.1 we will introduce the 'basic facts' surrounding presumed non-triggered scrambling in Dutch and German. Simultaneously, we will establish the basic tenets of Heck and Müller's (hereafter, H&M) analysis concerning repair-driven strategies for the local optimalization of scrambling structures. In section 2.2 we will expose three key flaws in H&M's account that we intend to address and improve upon in our analysis in section 2.3.

2.1 Non-triggered scrambling: basic facts

As stated above, the point of departure of our proposal is illustrated in the structures (1)–(2), repeated here as (6) and (7), where an otherwise non-scrambable indefinite pronoun, has undergone scrambling for the licensing of a pg in an adverbial embedded clause. (German examples in (6) from Heck and Müller; Dutch example in (7a) from Hans Broekhuis, *p.c.*; Dutch example in (7c) from Neeleman and Reinhart 1998):

(6) (a) *dass die Maria was$_i$ [ohne* pg$_i$ *zu lesen]   dem   Fritz* t_i
      that the Maria   something without to read   the   Fritz
      züruckgegeben   hat
      back-given   has
      'that Maria gave back something to Fritz without reading (it)'

  (b) *dass die Maria <*was> dem Fritz <was>   zurückgeben   hat*
      that the Maria   the Fritz   something   back-given   has
      'that Maria gave back something to Fritz'

(7) (a) *dat Marie iets   [zonder pg$_i$ te lezen] t$_i$ aan Frits heeft teruggegeven.*
      that Marie something without to read   to   Frits has   given back
      'that Marie has given back something to Fritz without reading'

  (b) *Heb je   <* iets> vanmorgen   <iets>   gegeten?*
      have you   this morning anything eaten?
      'Have you eaten anything this morning?'

In a paper with wider empirical coverage with complexities that fall outside the scope of the present work, H&M (2000) propose a hybrid MP-OT treatment of the grammatical (a)-examples as cases of untriggered scrambling, and address the issue of its interaction with pg licensing. H&M contend that (6) and (7) find a principled explanation if one assumes that the choice between the output of the derivation with scrambling (the structures in (a)) and the output of the derivation without scrambling (the structures in (b)) is made on the basis of a filtering device containing the two constraints in (8) below:

(8) (a) THE PARASITIC GAP CONSTRAINT (PGC)
      A parasitic gap is A-bar bound[6]
  (b) LAST RESORT (LR)
      Movement must result in feature checking

The PARASITIC GAP CONSTRAINT (PGC) is the OT reformulation of Chomsky's (1982) analysis of pgs as a [-pronoun, -anaphor] element that must be bound by an operator. Similarly, Last Resort (LR) can be understood as the violable counterpart of Chomsky's (1995) condition on movement operations. H&M analyze the grammatical structures in (6a) and (7a) above as the optimal candidates for pg construction with normally non-scrambable pronouns. They conclude on the basis of the (b)-examples that movement of the pronoun violates LR, but assume that it must nevertheless take place in the (a)-examples in order for the pg to comply with the PGC constraint. This is obtained by assuming that PGC outranks LR in German (and Dutch), which results in the choice of the candidate that violates the latter but satisfies the former, namely (6a) (and (7a) for Dutch). In this light, the ungrammaticality of the losing candidates is due to the fact that LR is fulfilled to the detriment of PGC.

T1 Repair-driven scrambling in parasitic gap contexts (from H&M 2000: 11 (T_4))

Input: $[_{VP}$ DP$_1$ V], v, NPSUBJ, $[_{CP}$ ... pg$_1$ ...]	PGC	LR
O$_1$: $[_{vP}$ $[_{CP}$ ... pg$_1$ ...] $[_{v'}$ NPSUBJ $[_{VP}$ ... *was*$_1$ ...]]]	*!	
☞O$_2$: $[_{vP}$ *was*$_1$ $[_{v'}[_{CP}$ ... pg$_1$ ...] $[_{v'}$ NPSUBJ $[_{VP}$ ...t_i...]]]]		*

Note that the use of the OT framework allows H&M's proposal to dispense with the pervasive problem of optional movement that any derivational account couched within the framework of Chomsky's (1993, 1995) Minimalist Program would face.[7] Nevertheless, it does not free it from some empirical problems, some of which will be presently discussed in the following sub-section.

2.2 Empirical problems with Heck and Müller's (2000) proposal

Here we elaborate in more detail on some of the empirical shortcomings of H&M's (2000) analysis of repair-driven movement and the local optimization of derivations. With respect to the connection between scrambling and the licensing of pgs, H&M's analysis exhibits the following shortcomings:

1. The conflict between *Webelhuth's Paradox* and the formulation of LR as a violable constraint. The crucial set of data here is that in (9), which serves as the basis for *Webelhuth's Paradox* (1989, 1992): a scrambled object licensing a pg can also be a binder of a pronoun or anaphor from that position. If, on standard assumptions, such binding is possible only from A-positions, the conclusion seems to be that, even in those cases like (9), in which scrambling licenses a pg, scrambling entails Case, or phi-feature checking.

(9) (a) ?*weil*   *Fritz jeden Gast$_i$ [ohne*   pg$_i$ *anzuschauen]*   *seinem*   *Nachbarn$_i$*
          because   Fritz every guest without   at-to-look   his   neighbor t$_i$
          vorgestellt   hat
          introduced   has
          'because Fritz introduced every guest to his neighbor without looking at (him)'

> (b) *dat Jan de rivalen₁   namens elkaar₁   [zonder pg₁ aan te kijken]* t₁
>   that Jan the rivals   on-behalf-of-each-other   without   at to look
>   *feliciteert*
>   congratulates
>   'that Jan congratulates the rivals on behalf of each other without looking at
>   (them)'

This simply means that there seem to be no such phenomena that violate LR. Additionally, note that *Webelhuth's Paradox* also makes the PGC constraint suspicious, given that the pgs in (9) are licensed by elements that are binders of pronouns/anaphors, that is elements that seem to occupy an A-position (or, at least, a non-standard A-bar one). In this respect, it must be noted that there is almost general agreement that scrambling is, in fact, A-movement: it feeds binding and secondary predication, does not give rise to weak crossover effects, and is clause-bounded (Neeleman 1994; Haider and Rosengren 1998; among many others).

2. The unavailability of parasitic gaps in relative clauses in German and Dutch, illustrated by examples like (10) below (from Kathol 2000):

> (10) (a) **Dies ist ein Umstand   wo/welcher₁ [jeder   [der* pg₁ *von gehört*
>   this is   an understanding where/which everyone who   of heard
>   *hat]]* t₁ *mit   rechnen muss*
>   has   with count   must
>   'This is an understanding which everyone who has heard of must count with'

> (b) **Dit is een vraag   waar₁ [iedereen [die* pg₁ *over   denkt]] een antwoord*
>   this is a   question which everyone who   about thinks   an answer
>   t₁ *op weet*
>   to knows
>   'This is a question which everyone who thinks about knows an answer to'

If pgs in German and Dutch are derived, as in Chomsky (1982), by means of the binding of a trace by an operator in an A-bar position, there is no explanation why the structures in (10) are ruled out: German *wo/welcher* 'where/which' as well as Dutch *waar* 'which' have uncontroversially undergone *wh*-movement, a canonical instance of A-bar movement. On this basis, there is no reason why the examples of subject pgs in (10) above should not be possible.[8]

3. The interplay between the two violable constraints LR and PGC does not tell us anything about the linear restrictions that, according to Kathol (2000), pg structures exhibit and which are illustrated in (3) and (4) above. Put differently, LR and PGC do not suffice for accounting for the contrast between structures, which minimally differ in the position that the matrix lexical verb occupies. In light of the discussion above, we conclude neither LR nor PGC are empirically motivated. On these grounds we dispense with both of these constraints in our analysis.

2.3 Non-triggered scrambling: an alternative account

The aim of the present section is to propose an account of German and Dutch pg structures that circumvents the three empirical obstacles that H&M's proposal faces. Such an account will adopt as a starting point Broekhuis' (2008) D&E hybrid model that imposes inviolable restrictions on syntactic derivations and violable restrictions on syntactic representations.

One of Broekhuis' main claims in his analysis of object displacement in Germanic languages is that Scandinavian OS and West Germanic scrambling basically reduce to the same derivational phenomenon, namely Case checking on v^*, and that cross-linguistic differences concerning OS/scrambling follow from language-specific constraint ranking. The constraints at stake belong to two basic types: constraints related to the computational system, or C_{HL} constraints, and constraints imposed by the interfaces, or interface (LF and PF) constraints. Two C_{HL} constraints that are relevant for our discussion are EPP (CASE) in (11a) and *MOVE in (11b), also called STAY in traditional OT (see Grimshaw 1997):

(11) (a) EPP (CASE)
           Unvalued case-features attract their goal

      (b) *MOVE (STAY)
           Don't apply internal merge

From this perspective, languages in which (full) OS or scrambling is possible are characterized by a sub-ranking EPP (CASE) >> *MOVE (STAY), which is reversed in the case of languages without OS or scrambling: (*MOVE (STAY) >> EPP (CASE)).[9] Interface constraints are responsible for the well-known semantic conditions involved with the application of OS and scrambling: given that only elements that are part of the presupposition of the clause may be shifted/scrambled, the assumption is that the semantic constraint ALIGNFOCUS (AF) in (12) outranks EPP (CASE) in both OS and scrambling languages: AF >> EPP (CASE).[10] In other words, constituents that are part of the focus of the clause must remain VP-internal.

(12) ALIGNFOCUS (AF)
      The prosodically unmarked focus is the rightmost constituent of the clause

The relevance for adopting Broekhuis' analysis of OS/scrambling for our account can be summed up as follows: if the only difference between scrambled and non-scrambled elements is the position where they have their Case-feature valued, H&M's violable LAST RESORT must be dispensed with. This is a welcome result in the light of the data connected to *Webelhuth's Paradox*: scrambling is invariably movement for the valuation of Case features. Furthermore, if AF may block scrambling due to the fact that it outranks EPP (CASE), nothing should preclude the possibility that AF fails to apply, if it is in its turn overruled by some higher constraint that favors scrambling. We contend that such a constraint is a sort of 'Parallelism Requirement' (PR)[11] that favors output representations in which the pg licenser in the matrix clause occupies exactly the same position as the pg in the embedded one. Our tentative assumption is that PR is an interface (PF) constraint of the class Broekhuis labels 'order preservation constraints':

(13)   THE PARALLELISM REQUIREMENT (PR)
       The position of a pg licenser in the matrix clause relative to its selecting head and its co-arguments must mimic in structural terms that of the pg in the embedded clause.

As a point of clarification, we interpret 'structural parallelism' to be (loosely) understood to mean that both the pg and the pg licenser must occupy a phase-edge, Spec,v*P in the case at stake.[12] As we will explain in what follows, this straightforwardly accounts for the non-triggered scrambling of the pg licenser in H&M's examples.

As repeatedly noted in several parts of the present work, even non-scrambable pg licensers must undergo scrambling in the presence of a pg. If PR in (13) is correct, this is due to the fact that the pg appears by default in the v*P-edge, that is, it has scrambled. From this perspective, the gist of our analysis is basically a return to the treatment of pgs as null weak pronominals, as argued by Cinque (1990) and especially Postal (1994, 2000). 1–3 below summarizes Postal's main arguments:

1. The P-gap licensing restriction: P-gaps are categorically limited to NPs (first noticed by Pesetsky 1982, Chomsky 1982, Postal 1994, and others).

(14)   (a) This is a topic$_i$ you should think about t$_i$ before talking about *pg*$_i$
       (b) *This is a topic [about which]$_i$ you should think t$_i$ before talking *pg*$_i$

2. The Pronominal Condition: P-gaps cannot occur in positions incompatible with weak definite pronoun (Postal 1994).

(15)   (a) He named his camel Ernie / *it
       (a′) *What$_i$ did he name his dog t$_i$ after naming his camel *pg*$_i$?
       (b) There are guns / *them in the cabinet
       (b′) *What$_i$ did he look for t$_i$ in the closet without knowing there were *pg*$_i$ on the table?
       (c) They touched (*him on) it
       (c′) [Which of his arms]$_i$ did they have to immobilize t$_i$ after accidentally touching (*him on) *pg*$_i$?
       (d) The government contains / includes Valdez / HIM / *him
       (d′) *What$_i$ every government which contains / includes *pg*$_i$ needs to worry about t$_i$ is spies.
       (e) [Which room]$_i$ did they hang out in t$_i$ so the children could play in *pg*$_i$?
       (e′) *Where$_i$ did they hang out t$_i$ so the children could play *pg*$_i$?

3. The Predicate Nominal Condition: neither a pg nor its 'licensing' category can be a predicate nominal (Postal 1994).

(16) (a) They turned into derelicts
      (a′) *[What kind of derelicts]$_i$ did they analyzed t_i after their children turned into
           pg_i?
      (a″) *[What kind of derelicts]$_i$ did they turn into t_i after their children analyzed pg_i?

The extension of Postal's analysis of English pgs to German and Dutch has important consequences, given that in those languages phonologically realized weak pronouns obligatorily undergo scrambling (17a, 18a), while strong (i.e. contrastively focused) ones preferably remain in their base-generation position (17b), (18b) (Dutch examples from Neeleman and Reinhart 1998):

(17) (a) *dass die Maria <ihn> gestern   <*ihn> gesehen hat*
          that the Maria   him   yesterday   seen   has
          'that Maria saw him yesterday'

      (b) *dass die Maria <*IHN> gestern   IHN gesehen hat*
          that the Maria   yesterday him seen   has
          'that Maria saw HIM yesterday'

(18) (a) *Ik   heb <hem> gisteren <*hem>   gezien*
          I   have   yesterday him   seen
          'I saw him yesterday'

      (b) *Ik   heb   <*HEM> gisteren   hem gezien*
          I   have   yesterday   him seen
          'I saw HIM yesterday'

The contrast between the two structures in the (a)-examples is generally viewed as the result of the inherent deictic nature of German and Dutch weak pronouns. From the perspective of Broekhuis' D&E analysis of OS, where AF outranks all relevant constraints, the contrast just reduces to the impossibility of interpreting a weak pronoun, that is an inherently discourse-given element, in its base-generation position, that is as a focus element. If, as expected on principled grounds, the null counterparts of West Germanic weak pronominals are also inherently deictic, the null assumption is that they will also scramble to a position preceding VP/*vP-adjoined adverbials (as is the case of *ihn* 'him' in (17b)). In other words, the embedded adverbial clause that appears in a structure such as (19a) below would look like (19b) at the vP-cycle, where *pro* stands for the null pronoun, that is the parasitic gap:

(19) (a) *dass Hans Maria$_i$ [ohne   pg$_i$ anzusehen]* t_i *geküsst hat*
          that Hans Maria   without   at-to-look   kissed   has
          'that Hans kissed Maria yesterday without looking at (her)'

      (b) [$_{vP}$ pro$_i$ [$_{vP}$ PRO [$_{VP}$ t_i *anzusehen*]]][13]

Based on this assumption, the PR requirement would force *Maria*, the internal argument of the matrix verb, to scramble to the vP-edge too, as illustrated in (20):

(20) $[_{vP}$ *Maria*$_i$ $[_{vP}$ *Hans* $[_{VP}$ t$_i$ *anzusehen*]]]

Note that, in an example such as (19a), where the internal argument/direct object *Maria* is interpreted as part of the presupposition of the clause, the only relevant constraint that is violated is *MOVE (STAY), which is outranked by both AF and EPP (CASE) in Broekhuis' analysis of scrambling, and additionally by PR in our proposal: PR $>>$ {AF , EPP (CASE) , *MOVE}:[14]

(21) (a) *dass Hans Maria$_i$ [ohne* pg$_i$ *anzusehen]* t$_i$ *geküsst hat*
       (b) **dass Hans [ohne* pg$_i$ *anzusehen] Maria geküsst hat*

T2 Triggered scrambling in parasitic gap contexts

Input: C, NP$_{SUBJ}$, NP$_{DO}$, [ohne *pg* …], *v*, geküsst, haben	PR	AF	EPP	*MOVE
☞ $[_{CP}$ C NP$_{SUBJ}$ NP$_{DO}$ [ohne *pg* …] $[_{vP}$ *v* t$_i$ geküsst hat]]				*
$[_{CP}$ C NP$_{SUBJ}$ [ohne *pg* …] $[_{vP}$ *v* NP$_{DO}$ geküsst hat]]	*!		*	

The situation is different, however, if the pg licenser is an element that does not belong to the class of elements that may undergo scrambling, such as the indefinite of the examples in (22), where scrambling entails the violation of AF, which nevertheless is outranked by PR:

(22) (a) *dass Hans wen$_i$ [ohne* pg$_i$ *anzusehen]* t$_i$ *geküsst hat*
       (b) **dass Hans [ohne* pg$_i$ *anzusehen] wen geküsst hat*

T3 Non-triggered scrambling in parasitic gap contexts

Input: C, NP$_{SUBJ}$, *wh*$_{ACC}$ [ohne pg …], *v*, geküsst, haben	PR	AF	EPP	*MOVE
☞ $[_{CP}$ C NP$_{SUBJ}$ *wh*$_{ACC}$ [ohne *pg* …] $[_{vP}$ *v* t$_i$ geküsst hat]]		*		*
$[_{CP}$ C NP$_{SUBJ}$ [ohne *pg* …] $[_{vP}$ *v* *wh*$_{ACC}$ geküsst hat]]	*!		*	

If tenable, the proposal we develop here presents an important empirical advantage with respect to those advanced by H&M. Recall that, as discussed above, the formulation of LAST RESORT (LR) as a constraint outranked by that responsible for pg licensing (PGC) could not accommodate *Webelhuth's Paradox*, which, nevertheless, falls into place in light of the interplay between Broekhuis' EPP (CASE) constraint and the PR. To put it differently, H&M's LR predicts that binding from a scrambling position may not be possible if the scrambled element is, at the same time, a pg licenser. However, under our approach, the possibility always exists for a non-scrambable element to have its Case feature valued in a scrambling position (namely, the *v**P-edge), when AF is outranked by PR.[15]

3   Beyond non-scrambling elements: Further advantages of our proposal

The following sections aim to show that our approach to West Germanic pg structures in terms of the PR also sheds some light on other data discussed in the preceding literature. Section 3.1 focuses on data already presented above, namely the unavailability of pgs in German and Dutch relative clauses ((10a), (10b)), and the data in (3) and (4), from Kathol (2000). Section 3.2 deals with the apparent asymmetry between German and Dutch in what concerns pg licensers other than DPs as well as the requirement that pg licensers and pgs appear adjacent in both languages.

3.1   On the absence of pgs in relative clauses and V2 structures

As shown in the preceding sections, German and Dutch pgs are impossible both in relative clauses ((10a), (10b)) and V2 structures ((3), (4)). With respect to the former, recall that, as pointed out in section 2.3 (footnote 11), the PR constraint we argue to play a critical role in our analysis here differs from Munn's (1993) in that we envisage it as a PF constraint. However, it shares with Munn's the restriction that it only applies to conjoined (or conjoined-like) structures. That adverbial clauses in which German pgs are licensed are semi-coordinating structures is shown in Fanselow (2001), on the basis of data such as those in (23), which illustrate that subordinators of the *ohne*-type[16] (23c) pattern with conjunctions (23a), but differ from true subordinators (23b), in that they can co-occur with declarative complementizers:[17]

(23) (a) *Er sagt, dass es regnet und dass es schneit*
       he says that it rains and that it snows
       'He says that it rains and that it snows'

    (b) *Es regnet bevor (*dass) es schneit*
       it rains before that it snows
       'It rains before (*that) it snows'

    (c) *Es regnet ohne dass es schneit*
       it rains without that it snows
       'It rains without snowing'

From this perspective, the impossibility of subject pgs just reduces to a trivial factor: the relative clauses in (10a), (10b) cannot host a pg simply because they are not (semi-)coordinating structures, which appears to be the only kind of structure that appears to allow for pg licensing in German and Dutch.[18]

Our proposal also has a straightforward response to the third set of empirical problems H&M's analysis confronts, namely the issue brought to light by the German data originally due to Kathol in (3) ((24) here),[19] which, as shown above in (4), are very similar in Dutch (25):

(24) (a) *?Hans hat Maria$_i$ [ohne   pg$_i$ anzusehen]* t$_i$ *geküsst*
       that Hans Maria   without   at-to-look   kissed
       'that Hans has kissed Maria without looking at (her)'

    (b) *??/*Hans küsste Maria$_i$ [ohne   pg$_i$ anzusehen]* t$_i$
       Hans kissed Maria   without   at-to-look
       'Hans kissed Maria without looking at her'

(25) (a) *?dat   Hans Maria$_i$ [zonder* pg$_i$ *aan te kijken]* t$_i$ *kuste*
       that   Hans Maria   without   at-to-look   kissed
       'that Hans kissed Maria without looking at (her)'

    (b) *??/*Hans kuste Maria [zonder* pg$_i$ *aan te kijken]* t$_i$
       Hans kissed Maria   without   at-to-look
       'Hans kissed Maria without looking at her'

As the reader will recall, the intriguing question the data above pose is why the licensing of a pg requires that the lexical verb of both the embedded and the matrix clause be final (a-examples vs. b-examples). Our answer is PR, which selects as optimal the representation in which the null weak pronominal (i.e. the pg) and the pg licenser precede its respective selecting head, that is, the lexical verb. The reasons why the null weak pronominal precedes the lexical verb in the embedded clause are straightforward: whereas the weak nature of the null pronominal forces it to scramble to the v*P-edge, the presence of the subordinator in C invariably blocks movement of the finite verb, which, consequently, remains on v*.[20] The situation is, however, different in the case of the matrix clause, where the presence of the subordinator is not obligatory: scrambling of the pg licenser does not suffice for rescuing a structure such as (24b), (25b), since Verb-second requires movement of the lexical verb to C, in flagrant violation of PR (the pg licenser would follow and not precede the lexical verb).

We would like to conclude this section by connecting the analysis we offer for the facts in (24) and (25) above with an interesting question posed by an anonymous reviewer. Given that, as it stands, our PR constraint appears to systematically outrank Broekhuis' AF, the reviewer asks why it cannot be treated as an inviolable constraint, that is, part of GEN. It is obvious that, since German and Dutch behave identically with respect to the two salient characteristics addressed in this chapter, the decision must be based on evidence drawn from a different language that, nevertheless, must share with German and Dutch similar conditions for pg licensing. On the one hand, since the application of PR is inextricably linked to (semi-)coordinating structures, the language at stake must allow for pg licensing in this kind of environment. Additionally, an alternative ranking of PR with respect to AF would necessarily require that, in such a language, both OS and V2 restricted to root clauses be available. Unfortunately, limitations of time and space have forced us to defer a detailed examination of the crucial sets of data of the potential candidates to future research.

3.2 Tying up some loose ends

This final section will address two additional sets of data that deserve some attention in light of the proposal defended here. The first one consists of the German example in (26a) and its Dutch counterpart in (26b), which shows that the two languages seem to differ in the availability of pg structures with a pg licenser other than a DP:

(26) (a) ?*Unsere Firma hat [mit dem Vertreter]ᵢ   [ohne   lange* pgᵢ *zu reden]*
our company   has with the representative without   long   to talk   tᵢ
einen Vertrag abgeschlossen
a contract   signed
'Our company signed a contract with the representative without talking (to him) for long'

(b) **Onze firma   heeft [met de vertegenwoordiger]ⱼ [zonder lang*
our company   has   with the representative   without long
pgᵢ *te overleggen]* tᵢ *een verdrag gesloten.*
to deliberate   a   contract signed
'Our company signed a contract with the representative without speaking (with him) for long.'

Note that our analysis, which defends the view that pgs are weak pronominals, straightforwardly accounts for the facts in Dutch, and even finds additional support in examples such as (27) below, where *er* 'there', the [R] pronominal complement of the postposition *mee* 'with', may indeed function as a pg licenser:[21]

(27) *Onze firma   heeft er*ᵢ *[zonder lang* pgᵢ *mee   te overleggen]*
our   company has   there without long   with   to deliberate
*een verdrag [t*ᵢ *mee] gesloten.*
a   contract with   signed
'Our company signed a contract with the representative without speaking (with him) for long.'

The argument is as follows: if, as we have argued, a pg is a null weak pronominal, one would expect it to be able to scramble only under the same conditions that apply for the scrambling of its phonologically realized counterpart. As observed by several researchers (Corver and van Riemsdijk 1996; Haider and Rosengren 1998, 2003; among many others), scrambling of pronominal (and nominal) DPs is possible only if it takes place out of a head-final projection, exactly the situation (27) depicts. Once the pronoun undergoes scrambling to the *v*P-edge of the embedded clause, PR selects the candidate in which the pg licenser also undergoes scrambling, resulting in exactly the kind of structure in (27). Stated differently, apparently 'untriggered' scrambling of pronominal *er* satisfies PR.[22]

The last set of data we will finally turn to comes from Fanselow (1993) and Bayer and Kornfilt (1994), where it is observed that no element may intervene between a scrambled pg licenser and the embedded adverbial clause ((28a) vs. (28b)), unless such an element is an adverbial (28c) or the pg licenser is a pronoun ((28d) vs. (28e)):[23]

(28) (a) *wenn jemand der Anette$_i$ [anstatt pg$_i$ zu helfen]* t$_i$ *das Buch von Jamal*
           if   someone   the Anette instead   to help   the book of Jamal
           wegnimmt
           away-takes
           'if someone takes away Jamal's book from Anette instead of helping (her)'

      (b) **wenn jemand   der Anette$_i$ das Buch von Jamal$_j$ [ansttat pg$_i$ zu helfen]*
           if   someone the Anette the book of   Jamal   instead   to help
           t$_i$ t$_j$ *wegnimmt*
              away-takes
           'if someone takes away Jamal's book from Anette instead of helping (her)'

      (c) *weil   er   der Anette$_i$ gestern   [ansttat pg$_i$ zu helfen]* t$_i$ *ein Buch$_i$ stahl*
           because he   the Anette yesterday instead   to help   a   book stole
           'because yesterday he stole a book from Anette, instead of helping (her)'

      (d) **Da   hat diesen Mann$_i$ der Polizist   [ohne pg$_i$ verwarnt zu haben]*
           there has this   man   the policeman without   warned   to have
           ins   Gefängnis t$_i$ *gesteckt*
           in-the prison   put
           'The policeman put this man in prison without having warned (him)'

      (e) *Da   hat ihn$_i$ der Polizist   [ohne   pg$_i$ verwant zu haben] ins*
           there has him the policeman without   warned   to have   in-the
           Gefägnis t$_i$ *gesteckt*
           prison   put
           'The policeman put him in prison without having warned (him)'

Since space limitations prevent us from developing a full argument here, we will restrict ourselves to pointing to some guidelines for a potential treatment of these kinds of structures. We suggest that the factor at stake is an issue regarding the notion of locality/closeness that exists between the pg and its potential licenser in Spec,v*P:[24] only the closest available constituent in Spec,v*P may serve as an antecedent for a pg. Bearing this in mind, the contrast between (28a) and (28b) simply reduces to the impossibility for *das Buch von Jamal* 'Jamal's book' in Spec,v*P to meet the thematic requirements that *helfen* 'help' imposes on its co-referent, namely the null weak pronominal. The same argument would explain the ungrammaticality of (28d), where the closest antecedent for the pg in the adverbial clause is the subject that resides on the innermost specifier of matrix v*P.

Intervention of a co-argument is, however, possible if this element is also a pg licenser (example from Kathol 2000):

(29) *?Karl hat   den Käfer$_i$ seiner$_j$ Tochter [ansttat pg$_i$ pg$_j$ zu schenken]*
      Karl   has   the VW Beetle his   daughter instead   to give
      teuer t$_i$ t$_j$ *verkauft*
      expensive   sold
      'Karl sold the VW Beetle to his daughter for much money instead of giving it to her'

We contend that (29) does not constitute an obstacle for the hypothesis sketched out here, since German allows a flexible order regarding the base generation of verbal internal complements, a possibility that seems to be supported by phenomena such VP-topicalization (Haider and Rosengren 1998, 2003; Fanselow 2001; Chocano 2007). In other words, the scrambled objects in (29) are the closest available antecedents for a multiple pg structure where the accusative object is base-generated higher than the dative one.

We would like to point out some guidelines to account for the grammaticality of (28c) and (28e). The grammaticality of (28c) is probably connected to those properties that, in a more general sense, distinguish arguments from adjuncts. On the other hand, the grammaticality of (28e) could most likely be related to the most salient difference between weak pronominals and regular DPs, namely that only the former have the ability to undergo phonological restructuring (cf. Cardinaletti and Starke 1996, 1999). The hypothesis is that restructuring makes the element that participate in the process 'invisible' for the purposes of the computation of linear order, although, admittedly, this speculative intuition requires much more research.

4. Conclusion

In this brief analysis of Dutch and German pg structures, we have demonstrated that *Move/Merge-α*-based explanatory attempts are inadequate in accounting for the licensing mechanisms involved in generating and evaluating pg structures in these languages. Here we argue that a hybrid MP-OT theory similar in scope and design to Broekhuis' D&E model is both conceptually simple while able to account for the diverse linearization requirements evidenced in the empirical data. Although this study presents only a novel sketch of two salient aspects of pg structures in Dutch and German, we are of the opinion that the simple design of the formalism coupled with the well-formed, limited number of linearization (PF) constraints is both conceptually and empirically appealing to linguists working in the MP, OT, or the ever-growing-in-interest hybrid (MP-OT) traditions, for example, the D&E framework.

Acknowledgments

The authors' names appear in alphabetic order and represent an equal contribution on both of their parts. We would like to thank the volume editors, Hans Broekhuis and Ralf Vogel, for the opportunity to submit our work on parasitic gaps to this volume. We are greatly indebted to John Hale, Martin Salzmann, and an anonymous reviewer for critical advice regarding our analysis. We would also like to thank Hans Broekhuis and Annemarie Toebosch for their willingness to provide Dutch data whenever called upon as well as Kleanthes Grohmann and Dorian Roehrs concerning German data. The usual disclaimers apply.

Notes

1. By 'pg licensers' we refer to those elements whose movement in the matrix clause makes the presence of a pg in the embedded one possible.
2. Indefinite wh-words in German normally have a non-specific, existential reading, which forces them to remain in their VP-internal, base-generated position (Haider, 1993; Frey and Pittner, 1998).

  (i) (a)   dass Peter gestern   dem Mann was   geschickt hat
              that Peter yesterday the man-D something-A sent   has
              'that Peter sent the man something yesterday'

        (b)   *dass Peter was$_i$ gestern   dem Mann t$_i$ geschickt hat
              that   Peter something-A yesterday the man-D   sent   has
              'that Peter sent something to the man yesterday'

3. While the contrast between the German root structures in (3) is also found in Dutch (Hans Broekhuis, p.c.), the German equivalent to the Dutch embedded clause in (4a) is notably worse (Ralf Vogel, p.c.). This is something that, admittedly, remains a mystery in our approach – and practically in every other alternative one as well.
4. This approach, of course, is not the first attempt at a hybrid formalism that fuses another established formalism (e.g., LFG and Minimalism) to function as the GEN component of the theory with the EVAL component of OT (see Bresnan (1996), (2001); Broekhuis and Dekkers (2000); Broekhuis (2008) among others). We concur with Kuhn's (2003: 28) observation that: "the value of the representations assumed can only be judged when looking at the interplay of all aspects of the theory. A special twist to the problem arises for OT syntax since the representations assumed are often inherited from another theoretical framework (GB, Minimalism, LFG). Obviously, some of the explanatory burden carried by some aspect of the original framework is now replaced by OT's mechanism of constraint interaction. This in turn may influence the 'grounding' of representations – or in other words, the same representation may be suitably motivated in the original framework, but may be foreign to the Optimality-Theoretic variant of the framework."
5. Broekhuis and Vogel (2010) point out that hybrid MP-OT approaches such as Broekhuis' (2008) D&E framework are not incompatible with versions of the MP that seek to be crash-proof (à la Frampton and Gutmann 2002) in design.
6. As far as a formal definition of A-bar movement is concerned, for H&M an 'A-bar position' is simply one occupied by an operator.
7. Most treatments of 'optional' movement in 'mainstream' (strictly derivational) versions of Minimalism are licensed by an optional EPP-feature (see Chomsky 2001; Biberauer, 2003; Biberauer and Roberts 2005; Biberauer and Richards, 2006). As Broekhuis (2008) and Broekhuis and Vogel (2010) point out in their discussion of Object Shift in Icelandic, that following Chomsky (2001), optional EPP-features are not inherent properties of Probes. Chomsky's notion; namely, that EPP-effects are added to Probes whenever a pragmatic/semantic effect is observed, can unfortunately be interpreted as a language-specific mechanism that is unfalsifiable. The D&E-framework circumvents this problem and eliminates this redundancy by introducing the Effect-on-Output condition and soft, violable pragmatic/semantic constraints such as ALIGNFOCUS (cf. (12)). Due to the fact that this constraint is: (a) violable; and (b) not argued to be part of the inviolable aspects (= GEN) of the C_{HL}, we no longer need 'optional' EPP-features in the narrow syntax.
8. The ungrammaticality of subject gaps in German and Dutch, as opposed to their counterparts in English, was capitalized on in seminal work by Bennis (1986), Bennis and Hoekstra (1985) and Huybregts and van Riemsdijk (1985), where pgs were viewed as the product of Across-the-Board extraction (ATB).
9. That is, languages like Icelandic, in which OS is possible for pronominal as well as nominal DPs. Our brief summary of Broekhuis' (2008) characterization of OS/scrambling abstracts away from the constraints responsible for the case of Mainland Scandinavian, where only pronouns are allowed to shift, since they are irrelevant for our analysis of Dutch and German pg constructions.

10. It is generally assumed in OT and hybrid formalisms such as OT-LFG that the GEN component produces candidates that do not vary semantically from the 'input' – although the notion of defining the 'input' in this approach is quite a debatable topic. Furthermore, the exact definition of semantic information is also unclear. Nonetheless, it appears that the D&E framework instituted by Broekhuis adheres (to some extent) to this general guiding principle.

11. Although our PF-constraint PARALLELISM REQUIREMENT takes its name from that in Munn (1993) and Hornstein and Nunes (2002), they are completely different requirements: whereas the former reduces to a semantic condition on well-formed coordinate structures that basically entails the semantic similarity of two conjuncts, the latter relates to similarity in precedence relations between the relevant elements in the two conjuncts.

12. On the other hand, the present formulation of the PR makes the prediction that pg licensers should also be allowed to appear in Spec, CP. This prediction is fulfilled in examples with wh-movement (i) (example from Kathol, 2000) and topicalization (ii) (example from Ralf Vogel, p.c.):

(i) Welches Mädchen$_i$ hat Hans [ohne   pg anzusehen] t$_i$ geküsst?
    which   girl   has Hans without   to-look-at   kissed
    'Which girl did Hans kiss without looking at?'

(ii) ?Die Maria$_i$ hat der Hans   [ohne   pg anzusehen] t$_i$ geküsst
     the   Maria has kissed the Hans   without   to-look-at
     'Maria, Hans kissed without looking at her'

Nevertheless, the facts in (a)–(b) are not surprising within a model of phasal derivation in which constituents that reach the CP-edge must necessarily pass through the v*P-edge. This raises the question whether CP or v*P is the domain relevant for evaluation of PR.

13. Hans Broekhuis (p.c) points out that replacing pro in (19b) with an operator would have the same effect as far as PR is concerned. However, it would be at odds with both Postal's (1994, 2000) data in (14)–(16) as well as with Webelhuth's Paradox.

14. Our rationale for maintaining the ordering AF >> EPP (CASE) >> *MOVE is that, in the absence of the PR constraint, these are crucially ranked.

15. In our account, it is clear that pg licensing is inextricably linked to movement of the pg licenser to the v*P-edge: if, as we argue, null weak pronominals obligatorily scramble to that position, PR will force the pg licenser to appear there too. However, Hans Broekhuis (p.c) points out that pgs are (marginally) possible in structures where A-movement targets other positions, which would suggest that their licensing can be tied to A-movement, irrespective of the structural position it targets. The main pieces of evidence he provides are given below ((i) (from Broekhuis, 1992); (ii) (from Hans Broekhuis, p.c.):

(i) ?dat [die boeken] [zonder pg$_i$ te bekijken] t$_i$ werden weggelegd
    that the books   without   to inspect   were   put away
    'that the books were put away without inspecting them'

(ii) dat Jan <*iets> waarschijnlijk <iets> [zonder pg$_i$ te lezen] aan Frits   heeft terug gegeven
     that Jan   probably something without   to read to   Frits has   back   given
     'that Jan has probably given back something to Frits without reading (it)'

Example (i) shows a Dutch passive structure in which movement of the internal argument die boeken 'the books' to Spec, T licenses the pg in the adverbial clause. With respect to (ii), Broekhuis (1992, 2008) assumes that sentence adverbs always follow the position in which Case-valuation takes place (i.e. Spec, v*P). From this perspective, (ii), in which both pg and pg licenser appear in their respective v*P-edges as PR demands, should be grammatical. Admittedly, these data pose a serious challenge to the approach that we adopt here; namely, the established connection between pg-licensing and movement to the v*P-edge. This caveat notwithstanding, the fact that pg-licensing could be (marginally) possible from A-positions in any language call many canonical assumptions about the A/A'-dichotomy into question.

Although we recognize that our current analysis cannot address example (i), it does not seem to be an insurmountable obstacle, given that corresponding structures seem to be impossible in both English and German (German example from Müller 1993; his judgment):

(iii) *dass [dieses Buch]$_i$ [ohne pg$_i$ zu lesen] dem Jungen t$_i$ gegeben wurde
       that this   book   without   to read   the boy-DAT   given   was
       'that the book was given to the boy without reading (it)'

(iv) *The book was filed without reading

On the other hand, we do not think that the data in (b), also attested in German (Ralf Vogel, p.c.), are incompatible with our hypothesis, especially if, as argued by Frey (2000, 2004, 2006) for German, scrambling past a sentential adverb is simply A-topicalization within the CP-domain. In other words, the ungrammaticality of (b) is due to the impossibility of interpreting the indefinite as a topic.

16. The subordinators at stake are, according to Parker (1999), ohne ('without'), anstatt ('instead of'), and um ('in order to') in German, and zonder ('without') and om ('in order to') in Dutch.

17. Although the (un)grammaticality of (23b) seems to be subject to dialectal variation (Ralf Vogel, p.c.).

18. In our view, the basic problem here, which is exactly the point that Kathol's (2000) study alludes to, is that we do not know if what we call a 'pg' in English is the same as what we observe in Dutch and German. In other words, the key question boils down to this: why does the semi-coordinating structure involved in pgs relevant for the grammars of Dutch and German but crucially not for English? Although we mention this previously in fn. 4 (for a more detailed treatment of this issue, see Parker (1999)), the treatment of Dutch and German pgs as ATB constructions extends back to the Government and Binding (GB) era, where they were ruled out on the basis of direction of recursion in these languages. Clearly, an adequate treatment of this issue transcends the scope of this current investigation and is something that must be left for future research. If, however, our current research is headed in the right direction, it is not too far-fetched to envisage that linearization (PF) constraints and their subsequent ranking lie at the heart of this parametric variation among Dutch, English, and German with regard to their (in)ability to license what Kathol calls 'true' p-gaps.

19. As pointed out to us by Martin Salzmann (p.c.) and also mentioned in Kathol (2000), in conjunction with the German data in (3/22) above, an example where the adverbial clause appears extraposed, that is, at the right edge of the sentence, is markedly worse than (22a) and (22b):

(iii) ??/*dass Hans Maria geküsst [ohne pg anzusehen] hat
            that Hans Maria kissed   without at-to-look   has
       'that Hans kissed Maria without looking at (her).'

For Salzmann (and other native German speakers we have consulted with) an overt pronoun sie 'she' is strongly preferred over the presence of a pg. The strong dispreference of example (iii) could be due to an adjacency requirement (similar to what we mention in conjunction with the data in (28) later in this chapter), however such a claim would have to be tested in the future with native speakers and Dutch and German to validate it.

20. In Broekhuis' (2008) D&E framework, Verb-second is tied to the constraint LEXICALLY FILL TOP F (LFTF) in (a):

(a) LEXICALLY FILL TOP F (LFTF)
    The highest head position in an extended projection must be lexically filled

Verb movement satisfies LFTF only if no complementizer or subordinator has been directly inserted in F.

21. Thanks to Hans Broekhuis (p.c.) for bringing this contrast to our attention.

22. Unfortunately, we cannot provide a fully-detailed, principled explanation for the grammaticality of (26a) in German in this current study. However, as mentioned to us by Martin Salzmann (p.c.), there may be an independent reason why (26a) is acceptable for some speakers of German, namely due

to the fact that the verb in the adverbial clause is used intransitively, this preventing any gap from appearing. To test this claim one would have to construct and test examples where the PP-complement is more or less obligatory, as shown in the following example from German:

(i) ??eine Frau,   an die ich [ohne häufig   zu denken] sofort   mein Herz verlor.
      a   woman in RP ich without frequently to think   immediately my heart   lost
    'a woman, whom whenever I think of (her), I lose my heart.'

Intuitively, such examples are only acceptable to the extent that the verb can be interpreted intransitively so that (26a) would be unproblematic for our analysis. One possibility would be to extend the notion of 'parallelism' to also include thematic relations (which is clearly not the case for the example above (cf. (i)). We leave these concerns for future research.

23. At this point, we would like to draw the reader's attention to the fact that there is no exact counterpart in Dutch to the structures in (28) due to reasons completely unrelated to a potential different behavior of the PR constraint in that language: a scrambled object can precede neither the higher base-generated dative nor the subject in the adverbial clause, therefore, there is no possibility for the PR constraint to evaluate candidates with those word orders in the matrix clause. However, the requirement that no argument intervenes between the pg and its licenser seems to hold also in that language, as Hans Broekhuis (p.c.) has confirmed to us on the basis of the contrast below:

(i) (a) ?Jan heeft zijn dochter$_i$ [in plaats van pg$_i$ een boek te geven] t$_i$ een maaltijd aangeboden
         Jan has   his daughter instead of   a book to give a   meal   offered
         'Jan offered his daughter a meal instead of giving (her) a book'

    (b) *Jan heeft zijn dochter$_i$ [in plaats van pg$_i$ een boek te geven] een maaltijd$_j$ t$_i$ t$_j$ aangeboden
         Jan has   his daughter instead of a book to give   a meal   offered
         'Jan offered his daughter a meal instead of giving (her) a book'

24. We thank Hans Broekhuis (p.c.) for this suggestion.

References

Bayer, J. and Kornfilt, J. (1994) Against scrambling as an instance of Move-alpha. In N. Corver and H. van Riemsdijk (eds) *Studies on Scrambling*, 17–60. Berlin: Mouton de Gruyter.

Bennis, H. (1986) *Gaps and Dummies*. Dordrecht: Foris.

Bennis, H. and Hoekstra, T. (1984) Gaps and parasitic gaps. *The Linguistic Review* 4 (1984–1985): 29–87.

Bennis, H. and Hoekstra, T. (1985) Parasitic gaps in Dutch. In *Proceedings of NELS* 151–14. GSLA, University of Massachusetts: Amherst.

Bresnan, J. (1996) LF in an OT setting: Modelling competition and economy. In M. Butt and T. King (eds) *Proceedings of the First LFG Conference*, CSLI Proceedings Online.

Biberauer, T. (2003) *Verb Second (V2) in Afrikaans: A Minimalist Investigation of Word Order Variation.* Doctoral dissertation, University of Cambridge.

Biberauer, T. and Richards, M. (2006) True optionality: When the grammar doesn't mind. In C. Boeckx (ed.) *Minimalist Essays*, 35–67. Amsterdam: Benjamins.

Biberauer, T. and Roberts, I. (2005) Changing EPP-parameters in the history of English: Accounting for variation and change. *English Language and Linguistics* 9: 5–46.

Broekhuis, H. (1992) *Chain-government: Issues in Dutch Syntax*, Doctoral dissertation, University of Amsterdam/HIL.

Broekhuis, H. (2008) *Derivations and Evaluations: Object Shift in Germanic Languages.* Berlin: Mouton de Gruyter.

Broekhuis, H. and Dekkers, J. (2000) The minimalist program and optimality theory: derivations and evaluations. In J. Dekkers, F. van der Leeuw and J. van de Weijer (eds) *Optimality Theory: Phonology, Syntax, Acquisition*, 386–422. Oxford: Oxford University Press.

Broekhuis, H. and Vogel, R. (2010) Crash-proof syntax and filters. In M. Putnam (eds) *Exploring Crash-Proof Grammars*, 245–67. Amsterdam: John Benjamins.

Cardinaletti, A. and Starke, M. (1996) Deficient pronouns. A view from Germanic. A study in the unified description of Germanic and Romance. In H. Thráinsson, S. D. Epstein and S. Peter (eds) *Studies in Comparative Germanic Syntax* vol. II, 21–65. Dordrecht: Kluwer.

Cardinaletti, A. and Starke, M. (1999) The typology of structural deficiency. A case study of three classes of pronouns. In H. van Riemsdijk (ed.) *Clitics in the Languages of Europe*, 145–233. Berlin: Mouton de Gruyter.

Chocano, G. (2007) *Narrow Syntax and Phonological Form: Scrambling in the Germanic Languages*. Amsterdam: John Benjamins.

Chomsky, N. (1977) On *wh*-movement. In P. Culicover, T. Wasow and A. Akmajian (eds) *Formal Syntax*, 71–132. New York: Academic Press.

Chomsky, N. (1982) *Lectures on Government and Binding*. Dordrecht: Foris.

Chomsky, N. (1993) A minimalist program for linguistic theory. In K. Hale and S. J. Keyser (eds) *The View from Building 20: Essays in Honor of Sylvain Bromberger*, 1–52. Cambridge, MA: MIT Press.

Chomsky, N. (1995) *The Minimalist Program*. Cambridge, MA: MIT Press.

Chomsky, N. (2000) Minimalist inquiries: The framework. In R. Martin, D. Michaels and J. Uriagereka (eds) *Step by Step: Essays in Minimalist Syntax in Honor of Howard Lasnik*, 85–155. Cambridge, MA: MIT Press.

Chomsky, N. (2001) Derivation by phase. In M. Kenstowicz (ed.) *Ken Hale: A Life in Language*, 1–52. Cambridge, MA: MIT Press.

Cinque, G. (1990) *Types of A-bar-dependencies*. Cambridge, MA: MIT Press.

Corver, N. and van Riemsdijk, H. (1996) The position of the head and the domain of scrambling. In B. Palek (ed.) *Typology: Prototypes, Item Orderings and Universals. Proceedings of the LP'96 Conference on Word Order*, 57–90. Prague: Charles University Press.

Culicover, P. (2000) Parasitic gaps: A history. In P. Postal and P. Culicover (eds) *Parasitic Gaps*, 3–68. Cambridge, MA: MIT Press.

Den Besten, H. (1983) On the interaction of root transformations and lexical deletive rules. In W. Abraham (ed.) *On the Formal Syntax of West Germania*, 47–131. Amsterdam: John Benjamins.

Diesing, M. (1992) *Indefinites*. Cambridge, MA: MIT Press.

Engdahl, E. (1983) Parasitic gaps. *Linguistics and Philosophy* 6: 5–34. Reprinted in P. Culicover and P. Postal (eds) *Parasitic Gaps*, 69–98. Cambridge, MA: MIT Press.

Fanselow, G. (1993) The return of the base generators. *Groninger Arbeiten zur Germanistischen Linguistik* 36: 1–74.

Fanselow, G. (2001) Features, theta-roles, and free constituent order. *Linguistic Inquiry* 32 (3): 405–37.

Felix, S. (1983) Parasitic gaps in German. *Groninger Arbeiten zur Germanistischen Linguistik* 22: 1–46.

Felix, S. (1985) Parasitic gaps in German. In W. Abraham (ed.) *Erklärende Syntax des Deutschen*, 173–201. Tübingen: Niemeyer.

Fox, D. and Pesetsky, D. (2005) Cyclic linearization of syntactic structure. *Theoretical Linguistics* 31: 1–46.

Frampton, J. and Gutmann, S. (2002) Crash-proof syntax. In S. D. Epstein and T. D. Seely (eds) *Derivations and Explanations in the Minimalist Program*, 90–105. Oxford: Blackwell.

Frey, W. (2000) Über die syntaktische Position der Satztopiks im Deutschen. *ZAS Papers in Linguistics* 20: 137–72.

Frey, W. (2004) The grammar-pragmatics interface and the German prefield. *Sprache und Pragmatik* 52: 1–39.

Frey, W. (2006) Contrast and movement to the German prefield. In V. Mólnar and S. Winkler (eds) *The Architecture of Focus*, 235–65. Berlin: Mouton de Gruyter.

Frey, W. and Pittner, K. (1998) Zur Positionierung von Adverbialen im deutschen Mittelfeld. *Linguistische Berichte* 176: 489–534.

Gazdar, G. (1981) Unbounded dependencies in coordinate structure. *Linguistic Inquiry* 12 (2): 155–84.

Grimshaw, J. (1997)   Projections, heads, and optimality. *Linguistic Inquiry* 28 (3): 373–422.

Grimshaw, J. (1998) *Constraints on Constraints in Optimality Theoretic Syntax*. Unpublished ms. Rutgers University.

Haider, H. (1993) *Deutsche Syntax Generativ*. Tübingen: Narr.

Haider, H. and Rosengren, I. (1998) Scrambling. *Sprache und Pragmatik* 49: 1–104.

Haider, H. and Rosengren, I. (2003) Scrambling. Non-triggered chain formation in OV languages. *Journal of Germanic Linguistics* 15 (3): 203–67.

Heck, F. and Müller, G. (2000) *Repair-driven Movement and the Local Optimization of Derivations*, ms., University of Tübingen and IDS Mannheim.

Hornstein, N. and Nunes, J. (2002) On asymmetries between parasitic gap and across-the-board constructions. *Syntax* 5 (1): 26–54.

Huybregts, R. and van Riemsdijk, H. (1985) Parasitic gaps and ATB. In *Proceedings of NELS 15*, 168–187. University of Massachusetts, Amherst: GSLA.

Kathol, A. (2000) On the nonexistence of true parasitic gaps in Standard German. In P. Culicover and P. Postal (eds) *Parasitic Gaps*, 315–38. Cambridge, MA: MIT Press.

Kuhn, J. (2003) *Optimality-theoretic Syntax: A Declarative Approach*. Stanford, CA: CSLI.

Legendre, G., Grimshaw, J. and Vikner, S. (1998) *Optimality-Theoretic Syntax*. Cambridge, MA: MIT Press.

Lenerz, J. (1977) *Zur Abfolge nominaler Satzglieder im Deutschen*. Tübingen: Narr.

Meinunger, A. (1995) *Discourse Dependent DP (De)placement*. Doctoral dissertation. Universität Postdam.

Müller, G. (1993) *On Deriving Movement Type Asymmetries*. Doctoral dissertation. Universität Tübingen.

Munn, A. (1993) *Topics in the Syntax and Semantics of Coordinate Structures*. Doctoral dissertation. University of Maryland, College Park.

Neeleman, A. (1994) Scrambling as a D-structure phenomenon. In N. Corver and H. van Riemsdijk (eds) *Studies on Scrambling. Movement and Non-movement Approaches to Free Word Order Phenomena*, 387–429. Berlin: Mouton de Gruyter.

Neeleman, A. and Reinhart, T. (1998) Scrambling and the PF interface. In M. Butt and W. Geuder (eds) *The Projection of Arguments: Lexical and Compositional Factors*, 309–52. Stanford, CA: CSLI Publications.

Parker, A. (1999) *Parasitic Gaps in Germanic Languages*, MA Thesis, National University of Ireland.

Pesetsky, D. (1982) *Paths and Categories*. Doctoral dissertation. Cambridge, MA: MIT.

Postal, S. (1994) Parasitic and pseudo-parasitic gaps. *Linguistic Inquiry* 25 (1): 63–117. Reprinted in P. Culicover and P. Postal (eds) *Parasitic Gaps*, 253–314. Cambridge, MA: MIT Press.

Postal, S. (2000) Further lacunae in the English parasitic gap paradigm. In P. Culicover and P. Postal (eds) *Parasitic Gaps*, 223–50. Cambridge, MA: MIT Press.

Putnam, M. (2007) *Scrambling and the Survive Principle*. Amsterdam: John Benjamins.

Salzmann, M. (2008) Variation in resumption requires violable constraints – a case study in Alemannic relativization. In H. Broekhuis and R. Vogel (eds) *Optimality Theory and Minimalism: Interface Theories. Linguistics in Postdam* 28: 99–132.

Webelhuth, G. (1989) *Syntactic Saturation Phenomena and the Modern Germanic Languages*. Doctoral dissertation. University of Massachusetts.

Webelhuth, G. (1992) *Principles and Parameters of Syntactic Saturation*. Oxford: Oxford University Press.

4 On three types of variation in resumption: evidence in favor of violable and ranked constraints

Martin Salzmann[*]

ABSTRACT Variation in the last resort nature of resumption cross-linguistically and variation in dative resumption among and within Alemannic varieties of German strongly favor an evaluator component that makes use of violable and rankable constraints as in Optimality Theory rather than filters as in the Minimalist Program. At the same time, the range of variation is best restrained in a model of syntax like the Derivations and Evaluations framework (Broekhuis 2008) that combines a restrictive MP-style generator with a flexible OT-evaluator.

KEYWORDS resumption; Swiss German; variation; evaluator; reference set; candidate set; dative; constraints; oblique case; relative clauses; last resort; elementary operation

1. Introduction

Optimality Theory (OT, Prince and Smolensky 2004) and the Minimalist Program (MP, Chomsky 1995, 2000, 2001, 2004, 2007, 2008) are usually seen as two mutually exclusive models of grammar that differ fundamentally in their architecture. Broekhuis (2008: chapter 1), however, shows convincingly that the similarities are in fact much closer than is normally assumed: Both models contain a generator which is responsible for the universal properties of language, and both make use of an evaluator which selects the grammatical form from among the members of the output. The two frameworks differ, however, in that they focus on different components: while MP tries to explain linguistic phenomena largely by reference to properties of the generator and tends to neglect output constraints, OT assumes a relatively unconstrained generator and puts most of its emphasis on the evaluator. As a consequence of this difference in focus, the two frameworks also have conflicting views on the locus of language variation: In OT, language variation is due to the evaluator, that is, different constraint

* Martin Salzmann, Universität Leipzig, Institut für Linguistik, Beethovenstr. 15, D-04107 Leipzig, Germany. E-mail: martin.salzmann@uni-leipzig.de

rankings. MP, on the other hand, attributes language variation largely to the lexicon (the so-called 'Borer-Chomsky-conjecture'), that is, to differences in the inventory of lexical items (especially of functional heads) and in the presence of movement-triggering EPP/edge-features on those items. However, as Broekhuis (2008: 28–31) has pointed out, recent versions of MP (Chomsky 2000ff.) also make use of language-specific output filters/interface constraints, as is clear from Chomsky's (2001) analysis of object shift. The difference in the treatment of language variation between OT and MP is thus narrowed down; in many cases it boils down to the question whether the evaluator takes recourse to output filters or to ranked constraints.[1] Language variation is thus a very important domain to test the validity of a given framework. To this end, I will investigate three variation phenomena obtaining with resumptive pronouns that all present different challenges for a theory of variation.

I will first introduce the basic facts about Swiss German relativization. In section 3 I will explain the distribution of resumptive pronouns as a last resort phenomenon. After that I show that resumptive relatives are best analyzed as involving base-generation. Section 5 introduces the variation facts. Section 6 discusses the implications of the variation facts and provides analyses for both OT and MP that show that an evaluator with ranked constraints is descriptively as well as explanatorily more adequate than one based on filters. Section 7 concludes the chapter. Since the argument requires a specific view on resumptive pronouns, the first part of the article will be devoted to many technicalities before the variation facts can be tackled. I therefore ask the reader to be patient.

2. Resumption in Swiss German relative clauses

Swiss German relative clauses are introduced by an invariant complementizer *wo* (*won* before unstressed vowels). There are no relative pronouns as in Standard German (except in certain adverbial relations).[2] In certain grammatical relations, a resumptive pronoun appears instead of a gap. In the default case the resumptives behave like weak personal pronouns and are fronted to the Wackernagel position or cliticized onto C (or, in the case of oblique objects, onto the governing preposition). According to earlier descriptions, the distribution of resumptive pronouns in restrictive local relativization follows the Accessibility Hierarchy by Keenan and Comrie (1977): Resumptive pronouns are used for dative objects and more oblique relations, but crucially not for subjects and direct objects. This is illustrated by the following examples from the High Alemannic dialect spoken in the Canton of Zurich (cf. Weber 1964; Van Riemsdijk 1989):[3]

(1) (a) d   Frau,   wo (***si**) immer z   spaat chunt
          the woman   C   (she)   always too late   comes
          'the woman who is always late'   (SU: gap)

     (b) es Bild,   wo niemert (***s**) cha   zale
          a   picture C   nobody   (it)   can   pay
          'a picture that nobody can afford'   (DO: gap)

(c) de Bueb, wo mer *(em)   es Velo   versproche händ
the boy   C   we   (he.DAT) a   bike   promised   have.1PL
'the boy we promised a bike'   (IO: res.)

(d) d   Frau,   won i von   *(ere)   es Buech   überchoo han
the woman C   I from   (she.DAT) a   book   got   have.1SG
'the woman from whom I got a book'   (P-object: res.)

Additionally, resumptive pronouns also occur inside islands, in positions from where regular *wh*-extraction is impossible (Salzmann 2006: 331, Salzmann 2011; islands are henceforth enclosed in angled brackets):

(2) (a) de Sänger, won i mi fröi,   <wänn i *(en) gsee>
the singer   C   I me be.happy.1SG when   I him   see.1SG
'the singer such that I am happy when I see him'

(b) * [Wele Sänger]₁ fröisch   di,   <wänn t__₁/en₁ gseesch>?
which   singer   be.happy.2SG you   when   you him see.2SG
lit.: 'Which singer are you happy when you see?'

As (2b) shows, extraction of *wh*-phrases does not improve with resumption. I will briefly come back to the incompatibility of regular *wh*-movement with resumption in 4.2 below. Gaps and resumptives are thus in complementary distribution. Whenever a gap is possible, a resumptive pronoun is not, and vice versa (although we will see in sections 6.2 and 6.3 below that things are more complex with datives).

3.   Explaining the distribution of resumptives in Swiss German

The distribution of resumptives in Swiss German can be related to two grammatical factors: one one hand, they occur to prevent violations of locality, on the other, they are a means of making oblique case visible. Resumptive pronouns can thus be understood as a last resort device that only comes into play when gap derivations fail (cf., e.g., Shlonsky 1992; Pesetsky 1998; Toman 1998; Boeckx 2003; Alexopoulou 2006; Guilliot 2006; Rouveret 2008).

3.1   Resumptive pronouns amnesty locality violations

As shown in (2), resumptive pronouns are obligatory in cases where relativization involves a position inside an island. They are thus a means of amnestying locality violations. Why resumptives have this property is not *a priori* clear and will be discussed in 4.1 below. The amnestying function also accounts for resumptive pronouns after prepositions as in (1d) since PPs form strong islands in German and its varieties (cf., e.g., Bayer 1996), as shown by example (3a): The PP *vo wem* cannot be extracted from the complement PP introduced by *a* 'at'. (3b) shows that extracting a PP from a direct object is fine:

(3) (a) *[Vo wem]₁ häsch <an e Schwöschter__₁> tänkt?
      of who.DAT have.2SG at a sister thought
      lit.: 'Who did think of a sister of?'

(b) [Vo wem]₁ häsch [e Schwöschter__₁] gsee?
      of who.DAT have.2SG a sister seen
      'Who did you see a sister of?'

This interpretation of the facts is strengthened by the observation that the same contrast obtains when contituents of semantic types other than <e> are relativized. The following pair involves relativization of a predicate; in (4a) it originates in a transparent position, in (4b) it originates within a PP (i.e., within an island). While resumption is impossible in the first example, it is obligatory in the second (Salzmann 2006):[4]

(4) (a) Er isch de **gliich Idiot,** wo scho sin Vatter **(*das)** gsii isch.
      he is the same idiot C already his father that been is
      'He is the same idiot his father already was.'

(b) Isch de Hans würkli de **Trottel,** won en all *(de)füür haltet?
      is the John really the idiot C him all there.for hold
      'Is John really the idiot everyone regards him as?'

Importantly, amnestying a locality violation is not to be understood in a processing sense: Relative clauses with resumptive pronouns inside islands are perfectly natural in Swiss German and do not have a repair flavor like intrusive pronouns in English, cf. Chao and Sells (1983).

3.2 Dative resumptive pronouns realize oblique case

Dative resumptive pronouns cannot be related to locality since they occur in positions from where extraction is in principle possible. The following examples show that while *wh*-extraction of an indirect object is unproblematic, the corresponding relative clause requires a resumptive pronoun:

(5) (a) [Welem Maa]₁ häsch__₁ es Buech ggëë?
      which.DAT man have.2s a book given?
      'To which man did man you give a book?'

(b) de Maa, won t *__/em es Buech ggëë häsch
      the man C you he.DAT a book given have.2s
      'the man to whom you gave a book'

Instead, the occurrence of dative resumptive pronouns can be related to a language-internal PF-constraint that requires the overt realization of oblique case: As in Standard German, dative, which is the only oblique case in the Swiss German case system (genitive has been lost), requires special morphological licensing. I illustrate this on the basis of two contexts here which were discussed earlier in Bayer *et al.* (2001).

First, complement clauses cannot directly fill the slot of a dative argument (Bayer *et al.* 2001: 471). Since CPs cannot realize morphological case in German, a DP has to be inserted to rescue example (6b). The non-oblique (i.e., direct) cases nominative and accusative do not require this extra licensing, and as a result a DP realizing such a case is optional (6a).

(6) (a) Wir bestritten, (die   Behauptung) [dass wir verreisen   wollten].
        we denied   the.ACC claim   that we travel.away wanted
        'We denied (the allegation) that we wanted to go away.'

    (b) Wir widersprachen *(**der   Behauptung**), [dass wir ... wollten].
        we rejected   the.DAT claim   that we ... wanted
        'We rejected the allegation that we wanted ... .'

Second, topic drop is possible with nominally-marked (subjects) and accusative-marked DPs (direct objects), but not with dative-marked DPs, cf. Bayer *et al.* (2001: 489). On topic drop and the role of PF, see also Sigurdsson and Maling (2010):

(7) (a) [$_{ACC}$] Hab' ich schon   gesehen.
            have I   already seen
        'I have already seen (it).'

    (b) *[$_{DAT}$] Würde ich nicht vertrauen.
             would I   not   trust
        'I wouldn't trust (him).'

The fact that the dative also stands out in Swiss German relativization is simply a consequence of the constraint that requires overt realization of oblique cases. The fact that there are no resumptive pronouns for subjects and direct objects and predicates like those in (4a), on the other hand, is little surprising: They are realized by non-oblique cases, which do not require any special morphological licensing so that resumptive pronouns are not necessary.[5] The direct/oblique-split in resumption is by no means exotic. It is found in a number of languages in the sample of Keenan and Comrie (1977: 93), Toman (1998: 305) reports the same pattern for colloquial Czech and Alexopoulou (2006: 63) for restrictive relatives in Greek.[6]

4.   Resumption in Swiss German as base-generation

4.1   Movement or base-generation?

While gap relatives can straightforwardly be analyzed as involving movement (but see Note 16), the analysis of resumptive relatives is less straightforward. While the literature up to the 1990s took a base-generation analysis for granted, movement analyses of resumption have become widespread in recent years.[7] It is important to distinguish two cases: Languages where resumption is sensitive to (certain) locality constraints and languages (like Swiss German) where resumptives can appear inside strong islands. For the first type of language, an analysis in terms of movement, or at least in terms of Agree, is straightforward; see Boeckx (2003: 108ff.) for Swedish and Vata, Goodluck and Stojanovic (1996) for Serbo-Croatian, Alexopoulou (2006) for restrictive relatives in Greek and Rouveret (2008) for Welsh.

For the second group of languages, things are less clear. Several linguists have argued in favor of a separation between resumptives that occur outside (strong) islands and those inside strong islands, cf. Aoun *et al.* (2001), Bianchi (2004), Alexopoulou (2006). Aoun *et al.* (2001), for instance, have termed the first type of resumptive 'apparent resumptives' and the second type 'true resumptives'. They posit a movement derivation for the first and a base-generation derivation for the second type and claim that movement is always preferred as the more economical option. Resumptives in transparent positions must therefore be motivated by reasons other than locality; resumptives inside islands must be base-generated. They further claim that this correlates with an asymmetry in reconstruction (see also Bianchi 2004: 97). Reconstruction is possible only if the resumptive is in a transparent position, but not if it is inside an island.

Demirdache (1991), Pesetsky (1998), Hornstein (2000), Boeckx (2003), Belletti (2006) and Boeckx and Hornstein (2008), on the other hand, have argued in favor of a uniform movement approach to resumptives and claim that movement out of islands is made possible by the presence of the resumptive. This predicts that we should also find reconstruction effects inside islands, contrary to what is claimed in Aoun *et al.* (2001).[8]

The proper analysis thus largely depends on the empirical question whether reconstruction is possible with resumptives inside islands. It is therefore important to look at the Swiss German facts: Reconstruction and Strong Crossover (SCO) effects systematically obtain in Swiss German relatives. The following pair illustrates reconstruction into transparent positions with a DO-gap relative and an IO-resumptive relative (the external head is enclosed in square brackets; the reconstruction site is indicated by means of underline):[9]

(8) (a) Ich wett s   [Fotti   vo sinen$_i$ Eltere] gsee,
          I   want the picture of   his   parents see
          wo jede Schüeler$_i$ __ am   beschte findt.
          C   every pupil   the best   likes
          'I would like to see the picture of his$_i$ parents that every pupil$_i$ likes best.'   DO

(b) de [Pricht über sini$_i$ Frau], won em   kän Politiker$_i$ __
   the story   about his wife C   he.DAT no politician
   würd   Glaube schänke
   would belief give
   'the story about his$_i$ wife that no politician$_i$ would believe'   IO

Crucially, reconstruction into islands is possible as well. Here are a few examples with resumptive pronouns inside strong PP-islands, some of which are even embedded in another island (for more data cf. Salzmann 2006, 2011); (9a/b) illustrate reconstruction and (9c) is an example of SCO. Of course, examples like (9b/c) are very complex and difficult to process, but their (potential) degradedness cannot be related to locality since (9a), where reconstruction is readily available, also involves a strong island.

(9) (a) D [Ziit vo sim$_i$ Läbe], wo niemert$_i$ gern   drüber   redt,
       the time of his life   C nobody likes.to there.about talks
       isch d   Pubertät.
       is   the puberty
       'The time of his$_i$ life that nobody$_i$ likes to talk about is puberty.'

     (b) de [Abschnitt vo sim$_i$ Läbe], won i <d Bhauptig,
       the period   of his life   C   I the claim
       dass jede Politiker$_i$ stolz druf   isch >, nöd cha   glaube
       that every politician proud there.on is   not can.1SG believe
       lit.: 'the period of his$_i$ life that I cannot believe the claim that every politician$_i$ is proud of'

     (c) *de [Bueb]$_i$, won er$_i$ für en Fründ vo <u>im</u>$_i$ es Auto gschtole hät
       the boy   C   he for a   friend of him a car   stolen   has
       lit.: 'the boy$_i$ who$_i$ he$_i$ stole a car for a friend of'   (SCO)

What these facts show is that reconstruction is systematic in Swiss German resumptive relatives. We thus arrive at a rather paradoxical situation: while resumption does not show the locality effects of movement dependencies, it does show the same reconstruction behavior.[10] Consequently, a movement analysis will need a special explanation for the absence of locality effects, whereas a base-generation analysis will need a new mechanism to account for movement effects like reconstruction and SCO. I will adopt a base-generation approach here because it is directly compatible with theories of locality which are independently needed: movement operations are subject to certain constraints no matter how they are captured theoretically. I therefore do not need to appeal to the somewhat exotic means proposed by the proponents of the movement analysis to explain why movement out of islands is possible.

Demirdache (1991), for example, attributes the island-voiding nature of resumption to LF-movement of the resumptive, Pesetsky (1998), Hornstein (2000: 178) and Belletti (2006: 132) link it to overtness of the trace while according to Boeckx (2003) and Boeckx and Hornstein (2008) it is the result of a movement operation without prior Agree.[11] I have argued against these proposals elsewhere in much detail

(Salzmann (2009a: 33–36; 2011: 156ff., 193ff.) so that I will not repeat the arguments here and conclude with McCloskey (2002) that to date there is no convincing explanation why resumptives make movement out of islands possible.[12]

Additionally, it has become clear in recent years that reconstruction effects are no waterproof diagnostic for movement. Reconstruction is also found in constructions without a direct movement relationship between the reconstructee and the reconstruction site. For instance, this generally holds for relative clauses (unless a Head Raising analysis is adopted) and pseudoclefts (Den Dikken *et al.* 2000: 42):

(10)   What nobody$_i$ bought was a picture of his$_i$ house.

Nobody and the bound pronoun *his* are not part of the same clause and there is no obvious movement relationship that could reconstruct *nobody* into the same clause as *his* (see Den Dikken 2006, section 6 for an overview over possible analyses).

Furthermore, certain instances of scope reconstruction in relative clauses must be explained without the interpretation of the bottom copy of a movement chain, see, for example, Sharvit (1999), Cecchetto (2005), Hulsey and Sauerland (2006):

(11)   The woman every man$_i$ loves is his$_i$ mother.

The multiple-individual reading (a different woman for every man) does not necessarily result from reconstructing the external head of the relative since the QP binds a pronoun in the matrix clause. Obviously, some other mechanism is available for the QP to c-command the bound pronoun in the matrix clause. This could be Quantifier Raising of the QP as in Hulsey and Sauerland (2006), or an analysis in terms of indirect binding, as in Sharvit (1999) and Cecchetto (2005). These mechanisms are also sufficient for the universal quantifier to gain wide scope with respect to the external head. But once such alternative mechanisms are available, it is no longer necessary to model variable-binding/scope reconstruction effects (also in cases without a bound pronoun in the matrix clause) by means of the interpretation of a lower copy of a movement chain.[13]

The parallel between movement and reconstruction is thus obviously not perfect so that alternative mechanisms are necessary anyway. This generally weakens the arguments for a movement analysis of resumption.

In principle, it would be possible to adopt base-generation for resumptives inside islands and movement for resumptives in transparent positions (i.e., the datives in (1c)), as in Aoun *et al.* (2001), Bianchi (2004) or Alexopoulou (2006). But at least for Swiss German this would be undesirable since there do not seem to be any fundamental differences concerning reconstruction possibilities. Since base-generation is needed independently (for resumptives inside islands), it is most economical to adopt base-generation for all resumptives.[14] In sum, a base-generation account allows one to maintain well-known generalizations about locality: the absence of locality effects in Swiss German resumption is due to the absence of a syntactic dependency between the operator and the resumptive. For reconstruction under resumption, alternative mechanisms are necessary. Before I turn to these I briefly need to sketch my assumptions about base-generation.

4.2   The syntax of movement and base-generation

The syntax of movement is that familiar from regular A′-movement: A relative operator bears an uninterpretable (unvalued) case-feature and an interpretable (valued) Op-/Wh-feature. Suppose we are relativizing a matrix direct object: The operator is merged in direct object position and then undergoes Agree with v. As a consequence it is assigned accusative. The matrix C has an uninterpretable (unvalued) Op-/Wh-feature which is associated with an EPP-feature (or, following the terminology of Chomsky (2008), an edge-feature). C undergoes Agree with the operator, which is subsequently moved to Spec, CP because of the EPP-feature. The derivation is sketched in (12):

(12)   [$_{CP}$ Op   C   [$_{vP}$ [$_{vP}$ O̶p V] v]]   movement

     *i*Op[x]   *u*Op[x]   *i*Op[x]

     *u*Case[acc] EPP   *u*Case [acc]

     *i*Phi[z]   *i*Phi[z]   *u*Phi[z]

The syntax of base-generation is somewhat different and translating the traditional base-generation account adopted here into the Agree-framework requires some care. McCloskey (2002: 203) and Alexopoulou (2006: 73ff., 88) both argue that base-generation does not involve Agree between the complementizer and the operator. Rather, they assume that the complementizer used in base-generation does not have an *u*Wh-/*u*Op-feature, but only an EPP-/edge-feature, which is then checked by the base-generated operator. Additionally, the silent relative operator cannot have an unvalued case-feature. This implies that the relative complementizer comes in two variants, one with and one without *u*Op. While this may be a desirable result for Irish where the complementizers are formally different (*aL* vs. *aN*), it is rather unattractive for Swiss German since the complementizer always appears as *wo* regardless of whether movement or base-generation is involved (the same problem obtains with Greek *pu*, cf. Alexopoulou 2006: 88). We therefore instead pursue the possibility that there is only one *wo*. Positing only one *wo* implies that base-generation must also involve feature checking. This can be done in at least two ways: Either – adopting a suggestion by Hans Broekhuis – one can assume that Merge is also triggered by feature checking so that the empty operator checks the *u*Op/*u*Wh on C (while the resumptive is only involved in agreement with v, T or a prepositional head). Alternatively, one can adopt the possibility of expansion of the search space of a probe (Rezac 2004: 66ff.). If it cannot find a matching goal in its c-command domain, it can exceptionally probe its specifier. If applied to base-generation, C first probes its complement domain; since it fails to find a matching goal, it can probe its specifier where it finds the base-generated operator (again, the resumptive does not agree with C). I will not choose between these two options here. What additionally has to be assumed in both cases is that the resumptive is bound by the operator:

(13) [$_{CP}$ Op$_i$ C   [$_{island}$ [$_{vP}$ [$_{vP}$ pron$_i$ V] v]]]   base-generation
      *i*Op[x] *u*Op[x]   *u*Case[acc]
      *i*Phi[z] EPP   *i*Phi[z]   *u*Phi[z]

4.3 Accounting for movement effects under base-generation

To my knowledge, there are basically two types of mechanisms that have been explored to handle movement effects for base-generated dependencies: semantic reconstruction (see Sternefeld 2000 for an overview) and the NP-ellipsis analysis of resumptive pronouns (Guilliot and Malkawi 2006, 2007, 2009; Rouveret 2008). In the latter, the resumptive is reanalyzed as a transitive determiner whose NP-complement has been elided under identity with an antecedent (PF-deletion is henceforth indicated by means of italics): [$_{DP}$ D *NP*]. This would give the following schematic representation for an example like (9a) (strikethrough indicates LF-deletion; English words are used for ease of presentation):

(14) the [~~time of his$_i$ life~~] [[Op ~~*time of his$_i$ life*~~] C nobody$_i$ likes to about
     [$_{DP}$ it [$_{NP}$ *time of his$_i$ life*]] talk]

Importantly, this only works in the present context if the Matching Analysis of relative clauses is adopted as in, for example, Salzmann (2006, 2011), where the relative operator is just a D-element with an NP complement that is elided under identity with the external head. Reconstruction effects are thus not per se a problem for a base-generation analysis.

The same holds for SCO effects, which can also be handled by means of the NP-ellipsis theory of resumptives. In examples like (9c), the resumptive *im* would have *Bueb* 'boy' as its NP complement. As it ends up in the c-command domain of the co-indexed *er* 'he', the sentence is out due to a violation of Principle C, just as it would be under a movement derivation. More traditional approaches like McCloskey (1990) and Shlonsky (1992) define SCO on the basis of the A′-chain linking the operator with the resumptive pronoun. An SCO effect in an example like (9c) would then be due to the fact that the chain between the base-generated operator and the resumptive crosses a pronoun with the same index (again, I use English words for ease of presentation):[15]

(15) *the boy$_i$, Op$_i$ C he$_i$ for a friend of him$_i$ a car has stolen
          L________________________________J $_i$

In conclusion, I adopt a base-generation approach for resumptive relatives in Swiss German because it is directly compatible with established generalizations about locality. The reconstruction effects that obtain in all Swiss German resumptive relatives can be accounted for by independently available non-movement alternatives.[16]

4.4 Definition of the reference set/candidate set

Recall that gap relatives are only possible for the relativization of subjects and direct objects (1a/b). Since the base-generation mechanism is in principle available and there is no obvious syntactic constraint that prevents resumptives for subjects and direct objects, we must conclude that resumptive derivations converge for these relations as well.[17] The question then is why only gap derivations are grammatical. In the explanation for the distribution of resumptives in 3.2 this was linked to the fact that subjects and direct objects do not have to be expressed overtly because they are not realized by means of oblique cases. In other words, resumptives would be superfluous. The resumptive derivation is thus blocked by the more economical gap derivation (we will come back to the issue of economy in 6.1.1 below). This statement is much less innocuous than it seems: The fact that resumptive derivations are blocked by gap derivations implies that the two types of derivations compete with each other. This in turn implies that they belong to the same reference set.

Normally, the reference set is based on identical numerations, but this cannot be correct for the case at hand because movement and base-generation derivations do not involve the same set of lexical items: the base-generation derivation has an additional pronoun (the resumptive); furthermore, the two operators differ in formal features. Rather, I take the competition of movement and base-generation derivations as evidence that the reference set is based on identical LFs (or perhaps rather LF-interpretations, cf. Salzmann 2009a: 44, fn. 26; 2009c: 75, fn. 6). This position is also advocated in Sternefeld (1997), Broekhuis and Dekkers (2000), Heck *et al.* (2002) and Broekhuis and Klooster (2007).[18]

At LF, a movement and a base-generation derivation will look very similar: Intermediate copies will have been deleted, and the bottom copy of the movement chain will be converted into a variable; the resumptive pronoun will likewise function as a variable through binding by the operator. By applying the preference principle (which favors minimally restricted quantifiers, cf. Chomsky 1995) to the movement derivation, the operator will be minimized and the restriction is kept in the bottom copy. Practically the same obtains in the base-generation derivation if the NP-ellipsis theory of resumptives is adopted (Guilliot and Malkawi 2006, 2007, 2009; Rouveret 2008, cf. 4.3):

(16) (a) $[_{CP} Op_i \ldots \quad [x_i NP]] \quad \rightarrow \lambda x \ldots \quad x \quad$ movement

(b) $[_{CP} Op_i \ldots \quad [pron_i NP]] \rightarrow \lambda x \ldots \quad x \quad$ base-generation

If the bottom copy of the movement chain is also interpreted as a definite description as in Fox (2002: 67f.), the parallelism will be almost perfect:

(17) (a) which boy Mary visited which boy $\rightarrow$ Trace Conversion

(b) which boy λx [Mary visited the boy x]   (= the boy identical to x)

I take these two LFs to be sufficiently similar for both to be part of the same candidate/reference set (see Salzmann 2009a: 43ff./c: 67f. for more detailed discussion).[19]

5. On three types of variation involving resumption

So far things seem quite straightforward in Swiss German: Resumptive pronouns, and thus base-generation, are a last resort that only becomes relevant when movement derivations fail. In all other contexts, movement is preferred. This would lend itself to a rather straightforward analysis in minimalist terms: Base-generation is the only converging derivation for relativization into islands and relativization of datives. For subjects and direct objects, some economy constraint (but see 6.1.1 below) prefers a movement derivation over a base-generation derivation.

This section will change this picture substantially, however, by showing that the last resort character of resumptives is not universal and that there is a fair amount of dialectal, inter-individual and even intra-speaker variation within Alemannic dative relativization.

5.1 Variation in the last resort character of resumptives

In the description of the Swiss German facts I have so far treated the last resort nature as an inherent property of resumption. While this seems to be correct for Swiss German and the other languages mentioned at the beginning of section 3, it is by no means universal. There are in fact quite a few languages where resumptive relatives exist side by side with gap relatives in identical environments, generally in transparent positions (but not in contexts such as islands where resumptives are unavoidable); that is, there is no complementary distribution and the choice between gap and resumptive is essentially free.[20] Examples can be found in Irish (McCloskey 1990), Hebrew (Shlonsky 1992), Slavic languages (Goodluck and Stojanovic 1996), varieties of Spanish (Suñer 1998), and several Italian dialects (Bianchi 2004). In these languages, resumptive pronouns represent a strategy that is in principle freely available and – contrary to what is the case in Swiss German – is not blocked by a gap derivation. In Irish, the optionality is found with matrix direct objects and embedded subjects/direct objects. (18) is an example with a matrix direct object (McCloskey 1990: 205). More examples can be found in Salzmann (2009a: 50f.).

(18)	(a)	an	fear	a	bhuail	tú	__		(b)	an	fear	ar	bhuail	tú	é
		the	man	aL	struck	you				the	man	aN	struck	you	him
		'the man that you struck'								'the man that you struck'					

5.2 Crosslinguistic/dialectal variation

Most traditional descriptions of Alemannic claim that dative relatives require a resumptive pronoun, see Bossard (1962: 141) for Zugovian, Fischer (1989: 429) for

Lucerne, Hodler (1969: 246) and Marti (1985: 235f.) for Bernese, Sonderegger and Gadmer (1999) for Appenzell, Suter (1992: 183) for Basel, and Weber (1964: 299) for Zurich German. However, there are exceptions: The Low Alemannic dialect of Oberrotweil (Germany), which is typologically very similar to the Swiss German varieties, has basically the same resumptive system as the Swiss German dialects, with gaps for subjects and direct objects and resumptive pronouns for PPs, but, crucially, there are no resumptive pronouns for datives, as shown in the grammatical description by Noth (1993: 418ff.):[21]

(19) (a) Alli, wun em __ ACC hab   wellá   machá, sí mr   vrgroodá.
           All C   he.DAT   have wanted make   are me.DAT failed
           'All (e.g. cakes) that I tried to make for him, turned out bad.'   DO

      (b) Sáli Fírma, wu dr Sebb noch __DAT   ebis   schulded,
           that firm   C the Sebb still   something owes
           hed scho   wíder aagruáfa.
           has already again called   IO
           'That company to which Sebb still owes something has called again.'

      (c) Dr áinzig,   wu si   vrhandlá **míd em**, ísch dr Aafíárer.
           the only.one C   they negotiate with him is   the leader
           'The only one with whom they negotiate is the leader.'   PP

The same seems to be the case in Glarus German. Bäbler (1949: 60) gives five examples with dative relativization all of which contain gaps. Otherwise, the resumption system is the same as in Zurich German. Here is one of the examples with dative relativization:

(20) Känntscht du der Bueb, ... wo me   ___DAT de es   Bremi gih   het?
      know.2sg you the boy   C   one then   a   prize given has
      'Do you know the boy to whom they then gave a prize?'

Importantly, the variation cannot be related to a different status of dative case in these varieties. As in Zurich German, dative has to be overtly realized in the contexts (6)–(7). Nor can the deviating behavior of dative relatives be attributed to the types of datives: Noth (1993) and Bäbler (1949) list examples in which datives of various types are relativized without resumptives: datives of ditransitive verbs, of intransitive verbs, subcategorized datives and non-subcategorized ones (bene-/malefactives). In other words, the dialectal variation is real.

More evidence for variation comes from the Idiotikon (1999, XV, 13f.), a dictionary of Swiss German dialects. The entry of the relative particle *wo* contains several examples with dative relatives, some of which are constructed with a resumptive pronoun and some without. All the examples are taken from carefully written sources such as textbooks, grammatical descriptions, dialect literature, and so on. The examples without resumptive pronoun come from the following dialects: Bernese, Appenzell, Glarus and Wallis German while those with resumptive pronoun are from Basel, Bernese, Zugovian and Lucerne German.

5.3   Inter-individual variation

The fact that we find both variants in Bernese suggests that the variation is not just between larger dialect areas but also occurs among individuals of the same variety; we are dealing with inter-speaker variation. More evidence for inter-speaker variation is found in Hodler (1969: 246), who notes that the resumptive pronoun is normally obligatory in Bernese, but (for reasons he does not specify) sometimes does not occur. Similarly, while Sonderegger and Gadmer (1999) explicitly state that dative resumptive pronouns are necessary in Appenzell German, one of the examples in the Idiotikon from the same dialect (by the author Jakob Hartmann) does not contain a resumptive pronoun.

Since the examples without resumptive pronouns occur in contexts where the grammatical descriptions normally take dative resumptive pronouns to be obligatory, the variation cannot be due to different types of dative. Rather, we seem to be dealing with true inter-speaker variation (in Salzmann 2009b: 145–50, the empirical situation is discussed in more detail).

5.4   Intra-speaker variation

The data presented so far show that the use of dative resumptive pronouns is much less systematic than suggested by earlier descriptions. Two recent studies (Salzmann (2009b) on Zurich German and Salzmann and Seiler (2010) on Swiss German) have not only confirmed this fact, but also showed that variation in dative resumption is pervasive. Speakers of the same variety do not only differ from each other in their use of dative resumptive pronouns, but there is also a lot of variation within the grammar of an individual: Most speakers judged both the gap and the resumptive version grammatical, so that we may conclude that the use of dative resumptive pronouns is essentially optional. Importantly, the variation is restricted to dative relativization in transparent contexts. In island contexts, dative resumptive pronouns are obligatory. In other grammatical relations, the result is also categorical and confirms the earlier descriptions: Resumptive pronouns are prohibited for subjects and direct objects, but necessary for PPs and islands.

There is no evidence that the variation is related to sociolinguistic factors like age, sex, education, and so on. One cannot simply say that younger people are less likely to use dative resumptive pronouns. In fact, some of the sources in the Idiotikon mentioned above without dative resumptive pronouns are 50–100 years old. Conversely, a quick Google search reveals that dative resumptive pronouns are used frequently in communicative contexts which are most likely to be frequented by younger people like news forums, chat-rooms, and so on. Nor is it the case that the variation can simply be attributed to processing factors, for example, that the resumptive pronoun is dropped in sloppy speech or conversely that the resumptive pronoun is inserted as some repair strategy. As shown in the previous subsection, gaps and resumptive pronouns for datives are found in very carefully written sources such as textbooks, traditional dialect literature, and so on. It is highly unlikely that they represent performance errors. But once gaps as well as resumptive relatives are a possibility in the grammar of many speakers of an Alemannic variety, it is unlikely that speakers who use gaps next to resumptive pronouns for dative relatives make performance errors when they use one of the variants. Furthermore, in the questionnaires, the majority of our informants explicitly marked both the gap and the resumptive variant as grammatical. Finally, a processing account would have to assume that one of the variants, the gap or the resumptive pronoun, is the basic variant while the other one is the result of a performance error. Given that both variants are attested in careful sources, both are equally good candidates for the basic variant. Choosing between the two seems not only arbitrary but plainly wrong. I conclude from this that intra-speaker variation in the use of dative resumptive pronouns is simply a fact one cannot deny. Both gap and resumptive pronoun are grammatical variants for one and the same speaker.[22]

6.   Implications of the variation: comparing MP and OT

In this section I will discuss the implications of the types of variation described in the previous section. It will be shown that a minimalist system is too rigid to accommodate them in a satisfactory way. Instead, I will argue in favor of a more flexible system that makes use of violable and rankable constraints as in Optimality Theory.

6.1   A crosslinguistically variable preference for elementary operations

6.1.1 Against a solution in terms of economy

In the description of the Swiss German facts (4.4) I concluded that movement and base-generation derivations belong to the same reference set and thus compete with each other. This conclusion is inevitable if resumptive derivations converge for subjects and direct objects, but are blocked by gap derivations. The question then is: Why does movement block base-generation? One possibility alluded to above is economy, but as we will see presently, there is good reason to be skeptical about such a solution. There are technical, conceptual, as well as empirical counterarguments.

First of all, it is far from trivial if not even impossible to find a (Minimalist) economy constraint that prefers a movement derivation over a base-generation derivation. Aoun *et al.* (2001) propose an account in terms of (global) derivational economy, arguing that a base-generation derivation involves more steps than a movement derivation. While this may be correct for their particular implementation of base-generation (see Salzmann 2009a: 39ff., 2009c: 66 for discussion), this is not obvious in the implementation adopted here (4.2) where at least the following operations are involved:

(21) (a)   Movement: Merge (operator) + Copy (operator) + Merge (operator)

     (b)   Resumption: Merge (operator) + Merge (pronoun)

Given this, one might in fact expect resumption to be more economical than movement. Even if we add the non-syntactic binding relationship linking the operator with the resumptive under base-generation, the number of steps will still be identical. Furthermore, successive cyclic movement will lead to additional copy (and deletion) operations that are not found under base-generation. Without going too much into detail here (but cf. Salzmann 2009a: 46, 2009c: 70f.) it should be clear that it is far from obvious that movement is more economical from a derivational perspective.

Turning to representational economy, there are two possibilities that suggest themselves: SILENTTRACE (Pesetsky 1998) and the Avoid Pronoun Principle (APP, cf. Chomsky 1982: 63f.; Van Riemsdijk 1989; Heck and Müller 2000: 44). However, the two constraints cannot be applied to the analysis of resumption here because they only work if the representations that are to be compared are based on more or less the same syntax. But this is crucially not the case here: SILENTTRACE fails to apply to resumptive derivations because on my account resumption does not involve the phonetic realization of a copy of a movement chain. Conversely, the APP fails to apply to traces/copies of movement because it only chooses between overt and zero pronouns.[23]

Furthermore, both constraints are inadequate because they refer to overtness. The possessor relativization facts discussed in Salzmann (2011) show, however, that what is crucial is not just a ban against variables with phonetic content, but against resumption/base-generation per se as there are also silent resumptive pronouns (see also Georgopoulos 1985, 1991; McCloskey 1990, for further evidence for silent resumptives). See Salzmann (2009a: 45–58, 2009c: 70ff.) for more details and additional evidence that resumption and representational economy are orthogonal dimensions.

There is one specific local economy constraint that is frequently appealed to, the Merge over Move principle (see McCloskey 2002: 204, for a particular case in Irish where it seems to be crucial). In its local form (i.e., applying at a particular stage in the derivation) it can arguably not be applied to the case at hand because the derivations are already too different after the initial merger of either verb + resumptive or verb + operator with *u*Case. In a global form it might in fact favor resumptives, but this would, of course, be the wrong result.

Postulating a Move over Merge principle instead may seem to be a possibility, but at least in a local form it would fail: as pointed out in the previous paragraph, the difference between movement and base-generation is already made when the verb is merged with the object. Insertion of an operator with *u*Case forces movement at a later stage while insertion of a resumptive forces merge of an operator later in the derivation. The selection of one derivation over the other thus can only be done trans-derivationally. A global principle favoring Move over Merge fares better, but it would fail to account for the language variation observed in 5.1, see the next subsection.

I conclude therefore that none of the minimalist economy constraints postulated to date can be used to explain why gap relatives block resumptive relatives in Swiss German. Next to these technical arguments, there are more general considerations that speak against an economy approach: Resumptive pronouns are unmarked in many languages of the world (cf. Comrie and Kuteva 2005) – treating them as marked with respect to movement is the result of a Eurocentric, standard language-based perspective. Furthermore, resumptive relatives often constitute the first relativization strategy acquired by children (cf. Goodluck and Stojanovic 1996). Even more importantly, the fact that the blocking effect is not found in languages like Irish casts principal doubts on the viability of an economy approach. Since economy constraints are normally taken to be universal and not subject to parameterization (Müller and Sternefeld 2001: 29), the putative constraint should favor movement over base-generation in all languages, contrary to what was found in 5.1.

6.1.2 Ranking the preference for Merge and Move

As a consequence, I would like to argue in favor of a very different perspective: Contrary to what is sometimes claimed in the literature, I submit that movement and base-generation are two inherently equally costly operations (see also Broekhuis 2008; Broekhuis and Klooster 2007).[24] Given free access to the lexicon the computational system is confronted with an indeterminacy as to which of the two should be applied. The empirical facts show that in languages like Irish this indeterminacy is not resolved in that both derivations are optionally available (as long as they converge). The facts from Swiss German, however, show that other languages resolve the indeterminacy in favor of one of the two operations. There is also a third type of language, which only uses resumption and thus resolves the indeterminacy differently than Swiss German. Possible candidates are Palestinian Arabic (Shlonsky 1992: 445), Palauan (Georgopoulos 1985, 1991), and (from Comrie and Kuteva 2005) probably Baka, Babungo, Ngemba, Youruba and Kayah Li.[25]

This variable preference for elementary operations cannot be modeled in an orthodox minimalist grammar. A system with violable and ranked constraints, however, has the necessary ingredients: I propose that the observed preferences are the result of the relative ranking of two constraints that each penalize an elementary operation. Following Broekhuis (2008), I adopt *MERGE and *MOVE. *MERGE penalizes external merge and thus also base-generation. *MOVE, on the other hand, penalizes internal merge and thus movement. Specifically, I argue that in languages where resumptives are a last resort *MERGE outranks *MOVE while in languages like Irish where resumptives and gaps occur in the same environment the two constraints are tied. In languages which only use resumption *MOVE outranks *MERGE:[26]

(22) (a) movement as a last resort (e.g. Swiss German):   *MERGE >> *MOVE

     (b) optionality (Irish/Hebrew):   *MERGE <> *MOVE

     (c) resumption only (e.g. Palestinian Arabic):   *MOVE >> * MERGE

The ranking for Swiss German receives independent support from negation facts where movement of a negative XP is preferred over merging a negative adverb, cf. Salzmann (2009a: 54ff., 2009c: 72) and Broekhuis and Klooster (2007). At this point I cannot assess the implications of the ranking in Irish/Hebrew and will leave it for further research.

The two constraints and their possible rankings can be interpreted as instantiating a kind of (macro-)parameter. The proposal advanced here is thus similar in spirit to that in Müller (2009) where the resolution of an indeterminacy in the order of rule application at the vP-cycle classifies languages into two types: ergative and accusative languages. There is one crucial difference, however: While the constraints in Müller (2009) and the more classical Merge over Move constraint are local derivational constraints, the two constraints adopted here are representational and translocal. The choice between movement or base-generation cannot be made locally, that is, at a particular derivational point, because, as pointed out in the previous subsection, the decision is already made when the verb is merged with an object, that is whether a resumptive pronoun or an operator with *u*Case is inserted. However, since in both cases Merge is involved (since movement is not yet an option, of course), there is no way of favoring one over the other option locally. Even if this could somehow be done, there would not be enough information available to make the right decision. If the ranking *MERGE >> *MOVE applied, it would invariably block base-generation. This would lead to the wrong result in case a gap derivation eventually fails, for example, because the operator ends up trapped inside an island. Rather, complete LF-representations must be compared in terms of how a given uninterpretable feature is valued, that is, whether it is valued by external or internal merge.

But could there be an account in terms of parameterization that is compatible with the MP? Part of the problem associated with the phenomenon under discussion is the fact that it seems to instantiate a rather fundamental difference between languages, reminiscent of a macro-parameter. Work on macro-parameters, however, has been largely abandoned in MP, and it is relatively unclear at this point whether they are formulable at all in (recent versions of) MP (see Richards 2008: 144ff. for discussion). There is one conceivable alternative to derive variable preference for movement and base-generation that is compatible with minimalist assumptions, a possibility first suggested in Sternefeld (1997: 97ff.): the parametrization of the reference set. For languages like Swiss German where resumptives are always a last resort, the reference set would be based on identical LFs (one would still need an economy constraint favoring movement over base-generation). For languages like Hebrew/Irish where gaps and resumptives exist side by side in certain contexts, however, the reference set would be based on identical numerations. It is indeed by reference to different numerations that Shlonsky (1992) and McCloskey (2002: 205) explain the optionality in Hebrew/Irish. This would be a possible albeit quite radical move whose implications are difficult to assess. At any rate, there are two strong counterarguments. First, as shown in the previous subsection, it is difficult if not impossible to come up with MP-compatible constraints that could be used to prefer movement over base-generation. Second, it would be unclear how to derive the third type of language with resumption only. Basing the reference set on identical LFs in that case would require the opposite type of economy constraint as in Swiss German. It is unclear how this could be done in an MP-system. Third, and this is the topic of the next subsection, such an approach fails to account for the variation facts observed in Alemannic.

6.2 Dialectal and inter-individual variation in dative resumption

6.2.1 A grammar with obligatory dative resumptives

Before analyzing the variation facts I will first sketch the analysis for a grammar with obligatory dative resumptive pronouns. The occurrence of dative resumptives can be linked to a representational PF-constraint that requires oblique case to receive phonetic realization, RealizeObl (OT-constraints will henceforth appear in small capitals, MP-constraints only with capitalized initials).

(23) RealizeObl: Oblique case must be phonetically realized

As shown in (6)–(7), such a constraint is independently necessary. It can in principle be employed in both an MP and an OT framework. As long as dative resumptives are obligatory, the MP grammar derives the correct result. The movement derivation, which leaves dative unrealized, simply crashes while the base-generation derivation is the only converging alternative. Importantly RealizeObl is an inviolable constraint.[27]

The corresponding constraint in an OT-framework would be essentially identical, the only difference being that it is in principle violable. In a grammar with obligatory dative resumptives, RealizeObl outranks *Merge, i.e., it overrides the preference for movement.

(24) Dative relatives

		RealizeObl	*Merge	*Move
☞ a.	Base-generation		*	
b.	Movement	*!		*

When non-oblique cases are involved, *Merge prefers the movement/gap derivation:

(25) DO-relatives

		RealizeObl	*Merge	*Move
a.	Base-generation		*!	
☞ b.	Movement			*

OT-accounts dealing with the left-periphery of relative clauses such as Pesetsky (1998) and Broekhuis and Dekkers (2000) assume that the syntactic basis of restrictive relative clauses universally involves an overt relative pronoun/operator + an overt complementizer both of which can be subject to deletion. Under such premises, the question arises why oblique case cannot be realized by a relative pronoun in Spec, CP in Alemannic relatives. One cannot say that there simply is a silent relative operator; the absence of overt relative pronouns should instead follow from constraint interaction. To put it differently: the inventory of relative elements is the result of evaluation and not just simply given by the lexicon. As suggested to me by Hans Broekhuis (p.c.), one possibility involves the constraint LE(CP), which favors CPs whose first element is an overt complementizer. If this constraint dominates REALIZEOBL, the possibility of realizing oblique case in Spec, CP is ruled out. Other things being equal, this basically implies that there are never overt relative pronouns in Alemannic dialects. RECOVERABILITY, which outranks LE (CP), is arguably only an issue for datives and PPs. Due to the ranking LE(CP) >> *MERGE recoverability is satisfied by means of resumption in these varieties. The following table shows the evaluation for the relativization of a dative object, the revised version of (24) (since we have no evidence for the relative ranking between LE(CP) and REALIZEOBL we use a tie for ease of illustration):[28]

(26) Dative relatives

		LE(CP)	REALIZEOBL	*MERGE	*Move
☞ a.	Base-generation			*	
b.	Movement + rel. pronoun	*!			*
c.	Movement – rel. pronoun		*!		*

6.2.2 A grammar without dative resumptives: problems for an MP-approach

Section 5.2 provided ample evidence for the existence of a grammar that is essentially identical to the one discussed in the previous section, but with one important difference: it does not use dative resumptives in non-island contexts.

In current minimalist work, crosslinguistic variation (including idiolectal variation) is usually reduced to differences in the inventory of lexical items or differences in the specification of lexical items. Languages differ as to whether a particular functional head is equipped with an EPP/edge-feature (or, as in older versions of MP, a strong or a weak feature) and thus will trigger overt movement in one language but not in another. Since in the case at hand we are not dealing with differences in displacement, presence or absence of an EPP-feature cannot be at stake. Alternatively then, the crosslinguistic variation must root in the presence vs. absence of a given lexical item.

At first sight, one might want to argue that the varieties without dative resumptive pronouns simply do not have the required operator without uCase so that a movement derivation is the only option for dative relatives. However, this does not work: first, dative resumptive pronouns do occur in all varieties when the dative is inside an island:

(27) de Maa, won i käs <Buech, won ***(em)** gib>, zrugg überchum
     the man C I no book C he.DAT give back get
     lit.: 'the man who I don't get any book back that I give to'

Second, since all varieties use base-generation whenever a (non-dative) variable is inside an island as in (1d) and (2), they all must have the operator without uCase posited in 4.2. This implies that varieties without dative resumptives in transparent contexts in principle have both derivations at their disposal for datives. The variation in dative resumption thus cannot be due to a difference in the inventory of operators. But how can the absence of dative resumption in transparent contexts be derived?

One possibility would be to assume that there is no RealizeObl in those varieties so that gap derivations converge and are preferred over resumptive derivations for reasons of economy (assuming for the sake of the argument that one could find an appropriate constraint). But this leads to serious problems, since then one can no longer account for the pattern in (6)–(7). We are thus forced to assume that the general requirement to realize dative case, i.e., RealizeObl, still holds in the respective variety. But then this PF-constraint will filter out all derivations where dative remains unexpressed, including dative gap relatives. In other words, dative relatives with gaps cannot be derived given that RealizeObl is inviolable. The only possible way out is to make RealizeObl more specific so that it no longer applies to relative clauses. In that case, both gap and resumptive derivations will converge. The gap variant, which is more economical, then emerges as grammatical. In a non-transparent context such as (27), on the other hand, only the base-generation derivation will converge, not because of RealizeObl, but because the movement derivation crashes.

This strategy of handling language variation by means of rather specific interface constraints is exactly what Broekhuis (2008) criticizes about Chomsky's (2001) treatment of object shift, where the cross-linguistic differences are handled by very specific filters. As pointed out in Broekhuis (2008), such a strategy is feasible, but amounts to a reformulation of the descriptive generalizations. The difference between varieties with dative resumptive pronouns and those without is then due to a slight difference in the PF-filter RealizeObl. It holds across the board in the first group, while in the second, it does not hold for relatives. An MP approach can thus handle the variation, but only at a very high cost.

6.2.3 A grammar without dative resumptives: in favor of violable constraints

Under an OT account, the variation can be handled straightforwardly: the fact that REALIZEOBL does not hold in all contexts is not a problem because it is a violable constraint. In the case at hand, we can argue that the absence of dative resumptive pronouns is due to a different ranking between REALIZEOBL and *MERGE. While REALIZEOBL dominates *MERGE in the varieties with dative resumptive pronouns, the reverse ranking obtains in the dialects/idiolects without dative resumptive pronouns. To rule out the possibility that the oblique case is realized by means of a relative pronoun in Spec, CP, we again include LE(CP):

(28)   Dative relatives without resumptive pronouns

			LE(CP)	*MERGE	REALIZEOBL	*MOVE
	a.	Base-generation		*!		
☞	b.	Movement – rel. pronoun			*	*
	c.	Movement + rel. pronoun	*!			*

The obligatoriness of dative resumptive pronouns in islands like (27) follows if *MERGE is dominated by a further constraint that penalizes locality violations (but see 6.4 below).

One might object that this solution is just as descriptive as the MP-analysis in the previous subsection. But this is certainly not correct. The OT approach fares better in a number of important aspects. First: in the OT-account, the variation is derived from primitive notions of grammar: all constraints are very general and independently needed while in the MP-account, the variation is handled by means of postulating two different filters, a general and a more specific one. Second, the OT description is more economical in that it only requires one version of REALIZEOBL while the MP-account requires two. Third, the OT approach makes interesting predictions about possible types of language: given the constraint set, one does not expect to find a language that consistently uses dative resumptive pronouns, but leaves dative unexpressed in contexts like (6)–(7). To my knowledge, this prediction is correct. Under an MP-account with very specific filters, it would be easy to formulate a constraint that leads to such an unattested pattern. I conclude, therefore, that an approach based on violable constraints is superior.

6.3 Intra-speaker variation in dative resumption

6.3.1 Problems for an MP-approach

The intra-speaker variation data are particularly interesting because they show a kind of optionality between gap and resumptive that is unexpected if resumptives are taken to be a last resort. Given that both the gap and the resumptive variants are grammatical for many speakers, we need a model of grammar that generates both variants. Importantly, we are dealing here with an instance of 'semantically vacuous optionality' (Biberauer and Richards 2006), in the sense that the two surface variants are identical in interpretation (only for wide-scope/specific readings, recall the discussion in Note 19).

The issue of optionality has generally been a difficult one for minimalist approaches (cf. Henry 2002, 2005). Unfortunately, the literature has almost exclusively been concerned with optionality of movement – a simple consequence of the fact that minimalism is mainly concerned with properties of the generator. Therefore, most minimalist approaches to optionality (optionally strong features/optional EPP-/edge-features, cf. Henry (2002: 275); optionality as an inherent property of movement, cf. Barbiers (2005: 254); Parallel Grammars, cf. Kroch (2000) or various pied-piping options, cf. Biberauer and Richards (2006)) cannot be applied to the optionality between gap and resumptive.

Within the lexical variation theory there is one recent approach by Adger and Smith (2005) and Adger (2006) that explicitly tackles intra-speaker variation. Simplifying somewhat, they propose that variation within a grammar arises if a grammar contains two featurally different, but semantically identical elements that – due to their feature difference – are realized differently in the morphological component. Depending on which element is chosen for a given derivation, we get either variant a or b.

The discussion on dialectal variation in 6.2.2 has shown, however, that the variation in dative resumption cannot be located in the inventory because all varieties have both gap and resumptive relatives and therefore require both an operator with *u*Case (for movement: SU/DO) and an operator without *u*Case (for base-generation: PPs, islands). The question is whether intra-speaker variation can be explained by the presence of both relative operators. In the case at hand it cannot, for principled reasons: in Adger's approach the differences in the numeration are taken to be significant enough to constitute two different reference sets so that two given (converging) derivations will not compete and can both emerge as grammatical, thereby leading to optionality. However, since 4.4 has shown that the candidate/reference set must be determined on the basis of LF in Swiss German to explain the impossibility of resumptives for SU/DO, there will always be competition between gap and resumptive derivations. The optionality thus cannot result from different inputs. Rather, it must somehow be the result of PF-constraints. As discussed in 6.2.2, the general version of the MP-constraint REALIZEOBL will be too strong when dative relatives contain gaps. Derivations with gaps violate REALIZEOBL and therefore crash so that only the resumptive variant should be grammatical. The same problem obtains in intra-speaker variation: with the general REALIZEOBL, derivations with gaps violate REALIZEOBL and therefore crash. Again, only the resumptive derivations should be grammatical, contrary to fact. The only alternative is to use the specific version of REALIZEOBL, which in principle allows both gaps and resumptive pronouns for datives. But even that will not do: even though both gap and resumptive relatives converge in that case, whichever economy constraint generally penalizes resumption (to rule out resumptive pronouns for subjects and direct objects) will favor the gap variant. In other words, it is simply not possible for this type of grammar to generate both variants. See Salzmann and Seiler (2010, section 7) for more discussion of alternative approaches to intra-speaker variation.

6.3.2 How an OT-approach succeeds

In an OT approach optionality in transparent contexts follows straightforwardly from a tie between REALIZEOBL and *MERGE. Both gap and resumptive pronoun can thus be optimal:

(29) Optional dative resumptive pronouns

			REALIZEOBL	*MERGE	*MOVE
☞	a.	Base-generation		*	
☞	b.	Movement	*		*

Importantly, this is a global tie (cf. Müller 2000 for an overview) so that lower-ranked constraints like *MOVE do not interfere. Within islands (27), the resumptive variant is the only possibility because, as in dialects without dative resumptives, a higher-ranked locality constraint forces base-generation (but see the next subsection).

Salzmann and Seiler (2010) have shown that the basic optionality can be affected by certain grammatical factors, such as the referentiality/definiteness of the head noun, narrow scope of the external head and case matching contexts (i.e., dative case on the external head noun). These factors all lead to a variable and non-categorical preference for the gap variant. The empirical facts thus seem very similar in nature to what Henry (2005) observes for idiolectal agreement patterns in *there*-sentences where various contextual factors (type of verb, type of associate) favor agreement. While Henry (2005) argues in favor of a return to the concept of rules that may be associated with probabilities, Salzmann and Seiler (2010) take this as evidence in favor of a stochastic model of grammar.

6.4   Why only datives? Arguments for a restrictive generator

As we have seen, only base-generation is possible if relativization targets a position inside an island (2). In the previous sections, I have argued that some locality constraint, call it LOCALITY for the sake of the argument, outranks *MERGE. This derives the right result for all Alemannic varieties and for all relations, i.e., also for relations like the direct objects in (2) or the dative resumptives inside islands in varieties that normally do not use dative resumptives (27):

(30)   Resumptives for dative inside an island in a variety without dative resumptives (27)

			LOCALITY	*MERGE	REALIZEOBL	*MOVE
☞	a.	Base-generation		*		
	b.	Movement	*!		*	*

However, there are two aspects that raise doubts about the validity of such an approach: Given the constraints LOCALITY, REALIZEOBL, *MERGE and *MOVE it is easy to come up with a ranking that will lead to a language that arguably does not exist: Suppose the following ranking: REALIZEOBL >> *MERGE >> LOCALITY >> *MOVE. This would lead to a typologically unattested language, which has dative resumptive pronouns in all contexts, but no resumptive pronouns for non-oblique relations even when the extraction site is inside an island (which implies that there would be movement out of islands). This is clearly undesirable.[29] An MP approach is not confronted with this problem because locality is hardwired into the derivational system so that derivations that violate locality will invariably crash.

Furthermore, it is completely arbitrary under the OT approach that variation is restricted to datives. With the OT formalism it is just as easy to model a language where resumptive pronouns inside islands are optional, e.g., with a tie between *MERGE and LOCALITY. Again, this problem does not arise under an MP-approach since the constraints that lead to variation (i.e., the versions of REALIZEOBL) do not apply to the computational system but to PF-representations. This captures the fact that the variation we find in Alemannic relatives is restricted to an interface phenomenon (the realization of oblique case) rather than fundamental syntactic properties, thereby echoing the dichotomy between core and periphery. This insight is completely lost in the present OT account.

Since I have shown that the violability of certain constraints is necessary for a correct description of the facts, I do not want to give up an account based on violable constraints altogether. Rather, I would like to propose an alternative that preserves the insight of the analysis while at the same time helps restrict the possible grammars (and thus the range of variation): locality constraints on movement, at least those banning movement from strong islands, are reanalyzed as part of the generator (e.g. some version of the CED or phase theory). As a result, the grammar will never generate sentences that violate such islands. In the case at hand, this will correctly limit the variation to the realization of oblique case (5.2, 5.3, 5.4), and to the preference for external or internal merge (5.1).

The Derivations and Evaluations model proposed by Broekhuis (2008) provides exactly the necessary architecture to implement such an approach. It combines an MP-generator with an OT-like evaluator that includes constraints expressing (macro-)parameters (such as *MERGE), interface constraints (like REALIZEOBL) and constraints triggering displacement (so-called EPP-constraints). Constraints that are never violated, for example, the prohibition to move out of strong islands, are built into the MP-generator. This accounts for the universal properties of human language while the evaluator is responsible for cross-linguistic, and as we have seen, also inter- and intra-speaker variation.[30]

7. Conclusion

I have investigated three types of variation involving resumption: (a) Variation in the last resort nature of resumption; (b) dialectal and inter-speaker variation in dative resumption in Alemannic; and finally (c) intra-speaker variation in Alemannic dative resumption. In all cases I came to the conclusion that a rigid minimalist system as it is generally assumed is ill-equipped to handle these types of variation. This largely has to do with MP's focus on constraints on the derivational system and the inviolability of the constraints. In the case at hand, however, what is at stake is macro-parameter-like variation and variation at PF, but not variation in terms of presence or absence of movement. The variation in the last resort nature of resumption requires a fundamental, macro-parameter-like division between languages, but the status and locus of macro-parameters and their possible format remains very much unclear in MP. Dialectal and inter-speaker variation in dative resumption requires sophisticated PF-constraints. Here it becomes obvious that this is a heavily underdeveloped aspect of minimalism. Postulating PF-constraints in minimalism is thus inevitable, but because of their inviolability they are not flexible enough to handle the variation in a straightforward way. Rather, to express the language variation, various very language-specific ad-hoc constraints are necessary. Intra-speaker variation, finally, also remains completely unaccounted for under an MP approach, mainly due to the lack of sophisticated PF-constraints and the general inviolability of the constraints.

Within OT, however, the types of variation can be formulated in a straightforward and non-arbitrary way in that the variation observed is the result of the interaction of general and independently needed constraints. At the same time, the range of variation can be better restrained if certain properties of language are not taken to be the result of constraint interaction, but rather of a restrictive generator. In this respect the facts discussed here argue for a combination of some elements of both the Minimalist Program and Optimality Theory, for example, as proposed in the Derivations and Evaluations framework by Broekhuis (2008).

Acknowledgments

Earlier versions of parts of this work were presented at DEAL II (Leiden, February 2008), at the workshop Perspektiven Minimalistischer Syntax (Leipzig, October 2008), at the syntax colloquium in Konstanz (November 2008), and at the TIN-dag 2009 (Utrecht, February 2009). I am grateful to the audiences at these occasions for helpful discussion, especially to Josef Bayer, Petr Biskup, Ellen Brandner, Hans Broekhuis, Hans-Martin Gärtner, Edward Göbbel, Günther Grewendorf, Kleanthes Grohmann, Fabian Heck, Joost Kremers, Antje Lahne, Gereon Müller, Doris Penka, Florian Schäfer, Wolfgang Sternefeld, Ralf Vogel, Susanne Winkler and Hedde Zeijlstra. Additionally, I thank Hans Broekhuis, Mike Putnam, and Ralf Vogel for detailed comments on an earlier version that have led to a substantial improvement of the paper. This research has been supported by a grant from the Swiss National Science Foundation Nr. PBSK1--119747/1.

Notes

1. It should be mentioned that in some minimalist approaches island constraints, sometimes even the Phase Impenetrability Condition, are taken to be interface constraints (cf., e.g., Boeckx 2008: chapter 7, for discussion). Such minimalist systems are clearly less derivational and thus even closer to OT-models.
2. See Salzmann (2009b: 155, fn. 1) for qualifications.
3. For the transcription see Salzmann (2006: 320, fn. 259). Long-distance relativization, where resumptive pronouns appear across the board, can be argued to instantiate a different construction, cf. Salzmann (2006: chapter 4.9), Van Riemsdijk (2008), and also Salzmann and Bayer (forthcoming). For possessor relativization, cf. Salzmann (2011). Free relatives require *wh*-relative pronouns that leave gaps, cf. Van Riemsdijk (1989). Appositive relatives behave like restrictive relatives with respect to resumption, except for the indirect object. Resumptive pronouns also occur in comparatives, but not, or at least not systematically, in topicalization and *wh*-movement, see Weber (1964: 304), Salzmann (2006: 376, fn. 297, Salzmann 2011: section 4) for details.
4. In the b-example the resumptive pronoun is an R-pronoun, the pronominal part of a pronominal adverb. Pronominal adverbs occur when prepositions take an inanimate pronominal complement (see Salzmann 2006: 325f. for details). This extends to resumption. In the present case, the resuming element for a predicate would be *das*, which is turned into *de-*.
5. Matching effects (Salzmann 2006: 348ff.; Salzmann 2009b: 150; Salzmann and Seiler 2010) provide additional evidence that resumption is related to the realization of oblique case. Problems with Bayer *et al.*'s generalization and other strategies to realize oblique case in German varieties are discussed in Salzmann (2009b: 156f., fn. 7/8).
6. There have been alternative – syntactic – proposals to explain resumptive pronouns for oblique cases most of which attempt to unify them with resumptive pronouns after prepositions. Some (e.g., Boeckx 2003; Bianchi 2004) have linked them to inherent case. As discussed in Salzmann (2006: 373; Salzmann 2009b: 140ff.), this does not work for Swiss German because datives require resumptive

pronouns irrespective of whether they are structural or inherent. Furthermore, inherent accusatives do not require resumptive pronouns. What is important in Swiss German is thus the morphological notion 'oblique case'. Van Riemsdijk (1989) argues that datives are in fact PPs so that dropping the resumptive pronoun would violate recoverability. See Salzmann (2006: 369ff., 2009b: 140ff.) for evidence that dative resumptive pronouns cannot be reanalyzed as PPs. The variation facts to be introduced in section 5.2 clearly show that dative resumptives require a separate explanation and cannot be subsumed under the account for resumptives within PPs.

7. A terminological remark is in order here: whenever I speak of base-generation, I assume that what links the operator and the resumptive is not a syntactic dependency, but rather a semantic one. This type of derivation is to be distinguished from non-movement accounts as in Adger and Ramchand (2005), Alexopoulou (2006) and Rouveret (2008) which are based on Agree and thus involve a syntactic dependency.

8. Unfortunately, the issue is only addressed partially in these works. Pesetsky (1998) and Hornstein (2000) do not discuss reconstruction at all, and Demirdache (1991: 97f.) only discusses reconstruction into a weak island. Belletti (2006: 135) indeed argues for reconstruction into islands on the basis of Italian data while Boeckx (2003: 155ff.) and Boeckx and Hornstein (2008) relate the non-reconstruction into islands to different mechanisms, viz. to a different resumption strategy (intrusion), and to properties of the reconstruction mechanism. Even though there is no general agreement and languages may differ from each other, it has become increasingly clear that reconstruction effects do not always pattern with locality. Guilliot and Malkawi (2006, 2007, 2009) and Guilliot (2007) have shown that reconstruction into islands is possible in Jordanian Arabic and French resumptive structures, respectively. Conversely, Adger and Ramchand (2005) have pointed out that island-sensitivity does not necessarily imply movement. They show for Scottish Gaelic that no reconstruction effects (or rather 'identity effects') obtain under resumption even though resumption is subject to locality constraints. For Greek and Welsh, on the other hand, for which pure agree-based analyses have been proposed, reconstruction effects under resumption have been documented, cf. Alexopoulou (2006: 82), Rouveret (2008: 182).

9. In (8b) the reconstruction site is indicated below the resumptive since this corresponds to the theta-position of the indirect object. The resumptive appears in a higher position because it undergoes weak pronoun fronting.

10. There is one important exception: Resumptive relatives tend to block scope reconstruction (at least pair-list, but not necessarily functional readings) in many languages, cf. Doron (1982), Suñer (1998), Sharvit (1999), Boeckx (2003), Bianchi (2004, 2008), Guilliot (2007), Guilliot and Malkawi (2009). For Swiss German, cf. Salzmann (2006: 355–66). For Welsh (Rouveret 2008: 181f.), Breton (Guilliot 2006: 1893), and Jordanian Arabic (Guilliot and Malkawi 2006, 2007) it has been observed that resumptive relatives do not show reconstruction for Principle C, contrary to gap relatives.

11. As pointed out to me by Mike Putnam, there seems to be an inherent conflict in Boeckx' assumption that movement without Agree voids island constraints (because Agree cannot penetrate islands) and his assumption in later work (Boeckx 2008) that intermediate movement steps are not feature-driven: Given the latter possibility it should always be possible for the movee to circumvent an island and come so close to the probe that it can be attracted.

12. Note that I assume that island constraints are structural, i.e., either derivational or representational/interface constraints. There have been claims in the literature, e.g., in Levine and Hukari (2006), that island violations are rather the result of pragmatic/semantic inconsistencies and parsing difficulties. It is indeed the case that even extractions from strong islands are sometimes quite acceptable; but the assumption that movement is essentially unbounded runs into difficulties when trying to account for contrasts as in (2). Even if (2b) is optimized w.r.t. semantic/pragmatic considerations, it will never come close to (2a) in acceptability. If movement is essentially unbounded, it remains unclear why resumptive structures are so much better (and why they are necessary in some cases).

13. See also Cecchetto (2005) for convincing arguments that reconstruction in relative clauses should generally not be accounted for in terms of the copy theory of movement.

14. I must admit that I do not understand why in some of the works cited in this paragraph resumptives for possessors and complements of prepositions are taken to be cases of apparent resumption which consequently involve Agree and movement. To my knowledge possessors and PPs are

islands for extraction in some of these languages (certainly in Italian). The only resumptives that occur in unambiguously transparent positions are those for subjects and direct objects.

15. The test case to tell apart movement and base-generation would involve reconstruction into intermediate positions. Such interpretations would be unexpected under base-generation since the reconstruction mechanisms for base-generation discussed above invariably lead to reconstruction to the tail of the A′-dependency since the external head is only related to the resumptive (mediated by the operator). With successive-cyclic movement, on the other hand, reconstruction into intermediate positions is expected to obtain. I discussed a number of cases in Salzmann (2006: 341–5), but the results are not clear enough to derive any conclusions from them. The problem is more general in that reconstruction into intermediate positions is generally degraded in German and its varieties, cf. Salzmann (2006: 92ff.). For resumption in Welsh, Rouveret (2008: 186) has claimed that cyclicity effects disappear, that is, reconstruction is always to the tail of the A′-dependency.

16. See Van Riemsdijk (1989) for an earlier proposal in terms of base-generation. There is one point where I crucially differ from Van Riemsdijk: Van Riemsdijk proposes that SU- and DO-relatives also involve resumptive pronouns, which, however, are fronted and then undergo deletion. In Salzmann (2009a: 41f., 2009b: 143ff., 2009c: 66f.) I rejected such an analysis among others because gap relatives allow scope reconstruction much more readily than resumptive relatives. This is unexpected if the difference between gap and resumptive relatives is only a matter of PF. Furthermore, relatives in which constituents of semantic types other than <e>, i.e. predicates or amounts are relativized, e.g., cases like (4a), cannot be analyzed as involving fronting and deletion of a weak pronoun: The only potential proform that could be used in such a case, *das* 'that', is arguably not weak enough to front and undergo deletion. In amount relativization there is no proper proform at all so that a movement analysis is the only option for those. But if movement is necessary anyway for certain gap relatives, it is most economical to assume movement for SU- and DO-relatives as well.

17. There is a line of research that argues that resumptives are barred from certain positions such as matrix subject/direct object due to A′-disjointness, that is, bound pronouns must be free in a certain domain. This means that resumptive derivations are taken to crash in such cases, contrary to what is claimed here, see Willis (2000: 545ff.) for discussion on Welsh and Irish. For Swiss German such a solution is inadequate because of the resumptives for indirect objects: since indirect objects (which can be shown to be DPs) do not differ with respect to the least Complete Functional Complex from direct objects (in both cases, it is the TP), the asymmetry cannot be derived by means of A′-disjointness.

18. Two possibilities need to be ruled out for the argument against identical numerations to be watertight: First, one has to exclude a resumptive basis for the relativization of subject and direct object with subsequent deletion of the resumptive (Van Riemsdijk 1989), cf. fn. 16. Second, one has to rule out the possibility that the resumptive is added during the derivation (Aoun *et al.* 2001). See Salzmann (2009a: 39–42, 2009c: 66f.) for critical remarks. For interesting discussion of the issue of candidate set within OT, see Kuhn (2003).

19. One caveat is in order here: As pointed out in fn. 10, resumptive pronouns often impose semantic restrictions on the external head, i.e., they block scope reconstruction. This has, of course, implications for the definition of the reference set if it is based on the notion of 'identical LF': There will not be any competition between movement and base-generation under the narrow-scope interpretation (only the gap derivation is possible in that case; the lower copy is then interpreted as an indefinite description unlike (17)). Competition is thus restricted to wide-scope readings, which are available in gap and resumptive derivations, see Salzmann (2009a: 52) for more details. I will briefly come back to this issue in 6.3.2 below.

20. But see Shlonsky (1992) who reinterprets the optionality as a last resort, see also 6.1.2. As discussed in the previous footnote, the freedom of choice is only found with wide-scope readings, but disappears under scope reconstruction.

21. Something similar seems to hold for the variety spoken in Stahringen on Lake Constance as described in Städele (1927) even though the description is not fully clear: He gives a gap example for an indirect object but notes that for the genitive an alternative construction based on a dative object is used (basically 'whose wife left' = 'to whom the wife left'), and in that case a dative resumptive is optional.

22. This is not to say that the distribution of gap vs. resumptive pronoun is completely random and free of processing effects. As discussed in Salzmann (2009b: 150) and Salzmann and Seiler (2010), there

are a number of configurations where the gap variant is preferred: in matching contexts and with inanimate/non-referential head nouns. To what extent those factors are hard grammatical constraints or just soft/processing-related constraints and how they should be integrated into a model of grammar is something I wish to investigate in future research. See Salzmann (2009b: 153f.) and Salzmann and Seiler (2010) for first results. See also Salzmann (2009c: 75, fn. 8).

23. As pointed out to me by Hans Broekhuis, the APP could in principle be reinterpreted as a constraint favoring traces over pronouns. The question just is whether such a constraint would be particularly natural since it would refer to different concepts: traces have something to do with overtness and movement chains while pronouns refer to the content of DPs. I consider it very unattractive to integrate heterogeneous concepts into the constraint formulation because this will in many cases lead to a restatement of the observational facts. I therefore reject this option.

24. The view on cost of operations has changed in recent MP-work (e.g. Chomsky 2008) where both external and internal merge are considered equally free.

25. The last five languages are those in the sample of the World Atlas of Language Structures that use resumptives in the relativization of subjects. I do not know, however, whether they also feature a movement/gap strategy.

26. Admittedly, the pattern in these languages could also be explained by assuming that they do not have operators with *u*Case so that a movement derivation is not possible in the first place. Watertight evidence for the ranking *Move >> *Merge would involve contexts where movement would emerge in such languages because resumption is impossible, for example, with semantic types other than <e> that often resist resumption, cf. ex. 4 above.

27. As pointed out to me by Mike Putnam, nothing in principle requires such minimalist PF-constraints to be inviolable, although this seems to be what is normally assumed. Once violability becomes a possibility, one will need to specify under which conditions constraints may be violable. Arguably, this will quickly lead to a system of conflicting and ranked constraints as we know them from OT even if the resulting system may be called differently. In essence then, once violability becomes an option, the difference between MP and OT becomes blurred. To bring out the differences between MP and OT it therefore seems best to adhere to the strongest possible position, namely violability (OT) vs. inviolability (MP).

28. I remain somewhat skeptical as to the necessity of such a step. The same result can also be derived by the assumption that Alemannic simply has silent relative pronouns/operators, without having to appeal to deletion. Eventually, the issue depends on whether the inventory is given or derived by means of constraint ranking and how empty elements are handled in syntax. If they are invariably the result of a deletion operation, as is assumed in much work on OT-syntax, an approach as sketched in the main text is inevitable.

29. Pesetsky's (1998) system is confronted with the same problem: Given that he adopts an OT-constraint for locality (which actually penalizes unpronounced traces within islands) and a constraint (SilentTrace) that penalizes the pronunciation of traces, undesirable rankings like those mentioned in the text become possible.

30. Languages like Standard German or Dutch cannot make use of resumptive pronouns and therefore do not have any options in island contexts; the result is absolute ungrammaticality/ineffability. Given the conclusion in this subsection, the most straightforward solution to this is to assume that the generator simply cannot generate any candidates in island contexts. In Salzmann (2011) this is related to the absence of operators without *u*Case in these languages.

References

Adger, D. (2006) Combinatorial variability. *Journal of Linguistics* 42: 503–30.

Adger, D. and Ramchand, G. (2005) Merge and move: Wh-dependencies revisited. *Linguistic Inquiry* 36 (2): 161–3.

Adger, D. and Smith, J. (2005) Variation and the minimalist program. In L. Cornips and K. P. Corrigan (eds) *Syntax and Variation. Reconciling the Biological and the Social,* 149–178. Amsterdam: John Benjamins.

Alexopoulou, T. (2006) Resumption in relative clauses. *Natural Language and Linguistic Theory* 24 (1): 57–111.

Aoun, Y, Choueiri, L. and Hornstein. N. (2001) Resumption, movement, and derivational economy. *Linguistic Inquiry* 32 (3): 371–403.

Bäbler, H. (1949) *Glarner Sprachschuel.* Glarus: Verlag der Erziehungsdirektion.

Barbiers, S. (2005) Word order variation in three verb clusters and the division of labor between generative linguistics and sociolinguistics. In L. Cornips and K. P. Corrigan (eds) *Syntax and Variation. Reconciling the Biological and the Social*, 233–64. Amsterdam: John Benjamins.

Bayer, J. (1996) *Directionality and Logical Form. On the Scope of Focusing Particles and Wh-in-situ.* Dordrecht: Kluwer.

Bayer, J., Bader, M. and Meng, M. (2001) Morphological underspecification meets oblique case: Syntactic and processing effects in German. *Lingua* 111 (4–7): 465–514.

Belletti, A. (2006) Extending doubling to non-local domains: complete vs. partial copying + deletion and related reconstruction issues. In P. Brandt and E. Fuss (eds) *Form, Structure and Grammar*, 129–36. Berlin: Akademie-Verlag.

Bianchi, V. (2004) Resumptive relatives and LF chains. In L. Rizzi (ed.) *The Cartography of Syntactic Structures. Volume 2*, 76–114. New York and Oxford: Oxford University Press.

Bianchi, V. (2008) Some notes on the 'Specificity effects' of optional resumptives. In A. Rouveret (ed.) *Resumptive Pronouns at the Interfaces*, 319–42. Amsterdam: John Benjamins.

Biberauer, T. and Richards, M. (2006) True optionality: When the grammar does not mind. In C. Boeckx (ed.) *Minimalist Essays*, 35–67. Amsterdam: John Benjamins.

Boeckx, C. (2003) *Islands and Chains.* Amsterdam: John Benjamins.

Boeckx, C. (2008) *Understanding Minimalist Syntax: Lessons from Locality in Long-distance Dependencies.* Malden, MA: Blackwell.

Boeckx, C. and Hornstein, N. (2008): Superiority, reconstruction and islands. In R. Freidin, C. P. Otero and M. L. Zubizarreta (eds) *Foundational Issues in Linguistic Theory. Essays in Honor of Jean-Roger Vergnaud*, 197–225. Cambridge, MA: MIT Press.

Bossard, H. (1962) *Zuger Mundartbuch.* Zürich: Schweizer Spiegel Verlag.

Broekhuis, H. (2008) *Derivations and Evaluations: Object Shift in the Germanic Languages.* Berlin: Mouton de Gruyter.

Broekhuis, H. and Dekkers, J. (2000) The minimalist program and optimality theory: Derivations and evaluations. In J. Dekkers, F. van der Leeuw and J. van der Weijer (eds) *Optimality Theory. Phonology, Syntax, and Acquisition*, 386–422. New York and Oxford: Oxford University Press.

Broekhuis, H. and Klooster, W. (2007) Merge and move as costly operations. *Groninger Arbeiten zur Germanistischen Linguistik* 45: 17–37.

Cecchetto, C. (2005) Reconstruction in relative clauses and the copy theory of traces. In P. Pica, J. Rooryck and J. van Craenenbroeck (eds) *Linguistic Variation Yearbook 2005*, 3–35. Amsterdam: John Benjamins.

Chao, W. and Sells, P. (1983) On the interpretation of resumptive pronouns. *NELS* 13: 47–61.

Chomsky, N. (1982) *Some Concepts and Consequences of the Theory of Government and Binding.* Cambridge, MA: MIT Press.

Chomsky, N. (1995) *The Minimalist Program.* Cambridge, MA: MIT Press.

Chomsky, N. (2000) Minimalist inquiries: The framework. In R. Martin, D. Michaels and J. Uriagereka (eds) *Step by Step. Essays on Minimalist Syntax in Honor of Howard Lasnik*, 89–156. Cambridge, MA: MIT Press.

Chomsky, N. (2001) Derivation by phase. In M. Kenstowicz (ed.) *Ken Hale: A Life in Language*, 1–52. Cambridge, MA: MIT Press.

Chomsky, N. (2004) Beyond explanatory adequacy. In A. Belletti (ed.) *Structures and Beyond. The Cartography of Syntactic Structures (Volume 3)*, 104–31. Oxford: Oxford University Press.

Chomsky, N. (2007) Approaching UG from below. In H.-M. Gärtner and U. Sauerland (eds) *Interfaces + Recursion = Language? Chomsky's Minimalism and the View from Syntax-Semantics*, 1–30. Berlin: De Gruyter.

Chomsky, N. (2008) On phases. In R. Freidin, C. Otero and M. L. Zubizarreta (eds) *Foundational Issues in Linguistic Theory. Essays in Honor of Jean-Roger Vergnaud*, 133–66. Cambridge, MA: MIT Press.

Comrie, B. and Kuteva, T. (2005) Relativization strategies. In M. Haspelmath, M. S. Dryer, D. Gil and B. Comrie (eds) *The World Atlas of Language Structures,* 494–501. New York and Oxford: Oxford University Press.

Demirdache, H. (1991) Resumptive Chains in Restrictive Relatives, Appositives and Dislocation Structures. Doctoral dissertation: MIT.

Den Dikken, M. (2006) Specificational copular sentences and pseudoclefts. In M. Everaert and H. van Riemsdijk (eds) *The Blackwell Companion to Syntax,* 292–409. Oxford: Blackwell.

Den Dikken, M., Meinunger, A. and Wilder, C. (2000) Pseudoclefts and ellipsis. *Studia Linguistica* 54 (1): 41–89.

Doron, E. (1982) On the syntax and semantics of resumptive pronouns. *Texas Linguistic Forum* 19: 1–48.

Fischer, L. (1989) *Luzerndeutsche Grammatik.* Hitzkirch: Comenius.

Georgopoulos, C. (1985) Variables in Palauan syntax. *Natural Language and Linguistic Theory* 3 (1): 59–94.

Georgopoulos, C. (1991) *Syntactic Variables: Resumptive Pronouns and A' Binding in Palauan.* Dordrecht, Boston, MA and London: Kluwer.

Goodluck, H. and Stojanovic, D. (1996) The structure and acquisition of relative clauses in Serbo-Croatian. *Language Acquisition* 5 (4): 285–315.

Guilliot, N. (2006) A top-down analysis for reconstruction. *Lingua* 116 (11): 1888–914.

Guilliot, N. (2007) Reconstructing resumption. Handout from the workshop on 'resumption at the interfaces'.

Guilliot, N. and Malkawi, N. (2006) When resumption determines reconstruction. *Proceedings of WCCFL* 25: 168–176.

Guilliot, N. and Malkawi, N. (2007) Reconstruction and islandhood in Jordanian Arabic. In M. A. Mughazy (ed.) *Perspectives on Arabic Linguistics XX,* 87–104. Amsterdam: John Benjamins.

Guilliot, N. and Malkawi, N. (2009) When movement fails to reconstruct. In J. M. Brucart (ed.) *Merging Features: Computation, Interpretation, and Acquisition,* 159–74. Oxford: Oxford University Press.

Heck, F. and Müller, G. (2000) *Repair-Driven Movement and the Local Optimization of Derivations.* Ms. Universities of Mannheim and Stuttgart.

Heck, F., Müller, G., Fischer, S., Vikner, S. and Schmid, T. (2002) On the nature of the input in Optimality Theory. *Linguistic Review* 19: 345–76.

Henry, A. (2002) Variation and syntactic theory. In P. Trudgill, N. Schilling-Estes and J. K. Chambers (eds) *The Handbook of Language Variation and Change,* 267–282. Oxford: Blackwell.

Henry, A. (2005) Idiolectal variation and syntactic theory. In L. Cornips and K. P. Corrigan (eds) *Syntax and Variation. Reconciling the Biological and the Social,* 109–22. Amsterdam: John Benjamins.

Hodler, W. (1969) *Berndeutsche Syntax.* Tübingen: Francke.

Hornstein, N. (2000) *Move! A Minimalist Theory of Construal.* Oxford: Blackwell.

Hulsey, S. and Sauerland, U. (2006) Sorting out relative clauses. *Natural Language Semantics,* 14: 111–37.

Idiotikon (1999) *Schweizerdeutsches Wörterbuch,* Frauenfeld: Huber, 1881ff.

Keenan, E. and Comrie, B. (1977) Noun phrase accessibility and universal grammar. *Linguistic Inquiry* 8 (1): 63–99.

Kroch, A. (2000) Syntactic change. In M. Baltin and C. Collins (eds) *The Handbook of Contemporary Syntactic Theory,* 699–720. Oxford: Blackwell.

Kuhn, J. (2003) *Optimality-theoretic Syntax: A Declarative Approach.* Stanford, CA: Center for the Study of Language and Information.

Levine, R. and Hukari, T. (2006) *The Unity of Unbounded Dependency Constructions.* Stanford, CA: Center for the Study of Language and Information.

Marti, W. (1985) *Berndeutsche Grammatik.* Bern: Cosmos.

McCloskey, J. (1990) Resumptive pronouns, A'-binding and levels of representation in Irish. In R. Hendrick (ed.) *The Syntax of the Modern Celtic Languages,* 199–248. New York and San Diego, CA: Academic Press.

McCloskey, J. (2002) Resumption, successive cyclicity, and the locality of operations. In S. D. Epstein and T. D. Seely (eds) *Derivation and Explanation in the Minimalist Program,* 184–226. Oxford: Blackwell.

Müller, G. (2000) *Elemente der optimalitätstheoretischen Syntax.* Tübingen: Stauffenburg.

Müler, G. (2009) Ergativity, accusativity, and the order of Merge and Agree. In K. Grohmann (ed.) *Exploring Features and Arguments*, 269–308. Berlin: Mouton de Gruyter.

Müller, G. and Sternefeld, W. (2001) The rise of competition in syntax: A synopsis. In G. Müller and W. Sternefeld (eds) *Competition in Syntax*, 1–68. De Gruyter: Berlin and New York.

Noth, H. (1993) *Alemannisches Dialekthandbuch vom Kaiserstuhl und seiner Umgebung*. Freiburg: Schillinger Verlag.

Pesetsky, D. (1998) Some Optimality principles of sentence pronunciation. In P. Barbosa, D. Fox, M. McGinnis and D. Pesetsky (eds) *Is the Best Good Enough? Optimality and Competition in Syntax*, 337–83. Cambridge, MA: MIT Press.

Prince, A. and Smolensky, P. (2004) *Optimality Theory Constraint Interaction in Generative Grammar*. Malden, MA: Blackwell Publishing.

Rezac, M. (2004) *Elements of Cyclic Syntax: Agree and Merge*. Doctoral dissertation, Department of Linguistics, University of Toronto.

Richards, M. (2008) Two kinds of variation in a Minimalist System. In F. Heck, G. Müller and J. Trommer (eds) *Varieties of Competition*, 133–62. Leipzig: University of Leipzig.

Rouveret, A. (2008) Phasal agreement and reconstruction. In R. Freidin, C. Otero and M. L. Zubizaretta (eds) *Foundational Issues in Linguistic Theory*, 167–95. Cambridge, MA: MIT Press.

Salzmann, M. (2006) *Resumptive Prolepsis. A Study in indirect A'-dependencies*. Utrecht: LOT (= LOT Dissertation Series 136).

Salzmann, M. (2008) Variation in resumption requires violable constraints – a case study in Alemannic relativization. In H. Broekhuis and R. Vogel (eds) *Optimality Theory and Minimalism: Interface Theories*, 99–32. Linguistics in Potsdam 28.

Salzmann, M. (2009a) When movement and base-generation compete – on the definition of the reference set, the typology of resumption, and ranked economy constraints. *Groninger Arbeiten zur Germanistischen Linguistik* 48: 27–63.

Salzmann, M. (2009b) Different notions of variation and their reflexes in Swiss German relativization. In A. Dufter, J. Fleischer and G. Seiler (eds) *Describing and Modeling Variation in Grammar*, 135–61. Berlin and New York: Mouton de Gruyter.

Salzmann, M. (2009c) When movement and base-generation compete. The definition of the reference set and parameterized preferences for elementary operations. *Linguistics in the Netherlands* 26: 64–77.

Salzmann, M. (2011) Silent resumptives in Zurich German possessor relativization. In P. Gallmann and M. Wratil (eds) *Null Pronouns*, 141–221. Berlin: Mouton de Gruyter.

Salzmann, M. and Seiler, G. (2010) Variation as the exception or the rule? Swiss relatives, revisited. *Sprachwissenschaft* 35: 79–117.

Salzmann, M. and Bayer, J. (forthcoming) That-trace effects and resumption: How Improper Movement can be repaired. In P. Brandt and E. Fuss (eds) *Repairs*. Berlin: Mouton de Gruyter.

Sharvit, Y. (1999) Resumptive pronouns in relative clauses. *Natural Language and Linguistic Theory* 17 (3): 587–612.

Shlonsky, U. (1992) Resumptive pronouns as a last resort. *Linguistic Inquiry* 23 (3): 443–68.

Sigurdsson H. and Maling, J. (2010) The Empty Left Edge Condition. In: Putnam, M. (ed.) *Exploring Crash-Proof Grammars*, 59–86. Amsterdam: John Benjamin.

Sonderegger, S. and Gadmer, T. (1999) *Appenzeller Sprachbuch*. Apenzell and Herisau: Erziehungsdirektion der Kantone A.Rh. and I.Rh..

Städele, A. (1927) *Syntax der Mundart von Stahringen*. Lahr i.B.: Schauenburg.

Sternefeld, W. (1997) Comparing reference sets. In C. Wilder, H.-M. Gärtner and M. Bierwisch (eds) *The Role of Economy Principles in Linguistic Theory*, 81–114. Berlin: Akademie-Verlag.

Sternefeld, W. (2000) *Semantic vs. Syntactic Reconstruction*. SfS-Report-02-00.

Suñer, M. (1998) Resumptive restrictive relatives: A crosslinguistic perspective. *Language* 74 (2): 335–64.

Suter, R. (1992) *Baseldeutsch-Grammatik*. Basel: Merian

Toman, J. (1998) A discussion of resumptives in colloquial Czech. In Z. Boskovic, S. Franks and W. Snyder (eds) *Formal Approaches to Slavic Linguistics 1997*, 303–18. Ann Arbor, MI: Michigan Slavic Publications.

Van Riemsdijk, H. (1989) Swiss relatives. In D. Jaspers, W. Klooster, Y. Putseys and P. Seuren (eds) *Sentential Complementation and the Lexicon,* 343–54. Berlin: Foris.

Van Riemsdijk, H. (2008) Identity avoidance: OCP effects in Swiss relatives. In R. Freidin, C. P. Otero and M. L. Zubizarreta (eds) *Foundational Issues in Linguistic Theory. Essays in Honor of Jean-Roger Vergnaud,* 227–50. Cambridge, MA: MIT Press.

Weber, A. (1964) *Zürichdeutsche Grammatik: Ein Wegweiser zur Guten Mundart.* Zürich: Schweizer Spiegel Verlag.

Willis, D. (2000) On the distribution of resumptive pronouns and wh-trace in Welsh. *Journal of Linguistics* 36 (3): 531–73.

II LOCAL AND GLOBAL OPTIMIZATION

5 Sources of phonological structure

John J. McCarthy[*] and Kathryn Pruitt[**]

ABSTRACT This chapter claims that phonology is like syntax in that the input consists of lexical items with little or no structure. Specifically, we argue that metrical foot structure is always absent from underlying representations. This argument is framed in a derivational version of Optimality Theory called Harmonic Serialism (HS). The natural assumption in HS is that metrical structures are built one foot at a time. This mode of structure building has desirable consequences for locality in stress patterns. But these results can be subverted if structures that the grammar cannot produce are already present in underlying representations. The chapter concludes with a further phonology-syntax parallel: exceptional stress patterns require uninterpretable features whose presence can influence the structures that are built.

KEYWORDS harmonic serialism; harmonic improvement; lexicon; derivations; locality; diacritic features; uninterpretable features; metrical structure; prosodic structure; lexical stress; exceptions; accent

1. Introduction

A generative grammar is a function from one level of representation to another, such as the phonologist's underlying and surface representations. It is the responsibility of a theory of language to define that function and the properties of those levels of representation. These two research questions – the nature of the grammar and the nature of the representations – are closely connected. That connection is a focus of this chapter.

In Optimality Theory (OT) (Prince and Smolensky 1993/2004), the input to the grammar is mapped to a set of candidate outputs by the GEN component, and the EVAL component applies a constraint hierarchy to select the optimal member of this set as the actual output. Two further assumptions have also been standard in the phonological literature: the grammar is parallel rather than serial, meaning that it

---

  * John J. McCarthy, Department of Linguistics, South College, University of Massachusetts, Amherst, MA, USA. E-mail: jmccarthy@linguist.umass.edu

** Kathryn Pruitt, Department of Linguistics, South College, University of Massachusetts, Amherst, MA, USA. E-mail: kathryn.pruitt@gmail.com

maps underlying to surface representations directly, without intermediate steps; and underlying and surface forms are homogeneous in the sense that they have identical representational systems. We refer to a theory with these properties as *classic OT*.

This chapter describes and argues for a version of OT called *Harmonic Serialism* (HS), in which the grammar is serial rather than parallel. We go on to show that HS requires a particular kind of *non*-homogeneity between underlying and surface representation: the phonological structure relevant to stress is necessarily absent from underlying representations, and so its presence in surface representations is always attributable to the workings of the grammar.

These aspects of HS recall two assumptions that have broad acceptance in work identified with the Minimalist Program (MP). First, the grammar is serial rather than parallel, meaning that it maps inputs to outputs through a succession of intermediate steps (a point emphasized by Chomsky 1995: 380 in his critique of OT). Second, according to the Bare Phrase Structure hypothesis in MP (BPS/MP) (Chomsky 1994), all pre-movement syntactic structure is produced by successive Merge operations. This too entails that the inputs and outputs of the grammar are non-homogeneous: the inputs lack structure, while the outputs are fully structured.

We will argue that this dual resemblance between HS and BPS/MP is no accident: there is a connection between serialism and the source of structure.

This chapter begins (section 2) with an introduction to HS and to those aspects of phonological theory that are essential to our argument. (Recognizing that readers of this chapter may not be phonologists, we have tried to make this material as accessible as possible.) Section 3 presents some of the evidence that supports HS over classic OT: HS's derivational architecture explains certain observations about the locality of phonological dependencies that are elusive in classic OT. Once these necessary preliminaries are out of the way, we arrive at our main point in section 4: in HS, as in BPS/MP, the properties of the grammar can explain the properties of the structure that the grammar creates only if that structure is never present in the input to the grammar. Section 5 completes this argument by showing how surface contrasts in metrical stress structure can be obtained without including that structure in the lexicon. This part of the analysis uses uninterpretable features, so it offers an opportunity for comparison with the role of uninterpretable features in MP. Section 6 concludes with a summary of our results.

2.   A brief introduction to Harmonic Serialism

HS is a variant of OT that combines optimization with a derivation. Prince and Smolensky (1993/2004) briefly consider HS in their original exposition of OT but decide in favor of the standard parallel version of the theory, referred to here as classic OT. The case for HS was reopened in McCarthy (2000, 2002: 159–63, 2007), where some general consequences of this theory are identified and discussed. This and subsequent work, mentioned in the next section, argues that HS is a better theory of many phonological phenomena than is classic OT. (See McCarthy 2010a for an overview.)

HS has the same grammatical components as classic OT: a candidate generator (GEN), a set of constraints (CON), a language-particular hierarchy of these constraints (*H*), and an evaluator (EVAL). The difference between classic OT and HS lies in GEN and its relationship to EVAL. While classic OT's GEN produces candidates that may differ from a given input in many ways simultaneously, the GEN component in HS is restricted to producing candidates that differ from the input by at most one application of one operation. This property of HS's GEN is known as *gradualness*. Because the ultimate output of a grammar can differ from the original input in more than one way, HS's restricted GEN has to have an altered relationship with EVAL. In HS, the output of EVAL is not necessarily the final output of the grammar. Rather, EVAL's chosen optimum is sent back to GEN for another iteration of candidate generation and comparison. This *GEN-EVAL loop* continues until the candidate selected by EVAL is identical with the most recent input to GEN, when the derivation is said to have *converged*. The optimal candidate at the point of convergence is the grammar's final output, such as a phonological surface form.

We will illustrate HS with an example of stress assignment. Since Liberman and Prince (1977), the process of stress assignment has been identified as a process of building metrical structure. The constituents most relevant to word stress are called feet, and they consist of a single syllable or two adjacent syllables. One of the syllables in a foot is always designated as its head, and that syllable is usually pronounced with a stress. Words that contain multiple stresses contain multiple feet.

For example, the data in (1) illustrate the stress pattern in the Australian language Pintupi (Hansen and Hansen 1969, 1978). Pintupi has stress, which is marked with the ' symbol, on the first, third, fifth, etc. syllables, except that it never has stress on the final syllable. (The strongest stress is on the first syllable.) The boundaries of feet are indicated by parentheses, and the boundaries of foot-internal syllables are marked with a period/full stop.

(1) Pintupi stress (Hansen and Hansen 1969: 163)

('pa.ŋa)	'earth'
('tʲu.ʈa)ya	'many'
('ma.ʆa)('wa.na)	'through (from) behind'
('pu.ʆiŋ)('ka.la)tʲu	'we (sat) on a hill'
('tʲa.mu)('lim.pa)('tʲuŋ.ku)	'our relation'
('ti.ʆi)('ri.ŋu)('lam.pa)tʲu	'the fire for our benefit flared up'

In classic OT, the stress of, say, /puʆiŋkalatʲu/ is determined by evaluating a candidate set that includes all of the ways of parsing this word into zero or more feet of one or two syllables (see (2)).[1]

(2) Some candidates from /puʆiŋkalatʲu/ in classic OT
  pu.ʆiŋ.ka.la.tʲu
  ('pu.ʆiŋ)ka('la.tʲu)
  pu('ʆiŋ.ka)('la.tʲu)
  ('pu.ʆiŋ)('ka.la)('tʲu)
  ('pu)('ʆiŋ)('ka)('la)('tʲu), etc.

In HS, on the other hand, gradualness limits GEN to creating one foot at a time. The candidate set from /puɭiŋkalatʲu/ is therefore limited to forms like those in (3):

(3)   Some candidates from /puɭiŋkalatʲu/ in HS
      pu.ɭiŋ.ka.la.tʲu
      (ˈpu)ɭiŋka.la.tʲu
      (ˈpu.ɭiŋ)ka.la.tʲu
      pu(ˈɭiŋ)ka.la.tʲu
      pu(ˈɭiŋ.ka)la.tʲu, etc.

In classic OT, the grammar of Pintupi is presented with the candidates in (2), and it identifies *(ˈpu.ɭiŋ)(ˈka.la)tʲu* as the optimum. This is the surface representation. In HS, the grammar of Pintupi is presented with the candidates in (3), and it identifies *(ˈpu.ɭiŋ)ka.la.tʲu* as the optimum. This intermediate form is submitted to GEN, which can again make at most a single change: removing the foot it has just constructed or building another foot. The result is in (4):

(4)   Some candidates from intermediate *(ˈpu.ɭiŋ)ka.la.tʲu* in HS
      (ˈpu.ɭiŋ)ka.la.tʲu
      pu.ɭiŋ.ka.la.tʲu
      (ˈpu.ɭiŋ)(ˈka)la.tʲu
      (ˈpu.ɭiŋ)(ˈka.la)tʲu
      (ˈpu.ɭiŋ)ka(ˈla)tʲu, etc.

The grammar of Pintupi is presented with this candidate set and selects *(ˈpu.ɭiŋ)(ˈka.la)tʲu* as the optimum. It is submitted to GEN, yielding the candidate set in (5):

(5)   Some candidates from intermediate *(ˈpu.ɭiŋ)(ˈka.la)tʲu* in HS
      (ˈpu.ɭiŋ)(ˈka.la)tʲu
      pu.ɭiŋ(ˈka.la)tʲu
      (ˈpu.ɭiŋ)ka.la.tʲu
      (ˈpu.ɭiŋ)(ˈka.la)(ˈtʲu)

The grammar of Pintupi once against selects *(ˈpu.ɭiŋ)(ˈka.la)tʲu* as the optimum. The derivation has therefore converged on the surface representation.

With standard metrical stress constraints (see, e.g., Kager 1999; McCarthy and Prince 1993), the grammar of Pintupi is nearly the same in classic OT and HS. These constraints include; ALIGN-LEFT(foot, word) (6), which requires every foot to be assigned as far to the left as possible; PARSE-SYLLABLE (7), which requires every syllable to be parsed into a foot; and FOOT-BINARITY (8), which is violated by any foot that consists of a single syllable with a short vowel.

(6)   ALIGN-LEFT(foot, word) (abbreviated AL-L(ft))
      For each foot in a word assign one violation mark for every syllable separating it from the left edge of the word.

(7) Parse-Syllable (Parse-Syll)
     Assign one violation mark for every syllable that is not a member of some foot.

(8) Foot-Binarity (Ft-Bin)
     Assign one violation mark for a foot with fewer than two moras.

If these constraints are ranked in the hierarchy Foot-Binarity >> Parse-Syllable >> Align-Left(foot, word), then the right result is obtained in classic OT, as shown in tableau (9).[2] This tableau and all of the others in this chapter are in the comparative format introduced by Prince (2002). When the number of violations of a constraint is greater than zero, it is indicated by an integer. In loser rows, a cell may contain **W**, **L**, or neither depending on whether the constraint favors the winner, the loser, or neither. Because every loser-favoring constraint must be dominated by some winner-favoring constraint, in a properly ranked tableau every **L** is preceded in the same row by a **W** across a solid line. For example, Parse-Syllable favors the fully-footed loser *('pu.[iŋ)('ka.la)('tʲu)* in (9b) over the winner, whose final syllable is unfooted. This loser-favoring constraint therefore has an **L** in row (9b). But this **L** is dominated by a **W**, because higher-ranking Foot-Binarity favors the winner. Next in the hierarchy, Parse-Syllable favors the winner over candidates like (9c) and (9d), with less than the full complement of disyllabic feet.

(9) Classic OT analysis of stress in Pintupi

	/pu[iŋkalatʲu/	Ft-Bin	Parse-Syll	Al-L(ft)
a. →	('pu.[iŋ)('ka.la)tʲu		1	2
b.	('pu.[iŋ)('ka.la)('tʲu)	1 W	L	6 W
c.	pu.[iŋ.ka.la.tʲu		5 W	L
d.	('pu.[iŋ)ka.la.tʲu		3 W	L
e.	pu.('[iŋ.ka)('la.tʲu)		1	4 W

Left-to-right foot parsing is ensured by Align-Left(foot, word). The winner incurs two violations of this constraint because only one of its feet is non-initial (the foot *('ka.la)*), and it is misaligned by just two syllables. Candidate (9e) does worse on this constraint: one of its feet is one syllable distant from the left edge and the other foot is three syllables distant, for a total of four violations.

The HS analysis of Pintupi works similarly, except that feet are constructed one at a time. Tableau (10) shows the first step in the derivation. Both Foot-Binarity and Parse-Syllable disfavor (10d)'s monosyllabic foot *('pu)*, so it is a sure loser. Parse-Syllable rules out the candidate with no feet at all, (10b). This leaves candidates with a disyllabic foot in various positions, including (10a) and (10c). Align-Left(foot, word) decides among them, favoring footing as far to the left as possible.

(10) Step 1 of stress assignment in Pintupi

	/pu.[iŋ.ka.la.tʲu/	Fᴛ-Bɪɴ	Pᴀʀsᴇ-Sʏʟʟ	Aʟ-L(ft)
a. →	('pu.[iŋ)ka.la.tʲu		3	
b.	pu.[iŋ.ka.la.tʲu		5 W	
c.	pu.('[iŋ.ka)la.tʲu		3	1 W
d.	('pu)[iŋ.ka.la.tʲu	1 W	4 W	

The derivation continues at the second step with *('pu.[iŋ)ka.la.tʲu* as the new input, as in (11). This step considers the new input as the faithful candidate, appearing in row (11b), and compares it to a new set of alternatives derived by Gᴇɴ's foot-structure operations. Since there is no reason to suppose that Gᴇɴ cannot remove feet as well as build them, we also include a candidate with the previously built feet removed, (11e). The candidate with another disyllabic foot adjacent to the first, *('pu.[iŋ)('ka.la)tʲu* in (11a), is chosen as optimal.

(11) Step 2

	('pu[iŋ)ka.la.tʲu	Fᴛ-Bɪɴ	Pᴀʀsᴇ-Sʏʟʟ	Aʟ-L(ft)
a. →	('pu.[iŋ)('ka.la)tʲu		1	2
b.	('pu.[iŋ)ka.la.tʲu		3 W	L
c.	('pu.[iŋ)ka('la.tʲu)		1	3 W
d.	('pu.[iŋ)('ka)la.tʲu	1 W	2 W	2
e.	pu.[iŋ.ka.la.tʲu		5 W	L

The first two steps of this derivation have succeeded in building the correct feet for this language, but one more step is required to satisfy the convergence requirement. The output of Step 2, *('pu.[iŋ)('ka.la)tʲu*, is fed back into another loop through Gᴇɴ and Eᴠᴀʟ, as shown in (12). This form has only one remaining footless syllable, so at this step there is only one candidate with further foot parsing, (12b). Fᴏᴏᴛ-Bɪɴᴀʀɪᴛʏ rules it out because of *('tʲu)*, while Pᴀʀsᴇ-Sʏʟʟᴀʙʟᴇ knocks out the candidates that have removed a foot, (12c) and (12d). None of these alternatives improves on *('pu.[iŋ)('ka.la)tʲu*, so the derivation converges at Step 3 with the correct stress placement for Pintupi.

(12) Step 3 – Convergence

	('pu.[iŋ)('ka.la)tʲu	Fᴛ-Bɪɴ	Pᴀʀsᴇ-Sʏʟʟ	Aʟ-L(ft)
a. →	('pu.[iŋ)('ka.la)tʲu		1	2
b.	('pu.[iŋ)('ka.la)('tʲu)	1 W	L	6 W
c.	('pu.[iŋ)ka.la.tʲu		3 W	L
d.	pu.[iŋ('ka.la)tʲu		3 W	2

This and all other HS derivations must show *monotonic harmonic improvement* until convergence. Harmony is the property that EVAL selects for: A is more harmonic than B if and only if the highest ranking constraint that distinguishes between A and B is a constraint that favors A. Harmonic improvement in an HS derivation refers to the relationship between the winner and input at each step. Because EVAL chooses the winner, the winner must be more harmonic than the most recent input to GEN (or else identical to it when there is convergence). Thus, harmony increases steadily in an HS derivation until convergence. This property of HS ensures that the derivations are finite: if CON is limited to markedness and faithfulness constraints, then every underlying representation has only finite potential for harmonic improvement in any grammar (Moreton 2000, 2003). Harmonic improvement is also crucial to the typological arguments for HS, as we will see in the next section.

3. Evidence for Harmonic Serialism

In the literature to date, the arguments in support of HS over classic OT are of two main types. Some are based on the fact that HS can state generalizations that are expressible only at the intermediate steps of a derivation, neither underlying nor surface: Elfner (2009), Jesney (to appear), Kimper (to appear), McCarthy (2008b, 2011), and Pater (2011). Other arguments are based on typological differences between HS and classic OT that follow from the harmonic improvement imperative: McCarthy (2007, 2008a, to appear), McCarthy *et al.* (2010), and Pruitt (2010). We will summarize one of Pruitt's typological results here.

First, though, a cautionary remark. In classic OT, typological claims follow from hypotheses about CON. In HS, typological claims follow from a combination of hypotheses about both GEN and CON. This would make the task of studying typology in HS notably harder for the analyst, but for two things. First, the relationship among GEN, CON, and typology is quite clear, so by holding two of these items constant it is relatively easy to draw inferences about the third (McCarthy 2010b). Second, the nature of GEN in HS makes it possible to implement a program that calculates typologies given only a list of underlying representations, GEN and CON. Such a program exists (Staubs *et al.* 2010), and it has been used to check the claims in this chapter.

The HS analysis of Pintupi above illustrates Iterative Foot Optimization in HS (IFO/HS), a derivational model of stress proposed by Pruitt (2010). As we just noted, any application of HS to some empirical domain must specify properties of both GEN and CON. In IFO/HS, GEN produces candidates with at most one metrical foot added or removed at a time, as in (10)–(12). The constraints are just exactly the standard stress constraints, such as (6)–(8).

Pruitt demonstrates that the typological predictions of IFO/HS are superior to those of classic OT with these same standard stress constraints. Hyde (2007) has shown that the standard stress constraints predict unattested stress patterns. According to Pruitt, the problem is not with the standard stress constraints but with the classic OT framework in which they are usually embedded. Because classic OT compares candidates that are completely parsed into feet, it predicts the existence of languages with unattested non-local dependencies. Because IFO/HS compares candidates that differ by the addition of a single foot, it does not predict these dependencies. In this respect, IFO/HS is a better fit to what is actually observed in languages.

Pintupi can be used to illustrate this point. The illustration begins with the observation that Pintupi allows long vowels in the first syllable of a word (Hansen and Hansen 1969: 161): *'muːɲu* 'fly'. A syllable with a long vowel satisfies the constraint FOOT-BINARITY as defined in (8). Therefore, this word could in principle be parsed as *('muː)ɲu*, with a monosyllabic bimoraic foot, or *('muː.ɲu)*, with a disyllabic foot. Which is it? In general, are Pintupi words that start with a long vowel parsed like (hypothetical) *('paː)('ta.ka)ma* or *('paː.ta)('ka.ma)*?[3] Since the decision about how to parse the first foot affects the placement of stress by the second and subsequent feet, this question is not merely academic. The grammar of Pintupi must choose the latter option in order to maintain the generalization that stress appears on every other syllable beginning with the first, regardless of vowel length.

Under the ranking that produces the Pintupi stress pattern in IFO/HS, classic OT makes a factually incorrect and typologically implausible prediction about the stress pattern of words with a long vowel in the first syllable. As tableaux (13) and (14) show, high-ranking FOOT-BINARITY and PARSE-SYLLABLE will cause the initial syllable to be parsed differently depending on whether it is followed by an odd or even number of syllables. If the number is odd, then the word will start with a disyllabic foot (13), and, if the number is even, the word will have a very different stress pattern because it will start with a monosyllabic foot (14):

(13)   Disyllabic foot when odd number of syllables follows (classic OT)

/paːtakama/		Ft-Bin	Parse-Syll	Al-L(ft)
a. →	('paː.ta)('ka.ma)			2
b.	('paː)('ta.ka)ma		1 W	1 L
c.	('paː)('ta.ka)('ma)	1 W		4 W

(14)   Monosyllabic foot when even number of syllables follows (classic OT)

/paːtakamana/		Ft-Bin	Parse-Syll	Al-L(ft)
a. →	('paː)('ta.ka)('ma.na)			4
b.	('paː.ta)('ka.ma)na		1 W	2 L
c.	('paː.ta)('ka.ma)('na)	1 W		6 W

In (13) and (14), the decision about how to parse at the beginning of the word is determined by the desire to avoid an unfooted syllable at the other end of the word. The optimal initial foot *('paː.ta)* in (13a) is a result of avoiding the final unfooted syllable in (13b). The optimal initial foot *('paː)* in (14a) is a result of avoiding the final unfooted syllable in (14b). This is a highly non-local dependency, given that the language's basic parsing direction is left to right, as we saw in (9). Classic OT predicts this non-local dependency because it evaluates full parses, in which all feet are created and therefore evaluated simultaneously. Neither Pintupi nor any other known language behaves in this way. In short, classic OT with this constraint set overgenerates.

One way of solving overgeneration problems in OT is to modify the constraint set. Of course, adding a constraint will not help with overgeneration. This leaves the possibility of redefining or eliminating a constraint. But all of these constraints, under the definitions operative in (13) and (14), are needed to analyze attested stress patterns under standard representational assumptions. FOOT-BINARITY, exactly as it is defined in (8), is required to analyze languages with the 'generalized trochee' stress pattern (Kager 1992; Prince 1980). In these languages, the condition on foot well-formedness is precisely a bimoraic minimum. PARSE-SYLLABLE or some equivalent is a necessity for analyzing languages with iterative, alternating stress. And although alternatives to ALIGN-LEFT(foot, word) have been discussed in the literature (Eisner 1999; Kager 2001; McCarthy 2003a), they will not affect this overgeneration problem.

In contrast to classic OT, IFO/HS does not predict these non-local dependencies under any ranking of the standard constraints. To show this, we begin by considering the derivations that this non-existent language would require. Words without an initial long vowel are parsed into disyllabic feet from left to right (15a). Words with an initial long vowel are also parsed from left to right, but they differ in whether the first foot is disyllabic (15b) or monosyllabic (15c):

(15)   Derivations for non-local language
      (a) /puɭiŋkalatʲu/ → ('pu.ɭiŋ)ka.la.tʲu → ('pu.ɭiŋ)('ka.la)tʲu
      (b) /paːtakama/ → ('paː.ta)ka.ma → ('paː.ta)('ka.ma)
      (c) /paːtakamana/ → ('paː)ta.ka.ma.na → ('paː)('ta.ka)ma.na → ('paː)('ta.ka)('ma.na)

The derivation in (15a) was already shown in (10)–(12). It requires the standard ranking for left-to-right iterative stress systems with minimally bimoraic feet: FOOT-BINARITY >> PARSE-SYLLABLE >> ALIGN-LEFT(foot, word). This ranking seals the fate of (15b) and (15c) as well. Because of ALIGN-LEFT(foot, word), they will both be parsed from left to right. And because of PARSE-SYLLABLE, *('paː.ta)* is preferred to *('paː)* at the first step in both derivations. Tableau (16) shows why:

(16)   Disyllabic foot preferred at step 1 of both derivations

	/paːtakamana/	FT-BIN	PARSE-SYLL	AL-L(ft)
a. →	('paː.ta)ka.ma.na		3	
b.	('paː)ta.ka.ma.na		4 W	
	/paːtakama/	FT-BIN	PARSE-SYLL	AL-L(ft)
c. →	('paː.ta)ka.ma		2	
d.	('paː)ta.ka.ma		3 W	

Tableau (16) illustrates our point about how IFO/HS – and HS in general – imposes locality restrictions that distinguish it from classic OT. An HS grammar has no foresight; it does not choose a suboptimal candidate like *('pa:)ta.ka.ma.na* in (16b) even though this candidate would eventually lead to a fully footed surface form, *('pa:)('ta.ka)('ma.na)*. An HS grammar has no way of knowing that this ultimate output would be 'better' because the derivation never reaches a point where *('pa:)('ta.ka)('ma.na)* is even a candidate. The result is that IFO/HS indirectly imposes a kind of locality restriction on the stress systems it can analyze. Each parsing decision is made individually and sequentially. Early decisions can affect later ones, but not the other way around. Arguably, all attested stress systems are local in this sense. In short, IFO/HS fits observed language typology better than classic OT does.[4]

Before concluding this argument for HS, it is worth noting a parallel in the development of syntactic theory. The insight of successive cyclic *wh*-movement (Chomsky 1977) is that the properties of long-distance dependencies between *wh* and its trace are best understood as the result of short *wh*-movement applied iteratively. In other words, the typological properties of long *wh*-movement make more sense if long movement is decomposed into short steps. Or, to put it yet another way, a restrictive theory of long-distance effects follows from the assumption that operations are local but they apply in a derivation. Abstractly, the argument for HS from metrical parsing is exactly the same.

4.   The source of metrical structure

This section has three parts. It begins in 4.1 by introducing the problem of exceptional or contrastive stress. As we will show, a fairly standard hypothesis about such stress systems – that they require metrical structure in underlying representations – will not work in IFO/HS. The argument continues in 4.2 with a critique of various ways of working around this consequence of our theory, such as allowing metrical structure in some languages but forbidding it in others. Finally, 4.3 draws the necessary conclusion: metrical structure is universally absent from the lexicon. We present conceptual arguments that reinforce this conclusion and we discuss the close parallel with BPS/MP.

4.1   Lexical metrical structure is incompatible with IFO/HS
Although stress is entirely predictable in some languages, in some others stress is contrastive, and in many more languages some words have exceptional stress patterns. For example, the usual pattern in Warao (Osborn 1966) is to put stress on all even numbered syllables counting from the right (17a),[5] but there are exceptional words where stress assignment begins on the last or third from last syllable (17b):

(17)   Stress in Warao (Osborn 1966)
      (a) Regular stress
          yi('wa.ra)('na.e)   'he finished it'
          ('ya.pu)('ri.ki)('ta.ne)('ha.se)   'verily to climb'

   (b) Exceptional stress
       he('su)   'Jesus'
       ('na.ho)('ro.a)e   'eaten'

A fairly standard assumption in the phonological literature is that unpredictable stress is marked by including metrical structure in lexical entries. The words in (18) would therefore have the following underlying representations:

(18) Stress in Warao lexicon
      /yiwaranae/
      /yapurikitanehase/
      /he('su)/
      /naho('ro.a)e/

On this view, words with predictable stress have no foot structure in their lexical entries. Words with unpredictable stress have as much metrical structure as is needed to account for their unpredictability.

This way of analyzing stress (un)predictability is inconsistent with IFO/HS, however. Tableau (19) illustrates this problem. Suppose that the lexicon of Pintupi includes a root with a lexically specified foot on the second and third syllables: /pa('taka)sana/. The location of this foot is inconsistent with the basic stress pattern of the language, and since Pintupi has no words with exceptional stress, we want the grammar to be unfaithful to this lexical foot. Under our assumption that GEN can only add or remove a foot, this requires the lexical foot to be eliminated before regular foot building begins. But ranking FAITH(stress) below all of the other stress constraints does not produce the desired result, as tableau (19) shows:

(19) Persistence of lexical foot despite low-ranking faithfulness

/pa('ta.ka)sa.na/	FT-BIN	PARSE-SYLL	AL-L(ft)	FAITH(stress)
a. → pa('ta.ka)('sa.na)		1	4	
b. pa('ta.ka)sa.na		3 W	1 L	
c. pa.ta.ka.sa.na		5 W	L	1 W
d. ('pa)('ta.ka)sa.na	1 W	2 W	1 L	

FAITH(stress) is ranked too low to matter, but still the lexical foot *('ta.ka)* is preserved by the winner in (19). Removing this unwanted foot, as in (19c), introduces additional violations of PARSE-SYLLABLE. Removing this foot does improve performance on ALIGN-LEFT(foot, word), but left-to-right iterative stress systems require the ranking PARSE-SYLLABLE >> ALIGN-LEFT(foot, word). (The reasoning: multiple feet obviously cannot all align perfectly with the left edge, so languages with iterative stress require high-ranking PARSE-SYLL to compel violations of ALIGN-L(foot, word).) In fact, PARSE-SYLL acts somewhat like a faithfulness constraint in IFO/HS, because removing a foot degrades harmony with respect to this constraint.

In general, IFO/HS predicts that in this and all iterative-stress languages, an underlying foot that would not arise in normal foot building will be kept if the only constraints it violates are ranked below PARSE-SYLL. As long as it meets other requirements of foot-form (e.g., in Pintupi it must be disyllabic and trochaic), it will never be harmonically improving to get rid of this foot. A misaligned lexical foot can then interfere with the grammar's ability to choose the desired stress pattern. As a result, it is impossible to analyze well-attested languages with predictable stress in IFO. The same rankings that get iterativity also predict preservation of underlying feet via PARSE-SYLL, regardless of the ranking of any genuine stress faithfulness constraint. This means that IFO's typology contains no language with predictable iterative stress. This is obviously a major problem.

4.2 Unsuccessful workarounds

There is an obvious but wrong solution to this problem. Why not assume that languages differ systematically in whether they allow lexical feet? Languages with fully predictable stress, such as Pintupi, would forbid lexical feet, while languages with partly or fully unpredictable stress, such as Warao, would permit them.

The encoding of systematic differences between languages in their lexicons was at one time standard in MP. As Samek-Lodovici (this volume) observes, this is one of the areas where OT and MP (according to some) differ. The central premise of OT is that languages differ in their constraint ranking. The null hypothesis is that languages differ *only* in their constraint ranking. From this it follows that no generalization about a language can be derived, in whole or in part, from some assumption about its lexicon – unless that assumption is made about the lexicons of *all* languages. For more on this point, see the conclusion of the next section.

The idea that Pintupi and Warao differ in whether they permit lexical feet is obviously inconsistent with this view. In OT, the distinction between Pintupi and Warao in tolerance for exceptional stress has to be derived from differences in their grammars, not their lexicons. Succinctly, the grammar of Warao must respect lexical feet, but the grammar of Pintupi must not. As we saw in (19), however, there is no way in IFO/HS to contrive a grammar for Pintupi that disrespects lexical feet.

A less obvious solution to the problem involves modifying GEN. In HS, predictions about typology emerge from hypotheses about *both* CON *and* GEN. Thus, a theory of GEN is an empirical claim in the same way as a theory of CON. We have hypothesized that GEN can add or remove one foot at a time, but other hypotheses are certainly possible. One might posit a more powerful GEN that is able to modify an existing foot while adding a new one, so that from underlying /pa('ta.ka)sana/ there could be a candidate *('pa.ta)ka.sa.na*, which has partially overwritten and modified the remainder of the input foot, and/or *('pa.ta)ka.sa.na*, which has overwritten and removed the input foot altogether.

This does not help. As shown in (20), an input /pa('ta.ka)sana/ is improved more by adding a disyllabic foot than by modifying existing feet, again because of the dominance of PARSE-SYLL.

(20) Expanded GEN with overwrite options does not solve the problem (step 1)

/pa('ta.ka)sa.na/	PARSE-SYLL	FT-BIN	ALL-FT-L	GEN operation
a. → pa('ta.ka)('sa.na)	1		4	foot added
b. pa('ta.ka)sa.na	3 W		1 L	none – faithful
c. ('pa.ta)ka.sa.na	3 W		L	overwritten foot removed
d. ('pa.ta)('ka)sa.na	2 W	1 W	2 L	overwritten foot modified
e. ('pa)('ta.ka)sa.na	2 W	1 W	1 L	foot added

From tableau (20), we can infer the minimum power that GEN would require to resolve this instance of the paradox: it must be able to rewrite /pa('taka)sana/ as *('pa.ta)('ka.sa)na* in a single step, removing one foot and building two others at the same time. This follows because *('pa.ta)('ka.sa)na* is the only form that would both beat (20a) and move toward the desired surface form. (In fact, it is the desired surface form.) This version of GEN is very powerful indeed – so powerful, in fact, that it subverts the typological results obtained in section 3, as we will now show.

The argument for IFO/HS in section 3 relies on GEN's limited power. The point of the argument is this: the IFO/HS grammar, but not the classic OT grammar, treats /paːtakama/ and /paːtakamana/ alike, parsing both into disyllabic feet: *('paː.ta)('ka.ma), ('paː.ta)('ka.ma)na*. A similar three-syllable input /paːtaka/ should be parsed as *('paː.ta)ka* under this ranking, and indeed it is when GEN has only the minimal foot-building and -deleting operations. But if GEN has the capacity to alter one foot and build another in a single step, then the derivation will converge on *('paː.)('ta.ka)* instead of *('paː.ta)ka*. This is shown in the derivation (21). (Convergence at step 3 is not shown.)

(21) Three-syllable input maps to wrong output with non-minimal GEN

Step 1

/paːtaka/	PARSE-SYLL	FT-BIN	AL-L(ft)
a. → ('paː.ta)ka	1		
b. ('paː)ta.ka	2 W		

Step 2

('paː.ta)ka	PARSE-SYLL	FT-BIN	AL-L(ft)
a. → ('paː)('ta.ka)			1
b. ('paː.ta)ka	1 W		L

In short, a GEN that is powerful enough to avoid the problem in (20) also undermines the results of section 3. This is clearly not a desirable move.

The failure of these various alternatives confirms our earlier conclusion: IFO/HS entails that in Pintupi and all iterative-stress languages, no foot present in the lexicon can be removed just because it is misaligned. IFO/HS therefore predicts that all languages with iterative stress will also have words with exceptional stress. Languages with totally regular iterative stress – which are in fact abundant – are predicted not to exist.

4.3   Metrical structure is never present in the lexicon

The argument in 4.1 and 4.2 shows that IFO/HS and lexical feet are incompatible hypotheses. Since there are good reasons to think that IFO/HS is correct (such as the one presented in section 3), we conclude that lexical feet are wrong. Specifically, we propose that lexical feet are banned not just in Pintupi but in every language, including languages with exceptional stress like Warao. The input to the phonology consists of representations that are devoid of metrical structure. Hence, all metrical structure is derived by the grammar.

Contrastive and exceptional stress, as in Warao, is an obvious challenge to this claim. We discuss it in section 5. But first we will present some conceptual arguments for thinking that it is right to assume a lexicon without metrical structure and we will discuss some parallels with BPS/MP.

The foot is a level in the prosodic hierarchy, dominating the syllable and dominated by the prosodic word, the phonological phrase, and so on. Lexical feet are suspect because there is no good evidence for lexical specification of any other prosodic constituent (except the mora). For example, if syllables could be lexically specified and if the grammar were faithful to this lexical specification, then we would expect to find a language that has a contrast morpheme-internally between *tab.la* and *ta.bla*. No such language is known to exist, leading to the conclusion that syllabification is never independently contrastive (Blevins 1995: 221; Clements 1986: 318; Hayes 1989: 260; McCarthy 2003b: 60–62). Syllabification is always determined by the grammar without influence from the lexicon. The analysis of sentences into higher-level prosodic constituents like prosodic words and phonological phrases is also decided by the grammar without lexical influence. These constituents are projected from the morphosyntactic representation by the grammar alone, unaided by the lexicon. In sum, lexical specification of foot structure is inconsistent with the lack of lexical specification at other levels of the prosodic hierarchy.

Lexical specification of foot structure has another conceptual problem, this one with empirical ramifications. Feet are composed of syllables, so a lexical foot must be composed of lexical syllables. As was just noted, however, lexical syllables are otherwise unnecessary. Indeed, lexical feet could become a way of sneaking in contrastive syllabification: *tab.la* could come from /('tab)la/ while *ta.bla* comes from /tabla/.

There is also a very general argument against lexical metrical structure, including lexical feet. The argument is of particular interest in the current context because it reveals an important similarity between HS and BPS/MP (Chomsky 1994).

The goal of BPS/MP is to derive the basic properties of syntactic structure from minimalist principles. Syntactic structures are binary-branching because the minimal structure-building operation, Merge, combines two elements. They are recursive because repeated applications of Merge produce embedded structures, again with consistent binary branching. The input to this system has no syntactic structure whatsoever; it is a numeration (a multiset) of lexical items.

The assumption that the input is devoid of structure is crucial to BPS/MP. A specific goal of BPS/MP is to derive the properties of syntactic structure from the properties of the grammatical system that creates it. Syntactic structure in the input could subvert that goal because it could have properties, such as ternary branching, that are impossible with grammatically derived structure.

From this perspective, BPS/MP bears a more than superficial resemblance to IFO/HS. This resemblance, we claim, is no accident. Both IFO/HS and BPS/MP are derivational theories of structure building. In a derivational theory, complex structures (such as the metrical parsing of an entire word or the phrase structure of an entire sentence) are derived by iterative application of processes that create simple structures (such as building a single foot or a single application of Merge). The very fact that complex structures are derived in this way imposes restrictions on them. These restrictions include binarity in BPS/MP and locality in IFO/HS. If these structures had some source other than the derivations, such as the lexicon, then those restrictions would no longer hold. For structure to be constrained by the fact that it is built up gradually in a derivation, it must *always* be built up gradually and derivationally.

5.   Exceptional and contrastive stress

5.1 Diacritic features

When a language has exceptions to its regular stress pattern, then not all words exhibit the default structure. There is a long tradition in generative phonology of attributing non-default behavior to the presence of *diacritic features*, as they are referred to in Chomsky and Halle (1968: 373–80). Diacritic features, unlike the familiar phonetic features, are phonetically uninterpretable. Their presence is always detected indirectly, by the effect they have on the grammar.

One application of this idea is the concept of diacritic *accent* in the study of tone. A diacritic accent is a phonetically uninterpretable lexical feature of a vowel (or mora) that attracts a particular tone (Goldsmith 1976, 1982, 1984; Haraguchi 1977; Hyman 1981, 1982; Hyman and Byarushengo 1980; Odden 1982, 1985). In a typical accentual analysis of Tokyo Japanese like the one in Haraguchi (1977), all words have the same LHL tone pattern[6] but they differ in the position of the diacritic accent, indicated by a superscripted ×: /kokǒro/ versus /atamǎ/. This difference in accent placement is reflected in differences in the alignment of the tones with the segments: the grammar associates H with the accented mora and all that precede it, except the first, as shown in (22b).

(22) Contrast in tonal association
    (a) Underlying
        /kokŏro/   /atamǎ/

    (b) Surface

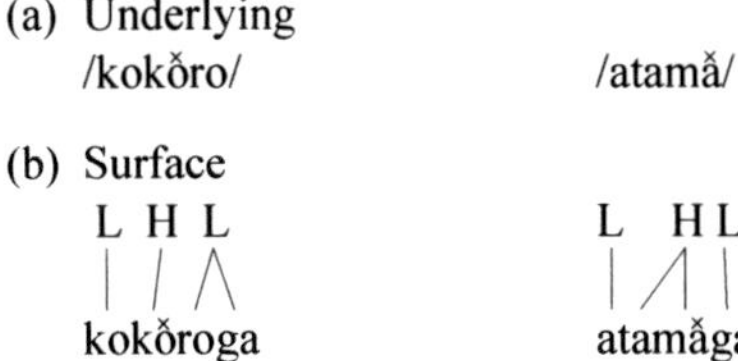

Accentual diacritics have received less attention in the stress literature, but a few analyses employ them (e.g., Hammond (1989) on Polish and Macedonian, Hayes (1980) on Aklan).

Here, we will present a theory of accentual diacritics in IFO/HS, using Turkish as an example (section 5.3). First, though, we will justify this move with some evidence from the Kansai dialect of Japanese (section 5.2), where the need for an accentual diacritic is particularly clear. Section 5.4 shows why a diacritic approach does not present the same problems for IFO/HS as lexical foot structure, and section 5.5 explores the parallels between phonology and syntax in the use of such uninterpretable features.

5.2 Evidence for accentual diacritics

To demonstrate the necessity of accentual diacritics, we will begin by introducing a competing hypothesis about Japanese that uses lexically associated tones rather than diacritics:

(23) Lexical contrast in tonal association (Poser 1984)

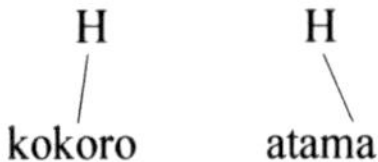

An argument offered in favor of lexically associated tones is based on a supposedly flawed prediction of the accentual theory (1986: 154–7). The accent diacritic and the tone that realizes it are distinct entities, so it should in principle be possible for a tone coming from one morpheme (morpheme A in (24)) to be realized on an accented syllable in a different morpheme (morpheme B in (24)). This process could be straightforwardly analyzed in a theory with diacritic accent, but not in a theory where accent is represented by a lexically linked tone.

(24) A truly accentual process (after Pulleyblank 1986: 157)

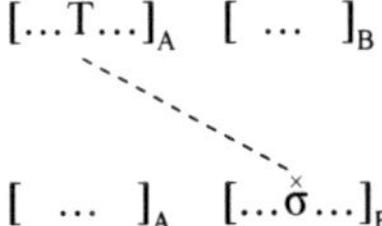

If this process is unattested, as Pulleyblank assumes, then we have here a strong argument against the diacritic accent theory.

In fact, the process schematized in (24) actually occurs in Kansai Japanese, and thus it constitutes a compelling argument *for* rather than *against* diacritic accents. In Kansai, nouns fall into two lexically specified tonal classes, HL and LHL. The location of accent must also be specified lexically for each noun:

(25)   Tonal and accentual contrasts in Kansai (Haraguchi 1999: 16–17)

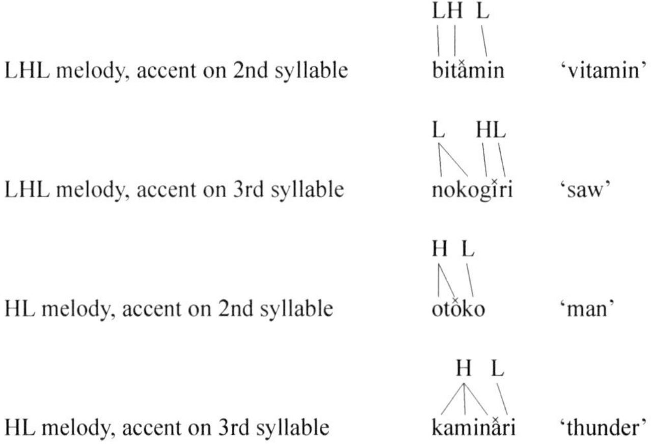

When two nouns are joined in a compound, the entire compound has just a single HL or LHL melody. The melody of the entire compound is determined by the melody of the first noun (Haraguchi 1977: 95). But the location of the accent in the entire compound is that of the *second* noun (unless that would put H on the final syllable).[7]

(26)   Kansai noun comp

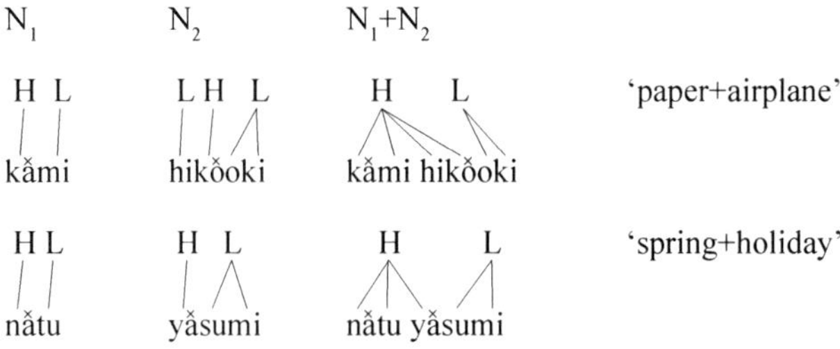

This is exactly the process depicted in (24). Because one morpheme contributes the tones and the other contributes the location of the tones, these must be separate pieces of information. Only the theory with diacritic accents allows for that possibility.

5.3 Stress diacritics in Turkish

With a little enrichment, the theory of accentual diacritics can be applied to exceptional stress patterns as well. The complexities of lexical stress in Turkish, studied by Inkelas (1999), will be used to exemplify the proposal.

The modal stress pattern in Turkish, illustrated in (27), puts stress on the final syllable of the word, thereby satisfying ALIGN-RIGHT('σ, word).

(27) Modal final stress
     gél   'come'
     gel-eǰék   'come-Fut'
     gel-eǰek-lér   'come-Fut-Pl'

Certain morphemes are lexically marked to have exceptional stress.[8] Both roots (28) and suffixes (29) may have fixed stress on a non-final syllable, usually the penult or antepenult. In addition, several one- and two-syllable suffixes in Turkish have the distinction of being prestressing – that is, they assign stress to the syllable preceding the affix (30).

(28) Fixed-stress roots
     penǰére   'window'
     ablúka   'blockade'
     Érzinǰan   a name

(29) Fixed-stress suffixes
     gid-íyor   'go-progressive'
     gid-érek   'go-by'
     gel-ínǰe   'come-when'

(30) Prestressing suffixes
     tekmelé-me   'kick-negative'
     arabá-mɨ   'car-interrogative'
     akšám-leyin   'evening-at'

In Inkelas's (1999) analysis, morphemes with fixed non-final stress like those in (28) and (29) are represented with a lexical disyllabic trochee, as in (31a). Prestressing suffixes are also represented with a lexical disyllabic trochee, but its head position is empty and its dependent position is associated with the first syllable of the suffix, as in (31b).[9]

(31) Lexical foot structure in Inkelas (1999: 169)
    (a) (x .)   (b) (x .)
        -iyor   -me

        (x .)
        abluka

If lexical metrical structure is impossible, as we have proposed here, then these exceptional behaviors must instead be analyzed with diacritic features. We posit diacritics of two types to account for the facts of Turkish:

(32) Lexical diacritics in Turkish
    (a) íyor   (b) -me^d
       abluka

The diacritic *h* is mnemonic for *head*, and the diacritic *d* is mnemonic for *dependent*. Like all diacritics, *h* and *d* are uninterpretable features; they have no necessary relationship to the phonetics, nor do they securely mark the head or dependent of a foot. Rather, the decision about whether and how *h* and *d* will influence the surface form is made by the grammar, specifically by ranked, violable markedness constraints that refer to them.

One constraint, h→HEAD, requires the bearer of the *h* diacritic to be parsed in foot head position:

(33) h→HEAD
    Assign one violation mark for every *h*-bearing segment that is not in the head syllable of a foot.

This constraint overrides the default final-stress pattern by dominating ALIGN-RIGHT('σ, word):

(34) Effect of *h* diacritic

/gid-íyor/	h→HEAD	ALIGN-R('σ, word)
a. → gi('díyor)		1
b. gidí('yor)	1 W	L

The other constraint, d→DEPENDENT, requires its bearer to be parsed in the non-head position of a foot:

(35) d→DEPENDENT (d→DEP)
    Assign one violation mark for every *d*-bearing segment that is not in the dependent syllable of a foot.

This constraint also overrides the default final-stress pattern by dominating ALIGN-RIGHT('σ, word). Given Inkelas's proposal that feet in Turkish are trochaic, this produces the desired prestressing behavior of suffixes like /-me/:

(36) Effect of *d* diacritic

/tekmele-me^d/	d→DEP	ALIGN-R('σ, word)
a. → tekme('leme^d)		1
b. tekmele('me^d)	1 W	L

In sum, with this theory of diacritic features, these Turkish exceptional stress patterns can be analyzed without lexical foot structure.

5.4   Stress diacritics in IFO/HS

The *h* and *d* diacritics are compatible with IFO/HS in a way that lexical metrical structure is not. As we showed in section 4, lexical metrical structure makes it impossible for IFO/HS to analyze regular iterative stress systems: iterative stress requires high-ranking PARSE-SYLL, but high-ranking PARSE-SYLL will not allow unwanted lexical metrical structure to be removed. Because the *h* and *d* diacritics are not themselves metrical structure, however, there is no need to remove them. Rather, for a language like Pintupi with completely predictable stress, it is enough if h→HEAD and d→DEPENDENT are ranked below other markedness constraints that are fully dispositive of stress in all words. The unwanted metrical structure is never built (except in losing candidates), so it need not be removed.

For example, tableau (19), repeated below in (37), shows that IFO/HS cannot analyze a completely regular left-to-right trochaic stress system because it is unable to remove an unwanted trochee on the second and third syllables:

(37)   Persistence of lexical foot despite low-ranking faithfulness

	/pa('ta.ka)sana/	FT-BIN	PARSE-SYLL	AL-L(ft)	FAITH(stress)
a. →	pa('ta.ka)('sa.na)		1	4	
b.	pa('ta.ka)sa.na		3 W	1 L	
c.	pa.ta.ka.sa.na		5 W	L	1 W
d.	('pa)('ta.ka)sa.na	1 W	2 W	1 L	

If lexical feet are prohibited and the *h* and *d* diacritics are adopted instead, this problem disappears. Tableau (38) shows the result of submitting underlying /pataʰkasana/ to a grammar where h→HEAD is ranked below all of the constraints responsible for a left-to-right trochaic stress pattern.

(38)   *h* diacritic ignored when h→HEAD ranked low

	/pataʰkasana/	FT-BIN	TROCHEE	PARSE-SYLL	AL-L(ft)	h→HEAD
a. →	('pa.taʰ)ka.sa.na			3		1
b.	pa('taʰ.ka)sa.na			3	1 W	L
c.	(pa'taʰ)ka.sa.na		1 W	3		L

The *h* diacritic is present in the surface form, but its presence is ignored because it has no intrinsic phonetic content and the only constraint that is sensitive to it, h→HEAD, is ranked too low to matter. This is why *h* must be an uninterpretable feature.[10]

5.5 Uninterpretable features in phonology and syntax

In sum, we have shown how head- and dependent-marking features can account for contrastive and exceptional stress. These features are uninterpretable: they are not metrical structure itself, but rather their presence can induce the creation of metrical structure through the agency of the grammar. From the perspective of IFO/HS, this is an important distinction. Because lexical marking of heads and dependents is done with uninterpretable features instead of metrical structure, it is possible for the grammar to disregard this lexical marking without degrading harmony by removing pre-existing metrical feet.

It is neither necessary nor desirable to assume that languages differ systematically in whether they allow uninterpretable features in the lexicon, which ones they have, and where those features can be placed. Because the grammar determines whether uninterpretable features have any effects, between-language differences in those effects can be accounted for by differences in ranking. A learner of the language whose grammar appears in (38) would never be disposed to set up any actual lexical representations with *h* diacritics, but that is irrelevant to our point. The important thing is that the grammar accounts for the observation that stress is fully predictable, and it does that by ranking h→HEAD so low that lexical *h* can have no effect under any circumstances.

Uninterpretable features are, if anything, even more important in MP than in HS. Their role is quite different in two respects, however. First, MP requires that uninterpreted features be checked (or valued); otherwise, the derivation will crash. In contrast, the analysis here sometimes allows head- and dependent-marking features to be 'unchecked' in the sense that they are not parsed into foot head or dependent position. This is a consequence of the assumption that 'checking' is done by violable constraints like h→HEAD and d→DEPENDENT. A second and related difference is that MP (in the view of some) allows for the possibility of systematic differences between languages in their lexical features. As we have argued, this assumption is unnecessary in OT, because grammars can differ in whether and how they respect lexical features.

Despite these differences, uninterpretable features are also a point of convergence between IFO/HS and MP. In both theories, the role of uninterpretable features is to force the creation of structures that would otherwise not be optimal. In IFO/HS, the standard markedness constraints on stress favor regular patterns anchored at an edge, like final stress in Turkish or directional alternating stress in Pintupi and Warao. The presence of an uninterpretable feature can override these default patterns and produce greater complexity and diversity in surface structures. In MP, checking of uninterpretable features is the impetus for structure-building by Merge. In a sense, then, the optimal structure in MP would be none at all, if not for the uninterpretable features. While it is true that MP and IFO/HS differ in how the features are checked

– via crashing derivations from unchecked features in MP versus violable constraints in IFO/HS – this is just the usual difference between OT and MP generally.

Why should this role for uninterpretable features be a point of convergence between MP and IFO/HS? Perhaps because it is a natural hypothesis about how inputs to the grammar can impose requirements on output structures without containing that structure themselves. As we have emphasized throughout, MP and IFO/HS share the goal of deriving the properties of their respective structures from the nature of the grammar and the derivation that builds them. Input structure would defeat this goal. Uninterpretable features provide a way of transmitting information from the input to the output structure while still maintaining grammatical control.

6. Conclusion

One of the biggest differences between classic OT and MP is that classic OT has a parallel architecture while most approaches to MP are derivational. In this chapter, we described Harmonic Serialism, a derivational version of OT. Focusing on the way that metrical structure is built in HS and phrase structure is built in MP, we found a major similarity: both are successful in their explanatory goals only under the assumption that the inputs to the grammar entirely lack the structure that the grammar is imposing. This similarity emerges, we argued, because both theories seek to explain the properties of complex structures by deriving them via repeated application of simple operations under the control of an optimizing grammar.

As we noted at the beginning of section 3, existing arguments for HS can be divided into two main categories. The material we have discussed here falls into one of those categories, arguments from language typology. The other category consists of arguments based on the need to refer to representations that exist only at the intermediate steps of a derivation. For example, deletion of unstressed vowels can be analyzed successfully only if there exists a point in the derivation after stress has been assigned but before vowels have been deleted (McCarthy 2008b). Likewise, the invisibility of inserted vowels to stress assignment requires a derivational step in which stress has been assigned but vowels have not yet been inserted (Elfner 2009). Abstractly similar arguments for derivations have also been made in MP (Takahashi 2006).

The case for HS in phonology is compelling, and the few extant arguments against HS have been challenged (McCarthy 2008b: 538–41; McCarthy *et al.* 2010; Pater 2011). Whether HS will prove equally valuable in syntax research remains to be seen, but the connections with MP identified here suggest that it may.

Acknowledgments

The authors' names are in alphabetical order. We are grateful for comments received from the editors and from Kyle Johnson, Ben Hermans, the McCarthy-Pater grant group at UMass Amherst, and the participants in ConSOLE XVIII at the Universitat Autònoma de Barcelona. This research was supported by grant BCS-0813829 from the National Science Foundation to the University of Massachusetts Amherst.

Notes

1. To simplify the exposition, we have omitted candidates with iambic (right-headed) feet from (2–5), and the subsequent tableaux. These candidates are ruled out by ranking TROCHEE over IAMB; see note 2.
2. To simplify the exposition, we have omitted some constraints from the tableaux. One is ALIGN-RIGHT(foot, word). Under the standard OT assumption that constraints are universally present, this constraint must be included in the grammar of Pintupi. It is ranked below ALIGN-LEFT(foot, word), to account for Pintupi's left-to-right foot assignment. And because Pintupi has trochaic (left-headed) feet rather than iambic (right-headed) ones, TROCHEE and PARSE-SYLLABLE have to dominate IAMB.
3. An actual example is *ŋuːŋwaraɲu* 'whining' (Hansen and Hansen 1969: 169).
4. See Hyde (2007) and Frampton (2007) for other views of this issue.
5. Warao has the opposite parsing direction than Pintupi because ALIGN-RIGHT(foot, word) >> ALIGN-LEFT(foot, word). Cf. note 2.
6. Subsequent research has shown that the initial L is not part of the basic tone melody. Rather, it is an utterance-level initial boundary tone (Pierrehumbert and Beckman 1988: 135–6).
7. This follows Kubozono's (2008, p.c.) statement of the generalization. Kubozono was also kind enough to provide the data in (26).
8. There is also a class of roots, consisting primarily of place names and loans, that respect a different generalization: stress falls on the antepenult if it is heavy and the penult is light; otherwise it falls on the penult. This sort of subregularity is best analyzed not with lexical structure but with the OT analogue of the traditional minor rule, a cophonology (Inkelas 1999: 143) or an indexed markedness constraint (Pater 2000, 2006).
9. The main point about Turkish in Inkelas (1999) is that the exceptional stress behavior of the morphemes in (28) and (29) has to be encoded in their lexical representations rather than the grammar. Lexical foot structure and lexical diacritic features are equally consistent with this result.

   Inkelas (1999) also observes that there is a connection between lexical prosodic structure, as in (31), and the existence of prosodic templates, whose lexical entries consist entirely of prosodic structure (McCarthy and Prince 1986/1996). Although there is a body of work arguing that prosodic templates in this sense do not exist (such as Gafos 1998; McCarthy and Prince 1994, 1995, 1999; Spaelti 1997; Urbanczyk 1996), more recent research claims that they are indispensible (Flack 2007; Gouskova 2007; McCarthy *et al.* 2010). The relevance of this debate to our proposals here is obvious.
10. The feature *h* is therefore *not* the same as the feature [+stress] of Chomsky and Halle (1968). The latter was conceived of as a phonetically interpretable feature: it is interpreted by the phonetic component as increased amplitude, greater duration, and/or a distinctive pitch excursion. In contemporary metrical theory, stress is understood in syntagmatic terms: a syllable is stressed because it is the head of a metrical foot. The feature *h* can induce a syllable to head a foot by way of the grammar, but it receives no interpretation as stress or any other phonetic property.

References

Blevins, J. (1995) The syllable in phonological theory. In J. A. Goldsmith (ed.) *The Handbook of Phonological Theory,* 206–44. Cambridge, MA and Oxford: Blackwell.

Chomsky, N. (1977) On *Wh*-movement. In P. Culicover, T. Wasow and A. Akmajian (eds) *Formal Syntax,* 77–132. New York: Academic Press.

Chomsky, N. (1994) *Bare Phrase Structure.* Cambridge, MA: Distributed by MIT Working Papers in Linguistics.

Chomsky, N. (1995) *The Minimalist Program.* Cambridge, MA: MIT Press.

Chomsky, N. and Halle, M. (1968) *The Sound Pattern of English.* New York: Harper & Row.

Clements, G. N. (1986) Syllabification and epenthesis in the Barra dialect of Gaelic. In K. Bogers, H. van der Hulst and M. Mous (eds) *The Phonological Representation of Suprasegmentals,* 317–36. Dordrecht: Foris.

Eisner, J. (1999) Doing OT in a straitjacket. Unpublished paper, Johns Hopkins University, Baltimore, MD. Retrieved from http://www.cs.jhu.edu/~jason/papers/eisner.ucla99.handout.large.pdf.

Elfner, E. (2009) Harmonic serialism and stress-epenthesis interactions in Levantine Arabic. Unpublished paper, University of Massachusetts Amherst, Amherst, MA. Retrieved from http://www.people.umass.edu/eelfner/elfner_arabic.pdf.

Flack, K. (2007) Templatic morphology and indexed markedness constraints. *Linguistic Inquiry* 38 (4): 749–58.

Frampton, J. (2007) Weak local parsing in a theory without foot inventories. Unpublished paper, Northeastern University, Boston. Retrieved from http://www.math.neu.edu/ling/pdffiles/WLP.pdf.

Gafos, A. (1998) A-templatic reduplication. *Linguistic Inquiry* 29 (3): 515–27.

Goldsmith, J. (1976) *Autosegmental Phonology*. Doctoral dissertation, MIT, Cambridge, MA. Published by Garland Press, New York, 1979.

Goldsmith, J. (1982) Accent systems. In H. van der Hulst and N. Smith (eds) *The Structure of Phonological Representations*, 47–63. Dordrecht: Foris.

Goldsmith, J. (1984) Tone and accent in Tonga. In G. N. Clements and J. Goldsmith (eds) *Autosegmental Studies in Bantu Tone*, 19–51. Dordrecht: Foris.

Gouskova, M. (2007) The reduplicative template in Tonkawa. *Phonology* 24: 367–96.

Hammond, M. (1989) Lexical stresses in Macedonian and Polish. *Phonology* 6: 19–38.

Hansen, K. C. and Hansen, L. E. (1969) Pintupi phonology. *Oceanic Linguistics* 8 (2): 153–70.

Hansen, K. C. and Hansen, L. E. (1978) *The Core of Pintupi Grammar*. Alice Springs, NT: Institute for Aboriginal Development.

Haraguchi, S. (1977) *The Tone Pattern of Japanese: An Autosegmental Theory of Tonology*. Tokyo: Kaitakusha.

Haraguchi, S. (1999) Accent. In N. Tsujimura (ed.) *The Handbook of Japanese Linguistics*, 1–30. Malden, MA and Oxford: Blackwell.

Hayes, B. (1980) *A Metrical Theory of Stress Rules*. Doctoral dissertation, MIT, Cambridge, MA. Published by Garland Press, New York, 1985.

Hayes, B. (1989) Compensatory lengthening in moraic phonology. *Linguistic Inquiry* 20 (2): 253–306.

Hyde, B. (2007) Non-finality and weight-sensitivity. *Phonology* 24: 287–334.

Hyman, L. (1981) Tonal accent in Somali. *Studies in African Linguistics* 12 (2): 169–203.

Hyman, L. (1982) Globality and the accentual analysis of Luganda tone. *Journal of Linguistic Research* 2: 1–40.

Hyman, L. and Byarushengo, E. (1980) Tonal accent in Haya: An autosegmental approach. Unpublished paper, University of Southern California, Los Angeles, CA.

Inkelas, S. (1999) Exceptional stress-attracting suffixes in Turkish: representation vs. the grammar. In R. Kager, H. van der Hulst and W. Zonneveld (eds) *The Prosody-Morphology Interface*, 134–87. Cambridge: Cambridge University Press. Available on Rutgers Optimality Archive, ROA-39.

Jesney, K. (to appear) Positional faithfulness, non-locality, and the Harmonic Serialism solution. In S. Lima, K. Mullin and B. Smith (eds) *Proceedings of the 39th Annual Meeting of the North East Linguistic Society*. Amherst, MA: GLSA Publications. Available on Rutgers Optimality Archive, ROA-1018.

Kager, R. (1992) Shapes of the generalized trochee. In J. Mead (ed.) *The Proceedings of the Eleventh West Coast Conference on Formal Linguistics*, 298–312. Stanford, CA: CSLI Publications.

Kager, R. (1999) *Optimality Theory*. Cambridge: Cambridge University Press.

Kager, R. (2001) Rhythmic directionality by positional licensing. University of Potsdam: Fifth HIL Phonology Conference (HILP 5). Available on Rutgers Optimality Archive, ROA-514.

Kimper, W. (to appear) Locality and globality in phonological variation. *Natural Language & Linguistic Theory*. Available on Rutgers Optimality Archive, ROA-988.

Kubozono, H. (2008) Japanese accent. In S. Miyagawa and M. Saito (eds) *The Oxford Handbook of Japanese Linguistics*, 163–89. New York: Oxford University Press.

Liberman, M. and Prince, A. (1977) On stress and linguistic rhythm. *Linguistic Inquiry* 8 (2): 249–336.

McCarthy, J. J. (2000) Harmonic serialism and parallelism. In M. Hirotani (ed.) *Proceedings of the North East Linguistics Society 30*, 501–24. Amherst, MA: GLSA Publications. Available on Rutgers Optimality Archive, ROA-357.

McCarthy, J. J. (2002) *A Thematic Guide to Optimality Theory*. Cambridge: Cambridge University Press.

McCarthy, J. J. (2003a) OT constraints are categorical. *Phonology* 20: 75–138. Retrieved from http://people.umass.edu/jjmccart/categorical.pdf.

McCarthy, J. J. (2003b) Sympathy, cumulativity and the Duke-of-York gambit. In C. Féry and R. van de Vijver (eds) *The Syllable in Optimality Theory*, 23–76. Cambridge: Cambridge University Press.

McCarthy, J. J. (2007) Restraint of analysis. In S. Blaho, P. Bye and M. Krämer (eds) *Freedom of Analysis*, 203–31. Berlin and New York: Mouton de Gruyter. Also appears in E. Bakovic, J. Ito, and J. J. McCarthy (eds) (2006) *Wondering at the Natural Fecundity of Things: Essays in Honor of Alan Prince*. Linguistics Research Center, UC Santa Cruz, CA. Retrieved from http://repositories.cdlib.org/lrc/prince/10.

McCarthy, J. J. (2008a) The gradual path to cluster simplification. *Phonology* 25: 271–319. doi:10.1017/S0952675708001486.

McCarthy, J. J. (2008b) The serial interaction of stress and syncope. *Natural Language & Linguistic Theory* 26: 499–546. doi: 10.1007/s11049-008-9051-3.

McCarthy, J. J. (2010a) An introduction to Harmonic Serialism. *Language and Linguistics Compass* 4 (10): 1–18.

McCarthy, J. J. (2010b) Studying Gen. *Journal of the Phonetic Society of Japan* 13: 3–12.

McCarthy, J. J. (2011) Perceptually grounded faithfulness in Harmonic Serialism. *Linguistic Inquiry* 42 (1): 171–83. Retrieved from http://works.bepress.com/john_j_mccarthy/104/.

McCarthy, J. J. (to appear) Autosegmental spreading in Optimality Theory. In J. Goldsmith, E. Hume and L. Wetzels (eds) *Tones and Features*. Berlin and New York: Mouton de Gruyter. Retrieved from http://works.bepress.com/john_j_mccarthy/100.

McCarthy, J. J., Kimper, W. and Mullin, K. (2010) Reduplication in Harmonic Serialism. Unpublished paper, University of Massachusetts Amherst, Amherst, MA.

McCarthy, J. J. and Prince, A. (1986/1996) *Prosodic Morphology*. New Brunswick, NJ: Rutgers University Center for Cognitive Science. Retrieved from http://ruccs.rutgers.edu/pub/papers/pm86all.pdf.

McCarthy, J. J. and Prince, A. (1993) Generalized Alignment. In G. Booij and J. van Marle (eds) *Yearbook of Morphology*, 79–153. Dordrecht: Kluwer. Available on Rutgers Optimality Archive, ROA-7.

McCarthy, J. J. and Prince, A. (1994) The emergence of the unmarked: Optimality in prosodic morphology. In M. Gonzàlez (ed.) *Proceedings of the North East Linguistic Society* 24, 333–79. Amherst, MA: GLSA Publications. Available on Rutgers Optimality Archive, ROA-13.

McCarthy, J. J. and Prince, A. (1995) Faithfulness and reduplicative identity. In J. Beckman, L. Walsh Dickey and S. Urbanczyk (eds) *University of Massachusetts Occasional Papers in Linguistics* 18, 249–384. Amherst, MA: GLSA Publications. Retrieved from Rutgers Optimality Archive, ROA-103.

McCarthy, J. J. and Prince, A. (1999) Faithfulness and identity in Prosodic Morphology. In R. Kager, H. van der Hulst and W. Zonneveld (eds) *The Prosody-Morphology Interface*, 218–309. Cambridge: Cambridge University Press.

Moreton, E. (2000) Faithfulness and potential. Unpublished paper, University of Massachusetts Amherst, Amherst, MA.

Moreton, E. (2003) Non-computable functions in Optimality Theory. In J. J. McCarthy (ed.) *Optimality Theory in Phonology: A Reader*, 141–63. Malden, MA and Oxford: Blackwell. Retrieved from Rutgers Optimality Archive, ROA-364.

Odden, D. (1982) Separating tone and accent: The case of Kimatuumbi. In D. Flickinger, M. Macken and N. Wiegand (eds) *The Proceedings of the West Coast Conference on Formal Linguistics 1*, 219–230. Stanford, CA: Stanford Linguistic Association.

Odden, D. (1985) An accentual approach to tone in Kimatuumbi. In D. Goyvaerts (ed.) *African Linguistics: Studies in memory of M. W. K. Seminenke*, 345–419. Amsterdam: John Benjamins.

Osborn, H. (1966) Warao I: Phonology and morphophonemics. *International Journal of American Linguistics* 32 (2): 108–23.

Pater, J. (2000) Nonuniformity in English secondary stress: The role of ranked and lexically specific constraints. *Phonology* 17: 237–74. Retrieved from Rutgers Optimality Archive, ROA-107.

Pater, J. (2006) The locus of exceptionality: Morpheme-specific phonology as constraint indexation. In L. Bateman, A. Werle, M. O'Keefe and E. Reilly (eds) *University of Massachusetts Occasional*

Papers in Linguistics 32: Papers in Optimality Theory III. Amherst, MA: GLSA. Available on Rutgers Optimality Archive, ROA-866.

Pater, J. (2011) Serial Harmonic Grammar and Berber syllabification. In T. Borowsky, S. Kawahara, T. Shinya and M. Sugahara (eds) *Prosody Matters: Essays in Honor of Lisa Selkirk*, 48–79. London: Equinox Publishing.

Pierrehumbert, J. and Beckman, M. (1988) *Japanese Tone Structure*. Cambridge, MA: MIT Press.

Poser, W. J. (1984) *The Phonetics and Phonology of Tone and Intonation in Japanese*. Doctoral dissertation, MIT, Cambridge, MA.

Prince, A. (1980) A metrical theory for Estonian quantity. *Linguistic Inquiry* 11 (3): 511–62.

Prince, A. (2002) Arguing optimality. In A. Carpenter, A. Coetzee and P. d. Lacy (eds) *University of Massachusetts Occasional Papers in Linguistics 26: Papers in Optimality Theory II*, 269–304. Amherst, MA: GLSA. Available on Rutgers Optimality Archive, ROA-562.

Prince, A. and Smolensky, P. (1993/2004) *Optimality Theory: Constraint Interaction in Generative Grammar*. Malden, MA and Oxford: Blackwell.

Pruitt, K. (2010) Serialism and locality in constraint-based metrical parsing. *Phonology* 27: 481–526.

Pulleyblank, D. (1986) *Tone in Lexical Phonology*. Dordrecht: D. Reidel.

Spaelti, P. (1997) *Dimensions of Variation in Multi-Pattern Reduplication*. Doctoral dissertation, University of California, Santa Cruz, CA. Available on Rutgers Optimality Archive, ROA-311.

Staubs, R., Becker, M., Potts, C., Pratt, P., McCarthy, J. J. and Pater, J. (2010) OT-Help 2.0 [computer program]. Computer program. Retrieved from http://web.linguist.umass.edu/~OTHelp/.

Takahashi, S. (2006) *Decompositionality and Identity*. Doctoral dissertation, MIT, Cambridge, MA.

Urbanczyk, S. (1996) *Patterns of Reduplication in Lushootseed*. Doctoral dissertation, University of Massachusetts, Amherst, MA.

6 Extremely local optimization

Fabian Heck[*] and Gereon Müller[**]

ABSTRACT In this chapter, we argue that a theory in which optimization procedures apply to the smallest domain possible (the derivational step), and which we therefore dub the theory of *extremely local optimization* (ELO), is not only a viable alternative to standard global optimization (or to less local optimization) but even proves to be empirically superior in some cases and under certain assumptions. We present four empirical arguments of this type, involving argument encoding, dative possessors, SpecC-expletives, and VP-topicalization.

KEYWORDS optimality theory; minimalist program; local optimization; last resort; inclusiveness; phase impenetrability condition; expletive; ergativity; VP-topicalization; dative possessors

1. Introduction

In this article, we pursue the idea that properties of the Minimalist Program (MP, Chomsky 1995, 2000, 2001) and Optimality Theory (OT, McCarthy and Prince 2004; Prince and Smolensky 2004) can be fruitfully combined. In doing so, we concentrate on two properties: (a) MP's tenet that syntactic structure is built up by repeated application of Merge, Move, and Agree;[1] (b) OT's assumption that the well-formedness of a syntactic object involves comparison with other objects, hence optimization. As a matter of fact, there exist proposals that combine properties of both frameworks (see Pesetsky 1998; Broekhuis and Dekkers 2000; Heck and Müller 2000a; Fanselow and Ćavar 2001, among others). Here, however, we will suggest a combination of the most radical kind. And we will argue that, *ceteris paribus*, this radical theory is empirically superior to less local alternatives.

In standard optimality theoretic syntax, Merge, Move, etc. are assumed to apply first, thereby creating a set of candidates that is then subject to optimization. Optimization is *global* in the sense that it applies once to complete structures (see

---

* Fabian Heck, Institut für Linguistik, Universität Leipzig, Beethovenstr. 15, Leipzig, Germany. E-mail: heck@uni-leipzig.de

** Gereon Müller, Institut für Linguistik, Universität Leipzig, Beethovenstr. 15, Leipzig, Germany. E-mail: gereon.mueller@uni-leipzig.de

Grimshaw 1997; Legendre *et al.* 1998; Pesetsky 1998, among others). Alternatively, one may assume that structure building operations and optimization apply in a cyclic interleaving fashion: Merge, Move, etc. create output candidates $\alpha_1, ..., \alpha_n$ which are subject to optimization. The optimal α_i serves as (part of) the input for the next cycle (which again involves structure building and optimization) and so on, until the numeration is empty. Optimization is *local* in the sense that it applies iteratively to small portions of structure (see Ackema and Neeleman 1998; Heck and Müller 2000a; Müller 2000c; Fanselow and Ćavar 2001, among others).[2]

The approach raises the natural question as to how large optimization domains are. Optimization has been suggested to apply to clauses (Ackema and Neeleman 1998), phases (Müller 2000a; Fanselow and Ćavar 2001), phrases (Heck and Müller 2000a; Müller 2000c; Fischer 2004; Heck 2009), or after each step (Chomsky 2000; Epstein and Seely 2002). Here, we pursue the consequences of the last, most radical position and refer to it as *extremely local optimization* (henceforth ELO).

Let us touch upon a conceptual consideration. On the one hand, small optimization domains imply a small number of derivations to be considered. This follows because derivations that are based on local sub-optima need not be pursued any further. On the other hand, however, one might argue that it is conceptually preferable for a derivation to involve as few optimization processes as possible. Under such a view, the global approach, which involves just one such process, is to be preferred. Thus there appears to be a conceptual trade-off between the global and the extremely local approach.

In section 4, we will provide empirical support for ELO, based on (a) argument encoding, (b) dative possessors, (c) SpecC-expletives and (d) VP-topicalization. The argument's structure is always the same: Sometimes, the relative order of Agree and Merge is under-determined at some particular point of the derivation. Provided that operations cannot apply simultaneously (see Epstein and Seely 2002; but cf. Pullum 1976; Chomsky 2008), this creates a conflict. Both operations are required to be executed immediately, but only one of them can. The conflict can be resolved by ranking the requirements: The higher ranked requirement is satisfied immediately; the lower ranked must remain unsatisfied, momentarily. As unsatisfiability does not lead to a crash of the derivation, this suggests an analysis in terms of violable constraints. Third, all things equal, larger optimization domains cannot preserve the order of operations induced by ELO. Empirically, this yields the wrong result, which in turn serves as an argument in favor of ELO.

We believe that many analyses that involve optimization of larger domains (e.g., successive-cyclic *wh*-movement, IPP-constructions, etc.) can be couched in terms of ELO, too, see section 3. There are, however, some analyses that arguably require larger optimization domains. In section 5 we tentatively speculate that they form a natural class in that they are analyzable in terms of post-syntactic morphological operations.[3]

2.   Constraints, features and operations

We assume that the derivation is driven by two types of features: (a) structure-building features, which trigger Merge;[4] (b) probe features, which trigger Agree. We write them as [•F•] and [*F*], respectively. Next, we assume that Move and Merge are dependent on the presence of [•F•]. This is ensured by the definitions in (1) and (2).

> (1)   Merge:
> α merges with β, yielding $\{\alpha, \beta\}$, if α bears [•β•].

> (2)   Move:
>   Move is Merge, with β internal to α.

Move, being an instance of Merge, is binary. Thus, Move(α, β) is well-defined. Moreover, we adapt Chomsky's (2001) operation Agree in (3).

> (3)   Agree:
> α can agree with β with respect to a feature bundle Γ if (a)–(c) hold:
>   (a) α bears a probe feature [*F*] in Γ.
>   (b) β bears a matching goal feature [F] in Γ.
>   (c) α m-commands β.

Unlike Chomsky, we permit Agree between a head and its specifier (see (3c)). This, perhaps controversial, assumption is crucial when we discuss the analyses in section 4.

We also assume that every [*F*] and every [•F•] is targeted once during the derivation by Agree or Merge respectively, see the constraints in (4) and (5).

> (4)   AGREE CONDITION (AC):
>   Probe features participate in Agree.

> (5)   MERGE CONDITION (MC):
>   Structure-building features participate in Merge.

Finally, we presuppose that the derivation unfolds cyclically and that movement is feature-driven, see the constraints (6) and (7). Suppose that a feature is active if it is a probe or a structure building feature that has not yet participated in Merge or Agree.

> (6)   STRICT CYCLE CONDITION (SCC, Chomsky 1973, 1993):
>   Merge(α, β) is possible only if β has no active features (but α does).

> (7)   LAST RESORT (LR, Chomsky 1995, 2001):
>   Move(α, β) requires previous Agree(α, β).

According to (7), Agree feeds Move (see Chomsky 2001). The gist of (6) is that since all operations are feature-driven (but cf. section 3), the internal structure of β cannot be tampered with if β does not contain active features. A structure building feature [•F•] that has participated in Merge is eliminated. A probe [*F*] that has participated in Agree is rendered inactive (becomes [F]) but remains visible for morphology.

With these assumptions in place, we can turn to the evidence in favor of ELO (section 4). But first, we suggest in section 3 that ELO cannot be generally dismissed.

3.   A case study

We now illustrate by means of a simple example how an analysis based on less local optimization is reconstructable in terms of ELO. To this end, we sketch an analysis of successive cyclic *wh*-movement based on a moderately local optimization procedure. Then we show how it can be rephrased in terms of ELO.

Successive cyclic *wh*-movement (as in (8), from German) poses a well-known problem for theories that incorporate LR (7). Namely, LR requires every instance of movement to be preceded by an Agree relation, but there is no obvious feature in the intermediate Specv/SpecC position that a *wh*-phrase could enter into Agree with (contra Collins 1997; Fanselow and Mahajan 2000, and others).

(8)   Successive-cyclic wh-movement in German:
    (a)   Fritz   fragt [$_{CP}$ wen$_1$ [$_{vP}$ t′$_1$ Maria t$_1$ liebt]].
           Fritz   asks   whom   Maria   loves
           'Fritz wants to know who Maria loves.'

    (b)   Wen$_1$ hat   er   gesagt [$_{CP}$ t′$_1$ dass Maria   t$_1$ liebt]?
           whom   has   he   said   that Maria   loves
           'Who did he say that Maria loves?'

A reviewer notes that the intermediate step in (8a) might be argued to satisfy LR via Φ-Agree of the *wh*-phrase with v. This is not an option in (8b), though.

3.1   Moderately local optimization

Heck and Müller (2000b) offer a solution to the problem above, which – as in other proposals – is based on the assumption that CP and vP are phases in the sense of Chomsky (2001). What is new is the idea that successive-cyclic *wh*-movement is not feature-driven, but violates LR in favor of the higher ranked constraint in (9):

(9)   PHASE BALANCE (PB):
    If P is a phase, then for every probe F in the numeration there must be a distinct
    matching goal that is accessible to F.

A goal is *accessible* within the current phase P in the sense of (9) if it is either part of the numeration or at the edge of P. As a consequence, a goal (a *wh*-phrase) from the current phase P (e.g. an embedded CP) that is supposed to enter into Agree with a probe (a *wh*-C head) from a higher phase P' (a dominating CP) is forced by PB to move to the edge of P, thereby (non-fatally) violating LR. By this, the goal becomes accessible to the higher probe and P counts as 'balanced'. Taking a look into the numeration provides some non-local information, namely, it informs the derivation whether there is such a higher probe in P' or not. Accordingly, PB triggers movement or not. Under this analysis, successive-cyclic *wh*-movement is a repair strategy, forced by PB under the ranking PB » LR. Derivations that involve non-successive cyclic *wh*-extraction from CP fatally violate the PHASE IMPENETRABILITY CONDITION of Chomsky (2001).

(10)   PHASE IMPENETRABILITY CONDITION (PIC):
       The domain of a head X of a phase XP is not accessible to operations at ZP (the next phase); only X and its edge are accessible to such operations.[5]

Crucially, the analysis is based on the assumption that optimization operates on the phase-level (it affects CP and vP), that is, optimization is moderately local.

3.2   Extremely local optimization

The analysis of Heck and Müller (2000b) can be rephrased in terms of ELO. The revised analysis differs from the less local version in that more optimization steps are involved.[6] Even in the extremely local approach, PB is exclusively relevant at the phase level, simply because it is defined for phases exclusively.

   Consider the derivation of (11). For reasons of simplicity, we ignore case- and Φ-features for the time being.

(11)   Successive-cyclic wh-movement in German:
       Wen$_1$ liebt [$_{vP}$ t'$_1$ Maria t$_1$]?
       whom   loves   Maria
       'Who does Maria love?'

We follow Grewendorf (1989) and Diesing (1992) in assuming that German T bears [•EPP•] optionally (*Maria* in (11) can stay within vP). Moreover, a *wh*-C of constituent questions in German obviously bears [•EPP•] obligatorily. A ranking that permits to derive (11) is given in (12).

(12)   Ranking:
       SCC » PB, AC » MC » LR   (German, English)

The ranking between PB and AC is underdetermined in the present context and is therefore left open in (12).

   The first step in the derivation of (11) involves Merge of the verb with the *wh*-phrase, creating a VP. As a consequence, the structure building feature [•D•] on V is eliminated, thereby satisfying MC. Once eliminated, [•D•] is no longer subject to the MC and is consequently ignored for the rest of the derivation. No movement applies, there is no probe feature, and VP is not a phase; therefore LR, AC and PB are satisfied vacuously. This is illustrated in tableau T1.[7]

T1 Optimization of step 1: Merge

Input: $V_{[\bullet D\bullet]} \oplus wh_1$ Workspace = $\{C_{[*\mathrm{WH}*]}, \ldots\}$	PB AC	MC	LR
☞ O_1: $[_{VP}\ wh_1\ V\ ]$			
O_2: $V_{[\bullet D\bullet]},\ wh_1$		*!	

Alternatively, the input may be returned unaltered, see candidate O_2 in T1. But then [•D•] on V remains and therefore incurs a violation of MC. This derives a ban on 'null'-transformations, i.e., a requirement that the derivation must not be idle.[8]

O_1 from T1 and v from the numeration constitute the input for the next optimization cycle, which is given in T2. Note that at this point only one of v's [•F•]-features can be satisfied by Merge in one step. The conflict is resolved by organizing the two features [•D•] and [•v•] on a stack, symbolized by >. Only the highest element of the stack (the leftmost element) can be accessed. This enforces Merge(v,VP).[9] [•D•] enters the structure on v and causes a non-fatal MC violation, see O_1 in T2.

T2 Optimization of step 2: Merge

Input: $v_{[\bullet v\bullet]>[\bullet D\bullet]} \oplus VP$ Workspace = $\{C_{[*\mathrm{WH}*]}, \ldots\}$	PB AC	MC	LR
☞ O_1: $[_{vP}\ [_{VP}\ wh_1\ V\ ]\ v_{[\bullet D\bullet]}\ ]$		*	
O_2: $v_{[\bullet v\bullet]>[\bullet D\bullet]},\ VP$		*!*	

The vP output of T2 serves as the input for the next optimization cycle. Being a phase, vP is subject to PB. To satisfy PB, wh_1 must move to the edge of vP (cf. O_1 and O_2 in T3). On the other hand, MC requires that the external argument be merged in Specv (v still bears [•D•]). The v-head thus has a dual role. But Move and Merge cannot apply simultaneously. The conflict is resolved by the ranking PB » MC, triggering movement of the *wh*-phrase first.[10] As no Agree relation precedes Move, LR is violated, although not fatally due to the ranking PB » LR, see O_1. The MC-violation that is incurred by procrastinating Merge of the external argument (DP_{ext}) is non-fatal either:

T3 Optimization of step 3: Move

Input: DP $\oplus$ [$_{vP}$ [$_{VP}$ *wh*$_1$ V] v$_{[\bullet D\bullet]}$] Workspace = {C$_{[*WH*]}$, …}	PB AC	MC	LR
☞ O$_1$: [$_{vP}$ *wh*$_1$ [$_{VP}$ t$_1$ V] v$_{[\bullet D\bullet]}$]		*	*
O$_2$: [$_{vP}$ DP [$_{VP}$ *wh*$_1$ V] v]	*!		

Next, DP$_{ext}$ is merged, thereby satisfying MC (see O$_1$ in T4). [$\bullet$D$\bullet$] on v is eliminated. Again, an idle derivation fatally violates MC, see O$_2$.

T4 Optimization of step 4: Merge

Input: DP $\oplus$ [$_{vP}$ *wh*$_1$ [$_{VP}$ t$_1$ V] v$_{[\bullet D\bullet]}$] Workspace = {C$_{[*WH*]}$, …}	PB AC	MC	LR
☞ O$_1$: [$_{vP}$ DP *wh*$_1$ [$_{VP}$ t$_1$ V] v]			
O$_2$: DP, [$_{vP}$ *wh*$_1$ [$_{VP}$ t$_1$ V] v$_{[\bullet D\bullet]}$]		*!	

In the following two steps T and C are merged (thereby eliminating [•v•] on T and [•T•] on C). We skip these (nothing interesting happens) and turn directly to the point of the derivation where CP becomes the input of the next optimization cycle.

CP is a phase. As there is no probe left in the numeration, PB is vacuously satisfied. Since C still bears [*WH*] and [•EPP•], it has a dual role. But again, Agree and Merge cannot apply simultaneously. The conflict is resolved by the ranking AC » MC. Therefore, the next step involves Agree(C[*WH*],*wh*$_1$), which renders [*WH*] on C inactive ([*WH*] turns into [WH]), see O$_1$ in T5. Movement of the *wh*-phrase, as with O$_2$, satisfies MC but fatally violates AC (LR is also violated, although this is irrelevant here).

T5 Optimization of step 7: Agree

Input: [$_{C'}$ C$_{[*WH*],[\bullet EPP\bullet]}$ [$_{TP}$ [$_{vP}$ *wh*$_1$ …] T]] Workspace = { }	PB AC	MC	LR
☞ O$_1$: [$_{C'}$ C$_{[WH],[\bullet EPP\bullet]}$ [$_{TP}$ [$_{vP}$ *wh*$_1$ …] T]]		*	
O$_2$: [$_{CP}$ *wh*$_1$ C$_{[*WH*]}$ [$_{TP}$ [$_{vP}$ t′$_1$ …] T]]	*!		*

The final step in the derivation involves elimination of [•EPP•] on C by moving the *wh*-phrase to SpecC. Note that movement of any other category to SpecC at this point is blocked by LR, cf. the definition in (7). By contrast, movement of the *wh*-phrase satisfies MC and vacuously fulfills all other constraints (see O$_1$ in T6). The null-transformation (see O$_2$) cannot satisfy MC and is therefore blocked.

T6 Optimization of step 8: Move

Input: $[_{C'}\, C_{\text{[WH]},[\bullet\text{EPP}\bullet]}\, [_{TP}\, [_{vP}\, wh_1\, ...]\, T\,]]$ Workspace = { }		PB AC	MC	LR
☞ $O_1{:}\ [_{CP}\, wh_1\, C_{\text{[WH]}}\, [_{TP}\, [_{vP}\, t'_1\, ...]\, T\,]$				
$O_2{:}\ [_{C'}\, C_{\text{[WH]},[\bullet\text{EPP}\bullet]}\, [_{TP}\, [_{vP}\, wh_1\, ...]\, T\,]]$			*!	

To conclude, the moderate local analysis of Heck and Müller (2000b) can be recast in terms of ELO. Although this is an interesting result by itself, the moderate and the extreme approach do not make different predictions here. But this is not always the case. In section 4 we present four studies where the predictions differ. As it turns out, ELO is superior in these cases. We take this to be an argument in favor of ELO (and, accordingly, against less local approaches).

4.   Empirical evidence

4.1   Argument encoding

The first piece of evidence is based on the fact that languages can differ with respect to how they encode the external and the internal argument.[11]

4.1.1 Data

To simplify matters, there are two basic patterns of argument encoding. In accusative languages, the internal argument (DP_{int}) of a transitive verb (V_t) bears accusative case. In contrast, DP_{int} of an intransitive verb (V_i) and external arguments (DP_{ext}) in general bear nominative case (see (13a)). In ergative languages, DP_{ext} of a V_t bears ergative, whereas its internal co-argument and the only argument of a V_i bear absolutive case (see (13b)).

(13)   Basic patterns of argument encoding:

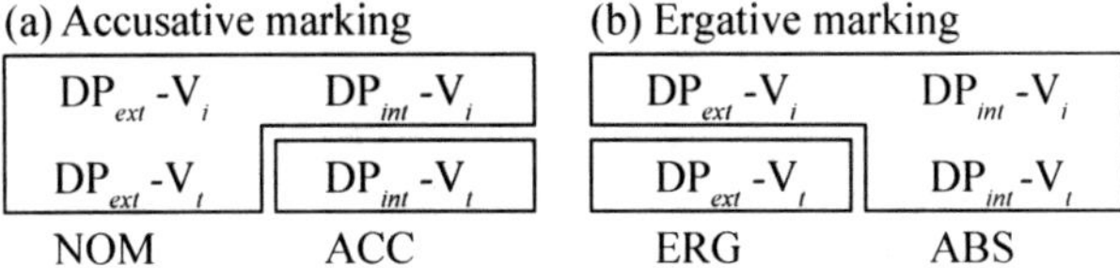

The two patterns are exemplified in (14) and (15) by Icelandic (Sigurðsson 2002: 698) and Archi (Kibrik 1979: 67), respectively.[12]

(14)   Accusative case-marking in Icelandic:

    (a) Sól-Ø-in   skín-Ø.
        sun-SG.NOM-DET.SG.FEM.NOM shine-3.SG
        'The sun is shining.'

   (b) Ólaf-ur   las-Ø   bók-Ø-ina.
       Olaf-SG.NOM   read.PAST-3.SG   book-SG.ACC-DET.SG.FEM.ACC
       'Olaf read the book.'

(15) Ergative case-marking in Archi:

   (a) Dija-Ø   w-irx̄ in.
       father.I-SG.ABS   I.SG-work
       'Father is working.'

   (b) Dija-mu   x̄ alli-Ø   b-ar-ši
       father.I-SG.ERG   bread.III-SG.ABS   III.SG-bake-GERb-i.III.SG-AUX
       'Father is baking the bread.'

4.1.2 Analysis

Our analysis requires the following assumptions. (a) There is one structural argument encoding feature: [CASE]. (b) [CASE] can have two values: ext(ernal) and int(ernal). (c) The valued feature [CASE:*ext*] expresses nominative/absolutive case, the valued feature [CASE:*int*] expresses accusative/ergative case (see Murasugi 1992). (d) Case features figure in Agree relations involving T/v on the one hand and DP on the other hand, as in (16).

(16) The role of T and v in argument encoding:
     (a) T bears [*CASE:*ext**] that instantiates [CASE:*ext*] on DP.
     (b) v bears [*CASE:*int**] that instantiates [CASE:*int*] on DP.

As the probe instantiates a case value on the goal, we assume that the case feature of the goal enters the derivation without a value. For this purpose, we introduce the convention that an unvalued feature [F] is written as [F:□]. We assume that there are valued and unvalued probes as well as valued and unvalued goals.

    Observe now that v has a dual role: It participates in a Merge operation with DP_{ext}, but it also participates in an Agree relation. This dual role has far-reaching consequences for the nature of argument encoding. To see why, consider a simple transitive context, with two arguments, DP_{int} and DP_{ext}. Suppose that the derivation has reached a stage Σ, where v has been merged with a VP containing DP_{int}, with DP_{ext} waiting to be merged with v in the workspace of the derivation. Due to the dual role of v, a conflict arises at this point: AC demands that the next operation is Agree(v, DP_{int}) whereas MC demands that it is Merge(DP_{ext}, v).

    Before we address the question of how the conflict is resolved, note that we assume that Agree is subject to the Minimal Link Condition, see (17).

(17) MINIMAL LINK CONDITION (MLC, Chomsky 1995, 2001):
     Agree(α, β) can only take place if there is no δ such that (a) and (b) hold:
     (a) δ is closer to α than β.
     (b) δ bears a feature that has not yet participated in Agree.

(18) Closeness:
     δ is closer to α than β if path(δ, α) is shorter than path(β, α).

(19) Path:[13]
    Path (α, β) is the set of categories Z such that (a) and (b) hold:
    (a) Z is reflexively dominated by the minimal XP that dominates α and β.
    (b) Z dominates α or β.
    The length of a path is determined by its cardinality.

The consequences of the MLC in (17), based on (18) and (19), are the following: (a) The specifier and the complement of a head qualify as equally close to the head. (b) The specifier of a head is closer to the head than a category that is further embedded in the complement of the head. Applied to the derivational stage Σ above, it follows that once DP_{ext} has undergone Merge with v in Σ, then it counts as closer to v than DP_{int}.

Returning to the main plot, we propose that the conflict is resolved by (language specific) ranking of the conflicting requirements AC and MC. The two possibilities of relative ranking yield the accusative and the ergative pattern of argument encoding:

(20) Rankings:

    (a) (MLC ») AC » MC   (Accusative pattern)
    (b) (MLC ») MC » AC   (Ergative pattern)

Let us trace the relevant stages of the derivation, starting with the accusative pattern. We enter the derivation at stage Σ. Since AC » MC, Agree takes priority over Merge. Agree targets the probe $[*CASE:int*]$ of v and thus instantiates $[CASE:int]$ on DP_{int}, see O_2 in T7.

T7 Accusative pattern, step 1 (Σ as input): Agree

Input: $[_{v'}\ v_{[*CASE:int*],[•D•]} \dots DP_{[CASE:\square]} \dots]$ Workspace $= \{DP_{[CASE:\square]},\ T_{[*CASE:ext*]},\ \dots\}$		MLC	AC	MC
	$O_1: [_{v'} DP_{[CASE:\square]} [_{v'}\ v_{[*CASE:int*]} \dots DP_{[CASE:\square]} \dots]]$		*!	
☞	$O_2: [_{v'}\ v_{[•D•]} \dots DP_{[CASE:int]} \dots]$			*

O_2 from T7 serves as the input for the next cycle. AC being satisfied, MC can now be fulfilled by applying Merge to DP_{ext}. This targets the $[•D•]$-feature on v, resulting in the optimal output O_1 in T8. Again, O_1 will serve as input for the next derivational cycle.

T8 Accusative pattern, step 2: Merge

Input: $DP_{[CASE:\square]} \oplus [_{v'}\ v_{[•D•]} \dots DP_{[CASE:int]} \dots]$ Workspace $= \{T_{[*CASE:ext*]},\ \dots\}$		MLC	AC	MC
☞	$O_1: [_{vP} DP_{[CASE:\square]} [_{v'}\ v \dots DP_{[CASE:int]} \dots]]$			

We skip step 3, which merges the T-head (bearing [*$\textsc{case}$:ext*]) with O_1 of T8. Once T is merged, AC demands T's [*$\textsc{case}$:ext*] to establish Agree, which instantiates [$\textsc{case}$:ext] on DP_{ext}, see O_1 in T9. The result is the accusative pattern.

T9 Accusative pattern, step 4: Agree

Input: $[_{T'} T_{[*\textsc{case}:ext*]} [_{vP} DP_{[\textsc{case}::\square]} \ldots DP_{[\textsc{case}:int]} \ldots]]$ Workspace $= \{\ldots\}$	MLC	AC	MC
☞ O_1: $[_{TP} T [_{vP} DP_{[\textsc{case}:ext]} [_{v'} v \ldots DP_{[\textsc{case}:int]} \ldots]]]$			

Now reenter the derivation at stage Σ with the ranking MC » AC. MC immediately forces Merge DP_{ext}, consuming v's [•$\textsc{d}$•]-feature at the cost of violating AC (v's [*$\textsc{case}$:int*] probe is still present), see O_1 in T10.

T10 Ergative pattern, step 1 (Σ as input): Merge

Input: $DP_{[\textsc{case}:\square]} \oplus [_{v'} v_{[*\textsc{case}:int*],[•\textsc{d}•]} \ldots \quad DP_{[\textsc{case}:\square]} \ldots]$ Workspace $= \{T_{[*\textsc{case}:ext*]}, \ldots\}$	MLC	MC	AC
☞ O_1: $[_{v'} DP_{[\textsc{case}:\square]} [_{v'} v_{[*\textsc{case}:int*]} \ldots DP_{[\textsc{case}:\square]} \ldots]]$			*
O_2: $[_{v'} v_{[•\textsc{d}•]} \ldots DP_{[\textsc{case}:int]} \ldots]$		*!	

At the next step, v's [*$\textsc{case}$:int*] probe must undergo Agree. Crucially, as DP_{ext} is present it counts as closer to v than DP_{int}. Therefore, v's probe instantiates [$\textsc{case}$:int] on DP_{ext} (see O_1 in T11). Valuation of DP_{int}'s goal fatally violates the MLC (see O_2).

T11 Ergative pattern, step 2: Agree (with DP_{ext})

Input: $[_{v'} DP_{[\textsc{case}:\square]} [_{v'} v_{[*\textsc{case}:int*]} \ldots DP_{[\textsc{case}:\square]} \ldots]]$ Workspace $= \{T_{[*\textsc{case}:ext*]}, \ldots\}$	MLC	MC	AC
☞ O_1: $[_{vP} DP_{[\textsc{case}:int]} [_{v'} v \ldots DP_{[\textsc{case}:\square]} \ldots]]$			
O_2: $[_{vP} DP_{[\textsc{case}:\square]} [_{v'} v \ldots DP_{[\textsc{case}:int]} \ldots]]$	*!		

We skip Merge of T. Once T with its [*$\textsc{case}$:ext*] has been merged, it instantiates [$\textsc{case}$:ext] on DP_{int}, deriving the ergative pattern, see O_1 in T12.

T12 Ergative pattern, step 4: Agree

Input: $[_{T'} T_{[*\textsc{case}:ext*]} [_{vP} DP_{[\textsc{case}:int]} [_{v'} v \ldots DP_{[\textsc{case}:\square]} \ldots]]]$ Workspace $= \{\ldots\}$	MLC	MC	AC
☞ O_1: $[_{T'} T [_{vP} DP_{[\textsc{case}:int]} [_{v'} v \ldots DP_{[\textsc{case}:ext]} \ldots]]]$			

Note in passing that Agree (T, DP_{int}) is just local enough to be in accordance with the PIC in Chomsky (2001: 14). DP_{ext} does not intervene between T and DP_{int} because DP_{ext}'s case feature has already participated in Agree (see (17)).[14]

The accusative pattern is the result of resolving the conflict between AC and MC in favor of AC. This makes the instantiation of the value [CASE:*int*] on DP_{int} possible (leaving valuation of DP_{ext}'s goal to the probe on T). If the conflict resolves in favor of Merge, then [CASE:*int*] must be instantiated on DP_{ext}, due to the MLC (leaving valuation of DP_{int}'s goal to the probe on T); this derives the ergative pattern.[15]

4.1.3 Less local optimization

Suppose that optimization targets complete phrases. Then it will not apply unless v has been Merged with DP_{ext}, forming a complete vP. As a consequence, less local optimization is able to derive the ergative pattern, as illustrated in T13.[16]

T13 vP optimization under MC » AC ('ergative') ranking: right result

Input: $DP_{[CASE:\square]} \oplus v_{[*CASE:int*]'[\bullet v\bullet]>[\bullet D\bullet]} \oplus [_{VP} \ldots DP_{[CASE:\square]} \ldots]$ Workspace = $\{T_{[*CASE:ext*]'} \ldots\}$	MLC	MC	AC
☞ O_1: $[_{vP} DP_{[CASE:int]} [_{v'} v \ldots DP_{[CASE:\square]} \ldots]]$			
O_2: $[_{vP} DP_{[CASE:\square]} [_{v'} v \ldots DP_{[CASE:int]} \ldots]]$	*!		

However, of more interest is the attempt to derive the accusative pattern under the ranking AC » MC: In a fully-fledged vP, DP_{ext} is always closer to [*CASE:*int**] on v. But then, given the MLC, [CASE:*int*] cannot be instantiated on DP_{int}, but must be instantiated on DP_{ext}. This yields again the ergative but not the accusative pattern (see O_1 in T14; the left-hand symbol ☜ marks the 'wrong' winner).

T14 vP optimization under AC » MC ('accusative') ranking: wrong result

Input: $DP_{[CASE:\square]} \oplus v_{[*CASE:int*]'[\bullet v\bullet]>[\bullet D\bullet]} \oplus [_{VP} \ldots DP_{[CASE:\square]} \ldots]$ Workspace = $\{T_{[*CASE:ext*]} \ldots\}$	MLC	AC	MC
☜ O_1: $[_{vP} DP_{[CASE:int]} [_{v'} v \ldots DP_{[CASE:\square]} \ldots]]$			
O_2: $[_{vP} DP_{[CASE:\square]} [_{v'} v \ldots DP_{[CASE:int]} \ldots]]$	*!		

Thus less local optimization undergenerates. The argument is independent of MLC's ranking relative to AC or MC.

4.2 Prenominal dative possessors in German

The second piece of evidence is based on the agreement pattern that is found in a construction involving dative possessors in German.

4.2.1 Data

German DPs can contain a dative-marked possessor (DP_{dat}) in SpecD (see Haider 1988; Zifonun 2004). The head of such DPs is realized by a possessive pronoun, which exhibits a twofold agreement pattern: (a) the root of the pronoun agrees with DP_{dat} with respect to number and gender; (b) the inflection of the pronoun agrees with its complement NP with respect to number, gender, and case. We focus here on agreement with respect to gender (written as [GEND]), see (21) vs. (22).

(21)   Gender agreement with dative possessor in German:

    (a) [$_{DP}$ dem   Fritz] sein-e   Schwester
         the.MASC.DAT Fritz his.MASC-FEM   sister.FEM
         'Fritz's sister'

    (b) [$_{DP}$ der   Maria] ihr-Ø   Bruder
         the.FEM.DAT Maria   her.FEM-MASC   brother.MASC
         'Maria's brother'

    (c) [$_{DP}$ dem   Fritz] sein-Ø   Buch
         the.MASC.DAT Fritz his.MASC-NEUT   book.NEUT
         'Fritz's book'

(22)   Ungrammatical gender agreement with dative possessor:

    (a) *[$_{DP}$ dem   Fritz] ihr-Ø   Schwester
         the.MASC.DAT Fritz her.FEM-MASC   sister.FEM
         'Fritz's sister'

    (b) *[$_{DP}$ dem   Fritz] sein-Ø   Schwester
         the.MASC.DAT Fritz his.MASC-MASC sister.FEM

    (c) *[$_{DP}$ dem   Fritz] ihr-e   Schwester
         the.MASC.DAT Fritz her.FEM-FEM   sister.FEM

We follow Georgi and Salzmann (2011) in assuming that DP_{dat} gets its case from the possessee NP. Note that the possessive D and NP show case agreement. As the probe that values this case is DP-external, one may expect NP to remain active (potentially intervening) while DP is derived, an unwanted result. We therefore assume that case agreement between D and NP in a first step involves feature sharing (cf. Pollard and Sag 1994; Frampton and Gutman 2000; Heck and Cuartero 2008) of the yet unvalued case features of D and NP. By assumption, feature sharing renders NP's case feature inactive, while D's case feature remains active. It is then D's case feature that becomes valued by the DP-external case probe in a second step and, via feature sharing, the case feature of NP agrees with it.[17]

4.2.2 Analysis

Suppose the following: (a) DP_{dat} is merged as a complement of the possessum (see De Vries 2005; cf. also Chomsky 1970) and undergoes [•EPP•]-driven movement to SpecD; (b) pronouns are realized by post-syntactic morphology (Halle and Marantz 1993); (c) the pronoun's inflectional features occupy a structurally higher position than its root features. To this end, we assume the following structure for the pronoun:

(23)   The internal structure of pronouns:
       $[_D [_D$ ROOT D] INFL]

It follows that the possessive pronoun has a dual role. First, it bears two probes that trigger Agree, namely [*GEND$_i$:□*] and [*GEND$_r$:□*], the gender probes of the inflection and the root of the possessive pronoun. Second, the possessive pronoun bears an [•EPP•] feature that triggers Move (possessor raising). This causes a conflict. Suppose the derivation has reached stage Σ, where the possessive pronoun has been merged with the possessum NP. DP_{dat} is still the complement of this NP. Then AC demands Agree (D, DP_{dat}) and Agree (D, NP); and MC demands movement of DP_{dat} to SpecD. The conflict can be resolved by ranking AC over MC, yielding the correct agreement pattern, see (24).

(24)   Ranking:
       MLC » AC » MC » LR   (German)

Let us say we want to derive (21a). We enter the derivation at stage Σ (see above). Due to AC » MC, Agree must apply first. Since [*GEND$_i$:□*] is, by assumption, structurally higher than [*GEND$_r$:□*] (see (23)), the former counts as closer to both NP and DP_{dat}. Thus the MLC constrains Agree to the inflectional probe [*GEND$_i$:□*]. Moreover, according to the definitions in (18) and (19), the NP, which bears [GEND:*fem*], counts as closer to the pronoun than DP_{dat}. Thus Agree (D, NP) instantiates [GEND$_i$:*fem*] on the pronoun (see O_1 in T15). Any Agree relation that involves the pronominal root or DP_{dat} violates the MLC (e.g., O_2); O_3, which seeks to satisfy MC by raising the possessor to SpecD, fatally violates AC.

T15 Valuation of inflection's gender, step 1 (Σ as input): Agree (with NP)

Input: $[_{D'1}$ D$_{[*GENDr:□*], [*GENDi:□*], [•EPP•]…}$ $…[_{NP}$ N$_{[GEND:fem]}$ DP$_{2[GEND:masc]}$]]	MLC	AC	MC	LR
☞ O_1: $[_{D'1}$ D$_{[*GENDr:□*], [GENDi:fem], [•EPP•]…}$ $…[_{NP}$ N$_{[GEND:fem]}$ DP$_{2[GEND:masc]}$]]		*	*	
O_2: $[_{D'1}$ D$_{[GENDr:fem], [*GENDi:□*], [•EPP•]…}$ $…[_{NP}$ N$_{[GEND:fem]}$ DP$_{2[GEND:masc]}$]]	*!	*	*	
O_3: $[_{DP1}$ DP$_{2[GEND:masc]}$ D$_{[*GENDr:□*], [*GENDi:□*]…}$ $…[_{NP}$ N$_{[GEND:fem]}$ t$_2$]]		**!		*

Having undergone Agree, the gender features on NP and D are rendered inactive ($[\text{GEND}_i]$ on D in O_1/T15 is no longer the probe $[{*}\text{GEND}_i{*}]$ from the input). Hence, Agree can next affect the pronoun's root probe $[{*}\text{GEND}_r{:}\square{*}]$ and $[\text{GEND}{:}masc]$ on DP_{dat}. This values $[{*}\text{GEND}_r{:}\square{*}]$ as $[\text{GEND}_r{:}masc]$ on the pronoun (see O_1 in T16). The MC-violation incurred is non-fatal.

T16 Valuation of root's gender, step 2: Agree (with DP)

	MLC	AC	MC	LR
Input: $[_{\text{D}'1}$ D $_{[{*}\text{GEND}r{:}\square{*}],\ [\text{GEND}i{:}fem],\ [{\cdot}\text{EPP}{\cdot}]}$ $\cdots$ $\cdots$ $[_{\text{NP}}$ N $_{[\text{GEND}{:}fem]}$ DP2$_{[\text{GEND}{:}masc]}$]]				
☞ O_1: $[_{\text{D}'1}$ D $_{[\text{GEND}r{:}masc],\ [\text{GEND}i{:}fem],\ [{\cdot}\text{EPP}{\cdot}]}$ $\cdots$ $\cdots$ $[_{\text{NP}}$ N $_{[\text{GEND}{:}fem]}$ DP$_{2[\text{GEND}{:}masc]}$]]			*	
O_2: $[_{\text{DP1}}$ DP$_{2[\text{GEND}{:}masc]}$ D $_{[{*}\text{GEND}r{:}\square{*}],\ [\text{GEND}i{:}fem]}$ $\cdots$ $\cdots$ $[_{\text{NP}}$ N $_{[\text{GEND}{:}fem]}$ t_2]		*!		

Finally, MC can be satisfied by movement of the possessor DP to SpecD, see T17. Since Move is preceded by Agree, LR is satisfied. The correct agreement pattern is derived.

T17 Possessor raising, step 3: Move

	MLC	AC	MC	LR
Input: $[_{\text{D}'1}$ D $_{[\text{GEND}r{:}masc],\ [\text{GEND}i{:}fem],\ [{\cdot}\text{EPP}{\cdot}]}$ $\cdots$ $\cdots$ $[_{\text{NP}}$ N $_{[\text{GEND}{:}fem]}$ DP$_{2[\text{GEND}{:}masc]}$]]				
☞ O_1: $[_{\text{DP1}}$ DP$_2$ D $_{[\text{GEND}r{:}masc],\ [\text{GEND}i{:}fem]}$ $\cdots$ $\cdots$ $[_{\text{NP}}$ N $_{[\text{GEND}{:}fem]}$ t_2]]				

4.2.3 Less local optimization

Suppose now that optimization applies to phrases. An optimal DP will always involve raising of DP_{dat} (due to MC). But with DP_{dat} raised, both DP_{dat} and NP are equally close to the pronoun. Then $[{*}\text{GEND}_i{:}\square{*}]$ can be valued $[\text{GEND}{:}masc]$ (leaving N's $[\text{GEND}{:}fem]$ to D's $[{*}\text{GEND}_r{:}\square{*}]$), thereby deriving the ungrammatical (22a) (see O_2 in T18).

T18 DP optimization: wrong result

	MLC	AC	MC	LR
Input: D$_{[{*}\text{GEND}r{:}\square{*}],\ [{*}\text{GEND}i{:}\square{*}],\ [{\cdot}\text{EPP}{\cdot}]}$ $\oplus$ $[_{\text{NP}}$ N $_{[\text{GEND}{:}fem]}$ DP$_{2[\text{GEND}{:}masc]}$]				
☞ O_1: $[_{\text{DP1}}$DP$_{2[\text{GEND}{:}masc]}$ D $_{[\text{GEND}r{:}masc],\ [\text{GEND}i{:}fem]}$ $\cdots$ $[_{\text{NP}}$ N $_{[\text{GEND}{:}fem]}$ t_2]				
☜ O_2: $[_{\text{DP1}}$DP$_{2[\text{GEND}{:}masc]}$ D $_{[\text{GEND}r{:}fem],\ [\text{GEND}i{:}masc]}$ $\cdots$ $[_{\text{NP}}$ N $_{[\text{GEND}{:}fem]}$ t_2]]				
O_3: $[_{\text{DP1}}$D $_{[\text{GEND}r{:}masc],\ [\text{GEND}i{:}fem],\ [{\cdot}\text{EPP}{\cdot}]}$ $\cdots$ $[_{\text{NP}}$ N $_{[\text{GEND}{:}fem]}$ DP$_{2[\text{GEND}{:}masc]}$]]			*!	
O_4: $[_{\text{DP1}}$DP$_{2[\text{GEND}{:}masc]}$ D $_{[{*}\text{GEND}r{:}\square{*}],\ [\text{GEND}i{:}fem]}$ $\cdots$ $[_{\text{NP}}$ N $_{[\text{GEND}{:}fem]}$ t_2]]		*!		

Thus the approach overgenerates. An additional constraint C is needed to block O_2. A naive interpretation of C could be as follows: the element that merges second with the possessive D must not value the higher feature within D. Of course, C is completely ad hoc. In fact, it mimics the derivational decision made by ELO.

4.3 SpecC-expletives in German

The third argument that we present involves SpecC-expletives in German V/2 clauses.

4.3.1 Data

SpecC-expletive insertion in verb second (V/2) clauses in German looks like a repair phenomenon: expletive *es* must and can only be inserted if no other element fills SpecC (see (25)) and if it is necessary at all to fill this position (see (26)).

(25) Expletives in V/2 clauses in German ('Vorfeld-es'):

    (a) Es   haben viele Leute   geschlafen.
        EXPL have   many people.NOM slept
        'Many people slept.'

    (b) Viele Leute   haben geschlafen.
        many people.NOM have   slept

    (c) *Haben viele Leute   geschlafen.
         have   many people.NOM slept

(26) Blocked expletives in verb-final clauses in German:

    (a) dass viele Leute   geschlafen haben
        that many people.NOM slept   have
        'that many people slept'

    (b) *dass es   viele Leute   geschlafen haben
        that EXPL many people.NOM slept   have

    (c) *es dass   viele Leute   geschlafen haben
        EXPL that many people.NOM slept   have

    (d) *viele Leute   dass geschlafen haben
        many people.NOM that slept   have

Es-insertion is optional. In Müller (2000b: 48–49), this is traced back to a tie of two crucial constraints: ECONOMY and FULL-INTERPRETATION are tied and ranked below SPECV/2 ('The specifier of V/2 must be filled').

Next, Bierwisch (1967: 111) observes that expletive insertion in SpecC is incompatible with a nominative pronoun (see also Erdmann 1886: §94): Another element moves to fill SpecC (see (27a)/(28a) vs. (27b)/(28b)).[18]

(27) Expletive/subject pronoun incompatibility:

    (a) *Es   habe   ich   geraucht.
         EXPL have.1.SG I.NOM   smoked
         'I smoked.'

    (b) Ich   habe   geraucht.
         I.NOM have.1.SG smoked

(28) (a) *Es   sahen   sie   den Zug kommen.
         EXPL saw.3.PL they.NOM the train come
         'They saw the train approaching.'

    (b) Sie   sahen   den Zug kommen.
         they.NOM saw.3.PL the train approaching

The intuition behind the analysis proposed below is that expletive *es* and subject pronouns compete for a person feature that is only present once.

4.3.2 Analysis

We follow Hornstein (2001) in assuming that expletives never show up in numerations. Then their insertion will violate the constraint in (29).

(29) INCLUSIVENESS CONDITION (IC, Chomsky 2001):
    Only material from the numeration can be used in a derivation.

If the IC is a violable constraint in the sense of OT, it follows that violations of the IC must be kept minimal. Hence, expletives are minimally specified categories that fit into a given context and satisfy structure-building features.

Note that the system of German personal pronouns strongly resembles that of determiners. Both paradigms involve underspecified vocabulary items (see Wiese 2001; Fischer 2006). The vocabulary item /s/ is the least specified (default) ending (see Bierwisch 1967; Wunderlich 1997). Similarly, /es/ is the least specified vocabulary item that can act as a personal pronoun. Therefore, it is the only pronoun that can be inserted in radically impoverished syntactic contexts (Halle and Marantz 1993, 1994). The reduced feature specification of *es* (lacking number) and the parallelism with other expletives is illustrated in (30).

(30) Some expletives:
    (a) Ø: {[D], [PERS:*3*]} $\rightarrow$ post-syntactic spell-out as /es/ in German
    (b) Ø: {[D], [PERS:*3*], [WH]} $\rightarrow$ post-syntactic spell-out as /was/ in German (Müller 1997)
    (c) Ø: {[V], [Φ], [TENSE]} $\rightarrow$ post-syntactic spell-out as /do/ in English (Grimshaw 1997)

Suppose now that AC and MC are actually relativized to phase domains. Thus there exist AC_v, AC_D, AC_C, MC_v, MC_D, and MC_C.[19] The different instances of AC (and MC) can occupy different positions in the constraint hierarchy. We assume here that

MC_C and AC_C are ranked via a global constraint tie (see, e.g., Müller 1999), written as $AC_C \circ MC_C$ (in contrast to the rankings $AC_v \gg MC_v$ and $AC_D \gg MC_D$ motivated above). The complete relevant ranking is shown in (31).

(31) Ranking:
       MLC » $AC_C \circ MC_C$ » LR » IC   (German)

Also, we follow Platzack (1987) (Holmberg and Platzack 1995; Chomsky 2008), assuming that C bears [Φ]/[CASE] relevant for subject agreement and nominative assignment (not T; cf. also Haider 1993).

It follows that a V/2 C has a dual role: It has an [•EPP•] feature that triggers Merge, and [Φ/CASE] features that trigger Agree. Consider a context with a V/2 C, and, to simplify things, assume that C does not have any information-structure related feature ([TOP], [FOC], [FORCE] etc. (see Rizzi 2004). Suppose that the derivation has reached a stage Σ where C has been merged with a TP containing DP_{ext}, with nothing waiting to be merged with C in the workspace. Then AC_C demands application of Agree (C, DP_{ext}), and MC_C demands insertion of an expletive pronoun in SpecC (Merge(DP_{expl}, C)): a conflict.[20] The conflict is resolved by ranking AC_C and MC_C, yielding expletive insertion and movement of DP_{ext} in *one* language (because of the tie), in interaction with IC, LR and MLC.

We enter the derivation at stage Σ. If $AC_C \gg MC_C$, then the probes of C enter into an Agree relation with DP_{ext}, thereby instantiating [Φ] on C and [CASE] on DP_{ext} (see O_2 in T19). Expletive insertion is blocked (cf. O_1; for ease of presentation only one AC-violation is indicated, cf. also O_3; in fact, there are several violations as C bears several probes).

T19 Subject movement, step 1 (Σ as input): Agree

Input: $[_{C'}\ C_{[*CASE:ext*], [*PERS:\square*],\dots, [•EPP•]}$ $\dots DP_{[CASE:\square], [PERS:x], [NUM:y], [GEND:z]} \dots]$	MLC	AC	MC	LR	IC
O_1: $[_{CP}\ DP_{[PERS:3]}\ [C'\ C_{[*CASE:ext*], [*PERS:\square*],\dots}$ $\dots DP_{[CASE:\square], [PERS:x], [NUM:y], [GEND:z]} \dots]]$		*!			*
☞ O_2: $[_{C'}\ C_{[PERS:x], [NUM:y], [GEND:z],\dots, [•EPP•]}$ $\dots DP_{[CASE:ext], [PERS:x],\dots} \dots]$			*		
O_3: $[_{CP}\ DP_{[CASE:\square], [PERS:x],\dots}$ $[_{C'}\ C_{[*PERS:\square*],\dots} \dots t_{DP} \dots]$		*!		*	

The second step involves movement of DP_{ext} to SpecC, satisfying MC_C and LR.[21] Note that expletive insertion is blocked at this point by IC (see O_2 vs. O_1 in T20).

T20 Subject movement, step 2: Move

Input: $[_{C'} C_{[PERS:x],\ldots,\,[\bullet EPP\bullet]} \ldots DP_{[CASE:ext],\,[PERS:x],\,\ldots\,\ldots}]$	MLC	AC	MC	LR	IC
O1: $[_{CP} DP_{[PERS:3]} [_{C'} C_{[PERS:x],\ldots}$ $\ldots DP_{[CASE:ext],\,[PERS:x],\,\ldots}\ \ldots]]$					*!
☞ O2: $[_{CP} DP_{[CASE:ext],\,[PERS:x]},\ \ldots$ $[_{C'} C_{[PERS:x],\,\ldots}\ \ldots t_{DP}\ \ldots]$					

If MC_C » AC_C, Merge applies first. As LR » IC, expletive insertion is favored over movement of DP_{ext} (see O_1 vs. O_3 in T21).

T21 Expletive insertion, step 1 (Σ as input): Merge

Input: $[_{C'} C_{[*CASE:ext*],\,[*PERS:\square*],\ldots,\,[\bullet EPP\bullet]} \ldots DP_{[CASE:\square],\,[PERS:x],\,[NUM:y],\,[GEND:z]}\ \ldots]$	MLC	MC	AC	LR	IC
☞ O_1: $[_{CP} DP_{[PERS:3]} [_{C'} C_{[*CASE:ext*],\,[*PERS:\square*],\ldots} \ldots DP_{[CASE:\square],\,[PERS:x],\ldots}\ \ldots]]$			*		*
O_2: $[_{C'} C_{[PERS:x],\ldots,\,[\bullet EPP\bullet]} \ldots DP_{[CASE:ext],\,[PERS:x],\ldots}\ \ldots]$		*!			
O_3: $[_{CP} DP_{[CASE:\square],\,[PERS:x],\ldots} [_{C'} C_{[*CASE:ext*],\,[*PERS:\square*],\ldots} \ldots t_{DP}\ \ldots]]$			*	*!	

Once the expletive occupies SpecC, it counts as closer to probes on C than DP_{ext} and thus values [PERSON:*3*] on the C-head (O_1 in T22). Agree (C,DP_{ext}) is blocked by the MLC (see O_2). Crucially, C can never check DP_{ext}'s person feature. If features that are required for post-syntactic spell-out must be checked in syntax, this derives the incompatibility of expletive *es* and subject pronouns (see (27)): A subject pronoun cannot be spelled out in the context of an expletive because its person feature has not been checked.[22]

T22 Expletive insertion, step 2: (Partial) Agree with expletive

Input: $[_{CP} DP_{[PERS:3]} [_{C'} C_{[*CASE:ext*],\,[*PERS:\square*],\ldots} \ldots DP_{[CASE:\square],\,[PERS:x],\ldots}\ \ldots]]$	MLC	MC	AC	LR	IC
☞ O_1: $[_{CP} DP_{[PERS:3]} [_{C'} C_{[*CASE:ext*],\,[PERS:3],\ldots} \ldots DP_{[CASE:\square],\,[PERS:x],\ldots}\ \ldots]]$			*		
O_2: $[_{CP} DP_{[PERS:3]} [_{C'} C_{[PERS:x],\ldots} \ldots DP_{[CASE:ext],\,[PERS:x],\ldots}\ \ldots]]$	*!				

In the last step C's remaining probes establish Agree with DP_{ext}. The person feature on the expletive is no obstacle, having participated in Agree at the preceding step. This is illustrated in T23.[23]

T23 Expletive insertion, step 3: Agree (with subject DP)

	MLC	MC	AC	LR	IC
Input: $[_{CP}$ DP$_{[PERS:3]}$ $[_{C'}$ C$_{[*CASE:ext*], [PERS:3], [*NUM:\square*],...}$ $...$ DP$_{[CASE:\square], [PERS:x], [NUM:y], [GEND:z]}$ $...]]$					
☞ O_1: $[_{CP}$ DP$_{[PERS:3]}$ $[_{C'}$ C$_{[PERS:3], [NUM:y], [GEND:z]}$ $...$ DP$_{[CASE:ext], [PERS:x], [NUM:y], [GEND:z]}$ $...]]$					

4.3.3 Less local optimization

Suppose that optimization affects the phrase. Note that a CP can perfectly satisfy AC, MC, MLC, and LR. Consequently, IC will be decisive, and will always block expletive insertion, irrespective of the ranking. Expletive insertion can be advantageous only at a certain specific stage in the derivation (where moving DP_{ext} is blocked by LR); after that stage, the advantage is gone. This is no problem under the ranking AC_C » MC_C, which correctly derives the configuration with subject movement, see T24.

T24 CP optimization under AC_C » MC_C (subject movement) ranking: right result

	MLC	AC	MC	LR	IC
Input: $C_{[*CASE:ext*], [*PERS:\square*],..., [\bullet EPP\bullet]}$ $\oplus$ $[_{TP} ...$ DP$_{[CASE:\square], [PERS:x], ...}$ $...]$					
O_1: $[_{CP}$ DP$_{[PERS:3]}$ $[_{C'}$ C$_{[PERS:3], [NUM:y], [GEND:z]}$ $...$ DP$_{[CASE:ext], [PERS:x], [NUM:y], [GEND:z]}$ $...]]$					*!
☞ O_2: $[_{CP}$ DP$_{[CASE:ext], [PERS:x], [NUM:y], [GEND:z]}$ $[_{C'}$ C$_{[PERS:x], [NUM:y], [GEND:z]}$ $...t_{DP} ...]$					

However, optimization under the ranking MC_C » AC_C yields subject movement, too, see O_2 in T25. O_1 with the expletive in SpecC, cannot be optimal.

T25 CP optimization under MC_C » AC_C (expletive) ranking: wrong result

	MLC	MC	AC	LR	IC
Input: $C_{[*CASE:ext*], [*PERS:\square*],..., [\bullet EPP\bullet]}$ $\oplus$ $[_{TP} ...$ DP$_{[CASE:\square], [PERS:x],...}$ $...]$					
O_1: $[_{CP}$ DP$_{[PERS:3]}$ $[_{C'}$ C$_{[PERS:3], [NUM:y], [GEND:z]}$ $...$ DP$_{[CASE:ext], [PERS:x], [NUM:y], [GEND:z]}$ $...]]$					*!
☞ O_2: $[_{CP}$ DP$_{[CASE:ext], [PERS:x], [NUM:y], [GEND:z]}$ $[_{C'}$ C$_{[PERS:x], [NUM:y], [GEND:z]}$ $...t_{DP} ...]$					

To conclude, less local optimization again undergenerates.[24]

4.4 VP-Topicalization

Our last argument involves *do*-support in English in the context of VP-topicalization.

4.4.1 Data

In the context of VP-topicalization in English, tense features do not appear on the main verb. If there is a modal verb or, in the absence of a modal, an auxiliary verb, then tense can be expressed on these elements (see (32a) for the auxiliary *will*). But if neither modal nor auxiliary are present, *do*-support has to apply, presumably in order to provide a host for the tense features, see (32b, c), adapted from Adger (2003: 161).

(32) VP-topicalization with auxiliary or do-support:

(a) Enkidu said he would free the animals and [$_{VP}$ free the animals] he will.
(b) Enkidu said he freed the animals and [$_{VP}$ free the animals] he did.
(c) *Enkidu said he freed the animals and [$_{VP}$ free(d) the animals] he.

But if there is no VP-topicalization, then (again in the absence of modal and auxiliary) tense must be expressed on the main verb, see (33a), while *do*-support is blocked (unless *do* bears emphatic stress), see (33b).

(33) Do-support blocked without VP-topicalization:

(a) Enkidu freed the animals.
(b) *Enkidu did free the animals.

We would like to propose an account of (32b, c) that is based on Adger's (2003) idea that tense marking on v is the result of Agree between T and v (and does not involve movement as in Chomsky (1957) and subsequent literature). But in contrast to Adger's analysis, our account locates the ultimate source of the problem of (32c) in the syntax, not the morphology (see Adger 2003: 192). The idea is that Agree between T and v necessarily applies after VP-topicalization, which is too late for the tense probe on T to establish Agree with the goal on v.[25]

4.4.2 Analysis

So far we have assumed that α establishes Agree with β under m-command (see (3c), section 2). Suppose now that Agree actually presupposes that α c-commands β (as assumed in Chomsky 2001), and that only in those cases, where α does not find β in its c-command domain, it may extend the search space to its m-command domain (as already suggested by Béjar and Řezáč (2009)). To this end, we propose that (3c) is completed by the violable constraint in (34) (with no unwanted consequences for the proposals in sections 4.1–4.3):

(34) COMMAND-CONDITION ON AGREE (CCA):
      Probe α cannot enter into Agree with goal β unless α c-commands β.

We follow Adger (2003) in assuming that T bears a probe [*TENSE:x*] (x a value for [TENSE]) and v a goal [TENSE:□]. Assume further that VP-topicalization in English targets an outer specifier of T and is triggered by [•v•] on T. As usual, the innermost SpecT is filled by subject raising (triggered by [•EPP•] on T). The order between the subject and a topicalized VP is derived by the feature stack [•EPP•] > [•v•] on T.[26]

As a consequence, the T-head that appears in the context of VP-topicalization has a dual role: it must enter into Agree with v and it must merge with vP. Again, T cannot perform both operations simultaneously. We propose that the conflict is resolved by the ranking MC » AC. This is the opposite of what has to be assumed for English in light of the analyses given in sections 3.2 and 4.1, respectively. Suppose therefore that AC and MC have to be relativized to categories in general (and not merely to the phase categories v, C and D, as proposed in section 4.3).[27]

The relevant ranking for English (including both CCA and MC$_T$, AC$_T$, the variants of MC and AC relativized to T) is given in (35).

(35) Ranking:

MLC » MC$_T$ » AC$_T$ » CCA » IC » LR   (English)

Consider a derivation with VP-topicalization. At its stage Σ, T has been merged with vP and subject raising has already applied. Due to [•v•] and [*TENSE:x*] on T, both MC and AC have to be satisfied. But T can only perform one operation at a time. Given the ranking MC$_T$ » AC$_T$, VP-topicalization applies first (see O$_1$ in T26). This incurs one violation of AC and one of LR because movement is not preceded by Agree. They are non-fatal, however, since leaving [•v•] unsatisfied (as in O$_2$) violates the higher ranked MC.

T26 VP-topicalization, step 1 (Σ as input): Move

Input: [$_{TP}$ DP$_2$ T$_{[\text{*TNS:}x\text{*}],\ [\text{•v•}]}$ [$_{vP}$ t$_2$ v$_{[\text{TNS:□}]}$ …]] Workspace = {…}		MLC	MC	AC	CCA	IC	LR
☞ O$_1$: [$_{TP}$ vP$_{3[\text{TNS:□}]}$ [$_{T'}$ DP$_2$ [$_{T'}$ T$_{[\text{*TNS:}x\text{*}]}$ t$_3$]]]				*			*
O$_2$: [$_{TP}$ DP$_2$ T$_{[\text{TNS:}x],\ [\text{•v•}]}$ [$_{vP}$ t$_2$ v$_{[\text{TNS:}x]}$ …]]			*!				

O$_1$ of T26 serves as the input for the next optimization cycle. There still remains the probe [*TENSE:x*] on T to be eliminated. The only available goal for [*TENSE:x*] within O$_1$ is vP$_3$. But in the last step, vP$_3$ was moved to SpecT and therefore occupies a position outside the c-command domain of T. Hence, Agree (T,vP$_3$) can only be established under violation of the CCA, see O$_1$ in T27.

At this point, an aside is in order. All along, we made the assumption that Merge and Agree are elementary operations. Technically speaking, however, they are complex. Merge, besides building a complex category, involves deletion of selectional features, and Agree involves inactivation of a probe, often in addition to valuation of features. Our interpretation of this is that Merge and Agree trigger deletion and valuation as a reflex. Now, Adger (2003) assumes that adjunction does not involve (the deletion of) selectional features. We would like to take this one step further by saying that, therefore, adjunction does not count as an elementary operation, at least not as far as optimization is concerned.

With this assumption in place, let us discuss a competitor to candidate O_1 mentioned above. As already indicated in (30c) (section 4.3), the English verbal expletive *do* bears [TENSE]. Suppose that *do*, when it enters the derivation, is adjoined to T. By assumption, adjunction is not an operation all by itself. But it places *do*'s tense feature within the c-command domain of [*TENSE:x*] on T. This enables [*TENSE:x*] on T to value [TENSE:□] on *do*, crucially without violating the CCA, see O_2 in T27. O_2 incurs a violation of the IC because *do*, as a verbal expletive, is not part of the numeration. But CCA outranks IC, and consequently candidate O_2 wins over O_1 in T27.[28] This derives *do*-support in the context of VP-topicalization in English.[29]

T27 VP-topicalization, step 2: Agree

Input: $[_{TP} vP_{3[TNS:□]} [_{T'} DP_2 [_{T'} T_{[*TNS:x*]} t_3]]]$ Workspace = {…}	MLC	MC	AC	CCA	IC	LR
O_1: $[_{TP} vP_{3[TNS:x]} DP_2 [_{T'} T_{[TNS:x]} t_3]]$				*!		
☞ O_2: $[_{TP} vP_{3[TNS:□]} DP_2 [_T V_{[TNS:x]} T_{[TNS:x]}] t_3]$					*	

If there is a modal or an auxiliary in T, *do*-support is superfluous, even in the context of VP-topicalization. The same holds if there is no VP-topicalization to begin with. In both cases, *do*-support is blocked by IC because Agree (T,v) does not violate CCA.

4.4.3 Less local optimization

O_2 from T27 is also a candidate if optimization operates on the phrase level, see O_1 in T28. A crucial difference between the two is that O_1 in T28 accumulates the IC-violation of O_2/T27 *and* the LR-violation of O_1/T26. This becomes relevant, once it is recognized that there is another candidate that has not been considered yet: O_3 in T28. O_3 involves Merge of an expletive VP headed by *do* in SpecT. As *do* is verbal but not part of the numeration, this eliminates [•v•] on T and incurs an IC-violation. Since vP in O_3 remains in-situ, it also avoids the fatal CCA violation of O_2: [*TENSE:x*] on T can establish Agree with [TENSE:□] on v under c-command. Most importantly, however, O_3 avoids the LR-violation of O_1 because vP has not moved. As a consequence, O_3 is more harmonic than O_1:

T28 TP-optimization: wrong result

Input: $T_{[*\text{TNS}:x*],[\bullet V\bullet]} \oplus [_{vP}\, DP_2\, v_{[\text{TNS}:\square]} \ldots]$ Workspace = {…}	MLC	MC	AC	CCA	IC	LR
O_1: $[_{TP}\, vP_{3[\text{TNS}:\square]}\, DP_2\, [_T\, V_{[\text{TNS}:x]}\, T_{[\text{TNS}:x]}\,]\, t_3\,]$					*	*!
O_2: $[_{TP}\, vP_{3[\text{TNS}:x]}\, DP_2\, [_{T'}\, T_{[\text{TNS}:x]}\, t_3\,]]$				*!		
☞ O_3: $[_{TP}\, VP\, [_{T'}\, DP_2\, [_{T'}\, T_{[\text{TNS}:x]}\, vP_{3[\text{TNS}:x]}\,]]]$					*	

Empirically, this is the wrong result. Namely, O_3 corresponds to the ungrammatical (36b), while the suboptimal O_1 corresponds to the grammatical (32b), repeated here as (36a). Therefore, less local optimization both over- and undergenerates.

(36) No VP-expletive in SpecT in English:
    (a) Enkidu said he freed the animals and $[_{\_\_vP}$ free the animals] he did.
    (b) *Enkidu said he freed the animals and $[_{vP}$ do] he freed the animals.

Do-insertion in SpecT is not optimal under ELO: The IC-violation incurred by a hypothetical candidate O_3 in T26 that involves *do*-insertion in SpecT would be fatal.[30] The reason is that the competing O_1 in T26 fulfills MC by vP-movement, which only violates LR. Since, by assumption, IC » LR, it follows that the hypothetical candidate O_3 in T26 is blocked by O_1. (Both O_1 in T26 and the hypothetical O_3 violate AC, which therefore cannot distinguish between the two.)

Put briefly, VP-topicalization in English requires the insertion of a verbal expletive. Under ELO, insertion is procrastinated, in order to get around an IC violation at the costs of violating LR. Ultimately, it turns out that IC *must* be violated (leading to *do*-support). But this cannot be anticipated on the basis of strictly local information. A less local approach forces expletive insertion in SpecT at an early point as this gets around the LR-violation and since it is clear that an IC-violation is unavoidable. Although this leads to an optimal result on the phrasal level, it is not attested empirically.

5. Conclusion

In this article, we have suggested that optimization in syntax is extremely local. The optimization domain is not the phrase, the phase, the clause, or the sentence; it is the syntactic operation. Syntax operates by constantly alternating between single applications of syntactic elementary operations (such as Merge, Move, Agree) producing derivational steps and choosing the optimal one among them.

We provided four empirical arguments for extremely local optimization (ELO) of the following shape: (a) the order of elementary operations in MP is sometimes underdetermined; (b) resulting conflicts can be resolved by assuming constraint violability and constraint ranking; (c) the evidence suggests that optimization is extremely local, affecting the single operation. Less local optimization loses distinctions that ELO can make.

Certain repair phenomena that lend themselves to an OT solution raise problems in a local optimization approach because they involve long dependencies, e.g., resumptive pronouns (Legendre *et al.* (1998), Pesetsky (1998)) or long-distance binding (Fischer (2004)). Our hunch is that these phenomena all involve issues of *morphological realization in chains*. In these cases (and only in these), optimization can be non-local: Somehow chains can trigger non-local post-syntactic spell-out (see Fischer 2004).

Acknowledgments

This is a revised and extended version of a paper that appeared in the proceedings of WECOL 2007. For various comments, we would like to thank Lennart Bierkandt, Joanna Błaszczak, Hans Broekhuis, Gisbert Fanselow, Werner Frey, Jane Grimshaw, Stefan Keine, Line Mikkelsen, Stefan Müller, Henk van Riemsdijk, Martin Salzmann, Peter Sells, Craig Thiersch, and Ralf Vogel. The paper is dedicated to Jeff Lynne.

Notes

1. But see Brody (1995), who takes a representational view.
2. Yet another alternative involves repeated optimization of complete structures. This has been proposed in OT phonology (McCarthy 2000, 2009) and is now known under the name of *harmonic serialism* (as opposed to harmonic parallelism).
3. A reviewer is sceptical about whether all less local analyses (of those that do not involve post-syntactic spell-out) can be recast in terms of ELO. As ELO is more restrictive than less local approaches (in the sense that the information taken into account by ELO is a proper subset of the information available to less local optimization), one would suspect that some state of affairs that can be expressed by less local optimization is not expressible by ELO. To confirm this suspicion, however, one would have to show for a particular analysis that a translation into ELO is either unavailable for principled reasons or would require unacceptable assumptions. To our knowledge, this has not been done yet.
4. See Svenonius (1994), Adger (2003), Sternefeld (2006), among others.
5. We follow standard practice in assuming that the edge of P includes the specifier(s) of P and its head.
6. Note that if constraints are evaluated after each derivational step, then this derives the effects of Pesetsky's (1989) Earliness Principle, see Chomsky (2001: 15). Evaluation at each step, in turn, will follow from the idea that constraint evaluation, hence optimization, is extremely local.
7. If several elements are part of the input, then, for reasons of readability, they are separated by the connective '$\oplus$'.
8. Another possible (suboptimal) competitor for O_1 in T1 is the empty output (or 'null parse', see Prince and Smolensky (2004)). Here (and in what follows), the empty output is omitted as it is irrelevant.
9. What happens if the input contains an element bearing [•D•]>[•v•] and no DP but only a VP instead? Then the derivation returns the input unaltered: [•v•] cannot be accessed and [•D•] cannot be eliminated as there is no DP in the input. The output serves as input for the next optimization cycle, which again returns the input unaltered, and so on, ad infinitum. To avoid this, suppose that if the derivation converges (i.e., the output of the last cycle is the same as the input of the last cycle; cf. also McCarthy 2009) and the numeration is non-empty, then the derivation crashes. For ease of exposition we will stick to the above practice, assuming that the numeration always contains an appropriate element.
10. See Müller (2010), who offers independent evidence for this order of operations.
11. Originally, the argument goes back to Müller (2004). Lahne (2008) offers an extension of Müller's (2004) theory.

12. Here and in what follows the glosses are: SG = singular, PL = plural, NOM = nominative, ACC = accusative, ABS = absolutive, ERG = ergative, DAT = dative, FEM = feminine, MASC = masculine, NEUT = neuter, I/III = noun classes, 1/2/3 = first/second/third person, PAST = past tense, DET = determiner, AUX = auxiliary, GER = gerund, EXPL = expletive, and WH.EXPL = *wh*-expletive.

13. See Müller (1998: 130); compare also Pesetsky (1982: 289) and Collins (1994: 56).

14. Chomsky (2000) proposes that valued DPs act as (defective) interveners. Here, we adopt the assumption that defective intervention does not exist (see, e.g., Broekhuis 2007; Richards 2008).

15. Intransitives in ergative and accusative languages can be dealt with by the assumption that v lacks [*CASE:*int*] (while [*CASE:*ext*] on T is retained) if there is only one argument in the numeration. Active ergative languages are derived (under the ergative ranking) if only the marked probe ([*CASE:*int*]) is retained in the context of a sole marked argument (DP_{ext}) and the unmarked probe ([*CASE:*ext*]) in the context of a sole unmarked argument (DP_{int}). An active accusative system results (under the accusative ranking) from preserving only [*CASE:*int*] for a sole DP_{int} and [*CASE:*ext*] for a sole DP_{ext}. Three way systems and tense/person based splits require more elaboration, perhaps also morphological operations.

16. Actually, less local optimization derives the ergative pattern under both rankings between AC and MC. T13 illustrates the ranking MC » AC, the 'ergative' ranking under ELO (but cf. T14).

17. It seems that every theory incorporating the SCC has to make special assumptions to account for the DP-internal agreement that holds with respect to case features that are valued by a DP-external probe.

18. As pointed out to us by Gisbert Fanselow and as is independently noted in Frey (2010) (see (1)), the incompatibility disappears as soon as the nominative pronoun is modified by a focus particle (as *nur* or *allein*):

(a) Es   kann nur   er   so klug   über Fußball sprechen.
    EXPL can   only he.NOM so knowledgeable about football talk
    'It's he (and only he) who can talk about football so knowledgeable.'

(b) Es   hat er   allein dieses Desaster zu verantworten.
    EXPL has he.NOM alone   this   disaster to be.responsible
    'It's he alone that is responsible for this disaster.'

For the analysis given in section 4.3.2, this means that pronouns that are accompanied by focus particles do not need their person features to be checked in order to be realized by post-syntactic spell-out. We have to leave open here why this should be the case.

19. We assume that, alongside vP and CP, DP constitutes a phase in the sense of Chomsky (2001).

20. We focus on [CASE] and [PERSON] here. V/2 does not interact and is consequently ignored.

21. Movement to SpecC of a category a other than DP_{ext} must be preceded by another Agree relation, arguably between an information-structure related probe on C, say [•TOP•], and the corresponding goal on α. Otherwise, movement of α incurs a LR-violation and is therefore always blocked by expletive insertion. Movement of DP_{ext} does not require such an Agree relation as DP_{ext} and C already have established Agree with respect to Φ and case. This asymmetry is empirically reflected by the fact that DP_{ext} is the only category whose fronting to SpecC is compatible with maximal focus projection (see Höhle 1982; Stechow and Uhmann 1986).

22. A determiner can be spelled out because it lacks [PERSON] to begin with. Although pronouns are specified for [PERSON], other DPs are assumed not to be. Interestingly, when a subject DP is headed by a local person determiner (cf. Postal 1970), it is incompatible with *es*, as expected, see (1):

(1) *Es   habt   ihr   Studenten geraucht.
     EXPL have.2.pl you.pl students   smoked
    'You students smoked.'

23. With MC_C » AC_C being an option, one would expect that an expletive can eliminate [•EPP•] on the C-head of a *wh*-clause, while [•WH•] is taken care of by the in-situ *wh*-phrase. In fact, a *wh*-C in German can have the *wh*-expletive *was* in its specifier (along with partial *wh*-movement), see (1). If Merge of expletives is subject to specificity-based competition, then *es* is blocked (correctly) by *was* in (1), *was* being more specific than *es* (in terms of the number of their features, see (30)).

(1) Was*ᵢ*   glaubst du,   wen*ᵢ* ich t*ᵢ* getroffen habe?
    WH.EXPL believe you who I   met   have?
    'Who do you believe I met?'

However, the compatibility of *was* with the nominative pronoun *du* in (1) suggests that *was* lacks [PERSON] (see the discussion around the tableaux T21, T22). Thus, specificity-based competition must refer to the types of the features of the expletives ([WH] counting as more specific than [PERSON]) rather than to the number of features (if *was* lacks [PERSON], then *es* and *was* bear the same number of features). Yet an additional assumption is needed to block insertion of *was* in monoclausal interrogatives, as the one in (2):

(2) *Was*ᵢ*   hast du   wen*ᵢ* getroffen?
     WH.EXPL have you who met
     'Who did you meet?'

What may be involved here is an anti-locality condition that militates against the *wh*-phrase and the *wh*-expletive showing up within the same minimal *wh*-clause.

24. Note that the probe [*TOP*] on C (needed to derive movement of categories other than DP*ₑₓₜ* to SpecC, see footnote 21) cannot be satisfied by *es*. The reason is that information-structure related features such as [TOP] are not lexical properties. That is, they must be added to elements in the numeration. Since *es*, being an expletive, is not part of the numeration, it can never bear [TOP]. Thus a derivation with [*TOP*] on C and no [TOP] in the numeration does not lead to Merge of *es* in SpecC. It follows that even under these conditions less local optimization cannot derive *es*-insertion.

25. It would, perhaps, be more appropriate to speak of vP (rather than VP) topicalization, provided that V always moves to v in English. We stick to the traditional term of VP-topicalization for expository reasons.

26. We ignore the interaction of the subject and T, leading to subject-verb agreement. Note in passing that the analysis of *do*-support in the context of VP-topicalization that is proposed below suggests that in English (as opposed to German; see section 4.3) the features for Φ-agreement are localized on T, not on C.

27. Although this comes close to postulating a separate feature hierarchy $F_1 > ... > F_n$ for every head, which would render optimization superfluous, it is not exactly the same. First, under such a theory every head of category X could have its features organized in a different hierarchy. Second, it would be possible in this theory to create 'mixed' hierarchies, with probes and structure building features alternating unpredictably within a hierarchy. Both possibilities are not an option under the present assumptions.

28. O_2 in T27 retains an unvalued feature [TENSE: □] on its fronted vP. We suppose that this is unproblematic and that the morphology can realize [TENSE: □] as an infinitival ending on the verb.

29. The same mechanism derives *do*-support in the context of VP-deletion provided the 'deleted' VP is structurally not present before LF (see Wasow 1972; Williams 1977). Other instances of *do*-support (e.g., in the context of negation or interrogatives) must receive a different analysis (see, e.g., Grimshaw 1997).

30. It is important to recall that since Merge of *do* in SpecT is accompanied by deletion of a selectional feature, it counts as a derivational step with respect to optimization.

References

Ackema, P. and Neeleman, A. (1998) Optimal questions. *Natural Language and Linguistic Theory* 16: 443–90.

Adger, D. (2003) *Core Syntax*. Oxford: Oxford University Press.

Béjar, S. and Řezáč, M. (2009) Cyclic Agree, *Linguistic Inquiry* 40 (1): 35–73.

Bierwisch, M. (1967) Syntactic features in morphology: General problems of so-called pronominal inflection in German. In O. Pritsak (ed.) *To Honour Roman Jakobson*, 239–70. The Hague and Paris: Mouton.

Broekhuis, H (2007) Does defective intervention exist? In B. Los and M. van Koppen (eds) *Linguistics in the Netherlands*, 49–61. Amsterdam: John Benjamins.

Broekhuis, H. and Dekkers, J. (2000) The Minimalist Program and Optimality Theory: Derivations and evaluation. In J. Dekkers, F. van der Leeuw and J van de Weijer (eds) *Optimality Theory: Phonology, Syntax and Acquisition*, 386–442. Oxford: Oxford University Press.

Chomsky, N. (1957) *Syntactic Structures*. The Hague: Mouton.

Chomsky, N. (1970) Remarks on nominalization. In R. Jacobs and P. Rosenbaum (eds) *Readings in English Transformational Grammar*, 184–221. Waltham MA: Ginn and Company.

Chomsky, N. (1973) Conditions on transformations. In S. Anderson and P. Kiparsky (eds) *A Festschrift for Morris Halle*, 232–86. New York: Holt, Reinhart and Winston.

Chomsky, N. (1993) A minimalist program for linguistic theory. In K. Hale and S. J. Keyser (eds) *The View from Building 20*, 1–52. Cambridge, MA: MIT Press.

Chomsky, N. (1995) *The Minimalist Program*. Cambridge, MA: MIT Press.

Chomsky, N. (2000) Minimalist inquiries: The framework. In R. Martin, D. Michaels and J. Uriagereka (eds) *Step by Step: Essays on Minimalist Syntax in Honor of Howard Lasnik*, 89–155. Cambridge, MA: MIT Press.

Chomsky, N. (2001) Derivation by phase. In M. Kenstowicz (ed.) *Ken Hale: A Life in Language*, 1–52. Cambridge, MA: MIT Press.

Chomsky, N. (2008) On phases. In R. Freidin, C. P. Otero and M. L. Zubizarreta (eds) *Foundational Issues in Linguistic Theory*, 133–66. Cambridge, MA: MIT Press.

Collins, C. (1994) Economy of derivation and the Generalized Proper Binding Condition. *Linguistic Inquiry* 25 (1): 45–61.

Collins, C. (1997) *Local Economy*. Cambridge, MA: MIT Press.

De Vries, M. (2005) Possessive relatives and (heavy) Pied-Piping. *Journal of Comparative Germanic Linguistics* 9 (1): 1–52.

Diesing, M. (1992) *Indefinites*. Cambridge, MA: MIT Press.

Epstein, S. D. and Seely T.D. (2002) Rule applications as cycles in a level-free syntax. In S. D. Epstein and T. D. Seely (eds) *Derivation and Explanation in the Minimalist Program*, 65–89. Oxford: Blackwell.

Erdmann, O. (1886) *Grundzüge der deutschen Syntax nach ihrer geschichtlichen Entwicklung*. Stuttgart: Cotta.

Fanselow, G. and Mahajan, A. (2000) Towards a Minimalist Theory of wh-expletives, wh-copying, and successive cyclicity. In U. Lutz, G. Müller and A. von Stechow (eds) *Wh-Scope Marking*, 195–230. Amsterdam: John Benjamins.

Fanselow, G. and Ćavar, D. (2001) Remarks on the economy of pronunciation. In G. Müller and W. Sternefeld (eds) *Competition in Syntax*, 107–150. Berlin and New York: Mouton de Gruyter.

Fischer, S. (2004) *Towards an Optimal Theory of Reflexivization*. PhD Thesis, Universität Tübingen.

Fischer, S. (2006) Zur Morphologie der deutschen Personalpronomina: eine Spaltungsanalyse. In G. Müller and J. Trommer (eds) *Subanalysis of Argument Encoding in Distributed Morphology: Linguistische Arbeitsberichte*, 84: 77–101. Leipzig: Universität Leipzig.

Frampton, J. and Gutman, S. (2000) Agreement is feature sharing. Ms., Northeastern University.

Frey, W. (2010) Zum *es* der Präsentativkonstruktion. Ms., Zentrum für allgemeine Sprachwissenschaft, Typologie und Universalienforschung, Berlin.

Georgi, D. and Salzmann, M. (2011) DP-internal double agreement is not double Agree: Consequences of Agree-based case assignment within DP. *Lingua* 121 (4): 2069–88.

Grewendorf, G. (1989) *Ergativity in German*. Dordrecht: Foris.

Grimshaw, J. (1997) Projection, heads, and optimality. *Linguistic Inquiry* 28: 373–422.

Haider, H. (1988) Zur Struktur der deutschen Nominalphrase. *Zeitschrift für Sprachwissenschaft* 7 (1): 32–59.

Haider, H. (1993) *Deutsche Syntax: Generativ*. Tübingen: Narr.

Halle, M. and Marantz, A. (1993) Distributed Morphology and the pieces of inflection. In K. Hale and S. J. Keyser (eds) *The View from Building 20*, 111–76. Cambridge, MA: MIT Press.

Halle, M. and Marantz, A. (1994) Some key features of Distributed Morphology. In A. Carnie and H. Harley (eds) *Papers on Phonology and Morphology 21*, 275–88. Cambridge, MA: MIT.

Heck, F. (2009) On certain properties of Pied-Piping, *Linguistic Inquiry* 40 (1): 75–111.

Heck, F. and Müller, G. (2000a) Repair-driven movement and the local optimization of derivations. Ms., Universität Stuttgart & IDS Mannheim.

Heck, F. and Müller, G. (2000b) Successive cyclicity, Long-distance superiority, and local optimization. In R. Billerey and B. D. Lillehaugen (eds) *Proccedings of WCCFL 19*, 218–31. Somerville, MA: Cascadilla Press.

Heck, F. and Cuartero, J. (2008) Long Distance Agreement in relative clauses. In F. Heck, G. Müller and J. Trommer (eds) *Varieties of Competition: Linguistische Arbeitsberichte 87*, 13–48. Leipzig: Universität Leipzig.

Höhle, T. (1982) Explikationen für 'normale Betonung' und 'normale Wortstellung'. In W. Abraham (ed.) *Satzglieder im Deutschen*, 75–153. Tübingen: Narr.

Holmberg, A. and Platzack, C. (1995) *The Role of Inflection in Scandinavian Syntax*. Oxford: Oxford University Press.

Hornstein, N. (2001) *Move: A Minimalist Theory of Construal*. Oxford: Blackwell.

Kibrik, A. (1979) Canonical ergativity and Daghestan languages. In F. Plank (ed.) *Ergativity*, 61–77. London: Academic Press.

Lahne, A. (2008) Excluding SVO in ergative languages. In F. Heck, G. Müller and J. Trommer (eds) *Varieties of Competition: Linguistische Arbeitsberichte 87*: 65–80. Leipzig: Universität Leipzig.

Legendre, G., Smolensky, P. and Wilson, C. (1998) When is less more? Faithfulness and minimal links in wh-chains. Cambridge, MA: MIT Press.

McCarthy, J. J. (2000) Harmonic serialism and parallelism. In M. Hirotani, A. Coetzee, N. Hall and J.-Y. Kim (eds) *Proceedings of NELS 30*, 501–24. Amherst, MA: GLSA.

McCarthy, J. J. (2009) *An Introduction to Harmonic Serialism*. Amherst, MA: University of Massachusetts.

McCarthy, J. J. and Prince, A. (2004) The emergence of the unmarked. In J. J. McCarthy (ed.) *Optimality Theory in Phonology: A Reader*, 483–94. Oxford: Blackwell.

Müller, G. (1997) Partial *wh*-movement and Optimality Theory. *The Linguistic Review* 14 (3): 249–306.

Müller, G. (1998) *Incomplete Category Fronting: A Derivational Approach to Remnant Movement in German*. Dordrecht: Kluwer.

Müller, G. (1999) Optionality in Optimality-Theoretic syntax. *GLOT International* 4 (5): 3–8.

Müller, G. (2000a) Das Pronominaladverb als Reparaturphänomen. *Linguistische Berichte* 182: 139–78.

Müller, G. (2000b) *Elemente der optimalitätstheoretischen Syntax*. Tübingen: Stauffenburg Verlag.

Müller, G. (2000c) Shape conservation and remnant movement. In M. Hirotani, A. Coetzee, N. Hall and J.-Y. Kim (eds) *Proceedings of NELS 30*, 525–39. Amherst, MA: GLSA.

Müller, G. (2004) Argument encoding and the order of elementary operations. Ms., IDS Mannheim.

Müller, G. (2010) On deriving CED effects from the PIC. *Linguistic Inquiry* 41 (1): 35–82.

Murasugi, K. (1992) *Crossing and Nested Paths: NP Movement in Accusative and Ergative Languages*. PhD thesis. Cambridge, MA: MIT Press.

Pesetsky, D. (1982) *Paths and Categories*. PhD thesis. MIT Cambridge, MA.

Pesetsky, D. (1989) *Language Particular Processes and the Earliness Principle*. Cambridge, MA: MIT Press.

Pesetsky, D. (1998) Optimality principles of sentence pronunciation. In P. Barbosa, D. Fox, P. Hagstrom, M. McGinnis and D. Pesetsky (eds) *Is the Best Good Enough? Optimality and Competition in Syntax*, 337–83. Cambridge, MA: MIT Press.

Platzack, C. (1987) The Scandinavian languages and the Null Subject Parameter. *Natural Language and Linguistic Theory* 5 (3): 377–402.

Pollard, C. and Sag, I. A. (1994) *Head Driven Phrase Structure Grammar*. Chicago, IL: University of Chicago Press.

Postal, P. (1970) On so-called pronouns in English. In R. A. Jacobs and P. S. Rosenbaum (eds) *Readings in English Transformational Grammar*, 56–82. Waltham, MA: Ginn and Company.

Prince, A. and Smolensky, P. (2004) Constraint interaction in Generative Grammar. In J. J. McCarthy (ed.) *Optimality Theory in Phonology: A Reader*, 3–71. Oxford: Blackwell.

Pullum, G. (1976) Sequential and simultaneous rule application in Spanish phonology, *Lingua* 38 (3–4): 221–62.

Richards, M. (2008) Quirky expletives. In R. d'Alessandro, G. H. Hrafnbjargarson and S. Fischer (eds) *Agreement Restrictions*, 181–213. Berlin: Mouton de Gruyter.

Rizzi, L. (2004) Locality and left periphery. In L. Rizzi (ed.) *The Structure of CP and IP: The Cartography of Syntactic Structures 2*. Oxford and New York: Oxford University Press.

Sigurðsson, H. Á. (2002) To be an oblique subject: Russian vs. Icelandic. *Natural Language and Linguistic Theory* 20 (4): 691–724.

Stechow, A. von and Susanne Uhmann (1986) Some remarks on Focus Projection. In W. Abraham and S. de Meij (eds) *Topic, Focus, and Configurationality*, 295–320. Amsterdam: John Benjamins.

Sternefeld, W. (2006) *Syntax: eine morphologisch motivierte generative Beschreibung des Deutschen*. Tübingen: Stauffenburg Verlag.

Svenonius, P. (1994) C-selection as feature-checking. *Studia Linguistica* 48 (2): 133–55.

Wasow, T. (1972) *Anaphoric Relations in English*. PhD thesis. MIT Cambridge, MA.

Wiese, B (2001) Pronominale Deklination. Ms., IDS Mannheim.

Williams, E. (1977) Discourse and Logical Form. *Linguistic Inquiry* 8 (1): 101–39.

Wunderlich, D. (1997) Der unterspezifizierte Artikel. In C. Dürscheid, K. H. Ramers and M. Schwarz (eds) *Sprache im Fokus* 47–55. Tübingen: Niemyer.

Zifonun, G. (2004) Dem Vater sein Hut: der Charme des Substandards und wie wir ihm gerecht werden. *Deutsche Sprache* 31 (S): 97–126.

7 Aspect splits and parasitic marking

Ellen Woolford[*]

ABSTRACT This chapter proposes both a formal and a functional theory of aspect splits, analyzing the ergative Case split in Hindi-Urdu, an agreement split in Yucatec Maya, and a split involving preposition insertion in Palauan. Aspect splits have a function: they mark aspect indirectly, by manipulating the distribution of an independent element to reflect aspect. The formal grammar produces aspect splits with contextually restricted faithfulness constraints within Optimality Theory. The combined effect of two such constraints produces a cross-cutting split, where the faithful environments are added together, as shown here in Nepali and Chontal.

KEYWORDS aspect split; ergative; contextual faithfulness; phases; preposition insertion; split agreement; marked objects

1. Introduction

The term *aspect split* is used in the typological literature to refer to a situation in which a grammatical element such as a particular Case or agreement pattern is restricted to one aspect. A well-known example occurs in Hindi-Urdu and related languages, where ergative Case is restricted to the perfective aspect. We see this in the minimal pair below from Butt and Deo (2005) where the external argument is marked with ergative Case only in the perfective aspect, as in (1), but not when the aspect is imperfective, as in (2):

(1) Ram-**ne**   gari   cala -ta   (hai).   [Hindi-Urdu]
     Ram-**ERGATIVE** car   drive-**PERFECTIVE** be.PRES
     'Ram has driven a/the car.'

(2) Ram gari cala -yi   (hai).
     Ram car   drive-**IMPERFECTIVE** be.PRES
     'Ram drives/is driving a car.'

---

*   Ellen Woolford, Department of Linguistics, University of Massachusetts, Amherst, MA 01003 USA.
    E-mail: woolford@linguist.umass.edu

Aspect splits are not limited to Case, nor do they have any inherent connection to ergativity. In this chapter, we will see aspect splits involving agreement (Yucatec Maya and Chontal), and preposition insertion (Palauan). Moreover, such splits are not limited to aspect; in this chapter we will examine cross-cutting splits involving negatives in Chontal and stage- versus individual-level predicates in Nepali.

There is no standard theory of aspect splits. The goal of this chapter is to develop a general theory of aspect splits, one which addresses not only the question of how such splits are produced in the formal grammar, but also the functional question of why they occur at all.

Taking the functional question first, I argue that aspect splits have an interesting and important function. Aspect splits provide an economical way of marking (or sometimes redundantly marking) aspect, without adding anything to the clause. Instead, they mark aspect indirectly, by blocking the use of an otherwise expected element in one aspect but preserving it in the other. I call this phenomenon *Parasitic Marking*, given that it involves manipulation of the distribution of an unrelated element (such as ergative Case) to indicate aspect. A real life example of Parasitic Marking is the 'shirts and skins' method that boys use to mark team membership when they play sports informally without uniforms: the boys on one team remove their shirts, while the boys on the other team keep their shirts on. The presence of an ordinary shirt thus comes to mark one team, while its absence marks the other team.

Parasitic marking in language is not as perfect as in the shirts and skins example, where the distribution of shirts is manipulated for both teams. In linguistic examples, it is as if one team removes their shirts, but the members of the other team do nothing (and may or may not happen to be wearing a shirt). That is, in parasitic marking in language, an element is blocked in one context (e.g. one aspect), but unaffected in the opposite context. For example, in Hindi, ergative Case is prohibited in the imperfective aspect, but the distribution of ergative subjects in the perfective aspect is unaffected.

Although not perfect, parasitic marking is cheap since it never involves adding anything. Instead it involves not using some element, often a marked element. Sometimes one aspect is only marked parasitically, with no aspect morpheme present, as we will see in Palauan. In other situations, parasitic marking of aspect occurs even if an aspect morpheme is present, and only redundantly marks aspect. This is what occurs in Hindi-Urdu.

Turning now to the formal grammar of aspect splits, I argue that the formal means for producing aspect splits already exists in the phonological literature. Although not called splits, similar contextual restrictions are observed in phonology. A well-known example is the situation in which [+voice] consonants are prohibited in codas but allowed in syllable onsets. This contextual restriction is analyzed by Beckman (1998) within Optimality Theory (Prince and Smolensky 1993, 2004) as involving positional faithfulness. The marked feature on consonants, [+voice], is protected in syllable onsets from the effect of a general constraint against [+voice] consonants that applies elsewhere. However, the contexts in which an element can be protected are not limited to positions, according to Smith (2001), and this is certainly true with respect to aspect splits. Thus I will use a more general term, *contextual faithfulness*, to refer to this phenomenon. In contextual faithfulness, a contextually restricted version of an independently motivated faithfulness constraint protects a marked element from an opposing markedness constraint that would otherwise eliminate it.[1]

The aspect split in Hindi-Urdu is produced by a contextually restricted version of the faithfulness constraint IDENT(ergative) which preserves an ergative Case feature once it has been licensed/valued on an argument by little v (Woolford 2001, 2007). Ergative Case is preserved in the perfective aspect in Hindi-Urdu, but is eliminated elsewhere by the general markedness constraint *ERGATIVE in favor of the less marked nominative Case (section 2). Supporting evidence for the contextual faithfulness approach comes from the additive nature of the overlapping split involving individual and stage-level predicates in Nepali, described in Butt and Poudel (2007) (section 3). In this section, we also see why other approaches such as contextual markedness and Case licensing parameters fail to predict the Nepali pattern. In section 4, we turn to a very different sort of aspect split that occurs in Palauan, where aspect is parasitically marked in terms of whether clitic doubling or preposition insertion is used in differential object marking constructions. Here the relevant contextual faithfulness constraint is a DEP constraint, prohibiting preposition insertion in perfective contexts. An aspect split involving agreement in Yucatec Maya is the topic of section 5. Here we see the effect of a contextually restricted version of the last of the three types of faithfulness constraints in OT, a Max constraint. The relevant Max constraint bars deletion of one of the two agreement series in the perfective aspect. This aspect split is produced at the syntax/PF interface, where the effect of the Max constraint is to require spell-out of the relevant agreement morpheme. A cross-cutting split in the related Mayan language, Chontal, involving positive versus negative contexts manifests an additive pattern, as predicted when the effects of faithfulness constraints are added together (section 6). Sections 7 and 8 are a discussion of some of the typological predictions of the contextual faithfulness approach to aspect splits proposed in this chapter.

2.   The ergative aspect split of Hindi-Urdu

In Hindi-Urdu and related languages, ergative Case is restricted to the perfective aspect (Bhatt 2005; Butt and Deo 2005), as shown in the examples above in (1) and (2) and in the similar minimal pair below in (3) and (4) from Bhatt (2005):

   (3) Rahul-**ne**   kitaab   par:h-ii   thii
         Rahul-ERGATIVE book.FEM   read-PERFECTIVE.fem be.PAST.FEM.SG
         'Rahul had read the book.'

   (4) Rahul   kitaab   par:h-taa   thaa
         Rahul.masc book.FEM   read-HABITUAL.MASC.SG be.PAST.MASC.SG
         'Rahul used to read a/the book.'

Because it is restricted to the perfective aspect, the presence of ergative Case in Hindi-Urdu is a reliable indicator of perfective aspect. This is an example of what I call parasitic marking, where manipulating the distribution of an unrelated element (ergative Case) can be used to indicate aspect. Now, aspect is also marked in Hindi-Urdu by an actual aspect morpheme suffixed to the verb, and one may wonder what the potential benefit is of redundantly marking aspect by means of the distribution of ergative Case. In addition to the general benefit of redundancy in insuring message transmission in noisy situations, it provides an early processing cue as to the presence of perfective aspect in this SOV language. Without this early cue, listeners would have to wait until the end of the clause to see the aspect morpheme suffixed to the verb.

The primary focus in this section is on the question of how the formal grammar produces this aspect split. The short answer to this question is with a contextually restricted version of the independently motivated faithfulness constraint that preserves the ergative Case. For this answer to be comprehensible, we need to see it in the context of the Optimality Theoretic approach to Case typology developed in Woolford (2001).

Let us begin with the basic question of why some languages use particular Cases such as the ergative Case and others do not. We cannot assume that this is simply the result of a lexical gap, e.g. the lack of an ergative Case morpheme in the lexicon. We know this because English has the nominative Case, although it has no morpheme in its lexicon to spell out this Case, and many languages have morphologically unmarked Cases whose identity can be deduced only from the agreement pattern. Instead, if a Case is not used in a language, the reason is to be found in the grammar of that language. In the Minimalist Program, for example, a possible answer to the question of why some languages have the ergative Case and others do not would be to posit a parameter such that the head that licenses ergative Case, little v, carries an ergative Case licensing feature in some languages, but not in others. However, we will see below that such an approach, which essentially turns ergative Case licensing 'on' or 'off' in a language, does not easily extend to languages with ergative splits where the ergative Case is available in some environments, but not others.

In the alternative approach to Case typology that I began to develop within Optimality Theory in Woolford (2001), there are no language-specific differences in the Case licensing abilities of heads.[2] The little v that theta-licenses external arguments always carries an ergative Case feature (Woolford 2006, 2007). However, all of the Cases that could potentially be licensed on any particular argument compete with each other. Two Cases compete to license an external argument, ergative licensed by little v and nominative licensed by T. This competition is regulated in the usual OT manner, by ranked markedness and faithfulness constraints. Ergative is a rather marked Case, and it will be ruled out by a markedness constraint, *ERGATIVE, unless it is protected by a higher ranked faithfulness constraint, IDENT (ergative).

(5) *ERGATIVE   No ergative Case.

(6) IDENT (ergative)   Preserve ergative Case

The idea that inherent Cases (e.g. dative, ergative) are licensed at a level before structural Cases, and cannot later be replaced by a structural Case, goes back at least to Chomsky (1981: 242); we keep this idea here, but change it from an inviolable assumption to a violable constraint.

The 'parameter' under this approach is the language particular ranking of these two constraints. In English, the markedness constraint is ranked higher, eliminating any instances of ergative Case. The opposite ranking produces an ergative language where all external arguments are marked with ergative Case.

(7)   *ERGATIVE >> IDENT (ergative)   [English ranking]

(8)   IDENT (ergative) >> *ERGATIVE   [Basque ranking]

With only these two constraints, this approach would only have the capacity to always preserve or always eliminate the ergative Case in a language. To capture the fact that languages such as Hindi-Urdu preserve the ergative Case in the perfective aspect, but prohibit it elsewhere, we need to add a contextually restricted faithfulness constraint, modeled after work in OT phonology (e.g. Beckman 1998). To capture phenomena such as the fact that consonant voice distinctions are preserved in onset position but not in coda position in some languages, Beckman argues that faithfulness constraints (but not markedness constraints) can come in contextually restricted versions. Building on this work, I propose that the aspect split in the ergative Case in Hindi is the result of a contextually restricted version of the IDENT (ergative) constraint, shown in (9):

(9)   IDENT $_{\text{perfective}}$ (ergative)   Preserve ergative Case in the perfective aspect.

This faithfulness constraint will have no effect if it is ranked below the unrestricted version of this constraint in (8), which preserves all ergatives, or below the markedness constraint in (7) that prohibits all ergatives. An aspect split will emerge only in the ranking in (10) where the contextually restricted faithfulness constraint is ranked above the markedness constraint which eliminates all (remaining) ergatives, which is in turn ranked above the unrestricted version of the faithfulness constraint that would otherwise preserve all ergatives:

(10)   Hindi-Urdu constraint ranking

IDENT $_{\text{perfective}}$ (ergative) >> *ERGATIVE >> IDENT (ergative)

These constraints apply in syntax (the CP phase), whose input is the earlier level where theta-marking and inherent Case licensing occurs (the argument structure level or vP phase).[3] As the tableau below shows, the high ranking contextually restricted faithfulness constraint eliminates the (b) candidate, which does not preserve an ergative Case from the input in this perfective context, leaving the (a) candidate which does preserve ergative as the winner (indicated here with →):

(11) An external argument in the perfective aspect in Hindi

input: DP-ergative perfective aspect	IDENT_{perfective} (ergative)	*ERGATIVE	IDENT (ergative)
→ a. DP-ergative		*	
b. DP-nominative	*!		*

In the imperfective aspect, shown in tableau (12) below, the contextually restricted constraint has no effect because the context is not perfective. Thus the next constraint, *ergative, applies and eliminates the (a) candidate containing an ergative Case. This leaves the (b) candidate with the nominative Case as the winning candidate.

(12) An external argument in the imperfective aspect in Hindi

input: DP-ergative imperfective aspect	IDENT_{perfective} (ergative)	*ERGATIVE	IDENT (ergative)
a. DP-ergative		*!	
→ b. DP-nominative			*

I maintain that UG will not allow a constraint that restricts the ergative Case to the imperfective aspect. This follows if constraints cannot make reference to the least marked element in a hierarchy (Gouskova 2003), and [+perfective] is more marked than [–perfective]. Alternatively, this would follow if perfective is a privative feature and there is no feature [–perfective] in the formal grammar.

Perfective is not the only context that can be referred to in a contextually restricted faithfulness constraint, as we see in Nepali in the next section.

3. Nepali and overlapping splits

Nepali also has the aspect split just described in Hindi-Urdu, but Nepali also has another, cross-cutting split involving ergative Case: Nepali preserves ergative Case with an individual-level predicate (Butt and Poudel 2007). In (13), the fact that Ram knows English is a property of Ram; not an event confined to a particular stage of time. With this individual-level predicate, Ram has ergative Case, even though the aspect is imperfective.

(13) Raam-**le**   (#aajaa)   angreji   jaan-da-cha.   [Nepali]
       Ram-**ERG**   (#today)   English   know-IMPF-NONPAST.3MASC.SG
       'Ram knows English (#today).'   (individual-level predicate)

In contrast, the event of Ram speaking in (14) will occur in one particular stage of time and thus the predicate is stage-level. Here Ram does not take ergative Case.

(14) Raam   (aajaa)   angreji   bol-da-cha.
      Ram   today   English   speak-IMPF-NONPAST.3MASC.SG
      'Ram will speak English (today).' (stage-level)   (Butt and Poudel 2007 (16))

Thus Nepali has two overlapping ergative splits and the effects of these splits are additive, in that ergative Case is preserved in both contexts, perfective aspect and with individual-level predicates:

(15) Additive pattern of overlapping ergative splits in Nepali

	Perfective aspect	Imperfective aspect
Individual-level	Ergative	Ergative
Stage-level	Ergative	**No ergative**

This additive pattern is just what we expect if such splits are the result of contextually restricted faithfulness constraints. These constraints specify a context in which ergative Case must be preserved. When two such constraints are active, as in Nepali, we expect preservation in both contexts. In Nepali, the constraint we saw above in Hindi-Urdu preserving ergative Case in the perfective is active, plus a similar constraint preserving ergative Case in clauses with individual-level predicates:

(16) IDENT$_{\text{perfective}}$ (ergative)   Preserve ergative Case in the perfective aspect.

(17) IDENT$_{\text{individual-level predicate}}$ (ergative)   Preserve ergative Case with individual-level
                                                            predicates.

As noted above for Hindi-Urdu, these contextually restricted faithfulness constraints will not produce the overlapping split of Nepali in (15) unless both constraints are ranked above *ERGATIVE, which is in turn ranked above the contextually unrestricted version of the faithfulness constraint:

(18) Nepali constraint ranking

      IDENT$_{\text{perfective}}$ (ergative), IDENT$_{\text{ind-level pred}}$ (ergative) >> *ERGATIVE >> IDENT (ergative)

The constraint preserving ergative in the perfective applies as shown above in section 2 in Hindi-Urdu. The effect of the constraint preserving ergative with individual-level predicates is similar, eliminating candidate (b) where the ergative in the input is replaced by a nominative, as shown in (19):

(19) An individual-level predicate in Nepali

input: DP-ergative ind-level predicate imperfective aspect	IDENT$_{ind\text{-}level\ pred}$ (erg)	IDENT$_{perfective}$ (erg)	*ERG	IDENT (erg)
→ a. DP-ergative			*	
b. DP-nominative	*!			*

In the perfective aspect, candidate (b) would violate both of these IDENT constraints. The only context in which neither constraint preserves the ergative Case is one with a stage-level predicate in the imperfect aspect. Here, the lower constraint, *ERGATIVE, makes the decision by eliminating the (a) candidate containing an ergative Case. This leaves the (b) candidate with nominative Case as the winner.

(20) A stage-level predicate in the imperfective aspect in Nepali

input: DP-ergative imperfective aspect Stage-level predicate	IDENT$_{ind\text{-}level\ pred}$(ergative) IDENT$_{perfective}$(ergative)	*ERGATIVE	IDENT(ergative)
a. DP-ergative		*!	
→ b. DP-nominative			*

3.1 Why a contextually restricted markedness approach fails for Nepali

An alternative OT approach which places the context restriction on the markedness constraint, *ERGATIVE, instead of on the faithfulness constraint, IDENT (ergative), would work for Hindi-Urdu, but in this section we will see why such an approach would fail for Nepali. In Nepali, using two contextually restricted markedness constraints would make the wrong prediction for the distribution of the ergative Case. The subtractive pattern produced by *ERGATIVE/STAGE-LEVEL PREDICATE plus *ERGATIVE/PERFECTIVE is shown in (21) below. The prediction is that ergative Case would only survive in clauses with individual predicates in the perfective aspect:

(21) *Incorrect* subtractive prediction of two contextually restricted markedness constraints for Nepali

	Perfective aspect	Imperfective aspect
Individual-level	Ergative	**No ergative**
Stage-level	**No ergative**	**No ergative**

We see the problem when we contrast this incorrect prediction with the actual Nepali pattern repeated below:

(22)   Actual pattern of overlapping additive ergative splits in Nepali

	Perfective aspect	imperfective aspect
Individual-level	Ergative	Ergative
Stage-level	Ergative	**No ergative**

The failure of contextual markedness here supports the contention of Bechman (1998) that only faithfulness constraints, and not markedness constrants, can be restricted to special contexts.

In the next section, we will see that a non-OT approach involving restricting the licensing of the ergative Case fails for the same reason: it *incorrectly* predicts a *reduction* of the contexts in which ergative Case can appear when two such restrictions are combined.

3.2   Against a restricted licensing approach to Nepali

In this section, we explore and reject another alternative approach to Nepali. The basic premise of this approach is the popular idea that if a language does not use a particular Case, it is because that language cannot *license* that Case. Such an approach is proposed in Davison (2004) to account for the aspect split in Hindi. Davison proposes that it is the aspect head which licenses the ergative Case in Hindi, and only if that head carries the [+perfective] feature.[4] Such an approach essentially introduces parameters governing Case licensing, since ergative languages without an aspect split can license the ergative Case in either aspect. The problem with a parameterized Case licensing approach emerges when we try to extend it to the overlapping splits in Nepali. Since Nepali manifests the same aspect split that we find in Hindi, we expect Davison's restriction to hold for Nepali:

(23)   Hindi: ergative is only licensed by [+perfective] aspect   (Davison 2004)

But this restriction does not hold in Nepali, since the ergative Case is also licensed in the *imperfective* aspect in Nepali when the predicate is individual-level as we saw above in (22), repeated below:

(24)   Additive pattern of ergative splits in Nepali

	Perfective aspect	Imperfective aspect
Individual-level	Ergative	Ergative
Stage-level	Ergative	**No ergative**

Under a restricted licensing approach, it would be possible to add a feature that must be present in order to license the ergative Case. For example, ergative Case licensing might require a head that carries both the [+perfective] feature and the [+individual level] feature. The problem is that this would only have the effect of further *reducing* the contexts in which the ergative can be licensed, incorrectly predicting the same reduced pattern that the contextual markedness approach produced, shown above in (21). Instead, what we need in order to account for the additive pattern in Nepali is a way of *expanding* the contexts in which the ergative is licensed, compared to Hindi. Under a parameterized licensing approach, this would require a disjunctive Case licensing parameter, allowing the ergative Case to be licensed by the perfective aspect AND/OR by a stage-level predicate in Nepali. While such a pattern is unexpected when parameters are involved, it is just what we expect when faithfulness constraints are involved, as we saw above.

To fully see the advantage of the idea that aspect splits result from contextual faithfulness constraints, we need to consider other types of splits which do not involve the ergative Case. In the next section we turn to Palauan, a language which manifests a very different sort of aspect split involving the possibility of preposition insertion.

4.   The aspect split in marked objects in Palauan

Palauan (Austronesian) also manifests an aspect split between the perfective and imperfective aspect; but the Palauan aspect split is very different from what we see in Hindi and Nepali. The Palauan aspect split involves two different ways of marking 'marked objects': with an inserted preposition in the imperfective aspect, but clitic doubling in the perfective aspect. Marked objects or differential object marking is a well-known typological phenomenon wherein objects with particular features (e.g. specific, human) are 'marked' in some way, for example with Case, agreement, a clitic or an inserted preposition (Comrie 1989; Woolford 1995; Aissen 2003).[5]

In Palauan, human objects must be marked, but there is an aspect split as to how they are marked. In the perfective aspect, human objects are clitic doubled.[6] The pronominal clitic is suffixed to the verb:

(25)   Ak   mils-**terir**   a retede el sensei.   [perfective aspect]
       I   saw-**3PL.CLITIC**   three   teacher
       'I saw three teachers.'   (Josephs 1975: 43)

In contrast, in the imperfective aspect, human objects are marked with an inserted preposition:[7]

(26)   A sensei   a mengelebed   **er**   a rengalek.   [imperfective aspect]
       teacher   hit   **P**   children
       'The teacher is hitting the children.'   (Georgopoulos 1991: 35 (27a))

The same aspect split pattern occurs with objects that are individuated (specific and singular), even if they are not human (Georgopoulos 1991). In the perfective aspect, such objects are marked by clitic doubling:[8]

(27) Te-'illebed-**ii**   a bilis   a rengalek.   [perfective aspect]
      3p-hit **-3sg.clitic**   dog   children
      'The kids hit the dog.'   (Georgopoulos 1991: 30 (15a))

In the imperfective aspect, such objects are marked by an inserted preposition:[9]

(28) Ng-milengelebed   er   a bilis.   [imperfective aspect]
      3s- imperf -hit   P   dog
      'S/he hit the dog.'   (Georgopoulos 1991: 29 (14a))

In contrast, objects that are neither human nor individuated (specific and singular) remain 'unmarked':

(29) Ng-milengelebed   a bilis.   [imperfective aspect]
      3s-imperf.hit   dog
      'He/she hit a dog /the dogs /some dogs.'   (Georgopoulos 1991: 29 (14b))

The analysis of this aspect split proposed here captures the idea that preposition insertion is a 'last resort' operation, in that when it is not needed, it does not occur. Any insertion violates a dep constraint. dep constraints, developed in OT phonology (McCarthy and Prince 1995), require that the output depend on the input; nothing can be inserted in the output that is not already present in the input. dep constraints are another kind of faithfulness constraint. Preposition insertion violates the dep constraint, dep (P).

(30) dep(P)   No preposition insertion.
               A preposition in the output must be present in the input.

However, what we need for Palauan is a contextually restricted version of this dep constraint, a version that blocks preposition insertion only in the perfective aspect

(31) $\mathrm{DEP}_{\mathrm{perfective}}(\mathrm{P})$ No preposition insertion in the perfective aspect.

This dep constraint prevents preposition insertion in the perfective aspect. Note that base generated prepositions are not affected by this dep constraint because the constraint does not block prepositions per se, but only the insertion of a preposition in the perfective aspect. Base-generated prepositions occur in both aspects in Palauan. In the following example, we see a base-generated preposition on the locative in a clause with perfective aspect:

(32) Ak mils-a   a Droteo   er   a party.   [perfective]
      I   saw-3sg.clitic   Droteo   at   party.
      'I saw Droteo at the party.'   (Josephs 1975: 324)

Preposition insertion is not used to mark the human object in the above example because preposition insertion is prohibited in the perfective aspect in Palauan. Instead, the human object is clitic doubled. We also see the contrast between base generated and inserted prepositions in the pair of examples below:

(33) Ak ousbech er a bilas er a klukuk.   [imperfective aspect]
      I   need   P   boat   P   tomorrow
      'I need the boat tomorrow.'   (Josephs 1975: 49)

(34) Ak ousbech a bilas er a klukuk.
      I   need   boat   P   tomorrow
      'I need a boat /the boats tomorrow.   (Josephs 1975: 49)

Now we turn to the question of why clitic doubling is not also used to 'mark' objects in the imperfective aspect. Here, all we need is the independently motivated markedness constraint against clitics, *CLITIC (e.g. Bresnan 2001). We do not need a contextually restricted version of this markedness constraint because the pattern falls out of the constraint ranking. The intuitive idea is that in Palauan, preposition insertion is actually the preferred way of 'marking' an object (and we set this preference by ranking *CLITIC above DEP(P)), but preposition insertion is prohibited in the perfective aspect.

To force object marking in Palauan despite violating either *CLITIC or DEP(P), we need a higher constraint that requires an object with 'marked' features to be 'marked'. I will refer to such constraints for our purposes here simply as MARK constraints:

(35) MARK (human)   A human object must be 'marked'.

(36) MARK (individuated) An object that is both specific and singular must be 'marked'.

The aspect split in how objects are marked in Palauan results from the following ranking where the two MARK constraints are at the top:

(37) Palauan constraint ranking
      MARK (human), MARK (individuated) >> DEP$_{perfective}$(P) >> *CLITIC >> DEP(P)

In the perfective aspect, the contextually restricted DEP constraint blocks preposition insertion, leaving clitic doubling as the only option for marking an object. In the imperfective aspect, that constraint has no effect. Instead, the ranking of *CLITIC above the unrestricted DEP(P) constraint in (37) has the effect of making it worse to clitic double an object than to 'mark' it by preposition insertion in the imperfect aspect.

Let us look at some tableaux to see how these constraints in this ranking produce the Palauan pattern. Let us begin with a human object in the perfective aspect. A human object must be 'marked' in some way in order to obey MARK (human). The tableau in (38) compares candidate (a) where the object remains unmarked, candidate (b) with an inserted preposition and candidate (c) with clitic doubling. Candidate (a) is eliminated because its unmarked human object violates MARK(HUMAN). In the perfective aspect, insertion of a preposition in candidate (b) is barred by DEP_{perfective}(P), which prohibits preposition insertion in the perfective aspect. This leaves candidate (c) as the winner:

(38) Pattern for a human object in the perfective aspect

input: V DP perfective [+human]	MARK(human)	DEP$_{perfective}$ (P)	*CLITIC	DEP(P)
a. V DP	*!			
b. V [P DP]		*!		*
→ c. V-cl DP			*	

In the imperfective aspect, the MARK constraint again eliminates candidate (a) with the unmarked human object. Here the next constraint, DEP$_{perfective}$(P), has no effect. The decision thus passes to the next constraint, *CLITIC, which rules out candidate (c) where the object is marked by clitic doubling. This leaves candidate (b) with an inserted preposition as the winner.

(39) Pattern for human objects in the imperfective aspect

input: V DP imperfective [+human]	MARK(human)	DEP$_{perfective}$(P)	*CLITIC	DEP(P)
a. V DP	*!			
→ b. V [P DP]				*
c. V-cl DP			*!	

The tableaux for non-human, but individuated (specific and singular) objects would be the same, except that the MARK(INDIVIDUATED) constraint would rule out the (a) candidate. In clauses where the object is neither human nor individuated, the two mark constraints have no effect. The tableau in (40) shows that regardless of the aspect, the (a) candidate wins, because *CLITIC rules out candidate (c) because of its clitic and DEP(P) (or DEP$_{perfective}$(P) in the perfective aspect) rules out candidate (b) because of its inserted preposition.

(40) Pattern for non-human, non-individuated objects

input: V DP [-human],[-ind]	MARK(human) MARK(INDIVID)	DEP$_{perfective}$(P)	*CLITIC	DEP(P)
→ a. V DP				
b. V [P DP]				*!
c. V-cl DP			*!	

The aspect split in Palauan is like the aspect split in Hindi in that both result from contextually restricted versions of an independently motivated faithfulness constraint where the restricting context is [+perfective]. The languages differ in which type of faithfulness constraint is involved, IDENT or DEP, and what these constraints apply to, ergative Case or prepositions.

Moving from the formal to the functional, this aspect split functions to parasitically mark aspect in Palauan. Preposition insertion redundantly marks aspect in the imperfective aspect. Because Palauan has no overt perfective aspect morpheme, clitic doubling is the *only* overt mark of perfective aspect in Palauan (Georgopoulos 1991: 25).

5.   Yucatec Maya

In this section, we turn to an aspect split involving agreement in Yucatec Maya. This split is unusual because it is limited to intransitive clauses (Nida and Romero 1950; Bricker 1981; Krämer and Wunderlich 1999; Bohnemeyer 2004). In transitive clauses, the cross-referencing pattern is identical in the two aspects: the subject of a transitive clause is cross-referenced with an agreement series traditionally labeled 'Set A', while the object is cross-referenced with the suffixing series traditionally labeled 'Set B':[10]

(41) Táan uy-   il -ik -en   [imperfective aspect]
     DUR   3rdSETA- see-IMPERFECTIVE-1stSETB
     'He is seeing me.'   (Bricker 1981 (1))

(42) T-   inw-   il- ah   -eč   [perfective aspect]
     COMPL-1stSETA- see-PERFECTIVE   -2ndSETB
     'I saw you.'   (Bricker 1981 (2))

The cross-referencing pattern in intransitive clauses shows the aspect split. Intransitive subjects are cross-referenced with Set A in the imperfective aspect, but with Set B in the perfective aspect:

(43) Táan in-   k'uč   -ul.   [imperfective aspect]
     DUR   1stSETA- arrive   -IMPERFECTIVE
     'I am arriving'   (Bricker 1981 (4))

(44) H-   k'uč   -eč   [perfective aspect]
     COMPL-arrive   -2ndSETB
     'You arrived.'   (Bricker 1981 (4))

This aspect split is not limited to unaccusatives, but also occurs with intransitive verbs that take an agentive subject (external argument):

(45) K-   u-   meyah   [imperfective aspect]
     IMPERF-3rdSETA- work
     'He works.'   Bohnemeyer 2004 (3a))

(46) H-   meyah -nah   -ih   [perfective aspect]
      PERF-   work   -COMPLETIVE -3rdSGSETB
      'He worked.'   (Bohnemeyer 2004 (3b))

In the account presented here, I identify Set A as ordinary subject agreement and Set B as a series of pronominal clitics (head clitics in the sense of Marantz (1988), which adjoin to V in syntax). In syntax, these forms are only bundles of features; the decision as to which features or feature bundles to spell out (by morpheme insertion) is made at the syntax/PF interface. I propose that both are generated in syntax even in intransitive clauses. Both must be spelled out in a transitive clause because they encode the features of different arguments. In intransitive clauses, the two series cross-reference the same argument. Since only one set of cross-referencing features needs to be spelled out, the choice of which to spell out at PF is available to be manipulated by contextual faithfulness to parasitically mark aspect.

5.1   Background on cross-referencing in OT syntax

The idea that different cross-referencing series compete with each other is proposed in earlier work in Optimality Theory in various forms. In Legendre and Rood (1992), violable mapping constraints compete. In Bresnan (2001), clitics and affixes compete to realize an argument. In Woolford (2003), I argue that languages differ with respect to whether they prefer to use agreement or pronominal clitics to cross-reference arguments; this preference is determined by the relative ranking of the two marked-ness constraints prohibiting these elements:

(47) *CLITIC No pronominal clitics.   (Bresnan 2001)

(48) *AGR   No agreement   (cf. Bresnan's *affix)

(49) Constraint Ranking and Cross-referencing Preference (from Woolford 2003)
      (a) *CLITIC >> *AGR   [language prefers to use agreement]
      (b) *AGR >> *CLITIC   [language prefers to use a clitic]

I revise this proposal slightly here, in order to maintain a more restrictive theory under which there is a universally fixed ranking of *CLITIC >> *AGR because clitics are the more marked cross-referencing form.[11] I assume here that both clitics and agreement are generated in syntax in some languages, and that what is actually responsible for the fact that some languages prefer to use clitics is a faithfulness constraint that preserves clitics at the syntax/PF interface, MAX (CLITIC). Max constraints are faithfulness constraints that block the deletion of an element (McCarthy and Prince 1995). At the syntax/PF interface, when applied to morphemes, they have the effect of requiring a morpheme to be spelled-out.[12]

(50) MAX(CLITIC)   Spell-out pronominal clitics.

When ranked above *CLITIC, MAX(CLITIC) will force all pronominal clitics from syntax to be spelled out at PF:

(51) Revised constraint ranking and cross-referencing preference
      (a) *CLITIC >> *AGR >> MAX(CLITIC)   [language prefers to use agreement]
      (b) MAX(CLITIC) >> *CLITIC >>*AGR   [language prefers to use a clitic]

As in Woolford (2003), there is a constraint, XRef, which requires that each argument be cross-referenced. When this constraint applies at PF, it requires that a cross-referencing morpheme be spelled out for each argument. XRef is violable, like the other constraints discussed here. If it is ranked above both *CLITIC and *AGR, all arguments will be cross-referenced; if it is ranked below *CLITIC, no argument will be cross-referenced by a pronominal clitic, and if it is ranked below both of these markedness constraints, no argument will be cross-referenced at all.

Although some languages allow clitic clusters, other languages limit pronominal clitics to one per clause, for example Chichewa (Bresnan and Mchombo 1986). In Woolford (2003), I show that a language that has subject agreement, but prefers to use clitics will use a clitic to cross-reference intransitive subjects. With a limit of one clitic per clause, transitive clauses will have the more familiar pattern where agreement cross-references the subject and a clitic is used to cross-reference the object. That pattern is characteristic of Selayarese and of many Mayan languages, where the pronominal clitic series is unspecified for Case, and can potentially cross-reference any argument, including the subject. Let us look at a tableau showing the competition for spelling out a cross-referencing form for an intransitive in the typical Mayan language. The constraint ranking for most Mayan languages is as in (52):

(52) XRef, MAX(CLITIC) >> *CLITIC >>*AGR

I will assume here that in syntax, both agreement (Set A) and one pronominal clitic (Set B) are always generated in Mayan languages, and when there is only one argument present, they both cross-reference that same argument.[13] This is the input to the PF competition to determine which of these cross-referencing forms is spelled out. The top two constraints in tableau (53) do not conflict and are therefore treated here as tied in the ranking. XRef eliminates the candidate in (d) where no cross-referencing element is spelled out for the intransitive subject. MAX(CLITIC) eliminates that candidate and also the one in (b) where the pronominal clitic from syntax is not spelled out. The remaining candidates (a) and (c) tie on the next lower constraint, *CLITIC, and thus neither is eliminated at this point. The decision thus passes to the lower ranked *AGREE constraint, which eliminates the (a) candidate, leaving the (c) candidate with just a pronominal clitic as the winner.[14]

(53) Intransitives in many Mayan languages

Input: agr-verb-clitic	XRef	MAX(CLITIC)	*CLITIC	*AGREE
a. agr-verb-clitic			*	*!
b. agr-verb		*!		*
→ c. verb-clitic			*	
d. verb	*!	*!		

In transitive clauses, the cross-referencing pattern in Mayan languages has a Set A form cross-referencing the subject (which I assume is agreement) and a Set B form cross-referencing the object (which I assume is a pronominal clitic). I assume here that Mayan languages have only subject agreement, and no true object agreement (as opposed to object clitics) and thus I will not include candidates with true object agreement in the tableaux.[15] Under the above constraint ranking, where the high ranking MAX-(CLITIC) requires the spell out of all pronominal clitics generated in syntax, we might expect a candidate with two clitics to win, one cross-referencing each argument in a transitive clause. However, Yucatec Maya is one of the languages mentioned above where pronominal clitics are limited to one per clause, and I will include in the tableaux only candidates with one clitic.[16] Considering only the four candidates in tableau (54) below, XRef eliminates every candidate except the one in (a) with both agreement and a clitic, because the other candidates do not cross-reference both arguments:

(54) Transitives in Mayan languages

Input: agr-verb-clitic	XRef	MAX(CLITIC)	*CLITIC	*AGREE
→ a. agr-verb-clitic			*	*
b. agr-verb	*!	*!		*
c. verb-clitic	*!		*	
d. verb	**!	*!		

This tableau is also correct for Yucatec Maya. However, intransitives in Yucatec Maya are different, manifesting an aspect split, to which we now turn.

5.2   An account of the aspect split in Yucatec Maya

The aspect split in Yucatec Maya is produced at the syntax/PF interface by a contextually restricted version of the MAX(CLITIC) constraint defined above. This contextually restricted version requires the spell-out of pronominal clitics in the perfective aspect:

(55) MAX$_{perfective}$ (CLITIC)   Spell out pronominal clitics in the perfective aspect.

In the following constraint ranking, applying at the syntax/PF interface, this constraint produces the aspect split in Yucatec Maya by forcing spell out of the clitic in the perfective aspect, but not in the imperfective:

(56) Yucatec Maya constraint ranking[17]
        XRef, MAX$_{perfective}$ (CLITIC) >> *CLITIC >> *AGREE >> MAX(clitic)

XRef requires each argument to be cross-referenced in the surface pattern. MAX$_{perfective}$ (CLITIC) requires that the pronominal clitic (Set B form) be spelled out at PF. Nothing other than XRef requires agreement (Set A) to be spelled out.

The tableau below in (57) shows the competition at spell-out for an intransitive in Yucatec Maya. The input from syntax has agreement and a pronominal clitic, both cross-referencing the subject. Only one of these cross referencing elements is needed to satisfy XRef, but XRef is not what eliminates this redundancy. As the tableau below shows, candidates (a) through (c) all satisfy XRef; XRef eliminates only candidate (d) where neither agreement nor the clitic is spelled out. We start in this tableau with what happens in the imperfective aspect. Here, the contextual faithfulness constraint, MAX-$_{perfective}$ (CLITIC) has no effect, and thus the decision is made by the next lower constraint, *CLITIC, which eliminates candidates (a) and (c) which contain a pronominal clitic. This leaves candidate (b), with just agreement, as the winner.

(57) Intransitives in the imperfective aspect

Input: agr-verb-clitic imperfective	XRef	MAX-PERF (CLITIC)	*CLITIC	*AGR	MAX(CL)
a. agr-verb-clitic			*!	*	
→ b. agr-verb				*	*
c. verb-clitic			*!		
d. verb	*!				*

This is why Yucatec Maya does not spell-out a clitic in intransitives in the imperfective aspect.

In the perfective aspect, shown in the tableau below, the contextually restricted Max constraint, MAX-$_{perfective}$ (CLITIC) alters the outcome. It eliminates candidates (b) and (d) because they do not spell out the pronominal clitic. The remaining candidates (a) and (c), which both have clitics, tie with respect to the next lower constraint, *CLITIC. The decision thus passes down to *AGREE, which eliminates the (a) candidate because it has agreement. This leaves the (c) candidate with just a pronominal clitic as the winner.

(58)   Intransitives in the perfective aspect

Input: agr-verb-clitic perfective aspect	XRef	MAX-$_{perf}$(CLITIC)	*CLITIC	*AGR	MAX(CL)
a. agr-verb-clitic			*	*!	
b. agr-verb		*!		*	*
→ c. verb-clitic			*		
d. verb	*!	*!			*

In the next section, we see this same aspect split co-occurring with a cross-cutting negative split in the Mayan language Chontal.

6.   A negative split in the related language Chontal

Chontal is a related Mayan language that manifests the same aspect split in intransitives that Yucatec Maya has, in that agreement (Set A) is not used in the perfective aspect. However, Chontal also has a cross-cutting negative split, which is also limited to intransitive clauses (Knowles-Berry 1987). This negative split is shown in the following pairs of examples in the imperfective aspect, where agreement is used in the positive form, but a clitic is used in the negative:

(59)   Kɨ   t   -e.   [Chontal]
       1stAGR come -IMPEFECTIVE
       'I come.'   (Knowles-Berry 1987 (67))

(60)   Mač   ʔu   t   -on.
       neg   particle come   -1stCL
       'I don't come.'   (Knowles-Berry 1987 (68))

(61)   Kɨ   wan –e
       1stagr jump-IMPERFECTIVE
       'I jump.'   (Knowles-Berry 1987 (63))

(62)   Mač   ʔu   wan   -on.
       NEG   particle jump   -1stCL
       'I don't jump.'   (Knowles-Berry 1987 (65))

The cross-cutting pattern that the two agreement splits produce together in Chontal is shown in the table below. Agreement (Set A) is reduced in intransitives to positive contexts in the imperfective aspect:

(63)   The intransitive pattern in Chontal

	Positive	Negative
Perfective	syntactic clitic	syntactic clitic
Imperfective	agreement	syntactic clitic

This intransitive pattern is the result of the additive effect of the following two contextually restricted MAX constraints that preserve syntactic clitics at the syntax/ PF interface. One preserves clitics in the perfective aspect while the other preserves pronominal clitics in negative clauses:

(64)   MAX$_{perfective}$ (CLITIC)   Spell out pronominal clitics in the perfective aspect.

(65)   MAX$_{negative}$ (CLITIC)   Spell out pronominal clitics in negative clauses.

The two MAX constraints that preserve clitics in Chontal are both ranked above the markedness constraint *CLITIC. Like Yucatec Maya, Chontal requires all arguments to be cross-referenced; and the high ranked XRef constraint enforces this.

(66)   Chontal constraint ranking
       XRef, MAX$_{perfective}$ (CLITIC), MAX$_{negative}$ (CLITIC) >> *CLITIC >> *AGR

The tableau in (67) below shows the competition in negative clauses in the imperfective aspect. XRef eliminates candidate (d) with no cross-referencing morpheme. Since the aspect is imperfective, the MAX$_{perfective}$ (CLITIC) constraint does nothing. The MAX$_{negative}$ (CLITIC) constraint eliminates candidate (b) because it has no clitic. This leaves candidates (a) and (c) in the running, and these tie on the next constraint, *CLITIC. The decision passes down to *AGREE, which eliminates candidate (a) because it has agreement. This leaves candidate (c) with just a clitic as the winner.

(67) Chontal intransitives (negative, imperfective aspect)

input: neg agr-verb-clitic imperfective	XRef	MAX$_{perf}$(CL)	MAX$_{neg}$ (CL)	*CL	*AGR
a. neg agr-verb-clitic				*	*!
b. neg agr-verb			*!		*
→ c. neg verb-clitic				*	
d. neg verb	*!		*!		

The tableau for a negative intransitive in the perfective aspect is similar, except that the MAX$_{perfective}$ (CLITIC) constraint also rules out candidates (b) and (d). This does not alter the outcome:

(68) Chontal intransitives (negative, perfective aspect)

input: neg agr-verb-clitic perfective	XRef	MAX$_{perf}$(CL)	MAX$_{neg}$(CL)	*CL	*AGR
a. neg agr-verb-clitic				*	*!
b. neg agr-verb		*!	*!		*
→ c. neg verb-clitic				*	
d. neg verb	*!	*!	*!		

It is only in positive intransitives in the imperfective aspect that neither of these MAX constraints applies. Instead, the decision is made by the lower ranked *CLITIC, which eliminates the candidates with a syntactic clitic in (a) and (c), leaving the candidate in (b) with agreement as the winner:

(69) Chontal intransitives (positive, imperfective aspect)

input: agr-verb-clitic imperfective	XRef	MAX$_{perf}$(CL)	MAX$_{neg}$(CL)	*CL	*AGR
a. agr-verb-clitic				*!	*
→ b. agr-verb					*
c. verb-clitic				*!	
d. verb	*!				

The competition in transitives in Chontal is exactly as in Yucatec Maya. Because there are two arguments to cross-reference, and only two cross-referencing forms available, agreement (restricted to subjects) and a pronominal clitic (restricted to one per clause), there is no choice. Only the candidate in (a) above, with subject agreement and an object clitic can satisfy XRef.

In the next section, we consider how these bits of information might be conceived of by someone used to thinking about cross-linguistic differences in terms of parameters.

7. Parameters and constraint ranking

For those who work in the Minimalist Program, one can think of the information about constraint ranking as parameters that set the priority relations among economy constraints. What children learn when they acquire language, according to the OT approach, is bits of information about constraint ranking. Under this view, the parameters that a child must set when learning Chontal are the relative ranking of the following pairs of constraints:

(70) Parameter settings of crucial priority relations among constraints in Chontal

*CLITIC >> *AGREE

XRef >> *CLITIC

MAX_{perf} (CL) >> *CLITIC

MAX_{neg} (CL) >> *CLITIC

Using this method of expressing the parameter settings makes it easy to compare the settings for complex patterns in related languages. For example, the parameter settings for Yucatec Maya are just like those for Chontal, except that MAX_{neg}(CLITIC) is ranked below *CLITIC instead of above it.

8. The limits of parasitic marking

Parasitic marking is possible only when the grammar independently allows a choice of elements in a particular context. Parasitic marking cannot add anything; it can only manipulate the distribution of independently available elements, so that one element comes to mark one context, e.g. perfective aspect, while another element marks the opposite context. In Hindi, parasitic marking manipulates the choice between ergative and nominative Case for a subject, in order to (redundantly) mark aspect. With verbs that do not license ergative Case, such parasitic marking is impossible. In Palauan, parasitic marking marks aspect by manipulating the choice between two ways to 'mark' an object with marked features. However, in clauses where there is no object, or the object has unmarked features, parasitic marking of aspect is not possible. In Yucatec Maya, parasitic marking manipulates the choice between cross-referencing a subject with agreement or a pronominal clitic in intransitives, and the presence of agreement (Set A) reliably indicates the imperfective aspect, while the presence of a pronominal clitic (Set B) reliably indicates the perfective aspect. However, parasitic marking of aspect does not occur in transitive clauses in Yucatec Maya because other constraints eliminate the possibility of using a clitic to cross-reference the subject.

If parasitic marking is formally implemented by contextually restricted faithfulness constraints, as argued here, the types that occur are limited by the types of such constraints that are available in UG. We have seen in this chapter an example of a contextually restricted version of all three of the types of faithfulness constraints in OT, IDENT, DEP and MAX. The question now is what range of contexts such faithfulness constraints can refer to. Since this chapter has focused on aspect splits, there has been no attempt to explore the full range of such contexts. However, the restricting contexts in this chapter are limited to properties of the verb (individual-level predicate) and the functional heads projected above the verb (aspect and neg).[18]

9. Conclusion

This chapter proposes both a formal and a functional account of aspect splits, demonstrating this theory with respect to the ergative split in Hindi, the split in Palauan with respect to whether 'marked' objects are marked with an inserted preposition or clitic doubling, and the split in Yucatec Maya as to whether agreement or a pronominal clitic cross-references intransitive subjects. The function of an aspect split is to mark aspect in an indirect way that is parasitic on another element of grammar, manipulating their distribution in order to (redundantly) indicate aspect. Such parasitic marking is economical because it never adds anything; it only suppresses an element in one aspect, while preserving it in the other aspect.

Aspect splits are produced by grammatical settings that prohibit an element (e.g. a particular Case, an inserted preposition, agreement) everywhere except in the perfective aspect. This is accomplished within Optimality Theory by a constraint ranking that places a contextually restricted faithfulness constraint preserving that element above the markedness constraint that would otherwise prohibit it. This approach builds on work in phonology such as Beckman (1998) who proposes that faithfulness constraints (but not markedness constraints) can be restricted to hold only in a special context such as the onset position of a syllable. In this chapter, we have seen that aspect splits can be produced by a contextually restricted version of each of the three types of faithfulness constraints that exist in Optimality Theory: IDENT constraints which preserve a marked feature, DEP constraints which prohibit the insertion of an element, and MAX constraints which prohibit the deletion of an element. Two of these constraints apply in syntax in the data discussed here, preserving an ergative Case licensed at vP structure at the CP phase, and prohibiting preposition insertion at the CP phase. The third constraint applies at the syntax/PF interface, requiring spell-out (by morpheme insertion) of a pronominal clitic.

The aspect splits discussed in this chapter are all produced by such faithfulness constraints restricted to apply only in the perfective aspect. It is hypothesized here that such constraints are never restricted to the context of the imperfective aspect. Evidence for this view comes from the pattern produced by two cross-cutting splits involving negatives in Chontal and stage-level predicates in Nepali. The effect of two active contextual faithfulness constraints is additive: they increase the contexts in which the relevant element is preserved. This evidence also provides further support for Beckman's contention that it is only faithfulness constraints, and not markedness constraints that can be restricted to special contexts; the operation of two active contextually restricted markedness constraints would be subtractive, reducing the surface distribution of the relevant element. Cross-cutting split patterns also provide evidence against a more conventional, non-OT approach involving restricted licensing of certain elements.

What remains to be determined is the range of contexts that can restrict faithfulness constraints. The contexts we have seen here all involve the verb or verbal projection (perfective aspect, negative, individual-level predicate).

Acknowledgments

This is a revised version of an earlier paper with the same title which appeared in the proceedings of the DEAL II Workshop on Interface Theories, published in *Linguistics* in Potsdam 2008.

Notes

1. There are three kinds of faithfulness constraints in Optimality Theory: IDENT constraints preserve features, MAX constraints prohibit deletion, and DEP constraints prohibit insertion.
2. Particular verbs and prepositions may lexically select a particular case for their objects, but the case licensing capabilities of heads such as T and v are universal.
3. This model is an updated version of the model in Chomsky (1981) where the inherent case is licensed at D-structure and preserved at the level of S-structure where the structural case is assigned.
4. As formulated, Davison's (2004) proposal would allow clauses without an external argument to have the ergative case. One might correct this problem by revising Davison's proposal so that, while little v alone can license the ergative case in many languages, in Hindi it is necessary for little v to raise to the aspect head, so that the combined forces of little v and the feature [+perfective] can license the ergative case.
5. There are two formal proposals within OT for the analysis of marked objects. Building on Diesing (1992), I argue in Woolford (1995) that objects with certain features (which vary cross-linguistically) are prohibited within the VP, paralleling the fact that consonants with certain features are disallowed in coda position in some languages. In that paper, I argued that objects that are 'marked' with a case or agreement change have moved out of the VP and that the case or agreement change is a secondary effect of that movement. To drive that object shift, I proposed what are essentially contextual markedness constraints to prohibit objects with such features in their base position inside VP, although these constraints might preferably be reformulated as contextual faithfulness constraints. Aissen (2003) takes a more traditional approach to marked objects, formalizing the iconic approach of Silverstein (1976) wherein the morphological case serves as a flag to mark an object with features that are atypical for objects. Aissen uses constraint conjunction to penalize objects with certain features if those objects lack the morphological case (where case is interpreted broadly to include prepositions).
6. It is likely that the clitic doubled objects have moved out of the VP, paralleling many Romance languages and Chichewa (Bresnan and Mchombo 1986) where objects in situ are not clitic doubled. If so, the verb has raised above the shifted object as in Icelandic (Holmberg 1986), given the lack of a change in the surface word order.
7. The *a* morpheme which precedes all arguments and some predicates in Palauan is not glossed in the original sources.
8. Subject and object pronouns are null in Palauan (not spelled out at PF). Null object pronouns that are human and/or specific and singular are also clitic doubled in the perfective aspect:

   (i)   te-'illebed-ii
         3pl-hit   -3sgclitic
         'They hit him/her/it.'   (Georgopoulos 1991: 43 (39c))

   Pronoun objects without these features are also null, even though they are not clitic doubled:

   (ii) te-'illebed
         3pl-hit
         'They hit them/something.'   (Georgopoulos 1991: 46 (15))

   Georgopoulos calls these suffixes object agreement to emphasize that Palauan is not a pronominal argument language. The distinction is not crucial here, but I gloss these as clitics because their distribution is not typical of agreement. (The distinction here is what Bresnan and Mchombo (1986) term anaphoric agreement versus grammatical agreement.)

9. Pronouns must be overt following a preposition in Palauan (Georgopoulos 1991: 30).

10. The identity of Set A and Set B forms which I will assume in the analysis below is that Set A (which only cross-references subjects) is agreement, while Set B (which cross-references objects in some clauses and subjects in others) is a pronominal clitic that is not morphologically marked for case.

11. Alternatively, these constraints are formulated following de Lacy (2002) to target sections of the hierarchy anchored at the marked end, so that the two constraints are *(clitic, agreement) and *(clitic). The *(clitic, agreement) constraint incurs a violation if either a clitic or agreement is present. De Lacy shows that this formulation will produce the empirical effect of a fixed ranking, without an actual fixed ranking.

12. Phonologists often use a Morph Real constraint to require morphemes to be spelled out. That is essentially a MAX (MORPHEME) constraint. Here we need a MAX constraint targeting a specific morpheme.

13. Although such double cross-referencing of the subject is usually filtered out at PF (by the markedness constraints against clitics and agreement), there are languages where it survives to the surface, because both forms are needed in order to fully cross-reference the features of that subject. For example, in Kashmiri, where agreement cross-references gender and number, but not person, and pronominal clitics cross-reference person and number, but not gender, both agreement and a nominative clitic are spelled out so that all three features are spelled out in the surface morphology:

(i)   BI   ch -**u**   -**s**   gatsha:n.   [Kashmiri]
      I(nom)   be -AGR(MASC.SG)   CLITIC(NOM.1SG)   go-PRESENT PARTICIPLE
      'I am going.'   (Wali and Koul 1997: 152)

14. The surface pattern of agreement in most Mayan languages thus fits the description in the typological literature of an ergative pattern: intransitive subjects and transitive objects are both cross-referenced with the same series (a head clitic), while transitive subjects are cross-referenced with a different series, subject agreement. It has been assumed in much of the Mayan literature that this pattern must be caused by the presence of a covert ergative case system, although there is no evidence for this from case morphology in any Mayan language, to my knowledge. The covert ergative approach does not easily extend to Yucatec Maya, as Krämer and Wunderlich (1999) and Bohnemeyer (2004) point out. Under the approach here, it is unnecessary to postulate a covert ergative case system in any Mayan language.

15. The evidence that any language has true object agreement, as opposed to participle agreement or cross-referencing by a head or phrasal pronominal clitic, is not strong in my opinion.

16. In Woolford (2003) I argue that clitic clusters are prohibited in some languages because two clitics cannot simultaneously align to the same edge, and thus an alignment constraint requiring this would be violated. I will assume that this or some other high ranking constraint bars clitic clusters in Mayan languages.

17. Yucatec Maya differs from the other Mayan languages in ranking *CLITIC above MAX(CLITIC). As a result, other Mayan languages always spell out a clitic (a Set B form), whereas Yucatec Maya does so only to satisfy XRef and/or MAX$_{\text{perfective}}$ (CLITIC).

18. A reviewer wonders whether the relevant contexts might be related to the set of c-commanding heads; this possibility remains to be investigated.

References

Aissen, J. (2003) Differential object marking: Iconicity vs economy. *Natural Language & Linguistic Theory* 21 (3): 435–83.

Beckman, J. (1998) *Positional Faithfulness*. Doctoral dissertation, University of Massachusetts, Amherst.

Bhatt, R. (2005) Long distance agreement in Hindi-Urdu. *Natural Language & Linguistic Theory* 23 (4): 757–807.

Bresnan, J. (2001) The emergence of the unmarked pronoun. In G. Legendre, J. Grimshaw and S. Vikner (eds) *Optimality-theoretic Syntax*, 113–42. Cambridge, MA: MIT Press.

Bresnan, J. and Mchombo, S. A. (1986) Grammatical and anaphoric agreement. In A.M. Farley *et al.* (eds) *CLS* 22 part 2, 278–97.

Bricker, V. (1981) The source of the ergative split in Yucatec Maya. *Journal of Mayan Linguistics* 2: 83–127.

Bohnemeyer, J. (2004) Split intransitivity, linking and lexical representation: The case of Yukatek Maya. *Linguistics* 42 (1): 67–107.

Butt, M. and Deo, A. (2005) Ergativity in Indo-Aryan. Ms., Konstanz and Stanford.

Butt, M. and Poudel, T. (2007) Distribution of the ergative in Nepali. Ms., Konstanz.

Chomsky, N. (1981) *Lectures on Government and Binding*. Dordrecht: Foris.

Comrie, B. (1989) *Language Universals and Linguistic Typology: Syntax and Morphology* (2nd edn). Chicago, IL: University of Chicago Press.

Davison, A. (2004) Structural case, lexical case, and the verbal projection. In V. Dayan and A. Mahajan (eds) *Clause Structure in South Asian Languages*, 199–225. Dordrecht: Kluwer.

de Lacy, P. (2002) *The Formal Expression of Markedness*. Doctoral dissertation, University of Massachusetts, Amherst.

Diesing, M. (1992) *Indefinites*. Cambridge, MA: MIT Press.

Georgopoulos, C. (1991) *Syntactic Variables: Resumptive Pronouns and A' binding in Palauan*. Dordrecht: Kluwer Academic Publishers.

Gouskova, M. (2003) *Deriving Economy: Syncope in Optimality Theory*. Doctoral dissertation, University of Massachusetts, Amherst.

Holmberg, A. (1986) *Word Order and Syntactic Features in the Scandinavian Languages and English*. Doctoral dissertation, University of Stockholm.

Josephs, L. S. (1975) *Palauan Reference Grammar*. PALI Language Texts: Micronesia. Honolulu: The University Press of Hawaii.

Knowles-Berry, S. (1987) Negation in Chontal Mayan. *International Journal of American Linguistics* 53 (3): 327–47.

Krämer, M. and Wunderlich, D. (1999) Transitivity alternations in Yucatec, and the correlation between aspect and argument roles. *Linguistics* 37 (3): 431–79.

Legendre, G. and Rood, D. (1992) On the interaction of grammar components in Lakhóta: Evidence from split intransitivity. *Proceedings of the Eighteenth Annual Meeting of the Berkeley Linguistics Society*, 380–394. University of California, Berkeley, CA.

Marantz, A. (1988) Clitics, morphological merger, and the mapping to phonological structure. In M. Hammond and M. Noonan (eds) *Theoretical Morphology: Approaches in Modern Linguistics*, 253–270. San Diego, CA: Academic Press.

McCarthy, J. and Prince, A. (1995) Faithfulness and reduplicative identity. In J. Beckman, L. Walsh Dickey and S. Urbanczyk (eds) *Papers in Optimality Theory*, 249–384. *University of Massachusetts Occasional Papers* 18. Amherst, MA: GLSA.

Nida, E. and Romero, M. (1950) The Pronominal Series in Maya (Yucatec). *International Journal of American Linguistics* 16 (4): 193–197.

Prince, A. and Smolensky, P. (1993) *Optimality Theory: Constraint Interaction in Generative Grammar*. RuCCS Technical Report #2, Rutgers University Center for Cognitive Science, Piscataway. [Published in 2004.]

Prince, A. and Smolensky, P. (2004) *Optimality Theory: Constraint Interaction in Generative Grammar*. Malden, MA and Oxford: Blackwell.

Silverstein, M. (1976) Hierarchy of features and ergativity. In R. M. W. Dixon (ed.) *Grammatical Categories in Australian Languages*, 112–71. Canberra: Australian Institute of Aboriginal Studies.

Smith, J. L. (2001) Lexical category and phonological contrast. In R. Kirchner, J. Pater and W. Wikely (eds) *PETL 6: Proceedings of the Workshop on the Lexicon in Phonetics and Phonology*, 61–72. Edmonton: University of Alberta.

Wali, K. and Koul, O. N. (1997) *Kashmiri*. New York: Routledge.

Woolford, E. (1995) Object agreement in Palauan. *UMOP 18: Papers in Optimality Theory*. University of Massachusetts, Amherst: GLSA.

Woolford, E. (2001) Case patterns. In G. Legendre, S. Vikner and J. Grimshaw (eds) *Optimality Theoretic Syntax,* 509–43. Cambridge, MA: MIT Press.

Woolford, E. (2003) Clitics and agreement in competition. *UMOP 26: Papers in Optimality Theory II.* University of Massachusetts: GLSA.

Woolford, E. (2006) Lexical case, inherent case, and argument structure. *Linguistic Inquiry* 37 (1): 111–30.

Woolford, E. (2007) Case locality: Pure domains and object shift. *Lingua* 117 (9): 1591–616.

8 Derivation of Scandinavian Object Shift and remnant VP-topicalization

Eva Engels* and Sten Vikner**

ABSTRACT Based on the examination of remnant VP-topicalization constructions, this chapter argues for an order preservation analysis to Scandinavian Object Shift. Reviewing Fox and Pesetsky's (2003, 2005) cyclic linearization approach and extending the empirical data base, we show that the phenomena are better accounted for in an Optimality Theoretic framework.

KEYWORDS Object Shift; VP-topicalization

1. Introduction

In the Scandinavian languages, an unfocused object may move from its base position right of the main verb to a position left of a sentential adverbial.[1] This movement operation is called Object Shift (OS). OS is restricted to weak pronouns in the Mainland Scandinavian languages (MSc), but may also optionally take place with full DPs in Icelandic; cf. (1) and (2). Note that pronominal OS is obligatory in Icelandic, Faroese, and Danish, (3)/(4), but optional in Norwegian and Swedish, (5).

(1) Ic (a) Af hverju <u>las</u> Pétur   aldrei ____ <u>þessa bók?</u>
           why   *read* *Pétur*   *never*   *this book*
        (b) Af hverju <u>las</u> Pétur <u>þessa bók</u> aldrei ____ ________?
                                                          (Vikner 2005: 394)

(2) Da (a) Hvorfor <u>læste</u> Peter   aldrig ____ <u>den her bog?</u>
           why   *read*   *Peter*   *never*   *this here book*
        (b) *Hvorfor <u>læste</u> Peter <u>den her bog</u> aldrig ____ ________?
                                                          (Vikner 2005: 394)

---

* Eva Engels, Department of Aesthetics and Communication, Section for English, Jens Chr. Skous Vej 4, DK-8000 Århus C, Denmark. E-mail: eva.engels@hum.au.dk

** Sten Vikner, Department of Aesthetics and Communication, Section for English, Jens Chr. Skous Vej 4, DK-8000 Århus C, Denmark. E-mail: engsv@hum.au.dk

(3) Ic (a) *Af hverju   <u>las</u>   Pétur   aldrei   ____   <u>hana</u>?
              why   *read*   *Pétur*   *never*   *it*
          (b) Af hverju   <u>las</u>   Pétur   <u>hana</u>   aldrei   ____   ____?

(Vikner 2005: 394)

(4) Da (a) *Hvorfor   <u>læste</u>   Peter   aldrig   ____   <u>den</u>?
              why   *read*   *Peter*   *never*   *it*
          (b) Hvorfor   <u>læste</u>   Peter   <u>den</u>   aldrig   ____   ___?

(Vikner 2005: 394)

(5) Sw (a) Varför   <u>läste</u>   Peter   aldrig   ____   <u>den</u>?
              why   *read*   *Peter*   *never*   *it*
          (b) Varför   <u>läste</u>   Peter   <u>den</u>   aldrig   ____   ___?

OS presupposes movement of the main verb; as shown in (6), it cannot cross a verb *in situ*.

(6) Da (a) Hvorfor   har   Peter   aldrig   <u>læst</u>   <u>den</u>?
              why   *has*   *Peter*   *never*   *read*   *it*
          (b) *Hvorfor   har   Peter   <u>den</u>   aldrig   <u>læst</u>   ___?

(Vikner 2005: 395)

However, the main verb does not have to undergo head movement (V°-to-I°-to-C° movement) as in (1)–(5). OS is also possible in clauses with a non-finite main verb if the verb occurs in clause-initial position, (7). In fact, OS has to take place in this case, (8).

(7) Sw (a) <u>Kysst</u>   har   jag   <u>henne</u>   inte   ___ ___   (bara hållit henne i handen).
              kissed   *have*   *I*   *her*   *not*   *only held her by hand-the*
                                                                          (Holmberg 1999: 7)
     Da (b) <u>Kysset</u>   har   jeg   <u>hende</u>   ikke   ___ ___   (bare holdt hende i hånden).
              kissed   *have*   *I*   *her*   *not*   *only held her in hand-the*
                                                                          (Vikner 2005: 407)
     Ic (c) <u>Kysst</u>   hef   ég   <u>hana</u>   ekki   ___ ___   (bara haldið í höndina á henni).
              kissed   *have*   *I*   *her*   *not*   *only held in hand-the on her*
                                                                          (Vikner 2005: 431)

(8) Sw (a) *<u>Kysst</u>   har   jag   inte   ___   <u>henne</u>.
              kissed   *have*   *I*   *not*   *her*   (Erteschik-Shir 2001: 59)
     Da (b) *<u>Kysset</u> har   jeg   ikke   ___   <u>hende</u>.
              kissed   *have*   *I*   *not*   *her*

The following sections concentrate on OS in constructions in which a non-finite main verb occurs in topic position. In section 2.1 we argue in favor of a remnant VP-topicalization approach, rejecting Holmberg's (1997, 1999) V°-topicalization approach. Section 2.2 presents Fox and Pesetsky's (2003, 2005a,b) cyclic linearization approach to OS and briefly addresses some theoretical and empirical problems this approach faces. In section 3, we set out the basics of our analysis which is couched in an Optimality Theoretic framework. Section 4 discusses two asymmetries related to OS during remnant topicalization: between OS of a direct object and OS of an indirect object (section 4.1) and between remnant topicalization out of a main clause and remnant topicalisation out of an embedded clause (section 4.2). Section 5 summarizes the main results.

2.   Holmberg's generalization: V°-topicalization vs. remnant VP-topicalization

2.1   Holmberg's (1997, 1999) V°-topicalization approach

The above observation that the object only moves if the main verb has moved forms the basis of Holmberg's generalization (Holmberg 1986: 165, 1997: 208). Holmberg's (1997) formulation is given in (9), where 'within VP' has to mean that only elements 'properly inside' VP (i.e. not adverbials or other elements adjoined to VP) may block object shift.

>   (9)   *Holmberg's Generalization (HG)*
>   Object Shift is blocked by any phonologically visible category preceding/
>   c-commanding the object position within VP.

The definition in (9) is vague with respect to whether precedence and/or c-command of a phonologically visible category blocks movement. In the 1999 version of the same paper, Holmberg formulates HG in terms of asymmetric c-command. For reasons that will become clear in section 3 below, the first option will be pursued here, that is, we will take HG to be the consequence of a violable condition on order preservation (cf. Déprez 1994; Müller 2001a; Sells 2001; Williams 2003; Fox and Pesetsky 2005a; Koeneman 2006).

Holmberg (1997, 1999) suggests that HG is a derivational condition, not a representational one. OS of an infinitival clause subject is possible as long as there is no intervening non-adverbial material; cf. (10a) and (10b). A violation of HG, as in (10c), cannot be repaired by subsequent operations, as in (10d), that place the blocking element to the left of the shifted object; in other words, HG may not be violated at any point in the course of derivation.

>   (10)   Sw   (a)   Jag   _såg_   _henne_   inte   [_VP_ ___ [_IP_ _____ arbeta]].
>   *I*   *saw*   *her*   *not*   *work*
>   (b)   Jag   har   inte   [_VP_ sett [_IP_ _henne_ arbeta]].
>   *I*   *have*   *not*   *seen*   *her*   *work*
>   (c)   *Jag har   _henne_ inte   [_VP_ sett [_IP_ _____ arbeta]].
>   (d)   *[_VP_ Sett [_IP_ _____ arbeta]] har jag   _henne_ inte_________.

(Holmberg 1997: 206)

Holmberg concludes that the grammatical sentences in (7) cannot involve OS prior to remnant VP-topicalization since that would violate HG in a parallel fashion,

196 *Eva Engels and Sten Vikner*

cf. (11). Rather, they must be derived by V°-topicalization, with subsequent OS, cf. (12).

(11) Deriving (7a) by remnant VP-topicalization

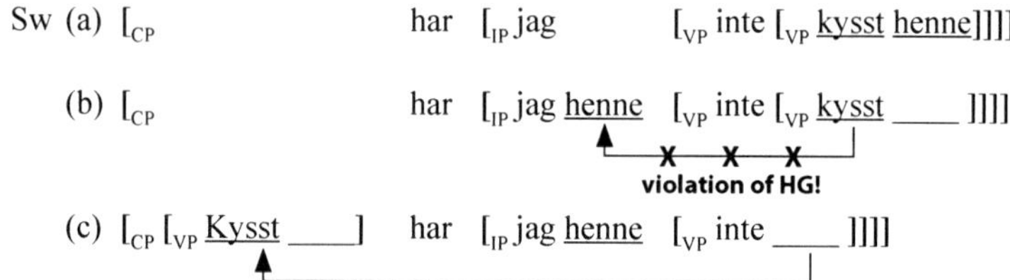

(12) Deriving (7a) by V°-topicalization

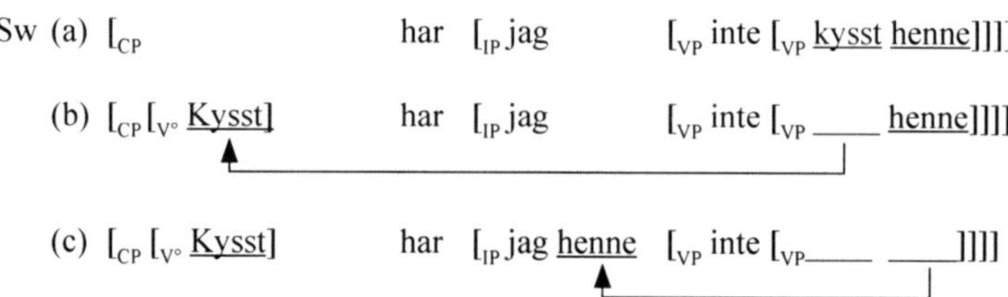

Note that the V°-topicalization analysis is theoretically somewhat problematic: It is counter-cyclic and it involves movement of an X° to an XP-position.[2] (See also Broekhuis 2008: section 4.3.3 for an extensive critique of Holmberg's (1999) proposal.)

Moreover, OS is usually optional in Swedish but it is obligatory if the verb occurs in topic position; cf. (7) and (8) above. This is unexpected under the V°-topicalization analysis, whereas it would follow under the remnant VP-topicalization analysis, where OS must apply to move the object out of VP prior to topicalization.

In addition, if V°-topicalization were possible, the sentences in (13b)/(14b) would be expected to be acceptable, contrary to fact. Furthermore, examples like (15) below show that remnant VP-topicalization is possible in Scandinavian, as admitted in Holmberg (2005: 148).

(13) Da (a) Jeg   har   ikke   smidt   den   ud.
         I   have   not   thrown   it   out
     (b) *Smidt har   jeg   den   ikke   ____   ___   ud.

(14) Da (a) Jeg   har   ikke   stillet   det   på bordet.
         I   have   not   put   it   on   table-the
     (b) *Stillet har   jeg   det   ikke   ____   ___   på bordet.

Against Holmberg (1997, 1999), remnant VP-topicalization will therefore be assumed to be possible, though it is subject to certain restrictions.

2.2 Fox and Pesetsky's (2003, 2005a,b) remnant VP-topicalization approach

As Fox and Pesetsky (2005a) observe, remnant VP-topicalization is possible in Swedish under certain conditions. In double object constructions, topicalization of a non-finite main verb may pied-pipe the indirect object (IO), stranding the direct object (DO) in shifted position, (15a). Even though (15a) is not completely perfect to all speakers, there is consensus that it is much better than stranding of an IO pronoun on its own, (15b), which simply is not possible.

(15) Sw (a) ?[$_{VP}$ Gett   <u>henne</u> ___]   har   jag   <u>den</u>   inte.
                  given *her*   *have* *I*   *it*   *not*
        (b) *[$_{VP}$ Gett   ____   den]   har   jag   <u>henne</u> inte.

                                          (Fox and Pesetsky 2005a: 25)

Fox and Pesetsky (2003, 2005a) suggest that the mapping between syntax and phonology, that is Spell-out, takes place at various points in the course of derivation (including at VP and at CP), whereby the material in the Spell-out domain D is linearized; see also Chomsky (2000, 2001). The crucial property of Spell-out is that it may only add information about the linearization of a newly constructed Spell-out domain D′ to the information cumulatively produced by previous applications of Spell-out. Established information cannot be deleted in the course of derivation, accounting for order preservation effects.

To Fox and Pesetsky (2005a), the fact that OS observes HG is a consequence of their 'linearization theory'. At the Spell-out domain VP, the ordering statement 'V precedes O' (hencefort 'V<O') is established, (16b). At CP, Spell-out adds information about the linearization of the new material, (16c); this information is consistent with the previously established information: The finite main verb moves to C° in the main clause and the pronominal object undergoes OS, maintaining their relative order V<O.

(16) Da (a) Jeg <u>kyssede</u> <u>hende</u> ikke ____ ____.
             I   *kissed*   *her*   *not*

        (b) Spell-out VP: [$_{VP}$ V <u>O</u>]
            <u>Ordering</u>:   **V<O**

        (c) Spell-out CP: [$_{CP}$ S V [$_{IP}$ t$_S$ <u>O</u> Adv [$_{VP}$ t$_V$ t$_O$]]]
            <u>Ordering</u>:   **S<V**   **V<O**
                           V<O
                           O<Adv
                           Adv<VP

Note that the adverbial is merged outside the VP Spell-out domain. Its position relative to the object (and the main verb) is thus not fixed until Spell-out of CP, thus predicting that OS can cross an adverb.

OS across a verb *in situ* as in (6b), repeated as (17a), gives rise to contradictory ordering statements. The ordering statements produced at Spell-out of CP, (17c), are in opposition to the statement 'V<O' established at Spell-out of VP, (17b). The statements O<Adv, Adv<V and V<O cannot simultaneously be satisfied.

(17) Da (a) *Jeg har   <u>hende</u> ikke kysset ____.
                 I   *have*   *her*   *not*   *kissed*

     (b) Spell-out VP: $[_{VP}$ V <u>O</u>$]$
        <u>Ordering</u>:   **V<O**

     (c) Spell-out CP: $[_{CP}$ S Aux $[_{IP}$ t$_S$ <u>O</u> Adv $[_{VP}$ t$_{Aux}$ $[_{VP}$ V t$_O]]]]$
        <u>Ordering</u>:   **S<Aux**   **V<O**
                   Aux<O
                   O<Adv
                   Adv<VP → Adv<V

Thus, Fox and Pesetsky (2005a) derive HG from ordering contradictions. OS cannot take place if it results in ordering statements at the Spell-out of CP that contradict those established at the Spell-out of VP. For our present purpose it is crucial to note that order preservation does not necessarily require that the main verb undergoes V°-to-I°-to-C° movement in all OS cases. Consistent ordering statements can also be obtained when OS applies across a non-finite verb *in situ* if subsequently remnant VP-topicalization takes place, as in (7b) repeated here as (18a).

(18) Da (a) Kysset har   jeg <u>hende</u> ikke ____.
                 kissed   *have*   *I*   *her*   *not*

     (b) Spell-out VP: $[_{VP}$ V <u>O</u>$]$
        <u>Ordering</u>:   **V<O**

     (c) Spell-out CP: $[_{CP}$ $[_{VP}$ V t$_O]$ Aux $[_{IP}$ S t$_{Aux}$ $[_{VP}$ <u>O</u> $[_{VP}$ Adv $[_{VP}$ t$_{Aux}$ t$_{VP}]]]]]$
        <u>Ordering</u>:   **V<Aux**   V<O
                   Aux<S
                   S<O
                   O<Adv
                   Adv<VP

Correspondingly, the asymmetry between stranding of an IO and stranding of a DO by remnant VP-topicalization illustrated in (15) above is expected by order preservation. Stranding of an IO, but not stranding of a DO gives rise to contradictory ordering statements at the various Spell-out domains: At VP, 'IO<DO' is established, which is consistent with the Spell-out of CP in (15a) but not in (15b).

Note that Fox and Pesetsky (2005a) predict that movement operations that do not obey HG have to proceed successive cyclically: the underlined constituents in (19) have to move via the edge of VP prior to linearization of the VP domain to prevent ordering contradictions at the Spell-out of CP; see (20). These movement operations comprise various instances of A-movement and A-bar-movement operations, such as Scandinavian Negative Shift (see Christensen 2005; Engels 2011, 2012), *wh*-movement, topicalization, passivization, and subject raising. The underlined constituents in (19) have to move via the edge of VP, giving rise to the order O<V at the VP-level; since the main verb remains *in situ*, we find the same order at the CP-level and the result is therefore acceptable, as illustrated in (20).

(19) Da (a) Måske   har han   <u>ingen bøger</u> solgt ____.
           probably   *has* *he*   *no books*   *sold*
     (b) <u>Hvad</u>   har du   solgt ____?
           what   *have* *you*   *sold*
     (c) <u>Bøgerne</u>   har jeg   solgt ____.
           books-the   *have* *I*   *sold*
     (d) Måske   blev <u>bøgerne</u>   solgt ____.
           perhaps   *were* *books-the*   *sold*
     (e) Efter min mening har <u>Poul</u> altid   set ud   til ____ at være intelligent.
           in my opinion   *has Paul always seemed to*   *to be   intelligent*

(20) Da (a) Måske   har han <u>ingen bøger</u> solgt ____.   = (19a)
           probably has he   no books   sold
     (b) Spell-out VP: $[_{VP}$ <u>O</u> $[_{VP}$ V $t_O]]$
         <u>Ordering</u>:   **O<V**
     (c) Spell-out CP: $[_{CP}$ Adv Aux $[_{IP}$ S t_{Aux} $[_{NegP}$ <u>O</u> $[_{AuxP}$ t_{Aux} $[_{VP}$ t_O V $t_O]]]]]$
         <u>Ordering</u>:   **Adv<Aux**   **O<V**
                          Aux<S
                          S<O
                          O<VP $\rightarrow$ O<V

Hence, the crucial difference between the various movement operations in (19) and OS is that the former may go via the edge of VP while OS cannot. Fox and Pesetsky (2005b: 245) propose that the motivation for movement through the edge of VP might be connected to semantics: phrases with a feature [+negative], [+wh], [+topic] or [+focus] cannot be interpreted in argument position and thus must undergo movement. 'It is possible that movement to the edge of VP is motivated by this semantic factor, and that there is no independent feature of *v* that could motivate such movement. In the case of [negative] phrases, it is the semantics that motivates the movement, and in the case of OS there is no motivation' (Fox and Pesetsky 2005b: 245).

However, the ability to move across a verb *in situ* may be subject to cross-linguistic variation (see also Broekhuis 2008: chapter 3). For instance, Negative Shift across a verb *in situ* is prohibited in Norwegian, (21a), but possible in the other Scandinavian varieties (see Engels 2011, 2012). In other words, movement of a negative object through the edge of VP is not possible in Norwegian; the semantic factor apparently does not apply in this language. Note that *in situ* occurrence of a negative phrase is not permitted under a sentential negation reading either, (21b); instead, the *ikke ... noen*-variant ('not ... any') must be used, (21c).

(21) No (a) *Han har   <u>ingen bøker</u> solgt   ____.
              he   *has* *no books*   *sold*
          (b) *Han har   solgt   <u>ingen bøker</u>.
          (c) Han   har   <u>ikke</u>   solgt   <u>noen bøker</u>.
              he   *has* *not*   *sold*   *any books*

In addition, if movement through the edge of VP were motivated by the feature [+negative], such a movement would be expected to be obligatory. However, this could not possibly be the case, given that string-vacuous Negative Shift is possible in all Scandinavian varieties, (22). The derivation of (22) would in fact have to be parallel to the one in (16) above; that is the object could not have gone through the edge of VP, since this would lead to an ordering contradiction.

(22) Da (a) Han sælger <u>ingen bøger</u>   ____.
      No (b) Han selger <u>ingen bøker</u>   ____.
              he   *sells*   *no books*

Fox and Pesetsky (2005b: 239–45) consider a range of options, including covert movement through the edge of VP, but if covert movement were possible, we would additionally expect that a negative object may occur *in situ*, contrary to fact; see (21b).

Note also that Fox and Pesetsky (2003, 2005a,b) make an incorrect prediction concerning remnant VP-topicalization in constructions with an auxiliary *in situ*. They assume that auxiliary verbs are merged outside *v*P, that is, after Spell-out of VP. As a consequence, the ordering of object and auxiliary verb is not fixed until Spell-out of CP, which incorrectly predicts that OS across an auxiliary is possible, (23a) = (24c). This is because it is consistent with the ordering statements previously established, none of which mention the auxiliary at all. (See also the examples in (24) and (25) below.)[3]

(23) Da (a) *Kysse har   jeg <u>hende</u> aldrig villet.
              kiss   *have* *I*   *her*   *never* *would*

          (b) Spell-out VP: $[_{VP}$ V <u>O</u>]]
               <u>Ordering:</u>   **V<O**

          (c) Spell-out CP:
               $[_{CP} [_{VP} V t_O]$ Aux2 $[_{IP} S t_{Aux} [_{AuxP2}$ <u>O</u> $[_{AuxP2}$ Adv$[_{AuxP2} t_{Aux} [_{AuxP1}$ Aux1 $t_{VP}]]]]]]]$
               <u>Ordering:</u>   **V<Aux2**   **V<O**
                                Aux2<S
                                S<O
                                O<Adv
                                Adv<Aux1
                                Aux1<VP $\rightarrow$ $\varnothing$

Fox and Pesetsky (2005b: 252) even go so far as to draw a tree diagram of the problematic structure, but then they claim, following Holmberg (2005: 151) that their prediction cannot be checked because VP-topicalization is impossible across an auxiliary *in situ*, regardless of whether or not OS out of the VP has taken place first. However, as shown in (24), this is incorrect: VP-topicalization is actually possible across an auxiliary *in situ*, but remnant VP-topicalization is not; the object can neither precede nor follow the auxiliary *in situ*.[4,5]

(24) Da (a) [$_{VP}$ Kysse <u>hende</u>] har jeg   aldrig villet.
            kiss   *her*   *have I*   *never would*
      (b) *[$_{VP}$ Kysse _____] har jeg   aldrig villet <u>hende</u>.
      (c) *[$_{VP}$ Kysse _____] har jeg <u>hende</u> aldrig villet.

(25) Sw (a) [$_{VP}$ Kyssa <u>henne</u>] har jag   aldrig velat.
            kiss   *her*   *have I*   *never would*
      (b) ??[$_{VP}$ Kyssa _____] har jag   aldrig velat <u>henne</u>.
      (c) *[$_{VP}$ Kyssa _____] har jag <u>henne</u> aldrig velat.

In order to account for the data in (24) and (25), another assumption might be added to Fox and Pesetsky's analysis, viz. that auxiliary phrases also constitute Spell-out domains (see also Bobaljik 2005): thus, VP-topicalization would have to proceed via the edge of the AuxP of *villet* and via the edge of the AuxP of *har* at points where OS could not possibly already have applied (as the target position of OS is not yet present at these points). In other words, remnant VP-topicalization would be expected to be ungrammatical; see (26). Movement of the entire VP, still including the object, via these two edge positions predicts that the object precedes both auxiliaries as in case of topicalization of the entire VP, (24a)/(25a).

(26) Da (a) *[$_{VP}$ Kysse _____] har jeg hende aldrig villet.
            kiss   *have I*   *her*   *never would*

      (b) Spell-out VP: [$_{VP}$ V <u>O</u>]]
           <u>Ordering</u>:   **V<O**

      (c) Spell-out AuxP1: [$_{AuxP1}$ [$_{VP}$ V <u>O</u>] [$_{AuxP1}$ Aux1 t$_{VP}$]]
           <u>Ordering</u>:   **V<O**   V<O
                        O<Aux1

      (d) Spell-out AuxP2: [$_{AuxP2}$ [$_{VP}$ V <u>O</u>] [$_{AuxP2}$ Aux2 [$_{AuxP2}$ t$_{VP}$ [$_{AuxP1}$ Aux1 t$_{VP}$]]]]
           <u>Ordering</u>:   **V<O**   V<O   V<O
                        O<Aux2   O<Aux1
                        Aux2<Aux1

      (e) Spell-out CP:
           [$_{CP}$ [$_{VP}$ V t$_O$] Aux2 [$_{IP}$ S t [$_{AuxP2}$ <u>O</u> [$_{AuxP2}$ Adv [$_{AuxP2}$ t$_{VP}$ [$_{AuxP2}$ t [$_{AuxP2}$ t$_{VP}$ [$_{AuxP1}$ Aux1 t$_{VP}$]]]]
            <u>Ordering</u>:   **V<Aux2**   V<O   V<O   V<O
                     Aux2<S   O<Aux2   O<Aux1
                     S<O   Aux2<Aux1
                     O<Adv
                     Adv<Aux1

However, with the additional assumption that auxiliary phrases also constitute Spell-out domains, it would no longer be possible to derive the remnant VP-topicalization of the grammatical sentence in (7), repeated in (27). Also here, (remnant) VP-topicalization would have to move via the edge of the AuxP of *har* at a point where OS could not possibly already have applied. Stranding of the object in OS position during VP-topicalization as in (27) would thus incorrectly be predicted to be ungrammatical.

(27) Da (a) <u>Kysset</u> har   jeg <u>hende</u> ikke ____ (bare holdt hende i hånden).
          kissed   have   I   her   not   only held her in hand-the
                                                          (Vikner 2005: 407)

The only way to derive (27) with the additional assumption that AuxPs also constitute Spell-out domains, would be to follow Holmberg (1997, 1999) and take it to be a case of V°-topicalization, but that in turn would incorrectly predict not only (27) but also (24c) and (25c) (as well as (13b) and (14b) above) to be grammatical.

In section 3 below we will outline an OT approach to OS and remnant VP-topicalization that also relies on order preservation. In section 4 we will then show how this approach can handle the problems discussed above: double object constructions in section 4.1, and auxiliaries *in situ* in section 4.2.

3.   An OT approach to Object Shift and remnant VP-topicalization

OS is motivated by the constraint SHIFT, which outranks the constraint STAY that prohibits movement. SHIFT is satisfied if the pronoun is adjoined to the top VP (see e.g. (33) below).

(28) SHIFT:
      A [-focus] constituent precedes and c-commands a VP (of the same clause) that
          contains all V° positions and all VP-adjoined adverbials.

(29) STAY:
      Don't move.

Recall that there is cross-linguistic variation as to the applicability of OS, depending on the syntactic complexity of the object. In Icelandic, both a pronominal object as well as a full DP can undergo OS, whereas OS is restricted to weak pronouns in Mainland Scandinavian; see the examples in (1)–(5) above. We therefore assume that the constraint STAY is differentiated as to syntactic complexity. In addition to the general constraint STAY, there exists a more specific constraint that prohibits movement of full DPs (see also Appendix 1).

(30) STAYBRANCH:
      Don't move a constituent that contains a branching node.

Differences in the ranking of Stay and StayBranch relative to Shift account for the cross-linguistic variation: Dominance of Shift over both Stay-constraints predicts that OS is possible with both pronominal objects and full DPs, as found in Icelandic, while the ranking StayBranch >> Shift >> Stay only permits weak pronouns but not full DPs to undergo OS, as observed in Mainland Scandinavian; see also *T1*.[6]

(31) Ic: Shift   >> StayBranch >> Stay
      Da: StayBranch >> Shift   >> Stay

T1 Full DP

Da:			Stay Branch	Shift	Stay	ex.
full DP	☞	a S <u>V</u> Adv t_v <u>DP-O</u>		*		(2a)
		b S <u>V</u> <u>DP-O</u> Adv t_v t_o	*!		*	(2b)
pronoun		a S <u>V</u> Adv t_v <u>Pron-O</u>		*!		(4a)
	☞	b S <u>V</u> <u>Pron-O</u> Adv t_v t_o			*	(4b)

In this and the following tableaux, only Stay-violations induced by OS are listed; Stay-violations induced by e.g. $V°$-to-$I°$-to-$C°$ movement or VP-topicalization are left out because they do not vary between competing candidates. The same holds for the violations of the constraint OrdPres, which we will turn to now.

Following Fox and Pesetsky (2005a,b), HG will be assumed here to result from a high ranking condition on order preservation (see also Müller 2001).

(32) Order Preservation (OrdPres):
     An independently moved constituent must not precede a non-adverbial constituent that it (or parts of it) followed at base level.

Dominance of OrdPres over Shift predicts that OS is only possible if it maintains the base order of certain constituents. What is crucial for OS to be possible is that the main verb occurs in a position to the left of the target position of OS, such that the relative order between verb and object is preserved. This is guaranteed if the verb undergoes movement to a position to the left of the target position of OS such as $V°$-to-$I°$-to-$C°$ movement or embedded $V°$-to-$I°$ movement in Icelandic (see section 4.2). The former case is illustrated in *T2*. However, if the main verb stays *in situ*, OS gives rise to a fatal violation of OrdPres and is thus excluded; the object must remain *in situ* to the right of the main verb, as shown by the optimal candidate in *T3*. (The restriction to *non-adverbial* constituents is necessary to permit OS across clause-medial adverbials.)

T2 OS & V°-to-I°-to-C° movement

Da:			ORD PRES	SHIFT	STAY	ex.
V in C°	a	S $\underline{V}$ Adv t_V <u>Pron-O</u>		*!		(4a)
	☞ b	S $\underline{V}$ <u>Pron-O</u> Adv t_V t_O			*	(4b)

T3 OS & in situ verb

Da:			ORD PRES	SHIFT	STAY	ex.
V *in situ*	☞ a	S Aux Adv $\underline{V}$ <u>Pron-O</u>		*		(6a)
	b	S Aux <u>Pron-O</u> Adv $\underline{V}$ t_O	*!		*	(6b)

However, the main verb does not necessarily have to undergo V°-to-I°-to-C° movement for OS to be possible; ORDPRES is also satisfied if the main verb occurs in topic position as in (7) above; see *T4*.

T4 OS and verb in SpecCP

Da:			ORD PRES	SHIFT	STAY	ex.
V in SpecCP	a	$[_{VP}\,\underline{V}\,t_O]$ Aux S Adv <u>Pron-O</u> t_{VP}		*!	**	(8b)
	☞ b	$[_{VP}\,\underline{V}\,t_O]$ Aux S <u>Pron-O</u> Adv t_{VP}			**	(7b)

As argued for in section 2, we consider occurrence of a non-finite verb in topic position to involve OS of the pronominal object prior to remnant VP-topicalization, as illustrated in (33). We saw in (11) that in Holmberg's (1997, 1999) approach, such remnant VP- topicalization is ruled out by the assumption that HG is derivational, that is it cannot be violated at any point in the derivation. The OT constraint ORDPRES, by contrast, is representational: constraint violations are computed based on the final structure of the candidates. Hence, although the individual steps of OS might violate ORDPRES, this is of no consequence as long as the verb is subsequently placed to the left of the shifted object such that their original precedence relation is re-established.

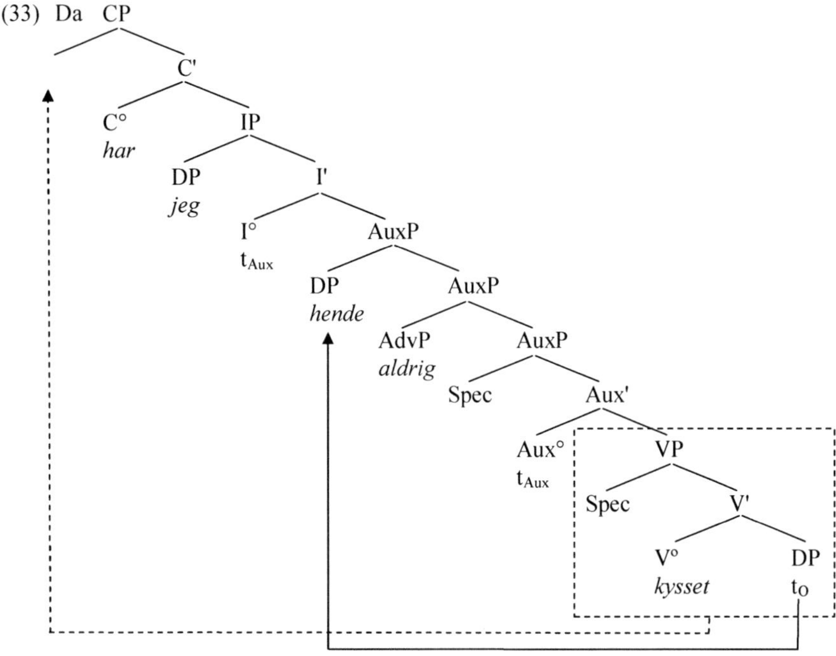

Section 2.2 showed that other types of object movement such as topicalization may cross a verb *in situ*, that is they need not preserve the base order (cf. (34) repeated from (19c) above). Under the OT approach adopted here, this follows if the relevant constraint that motivates movement, for example Topic, outranks OrdPres (see *T5*).

(34) Da <u>Bøgerne</u> har   jeg solgt ____.
     books-the have   I   sold

(35) Topic: Elements with a [+topic] feature occur in Spec,CP.

T5 Object topicalization

Da:		Topic	OrdPres	Shift	Stay	ex.
a	S Aux t$_s$ V O$_{[+top]}$	*!		*	*	-
☞ b	O$_{[+top]}$ Aux S V t$_o$		***	*	*	(34)

The following section focuses on two asymmetries related to OS during remnant VP-topicalization (namely, between OS of a direct object and OS of an indirect object, section 4.1, and between remnant topicalization out of a main clause and remnant topicalization out of an embedded clause, section 4.2). These support the OT approach presented here.

4   Asymmetries in Object Shift and remnant VP-topicalization

4.1   Stranding of a DO vs. stranding of an IO

As mentioned in section 2.2 above, there is an asymmetry between stranding of an IO and stranding of a DO during remnant VP-topicalization; see (36), the Danish version of the Swedish example in (15). This asymmetry follows from the ranking ORDPRES >> SHIFT.[7]

(36) Da (a) ?[$_{VP}$ Givet   <u>hende</u> ___] har   jeg   <u>den</u>   ikke.
                            given   her   have I   it   not
        (b) *[$_{VP}$ Givet   ___ <u>den</u>] har   jeg   <u>hende</u> ikke.

(Fox and Pesetsky 2005a: 25)

Note that also both objects of a double object construction may be taken along, (37a), or both of them may be stranded by remnant VP-topicalization, (37b).

(37) Da (a) [$_{VP}$ Givet   <u>hende</u> <u>den</u>]   har   jeg   ikke.
                            given   her   it   have I   not
        (b) ?[$_{VP}$ Givet   ___   ___] har   jeg   <u>hende</u> <u>den</u> ikke.

Because of these alternatives, it is necessary to assume that it is specified in the input which constituents are to be placed in topic position (= bold in the tableaux below). Stranding of an element that should appear in topic position then violates TOPIC whereas pied-piping (i.e. taking along) extra material does not violate this constraint, see *T6* and *T7*.

T6 Remnant VP-topicalization that strands both IO and DO

Da	Topic: V	TOPIC	ORD PRES	SHIFT	STAY	ex.
a	[$_{VP}$ V <u>Pron-IO</u> <u>Pron-DO</u>] Aux S Adv t$_{VP}$			*!*		(37a)
b	[$_{VP}$ V <u>Pron-IO</u> t$_{DO}$] Aux S <u>Pron-DO</u> Adv t$_{VP}$			*!	*	(36a)
c	[$_{VP}$ V t$_{IO}$ <u>Pron-DO</u>] Aux S <u>Pron-IO</u> Adv t$_{VP}$		*!	*	*	(36b)
☞ d	[$_{VP}$ V t$_{IO}$ t$_{DO}$] Aux S <u>Pron-IO</u> <u>Pron-DO</u> Adv t$_{VP}$				**	(37b)

T7 VP-topicalization that takes along both IO and DO

Da	Topic: V & Pron-IO & Pron-DO	TOPIC	ORD PRES	SHIFT	STAY	ex.
☞ a	[$_{VP}$ V **<u>Pron-IO</u>** **<u>Pron-DO</u>**] Aux S Adv t$_{VP}$			**		(37a)
b	[$_{VP}$ V **<u>Pron-IO</u>** t$_{DO}$] Aux S **<u>Pron-DO</u>** Adv t$_{VP}$	*!		*	*	(36a)
c	[$_{VP}$ V t$_{IO}$ **<u>Pron-DO</u>**] Aux S **<u>Pron-IO</u>** Adv t$_{VP}$	*!	*	*	*	(36b)
d	[$_{VP}$ V t$_{IO}$ t$_{DO}$] Aux S **<u>Pron-IO</u>** **<u>Pron-DO</u>** Adv t$_{VP}$	*!*			**	(37b)

Recall that ORDPRES, (32), refers to *independently moved constituents*. As a consequence, the number of ORDPRES-violations (namely, one for each crossed constituent) induced by VP-topicalization is independent of how many constituents are included in the topicalized VP.[8]

As *T6* and *T7* show, SHIFT favors stranding of a pronoun, but this is only possible if the pronoun is not marked [+topic], due to the higher ranking constraint TOPIC. The asymmetry between stranding of a DO and stranding of an IO is expected by the ranking ORDPRES >> SHIFT. Remnant VP-topicalization with OS of a DO maintains the VP-internal ordering relations, satisfying ORDPRES (see *T8*). Note that it is crucial for the remnant VP-topicalization constructions that ORDPRES refers to precedence rather than c-command relations: While the precedence relations are maintained in (36a), the c-command relations are not: Neither the verb nor the IO c-commands favours the shifted DO.

T8 Remnant VP-topicalization that strands DO

Da		Topic: V & Pron-IO	TOPIC	ORD PRES	SHIFT	STAY	ex.
	a	$[_{VP}$ **V Pron-IO** Pron-DO] Aux S Adv t_{VP}			**!		(37a)
☞	b	$[_{VP}$ **V Pron-IO** t_{DO}] Aux S Pron-DO Adv t_{VP}			*	*	(36a)
	c	$[_{VP}$ **V** t_{IO} Pron-DO] Aux S **Pron-IO** Adv t_{VP}	*!	*	*	*	(36b)
	d	$[_{VP}$ **V** t_{IO} t_{DO}] Aux S **Pron-IO** Pron-DO Adv t_{VP}	*!			**	(37b)

In contrast, remnant VP-topicalization with OS of an IO does not re-establish the base order relations: The topicalized VP precedes the shifted IO although parts of it (namely, the DO) followed the IO at base level. The violation of ORDPRES therefore rules out stranding of the IO in OS position, see *T9* below. Instead, the IO has to be pied-piped by VP-topicalization, giving rise to neutralization: Despite the different input specifications with regard to topichood, the same candidate (namely, candidate a) arises as output in *T7* and *T9*. (But stranding of the IO is possible if it does not result in a violation of ORDPRES, namely if both objects are stranded as in (37b), *T6*.)

T9 No remnant VP-topicalization that strands IO

Da		Topic: V & Pron-DO	TOPIC	ORD PRES	SHIFT	STAY	ex.
☞	a	$[_{VP}$ **V** Pron-IO **Pron-DO**] Aux S Adv t_{VP}			**		(37a)
	b	$[_{VP}$ **V** Pron-IO t_{DO}] Aux S **Pron-DO** Adv t_{VP}	*!		*	*	(36a)
	c	$[_{VP}$ **V** t_{IO} **Pron-DO**] Aux S Pron-IO Adv t_{VP}		*!	*	*	(36b)
	d	$[_{VP}$ **V** t_{IO} t_{DO}] Aux S Pron-IO **Pron-DO** Adv t_{VP}	*!			**	(37b)

More generally, the ranking OrdPres >> Shift predicts that stranding of an object during remnant VP-topicalization is only acceptable if the object is right-peripheral within VP. As shown in (38)–(40), topicalization of the entire VP but not remnant topicalization with stranding of the pronoun is possible in constructions in which the object is followed by other elements within VP, for example in constructions with an infinitival clause, (38), with a verb and an additional PP-complement, (39), or with a verb and a particle, (40); see Appendix 2. Recall that the unacceptable sentence in (38b), repeated from (10d), led Holmberg (1997, 1999) to assume that remnant VP-topicalization is not possible.

(38) Sw (a) [$_{VP}$ Sett   <u>henne</u> arbeta]   har   jag   inte.
                      seen   *her*   *work*   *have* *I*   *not*
          (b) *[$_{VP}$ Sett   ____   arbeta]   har   jag   <u>henne</u> inte.
                                                                  (Holmberg 1997: 206)

(39) Da (a) [$_{VP}$ Stillet   <u>det</u>   på bordet]   har   jeg   ikke.
                      put   *it*   *on table-the* *have* *I*   *not*
          (b) *[$_{VP}$ Stillet   ____   på bordet]   har   jeg   <u>det</u>   ikke.

(40) Da (a) [$_{VP}$ Smidt   <u>den</u>   ud]   har   jeg   ikke.
                      thrown   *it*   *out*   *have* *I*   *not*
          (b) *[$_{VP}$ Smidt   ____   ud]   har   jeg   <u>den</u>   ikke.

As mentioned above, HG only prohibits OS across constituents to the left. This section has shown that the condition on order preservation is more general: OS is only grammatical if the VP-internal ordering relations are retained. Only right-peripheral objects may be stranded during remnant VP-topicalization. In the present OT-analysis, this follows from the constraint OrdPres and its dominance over Shift.

4.2   Remnant VP-topicalization out of a main vs. an embedded clause

Apart from the asymmetry between stranding of an IO and stranding of a DO, there is an asymmetry between remnant VP-topicalization out of a main clause and remnant VP-topicalization out of an embedded clause in Mainland Scandinavian.

While the finite verb undergoes V°-to-I°-to-C° movement in main clauses, it stays *in situ* in embedded clauses in Mainland Scandinavian, (41). As a consequence, OS is not possible in embedded clauses (OrdPres >> Shift); see (42).

(41) Da (a) Jeg   spurgte hvorfor Peter   aldrig <u>læste</u> bogen.
               I   *asked*   *why*   *Peter*   *never* *read*   *book-the*
          (b) *Jeg   spurgte hvorfor Peter   <u>læste</u> aldrig   ____   bogen.

(42) Da (a) Jeg   spurgte hvorfor Peter   aldrig læste   <u>den</u>.
               I   *asked*   *why*   *Peter*   *never* *read*   *it*
          (b) *Jeg   spurgte hvorfor Peter   <u>den</u>   aldrig læste   ____.

As shown in (43), a full VP may be topicalized from both main clauses and embedded clauses.

(43) Da (a) [$_{VP}$ Set <u>ham</u>] har jeg ikke, ...
seen him have I not
... hvis jeg skal være helt ærlig, men jeg har talt i telefon med ham.
if I should be totally honest but I have spoken in phone with him

(b) [$_{VP}$ Set <u>ham</u>] tror jeg ikke at hun har, ...
seen him believe I not that she has
... men hun kan måske nok have talt i telefon med ham.
but she may perhaps well have spoken in phone with him

Topicalization of a remnant VP, by contrast, is only possible out of a main clause, (44a), not out of an embedded clause in Danish: The stranded object may neither follow the finite auxiliary (in its base position), (44b), nor may it precede it, (44c).

(44) Da (a) ?[$_{VP}$ Set ____] har jeg <u>ham</u> ikke, ...
seen have I him not
... hvis jeg skal være helt ærlig, men jeg har talt i telefon med ham.
if I should be totally honest but I have spoken on phone-the with him

(b) *[$_{VP}$ Set ____] tror jeg ikke at hun [$_{V°}$ har] <u>ham</u>, ...
seen believe I not that she has him

(c) *[$_{VP}$ Set ____] tror jeg ikke at hun <u>ham</u> [$_{V°}$ har] , ...
seen believe I not that she him has
... men hun kan måske nok have talt i telefon med ham.
but she may perhaps well have spoken in phone with him

This asymmetry shows that stranding must involve OS, because OS requires the (stranded) object to occur in a position to the left of the base position of a finite verb (SHIFT is violated in candidate b below as the object is adjoined to a lower VP), but it can only do so if this verb has itself left its base position (ORDPRES). In other words, stranding is only possible if motivated independently, in this case by SHIFT, and if it does not violate higher ranking principles (ORDPRES, STAYBRANCH).

T10 Remnant VP-topicalization out of a main clause

Da	Topic: V	ORDPRES	SHIFT	STAY	ex.
a	[$_{VP}$ **V** <u>Pron-O</u>] Aux S Adv t$_{VP}$		*!		(43a)[9]
b	[$_{VP}$ **V** t$_{O}$] Aux S Adv <u>Pron-O</u> t$_{VP}$		*!	*	(8b)
☞ c	[$_{VP}$ **V** t$_{O}$] Aux S <u>Pron-O</u> Adv t$_{VP}$			*	(7b)/(44a)

(45)

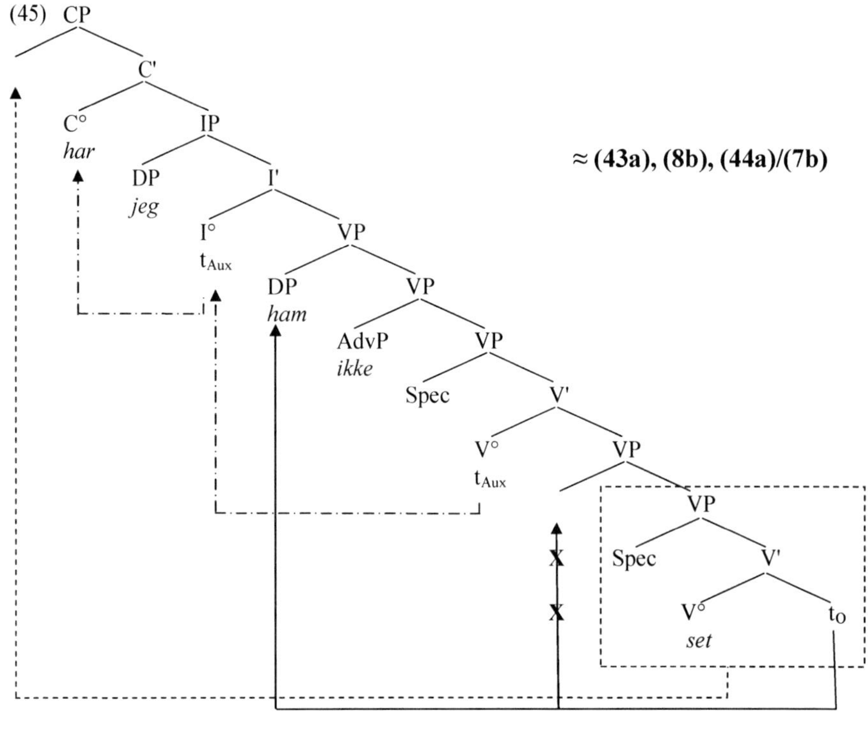

$\approx$ **(43a), (8b), (44a)/(7b)**

(46)

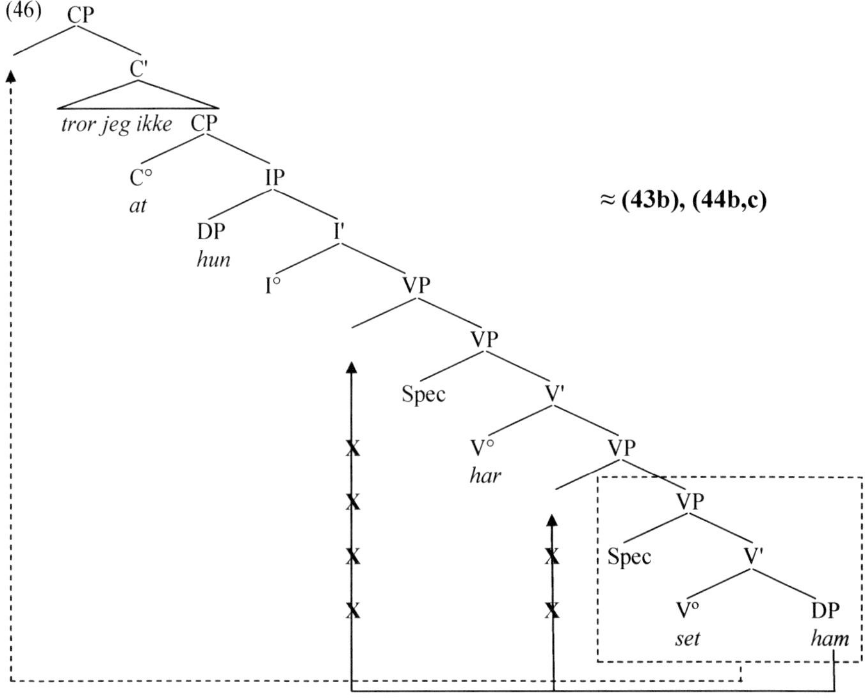

$\approx$ **(43b), (44b,c)**

T11 No remnant VP-topicalization out of an embedded clause

Da	Topic: V	OrdPres	Shift	Stay		ex.
☞ a	$[_{VP}$ **V** <u>Pron-O</u>] V S Adv Comp S Aux t_{VP}		*			(43b)
b	$[_{VP}$ **V** t_o] V S Adv Comp S Aux <u>Pron-O</u> t_{VP}		*	*!		(44b)
c	$[_{VP}$ **V** t_o] V S Adv Comp S <u>Pron-O</u> Aux t_{VP}	*!		*		(44c)

VP-topicalization out of an embedded clause with finite auxiliary *in situ* is completely parallel to the examples of VP-topicalization out of a main clause with non-finite auxiliary *in situ* in (24) and (25) above, repeated here as (47). In both cases, the presence of an auxiliary *in situ* means that OrdPres makes it impossible to comply with Shift (the object would have to adjoin to the top VP to satisfy Shift, where it precedes the auxiliary *in situ*), and there is therefore no reason for the object to leave the VP at all (see also that *T11* and *T12* are completely parallel).

(47) Da (a) $[_{VP}$ Kysse <u>hende</u>] har jeg aldrig villet.
  kiss her have I never would
  (b) *$[_{VP}$ Kysse _____] har jeg aldrig villet <u>hende</u>.
  (c) *$[_{VP}$ Kysse _____] har jeg <u>hende</u> aldrig villet.

T12 No remnant VP-topicalization across auxiliary in situ

Da	Topic: V	OrdPres	Shift	Stay		ex.
☞ a	$[_{VP}$ **V** <u>Pron-O</u>] Aux2 S Adv Aux1 t_{VP}		*			(47a)
b	$[_{VP}$ **V** t_o] Aux2 S Adv Aux1 <u>Pron-O</u> t_{VP}		*	*!		(47b)
c	$[_{VP}$ **V** t_o] Aux2 S Adv <u>Pron-O</u> Aux1 t_{VP}	*!		*		(47c)

The hypothesis that OS has to take place, i.e., that (a) a stranded object has to undergo movement to some position to the left of the finite verb, and (b) this movement is only possible if the finite verb itself has left its base position, would seem to be supported by phenomena of remnant VP-topicalization in Icelandic. Icelandic which has V°-to-I° movement and therefore also OS in embedded clauses, (48), permits a remnant object in VP-topicalization out of an embedded clause; compare (49) with the Danish examples in (44b,c), which are completely ungrammatical).

(48) Ic (a) *Ég spurði af hverju Pétur aldrei <u>læsi</u> <u>hana</u>.
  I asked why Pétur never read it
  (b) Ég spurði af hverju Pétur <u>læsi</u> <u>hana</u> aldrei _____ _____ .

(Vikner 2005: 396)

(49) Ic ?[$_{VP}$ Kysst ____] hélt   ég   ekki   að   þú   [$_{I^\circ}$ hefðir] <u>hana</u> oft, ...
          kissed   *think   I   not   that you   have*   *her   often*
                               ... bara haldið í höndina á henni.
                               only held in hand-the on her
                                              (Gunnar Hrafn Hrafnbjargarson, p.c.)

Stranding of the object is expected to be possible under the present approach since SHIFT can be satisfied without violating the higher ranking constraint ORDPRES due to movement of the finite auxiliary: OS is order-preserving; see *T13* below.

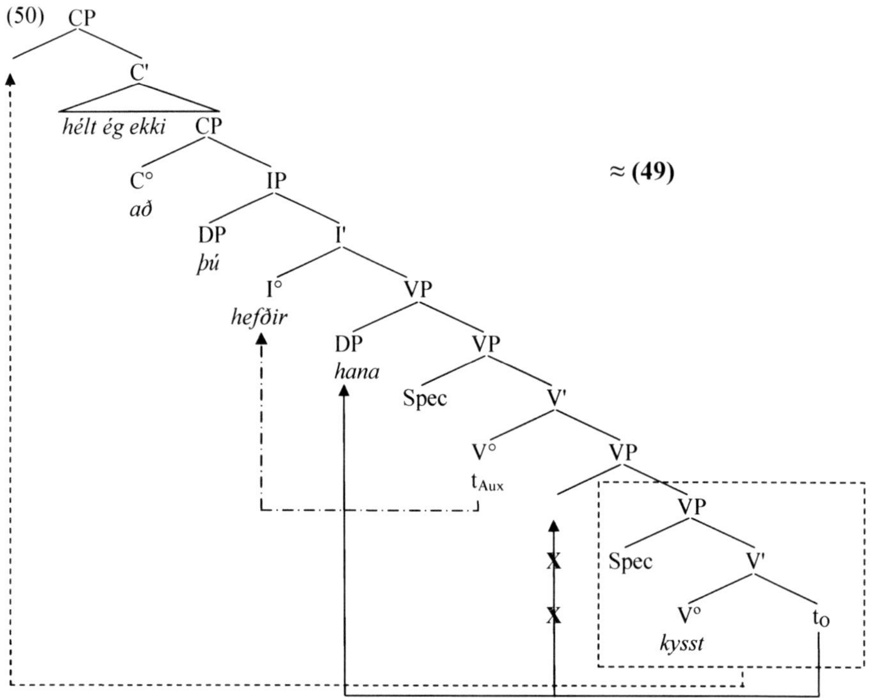

T13 Remnant VP-topicalization out of an embedded clause in Icelandic

Ic Topic: V	ORDPRES	SHIFT	STAY	ex.
a [$_{VP}$ **V** <u>Pron-O</u>] V S Adv Comp S Aux t$_{Aux}$ t$_{VP}$		*!		-
b [$_{VP}$ **V** t$_{O}$] V S Adv Comp S Aux t$_{Aux}$ <u>Pron-O</u> t$_{VP}$		*!	*	(49)
☞ c [$_{VP}$ **V** t$_{O}$] V S Adv Comp S Aux <u>Pron-O</u> t$_{Aux}$ t$_{VP}$			*	(49)

As in Mainland Scandinavian, remnant VP-topicalization is not possible in Icelandic in the presence of a non-finite auxiliary *in situ*, which prevents OS from complying with order preservation.

(51) Ic (a) [_{VP} Kyssa <u>hana</u>] hef ég aldrei viljað ...
            kiss   *her*   *have* *I*   *never* *would*
      (b) *[_{VP} Kyssa ____] hef ég aldrei viljað   <u>hana</u> ...
      (c) *[_{VP} Kyssa ____] hef ég <u>hana</u> aldrei viljað ...
                     ... bara haldið í höndina á henni.
                     only held in hand-the on her
                           (Gunnar Hrafn Hrafnbjargarson, p.c.)

Finally, note that long-distance topicalization of a VP that contains a trace of a *wh*-moved object is possible, (52). The fact that *wh*-movement is not subject to order preservation indicates that the constraint motivating *wh*-movement (WHSPEC) outranks ORDPRES, much like the constraint TOPIC in *T5*. Accordingly, stranding of a *wh*-object in SpecCP is predicted to be possible under the present approach – even if the object is non-peripheral within VP.

(52) Da (a) ?[_{VP} Læst __] ved jeg ikke <u>hvad for nogen bøger</u> Poul har, ...
           read   *know* *I*   *not*   *what for some books* *Poul* *has*
                 ... men jeg ved hvad for nogle han har købt.
                 but I know what for some he has bought

      (b) ?[_{VP} Smidt ___ ud] ved jeg ikke <u>hvor mange bøger</u> Poul har, ...
          thrown   *out* *know* *I*   *not*   *how many books* *Poul* *has*
                 ... men jeg ved hvor mange han har foræret væk.
                 but I know how many he has given away

The Mainland Scandinavian asymmetry between remnant VP-topicalization out of a main clause and remnant VP-topicalization out of an embedded clause discussed in the present subsection shows that stranding of an object must be motivated independently. Only if object extraction out of VP is required by some constraint (e.g. SHIFT) and complies with higher ranking principles (e.g. ORDPRES) is stranding during VP-topicalization possible.

5. Conclusion

Holmberg (1997, 1999) considers occurrences of a non-finite verb in topic position such as (7) to result from V°-topicalization. He assumes that HG is a matter of derivation rather than of representation, that is, a violation of HG cannot be rescued by some subsequent operation, and hence the non-finite verb has to move before OS can take place, ruling out remnant VP-topicalizations altogether.

Section 2.1 has shown, however, that there are theoretical as well as empirical problems with the V°-topicalization analysis. It is counter-cyclic and involves movement of an X° to an XP position. And it falsely predicts topicalization of a verb in constructions with a particle, PP-complement or infinitival clause to be grammatical.

Moreover, Fox and Pesetsky (2005a) present data from double object constructions that clearly show that remnant VP-topicalization is possible, as long as it does not involve a reversal of the base order of elements, which suggests that HG is representational. Their approach builds on the assumption that Spell-out applies at various points in the derivation (in particular, at VP and at CP) and that the information about the linearization of the material of a newly constructed Spell-out domain must not contradict the cumulated information of previous applications of Spell-out. In this way, Fox and Pesetsky (2005a) predict that OS differs radically from other types of (A- and A-bar-) movement that can result in a reversal of the order of elements, such as *wh*-movement or subject raising, in that the latter have to proceed successive cyclically via the left edge of VP while this is impossible for OS. In addition, Fox and Pesetsky's (2005a,b) approach makes incorrect predictions as to remnant VP-topicalization in constructions with an auxiliary verb *in situ.*

Based on an extended set of data concerning remnant VP-topicalization, the present OT approach agrees with Fox and Pesetsky (2005a,b) in the assumption that HG is to be accounted for in terms of order preservation, as required by the violable constraint ORDPRES. The ranking of ORDPRES relative to the constraints that motivate the various types of movement accounts for the contrast as to whether or not a certain movement operation has to be order preserving. Hence, OS does not receive a special treatment in the present approach; the properties distinguishing it from other movement types result from constraint interaction.

The linear conception of HG as expressed by the constraint ORDPRES and its dominance over the constraint that triggers OS, SHIFT, predicts that only objects that originate in a right-peripheral position within VP might be left behind in OS position during remnant VP-topicalization, accounting for the asymmetry in stranding of an IO and stranding of a DO observed by Fox and Pesetsky (2005a).

Finally, the asymmetry between main clauses and embedded clauses as to the applicability of remnant VP-topicalization in Mainland Scandinavian illustrates that object stranding has to involve OS. Object stranding is only possible in sentences in which there are no intervening verbs, something that would be expected if any object left behind during remnant VP-topicalization would have to undergo OS.

APPENDIX 1: Syntactic complexity of pronouns

The examples in (1)–(4) repeated below have shown that in Mainland Scandinavian, OS is restricted to weak pronouns whereas in Icelandic, also full DPs may undergo OS. In this connection note that not only a full DP like *den her bog* 'this book', (53), but also syntactically complex pronouns, that is modified or conjoined ones as in (54) and (55), are excluded from OS in Mainland Scandinavian. In Icelandic, in contrast, they can undergo OS, (58) and (59).

(53) Da (a) Hvorfor <u>læste</u> Peter   aldrig ____ <u>den her bog</u>?
         why   *read*   *Peter*   *never*   *this here book*
     (b) *Hvorfor <u>læste</u> Peter <u>den her bog</u> aldrig ____ ____?

(Vikner 2005: 394)

(54) Da (a) Hvorfor læste Peter   aldrig ____ <u>den her</u>?
             why   *read* *Peter*   *never*   *this here*
         (b) *Hvorfor læste Peter <u>den her</u> aldrig ____ ____?
                                                        (Vikner 2005: 417)

(55) Da (a) Han   så   ikke ____ <u>dig og hende</u> sammen.
             he *saw*   *not*   *you and her*   *together*
         (b) *Han   så <u>dig og hende</u> ikke ____ ____ sammen.
                                                        (Diesing and Jelinek 1993: 27)

(56) Da (a) *Jeg <u>kyssede</u>   ikke ____ <u>hende</u>.
             I   *kissed*   *not*   *her*
         (b) Jeg <u>kyssede</u> <u>hende</u> ikke ____ ____.

(57) Ic (a) Af hverju las Pétur   aldrei ____ <u>þessa bók</u>?
             why   *read* *Pétur*   *never*   *this book*
         (b) Af hverju las Pétur <u>þessa bók</u> aldrei ____ ____?
                                                        (Vikner 2005: 394)

(58) Ic (a) Af hverju las Pétur   aldrei <u>þessa hérna</u>?
             why   *read* *Pétur*   *never* *this here*
         (b) Af hverju las Pétur <u>þessa hérna</u> aldrei ____?
                                                        (Vikner 2005: 417)

(59) Ic (a) Ég   þekki   ekki <u>hann og hana</u>.
             I *know*   *not* *him and her*
         (b) Ég   þekki <u>hann og hana</u> ekki ____.
                                                        (Diesing and Jelinek 1993: 27)

(60) Ic (a) *Af hverju <u>las</u> Pétur   aldrei ____ <u>hana</u>?
             why   *read* *Pétur*   *never*   *it*
         (b) Af hverju <u>las</u> Pétur <u>hana</u> aldrei ____ ____?
                                                        (Vikner 2005: 394)

The difference between simple pronouns and all other DPs is that the former are DPs that do not contain a branching node whereas the latter are DPs that contain a branching node (compare (61a) with (61b,c) and (62a,b,c) below).[10,11]

(61) a. **simple pronoun**   b. **modified pronoun**   c. **conjoined pronoun**

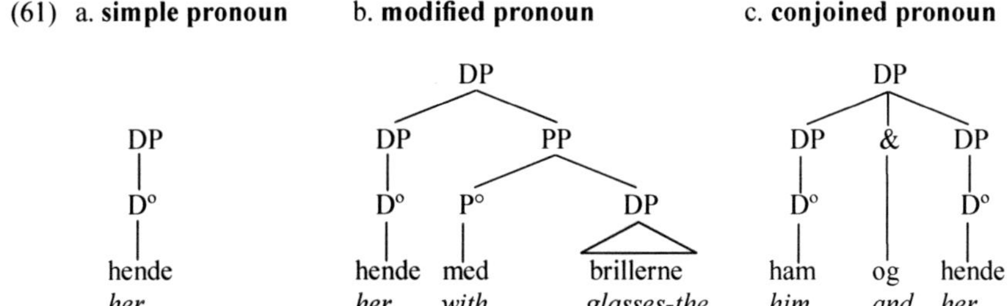

(62) **full DPs**

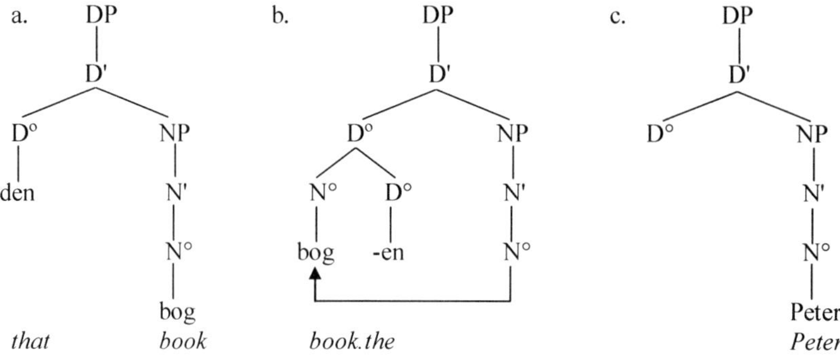

Thus, the ranking SHIFT >> STAYBRANCH permits OS of full DPs and more complex pronouns whereas the reverse ranking STAYBRANCH >> SHIFT prohibits it. Simultaneously, dominance of SHIFT over the more general constraint STAY predicts OS of weak (i.e. unstressed, non-modified, non-conjoined) pronouns to be possible even in cases where SHIFT is dominated by STAYBRANCH (STAYBRANCH >> SHIFT >> STAY).

APPENDIX 2: Differentiation according to syntactic complexity: Stay, Shift, or both?

In earlier versions (see for example Engels and Vikner 2006; Vikner and Engels 2006), we accounted for the contrasts as to the applicability of OS to pronouns and full DPs by a differentiation of the constraint SHIFT according to syntactic complexity, SHIFT, (63) repeated from (28), and SHIFTPRONOUN, (64).

(63) SHIFT:
      A [-focus] constituent precedes and c-commands a VP (of the same clause) that
      contains all V° positions and all VP-adjoined adverbials.

(64) SHIFTPRONOUN (SHIFTPRON):
      A [-focus] proform that is 'min = max' precedes and c-commands the lowest VP (of
      the same clause) that contains all other VPs and all VP-adjoined adverbials.

The ranking SHIFTPRON >> STAY >> SHIFT predicts that weak pronouns but not full DPs can undergo OS as observed in Mainland Scandinavian, while dominance of both SHIFT-constraints over STAY permits OS independent of syntactic complexity as found in Icelandic; see Appendix 1.

The change from the differentiation of SHIFT to the differentiation of STAY according to syntactic complexity made it possible to account for the fact that OS cannot force stranding of other right-peripheral constituents such as the PP-complement in (65) under remnant VP-topicalization, which was incorrectly predicted to be possible in the SHIFTPRON/SHIFT analysis (compare *T14* with *T15*, where the ungrammatical candidate d is incorrectly predicted to be optimal, as marked by L).

(65) Da (a) [$_{VP}$ Stillet <u>det</u> <u>på bordet</u>] har jeg   ikke.
             put *it* *on table-the* *have* *I*   *not*
     (b) *[$_{VP}$ Stillet ___ <u>på bordet</u>] har jeg <u>det</u> ikke.
     (c) *[$_{VP}$ Stillet <u>det</u> _______] har jeg   ikke <u>på bordet</u>.
     (d) *[$_{VP}$ Stillet ___ _______] har jeg det ikke <u>på bordet</u>

T14

Da:	Topic: V	ORD PRES	STAY BRANCH	SHIFT	STAY	ex.
☞ a	[$_{VP}$ **V** <u>Pron-O</u> PP] Aux Sub Adv t$_{VP}$			**		(65a)
b	[$_{VP}$ **V** t$_{Pron}$ <u>PP</u>] Aux Sub <u>Pron-O</u> Adv t$_{VP}$	*!		*	*	(65b)
c	[$_{VP}$ **V** <u>Pron-O</u> t$_{PP}$] Aux Sub Adv <u>PP</u> t$_{VP}$		*!	*	*	(65c)
d	[$_{VP}$ **V** t$_{Pron}$ t$_{PP}$] Aux Sub <u>Pron-O</u> Adv <u>PP</u> t$_{VP}$		*!		**	(65d)

T15

Da:	Topic: V	ORD PRES	SHIFT PRON	STAY	ex.
a	[$_{VP}$ **V** <u>Pron-O</u> PP] Aux Sub Adv t$_{VP}$		*!		(65a)
b	[$_{VP}$ **V** t$_{Pron}$ <u>PP</u>] Aux Sub <u>Pron-O</u> Adv t$_{VP}$	*!		*	(65b)
c	[$_{VP}$ **V** <u>Pron-O</u> t$_{PP}$] Aux Sub Adv <u>PP</u> t$_{VP}$		*!	*	(65c)
☹ d	[$_{VP}$ **V** t$_{Pron}$ t$_{PP}$] Aux Sub <u>Pron-O</u> Adv <u>PP</u> t$_{VP}$			**	(65d)

However, a distinction between STAY and STAYBRANCH would seem not to be quite sufficient. Although the cross-linguistic variation as to the mobility of pronouns and more complex DPs might be accounted for by the differentiation of STAY suggested in the main text above, the distinction between SHIFT and SHIFTPRON would seem to be necessary as well. In Vikner and Engels (2006), we argued that Scrambling in the West Germanic languages should be treated on a par with OS in the Scandinavian languages by considering both movements to be triggered by SHIFT (and SHIFTPRON). Though both pronouns and complex phrases may undergo movement in Dutch (SHIFT >> STAY, STAYBRANCH), they differ in their ability to scramble across an intervening argument, that is, whether or not the movement has to maintain the ordering relations (ORDPRES). In other words, whereas a pronominal DO may scramble across an IO, (66b), a non-pronominal DO may not, (67b), even though a non-pronominal DO may scramble across an adverb, (68b).

(66) Du (a) *... dat Jan   waarschijnlijk   <u>Marie</u> <u>'t</u>   gegeven   heeft.
            that Jan   *probably*   *Marie*   *it*   *given*   *has*
     (b)   ... dat Jan   <u>'t</u>   waarschijnlijk   <u>Marie</u>   __   gegeven   heeft.

(67) Du (a)   ... dat ik   gisteren   <u>de jongen</u> <u>het boek</u>   gegeven   heb.
            that I   *yesterday* *the boys*   *the book* *given*   *have*
     (b) *... dat ik   <u>het boek</u>   gisteren   <u>de jongen</u> ______   gegeven   heb.

                                         (De Hoop & Kosmeijer 1995:150)

(68) Du (a)   ... dat ik   gisteren   <u>het boek</u>   gelezen   heb.
            that I   *yesterday* *the book* *read*   *have*
     (b)   ... dat ik   <u>het boek</u>   gisteren   ______   gelezen   heb.

This asymmetry may only be accounted for if movement of pronouns and movement of more complex phrases are motivated by distinct constraints, SHIFTPRON and SHIFT. Only if pronominal movement is additionally triggered by some other constraint than movement of full DPs, this asymmetry might be derived from differences in the constraint ranking relative to ORDPRES: SHIFTPRON >> ORDPRES >> SHIFT.

Hence, we would seem to end up with differentiation according to syntactic complexity twice, for SHIFT and for STAY.[12]

Notes

1. We are grateful for helpful comments and suggestions to Ken Ramshøj Christensen, Gunlög Josefsson, Henrik Jørgensen, Gereon Müller, Martin Salzmann, Johanna Wood and the editors of this volume, as well as to audiences at the universities of Aarhus, Berlin (ZAS), Cambridge, Leipzig, London (UCL), Lund, Newcastle and Stuttgart. This work was carried out as part of the project 'Object positions – comparative syntax in a cross-theoretical perspective' financed by Forskningsrådet for Kultur og Kommunikation (Danish Research Council for Culture and Communication).
2. In addition, note that OS in verb topicalization contexts is unexpected under an equidistance approach to OS; see Chomsky (1993: 15–19), Bobaljik and Jonas (1996: 200–3) and the discussion in Broekhuis (2000). A very different approach that we shall not pursue here is one of trying to do away with the differences between X°- and XP-movement, as for example in Vicente (2009).
3. Note that OS targets a position to the left of the base position of the finite verb: A shifted object precedes a clause-medial adverbial, (4), which in turn precedes the finite verb in embedded clauses in Mainland Scandinavian, where verb movement (and thus OS) is not possible.

(i) Da (a)   Hun   spurgte   hvorfor   han   aldrig   <u>havde</u>   læst   den her bog.
           she   *asked*   *why*   *he*   *never*   *had*   *read*   *this here book*
     (b)   *Hun   spurgte   hvorfor   han <u>havde</u>   aldrig   ____   læst   bogen.

4. Notice further that although these examples, (24) and (25), have a non-finite auxiliary *in situ* (as do the ungrammatical examples in Holmberg (2005: 151) that Fox and Pesetsky (2005b: 252) refer to), this is not the only possible case of auxiliaries *in situ*. In embedded clauses, finite auxiliaries remain *in situ* in Mainland Scandinavian, and also here topicalization of the entire VP (but not of a remnant VP) is possible, and also here Fox and Pesetsky (2005b: 252) make the wrong prediction, as discussed in section 4.2 below.
5. There is a slight difference between (25)b and (25)c, which we cannot account for. What we can account for is the much clearer difference between (25)a on the one hand and (25)b and (25)c on the other hand.

6. The ranking SHIFT >> STAY predicts that OS is obligatory (unless it is blocked by an intervening category; see below). In Swedish and Norwegian, where pronominal OS is optional, STAY and SHIFT might be tied, STAY <> SHIFT: Both relative rankings of the two constraints, STAY >> SHIFT and SHIFT >> STAY, co-exist in these languages; depending on the actual ranking, movement is required or prohibited, accounting for its optionality. Likewise, a constraint tie between SHIFT and STAYBRANCH would predict that OS of unfocused full DPs is optional in Icelandic. (In terms of Müller's (2001b) classification of constraint ties, we are here dealing with an ordered global tie.)

7. Crucially, the order at *base level* referred to in the definition of ORDPRES in (32) cannot correspond to the base-generated order but instead, we would like to tentatively suggest that it corresponds to the order at an intermediate level at which all cases and all thematic roles assigned by lexical $V°$ have been assigned. This is important for double object constructions if these are considered to involve a Larsonian shell structure. The IO precedes the verb in the base-generated order but follows it at the intermediate level. As (i) shows, an IO cannot undergo OS across a verb *in situ*, as expected if it is the order at the intermediate level that has to be preserved.

  (i) Da (a) Jeg har   ikke [$_{VP}$ givet [$_{VP}$ <u>hende</u> t$_v$ den]]
                I   *have*   *not* *given*   *her*   *it*
           (b) *Jeg har <u>hende</u> ikke [$_{VP}$ givet [$_{VP}$ _____ t$_v$ den]]

8. Note that OS of two objects takes place as two independent movements. The ranking STAYBRANCH >> SHIFT >> STAY predicts that the two pronouns cannot be moved together in a complex constituent but must each move individually. Thereby, reversal of the two objects is prohibited by ORDPRES.

9. Candidate a (which also corresponds to a grammatical sentence, (43)a), presumably wins a different competition, namely the one where the object is also marked for topic-hood. In the competitions discussed in this subsection, the object is not marked for topic-hood, only the verb is.

10. Note that although they are syntactically simple (i.e. do not contain a branching node), focused pronouns do not undergo OS, neither in Mainland Scandinavian nor in Icelandic.

  (i) Da (a) Hvorfor læste Peter   aldrig ____ <u>DEN</u>?
                why   *read* *Peter*   *never*   *it*
           (b) *Hvorfor læste Peter <u>DEN</u> aldrig ____ ____?

                                        (Vikner 2005: 417)

  (ii) Ic (a) Af hverju las Pétur   aldrei ____ <u>HANA</u>?
                why   *read* *Peter*   *never*   *it*
           (b) ?*Af hverju las Pétur <u>HANA</u> aldrei ____ ____?

                                  (Gunnar Hrafn Hrafnbjargarson, p.c.)

This is captured by the restriction of SHIFT to [-focus] constituents. As these are not required to undergo OS by SHIFT, they are prohibited from doing so by STAY.

11. This attempt to capture the difference between simple pronouns and all other DPs is thus purely syntactic, as opposed to e.g. Vogel (2006), which also employs phonological constraints.

12. Note that SHIFTPRON would have to be ranked below STAYBRANCH in Mainland Scandinavian to avoid the problem illustrated in *T15* above.

References

Bobaljik, Jonathan (2005) Re: CycLin and the role of PF in Object Shift. *Theoretical Linguistics* 31 (1–2): 111–25.

Bobaljik, Jonathan and Jonas, Dianne (1996) Subject positions and the roles of TP. *Linguistic Inquiry* 27 (2): 195–236.

Broekhuis, Hans (2000) Against feature strength: The case of Scandinavian Object Shift. *Natural Language and Linguistic Theory* 18 (4): 673–721.

Broekhuis, Hans (2008) *Derivations and Evaluations: Object Shift in the Germanic Languages.* Berlin: de Gruyter.

Chomsky, Noam (1993) A minimalist program for linguistic theory. In Kenneth Hale and Samuel J. Keyser (eds) *The View from Building 20,* 1–52. Cambridge, MA: MIT Press.

Chomsky, Noam (2000) Minimalist inquiries. In Roger Martin, David Michaels and Juan Uriagereka (eds) *Step by Step: Essays on Minimalist Syntax in Honor of Howard Lasnik,* 89–156. Cambridge, MA: MIT Press.

Chomsky, Noam (2001) Beyond explanatory adequacy. *MIT Working Papers in Linguistics* 20: 1–28.

Christensen, Ken Ramshøj (2005) *Interfaces: Negation – Syntax – Brain.* PhD dissertation, University of Aarhus, Denmark. (www.hum.au.dk/engelsk/engkrc/Papers/krc-phd.pdf)

De Hoop, Helen and Kosmeijer, Wim (1995) Case and scrambling: D-structure versus S-structure. In Hubert Haider, Susan Olsen and Sten Vikner (eds) *Studies in Comparative Germanic Syntax,* 139–58. Dordrecht: Kluwer Academic Publishers.

Déprez, Viviane (1994) Parameters of object movement. In Norbert Corver and Henk van Riemsdijk (eds) *Studies on Scrambling,* 101–52. Berlin: Mouton de Gruyter.

Engels, Eva (2011) Microvariation in object positions: Negative Shift in Scandinavian. *Nordic Journal of Linguistics* 34 (2): 133–55.

Engels, Eva (2012) Scandinavian negative indefinites and cyclic linearization. *Syntax* 15 (2): 109–41.

Engels, Eva and Vikner, Sten (2006) An Optimality–Theoretic analysis of Scandinavian Object Shift and remnant VP-topicalisation. *Linguistics in Potsdam* 25: 195–231. (http://opus.kobv.de/ubp/volltexte/2007/1190/pdf/linguistics25.pdf)

Erteschik-Shir, Nomi (2001) P-syntactic motivation for movement: Imperfect alignment in Object Shift. *Working Papers in Scandinavian Syntax* 68: 49–73.

Fox, Danny and Pesetsky, David (2003) Cyclic linearization and the typology of movement. Ms., MIT. (http://web.mit.edu/linguistics/www/fox/July_19_handout.pdf)

Fox, Danny and Pesetsky, David (2005a) Cyclic linearization of syntactic structure. *Theoretical Linguistics* 31: 1–45.

Fox, Danny and Pesetsky, David (2005b) Cyclic linearization and its interaction with other aspects of grammar: A reply. *Theoretical Linguistics* 31: 235–62.

Holmberg, Anders (1986) *Word Order and Syntactic Features in the Scandinavian Languages and English.* PhD dissertation, University of Stockholm.

Holmberg, Anders (1997) The true nature of Holmberg's generalization. *NELS* 27: 203–17.

Holmberg, Anders (1999) Remarks on Holmberg's generalization. *Studia Linguistica* 53 (1): 1–39.

Holmberg, Anders (2005) Linearization in two ways. *Theoretical Linguistics* 31 (1–2): 147–57.

Koeneman, Olaf (2006) Shape conservation, Holmberg's generalization and predication. In Jutta Hartmann and Laszlo Molnárfi (eds) *Comparative Studies in Germanic Syntax,* 51–87. Amsterdam: Benjamins.

Müller, Gereon (2001a) Order preservation, parallel movement, and the emergence of the unmarked. In Jane Grimshaw, Géraldine Legendre and Sten Vikner (eds) *Optimality Theoretic Syntax,* 279–313. Cambridge, MA: MIT Press.

Müller, Gereon (2001b) Optionality in Optimality–Theoretic syntax. In Lisa Cheng and Rint Sybesma (eds) *The Second Glot International State-of-the-Article Book,* 289–321. Berlin: Mouton.

Sells, Peter (2001) *Structure, Alignment and Optimality in Swedish.* Stanford, CA: CSLI Publications.

Vicente, Luis (200). An alternative to remnant movement for partial predicate fronting. *Syntax* 12 (2): 180–213.

Vikner, Sten (2005) Object Shift. In Henk van Riemsdijk and Martin Everaert (eds) *The Blackwell Companion to Syntax,* 392–436. Oxford: Blackwell.

Vikner, Sten and Engels, Eva (2006) The Germanic languages and the SOV/SVO difference, Part VII: Object Shift and Scrambling – An Optimality Theoretic approach. DGfS/GLOW Summer School: Micro- & Macrovariation, University of Stuttgart, 14 August–2 September. Ms., University of Aarhus. (www.hum.au.dk/engelsk/engsv/papers/stuttgart/vikner-stgt7.pdf)

Vogel, Ralf (2006) Weak function word shift. *Linguistics* 44 (5): 1059–93.

Williams, Edwin (2003) *Representation Theory.* Cambridge, MA: MIT Press.

III OPTIMAL DESIGN, ECONOMY AND LAST RESORT IN OT

9 Optimality theory and the minimalist program

Vieri Samek-Lodovici*

ABSTRACT This chapter examines the relation between Optimality Theory and the Minimalist Program, arguing that OT and Minimalism are not alternative, incompatible theories and that a theory of constraint conflict like OT offers an ideal framework to model the central thesis of the Minimalist Program, namely that syntax constitutes an optimal solution for meeting constraints at the Sensory-Motor and Conceptual interfaces. The chapter examines three linguistic phenomena where OT can provide a detailed and precise understanding of how such a central Minimalist thesis is realized: (i) the existence of crosslinguistic variation, which under OT stems from the very content of UG constraints; (ii) the effects of prosodic constraints on the syntax of focus in Italian (Zubizarreta 1998), which constitutes one of the clearest cases of interface constraints shaping syntax, provided the import of constraint conflict is recognized; (iii) the presence of constraint conflict even amongst minimalist principles originally conceived as non-conflicting, as is the case for the movement and structure economy principles proposed in the analysis of pronominals by Cardinaletti and Starke (1994, 1999).

KEYWORDS Optimality Theory; constraint conflict; minimalist program; prosody-syntax interface

1. Introduction

The Minimalist Program (Chomsky 1995, 2000) and Optimality Theory (Prince and Smolensky 1993, 2004) are not alternative theories logically inconsistent with each other. Optimality Theory is a theory of how universal constraints of grammar interact (Prince and Smolensky 1993; Grimshaw 2005). Minimalism, as Chomsky (2000: 41) notes, is a research *program* – not a theory – investigating to what extent the language faculty provides an optimal design for the satisfaction of conditions at the interface with the sensory-motor system (PF) and the system of thought (LF). It

* Vieri Samek-Lodovici, Department of Italian, University College London, Gower Street, London WC1E 6BT. E-mail: ucljvsl@ucl.ac.uk

is thus possible to pursue an OT-perspective of human grammar while maintaining minimalist goals, a fact highlighted by many contributors to the DEAL 2005 conference at ZAS (Berlin) on the relation between OT and Minimalism and also explicitly pointed out by Chomsky (2000: 141). In this chapter, I argue that an OT-approach to grammar is essential to minimalist investigations, because it dramatically widens the set of linguistic properties potentially reducible to interface conditions while at the same time dispensing with interface-external language-specific provisos. The discussion will hopefully also dispel some common misconceptions about OT.

2.   Crosslinguistic variation

One of the most evident empirical properties of human language is its crosslinguistic variation. Minimalism, as described in Chomsky (1995, 2000), excludes crosslinguistic variation from the set of properties and imperfections that call for a minimalist explanation.

Variation is instead assumed to follow from differences in the feature-bundles associated with lexical items in the lexicon of each language, allowing for parametric variation in feature strength (weak vs. strong) and/or variation in feature distribution (presence of EPP-features, presence of dislocating features).

Some important consequences follow from this assumption. To begin with, variation is left unrelated to interface conditions. Interface conditions might possibly motivate the existence of interpretable and even uninterpretable features as part of the optimal design of grammar, but they cannot derive the differences in strength and distribution associated with crosslinguistic variation. Variation is treated as if it were accidental. The parametric properties of features could be eliminated with no consequences for the optimal design of C_{HL}. The existence of variation is thus unexpected: since a relation with interface conditions is excluded a priori, the parametric properties responsible for it are left with no linguistic motivation. It is left unexplained why variation occurs at all. This state of affairs appears at odds with minimalist goals. In its strictest possible interpretation a minimalist approach to language should see a pervasive property like crosslinguistic variation emerge naturally from interface conditions.

Whether this ambitious goal can be achieved or not depends on what assumptions are made about the nature of grammar constraints and their interaction. If the universal constraints of grammar never conflict with each other, then grammaticality inevitably requires their simultaneous satisfaction, and since the structures that satisfy all constraints in one language would also do so in another language when available, it becomes inevitable to account for crosslinguistic variation via stipulated language-specific properties governing which structures are available in each language.

If on the other hand universal constraints are allowed to conflict with one another, as maintained by OT, crosslinguistic variation becomes a predicted outcome, merely reflecting all the possible alternative resolutions of the conflicts among UG constraints.[1] Under this view, crosslinguistic variation is no longer accidental. Rather, it is entailed by the universal constraints of grammar themselves, which directly determine: (i) *whether* variation occurs: it only occurs whenever two or more constraints conflict, never when constraints do not conflict; (ii) *where* it occurs: it occurs only with respect to those structures and properties on which constraints conflict; (iii) *how* it occurs: the different structural aspects and properties found across distinct languages are themselves entirely determined by universal constraints, not by language-specific provisos.[2]

Deriving crosslinguistic variation as an inevitable consequence of constraint interaction is highly desirable because it deepens the explanatory power of our generative models. As concisely but effectively stated by Edwin Williams in his DEAL 2005 contribution, '*deepening explanation* [...] *arises when previously unrelated parts of a theory become predictively interrelated – the "constants" of the theory are thereby reduced, making the correct theory more inevitable*' (Williams 2005). By making crosslinguistic variation a predicted property, OT relates it to UG constraints in the strictest possible way, reducing the need for unnecessary theoretical constants such as language-specific devices and provisos.

The explanatory power of constraint conflict also emerges when considering the number of distinct languages derived by a set of N conditions. With N binary parameters we may at most derive 2^N distinct languages, whereas N conflicting constraints may give rise to $N!$ languages.[3] As N increases, $N!$ rapidly becomes a vastly larger number than 2^N. For example six conditions determine $2^6 = 64$ languages with binary parameters against $6! = 720$ potential languages with conflicting constraints. With eight conditions the numbers become 256 vs. 40,320. Conversely, this means that deriving a fixed number of languages requires a smaller number of conflicting constraints than parameters. For example, 5,040 languages could be potentially derived by seven conflicting constraints, but would require at least 13 binary parameters.[4] It follows that on purely formal grounds an OT approach to constraint interaction may potentially account for the variation manifested across human languages through a much more restricted number of principled conditions than would be necessary with parametric devices, thus showing a higher degree of explanatory power.[5]

The above arguments provide a compelling theoretical motivation for investigating an OT approach to constraint interaction. They hold independently of minimalist goals, yet they appear essential to a minimalist perspective given their potential for reducing all aspects of human grammar, crosslinguistic variation included, to the conflicting interaction of universal constraints, including constraints at the PF and LF interfaces.[6]

3.   Constraint conflict

Having considered the above theoretical motivation favoring an OT perspective, we may ask whether it is supported by any empirical evidence. Obviously, the very existence of crosslinguistic variation provides a first important piece of empirical support since, as we have seen, variation is expected if constraints conflict and unexpected if they do not. There is also a great variety of highly complex linguistic paradigms that find a simple and principled explanation once examined in terms of constraint conflict. See for example the numerous OT-syntax analyses downloadable at the Rutgers Optimality Archives at roa.rutgers.edu. Several analyses are also available in the following volumes: Barbosa *et al.* (1998); Beckman *et al.* (1995); Fanselow and Féry (2002); Legendre *et al.* (2001); and Samek-Lodovici (2007). Here, I will only consider two specific cases that I find particularly significant for the kind of constraint conflicts involved. The first shows how syntactic properties could be genuinely reduced to interface constraints – here prosodic constraints governing the position of stress – once a constraint conflict perspective is adopted. The second examines an important case of constraint conflict within a minimalist analysis, showing how a theory of constraint conflict is often implicit and inevitable even in non-OT analyses.

3.1 Conflict between prosody and syntax

Verb movement aside, the syntactic and prosodic properties of simple clauses with overt subjects in Italian and English are very similar. When the entire clause constitutes new information focus, occurring as an answer to the general question '*any news?*', we observe SVO order with rightmost prosodic prominence in both languages, as shown in (1) (I am abstracting away from the idiosyncratic properties of English unaccusatives, where stress may fall on the subject. Focused phrases are subscripted by 'F'. The word carrying prosodic prominence is marked as 'x' and constitutes the head of the intonational phrase 'IP' that encompasses the entire clause.)

(1) (a) (x   )$_{ip}$
   [Gianni ha cantato]$_F$ (focusing context: Any news?)
   John   has   sung
   'John has sung'

  (b) (x   )$_{ip}$
   [John has sung]$_F$ (focusing context: Any news?)

This similarity is disrupted as soon as non-final constituents are focused. In this case, Italian can preserve its rightmost prosodic prominence by rearranging the syntactic structure so as to let focus occur rightmost; see for example the postverbal focused subject in specVP in (2a) below. English instead leaves its syntactic structure unaffected, but it retracts prosodic prominence onto the focused constituent; see for example the stressed clause-initial focused subject in (2b).

(2) (a) (x   )$_{ip}$
   [Ha cantato   Gianni$_F$]   (focusing context: Who, among them, has sung?)
   has sung   John
   'JOHN has sung'

  (b) (x   )$_{ip}$
   [JOHN$_F$ has sung]   (focusing context: Who, among them, has sung?)

The challenge is to derive the divergence in (2a) and (2b) from the same constraints that determine the convergence in (1a) and (1b). Note the minimalist nature of this challenge, which aims at analyzing all above sentences as optimal solutions dictated by a single set of universal constraints rather than resorting to language-specific stipulations to derive the divergence in (2).[7]

The crucial insight was provided by Zubizarreta (1998), who analyzed rightmost focus in Romance as arising from the need to keep prosodic prominence rightmost while stressing the focused constituent. Armed with this insight and constraint conflict, we may account for the entire paradigm in terms of three simple constraints: (i) the syntactic constraint EPP, forcing subjects to raise to specTP (Chomsky 1982; Grimshaw 1997); (ii) the prosodic constraint HipRt requiring the prosodic head of an intonational phrase ip to align with that ip's right boundary (Selkirk 1995; Truckenbrodt 1995); and (iii) the constraint Stress-Focus requiring focused phrases to carry the highest prominence in their domain (Jackendoff 1972; Truckenbrodt, 1995; Zubizarreta 1998. In all above examples the focus domain coincides with the entire clause.)

When the entire clause is focused, as is the case in (1a) and (1b), Stress-Focus is trivially satisfied independently of the position of prosodic prominence. Consequently EPP and HipRt can be satisfied independently of one another, giving rise to the preverbal subject and rightmost stress of sentences (1a) and (1b) represented in structure a in tableau T1 below. Having a rightmost subject as in structure b violates the EPP constraint and therefore yields a suboptimal structure independently of the constraint ranking (in T1 below, 'x' represents main stress and each '*' represents one constraint violation).

T1 Clause-wide focus

	Stress Focus	HipRt	EPP
a. ☞ $\begin{array}{c}(\quad\quad x)_{ip}\\ [\text{ S aux V}]_F\end{array}$			
b. $\begin{array}{c}(\quad\quad x\ )_{ip}\\ [\_\text{ aux V S}]_F\end{array}$			*

When the subject is focused, however, the need to satisfy Stress-Focus – here ranked highest – unleashes a conflict between EPP and HipRt. Grammars ranking HipRt higher than EPP, like Italian, place the subject in rightmost position to satisfy HipRt, as in (2a), even though this forces a violation of the lower ranked EPP constraint. Grammars ranking EPP higher than HipRt, like English, raise the subject to specTP to satisfy EPP, as in (2b), even though this forces a non-rightmost prosodic peak in the intonational phrase encompassing the clause, violating the lower ranked HipRt. The conflict is also schematically represented in tableau T2. For a more detailed analysis, see Samek-Lodovici (2005).[8]

T2 Focused subjects

	Stress Focus	HipRt	EPP
a. $\begin{array}{c}(\qquad\text{x})_{ip}\\ [\,\_\,\text{aux V S}_F]\end{array}$			*
b. $\begin{array}{c}(\ \text{x}\qquad)_{ip}\\ [\,\text{S}_F\,\text{aux V}]\end{array}$		*	

The conflict between EPP and HipRt predicts *where* the focus patterns converge and diverge, while its possible resolutions determine *how* the structures diverge when they diverge. All these predictions follow with no appeal to language-specific properties and devices. The relevant constraints remain invariant in both languages and are fairly non-controversial, rooted in a long tradition of generative analysis. They are also clearly active in both languages, since they are necessary in both to determine the location of subjects and main stress when focus encompasses the entire clause.

These desirable properties of the analysis follow from constraint conflict. If we assume that constraints do not conflict, we immediately lose the potential for a unified analysis rooted in UG-constraints alone. Non-violable counterparts of EPP and HipRt would still be necessary to derive the preverbal subject and rightmost stress of (1a) and (1b). Being non-violable, they would have to be satisfied by sentences (2a) and (2b) as well, since these sentences are grammatical. Yet these sentences appear to clearly violate them. Therefore, some further provisos will have to be introduced to avoid these violations.

This is exactly the problem faced by the analysis in Zubizarreta (1998), where the lack of a theory of constraint conflict forces the introduction of two language specific stipulations. The first makes unfocused phrases prosodically invisible in English (Zubizarreta 1998: 49). This is necessary to prevent English from resembling Italian, where the prosodic visibility of unfocused phrases together with rightmost stress forces focus in rightmost position. The second introduces in the grammar of Italian a device that detects the potential conflict between (the inviolable counterparts of) EPP and HipRt when focus is non-final and forces a re-arrangement of the syntactic structure in order to solve it (Zubizarreta 1998: 140). Without this device, the syntactic re-arrangement would not happen and focus would not occur rightmost.

These two stipulations are the theoretical price paid to the lack of constraint conflict. Because the conflict between EPP and HipRt cannot be exploited, English and Italian must be made different via language-specific provisos, or else they would behave the same way because both must satisfy the non-violable versions of the constraints. This is a general problem that inevitably arises whenever conflicting constraints responsible for crosslinguistic variation are sufficiently essential to have non-violable counterparts in non-OT frameworks. The work done by constraint conflict in determining variation will have to be addressed by special provisos, as the non-violable constraints would otherwise impose uniformity.

The benefits of a conflict based approach in the above analysis are apparent, since it provides a unified account of the attested convergent and divergent focus patterns of English and Italian with no appeal to language-specific provisos. Taking a minimalist perspective, however, we may also ask whether the conflict-based analysis is consistent with minimalist criteria. In this respect, we may wonder how Stress-Focus, EPP, and HiPRt relate to the PF and LF interfaces. The same minimalist criteria, however, do not entail the absence of constraint conflict. Since the sensory-motor and conceptual system serve largely independent goals, there is no reason to exclude a priori the possibility of conflicting interface conditions. As far as I can see minimalist goals would remain best served by an analysis based on constraint conflict.

Zubizarreta's insights on Romance focus also show that constraints governing prosodic prominence may affect syntactic structures. It follows that PF should not be insulated in a sub-system of its own external to narrow syntax as proposed in Chomsky (2000: 118). In my opinion, this ought to be considered a welcome result under a minimalist perspective, because it ties syntactic dislocation to constraints governing prosody, thus identifying a linguistic pattern where non-syntactic interface conditions affect syntax, as is predicted by a strict interface-based minimalist approach to grammar.

3.2   Conflict between economy principles

Economy principles impose an order on grammatical structures, favoring the one that is most economic according to a given criterion (e.g. the shortest movement chain). When distinct economy principles are at play, they may conflict with each other, each favoring a distinct structure. In OT, the ranking between the two constraints determines how the conflict is resolved, but this solution is only available if constraint violation is allowed. When constraints are turned into inviolable principles, conflicts must be resolved by some other means. It is useful to understand what these means are and their theoretical cost.

An interesting case of this kind occurs between the principles for structural and movement economy discussed in Cardinaletti and Starke (1994, 1999) in their study of pronominal forms. Using data from a great variety of languages, they make four important observations: (i) weak pronominal forms are structurally simpler than their strong counterparts, lacking one or more of the functional projections that top the structural representation of strong forms; (ii) weak forms must obtain/check the functional features encoded in the projections that they lack by raising to appropriate positions of the clause (e.g. movement to spec AgrP to get Case); (iii) there is thus an inverse relation between the richness of a pronominal form's structural representation and the length of its movement chain, with weak pronominal forms involving less structure but requiring longer chains; (iv) despite their longer chains, weak forms are always preferred to strong forms. Strong forms however remain possible whenever weak forms are excluded by independent factors.

On the basis of (iv), Cardinaletti and Starke propose an 'Economy of Representation' principle requiring minimal structures. But as the inverse relation between structure and chain-length in (iii) above shows, the Economy of Representation principle conflicts with the Economy of Movement principle. How should this conflict be modeled and (iii) derived?

Under a conflict based theory like OT, the solution is straightforward. Economy is an inevitable property of the optimality theoretic interaction of the universal constraints of grammar (Grimshaw 1997, 2005; Prince 1997: 2; Burzio 2000: 209, 216; McCarthy 2002: 40; Smolensky *et al.* 2006: 505, 531). The effects associated with Economy of Movement, for example, emerge from the conflict between constraints requiring movement to specific positions of the clause to obtain/check the relevant features – let me identify them collectively as a single 'Check-F' constraint – and the constraint Stay violated once per movement operation (Grimshaw 1997). When Stay is ranked lower than Check-F, the optimal structure is the one that best meets Check-F, for example by raising a weak pronoun to spec AgrP to get Case, while ensuring the lowest number of Stay violations, effectively minimizing movement (or more precisely, avoiding any movement not required by Check-F).[9,10]

A similar analysis can be given for Cardinaletti and Starke's Economy of Structure, with a general constraint *Struc (Zoll 1993, Prince and Smolensky 1993/2004) that penalizes all structure. Cardinaletti and Starke's observed preference for weaker pronominal forms simply reflects the ranking Check-F » *Struc » Stay (i.e. Check-F outranking *Struc, and *Struc outranking Stay). In accord with Cardinaletti and Starke's points (iii) and (iv), this ranking favors weaker forms with less structure, and hence fewer violations of *Struc, over strong forms that violate *Struc more times, even though the strong forms perform better than the weak forms on the lower ranked Stay constraint. Crucially, the weaker form can beat the strong one on *Struc because both perform equally well on Check-F, here representing general requirements other than structural and movement economy. This is illustrated schematically in tableaux T3. The actual number of violations for each constraint depends on the specific data being examined, but boxes marked with a star '*' would still contain more violations than boxes with no stars.

T3 Pronominal forms

	Check-F	*Struc	Stay
a. ☞ weak form			*
b. strong form		*	

The preference for weaker pronominal forms is subordinated to the satisfaction of the general requirement represented by Check-F. Whenever the weaker form underperforms a strong form on some property assessed by Check-F – such as being available in conjunctions, which weak forms disallow, or allowing for focusing, which weak forms also generally disallow due to their clitic nature – the stronger form is preferred, in accord with point (iv); see T4.

T4 Pronominal forms

	Check-F	*Struc	Stay
a. weak form	*		*
b. ☞ strong form		*	

The conflict between structural and movement economy is not as adequately and transparently characterized in models that disallow constraint conflict. Consider for example Cardinaletti and Starke's analysis, cast in terms of the interaction between feature checking and economy principles in accord with Chomsky (1995). While they acknowledge the conflicting nature of the principles under discussion, they address it by letting Economy of Representation (henceforth ER) apply at the point of lexical insertion, which would appear to precede any movement and hence also the effects of Economy of Movement (EM) (Cardinaletti and Starke 1999: 202).

At first sight, the assumed serialization might appear to deliver the desired result: first ER selects the least structured pronoun – favoring weaker forms over strong ones – and then EM imposes the derivation with the shortest possible chain to the selected pronominal form. Since EM examines derivations involving the same pronoun, the one selected by ER, the conflict between the two principles appears to have been dissolved.

The problems emerge when examining how ER makes its choice, which, as it turns out, cannot occur prior and independently of EM. The choice between a weak and a strong form depends on the availability of a non-crashing derivation for the weak form (one satisfying all the requirements represented by Check-F), since only in this case should the weak form be preferred to the strong one by ER. But assessing the existence of a non-crashing derivation for the weak form requires the assessment of EM, since weak forms must check their features with minimal movement.

Consequently, ER cannot truly be assessed before and independently of EM, because EM is part of the assessment of ER. This means that there is no straightforward serialization solution to the conflict of these two principles: EM cannot be assessed before ER, because it favors stronger forms that do not need movement (whereas we want weaker forms to win), yet ER cannot be assessed before EM either, because it has EM's assessment as a prerequisite of its own assessment. A simple serialization between ER and EM where each constraint compares all competing pronominal forms against each other cannot be construed.

A less straightforward formal solution to the underlying conflict can be provided through an explicit definition of how ER and EM are assessed. The supplied algorithm would be defined along the lines described above, with EM incorporated in the assessment of ER. It would restrict EM's assessment to derivations that share the same pronominal form, thus eliminating the conflict: given a weak and a strong pronominal forms, EM assesses whether a grammatical derivation that satisfies economy of movement exists for *each* form, never comparing them against each others, then among the derivations that satisfy EM, ER selects the one where the pronoun has the least structure.

Under the above solution, EM and ER are fundamentally different: only ER is allowed to compare distinct forms against each other. EM must be prevented from making similar comparisons, or else the conflict between EM and ER would not be solved in favor of ER. The impossibility to explicitly model constraint conflict via constraint ranking thus forces the introduction of fundamentally different constraint classes. Furthermore, unlike the OT analysis, the described algorithm does not transparently represent the very conflict that makes its existence necessary.

Cardinaletti and Starke's analysis was conceived under the early minimalist system of Chomsky (1995) which allowed for economy principles. The revised crash-proof model in Chomsky (2000) aims at disposing of economy principles and transderivational comparisons by carefully designing the operations involved in syntactic derivations, the domain to which they apply, and the order in which they occur. For example, Move is defined in terms of the Agree and Merge operations plus an additional operation selecting the phrase that pied-pipes with the moving head (Chomsky 2000: 135). The higher complexity of Move relative to Agree and Merge is also assumed to prevent unnecessary movement. For example, '*a proof*' will not move to specTP in '*there was a proof discovered*' whenever the expletive '*there*' is present in the initial array because merging of '*there*' only requires Agree and Merge alone and no additional projection selection (Chomsky 2000: 138).[11]

Even this revised system, however, does not seem able to provide an adequate and transparent characterization for the conflict between movement and structural economy uncovered by Cardinaletti and Starke. The conceivable solutions appear to run against significant aspects of the design of C_{HL} in Chomsky (2000). The most obvious solution, for example, would appear to involve a (possibly phase internal) explicit comparison of distinct derivations, eventually selecting the non-crashing derivation with the least structured pronominal form. However this solution still relies on transderivational comparisons.

Another conceivable solution, possibly more in tune with the spirit of the model proposed in Chomsky (2000), could assume some degree of freedom in the merging of the feature bundles represented by the items in the lexical array. Weak pronominal forms that leave the feature bundles associated with higher functional projections unparsed would proceed with their derivation. The overall derivation would backtrack to the structurally more complex strong pronominal forms that do parse those same feature bundles whenever the derivation of the weak forms does not converge. Transderivational comparisons are here avoided at the cost of backtracking and a stipulation about which pronominal forms should be tried first.

While the details of these two solutions would have to be further investigated,[12] neither of them accounts in a uniform, principled, and transparent manner for the property of economy shared by the two principles proposed by Cardinaletti and Starke. Economy of movement is assumed to follow from the relation holding between Move, Agree and Merge, whereas structural economy would have to follow from transderivational comparisons or backtracking within an overall more complex derivation as mentioned above. The conflict between the two economy principles, so readily observable in the inverse relation between structure and movement in (iii), is also lost, buried in analysis-specific stipulations necessary to determine the right results.

In conclusion, the attempts to model conflicts between economy principles without a principled formalization of constraint conflict appear unable to provide an adequate analysis of the linguistic patterns such conflicts determine. In contrast, allowing for constraint conflict and defining grammaticality accordingly, enables OT to represent the underlying conflict adequately and transparently, letting related linguistic patterns emerge from very simple constraints whose dominance relations are explicitly encoded in the constraint ranking of each language. Paradigm specific assumptions and provisos are dispensed with; all constraints are assessed in exactly the same way, examining only the structures at hand with no reference to the evaluation of other constraints. These appear to be highly desirable properties for a minimalist perspective, as they make it possible to pursue a view of UG where universal constraints are potentially rooted in legibility conditions at the PF and LF interfaces, while economy in its various manifestations emerges naturally and freely from their interaction.

4.   OT and minimalism

The above sections provided some theoretical and empirical reasons for pursuing the minimalist program under a formal theory of constraint conflict and interaction, such as OT. Conversely, we may ask what a minimalist perspective could bring to OT-based inquiries.

A minimalist perspective encourages a deeper understanding of conflicting constraints, with the ultimate goal of linking them directly to interface conditions. OT's fundamental tenet that crosslinguistic variation follows from constraint conflict already forces a better modeling of UG constraints, because it disallows language-specific properties and devices. Successive analyses of similar phenomena within the OT-literature show a welcome trend towards ever simpler constraints; this increases the explanatory power of the analysis and, at least in some instances, comes closer to identifying constraints dictated by interface conditions alone as required by minimalism.[13]

A particularly clear example of this trend is provided by Grimshaw's (2001, 2002) analysis of structural and movement economy. Rather than viewing them as separate phenomena emerging from the constraints Stay and *Struc introduced above, Grimshaw derives both from a fixed set of five simple constraints: two of them respectively require the presence of specifiers and heads in phrasal projections, while the remaining three require specifiers, heads, and complements to occur leftmost in their projection. As a result, every projection is bound to violate some constraints, either because a specifier or a head is missing or because a specifier, head, or complement is not perfectly aligned due to the presence of another item in the same projection. It follows that structures involving projections not benefiting higher ranked constraints inevitably lose against competing structures that do without those same projections, yielding economy of representation. Likewise, since movement increases structure by adding additional copies of a constituent, it too inevitably adds violations to the proposed constraints. Therefore, movement operations that do not benefit any higher ranked constraints are suboptimal too, deriving economy of movement. Under Grimshaw's analysis, economy of structure and economy of representation become predictable epiphenomena of constraint conflict.

A minimalist perspective on OT also invites us to examine exactly how the form selected as optimal by OT-optimization is identified. In this respect many linguists incorrectly believe that OT-optimization requires the human mind to actively generate an infinite number of competing structures, an impossible task in the finite time of linguistic exchanges. The misconception lies in interpreting optimization tableaux as procedures to compute optimal structures – involving the generation of all suboptimal alternatives – rather than as demonstrations of the optimal status of the selected form relative to any other conceivable alternative potentially generated by a maximally unconstrained procedure 'GEN' responsible for structural assemblage. The real issue is whether computing optimal status relative to an infinite set of potential (but not necessarily generated) alternatives with finite means and within finite time is psychologically feasible. Humans are clearly able to do that with numbers. For example, we know that zero is lower than any other positive integer with no need to first enumerate all positive integers. We can also easily determine the least common multiple of any two numbers without calculating the infinitely many other common multiples available. We even know that even numbers are a subset of all integers despite both sets being infinite.

In all these cases, and the many others that can be conceived, our mind appears to work in terms of the invariant properties and relations of the objects involved rather than by enumeration and comparison. The identification of grammatical expressions as optimal solutions to possible rankings of UG constraints is likely to follow from the same kind of reasoning. For example, a ranking with Stay placed highest necessarily selects structures lacking movement; this property is sufficient to confine to suboptimal status every possible structure involving movement. There are infinitively many of them, but none of them needs to be actively generated to determine their suboptimal status (on the misconception of infinite generation and other common misconceptions see also Prince and Smolensky 1993: 197, and Smolensky *et al.* 2006: 523).

Misconceptions aside, the issue of how optimal structures are identified is a valid one and has repeatedly been addressed by the OT literature. The properties of OT-optimization already provide useful conceptual tools in guiding the identification process. For example, any given set of structures identifies an infinite set of harmonically bounded alternatives that are necessarily suboptimal because inevitably beaten by one or more of the original structures on any constraint ranking (Samek-Lodovici and Prince 1999, 2002). These alternatives need not be generated since the optimal form cannot be among them.[14] Tesar (1995), in turn, showed that dynamic programming provides a solution to the identification problem provided specific conditions on the complexity of the constraints involved are satisfied. He applied this technique to the theory of syllable structure, providing an algorithm that computes the optimal structure among an infinite set of potential competitors for any given ranking of five constraints. Riggle (2004) went even further, providing a fully general solution to the above issue cast in terms of finite state automata (FSA).

FSAs representing OT-constraints combine together into a single, larger, FSA which is used by a general algorithm to efficiently compute the optimal forms associated with every constraint ranking.

In conclusion, whether UG constraints conflict or not is an empirical issue. If they do, as they appear to, a formally precise theory of their interaction becomes necessary, because simultaneous satisfaction of all constraints ceases to be a viable definition of grammaticality. This reason alone provides a strong motivation for pursuing an OT-perspective of human grammar, while further theoretical and empirical reasons have been offered in the above sections and in the OT-syntax literature. Such pursuit is compatible with the parallel pursuit of minimalist goals, since these goals do not presuppose a specific type of constraint interaction. The Minimalist Program is fully consistent with an OT approach to constraint interaction, and, as discussed in this chapter, it can significantly benefit from it to rigorously yet transparently characterize which constraints conflict, which structural components or derivational steps are affected by each conflict, and how the conflict is resolved. This in turn would greatly help minimalist analysts in addressing essential aspects of human grammar, such as crosslinguistic variation, the syntactic effects of constraints at the phonological and semantic interfaces, and economy in all its manifestations.

Notes

1. Variation is contingent on the assumption that the conflicting constraints, or at least some of them, can be reranked. The availability of reranking follows from the null hypothesis that no ranking is superior to any other.

2. Under OT, individual grammars are identified by rankings of UG-constraints. The structure selected as grammatical by each grammar is the one that best satisfies UG-constraints under the corresponding ranking. More precisely, it is that structure A that beats any conceivable alternative B on the ranking at hand, that is that structure A such that for any B, A beats B on the highest constraint on which the two perform differently (Prince and Smolensky 1993, 2004; Grimshaw 2006a). When two constraints conflict, their possible rankings determine the available conflict resolutions, with each ranking selecting a distinct optimal structure. The properties of the optimal structure are thus shaped by the ranked constraints that selected it.

3. The '$N!$' figure presupposes N constraints each conflicting with all the others. If some constraints do not conflict with each other, the number of distinct optimal forms will be lower than $N!$. For example, constraints governing phrase structure do not directly conflict with constraints governing syllable structure, since they are satisfied or violated independently (Jane Grimshaw, p.c.).

4. Twelve binary parameters may yield 2^{12} languages, that is 4,096 languages. Seven conflicting constraints may yield $7! = 5,040$ distinct languages.

5. The observation that 2^N and $N!$ are very different quantities should also dispel the misconception that reranked constraints are parameters in disguise. On the non-equivalence between parameters and pairs of opposite constraints see also Grimshaw (1997) and Samek-Lodovici (1998).

6. An even more ambitious project is pursued in Smolensky and Legendre (2006), where the OT articulation of human grammar is viewed as directly emerging from the connectionist architecture of the human brain.

7. Jane Grimshaw (p.c.) notes that constraint rankings are themselves language specific, but that unlike parametric values the set of possible rankings is mathematically derived once the set of universal constraints is known.

8. The complete analysis employs finer grained prosodic and syntactic structures and it derives a wider range of empirical data from Italian, English, German, French and Bantu languages. Clause-initial

and clause-internal focus can be reduced to cases where focus is prosodically final provided right-dislocation is taken into account; see Samek-Lodovici (2006).

9. Interestingly Chomsky (2000:132) describes 'feature strength' in the model developed in Chomsky (1995) as a concept 'introduced to force *violation* of Procrastinate' (my italics), confirming the violable nature of early minimalist economy principles. Optimality accounts like the one sketched here must explicitly identify the constraint that is violated and the higher ranked constraints that force its violation. Accounts of this kind have constraint conflict and constraint violability as their prerequisite and are thus precluded within any theory of grammaticality based on the simultaneous satisfaction of all UG constraints.

10. Grimshaw (2001, 2002) further enhanced the analysis of movement economy, replacing Stay with constraints that never refer to either movement or economy and deriving both economy of movement and economy of structure. Her analysis is briefly described at the beginning of section 4. See also Grimshaw (2006b), arguing that chains necessarily violate faithfulness constraints, thus deriving economy of movement even when competing candidates have the same structure.

11. The definition of Move β in Chomsky (2000), repeated below, has Agree followed by the selection operation [b], followed by Merge. It remains unclear exactly how the complexity of Move alone can favor merging of the expletive over raising of '*a proof*' in the derivation of '*there was a proof discovered*'. The initial Agree operation, step [a], is shared by both derivations (Chomsky 2000: 123, 135). Once step [a] has been performed the correct derivation is contingent on proceeding with Merge of the expletive rather than performing the selection operation in step [b], which would eventually yield the raised subject in '*a proof was discovered*'. The correct choice does not appear entailed by the complexity of Move, but rather by the assumption that Merge of array items always precedes the phrase selection operation in [b].

    (i) Definition of Move β (Chomsky 2000: 135).
        (a)   A Probe P in the label L of β locates the closest matching [goal] G in its domain.
        (b)   A feature G' of the label containing G selects a phrase b as a candidate for 'pied-piping'.
        (c) β is merged to a category K.

12. This is particularly true for the second solution, where Merge of array items has to wait past the attempted derivation of the weak pronoun. This contradicts the crucial assumption that Merge preempts Move (Chomsky 2000). See also the above footnote.

13. Jane Grimshaw (p.c.) notes how many constraints used in OT syntax are eminently syntactic, not straightforwardly related to the PF and LF interfaces, and that the same appears true, to a good degree, of minimalist analyses as well. The article, however, is mainly concerned with the potential use of OT as a framework for pursuing minimalist goals. When considered from this perspective, many OT analyses of syntactic phenomena have provided content to minimalist goals by detailing how PF and LF constraints affect syntax. See for example the papers concerning semantic constraints collected in Samek-Lodovici (2007) or the studies in Szendröi (2001), Büring and Gutierrez-Bravo (2002), Dehé (2005), Samek-Lodovici (2005) on the relation between prosody and focus in different languages, with the prosodic constraints being increasingly replaced by the actual constraints used in prosodic studies.

14. The above discussion also illustrates a fundamental difference between GEN and C_{HL} as defined in Chomsky (2000). GEN defines the set of possible linguistic structures among which a constraint ranking selects the grammatical ones; it does not itself identifies the optimal structure. C_{HL} on the other hand is expected to do just that, building the grammatical structure once provided with a suitable array of lexical items. But see also Broekhuis (2006) and Broekhuis and Woolford (to appear) for an analysis combining OT with Minimalism and where C_{HL} replaces GEN.

References

Barbosa, P., Fox, D., Hagstrom, P., McGinnis, M. and Pesetsky, D. (eds) (1998) *Is the Best Good Enough. Optimality and Competition in Syntax.* Cambridge, MA: MIT Press.

Beckman, J., Walsh Dickey, L. and Urbanczyk, S. (eds) (1995) *Papers in Optimality Theory*. University of Massachusetts Occasional Papers 18. Amherst, MA: GLSA, UMASS.

Broekhuis, H. (2006) Derivations (MP) and evaluations (OT). In H. Broekhuis and R. Vogel (eds) *Optimality Theory and Minimalism: A Possible Convergence? Linguistics in Postdam 25*: 137–93.

Broekhuis, H. and Woolford, E. (to appear) Minimalism and Optimality Theory. In M. den Dikken (ed.) *The Cambridge Handbook of Generative Syntax*. Cambridge: Cambridge University Press.

Burzio, L. (2000) The Rise of Optimality Theory. In L. Cheng and R. Sybesma (eds) *The First Glot International State-of-the-Article Book*, 199–220. New York: Mouton de Gruyter.

Büring, D. and Gutiérrez-Bravo, R. (2002) Focus-related word order variation without the NSR. A Prosody-based crosslinguistic analysis. In S. Mac Bloscaidh (ed.) *Syntax at Santa Cruz 3*, 41–58. Santa Cruz, CA: ICSC.

Cardinaletti, A. and Starke, M. (1994) The typology of structural deficiency. A case study of the three classes of pronouns. Ms., MIT, Boston, MA.

Cardinaletti, A. and Starke, M. (1999) The typology of structural deficiency. A case study of the three classes of pronouns. In H. van Riemsdijk (ed.) *Clitics in the Languages of Europe*, 145–234. New York: Mouton de Gruyter.

Chomsky, N. (1982) *Some Concepts and Consequences of the Theory of Government and Binding*. Cambridge, MA: MIT Press.

Chomsky, N. (1995) *The Minimalist Program*. Cambridge, MA: MIT Press.

Chomsky, N. (2000) Minimalist inquiries: The framework. In R. Martin, D. Michaels and J. Uriagereka (eds) *Step by Step. Essay on Minimalist Syntax in Honor of Howard Lasnik*, 89–156. Cambridge, MA: MIT Press.

Dehé, N. (2005) The optimal placement of *ab* and *up* – a comparison. *The Journal of Comparative Germanic Linguistics* 8 (3): 185–224.

Fanselow, G. and Féry. C. (eds) (2002) Resolving conflicts in grammar. *Linguistiche Berichte Sonderheft* 11. Hamburg: Helmut Buske Verlag.

Grimshaw, J. (1997) Projections, heads, and optimality. *Linguistic Inquiry* 28 (3): 373–422.

Grimshaw, J. (2001) Economy of structure in OT. Ms., Rutgers University. Retrieved on 2 April 2010 from http://roa.rutgers.edu/files/434-0601/434-0601-GRIMSHAW-0-0.PDF.

Grimshaw, J. (2002) Economy of structure in OT. In Carpenter, A., Coetzee, A. and de Lacy, P. (eds) *Papers in Optimality Theory II. University of Massachusetts Occasional Papers 26*, 81–120. Amherst, Massachusetts: GLSA, UMASS.

Grimshaw, J. (2005) How OT Works: Questions and Answers, Descriptions and Explanations. Talk given at DEAL Conference, Zentrum für allgemeine Sprachwissenschaft, Berlin.

Grimshaw, J. (2006a) Last resort and grammaticality. In H. Broekhuis and R. Vogel (eds) *Optimality Theory and Minimalism: A Possible Convergence? Linguistics in Postdam 25*: 33–41.

Grimshaw, J. (2006b) Chains as unfaithful optima. In E. Bakovic, J. Ito and J. McCarthy (eds) *Wondering at the Natural Fecundity of Things: Essays in Honor of Alan Prince*, 97–109. Santa Cruz, CA: Linguistics Research Center, University of California, Santa Cruz.

Jackendoff, R. (1972) *Semantic Interpretation in Generative Grammar*. Cambridge, MA: MIT Press.

Legendre, G., Grimshaw, J. and Vikner. S. (eds) (2001) *Optimality-Theoretic Syntax*. Cambridge, MA: MIT Press.

McCarthy, J. (2002) *A Thematic Guide to Optimality Theory*. Cambridge: Cambridge University Press.

Prince, A. (1997) *Endogenous Constraints in Optimality Theory*. Talk handout, LSA-Institute, Cornell.

Prince, A. and Smolensky, P. (1993/2004) *Optimality Theory: Constraint Interaction in Generative Grammar*. Oxford: Blackwell.

Riggle, J. (2004) Contenders and learning. In B. Schmeiser, V. Chand, A. Kelleher, A. and A. Rodriguez (eds) *WCCFL 23 Proceedings*, 101–14. Somerville, MA: Cascadilla Press.

Samek-Lodovici. V. (1998) Opposite constraints: left and right focus-alignment in Kanakuru. *Lingua* 104 (1–2): 111–30.

Samek-Lodovici, V. (2005) Prosody-Syntax interaction in the expression of focus. *Natural Language & Linguistic Theory* 23 (3): 687–755.

Samek-Lodovici, V. (2006) When right dislocation meets the left-periphery. A unified analysis of Italian non-final focus. *Lingua* 116 (6): 836–73.

Samek-Lodovici, V. (ed.) (2007) Studies in OT syntax and semantics. *Lingua* 117 (9): 1513–676.

Samek-Lodovici, V. and Prince, A. (1999) *Optima*. Technical reports of the Rutgers Center for Cognitive Science RuCCS TR-57. Rutgers University. Retrieved on 2 April 2010 from http://roa.rutgers.edu/files/785-1205/785-SAMEK-LODOVICI-0-0.PDF

Samek-Lodovici, V. and Prince, A. (2002) *Fundamental Properties of Harmonic Bounding*. Technical reports of the Rutgers Center for Cognitive Science RuCCS TR-71. Rutgers University. Retrieved on 2 April 2010 from http://roa.rutgers.edu/files/785-1205/785-SAMEK-LODOVICI-0-0.PDF

Selkirk, E. (1995) Sentence prosody: intonation, stress and phrasing. In J. A. Goldsmith (ed.) *The Handbook of Phonological Theory*, 550–69. Cambridge, MA: Blackwell.

Smolensky, P. and Legendre, G. (2006) *The Harmonic Mind*. Cambridge, MA: MIT Press.

Smolensky, P., Legendre, G. and Tesar, B. (2006) Optimality Theory: The structure, use and acquisition of grammatical knowledge. In P. Smolensky and G. Legendre (eds) *The Harmonic Mind,* 453–544, Vol. 1. Cambridge, MA: MIT Press.

Szendröi, K. (2001) *Focus and the Syntax-Phonology Interface*. Doctoral dissertation. University College London.

Tesar, B. (1995) *Computational Optimality Theory*. Doctoral dissertation. University of Colorado.

Truckenbrodt, H. (1995) *Phonological Phrases: Their Relation to Syntax, Focus, and Prominence*. Doctoral dissertation. Cambridge, MA: MIT Press.

Williams, E. (2005) '*My Theses.* ' Handout, DEAL Conference, Zentrum für allgemeine Sprachwissenschaft, Berlin.

Zoll, C. (1993) Directionless syllabification and ghosts in Yawelmani. Ms. Berkeley, CA. ROA-28.

Zubizarreta, M. L. (1998) *Prosody, Focus and Word Order*. Cambridge, MA: MIT Press.

10 The trivial generator

Ralf Vogel*

ABSTRACT I discuss a proposal for Optimality theoretic syntax that relies on the mechanisms provided by OT as much as possible. The proposal contains a particular application of OT's core concepts, markedness and faithfulness. Faithfulness is used in its correspondence theoretic version. Faithfulness constraints organize isomorphic mappings between semantic, syntactic and phonological representations. The model therefore has a strong focus on the interfaces. The three representations each have their own generator. With respect to the syntactic generator it is argued that it can and should be much simpler than the computational system used in minimalist syntax. Economy, another concept from minimalist syntax that has often been taken over in OT syntactic analyses, is argued to better be replaced by the OT genuine conception of markedness which does not simply reward the smallest structure but rather evaluates structures relative to the purpose they are supposed to serve.

KEYWORDS analytic and synthetic constructions; correspondence; syntactic markedness; syntax-semantics interface; *wh*-movement

1. Introduction

Taking the OT perspective can have radical consequences for the architecture of the grammar and for our view of what counts as an explanation in linguistic theory.

Minimalism and (mainstream) OT syntax both descend from the generative syntax of the 1980s and early 1990s. But they have taken opposite directions. The GB model and its predecessors, starting at latest with Chomsky and Lasnik (1977)[1] divides the labour between two components, a generator (derivational mechanism, phrase structure component, etc.) and a constraint system (filters, principles, etc.). The two components constitute the grammar which, as a whole, strives for explanatory adequacy.

Minimalism emphasizes the generator component of the grammar and seeks to eliminate the explanatory contribution of the filter component to a minimum.

---

*   Ralf Vogel, Universität Bielefeld, Fakultät für Linguistik und Literaturwissenschaft, Bielefeld, Germany. E-mail: rvogel@uni-bielefeld.de

The opposite is true of optimality theory which in its classical version claims that linguistic generalizations are about the surface forms, the outputs of the grammar, while the generator component undergoes *trivialization*, being merely more than a logical necessity of the model (see Prince and Smolensky 1993: 5). Therefore, OT in fact has a very minimalist spirit – just taking the direction opposite to that of the Minimalist Program.

In early OT phonology, this trivialization could indeed be observed. Recent years have seen a return of derivational aspects in the guise of serial optimization, but they do not so much concern the functioning of the generator component itself.[2]

Nevertheless, little work in OT syntax has strived for a maximally trivialized syntactic generator. Even more so, it might not be unfair to state that most work in OT syntax rather than elaborating a genuine OT perspective on syntax applies OT as an additional tool within already established non-OT frameworks. For instance, most of the papers in Legendre *et al.* (2001) implicitly take over core assumptions about grammar familiar from the Chomskyan branch of generative syntax, just as the papers in Sells (2001a) adapt OT to LFG without significant changes to the overall view on grammar.

What is rare, is work that explores more radical ways of applying OT to syntax. To execute a radical OT perspective in syntax means to make critical use of OT's core concepts, *markedness* and *faithfulness*, as paradigmatically demonstrated by Baković and Keer (2001). This chapter is dedicated to such an exploration. It is organized as follows: section 2 discusses the main differences between the OT architecture of grammar that I have in mind and the model of Chomskyan generative syntax. Section 3 elaborates particularly on the syntax generator. Section 4 elaborates on the syntax-semantics interface. Having established an extremely trivial version of the syntactic generator, I will discuss in section 5, how OT's notion of markedness correlates with the concept of syntactic simplicity used here. I will especially focus on the relation of syntax and morphology as a test case for syntactic markedness in the OT sense.

2. Syntax from an OT perspective

OT is not the first approach that views grammars as <input, output> mappings. In fact, all versions in the Chomskyan tradition view syntax that way. The difference lies in what are considered as input and output.

The Chomskyan tradition, as quite clearly stated in the minimalist programme, sees syntax as a procedure to generate an output pair <p,m> (for 'phonetic form' and 'meaning') from a set of lexical items, the numeration in minimalism. The semantic and phonetic subsystems are independent of each other – mediated by syntax. Syntactic structures are fed into these interfacing systems.

So, what we have is a two-step procedure, where syntax proper only plays a role in the first step, the generation of two syntactic interface representations – in the minimalist programme they are called Logical Form (LF) and spell-out. The second step consists in the two interpretive processes at the interfaces which lead to a semantic representation and Phonetic Form (PF).

In one of the earliest examples of OT syntactic work, Pesetsky's (1997) discussion of the syntax-PF interface, the author showed that minimalism and OT could coexist well, if minimalism was used for syntax proper and OT for the syntax-PF interface. The generator in this work produces a set of candidate PF's.

Subsequently, OT has been applied quite successfully in syntax-prosody mapping (see for example Selkirk 1996; Truckenbrodt 1999, 2000; Büring 2001; Szendröi 2001, 2003; Samek-Lodovici 2005; Féry and Samek-Lodovici 2006; Vogel 2006b). In some of these papers, the optimal syntactic structure is made dependent on prosodic well-formedness to a limited extent. In Samek-Lodovici (2005) and Büring (2001), for instance, the candidates are <syntax, prosody> pairs. Thus, syntax and prosody are optimized in parallel. PF is here not simply an interpretation of syntactic structure, but syntactic structure is also restricted by prosodic wellformedness constraints.

The syntactic generator in OT in such analyses has a different job to do than in minimalism. In minimalism, the generator is designed in such a way that for each numeration there is only one converging syntactic structure for each interface. In OT, exactly this has to be avoided. For each syntactic structure that one might generate in the minimalist way, an OT syntax evaluator also considers a small set of usually quite similar alternative structures and chooses the structure that performs best in the evaluation. Furthermore, a pair of a syntactic structure and its prosodic interface interpretation can be a candidate which requires a very different and especially more complex generator function.

The syntactic part of the generator can be quite minimalist, still. For instance, in the 'derivation and evaluation' approach (see for example Part I of Broekhuis, this volume), the reason why there is a candidate set lies in a kind of underspecification of the generator: if, under a feature-checking approach, syntactic elements may occur in their checking positions or in their base positions, then the candidate set contains a fixed number of structures generated with the same numeration that each differ in which elements occupy their checking positions.

A notorious difficulty of this kind of approach lies in syntactic problems that seem to require lexical variation, too, as for example in the case of 'do'-support which has played a prominent role in Grimshaw (1997) where it seems necessary for the numeration in a minimalist analysis to optionally contain 'do' in order to construct the appropriate candidate set.

The usual criterion for the selection of the candidate set in OT syntax papers is a bit more liberal, and basically a semantic one: output candidates are equivalent in terms of argument structure, aspect, tense, lexical items, information structure, operator scope. Legendre *et al.* (1998) use a candidate set where candidates 'target the same LF' but might fail – in particular, in the case of Italian multiple *wh*-questions.

What Legendre *et al.* (1998) make crucial use of, is *faithfulness*, a genuine OT concept that evaluates how much the input is preserved in the output. It allows unfaithful candidates – that is candidates that differ syntactically and/or semantically from the input – to compete.

The approach by Legendre *et al.* (1998) seems to assume a non-OT syntax-semantics interface where meanings are part of the candidates in syntactic optimization. But OT has been used for the syntax-semantics interface, too, and under the heading of *bidirectional optimization* (see in particular Blutner 2001) it played an important role for the solution of certain problems of the syntax-semantics interface. Wilson (2001), for example, explored this for binding theory.

Meaning has always played a crucial role in transformational syntax. While the strong requirement from early transformational grammar that transformations should be meaning preserving had to be abandoned, certain semantic aspects, especially argument structure, are still assumed to be unaffected by syntactic movement – because there are genuine syntactic positions where semantic roles are assigned.

This becomes superfluous in OT. Syntax is meaning preserving in OT per se in the sense that the input cannot be changed by whatever the syntactic generator component is doing. Because the output of the grammar is an <input, output> pair, whichever expression is the optimal candidate will be the optimal expression for the meaning given in the input.

However, an OT conception of both directions of the syntax-semantics interface might lead to a situation like the following:

(1)   Optimization mismatch in bidirectional optimization:

syntax optimization:	input: $meaning_1$	output: $expression_1$
semantics optimization:	input: $expression_1$	output: $meaning_2$

The consequence of the scenario in (1) is that $meaning_1$ is ineffable in the language at hand: the expression that would be ideal for its expression has a more optimal alternative meaning, $meaning_2$. In this way, bidirectional OT can derive ineffability and ungrammaticality. Bidirectional conceptions of OT syntax use a definition of grammaticality that takes into account both directions of the interface:

(2)   **Grammaticality:** A pair $<m_i,e_i>$ is grammatical iff the expression e_i is the optimal candidate for the input m_i and the meaning m_i is the optimal candidate for the input e_i. (See Vogel 2004a, 2004b, for a detailed elaboration of bidirectional OT syntax.)

It is important to note that we are *not* dealing with an interpretive semantics here. This is an important departure from standard Chomskyan conceptions of the syntax-semantics interface. Instead, syntax and semantics are in a *correspondence* relation that is established by the OT grammar. The syntax-semantics relation is therefore potentially non-compositional. In fact, applying OT to semantics, as in OT semantics,[3] *only* makes sense if the syntax-semantics relation is conceived as (partly) non-deterministic – otherwise, there could not be more than one candidate meaning for a given expression. Typical phenomena dealt with here are at the semantics-pragmatics transition, for example blocking phenomena, contextual enrichment, anaphora resolution, ambiguity resolution, etc.

This fundamental difference in the syntax-semantics relation has consequences for the OT view on syntax. To be more precise: it *should* have. The reality is different, as OT semantics is rarely adapted in OT syntax.

The main idea for my correspondence theoretic conception of OT syntax[4] is that the grammar organizes the syntax-semantics-PF mapping by way of constraints that require isomorphic mappings from one kind of structure into the other. For instance, semantic scope translates into asymmetric c-command in syntax, which in turn translates into precedence at PF.

Such constraints are potentially conflicting and so we expect mismatches between syntax and semantics (i.e. phenomena of 'covert movement' and non-compositional meaning) and syntax and phonology (i.e. phenomena of 'PF reordering') to occur. The syntactic generator that we need for such a grammar conception should be much simpler than the minimalist apparatus which is designed for a very different conception of the interfaces. Among the ingredients prominent in (some versions of) minimalist syntax that will not be made use of, are feature checking, movement, a rich inventory of functional categories just for deriving word order, and adjunction.

In the sections below, I will show how this can be made to work. The languages discussed are German and English. As the discussion has a programmatic character, much of what is said here requires empirical exploration and application in a wider range of languages and phenomena.

3.   Simplifying the syntactic apparatus

3.1   Conditioned feature checking

In early minimalism, movement of *wh*-items is triggered by strong features (alternatively, nowadays, a *wh*-feature on a head with an EPP-feature). The dimension of feature strength (strong vs. weak feature) or the optional presence of EPP-features is not necessary under an OT approach where movement is regulated by the relative rank of the derivational economy constraint STAY. This has been demonstrated, among others, in minimalist work on *wh*-movement (Grimshaw 1997; Ackema and Neeleman 1998; Legendre *et al.* 1998) and Object Shift (Broekhuis 2000, 2008).

The OT generator generates a set of candidate structures for a given input. In minimalist terms, this means that structures with strong features and structures with weak features are generated in parallel. It is the task of the well-formedness constraints to select the optimal output. The ideal of a minimalist grammar is that one input (or: numeration) can only lead to one single well-formed output. Assuming feature strength (or, nowadays, EPP features) is one way to ensure this.

Broekhuis (2000) argues that one advantage of the OT model lies in the ability to derive what may be called *conditioned feature checking*. In Scandinavian, object shift, the movement of an object noun phrase outside or to the left edge of VP, applies if three conditions are met:

(a)   the verb has left the verb phrase,
(b)   the object is an unstressed pronoun,
(c)   no other material c-commanding the object is left within VP.

(3) Object shift in Swedish: (Holmberg 1999)
   (a) Jag kysste henne inte
        I   kissed   her   not

   (b) ?Jag kysste inte henne

   (c) Jag kysste inte Marit
        I   kissed   not   Marit

   (d) *Jag kysste Marit inte

Broekhuis (2000) follows earlier analyses of this phenomenon in that he assumes that the object pronoun in (3a) moves to its case position, that is in a position where it checks its case feature. An early minimalist analysis would assume here that the case feature either on the noun or on the head AGR-O, which checks the case feature, must be strong in order to evoke this movement. But then there must be an unchecked strong case feature in (4a) and (3c), which should, erroneously, lead to ungrammaticality. It further remains unclear why (4b) is ill-formed.

(4) (a) Jag har inte kysst henne
        I   have not   kissed her

   (b) *Jag har henne inte kysst
        I   have her   not   kissed

Broekhuis (2000) shows how OT offers a way out: case is unchecked in Swedish in principle, but case movement can be triggered by another factor, here it is the constraint D-PRONOUN which requires definite pronouns to leave VP.[5]

Broekhuis further assumes that the minimal link condition is an inviolable constraint on the generator: there will only be candidates that fulfil the MLC. This explains why (4b) is ungrammatical: although this structure would fulfil D-PRONOUN, it will not even be generated since the object's movement outside VP violates the MLC if the verbal head has not moved out of VP itself. Broekhuis assumes the constraints CASE, which requires case features to be checked and STAY, which penalizes syntactic movement (Grimshaw 1997). The ranking that derives the above observations about object shift is as follows:

(5) D-PRONOUN » STAY » CASE

The minimalist conception of feature strength is in this account replaced by the relative rank of the constraint that requires feature checking, CASE, and STAY. The high rank of D-PRONOUN leads to 'conditioned feature checking': case movement might apply for a different reason than the checking of the case feature.

Such a reformulation of feature strength as relative constraint ranking has also been used in various OT accounts of *wh*-movement (Grimshaw 1997; Ackema and Neeleman 1998; Legendre *et al.* 1998). The general picture that these accounts draw can be sketched as in (6).

(6) Simple economy-of-movement account of *wh*-fronting vs. *wh*-in-situ within OT:
    (a) CHECK-WH » STAY yields *wh*-movement.
    (b) STAY » CHECK-WH yields *wh*-in-situ.

One might object that this is hardly more than a reformulation of the minimalist approach. This even holds, for example, in Ackema and Neeleman's (1998) account of multiple questions, as in (7a):

(7) (a) Who bought what?
    (b) What did you buy?

Despite the fact that the *wh*-feature on '*what*' remains unchecked, and would have to be checked in a single question as in (7b), (7a) is grammatical. In minimalism, a solution suggests itself that exploits the distinction between the checker and the checkee of a formal feature: if the [+*wh*] feature on the clause-initial head C is strong, while that on the *wh*-phrase is weak, then we expect just one *wh*-phrase to be fronted. The OT approach by Ackema and Neeleman (1998) mimicks this by assuming a three-constraint system, including STAY, Q-SCOPE (for the *wh*-phrase) and Q-MARKING (for the C head).

3.2 Against economy of movement as a violable constraint

It is typical of analyses like the one discussed in section 3.1 that they take over background assumptions from other frameworks without considering their usefulness in OT. One concern that I have is the question how to rule out a candidate structure like the following one:

(8) What did John say?

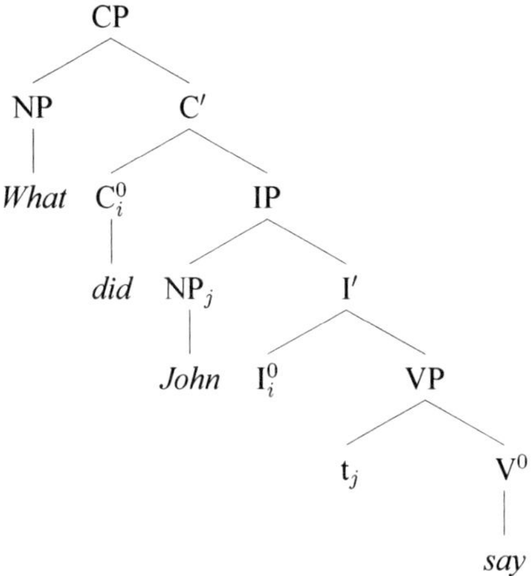

A violation of STAY can be avoided by simply inserting the *wh*-phrase directly in [Spec,CP]. This candidate fulfils both Q-MARKING and Q-SCOPE, hence it should be optimal even (wrongly) in in-situ languages.

In minimalism and its predecessors, structure (8) is usually ruled out by interpretive and case requirements: an NP is assigned its Θ-role inside VP, and uninterpretable otherwise. Likewise, case is assigned into that position, or another one designated for object case assignment, hence an NP inserted into [Spec, CP] has no case, or its case feature unchecked.

These options are not as straightforwardly applicable in OT. Among most varieties of OT syntax that are on the market, there is consensus at least with respect to one issue: *the input contains an argument structure specification.*

For this reason, an argument against the structure in (8) in terms of a violation of the Θ-criterion is much less forceful than in a purely derivational system: failure to merge into Θ-position does not lead to a loss of semantic information, if the latter is given in the input.

One principal difference between minimalism (and other purely derivational systems) and OT syntax is the construction of the interfaces between syntax, on the one hand, and semantics and phonology, on the other. In the usual generative conception, syntactic structures are fed into the semantic and phonological modules which *interpret* the 'instructions' the syntactic structure provides.

The OT conception of the interfaces I am advocating brings syntactic, semantic and phonological/prosodic representations into *correspondence*. It organizes their *mappings*. Semantic and phonological structures are generated independent of the syntactic structure, and they serve as candidates in an OT competition for the optimal syntax↔semantics and syntax↔phonology mappings.

Mapping requirements are typical candidates for violable OT constraints. Examples for constraints on syntax↔semantics mapping are the constraints D-PRONOUN, Q-SCOPE and Q-MARKING, mentioned above. Such constraints can easily come into conflict, and therefore imperfect mappings are expected to be the rule rather than the exception in OT.

Hence, from the logic of an OT model, it would be a mere stipulation to claim that a constraint like Θ-MARKING requiring arguments to be inserted in their Θ-position is inviolable and part of the generator.

A similar argument can be made with respect to case assignment: an NP might be faced with particular syntactic ordering constraints because it has a particular case, but not necessarily in order to receive case. It might bring its case, being a morphological property, already with it.

It is thus difficult to argue that candidate (8) is ruled out by Gen, as the inviolable principle supposed to hold in Gen can hardly be motivated. Hence, economy of movement cannot help us prevent the candidate in (8) from being optimal in in-situ languages. In other words, *wh*-in-situ does not equal absence of *wh*-movement, if base generation into 'derived' positions is allowed for by Gen.

I therefore want to propose that there is no place for constraints like STAY. Syntactic movement, if we want to use it at all in OT syntax, should be evaluated by its effects *only*. It is welcome if it helps fulfilling highly ranked constraints, and disadvantageous if it leads to their violation. But these constraints should not be about movement itself, rather, they should require certain *syntactic consequences* of semantic, morphological and phonological relations among words and constituents, like, for instance, *wh*-phrase placement, syntactic conditions for case licensing and agreement, prosodic structuring, and so on. The impression that we have of syntax as being an economically designed system should be an emergent by-product of this, if anything.[6]

This does not yet imply abandoning syntactic movement per se. However, one conceptual issue might arise. Given that movement as such is not subject to well-formedness constraints, we might find a situation where two structurally different candidates have an identical constraint violation profile. The case I discussed above could be of this kind, or, more schematically, the following pair of trees:

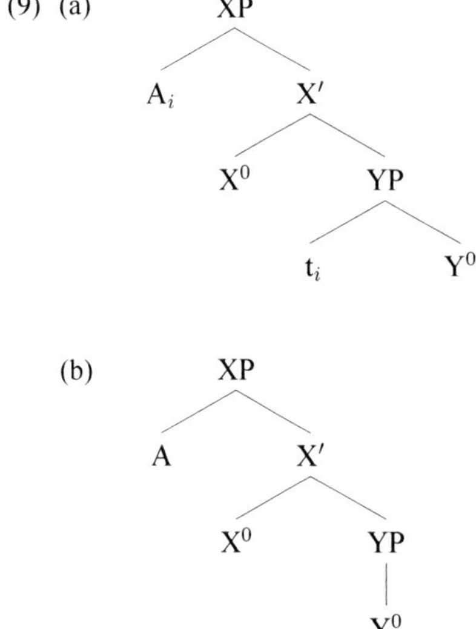

This situation would be an artefact of the way the generator is defined. It would not be an empirical issue in any sense. We are well advised to avoid such candidate pairs for conceptual reasons. The question then would be which of the two trees should be given up. I vote for the 'minimalist' solution here to get rid of the conceptually more complicated structure, that is, (9a). Further arguments are given in the following subsection.

3.3 OT syntax without movement

The main motivation for syntactic movement is a particular strategy to solve a design problem for syntactic representations within the Chomskyan tradition: syntactic structures shall at the same time represent word order, constituency and dependency relations among syntactic units. Dependency is expressed locally within a phrase as relation between the phrase's head and other material within its phrase. Movement is necessary whenever a certain dependency of some element requires a position within the tree that differs from its surface position. For instance, an English object *wh*-phrase receives case within VP, right adjacent to the verb, but occupies the clause-initial position at the surface in simple questions.

There is no intrinsic need to represent, for example, dependency as local relation within a syntactic structure. Alternative frameworks that do not use movement – LFG and HPSG – separate word order from such dependency relations. Dependency is a good predictor for word order, though, but not without exception, as *wh*-questions show.

Let us now discuss the consequences of a model that gets rid of the three types of syntactic movement: adjunction, head movement and movement into specifier position. We start with adjunction.

In Vogel (2004a, b) I already argued for a grammar that does not use syntactic adjunction. The argument relies on the fact that PF is a complete representation of linear order already, and that the heuristics that is used for the detection of adjunction sites is first of all linear order.[7] Therefore, the abstract syntactic device of adjunction does not add new information. By Occam's razor, it can and should be omitted, if possible. As a consequence, the syntactic representation of a clause now is a set of phrase structure trees, the matrix clause and its adjuncts. The (linear) position of an adjunct follows from violable syntax-PF mapping constraints.

Movement into adjunct position is already abandoned, too, under this assumption. Let me briefly show how it works in this framework. Consider a typical case of leftwards adjunction, English left dislocation which is usually represented as in (10).

(10)   [$_{ip}$ Such a book, [$_{ip}$ I would never read.]]

The direct object, 'such a book', under standard assumptions is left adjoined to the clause, traditionally IP. The syntactic structure for this clause that I am assuming is the non-dislocated one:

(11)   [$_{ip}$ I would never read such a book]

The placement of 'such a book' at the left edge is now a case of PF reordering only, which is induced by a semantics-PF ordering constraint that requires topics to occur at the left edge. It is ranked higher than a syntax-PF mapping constraint that requires sister constituents to be adjacent at PF; 'read' and 'such a book' are sisters, but non-adjacent.

We are left with movement into specifier position and head movement. In the previous section, I already showed that a base generation account of *wh*-placement – a typical instance of movement into specifier position – is promising. I will leave this as it is here.

How about head movement? In our work on the dialectal variation in German verbal complexes (Vogel 2003; Schmid and Vogel 2004; Schmid 2005), Tanja Schmid and I already argued that a PF linearization based account that does not rely on syntactic head movement is conceptually simpler and empirically more satisfactory.

Another phenomenon that is typical of Germanic syntax and calls for a treatment in terms of head movement is the verb-second phenomenon. In German and other continental West Germanic languages, this is even more apparent than in other Germanic languages, as these show an asymmetry between main and subordinate clauses:

(12) (a) Peter hat   ein   Buch   gelesen.
           P.   has   a   book   read
           'Peter has read a book.'

      (b) ... weil   Peter ein   Buch   gelesen hat.
                Because P.   a   book   read   has
           '... because Peter has read a book.'

      (c) [$_{VP}$ Bücher lesen]   macht Spaß.
                Books   reading   is   fun
           'Reading books is fun.'

      (d) [$_{AUXP}$ [$_{VP}$ Bücher gelesen] zu haben] ist wichtig
                    books   read   to have   is   important

Whereas the auxiliary 'hat' in (12a) is in V2 position, the second constituent of the clause, it remains in clause-final position in the subordinate clause (12b). Because of the ordering facts in German verb phrases – as also exemplified in (12c) and (12d), the German verb phrase is assumed to have head-final word order. V2 then arises by movement into the head of a higher head-initial projection, which nowadays is widely assumed to be CP.[8] That is, the finite verb in (12a) occupies the same position as the complementizer in (12b) and can only get there by syntactic movement:

(13)

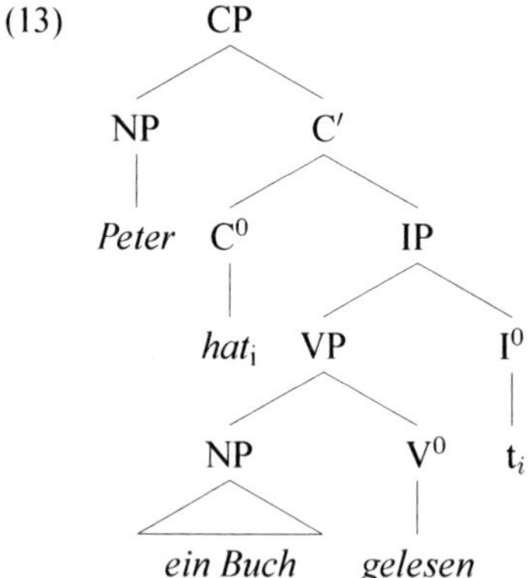

Head-complement order is subject to violable constraints in OT syntax, and variation in their relative ranking is a basic parameter in reconstructing syntactic typology within OT. However, this also means that dispreferred candidates are competitors in each language. A route of analysis for (12a) could then be that we here have a head-initial order that is triggered by a particular syntactic configuration. The analysis then involves no head movement:

(14)

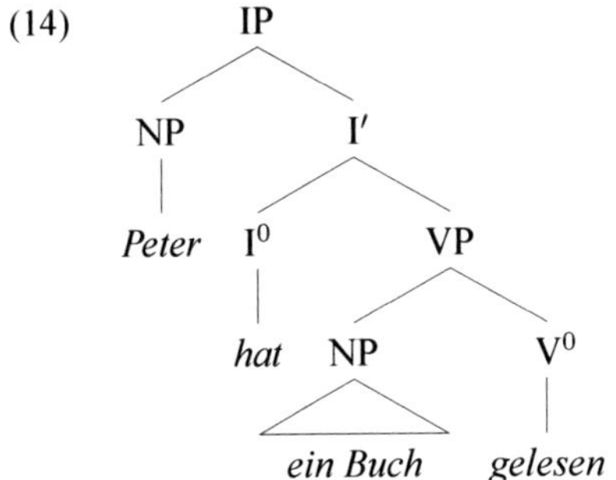

In Vogel (2004*a*), I argue that this structure is preferred by a constraint that requires the topmost projection to have the head to the left of the complement:

(15) **Hd-Comp/Top**
      The head of the topmost projection precedes its complement.

Given the constraint ranking in (16), the winning structures (12a) and (12b) are correctly derived:[9]

(16) Hd-Comp/Top » Comp-Hd » Hd-Comp

Simply put, the constraint ranking has the effect that IP is right-headed within CP, but left-headed in main clauses. This derives the V2 effect without having to assume that the auxiliary occupies a different syntactic position.

The candidates in this conception are [syntax, PF] pairs, where PF is the only locus of linear order, and syntax is a set of syntactic objects, a matrix and adjunct phrases. Constraints require correspondence among semantics and syntax, semantics and PF, as well as syntax and PF. Such correspondence relations usually hold, for instance between relative scope (semantics), asymmetric c-command (syntax) and precedence (PF, linear order), or predication (semantics), head-dependent relation (e.g. sisterhood in syntax) and adjacency (PF). Being OT constraints, they are, of course, violable.

The possibility of mismatches between those structures is therefore systematically taken advantage of. I did so, for instance, in my analysis of pronominal object shift in Germanic (Vogel 2006b) which I analysed as a mismatch between syntactic structure and linear order which is prosodically triggered. Our aforementioned account of the syntax of German verb clusters is another case in point.

4.   An alternative account of *wh*-movement in terms of syntax-semantics correspondence

This section introduces an alternative account of the typology of *wh*-movement that does without economy of movement. It is based on the correspondence between semantics and syntax and can be sketched as in (17).

(17)   Alternative OT account of *wh*-movement:
  - An object *wh*-phrase as in 'What did you say?' has a couple of semantic and morphological properties (*wh*-, case, Θ-role, a.o.) which are syntactically relevant.
  - The *wh*-item is in conflict between which of its semantic properties determines its position, [WH-SCOPE] or [Θ-role]. We assume two constraints, WH-SCOPE and Θ, requiring placement in scope or Θ position, respectively.
  - WH-SCOPE is essentially the demand to have a *wh*-operator c-command its scope domain.
  - Θ is the demand for an argument to occur within the phrase headed by its predicate.
  - No *wh*- or Θ features are necessary. Both constraints are formulated purely relationally.
  - WH-SCOPE » Θ derives *wh*-movement.
  - Θ » WH-SCOPE derives *wh*-in-situ.

This derives a core aspect of the typological variation in *wh*-movement in terms of conflicting semantics↔syntax mapping demands (*wh*-scope, Θ-role). It might be the conceptually stronger analysis in the sense that it also has something to say about the in-situ position.

   Furthermore, I think this kind of approach has an empirical advantage. Note the following problem with Turkish:

> It should be noted that, although Turkish is an SOV language, the basic word order is overridden by various other factors. For example, the most unmarked position for a WH-element is to the immediate left of the verb, irrespective of the grammatical relation. The second-best alternative is for the WH-element to be placed in its original position …
>
> (Kornfilt 1997)

(By 'original position' it is obviously meant what in generative terms is the theta or case position, that is the default position for non-*wh* items of the same type.)

(18)   (a)   bu   kitab-ı   kim   oku-du?
          This   book-ACC   who   read-Past

    (b)   kim   bu   kitab-ı   oku-du?
          Who   this   book-ACC   read-Past
          'Who read this book?'

As the position left adjacent to the verb is the focus position in Turkish, it is easy to integrate Turkish into our alternative account, assuming that focus is on the *wh*-phrase in (18a), and on the direct object in (18b):[10]

> (19) Constraint ranking for Turkish:
> Focus » Θ » Wh-scope

The Focus constraint can best be formulated as a constraint on semantics-prosody mapping. Different accounts have been developed by Truckenbrodt (1999), Büring (2001), Samek-Lodovici (2005), and so on. These accounts derive right-aligned focus placement from typologically well-confirmed prosodic well-formedness constraints that require the prosodic head of the intonation phrase to be phrase-final.

An analysis in terms of economy can be extended in the same way, of course. However, Turkish shows that the positioning of *wh*-items is not simply a matter of having *wh*-movement or not. The spirit of the Stay-based analysis as such is called into question here.

To sum up: the surface position of the *wh*-item is *always* determined by some semantic property, no matter which position it is. The *wh*-item bears several semantic properties with conflicting placement requirements (Θ-role, scope, focus), and the conflict is resolved in the usual OT way. We do not need to specify particular positions for these properties. Their syntactic consequences are always *relational*, that is the placement requirements can completely be stated in terms of the item's position relative to other elements.

4.1 Reinhart (1995): Syntactic economy relativized by syntax-semantics interface needs

This subsection deals with a phenomenon that has been discussed by Reinhart (1995). She notes the following grammaticality contrast for English:

> (20) (a) *Bill$_1$ wonders what$_3$ who$_2$ bought.
> (b) Who$_1$ wonders what$_3$ who$_2$ bought?
> (c) Who$_1$ wonders what$_3$ Bill$_2$ bought?

This is a problem for economy of movement, as the order of the *wh*-items in the subordinate clause in (20b) violates superiority, and hence it should be ruled out for the same reason as (20a). But, surprisingly, the subordinate clause's subject NP does not induce a superiority violation here, just as in (20c).

This observation about (20b) is only correct, as long as the two embedded *wh*-phrases do not compete for the embedded [Spec,CP] position in (20b). 'Who$_2$' has matrix scope. This distinction is difficult to integrate into a minimalist analysis, if [WH] is a purely formal syntactic feature:

(21)

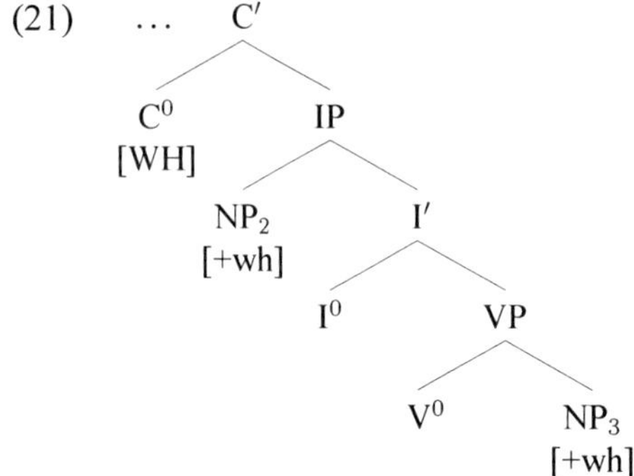

The [WH] Comp of the embedded clause should attract the closest [+wh] element, which is who$_2$ in both (20a,b). The main problem for the analysis lies in the fact that the [WH] Comp is blind for the semantic scope of the *wh*-elements it attracts.

Reinhart's solution relativizes the Minimal Link Condition (MLC) to semantically equivalent syntactic structures. This interpretation of the MLC in terms of competition and blocking is already close to an OT account.

Reinhart's idea can be implemented quite nicely in OT. Assume that there is no formal [WH] feature, no attraction of such features, and no checking. Assume further that *wh*-elements have scope over whatever they c-command, and need not stand in an A-bar position. Take the constraints WH-SCOPE and τ from above. Consider the following OT competition:

(22)   *input*: Qxy [x wonders Qz [y bought z]]
       Candidate structures:
       (a) *Who$_x$ wonders who$_y$ bought what$_z$
       (b) *Who$_y$ does who$_x$ wonder what$_z$ bought
       (c) √Who$_x$ wonders what$_z$ who$_y$ bought

The three candidates are Reinhart's examples in (20). The input specifies the reading where both the matrix subject and the embedded subject have matrix scope. Which is the optimal syntactic structure for this reading?

(23) OT tableau for (22):

Qxy [x wonders Qz [y bought z]]	WH-SCOPE	Θ
(22a)	*(y) *(z)	
(22b)	*(x)	*(y)*(z)
☞ (22c)	*(y)	*(z)

Structure (22a) has two violations of WH-SCOPE, because neither the embedded object nor the embedded subject occupy their scope positions. Structure (22b) has only one violation of Wh-scope, because the matrix subject *wh*-phrase remains *in situ*. However, both the embedded object and the embedded subject occupy their scope positions and therefore incur violations of Θ. The candidate in (22c) exploits the fact that the matrix subject *wh*-phrase simultaneously satisfies both Wh-scope and Θ in the same syntactic position. This gives this structure the advantage of having one violation of Θ less than (22b), for the embedded *wh*-object, '*what*'. The only element that violates Wh-scope is the embedded '*who*'. This is the optimal candidate.

(22b) might even be worse under a definition of Wh-scope that requires a *wh*-operator to c-command *all* elements that belong to its scope domain. This is not met, though $what_z$ is in the embedded [Spec,CP], because one element of this domain, who_y, has moved higher – such a definition of Wh-scope is thus even able to derive *wh*-island effects.[11] Let me summarize the claims I have made so far:

- Syntactic constraints should formulate placement requirements as *purely relational consequences* of particular semantic, morphological, or (perhaps) phonological properties of syntactic elements.
- Gen does not contain any checking operations.
- Consequently, the respective features and their (functional) projections are unnecessary.
- So, Gen simply consists of one operation, Merge, which is used to construct structures from lexical items that are conform with X-bar theory.

We can go one step further in excluding multiple specifiers and complements. As the heuristics for the relative relation of such elements would again only be their linear order which is already represented at PF, we are left with four phrase structure rules:[12]

(24) (a) XP → [$_{x'}$ X]
     (b) XP → [$_{x'}$ X ZP]
     (c) XP → YP [$_{x'}$ X]
     (d) XP → YP [$_{x'}$ X ZP]

The syntax of an output candidate is a forest, that is a set of X-bar conform binary branching trees with at most one X′ node including a matrix and its adjuncts.

5. Syntactic simplicity and markedness

Both minimalism and Optimality Theory use meta-principles. In minimalism, one such principle is *economy*, both derivational and representational. Optimality Theory relies on the principle of *markedness*. This section discusses how these two concepts relate.

OT's notion of markedness is close to the traditional understanding of this term. Typical claims about the differences between marked and unmarked versions of an expression are the following:

- The unmarked expression is typologically more frequent than the marked one.
- When a language has the marked expression, it also has the unmarked expression.
- In languages that have both the marked and the unmarked expression, the contexts in which the marked expression can occur build a proper subset of the contexts in which the unmarked expression can occur.

How does syntactic simplicity correlate with this traditional conception of markedness? Optimality Theory is good at modelling so-called 'repair strategies'. A typical case in phonology is the *neutralization* of a marked feature, which happens under particular conditions, as, for example, in German final devoicing – where syllable-final obstruents lose voice, for example, /rad/ → [rat]:

(25)   German final devoicing (after Wiese 1996):
       [+ obstruent] → [– voice] /__]$_\sigma$

As we will see in the following subsection, *syntactic* repair strategies are not always the unmarked option, and the unmarked option is not always the structure that is less complex. A further issue is the relationship between analytical and synthetic expressions. Sometimes, we use syntactic means in order to fill a 'morphological gap'. Are these syntactic means therefore less marked? And if so, why is the syntactic route often blocked when the morphological route is available, and how can this all be integrated in a theory of syntactic markedness?

5.1   Optional and obligatory complementisers

A nice example of an unmarked-marked pair of two syntactic expressions are the two versions of English subordinate clauses, with and without complementizer, here not quite precisely called CP and IP, respectively. Their division of labour has been subject to several OT analyses (see for example Baković and Keer 2001; Grimshaw 1997).

Interestingly, '*that*'-clauses, that is CPs, have to be seen as the unmarked option in the classical sense. The contexts where they are possible are a proper superset of those where the '*that*'-less (IP) variant is possible. For instance, when the clause is fronted, only *that*-clauses are possible, while both forms are legitimate in final position:

(26)   (a) I would never say John should leave
       (b) I would never say that John should leave
       (c) That John should leave, I would never say
       (d) *John should leave, I would never say

The complementizer becomes obligatory with the insertion of an adverbial preceding the subject (Grimshaw 1997):

(27)   (a) *She swore/insisted/thought, most of the time, they accepted this solution.
       (b) She swore/insisted/thought that, most of the time, they accepted this solution.

The possibility of complementizer-less clauses is restricted to complements of so-called bridge verbs. Many verbs only allow for a clause with complementizer:

(28) (a) I regret that John left
      (b) *I regret John left

Considerations about the economy of representation would suggest that the version with the complementizer is the marked option, because it has more structure. This is clearly not the case. We thus conclude that the grammatically unmarked form is not always the shortest (or literally unmarked) form. There is a discrepancy between economy of structure and syntactic markedness.

The complementizer can also be understood as a marker for subordination. We can then say that it is the unmarked case for a subordinate clause to have a complementizer. This observation seems to stand in opposition to the traditional notion of markedness. However, this is also a matter of perspective. If we see the two forms as possible variants of English clauses in general, we find that *that*-less clauses can serve as both main and subordinate clauses, while *that*-clauses can only serve as subordinate clauses. *That*-less clauses, from this perspective, have the wider distribution.

All of this suggests that, especially in syntax, expressions are not marked or unmarked as such. They count as (un)marked *for a particular purpose*:

(i)   The unmarked main clause has no complementizer.
(ii) The unmarked subordinate clause has a complementizer.
(iii) We can nevertheless make the following two statements:
      – Subordinate clauses are more marked than main clauses.
      – Clauses with a complementizer are more complex than those without one.

The statements in (i) and (ii) can be interpreted as the result of the interaction of the two markedness tendencies expressed in (iii) and (iv). The latter statements can be reinterpreted as scales:[13]

(29) main clause < subordinate clause
      IP < CP

By using the method of harmonic alignment, as established by Prince and Smolensky (1993, 2004), we can construct two universally fixed sub-rankings of constraints composed by aligning the two scales appropriately:

(30) (a) *MainCl/CP » *MainCl/IP
      (b) *SubCl/IP » *SubCl/CP

The typological claim is that it is universally more harmonic for a main clause not to have a complementizer, and for a subordinate clause to have one. The interleaving of these two subrankings is open to typological variation. For English, it is crucial that *MainCl/CP is ranked higher than all the other constraints, as this is the structure that never occurs.

As this analysis shows, economy of structure does indeed play a role, but perhaps not in a pure way, but only indirectly as part of a constraint subsystem that is derived by harmonic alignment. More complex structures are sometimes preferred, in particular, in order to maintain a contrast.

This is a reminder of Horn's (1984) 'division of pragmatic labour', the observation that unmarked forms tend to be used for unmarked situations and marked forms for marked situations. When a pair of two forms stands in such a relation, the more general form will be blocked by the more specific one in a 'neutral' context. This is not the case with our two sentence types, but the next section will discuss a candidate for such an interaction, English *do*-support.

5.2 *Do*-support, periphrasis, and markedness

As we saw in the previous section, the decision which of two syntactic structures has to be considered as less marked is not necessarily decided simply by considering structural complexity. This also holds for the second example I would like to discuss, English *do*-support. Consider the following examples:[14]

(31) (a) John left.
   (b) *John did leave.
   (c) John DID leave.
   (d) John didn't leave. / *John left not.
   (e) Why did John leave? / *Why left John?

Do-support is the analytic version of a simple tense form, it alternates with the tense inflection on the verb. A couple of contexts make it obligatory – in (31), we have contrastive verum focus (31c), negation (31d) and non-subject questions (31e). Which is the unmarked form, *do*-support or tense inflection? If we follow the reasoning above, then the unmarked form is the one which is more widely applicable and which occurs especially in difficult environments. This is clearly the case with *do*-support. However, the unmarked expression should also be possible in an unproblematic environment. But as the judgement in (31b) indicates, this is not the case for *do*-support.

These observations thus do not fit the picture of markedness in syntax that we developed thus far. I see two possible explanations for the oddity of (31b) which are in line with our theory of syntactic markedness:

(i) The non-acceptability of (31b) is not an instance of syntactic ill-formedness, but due to pragmatic blocking.
(ii) (31b) is well-formed, its low acceptability is due to a prescriptive norm within the speech community.

Explanation (i), pragmatic blocking, could rely on the theory of conventional implicatures, as founded by Grice (1975), and further developed, for example, by Levinson (2000). It can happen that two semantically equivalent forms stand in a scalar opposition. These scales are called Horn-scales after Horn (1984) who was the first to give a systematic account of such phenomena. It was originally developed to derive pragmatic effects of the usage of quantitative expressions: the use of 'some', for instance, pragmatically excludes the meaning 'many' though semantically it doesn't. Levinson extended this to oppositions of grammatical forms, thus developing a pragmatic theory of grammaticalization.

The example that Levinson has studied in detail is the English system of pronominal and anaphoric reference. The SELF-anaphora (*himself, herself, itself, myself,* etc.) are nowadays the only option for a locally bound pronoun in English. But in Old High English, the simple pronouns *him, her, it* were still possible, that is, 'John shaved him' could mean that John shaved himself. What has changed since then, according to Levinson, is the *conventionalization* of the scale 'SELF-pronoun – pronoun'. This had the consequence that in contexts where the SELF pronoun is used, the simple pronoun is blocked.

The oddity of (31b) might result from another instance of such a division of pragmatic labour. The first assumption that I make is that the synthetic form is preferred over the analytic form in general:

> **Blocking of analytic forms:** If two forms differ only in whether they express a feature by a morpheme or by a function word and build a Horn-scale, then the form that uses the morpheme blocks the form that uses the function word.

It is striking that the syntactic structure of (31b) is not unacceptable per se, but, as we see in (31c), requires, or induces, an additional semantic feature, verum focus. This is in fact a precondition for the building of a Horn-scale in Levinson's sense: the forms involved in a Horn-scale are well-formed according to core grammatical criteria. Thus, *do*-support is syntactically well-formed, even in (31b), but because of the division of pragmatic labour, its use induces a semantic contrast – if no such contrast is intended, the use of the dispreferred form is not justified.

While in Standard English the scale '*do*-support – morphological tense' is conventionalized, there exist English dialects which are in a state comparable to Old English in Levinson's example: they use *do*-support even in neutral environments. This has been reported by Kortmann (2002) for the southwest counties of England[15] where 'unstressed' *do* [occurs] as simple tense-carrier in affirmative sentences:

> We do breed our own cows. This man what do own this, …
>   We've been up milking at 6 o'clock in the morning, and then we did
> go on haymaking, …   (Kortmann 2002: 197)

Among German dialects, this phenomenon is even more widely spread, though also most German speakers will presumably agree that (32) is ill-formed as a Standard German sentence:

(32) ?* Maria   tut   schlafen
         M.   does   sleep
      'Maria is sleeping'

(32) probably sounds to most Germans as colloquial, dialectal, or child speech. For Standard German, a sociolinguistic explanation for the low acceptability of (32) seems plausible – it is the result of the exposition to prescriptive pressure by language norms put forward for centuries in the media, the literal and academic world, and at school.[16]

5.3   Comparative adjective formation

The two versions of comparative adjective formation in English follow a pattern similar to *do*-support: short adjectives are formed with *-er*, those with 3+ syllables are built with *more*. The two options have nearly complementary distribution:

(33) (a) easier, *more easy
      (b) *intelligenter, more intelligent
      (c) luckier, more lucky

Adjectives with two syllables are somewhat in between. Via a *Google* search, it is possible to find both versions for '*lucky*':

(34) (a) http://www.omgclothing.com/score/36052/Liberals_are_**luckier**_in_love!
      (b) 'How You Can Be **More Lucky**' (http://www.somethingyoushouldknow.net/
           transcript8_13_03.htm)

Analytic comparatives of '*easy*' can be found in coordinated adjectives:

(35) Periphrastric comparative adjectives with a disyllabic adjective:
      (a) 'But then turn to an open source language, inspired by Unix shell
           programming, but, oh, so much **more easy and powerful**.'
           (http://www.awaretek.com/programming.html)
      (b) 'AOSell integrates with America Online software to make researching stocks
           with AOL **more easy and productive**.'
           (http://www.softdepia.com/business_solutions_sub_155_1.html)
      (c) 'Act for the **more easy and speedy** recovery of small debts, within the city of
           Rochester, and the parishes of Strood [etc.] and the ville of Sheerness.
           (http://library.kent.ac.uk/library/special/html/specoll/acts.htm)

This can even be observed with monosyllabic adjectives:

(36) Analytic comparatives with a coordinated monosyllabic adjective:
      (a) 'Just hope that the script kiddie graphic interface will be **more nice and sober**
           in the future.'
           (forum.sysinternals.com/forum_posts.asp?TID=7003andPN=1andTPN=57)

  (b) 'Being the North the poor area, the South the **more nice and old** area, with medium class all over it and some old rich people also.'
(geoimages.berkeley.edu/wwp904/html/AYRTON.html)

  (c) 'I spent around thirty hours or so working on the Everything Engine, trying to refactor it into something a little **more nice and usable.**'
(www.oreillynet.com/onlamp/blog/2006/06/refactoring_everything_retrosp.html)

As in the case of *do*-support, periphrasis is an option the system can 'fall back' to in a non-trivial syntactic context. Although the expressions 'easier and speedier' and 'nicer and older' are available, the analytic 'more easy and speedy' and 'more nice and old' are not blocked any more. Hence, in the context of our discussion about markedness we again notice that the analytic form, the *'more'*-comparative is the one that is more widely applicable, and, thus, should count as the less marked form, despite its being blocked in the case of small adjectives in unproblematic contexts.

In the absence of a morphological strategy, the analytic form is even obligatory in the simple cases. This can be seen with *less*-comparatives:

(37) (a) 'That's less nice. And we hope.' (www.aquinas.ac.uk/documents/download.asp?nodeid=2631andlibraryversionid=1719)

  (b) 'A little less nice and a lot more nasty would have made Shallow Hal twice the film.'
(www.totalfilm.com/cinema_reviews/shallow_hal)

  (c) 'I had to make her a bit less nice and a bit more willing to make mistakes and get involved with people.'
(fictionwriting.about.com/od/interviews/a/alixohlin_2.htm)

This is expected: without a morphological alternative, no pragmatic blocking can apply. If there was a genuinely morpho-phonological or morpho-syntactic constraint ruling out analytic comparatives with small adjectives, we would expect this constraint to also apply with the *less*-comparative. *'Less nice'* should then be ill-formed. As we see, this is false. The ill-formedness of *'more nice'* in unproblematic contexts is thus indeed dependent on the existence of a morphological alternative – the two forms build a Levinsonian Horn-scale.

Summarizing the discussion in the last two sections, we can state that from a purely formal perspective, analytic forms are less marked than synthetic forms, because they are more generally applicable. But whenever we have an alternation between morpheme and function word, and this relation has become conventionalized in the form of a Levinsonian Horn-scale, the less marked analytic form is blocked in neutral environments, due to the principle of the 'division of pragmatic labour'.

Furthermore, whether a morphological variant is present must be determined by the language's particular lexicon. Though it might be a universal possibility to have such structures in the candidate set, the lexicon of the language and its morphological subsystem have to provide it. Thus, candidate sets – and maybe Gen with respect at least to its morphological component – may indeed vary from language to language precisely in whether they offer morphological variants that induce blocking due to conventionalization in the form of a Levinsonian-Horn scale.

Assuming such a language particular (morphological) Gen would not mean giving up the idea of universal grammar: in OT, first of all Eval and the constraint set are universal, whereas Gen might not necessarily be universal in all respects, with the lexicon including the systems of morphological inflection as one major source of language particular restrictions on the candidate set. The blocking mechanism described in this section should also be a universal property of languages.

5.4   Agreement with first and second person in relative clauses

Thus far, the results of our discussion on the relation between markedness and structural simplicity showed that analytic forms are the less marked forms, i.e., those forms that are more widely applicable, and the last resort the system can fall back to under difficult circumstances. Thus, richer, more explicit structures are less marked than those which are more condensed.

However, this should not mean that structural richness is less marked in general. One example of a richer, but more marked structure that occurs only as repair form are resumptive pronouns in German relative clauses. German relative pronouns are marked for third person and agree with their head noun in the φ-features person, number and gender:

(38) (a) Der   Mann,   der   da   steht …
          the   man-3SgMasc   the-3SgMasc   there   stands
      (b) Die   Frau,   die   da   steht …
          the   woman-3SgFem   the-3SgFem   there   stands
      (c) Die   Leute,   die   da   stehen
          the   people-3Pl   the-3Pl   there   stand

But German lacks relative pronouns for first and second person. Using the third person relative pronoun alone leads to ill-formedness, especially when an appositive relative clause is extraposed (39a), (39b). The structure is repaired by inserting a resumptive pronoun that bears the missing person features (39c). This option is ruled out in third person (39d) (underlining indicates relativizer and its antecedent, the additional pronoun is in boldface):

(39)   Relative pronoun agreement with first/second person in German:
       (a) *<u>Ich</u> gehe zu ihr, <u>der</u>   sie   am   besten   kennt.
            I   go   to   her the-3SgNomMasc her   at-the   best   knows-3Sg
           'I'll go to her, who (i.e., me) knows her best.'

       (b) *<u>Ich</u> gehe zu ihr, <u>der</u>   sie   am   besten   kenne.
            I   go   to   her the-3SgNomMasc her   at-the   best   know-1Sg

   (c) <u>Ich</u>   gehe zu ihr, <u>der</u>   **ich** sie   am   besten kenne.
        I   go   to   her the-3SgNomMasc I   her   at-the best   know-1Sg

   (d) *<u>Peter</u> geht zu ihr, <u>der</u>   **er** sie   am   besten kennt.
        P.   goes to her the-3SgNomMasc he her   at-the best   knows-3Sg

   (e) Peter geht zu ihr, <u>der</u>   sie   am   besten kennt.
        P.   goes to her the-3SgNomMasc   her   at-the best   knows-3Sg

While (39a), (39b) are clearly odd examples, (39d) sounds first of all 'archaic', as if it stemmed from an eighteenth-century Shakespeare translation. Nevertheless, leaving the resumptive pronoun out, as in (39e) is clearly the preferred and fully acceptable option, and this strongly contrasts with (39a), (39b).

Using such a resumptive pronoun is totally ruled out in restrictive relative clauses:

  (40) *Ich kenne <u>einen</u> <u>Mann,</u> <u>der</u>   **er** Maria kennt
       I   know   a   man   the-3SgNomMasc he M.   knows
     'I know a man who (he) knows Maria'

I conclude that the resumptive pronoun in (39c) is a repair form that is invoked by agreement requirements. There is an agreement chain starting from the head noun of the relative pronoun, 'Ich', via the relative pronoun to the finite verb of the relative clause. Especially in order to avoid an agreement clash with the finite verb of the relative clause, the resumptive pronoun is required.

(39c) is the syntactically more complex expression, but in this case it is also the more marked expression. Use of an additional pronoun is restricted to cases like (39c). There is also another important difference: while in all examples that we discussed we are dealing with function words that express a feature that could be expressed by a morpheme, the feature in this latter case is agreement, that is, a purely formal property of the relative pronoun – of course, one that it is unable to express. In the other cases above, the expressed properties were tense and comparative, that is, semantically relevant properties.

5.5 Summary

Let me briefly sum up the results of this section.

Analytic forms where a function word expresses a semantically relevant feature are less marked than their synthetic alternatives, because they have broader application. Their avoidance in unproblematic contexts is due to the division of pragmatic labour. There has been a considerable debate about the integration of these pragmatic aspects into optimality theory, especially in the context of bidirectional OT, see for instance the paper by Blutner (2001), and the collection by Blutner and Zeevat (2004). I sketched a bidirectional model of OT syntax that is able to capture relevant aspects of Horn's division of pragmatic labour, as they are relevant for syntactic analyses, in Vogel (2004a,b).

Pronominal or clitic doubling, as we find it in the preceding subsection, is used to fulfil agreement requirements. It does not serve a semantic purpose in such cases, has an isolated range of application, and is therefore the marked option.

Structural economy in the strict sense seems to hold when function words are used to express a purely morpho-syntactic property like agreement, but not when they express semantically relevant properties like tense or comparative. Thus, it seems that the unmarked syntactic expressions are typically analytic constructions. These unmarked analytic constructions can be seen as standing in a balance between *compression* (synthetic constructions) and *redundancy* (doubling). However, this is counterbalanced by the pragmatic constraints governing language use.

6.   Conclusion

The starting point of my discussion was the shift of explanatory burden from Gen to Eval within OT. One consequence of this shift should lie in a simplification of the syntactic generator, compared to a purely derivational system like minimalism. I argued that OT's syntax generator can indeed do without a couple of important ingredients of minimalist theory: features, feature strength, functional projections, movement, and also, to a certain extent, economy of representation. Much of this still requires further evaluation and critical examination.

A genuine OT model makes crucial use of faithfulness and markedness. I proposed that faithfulness should be used for the OT account of the interfaces in a correspondence theoretic fashion.

Markedness is OT's replacement for economy. Representational economy is called into question from an empirical perspective: the syntactic structures that count as unmarked, according to typological and distributional criteria, often are not the 'shortest' ones. Syntactically unmarked structures tend to be non-redundantly analytic.

Analytic constructions are those with the broadest applicability. We further found that the situations where analytic constructions are ruled out have two characteristics: we have a syntactically unproblematic context, and a synthetic alternative is available. I argued that these cases should be treated as instances of the pragmatic blocking of the analytic form by the synthetic one. However, the (syntactic) well-formedness of the involved expressions is a prerequisite for such pragmatic blocking to apply.

What is left of minimalism in this approach? To be honest, not much. The properties of the generator component that the presented account needs can be found in most syntax formalisms. Properties specific of minimalism, like movement, feature checking and economy of derivation and representation are not very useful from a consequent OT perspective. This trivialization of the generator is a consequence of the radical execution of OT's output orientation as a theory of the interfaces. But still, such a radical trivialization of the generator is – to my mind – very much in the spirit of the Minimalist Program.

Acknowledgements

This chapter is a revised version of Vogel (2006a). I thank Hans Broekhuis and an anonymous reviewer and the audience at the DEAL conference in Berlin, 17–19 December 2005, for helpful comments and discussion.

Notes

1. For a detailed discussion of the traces of the 'Filters and Control' approach within current theorizing see Broekhuis (2008), Broekhuis and Vogel (2011).
2. But it is important to note that the mechanisms of derivational OT still are quite different from those of derivational syntax. See the contribution by McCarthy and Pruitt in this volume.
3. See Blutner *et al.* (2006) for an overview.
4. I laid out this model in Vogel (2004a), applying core ideas of McCarthy and Prince (1995) in their reconstruction of faithfulness as *correspondence* between an input and an output representation.
5. Note that Hans Broekhuis has revised his earlier account, adopting an approach in terms of 'shape conservation' which no longer assumes inviolability of the MLC. See Broekhuis (2008) and also Broekhuis (this volume). The constraint CASE is renamed as EPP(CASE) in these more recent proposals.
6. This is very much in line with recent proposals by Grimshaw (2001), Grimshaw (2006) though she takes a different avenue to fulfil this goal.
7. Semantic considerations are another indicator of adjunction sites – in particular for base positions of adverbials.
8. See Besten (1983) and more recently Sternefeld (2006), Haider (2010) for detailed discussion.
9. The two constraints 'Comp-Hd' and 'Hd-Comp' require 'complement before head' and 'head before complement', respectively. The definition of 'Hd-Comp/Top' is an informal version of the one given in Vogel (2004a).
10. The latter assumption has been confirmed to me by Orhan Orgun, p.c.
11. I carried out this analysis in Vogel (2010).
12. That the X' node in some of these structures is redundant, is an independent issue that is not relevant here.
13. Recall that we use use the labels CP and IP for clauses with and without complementizer. Traditional analyses of non-subject wh-fronting in English assume a CP structure. These cases have to be distinguished from what is at issue here.
14. See also the detailed analysis by Grimshaw (this Volume) for another view on *do*-support.
15. Kortmann quotes Wakelin (1986), according to whom this region is mainly constituted by the counties of Cornwall, Devon, Somerset, South Avon, Wiltshire and Dorset, with East Cornwall, Devon and (West) Somerset forming its core.
16. The history of the stigmatization of auxiliary 'tun' in the course of the creation of standard German has been reconstructed by Langer (2001).

References

Ackema, P. and Neeleman, A. (1998) WHOT. In P. Barbosa, D. Fox, P. Hagstrom, M. McGinnis and D. Pesetsky (eds) *Is the Best Good Rnough? Optimality and Competition in Syntax*, 15–34. Cambridge, MA: MIT Press.

Archangeli, D. and Langendoen, D. T. (eds) (1997) *Optimality Theory. An Overview*. Malden, MA and Oxford: Blackwell.

Baković, E. and Keer, E. (2001) Optionality and ineffability. In G. Legendre, J. Grimshaw and S. Vikner (eds) *Optimality-Theoretic Syntax*, 97–112. Cambridge, MA: MIT Press.

Barbosa, D., Fox, D., Hagstrom, P., McGinnis, M. and Pesetsky, D. (eds) (1998) *Is the Best Good Enough? Optimality and Competition in Syntax*. Cambridge, MA: MIT Press.

den Besten, H. (1983) On the interaction of root transformations and lexical deletive rules. In W. Abraham (ed.) *On the Formal Syntax of the Westgermania*, 47–138. Amsterdam: John Benjamins.

Blutner, R. (2001) Some aspects of optimality in natural language interpretation. *Journal of Semantics* 17 (3): 189–216.

Blutner, R., de Hoop, H. and Hendricks, P. (2006) *Optimal Communication*. Stanford, CA: CSLI Publications.

Blutner, R. and Zeevat, H. (eds) (2004) *Optimality Theory and Pragmatics*. Basingstoke: Palgrave Macmillan.

Broekhuis, H. (2000). Against feature strength: The case of Scandinavian object shift. *Natural Language and Linguistic Theory* 18 (4): 673–721.

Broekhuis, H. (2008) *Derivations and Evaluations: Object Shift in the Germanic Languages*. Berlin: Mouton de Gruyter.

Broekhuis, H. and R. Vogel (2011) Crash-proof syntax and filters. In: M. Putnam (ed.), *Exploring Crash-Proof Grammars*, 245–68. Amsterdam: John Benjamins.

Büring, D. (2001) Lets's phrase it. Focus, word order, and prosodic phrasing in German double object constructions. In G. Müller and W. Sternefeld (eds), *Competition in Syntax*, 69–106. Berlin: Mouton de Gruyter.

Chomsky, N. (1981) *Lectures on Government and Binding*. Dordrecht: Foris.

Chomsky, N. (1995) *The Minimalist Program*. Cambridge, MA: MIT Press.

Chomsky, N. and Lasnik, H. (1977) Filters and control. *Linguistic Inquiry* 8 (3): 425–504.

Chomsky, N. and Lasnik, H. (1993) Principles and parameters theory. In J. Jacobs, A. von Stechow, W. Sternefeld and T. Vennemann (eds) *Syntax. Ein internationales Handbuch zeitgenössischer Forschung*, 506–69. Berlin: Walter De Gruyter.

Culicover, P. W. and Jackendoff, R. (2005) *Simpler Syntax*. Oxford and New York: Oxford University Press.

Féry, Caroline and Samek-Lodovici, V. (2006) Focus projection and prosodic prominence in nested foci. *Language* 82 (1): 131–50.

Grice, H. Paul (1975) Logic and conversation. In P. Cole and J. Morgan (eds), *Speech Acts. Syntax and Semantics, vol. 3*, 41–58. New York: Academic Press.

Grimshaw, J. (1997) Projection, heads, and optimality. *Linguistic Inquiry* 28 (3): 373–422.

Grimshaw, J. (2001) 'Economy of Structure in OT.' Rutgers Optimality Archive (ROA). URL:http://roa.rutgers.edu/view.php3?id=479

Grimshaw, J. (2006) Chains as unfaithful optima. In: E. Bakovic, J. J. McCarthy and J. Junko (eds), *Wondering at the Natural Fecundity of Things: Essays in Honor of Alan Prince*, 97–109. Charleston, SC: BookSurge Publishing. URL:http://repositories.cdlib.org/lrc/prince/6/

Haider, H. (2010) *The Syntax of German*. Cambridge: Cambridge University Press.

Heck, F. and Müller, G. (2000) Successive cyclicity, long-distance superiority, and local optimization. *Proceedings of WCCFL* 19: 218–31.

Holmberg, A. (1999) Remarks on Holmberg's generalization. *Studia Linguistica* 53 (1): 1–39.

Horn, L. R. (1984) Toward a new taxonomy for pragmatic inference: Q-based and R-based implicatures. In D. Schiffrin (ed.), *Meaning, Form and Use in Context*, 11–42. Washington, DC: Georgetown University Press.

Kornfilt, J. (1997) *Turkish. Descriptive Grammmars*. London: Routledge.

Kortmann, B. (2002) New prospects for the study of English dialect syntax: Impetus from syntactic theory and language typology. In S. Barbiers, L. Cornips and S. van der Kleij (eds), *Syntactic Microvariation*, 185–213. Amsterdam: Meertens Instituut. URL:http://www.meertens.knaw.nl/projecten/sand/synmic/

Langer, N. (2001) *Linguistic Purism in Action – How Auxiliary 'tun' was Stigmatized in Early New High German*. Berlin: Walter de Gruyter.

Legendre, G., Grimshaw, J. and Vikner, S. (eds.) (2001) *Optimality Theoretic Syntax*. Cambridge, MA: MIT Press.

Legendre, G., Smolensky, P. and Wilson, C. (1998) When is less more? Faithfulness and minimal links in

WH-chains. In P. Barbosa, D. Fox, P. Hagstrom, M. McGinnis and D. Pesetsky (eds) *Is the Best Good Enough? Optimality and Competition in Syntax*, 249–289. Cambridge, MA: MIT Press.

Levinson, S. C. (2000). *Presumptive Meanings. The Theory of Generalized Conversational Implicature*. Cambridge, MA: MIT Press.

McCarthy, J. J. and Prince, A. (1995) Faithfulness and reduplicative identity. In J. Beckman, L. Walsh-Dickie and S. Urbanczyk (eds) *Papers in Optimality Theory*, vol. 18, 249–384. Amherst, MA: UMass Occasional Papers in Linguistics.

Pesetsky, D. (1997) Optimality theory and syntax: movement and pronunciation. In D. Archangeli and T. D. Langendoen (eds) *Optimality Theory. An Overview*, 134–70. Cambridge, MA: MIT Press.

Pesetsky, D. (1998) Some optimality principles of sentence pronunciation. In P. Barbosa, D. Fox, P. Hagstrom, M. McGinnis and D. Pesetsky (eds) *Is the Best Good Enough? Optimality and Competition in Syntax*, 337–83. Cambridge, MA: MIT Press.

Prince, A. and Smolensky, P. (1993) Optimality Theory. Constraint interaction in generative grammar. Rutgers Optimality Archive: ROA-537. Published as Prince and Smolensky 2004. URL:http://roa. rutgers.edu/view.php3?roa=537

Prince, A. and Smolensky, P. (2004) *Optimality Theory: Constraint Interaction in Generative Grammar*. Oxford: Blackwell.

Reinhart, T. (1995) Interface Strategies. OTS Working Papers, University of Utrecht.

Samek-Lodovici, V. (2005) Prosody syntax interaction in the expression of focus. *Natural Language and Linguistic Theory* 23 (3): 687–755.

Schmid, T. (2005) *Infinitival Syntax. Infinitivus Pro Participio as a Repair Strategy*. Amsterdam: John Benjamins.

Schmid, T. and Vogel, R. (2004) Dialectal variation in German 3-verb clusters. A surface-oriented optimality theoretic account. *Journal of Comparative Germanic Syntax* 7 (3): 235–74.

Selkirk, E. (1986) On derived domains in sentence phonology. *Phonology Yearbook* 3: 371–405.

Selkirk, E. (1996). The prosodic structure of function words. In J. Morgan and K. Demuth (eds), *Signal to Syntax: Bootstrapping from Speech to Grammar in Early Acquisition*, 187–213. Mahwah, NJ: Lawrence Erlbaum Associates.

Selkirk, E. (2000) The interaction of constraints on prosodic phrasing. In M. Horne (ed.) *Prosody: Theory and Experiment*, 231–61. Dordrecht: Kluwer.

Sells, P. (ed.) (2001a) *Formal and Empirical Issues in Optimality-Theoretic Syntax*. Stanford, CA: CSLI Publications.

Sells, P. (2001b) *Structure, Alignment and Optimality in Swedish*. Stanford Monographs in Linguistics. Stanford, CA: CSLI Publications.

Sternefeld, W. (2006) *Syntax. Eine morphologisch motivierte generative Beschreibung des Deutschen*. Tübingen: Stauffenburg.

Szendröi, K. (2001) *Focus and the Syntax-Phonology Interface*. Ph.D. thesis, University College London.

Szendröi, K. (2003) A stress-based approach to the syntax of Hungarian focus. *The Linguistic Review* 20 (1): 37–78.

Truckenbrodt, H. (1995) *Phonological Phrases: Their Relation to Syntax, Focus, and Prominence*. Ph.D. thesis, MIT, Cambridge, MA.

Truckenbrodt, H. (1999) On the relation between syntactic phrases and phonological phrases. *Linguistic Inquiry* 30 (2): 219–55.

Vogel, R. (2003) Dialectal variation in German 3-verb clusters. Looking for the best analysis. In A. Mahajan (ed.) *Syntax at Sunset 3. Head Movement and Syntactic Theory. UCLA working papers in Linguistics 10*, 199–235. Los Angeles, CA: UCLA.

Vogel, R. (2004a) Correspondence in OT syntax and minimal link effects. In A. Stepanov, G. Fanselow and R. Vogel (eds) *Minimality Effects in Syntax*, 401–41. Berlin: Mouton de Gruyter.

Vogel, R. (2004b). Remarks on the architecture of Optimality Theoretic syntax grammars. In R. Blutner and H. Zeevat, H. (eds) *Optimality Theory and Pragmatics*, 211–27. Basingstoke: Palgrave Macmillan.

Vogel, R. (2006a). The simple generator. In H. Broekhuis and R. Vogel (eds) *Optimality Theory and Minimalism: A Possible Convergence?*, Linguistics in Potsdam 25, 99–136, University of Potsdam.

Vogel, R. (2006b) Weak function word shift. *Linguistics* 44 (5): 1059–93.

Vogel, R. (2010) Wh-islands: A view from correspondence theory. In C. Rice and S. Blaho (eds), *Modelling Ungrammaticality in Optimality Theory*, 267–92. London: Equinox.

Wakelin, M. F. (1986) *The Southwest of England*. Amsterdam: John Benjamins.

Wiese, R. (1996) *The Phonology of German*. Oxford: Oxford University Press.

Williams, E. (2003) *Representation Theory*. Cambridge, MA: MIT Press.

Wilson, C. (2001) Bidirectional opimization and the theory of anaphora. In G. Legendre, J. Grimshaw and S. Vikner (eds) *Optimality Theoretic Syntax*, 465–507. Cambridge, MA: MIT Press.

11 Last resorts: a typology of *do*-support

Jane Grimshaw[*]

ABSTRACT The notion of a 'last resort' figures prominently in linguistic discussion within the last 25 years. This investigation suggests it is coherent only within a theory of grammatical optimization, such as that provided by Optimality Theory (Prince and Smolensky 2004). In this theory, every grammatical candidate is a last resort, in a sense which is both theoretically and empirically definable. This chapter explores the phenomenon of *do*-support and argues that it is indeed a last resort, as are all grammatical alternatives such as raising V or realizing a tense as a free morpheme. The predicted typology is shown to be highly structured, allowing only tightly restricted combinations of optima.

KEYWORDS Last resort; *do*-support; V-raising; free tense; interrogative clauses; negative clauses; VP-displacement; factorial typology

1. Introduction

The notion of a 'last resort' figures prominently in linguistic discussion within the last 25 years.[1] The present investigation suggests that it is both fundamentally right and fundamentally incoherent. It can be right and coherent only within a theory of grammatical optimization, such as that provided by Optimality Theory (Prince and Smolensky 2004). In this theory, every grammatical candidate is a last resort, in a sense which is both theoretically and empirically definable. This chapter explores the phenomenon of *do*-support, a frequently cited example of a last resort grammatical device, and argues that it is indeed a last resort, but so is every grammatical alternative. It is nothing more than an option made available by universal grammar and selected in a particular configuration by universal constraints as ranked in a grammar. It is no more language-particular than, say, moving V to T. It is simply the best grammatical structure that the language can construct.

---

* Jane Grimshaw, Department of Linguistics, Rutgers University, New Brunswick NJ, USA. E.mail:grimshaw@ruccs.rutgers.edu

When some grammatical structure is said to be a 'last resort', what does it mean? It is a meaningful claim in cases where some principle allows alternatives to be systematically assessed. This is the case where a universal markedness hierarchy governs a phenomenon: the most marked member is guaranteed never to occur unless requirements such as faithfulness or conflicting markedness constraints force it to occur. (See the discussion of markedness in Prince and Smolensky 2004, for example.) However, no markedness hierarchy lies behind the last resort status of *do*-support. Perhaps a universal hierarchy in which *do*-support appears as the most marked member could be posited. This doesn't seem very promising, though, given that much current research holds that movement is a last resort, and the two frequently compete.

Perhaps it is possible to state for each grammar what its last resort is. The problem is that a language can choose different 'last resorts' in different situations. Monnese, for example, as analysed in Benincà and Poletto (2004), prefers V-raising to *do*-support when it is movement to T that is at issue, but prefers *do*-support to V-raising when movement to C is at stake. German (Bader and Schmid 2006) chooses V-raising in negative and interrogative clauses, but *do*-support with VP-preposing. English, I will argue, chooses to strand T in the future, realizing it as a free tense, and chooses *do*-support in the present and past. This is not a good fit with the concept of a last resort: a given choice either is, or is not, last. We do not want a theory that lists the choice of grammatical devices for each configuration or 'construction': English past tense interrogatives use *do*-support, Korean negatives use *do*-support, German negatives use V-raising, etc. The choices are not independent but are systematically related to each other, as explored in Anttila and Andrus (2006), Prince (2006) and the present work. In fact the constraints investigated here, numbering nine if we collapse the present and future tense constraints, generate a typology which includes only 28 languages, because most combinations of optima for negation, *wh* questions and VP displacement require inconsistent rankings and thus cannot co-occur in a single language. I will show, for example, that 'Anti-Monnese', a language which is just like Monnese except for having V-raising to C and *do*-support in T, cannot be derived given the universal constraints proposed here. Neither can 'Anti-German', a language with *do*-support winning in the negation and *wh* question candidate-sets and V-raising in the VP displacement competition.

Within this perspective, *do*-support is no more language-particular than any other grammatical option. This contradicts the frequently found characterization of it as language-particular or unique to English. Lying behind the last resort theme is the assumption that *do*-support is an odd phenomenon from some perspective. It is not found in positive declarative main clauses in neutral focus contexts, for example. However, far from being language-particular, *do*-support is widespread. It is found in many languages and language families. In addition to the cases analysed below, which come from Germanic, Romance and Panoan languages, many others have been discussed. French has cases of pleonastic *faire* (see Miller 1997; Meinunger 2001). Celtic languages exhibit it also: see Newton (2009) on *do*-support in Old Irish complementizers, and Legendre (2001) and references therein on *do*-support in Breton. Kandybowicz (2010) argues that Twi has *do*-support. Korean exhibits *do*-support with the negative *ani* and the 'nominalizer' *ci* (see Hagstrom 1996). Basque VP focalization induces *do*-support (see Haddican 2007). Japanese 'emphatics' trigger *do*-support (Kuroda 1965; Miyagawa 2001). Korean and Japanese offer a rather different case analysed in Grimshaw and Mester (1988), Saito and Hoshi (2000), among others. Here a noun which bears thematic argument structure occurs in an outer framework consisting of tense and the light verb *do* (*suru* in Japanese and *ha* in Korean).

Within English there are numerous instances of *do*-support beyond interrogatives and negatives. It appears in positive imperatives: *Do come in.* It appears in VP ellipsis. It appears emphatically, for example in contradictions: *They said I hadn't paid but I DID pay.* It occurs in evasive answers to questions: *Is he a good doctor? Well he does have a lot of patients.* Its presence is a response to a cluster of prosodic and syntactic factors, as well as polarity and focus. It appears to be a favourite resource of the language, rather than a last resort. (Children learning English use *do*-support with enthusiasm: see Hollebrandse and Roeper 1996.)

Of course *do*-support is irreducibly language-particular in one sense: it involves a particular morpheme of a particular language. But it is language-particular only in the most shallow way: the choice of morpheme is predictable given the vocabulary of the language. In all cases discussed here the verb used in support is the morpheme corresponding to the verb translating *do*. Setting the morpheme itself aside, there is no evidence I can see to favour the view that *do*-support has a special status *vis-à-vis* other grammatical options like verb movement.[2] Both are language-particular choices: they depend on constraint ranking. Both are universal: they follow from the interaction of universal constraints. The last resort status of *do*-support is both genuine and spurious: a *do*-support candidate will always have competitor(s) which satisfy constraints violated by the presence of *do*. In this sense *do*-support is a genuine last resort: the candidate wins if and only if all the alternatives lose. On the other hand, the same is true for any other winning candidate. They are all last resorts.

In sum, the notion 'last resort' is entirely central to grammatical theory. Every optimal candidate is a last resort, the best in the circumstances, the last candidate standing. The set of last resorts is identical to the set of potential winners – candidates which are not harmonically bounded. (A candidate is harmonically bounded if for every ranking of the constraints, there is a better candidate; see Samek-Lodovici and Prince 2005.)[3] The fact that every language does the best it can with what it has available is a result of the very way that grammaticality is decided. Grammaticality itself is irreducibly comparative and a theory of how candidates are compared is required to render the concept of a last resort coherent.

OT does not include 'last resort' principles or constraints, or lists of last resort 'devices'. The last resort property of optima is a direct consequence of the theory of grammar, and does not need to be stipulated by auxiliary, external statements. Last resort effects, of which economy effects are one example, are entailed by the theory of constraints and constraint interaction. This is the argument of Grimshaw (2001, 2002) with respect to economy of structure and Grimshaw (2006a) with respect to chains, that is movement.

The massive literature which appeals to last resorts has several striking properties which suggest that the concept of a last resort lacks theoretical content in the absence of a theory of constraint conflict, candidate sets and optimization. First of all, the frequent use of scare quotes in punctuation suggests a certain lack of commitment to the notion. (In Lasnik *et al.* (2005: 269) the term appears in this form five times in the penultimate paragraph.) Second, while last resort analyses are extremely common, they generally appeal to the last resort idea by word and not by deed. For instance, in many variants of 'movement as a last resort' the theory says that if a particular kind of feature is present movement is required. If it is absent, movement is disallowed. If we remove the 'last resort' concept from this, we get exactly the same results. In fact, if we claim that no-movement is a last resort and is possible only when a particular (type of) feature is absent, we get exactly the same result, at least in the absence of a substantive theory of features. The words 'last resort' are employed but the concept plays no role in the analysis. An example that is directly relevant here is the Benincà and Poletto (2004) account of *do*-support in Monnese, in which the presence of a feature on C forces a head to be filled, and the head cannot be filled by a lexical V. The theory simply imposes these two requirements. It in no way relies upon or uses a special status for *do*-support, however encoded. However, like many researchers discussing the last resort 'flavour' of an analysis Benincà and Poletto elect to use language which is precisely that of OT, and refers to concepts defined within OT. On p. 79 they comment of English and Monnese: 'Hence, both languages react to the same tension between two conflicting constraints, the necessity to check a strong feature and the fact that the position hosting the feature has become thematically opaque in Pollock's terms; for both languages the problem is solved by inserting a dummy verb.' The language of constraint conflict and competition between candidates is valuable in conceptualizing the problem, despite the fact that the proposed analysis involves neither. A similar point is made in Samek-Lodovici (this volume, ch. 9): constraint conflict is appealed to in analyses framed within theories which have no way to accommodate it.

In sum:

- The notion of a last resort is explicated only by a theory of optimization with constraint interaction.
- The last resort character of grammatical structures is attributable to the determination of well-formedness itself, not to additional principles.
- Every grammatically possible structure is a last resort. The set of last resorts is the same as the set of possible winning candidates (i.e. grammatical sentences).
- *Do*-support is a last resort in exactly the same sense as any other grammatical strategy is. It is the best that can be done in the circumstances.

2.   The cost and benefit of *do*-support

Certain grammatical demands can be satisfied by the presence of *do*: it can carry tense and it can fill a head position. The cost of expletive *do* is that it has no meaning. Like other expletives such as *it* and *of* it appears to be the least-marked member of its category; see Halle and Marantz (1993), Grimshaw (1997), Schütze (2001). Many theories of verb meaning (e.g. Dowty 1979) posit a semantic prime which corresponds closely to the meaning of *do* and corresponding predicates in other languages. The idea that some languages have the right kind of *do* to allow *do*-support, while others do not, plays no role in the explanation for the distribution of *do*, as I argued in Grimshaw (1997). The presence or absence of *do* in grammatical sentences is a consequence of the grammar of the language, not a matter of lexical stipulation.

The constraints which evaluate *do*-support and its competitors are in (1):

(1) $V+T_P$ Present/Past T is affixed to a V
     $V+T_F$ Future T is affixed to a V
     OBHD   A phrase has a head
     FULLINT   No meaningless element
     *LINA′   No lexical head within an A′ functional head
     *LINF   No lexical head within a functional head[4]
     CCOM   The overt member of a chain c-commands null copies
     UNIQUE   An element in the input has no more than one correspondent in the output

I assume here that the constraints FULLINT, V+T, *LINF, and *LINA′ are violated at most once per chain, by the head of the chain. Thus, for example, a chain containing *do*+T and a copy receives one violation of FULLINT and not two.

Two additional constraints divide the set of VP displacements into those in which VP occupies a specifier projection and those in which it is adjoined. This is discussed further in Section 4.

(2) VPSPEC   A displaced VP is a specifier
     VPADJ   A displaced VP is an adjunct

Inputs are represented in a highly simplified form, specifying that they contain a verb, a subject and a tense. An internal argument ('int') is included in the inputs for VP displacement, because its position shows the location of the VP if the V has moved outside it. Since all candidates under consideration are faithful (aside from the unfaithful character of chains, which violate UNIQUE) no faithfulness constraints are at play, so such inputs suffice for present purposes. The order in which elements appear in the input is not significant, since the constraints themselves determine order in winning candidates, although the constraints responsible are not discussed here.

The constraints in (1) are chosen in part because their properties have been explored in earlier work. The constraint *LINA′ is important in distinguishing a lexical head raised to C, which violates it, from a lexical head raised to T, which does not. Quite possibly this constraint and *LINF are members of a set of such constraints which together prefer the lexical head to be as close to the lexical projection as possible. OBHD was posited in Grimshaw (1997) to force T-to-C movement in interrogatives. For the present purpose it is not crucial that this is the constraint at issue as opposed to one relating to feature specifications as in, for example Pesetsky and Torrego (2001, 2007). UNIQUE is a faithfulness constraint based on McCarthy and Prince (1997/1999). Grimshaw (2006a) argues that this constraint entails economy of movement effects, which thus reduce to the theory of faithfulness. (See Grimshaw (2001, 2002) for an argument that markedness constraints can entail economy of movement under certain circumstances.)

FULLINT is crucial in selecting an optimum with raising of a meaningful auxiliary verb over a candidate in which the auxiliary stays in place and *do* occupies the higher head position. This is demonstrated in Grimshaw (2011). A different view of the constraint violated in *do*-support is put forward in Vikner (2001). He proposes that *do*-support violates a constraint VV^0, which is violated by any verb that is not inserted in V. Since *do* is inserted directly into T when it is present for *do*-support, it violate this constraint. A final point: I do not try to analyse restrictions on *do* as due to a faithfulness constraint. This is because occurrences of *do* would not be penalized by such a constraint if *do* were in the input. Given 'richness of the base' (Prince and Smolensky 2004), there is no way to exclude *do* from inputs entirely. Nor is there any need to, as far as I can see.

3.   Which resort is the last?

Cross-linguistically *do*-support is often associated with negation and with *wh*-interrogatives. This is because, when no meaningful auxiliary or modal verb is present, these configurations lead to inevitable violations of the constraints in (1).[5] The present analysis proposes, following many others, that negation can cause *do*-support because it separates the verb from tense.[6] *Wh*-movement induces the presence of a head position in the structure which needs to be filled. See for example Chomsky (1957, 1991), Halle and Marantz (1993), Bobaljik (1995), Grimshaw (1997) and Vikner (2001). One resolution to these crises is to raise a main verb out of its position inside VP, violating *LINF, and another is to use *do*-support, violating FULLINT. A third option is to allow the tense to remain separate from V, resulting in a free tense morpheme, which violates V+T. This candidate is optimal in the English future tense, as analysed in Section 5.[7] Until that point I will discuss only the patterns of *do*-support found with present and past tenses in English.

The three options, which I will abbreviate for the remainder of the chapter as DS (for *do*-support), VR (for verb raising) and FT (for free tense), form the core of the candidates in the Negation c(andidate)-set. Can one of them be identified as a last resort in some meaningful way? This section shows that within a single language, one of the options can be selected in one structure and another elsewhere, and that that this follows from the interaction of the constraints in (1).

3.1   The Negation candidate set

The Northern Italian dialect spoken in Monno, reported in Benincà and Poletto (2004), prohibits the expletive verb *fa* 'do' from appearing in negated clauses (Benincà and Poletto 2004: 70–71).

(3) (a) l so   mìa
        It I know not
    (b) *fo mìa savè-l
        I do not know-it

Benincà and Poletto hypothesize that main verbs raise to T, observing that V always raises across 'low adverbs' as in (4) (their (7a)), and hence across *mìa*, the negation, as shown by (3) above. In the terms of the present analysis, Monnese thus presents a case in which a constraint ranking allows violation of *LinF, and hence allows V-to-T movement.

(4) l tʃàkola semper
    he speaks   always
    'He always speaks'

German patterns like Monnese, as shown in (5) and (6).[8] (These examples were provided by Fabian Heck.) The main verb precedes negation and the adverb *immer*.

(5) (a) Ich weiß   es nicht
        I   know   it not
    (b) *Ich tu(e) es nicht wissen
        I   do   it not   know
        'I do not know it'

(6) (a) Er spricht immer
        'He speaks always'
    (b) *Er immer spricht
        'He always speaks'

In contrast, English, in accordance with the hypothesis first put forward in Pollock (1989), does not allow V-to-T movement, and thus disallows a lexical V before *always* and requires *do*-support with negation.

(7) (a) *I know not it
    (b) I do not know it

(8) (a) He always speaks
    (b) *He speaks always

The analysis of the Negation c-set that I present here is based on the analysis of English in Grimshaw (1997), but restricted in scope and limited to very small candidate sets. Vast, in fact infinite, numbers of candidates cannot be generated in this system, because they are harmonically bounded, see Grimshaw (1997) and Vikner (2001). Candidates with *do*-support which also contain auxiliary *have* or the verb *be* are harmonically bounded, as is every candidate containing more than one occurrence of *do*-support. This is demonstrated in Grimshaw (2011). A similar argument with respect to multiple occurrences of the complementizer *that* in English is developed in Grimshaw (2008). The table in (9) shows the number of violations that each candidate incurs on the five constraints that are relevant in assessing present and past tense forms. (I include OBHD and *LINA' in the table because they can be violated in interrogatives, which are discussed later in this section. The constraints CCOM, VPSPEC and VPADJ are unviolated in the members of the negation and interrogative c-sets considered here, and are omitted.) The first candidate, which is optimal in German and Monnese, raises V to T, in violation of *LINF. The second candidate, which is optimal in English, violates FULLINT by virtue of the presence of *do*. The third candidate realizes tense as a free morpheme, violating V+T$_\text{p}$.

(9)   Violation table: Negation

Input: {V Subj P Neg}	V+T$_\text{p}$	OBHD	FULLINT	*LINA'	*LINF	UNIQUE
a. VR [$_\text{TP}$ Subj V-P Neg [$_\text{VP}$ <V> ...]]					1	1
b. DS [$_\text{TP}$ Subj do-P Neg [$_\text{VP}$ V ...]]			1			
c. FT [$_\text{TP}$ Subj P Neg [$_\text{VP}$ V ...]]	1					

The candidates and the violation profiles are necessarily identical in all three languages. The only difference lies in the ranking and hence the optimum. (I gloss over many important issues such as exactly where negation is located, whether it is a head and so forth.) The three comparative tableaux in (10)–(12) show how the optima are selected, and allow us to determine which rankings generate the languages; see Prince (2002 a,b), Brasoveanu and Prince (2011). All comparative tableaux in this chapter have the winning candidate bolded, and annotated with 'W'.

(10)   VR-Neg winner

Input: {V Subj P Neg}	V+T$_\text{p}$	OBHD	FULLINT	*LINA'	*LINF	UNIQUE
a. W VR [$_\text{TP}$Subj V-PNeg [$_\text{VP}$<V>...]]						
b. DS [$_\text{TP}$ Subj do-P Neg[$_\text{VP}$ V ...]]			W		L	L
c. FT [$_\text{TP}$ Subj P Neg [$_\text{VP}$ V ...]]	W				L	L

When the winner is the VR optimum, *LINF and UNIQUE prefer the loser in both competitions, (a vs. b, and a vs. c) and they must each be subordinated to both V+T$_\text{p}$ and FULLINT.

When the DS candidate is the winner (below) FULLINT prefers the losing FT candidate (b vs. c). Since only V+T$_\text{p}$ prefers the winner, V+T$_\text{p}$ must dominate FULLINT. In the competition between DS and VR (b vs. a) *LINF and UNIQUE prefer the winner. One of these must dominate FULLINT, since it prefers the VR loser to the DS winner.

(11) DS-Neg winner

Input: {V Subj P Neg}	$V+T_p$	ObHd	FullInt	*LinA′	*LinF	Unique
a. VR $[_{TP}$ Subj V-P Neg $[_{VP}$ <V> ...]]			L		W	W
b. W DS $[_{TP}$ Subj do-P Neg $[_{VP}$ V ...]]						
c. FT $[_{TP}$ Subj P Neg $[_{VP}$ V ...]]	W		L			

When the optimum has a free tense as in (12), $V+T_p$ prefers both of the losing candidates over the winner. Hence FullInt must dominate $V+T_p$ in order for FT to beat DS (c vs. b), and either Unique or *LinF must dominate $V+T_p$ in order for FT to beat VR (c vs. a). The FT candidate is the winner in the English future tense as discussed in Section 5.

(12) FT-Neg winner

Input: {V Subj P Neg}	$V+T_p$	ObHd	FullInt	*LinA′	*LinF	Unique
a. VR $[_{TP}$ Subj V-P Neg $[_{VP}$ <V> ...]]	L				W	W
b. DS $[_{TP}$ Subj do-P Neg $[_{VP}$ V ...]]	L		W			
c. W FT $[_{TP}$ Subj P Neg $[_{VP}$ V ...]]						

The rankings in (13) are thus required to select the optima from the Negation c-set.

(13) VR-Neg FullInt, $V+T_p$ >> *LinF, Unique
     DS-Neg $V+T_p$ >> FullInt   *LinF or Unique >> FullInt
     FT-Neg FullInt >> $V+T_p$ *LinF or Unique >> $V+T_p$

The violation table and rankings already suggest that there is no asymmetry in the status of the three candidates. Each is both 'better' and 'worse' than the others. Each violates at least one of the constraints under discussion. Each option is chosen by several rankings (all rankings that are consistent with (13)). There is, as far as I can see, no basis for identifying the solution of *do*-support, as opposed to leaving T as a free morpheme or V-to-T movement, as a last resort.

3.2 The *Wh*-question candidate set

The theory presented here predicts the possibility of a language with *do*-support in interrogatives but not with negation. In such a language is *do*-support a last resort or not? The reason for the non-uniform pattern is that there is a stringency relationship (Prince 1997) between two of the constraints posited in (1). *LinA′ is violated by a high lexical head in a projection with A-bar properties, such as CP. However, *LinF is violated there *and* in functional projections with A properties such as those in the IP 'region'. Hence *LinF is violated wherever *LinA′ is violated, but not vice versa. In particular, a V in T violates *LinF but a V in C violates *LinF and *LinA′.[9]

Benincà and Poletto demonstrate that Monnese is a language which has a non-uniform pattern of *do*-support. In interrogatives it patterns with English, instead of with German, having *do*-support in matrix questions. The grammaticality of *fa*-support is illustrated for *wh* interrogatives in (14) (Benincà and Poletto (1b) and (1d) p. 52).

(14) (a) ke   fa-l   majà?
           What does-he eat
     (b) *ke   majà-l?
          What eats he

The corresponding German examples in (15) were provided by Fabian Heck.

(15) (a) Was   isst   er?
          What eats   he
     (b) ?*Was tut   er essen?
          What does he eat

(16) (a) What does he eat?
     (b) *What eats he?

Again we begin by examining the violation table for the candidates under consideration. There are two decisions to be made in selecting the optimum within the c-set. The first is the choice between the VR, DS and FT structures. The second is the location of the V, *do* and T, which might be in C or in some lower head position such as T, with C being empty. As a representative of the empty C options I have included the ∅C candidate d in (17), which has V-raising to T.[10]

Since I am making the simplifying assumption that all *wh*-movement candidates have a *wh* chain of the same length I do not include violations of UNIQUE caused by these chains in the analysis, and I follow the same strategy for VP displacement candidates in Section 4.

(17) Violation table: *wh*-questions

Input: {V Subj P Wh}	$V+T_p$	OBHD	FULLINT	*LINA'	*LINF	UNIQUE
a. VR [$_{CP}$ Wh V-P [$_{TP}$ Subj <V-P> [$_{VP}$ <V> …]]]				1	1	2
b. DS [$_{CP}$ Wh do-P [$_{TP}$ Subj <do-P> VP]]			1			1
c. FT [$_{CP}$ Wh P [$_{TP}$ Subj <P> VP]]	1					1
d. ∅C [$_{CP}$ Wh __ [$_{TP}$ Subj V-P [$_{VP}$ <V> …]]]		1			1	1

The VR candidate violates both *LINF and *LINA', while the DS and TS candidates violate neither. Again, I present the comparative tableaux for the VR, DS and TS candidates as winners.

(18) VR-WhQ winner

Input: {V Subj P Wh}	$V+T_p$	ObHd	FullInt	*LinA′	*LinF	Unique
a. W VR [$_{CP}$Wh V-P[$_{TP}$Subj <V-P>[$_{VP}$<V>…]]]						
b. DS [$_{CP}$ Wh do-P [$_{TP}$ Subj <do-P> VP]]			W	L	L	L
c. FT [$_{CP}$ Wh P [$_{TP}$ Subj <P> VP]]	W			L	L	L
d. ∅C [$_{CP}$ Wh __ [$_{TP}$ Subj V-P [$_{VP}$ <V> …]]]		W		L		L

The rankings required to select the VR winner are those in (19), which in fact select the VR winner in both c-sets discussed so far, that is they correspond to German.

(19) VR-WhQ   ObHd >> *LinA′, Unique
            FullInt, $V+T_p$ >> *LinF, *LinA′, Unique

The FT comparative tableau establishes the rankings in (21).

(20) FT-WhQ winner

Input: {V Subj P Wh}	$V+T_p$	ObHd	FullInt	*LinA′	*LinF	Unique
a. VR [$_{CP}$Wh V-P[$_{TP}$Subj <V-P>[$_{VP}$<V>…]]]	L			W	W	W
b. DS [$_{CP}$ Wh do-P [$_{TP}$ Subj <do-P> VP]]	L		W			
c. W FT [$_{CP}$ Wh P [$_{TP}$ Subj <P> VP]]						
d. ∅C [$_{CP}$ Wh __ [$_{TP}$ Subj V-P [$_{VP}$ <V> …]]]	L	W			W	

(21) FT-WhQ   FullInt >> $V+T_p$
            ObHd or *LinF >> $V+T_p$
            *LinA′ or *LinF or Unique >> $V+T_p$

The comparative tableau for the DS optimum motivates the rankings in (23):

(22) DS-WhQ winner

Input: {V Subj P Wh}	$V+T_p$	ObHd	FullInt	*LinA′	*LinF	Unique
a. VR [$_{CP}$Wh V-P[$_{TP}$Subj <V-P>[$_{VP}$<V>…]]]			L	W	W	W
b. W DS [$_{CP}$Wh do-P [$_{TP}$Subj <do-P> VP]]						
c. FT [$_{CP}$Wh P[$_{TP}$Subj <P> VP]]	W		L			
d. ∅C [$_{CP}$Wh __ [$_{TP}$Subj V-P[$_{VP}$<V>…]]]		W	L		W	

(23) DS-WhQ $V+T_p$ >> FullInt
            ObHd or *LinF >> FullInt
            ***LinA′ or *LinF or Unique >> FullInt**

We can see that the DS-WhQ rankings do not enforce the choice of DS as the optimum in the Negation c-set. The rankings which select the DS candidate for negation are repeated in (24):

(24)   DS-Neg $V+T_p >> $ FULLINT
                ***LINF or UNIQUE** $>>$ FULLINT

The Negation c-set ranking requires *LINF or UNIQUE $>>$ FULLINT, while the WhQ competition is won by DS if *either* one of these two constraints *or* *LINA' dominates FULLINT. (The critical parts of (23) and (24) are bolded.) Hence the DS winner in WhQ is compatible with a ranking in which DS does not win in the Negation c-set, namely one in which *LINA' dominates FULLINT but neither *LINF or UNIQUE does. This is the Monnese ranking. In Monnese, *do*-support is preferred when it avoids a violation of *LINA', even though it is not preferred when just a violation of *LINF or UNIQUE is at issue. Monnese does not tolerate a lexical verb in C even though it tolerates one in T.

3.3   Interim conclusion

The case of Monnese demonstrates that it is not possible to declare a 'last resort' for a language. If *do*-support is the last resort for English, and not for German, then what can we usefully say about Monnese? The fact is simply that the Monnese grammar chooses *do*-support for interrogatives but not for negation, because its constraint ranking gives DS as the optimum in interrogatives only. In contrast, English prefers *do* in both cases, and German prefers to raise the lexical verb in both cases. It is interesting to note that the non-uniform distribution of DS in Monnese leads Culicover (2008: 32) to consider that it is not a real case of DS: 'However, as Benincà and Poletto (2004) suggest, *do*-support in Monnese can be seen as a type of light-verb construction, which has generalized to most of the lexicon and which is restricted to questions.'[11] The fact that it is restricted to questions is simply a consequence of ranking, in the present account. It is not necessary to appeal to a construction-related restriction, or to separate cases into 'real' *do*-support versus *do*-periphrasis, as Culicover does.

Since the existence of non-uniform systems, such as that of Monnese, is predicted by the constraint system, the obvious question is whether all non-uniform systems are possible. Are we predicting the existence of 'Anti-Monnese', a language with *do*-support in T (i.e. with negation) but with a lexical V occurring in the C position? The answer is that Anti-Monnese cannot be generated, as I will show in Section 6. No language can pick *do*-support as the optimum in negation and V-raising as the optimum in *wh* questions.

4. VP displacement

When a VP is displaced, tense is again potentially separated from the verb, and we find the familiar resolutions of the crisis, with the ranking of the constraints in (1) and (2) critical in determining the optimal structure for a given language. As elsewhere, *do*-support occurs in English when no other auxiliary verb is present.

(25)   He was supposed to read the book and *read the book he will/did.*

However English poses a puzzle. With *wh*-movement in main clauses, and with negative preposing everywhere, the raising of an auxiliary verb across the subject is required, but with VP-preposing and topicalization raising is neither allowed nor required. The examples in (26) differ precisely in this respect.

(26)   (a) Which book *will/did he* read?   *Which book he *will/did* read?
      (b) Read the book *he will/did.*   *Read the book *will/did* he.

Similarly, under the complementizer in complement clauses a displaced VP is immediately followed by the subject, while a preposed negative phrase is followed by a raised auxiliary.[12]

(27)   He was supposed to read the books from cover to cover …
      (a) but he said that only rarely *did he* read more than one chapter.
      (b) and he said that read the book from cover to cover *he did.*

Why is inversion and DS observed in (matrix) interrogatives and with negative preposing, and not with VP-preposing? This pattern cannot be derived in the present system if the VPs are preposed to specifier position. Every member of the typology in (54) which has DS in C in the WhQ c-set also has DS in C in the VP displacement c-set, if its VP is displaced into specifier position. No language can combine a filled head with a *wh* specifier and an empty head with a VP specifier, because these optima require contradictory rankings.

I conclude from this that the difference between questions and VP displacement stems from a difference in structure. In English the VP is adjoined (like a topicalized phrase in Zepter (2000)), and hence has no associated head position. (See Kiss (2010) and Thrainsson (2010) for recent arguments in favour of a specifier-adjunct distinction.) Therefore, OBHD is not violated in the grammatical sentences in (25)–(27).[13]

The choice between the specifier analysis of the displaced VP and the adjunct analysis is made by the ranking of the constraints in (2), VPSPEC and VPADJ. We can partition the c-set into three: candidates which satisfy VPSPEC and violate VPADJ, those with the opposite violation pattern, and those that violate both or neither, which will not be under consideration here.

4.1 Adjoined VPs

Let us consider first the candidates which satisfy the constraint VPADJ and violate the constraint VPSPEC. (28) is the violation table for the three candidates of interest.[14] 'Int' is an internal argument of the verb.

(28) Violation Table: Adjoined VPs

Input: {V int Subj P}	V+T$_p$	OBHD	FULLINT	*LINA'	*LINF	UNIQUE	CCOM
a. VR: V in T [$_{TP}$ VP[$_{TP}$ Subj V-P<[$_{VP}$ <V> int]>]]					1	1	1
b. DS: do in T [$_{TP}$ VP[$_{TP}$ Subj do-P<VP>]]			1				
c. FT: T in T [$_{TP}$ VP[$_{TP}$ Subj P <VP>]]	1						

In the VR candidate V raises from within the VP into the tense position, and the VP which contains the original V position moves away. I have not identified any such cases with leftward movement of the VP, which should exist if the proposal is correct. However, rightward movement of the critical type is posited in Bhatt and Dayal (2007). They propose an analysis of Hindi-Urdu in which the V raises rightward and the remnant VP scrambles further to the right. The example in (29) from Bhatt and Dayal (2007) is their (13c), which has the observed order 'S V Aux IO DO'. In their analysis, the IO+DO is a VP from which the V has been raised. The trace of the VP is between the subject and the verb. Example (30), which contains no auxiliary verbal material, was provided by V. Dayal.

(29) [[Ram-ne t$_j$ dii$_i$ thii]   [$_{VP1}$ Sita-ko   [$_{VP2}$ kitaab   t$_i$]]$_j$]
       Ram-ERG   give.PFV.F be.PST.FSG   Sita-DAT   book.F
       'Ram had given a book to Sita.'

(30) [[kis-ne t$_j$ dii$_i$]   [$_{VP1}$ Sita-ko   [$_{VP2}$ kitaab   t$_i$]]$_j$]
       Who-ERG   give.PFV.F   Sita-DAT   book.F
       'Who gave a book to Sita?'

Abstracting away from the direction of VP displacement, Hindi-Urdu is an instance of the VR candidate in (28), in the Bhatt and Dayal analysis. It violates *LINF and Unique as all VR structures do. It also violates CCOM if the trace of V, which is inside the displaced VP, is not c-commanded by the raised V. I assume that this is the situation in all V-raising candidates with displaced VPs. No other constraint is violated.

(31) VR-AdjVP winner

Input: {V int Subj P}	V+T$_p$	OBHD	FULLINT	*LINA'	*LINF	UNIQUE	CCOM
a. W VR [$_{TP}$ VP[$_{TP}$ Subj V-P<[$_{VP}$ <V> int]>]]							
b. DS [$_{TP}$ VP[$_{TP}$ Subj do-P<VP>]]			W		L	L	L
c. FT [$_{TP}$ VP[$_{TP}$ Subj P <VP>]]	W				L	L	L

The V-to-T optimum, we see, is generated by any ranking consistent with the rankings in (32).

(32) $V+T_p$, FULLINT >> *LINF, UNIQUE, CCOM

The DS candidate wins in English, where the VP adjoins to the left of TP, as in (25) and (27) above. The crucial rankings for English are revealed by the comparative tableau:

(33) DS-AdjVP winner

Input: {V int Subj P}	$V+T_p$	OBHD	FULLINT	*LINA'	*LINF	UNIQUE	CCOM
a. VR $[_{TP}VP[_{TP}Subj V\text{-}P<[_{VP}<V>int]>]]$			L		W	W	W
b. W DS $[_{TP}VP[_{TP}Subj do\text{-}P <VP>]]$							
c. FT $[_{TP}VP[_{TP}Subj P <VP>]]$	W		L				

(34) $V+T_p$ >> FULLINT
      *LINF or UNIQUE or CCOM >> FULLINT

The third possibility is for the FT candidate to win. The comparative tableau shows that the ranking required for T to be realized as a free morpheme is (36).

(35) FT-AdjVP winner

Input: {V int Subj P}	$V+T_p$	OBHD	FULLINT	*LINA'	*LINF	UNIQUE	CCOM
a. VR $[_{TP}VP[_{TP}Subj V\text{-}P <[_{VP}<V>int]>]]$	L				W	W	W
b. DS $[_{TP}VP[_{TP}Subj do\text{-}P <VP>]]$	L		W				
c. W FT $[_{TP}VP[_{TP}Subj P <VP>]]$							

(36) *LINF or UNIQUE or CCOM >> $V+T_p$
      FULLINT >> $V+T_p$

4.2 Specifier VPs

Moving now to candidates with specifier VPs, the critical candidate set is twice as large. The reason is the presence of an additional head in the structure. This is the head of the projection containing the preposed VP as its specifier. Since the exact identity of the projection varies from case to case, I label it XP here. As for the Wh-Q c-set, it is necessary to consider the location of the free T, the raised V or the *do*, which might be in T or in X, so there are two candidates for each of DS, VR and FT. The constraint UNIQUE prevents harmonic bounding of the DS and FT candidates where *do* or T is in the T position by candidates in which it is in X, satisfying OBHD. Cf. n. 10. (There is no such potential harmonic bounding in the VR pair, since each violates a constraint which the other satisfies.)

(37)   Violation Table: Specifier VP

Input: {V int Subj P}	V+T$_P$	ObHd	FullInt	*LinA'	*LinF	Unique	Ccom
a. VR: V in X [$_{XP}$ VP V-P-X [$_{TP}$Subj <V-P> <[$_{VP}$<V>int]>]]				1	1	2	1
b. VR: V in T [$_{XP}$VP __ [$_{TP}$ Subj V-P <[$_{VP}$<V> int]>]]		1			1	1	1
c. DS: do in X [$_{XP}$ VP do-P-X [$_{TP}$Subj <do-P> <VP>]]			1			1	
d. DS: do in T [$_{XP}$ VP __ [$_{TP}$ Subj do-P <VP>]]		1	1				
e. FT: T in X [$_{XP}$ VP P-X [$_{TP}$ Subj <P> <VP>]]	1					1	
f. FT: T in T [$_{XP}$ VP __ [$_{TP}$ Subj P <VP>]]	1	1					

I will not show the comparative tableaux for the VR candidates in (37), since I have not identified examples. The tableaux are given in Grimshaw (2011), and the candidates are included in the typology analysed in Section 6.

It has been suggested that the VR candidates are always ungrammatical, because a phrase from which a head has been removed cannot undergo remnant movement. See Müller (1998) and Hinterhölzl (2006) for discussion and references. (In contrast Müller (2002) proposes that VPs with an empty V can occur in initial position in German.) If the VR candidates are indeed impossible, the present theory requires modification, and the analysis of Hindi-Urdu cannot be sustained. However, within the theoretical assumptions of OT the fact that a structure is ungrammatical in a language (as VR is in German VP displacements) does not license the conclusion that it is not a possible optimum. In the present analysis, this candidate is ungrammatical in German because the rankings of the language eliminate it.

German switches to the DS structure with VP displacement. It thus exemplifies non-uniform distribution of DS, as Bader and Schmid (2006) show. Dutch also has *do*-support with VP displacement (E. Reuland, p.c.). In a main clause, the displaced VP occupies the position usually characterized as 'specifier of CP', and *do* raises from T across the subject into C, creating a verb second configuration. This is in essence the analysis of Bader and Schmid, who give (38), their (14a).

(38)   Tanzen tut   Katja   immer noch häufig.
      Dance *does* Katja   still   often

Elías-Ulloa (2001) demonstrates DS in Capanahua, an SOV Amazonian language belonging to the Pano linguistic family, spoken in Eastern Peru. He proposes that a displaced VP occupies the specifier of an Evidential Phrase, matching the related language Shipibo, which has an overt evidential morpheme as the head of this phrase. Information-prominent constituents can front to first position, before the second position clitic. The examples in (39)–(41) are examples (72), (74) and (76) in his paper:

(39) ʔin-taʔ   ʔin   yoʔa   βana-ni-ʔ-ki
    I-Cl2   I   yucca   plant-past_tense-1/2p-evidential
    'I planted yucca (long ago)'

When the subject is null, the object is initial, as in (40). When both the subject and the object are null, the VP fronts and *ha* 'do' appears in X, as in (41). (Adverbial and aspectual suffixes move with the V, only tense is left behind; Elías-Ulloa (p.c.).)

(40) yoʔa-taʔ   βana-ni-ʃ-ki
    yucca-Cl2   plant-past_tense-3p-evidential
    '(He) planted yucca'

(41) βana-taʔ   ha-ni-ʃ-ki
    plant-Cl2   ha_support-past_tense-3p-evidential
    '(He) planted (it)'

The analysis of Capanahua and German in (43) is modified from Bader and Schmid (2006) and Elías-Ulloa (2001). As the comparative tableau shows, FULLINT must be dominated by at least one of *LINA′, *LINF, and CCOM, to choose the DS winner over the VR candidate a, with V in X. FULL INT must be dominated by OBHD or CCOM or *LINF to eliminate the VR candidate b, with V in T. To eliminate the DS candidate d, OBHD must dominate UNIQUE. To eliminate the FT candidate in e, with T in X, V+T$_p$ must dominate FULLINT. These last two rankings will correctly eliminate candidate f.

(42) *LINA′ or *LINF or UNIQUE or CCOM >> FULLINT
    OBHD or *LINF or CCOM >> FULLINT
    OBHD >> UNIQUE
    V+T$_p$ >> FULLINT

(43) DS-SpecVP winner[16]

Input: {V int Subj P}	V+T$_p$	OBHD	FULLINT	*LINA′	*LINF	UNIQUE	CCOM
a. VR: V in X [$_{XP}$ VP V-P-X [$_{TP}$Subj ‹V-P›‹[$_{VP}$‹V› int]›]]			L	W	W	L	W
b. VR: V in T [$_{XP}$ VP __ [$_{TP}$ Subj V-P ‹[$_{VP}$ ‹V› int]›]]		W	L		W		W
c. W DS: do in X [$_{XP}$ VP do-P-X [$_{TP}$ Subj ‹do-P› ‹VP›]]							
d. DS: do in T [$_{XP}$ VP __ [$_{TP}$ Subj do-P ‹VP›]]		W				L	
e. FT: T in X [$_{XP}$ VP P-X [$_{TP}$ Subj ‹P› ‹VP›]]	W		L				
f. FT: T in T [$_{XP}$ VP __ [$_{TP}$ Subj P ‹VP›]]	W	W	L			L	

The comparative tableau for a FT winner is given in (44). (Since English is the only free tense language considered here, and it chooses to adjoin displaced VPs, I do not provide an example of a FT optimum with a VP preposed to specifier.) The comparative tableau yields the rankings in (45).

(44)   FT-SpecVP Winner

Input: {V int Subj P}	V+T$_p$	ObHd	FullInt	*LinA'	*LinF	Unique	Ccom
a. VR: V in X [$_{XP}$ VP V-P-X [$_{TP}$ Subj <V-P> <[$_{VP}$ <V> int]>]]	L				W	W	W	W
b. VR: V in T [$_{XP}$ VP __ [$_{TP}$ Subj V-P <[$_{VP}$ <V> int]>]]	L	W			W		W
c. DS: do in X [$_{XP}$ VP do-P-X [$_{TP}$ Subj <do-P> <VP>]]	L		W				
d. DS: do in T [$_{XP}$ VP __ [$_{TP}$ Subj *do*-P <VP>]]	L	W	W			L	
e. W FT: T in X **[$_{XP}$ VP P-X [$_{TP}$ Subj <P> <VP>]]**							
f. FT: T in T [$_{XP}$ VP __ [$_{TP}$ Subj P <VP>]]		W				L	

(45)   *LinA' or *LinF or Unique or Ccom >> V+T$_p$
   *LinF or Ccom or ObHd >> V+T$_p$
   FullInt >> V+T$_p$
   ObHd >> Unique

The optima for VP displacement illustrate again the important point that the choice of whether *do*-support is allowed is not made by the language as a whole. We have already seen this for interrogatives and negation, where Monnese chooses *do*-support in one and not the other, while both English and German are uniform. Now we see it again in the case of German, which chooses *do*-support for VP-preposing but not elsewhere. No inherent asymmetry is detectable between *do*-support and V-raising or free T realization.

5.   Free Tense realization: non-uniform *do*-support in English

When the input is present or past tense, *do*-support is the optimum in English in all c-sets discussed. However when the input is specified as future, *will* appears in the positions that are occupied by *do* in DS optima.[16] When *will* is present, *do*-support is ungrammatical. Compare the examples in (46) with the *do*-support examples cited earlier. There is no word order which will make the starred versions of these sentences grammatical: *do* and *will* simply cannot co-occur.

(46) (a) I will not know it.   *I do will not know it.
      (b) What will he eat?   *What does will he eat?
      (c) Read the book he will.   *Read the book he does will

The contrast between the present/past and future tenses gives evidence for positing (at least) two constraints governing tense realization: $V+T_P$ and $V+T_F$. $V+T_F$ is vacuously satisfied in all the cases presented so far. Because these constraints can be ranked separately, a language may choose free realization for neither tense, one tense or both.

The violation tables given above are valid for the future tense versions of the candidate sets *mutatis mutandis*. Replacing P in (12) with F yields (47).

(47) FT-Neg winner

Input: {V Subj F Neg}	$V+T_F$	OBHD	FULLINT	*LINA'	*LINF	UNIQUE
a. VR [$_{TP}$ Subj V-F Neg [$_{VP}$ <V> ...]]	L				W	W
b. DS [$_{TP}$ Subj do-F Neg [$_{VP}$ V ...]]	L		W			
c. W FT [$_{TP}$ Subj F Neg [$_{VP}$ V ...]]						

The rankings in (48) select the FT optimum from the future tense Negation c-set.

(48) FULLINT >> $V+T_F$ *LINF or UNIQUE >> $V+T_F$

The comparative tableaux for the WhQ c-set and the VP displacement c-sets can be similarly modified to yield the analysis for the future. The FT-WhQ winner (identical to (20) in all but the tense) is in (49). It establishes the rankings in (50), which are those in (21) with F replacing P. This optimum corresponds to the grammatical question in (46).

(49) FT-WhQ winner

Input: {V Subj F Wh}	$V+T_F$	OBHD	FULLINT	*LINA'	*LINF	UNIQUE
a. VR [$_{CP}$ Wh V-F [$_{TP}$ Subj <V-F> [$_{VP}$ <V> ...]]]	L			W	W	W
b. DS [$_{CP}$ Wh do-F [$_{TP}$ Subj <do-F> VP]]	L		W			
c. W FT [$_{CP}$ Wh F [$_{TP}$ Subj <F> VP]]						
d. ØC [$_{CP}$ Wh __ [$_{TP}$ Subj V-F [$_{VP}$ <V> ...]]]	L	W			W	

(50) FT-WhQ   FULLINT >> $V+T_F$
                OBHD or *LINF >> $V+T_F$
                *LINA' or *LINF or UNIQUE >> $V+T_F$

Apart from tense-related changes, the FT AdjVP winner is identical to (35) and the rankings are identical to those in (36). The winning candidate corresponds to the grammatical VP displacement in (46).

(51) FT-AdjVP winner

Input: {V int Subj T}	$V+T_F$	ObHd	FullInt	*LinA′	*LinF	Unique	Ccom
a. VR: V in T [$_{TP}$VP[$_{TP}$Subj V-F <[$_{VP}$<V>int]>]]	L				W	W	W
b. DS: do in T [$_{TP}$VP [$_{TP}$Subj do-F <VP>]]	L		W				
c. **FT: T in T** **[$_{TP}$VP [$_{TP}$Subj F <VP>]]**							

(52)   Ccom or *LinF or Unique or Ccom $>>$ $V+T_F$
     FullInt $>>$ $V+T_F$

What remains to be shown is that the ranking of $V+T_F$ is consistent with the ranking of $V+T_P$ for English. What total rankings of the constraints choose DS in the past (and present) c-sets but realize *will* as a free morpheme in the future? The answer is: any ranking in which all constraints in stratum A in (53) dominate all those in B, which in turn dominate all those in C.

(53)   Stratum A: *LinA′, **$V+T_P$**, Ccom, ObHd, *LinF, VPAdj
     Stratum B: VPSpec, Unique, FullInt
     Stratum C: **$V+T_F$**

This information was arrived at by performing Recursive Constraint Demotion (Tesar and Smolensky 1998) using OTWorkplace (Prince and Tesar 2012) over all six candidate sets (the three considered earlier plus their future counterparts) and including two additional candidates in the WhQ c-set, as described below. The result can be found in Grimshaw (2011).

The idea that a free tense morpheme might result from violation of a constraint requiring bound realization is due to Elías-Ulloa (p.c.). See Declerck *et al.* (2006) for a similar hypothesis from a different perspective. Such a hypothesis is of course only possible in a theory in which constraints are violable, hence 'isolated' grammatical material is not widely analysed in this way.[17]

In sum English shows non-uniform distribution in *do*-support, like German and Monnese. This is the result of a decision made by constraint ranking, not due to a lexical stipulation. The choice of a free morpheme for the future tense is governed by the entire grammar: the ranking of the critical constraints on tense must be consistent with the grammar as a whole.

6.   The typology

The typology for uniform tense systems, generated by a constraint set containing a single constraint V+T (or equivalently by every ranking in which $V+T_P$ and $V+T_F$ are not separated), is given in (54). The core structural properties of this typology are preserved in the larger one in which $V+T_P$ and $V+T_F$ are separable.

The candidates are those from the three c-sets analysed above. Two additional WhQ candidates are included, one with *do*-support in T and an empty C, and one with a free tense in T and an empty C. (These are included in (37), which is the violation table for VPs displaced to specifier position.) There are thus three candidates for negation, six for *wh*-questions, and nine for VP displacement, combining those with adjoined and specifier VPs. The violation table constructed from merging all the violation tables in this chapter and adding the two extra candidates just mentioned can be found in Grimshaw (2011).[18]

Since the system under investigation posits nine constraints, there are 9! (362,880) possible rankings. There are 162 logically possible combinations of candidates (3 × 6 × 9), taking one from each of the three c-sets. The factorial typology is calculated using OTWorkplace (Prince and Tesar 2012). It contains 28 distinct languages, that is, combinations of optima. The rankings for each language are reported in Grimshaw (2011). To make the patterns as easily visible as possible, I have labelled the optima as VR, DS or FT and used these labels in the table. The candidates are directly represented in the factorial typology in Grimshaw (2011). 'A-VP' and 'S-VP' abbreviate 'Adjunct-VP' and 'Specifier-VP' respectively.

(54)   The Factorial Typology

Lge	Negation	*Wh* Question	VP	Displacement
1	VR	VR to C	A-VP	VR
2	VR	VR to C	A-VP	*DS*
3	VR	VR to C	A-VP	FT
4	VR	VR to C	S-VP	VR to C
5	VR	VR to C	S-VP	*DS* in C
6	VR	VR to C	S-VP	FT in C
7	VR	VR to T	A-VP	VR
8	VR	VR to T	A-VP	*DS*
9	VR	VR to T	A-VP	FT
10	VR	VR to T	S-VP	VR to T
11	VR	VR to T	S-VP	*DS* in C
12	VR	VR to T	S-VP	*DS* in T
13	VR	VR to T	S-VP	FT in C
14	VR	VR to T	S-VP	FT in T
15	VR	*DS* in C	A-VP	VR
16	VR	*DS* in C	A-VP	*DS*
17	VR	*DS* in C	S-VP	*DS* in C
18	VR	FT in C	A-VP	VR
19	VR	FT in C	A-VP	FT

Lge	Negation	*Wh* Question	VP	Displacement
20	**VR**	FT in C	**S-VP**	FT in C
21	*DS*	*DS* in C	**A-VP**	*DS*
22	*DS*	*DS* in C	**S-VP**	*DS* in C
23	*DS*	*DS* in T	**A-VP**	*DS*
24	*DS*	*DS* in T	**S-VP**	*DS* in T
25	FT	FT in C	**A-VP**	FT
26	FT	FT in C	**S-VP**	FT in C
27	FT	FT in T	**A-VP**	FT
28	FT	FT in T	**S-VP**	FT in T

Twelve of the languages are uniform with respect to structure. Four have VR everywhere: (1, 4, 7, 10). Four have DS everywhere (21–24). Four have FT everywhere (25–28). Each structure is used by several languages. The languages vary in where V, *do* and T occur, as well as in whether displaced VPs are specifiers or adjuncts. Twelve of the languages have DS somewhere, and 12 have FT somewhere. English is #21: DS with negation, DS in C in the WhQ winner and an adjoined VP with DS in T in the VP displacement competition. Twenty languages have VR somewhere. All of these have it in the Negation c-set, as discussed below. There doesn't seem to be any way in which the notion of a last resort sheds light on the patterns.

Sixteen of the languages are non-uniform, like German and Monnese, following from the fact that compatible rankings can yield non-uniform results. The rankings which choose VR with negation are compatible with rankings which choose DS in the WhQ c-set, hence Monnese is generated, as language 15, 16 or 17.[19] The same logic holds for German, which is language #5. The rankings established for German for VP-preposing, negation and interrogatives are all compatible with each other, and any total ranking compatible with the domination relationships in Figure 11.1 will choose the correct optima for German.

In contrast, neither Anti-Monnese nor Anti-German is among the languages listed in (54). Anti-Monnese would have a VR winner in the WhQ c-set and a DS winner

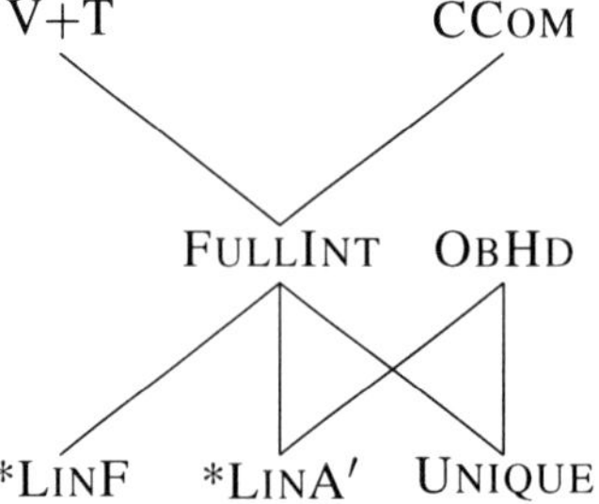

Figure 11.1

in the Negation c-set. Anti-German would have DS with negation and in the WhQ c-set and VR with VP displacement. In (54) all languages with DS winners in the Negation c-set have DS in all c-sets.[20]

Why is this so? The answer is that in order to have a DS winner in the Negation c-set, the language must have a ranking in which V+T and either *LinF or Unique dominate FullInt. Such a ranking can never choose VR to C in the WhQ c-set, because this choice requires that FullInt dominate *LinF, *LinA' and Unique, as (18) showed. Moreover, a language in which DS is optimal with negation cannot choose VR in the VP displacement c-set. The only language with a VP displaced as a specifier and VR into C is #4, which has a ranking in which FullInt dominates *LinF *LinA', Ccom and Unique. (These calculations are in Grimshaw (2011).)

The prediction is not that any language which has DS optima with negation must have DS in *wh*-questions. Korean, for example, has DS with negation (see Section 1) but not in questions, because it doesn't have the relevant *kind* of question, that is its other rankings are not the same as those for the languages looked at here. The prediction is that any language where the same constraints make the decisions as in the cases studied here must make the same choices. Bader and Schmid (2006) make this point in response to a carelessly worded claim made in Grimshaw (1997), to the effect that no language with the rankings of German could have DS optima. A more accurate wording would say that no language with the critical rankings of German could have DS optima in the Negation or WhQ c-sets, because the choice between DS and some alternative is not made by the lexicon (i.e. arbitrarily) but by the grammar of the language.

There are several general points to be made about the typology. Most obviously, the number of languages generated is not 9!. The number of possible combinations of optima is not 162. The reason is that the typology is highly structured. There are many entailments between optima in one candidate set and optima in others (see Anttila and Andrus 2006; Prince 2006).

(55) Typological patterns
- No language uses all three structures
- Languages (21–28), which choose DS or FT optima in the Negation c-set, preserve the choice in the other two c-sets.
- Given that there are only three alternative structures, it follows from this that any language with VR in the WhQ c-set must have VR in the Negation c-set, and any language with VR in the VP displacement c-set must have VR in the Negation c-set.
- It also follows that all non-uniform languages have VR in the Negation c-set. Only VR in the Negation c-set is compatible with more than one choice in the WhQ and VP displacement c-sets.

In the larger typology generated by splitting the V+T constraint into two, there are six c-sets. Negation past/present, Negation future, WhQ past/present, WhQ future, VP Displacement past/present and VP Displacement future. There are thus twice as many candidates as in the compressed typology, that is $3+3+6+6+9+9$. There are therefore 26,244 logically possible combinations of optima. Since there are 11 constraints the number of rankings is almost 40 million. The system generates 162 languages. The typology is presented in Grimshaw (2011).

All structural properties listed in (55) are preserved in the expanded typology, relative to the tense. Forty-eight languages use all three structures in optima, but in every case this is due to tense split. That is, none of them uses one optimum in the Negation c-sets, a different one in the WhQ c-sets and yet another in the VP displacement c-sets, for a fixed choice of tense. The second point is preserved also, relative to tense. Thus a language which chooses a DS or FT optimum in the Negation c-set for a particular tense must choose the same in the other c-sets for the same tense.

The third point also holds, relative to tense. For example, if a language has VR in the WhQ c-set with the past tense, it must also have VR in the Negation c-set for the past tense. Finally, we continue to observe the general distribution in which VR is most frequent in the Negation c-sets (it occurs in 118 of the languages in both of the Negation c-sets) and compatible with all three choices in the others.

These patterns bear in an interesting way on the question of whether DS, or any of the alternative strategies, can be identified as being highly marked or a 'last resort'. It is clear that what might seem like a particularly marked grammatical device in one c-set may seem much less so in another. For example, VR with negation is highly unmarked in the sense that it is optimal in 20 languages in the 28 system typology. However, it is optimal in the WhQ c-set in only 14 languages and in the VP displacement c-set in only 6. So if the number of languages which use a particular device is a measure of its last resort status, there doesn't seem to be a clear answer to the question of whether a particular strategy is a last resort or not.

Let us consider why DS and FT are so much more prominent in the WhQ and VP displacement c-sets than in the Negation c-set. DS is found in 4 languages in the Negation c-set, in 7 in the WhQ c-set and in 11 in the VP displacement c-set. FT shows exactly the same numbers. The explanation is as follows. Each of FT and DS violates exactly one constraint within this system, namely V+T or FULLINT. These constraints are relevant in all three c-sets. Two additional constraints are relevant for the WhQ c-set, namely OBHD and *LINA'. While OBHD is insensitive to the difference between a head occupied by a V, a T or a *do*, *LINA' is not. It prefers T or *do* over V in the C position. Hence its ranking can force the choice of T or *do* in those candidates in which C is filled. Finally, for the VP displacement c-set, CCOM is relevant because it is violated in some candidates. Again it prefers T or *do* over V since VR leads to CCOM violations. Thus as we move from left to right through the candidate sets in (54) we find that VR is increasingly disfavoured and hence the two alternatives, FT and DS, are increasingly favoured. (Only two languages (#4 and #10) allow VR with a VP in specifier position, and they have VR optima in all c-sets.) What emerges is that the languages which have VR optima for the VP displacement c-set are a proper subset of those which have VR optima for the WhQ c-set, which in turn are a proper subset of those that have VR for the Negation c-set.

Does the notion of last resort play any role in our understanding of the system? We can identify a structure that, as the optimum for a given c-set, is compatible with fewer optima in other c-sets. To put it another way, it is the optimum for a smaller set of combinations of optima, that is languages. For example DS and FT in the Negation c-set are compatible with fewer optima for the WhQ c-set and the VP displacement c-set than VR. We could agree to call DS or FT a last resort for the Negation c-set. However, nothing is gained by doing so. The work is being done by the theory of constraint interaction and comparison among members of the candidate sets, and the label 'last resort' adds nothing.

Acknowledgements

This chapter is a major extension and development of Grimshaw (2006b). Veneeta Dayal and José (Beto) Elías-Ulloa provided me with key examples, and much help in understanding how they work. Sabine Mohr, and Susanne Lohrmann explained *do*-support in Swabian to me along with Britta Sauereisen, who kindly translated many examples in addition. Brian Smith and Alan Prince helped with OTWorkplace calculations, and Fabian Heck constructed paradigms in German. Sara O'Neill's expertise turned a manuscript into a paper. Many others, including audiences at UMass Amherst, the University of Stuttgart, RuLing II, RORG and St@r, raised questions which sharpened the argument and analysis presented in the paper. Many helpful people discussed *do*-support or the analysis with me: Birgit Alber, Artemis Alexiadou, Daniel Altshuler, Will Bennett, James Bruno, José Camacho, Nick Danis, Christa Gordon, Bart Hollebrandse, Patrick Houghton, Paula Houghton, Carlo Linares, Sara O'Neill, Alan Prince, Ljiljana Progovac, Tanja Schmid and Brute Tesar. Special thanks to Alan Prince and Vieri Samek-Lodovici, whose input and insights had a major impact on this research. Finally, thanks are due to Hans Broekhuis and Ralf Vogel for detailed comments on an earlier version of the paper and for making things happen.

Notes

1. It is impossible to cite all works which rely on or address the notion of a last resort, which has been prominent since Chomsky (1957). Here are a few which represent or review a variety of different applications: Chomsky (1991), Corver (1997), Rizzi (1997), Bosković and Takahashi (1998), Harley and Noyer (1998), Collins (2001), Benincá and Poletto (2004), Schmid (2005) and several papers in Bosković and Lasnik eds (2006).
2. Interesting analyses of *do*-support which do not make any appeal to it being a last resort are given by Embick and Noyer (2001: 584-591), Schütze (2004) and Haddican (2007).
3. See Grimshaw (2011) for the analysis of some of the harmonically bounded candidates of relevance here.
4. Since many analyses stemming from Larson (1988), posit movement of a lexical V to a head position below T, I assume that *LinF is not violated by such movements, because the target positions are too low. It is likely that such movement violates other constraints, so this point needs further technical development.
5. The candidate sets for positive declaratives with no VP displacement are not analysed here, although they are a crucial part of the overall analysis. See Grimshaw (1997), Ackema (2001) and Vikner (2001) for OT analyses of how V and T combine.
6. I do not address the analysis of negative imperatives, which have *do*, and subjunctives, which do not. See Haiman (2010) on the nature of *do* in negative imperatives.
7. Another possible resolution repeats the V. See Landau (2006), Cheng (2007), Martins (2007), Aboh (2009) and Trinh (2009) for recent discussion of doubling.
8. The judgements in (5) and (15) are controversial, with some speakers of German and Dutch accepting both DS and non-DS with negation, and even in positive declarative clauses. See Ackema (2001), Vikner (2001), Erb (2001) and also Schütze (2004) on English *do* and Soh (2007) on Chinese *shi*. Bader and Schmid (2006) analyse the choice between the two as a case of optionality attributable to tied constraints. I will proceed in accordance with the judgements given in (5) and (15), noting

that there seems to be a significant difference between speaker reaction to DS in the case of VP Displacement (Section 4) and to DS elsewhere, motivating an analysis which distinguishes the cases. Other research such as Erb (2001) raises the possibility that the discourse status of a clause determines the presence of *do*. Moreover, once we recognize speakers' control of multiple grammars, as discussed recently in Anttila (2007), different accounts of apparent optionality become available. Grimshaw (in prep.) presents an analysis of *that* omission in English complement sentences in which it results from two register-connected grammars, one with and one without *that* in complement clauses. Omission is not optional in either grammar. An analysis along these lines may prove to be correct for the German/ Dutch case as well.

9. This holds regardless of whether there is a trace in all head positions between the VP and the CP, since the V is in C, which is both a functional head and an A′ position.

10. Candidates with an empty C are optimal for subordinate clauses in both English (Grimshaw 1997, 2006c) and Monnese (Benincà and Poletto 2004). In main clauses they do not win, so I have not analysed them here. Optima with empty C positions motivate (under certain assumptions) the constraint Unique, which prefers candidates with empty C positions to those in which the C position is filled by movement. Without Unique, candidates like d in (17), with VR, FT or DS in the T position, are harmonically bounded by those with VR, FT and DS in the C position, which do not violate ObHd. Grimshaw (2011) includes WhQ candidates with empty C as well as some with multiple auxiliaries. Since the WhQ c-set there is larger than the one presented here, it establishes some rankings above and beyond what can be determined from (18), (20) and (22).

11. Benincà and Poletto (2004) show that *do*-support is slightly broader than in English: the verbs *fa* 'do' and *nda* 'go' optionally occur with *do*-support (p. 73) whether they are used as auxiliaries or as main verbs with thematic complements. Benincà and Poletto (81–84) analyse these verbs as 'semi-auxiliaries'.

12. See Grimshaw (1997) for an analysis of Negative Preposing and inversion.

13. An alternative way to address the difference between VP-preposing and *wh*-movement would posit a specifier position in both cases but treat the heads differently. For example, the head of the projection containing the *wh* phrase would be governed by an ObHd constraint or associated with a strong feature, while that for VP displacement would not. In a theory which disallows adjunction some solution along these lines must be posited.

14. As for *wh*-movement above, I will consider only candidates in which the VP is displaced. None of the constraints discussed here is sensitive to whether the displaced VP is on the left or the right, so I will only show leftward displacement in tables and tableaux. Other constraints, in particular the alignment constraints discussed in Grimshaw (2001, 2002), govern the order of heads and phrases.

15. Haddican (2007) proposes a rather different account for Basque, in which focalized VPs must be headed by a nominalizing affix. In such cases the verb *egin* 'do' appears in *v* and raises through the higher inflectional heads to Asp^0. Haddican argues that *egin* does not occur freely because in all other circumstances the noun feature on the infinitive goes unvalued. As he points out, this is not a last resort analysis.

16. It is of course a significant over-simplification to treat *will* as just a future tense. The ideal analysis covers all cases of *will* and potentially extends to other modals.

17. Note that languages in which Infl heads take complements other than VPs (such as Chamorro as analysed in Chung (1990)) necessarily violate V+T whenever the complement is not a VP.

18. While candidates with remnant movement of the VP are in the Negation and WhQ c-sets I do not consider them here.

19. The typology predicts that Monnese could have either DS or VR with VP displacement if it has the structures at all. Benincà and Poletto mention that it lacks VP ellipsis after auxiliaries, so it may also lack VP displacement.

20. Provided that movement through T is a prerequisite for movement to C, the Benincà and Poletto analysis might not generate Anti-Monnese. (I am not sure about Anti-German.) Under this assumption, a language which does not allow V to raise to T could not allow it to raise to C. Benincà and Poletto do not discuss this question, but the theory of features which regulate movement might restrict the options in this way. Anti-Monnese and Anti-German are clearly generable under the construction based approach of Culicover (2008), in which 'every construction in which there is *do*-support must

explicitly mention Vaux. This includes not only SAI and negation, but ellipsis and related constructions, and VP-topicalization.'

References

Aboh, E. (2009) Delete: a phase-level property. *Theoretical Linguistics* 35 (2–3): 229–37.

Ackema, P. (2001) On the relation between V-to-I and the structure of the inflectional paradigm. *The Linguistic Review* 18 (3): 233–63.

Anttila, A. (2007) Variation and optionality. In P. de Lacy (ed.) *The Cambridge Handbook of Phonology*, 519–36. Cambridge: Cambridge University Press.

Anttila, A. and Andrus, C. (2006) T-orders. ROA-873, Rutgers Optimality Archive. Retrieved on 26 May 2012 from http://roa.rutgers.edu/

Bader, M. and Schmid, T. (2006) An OT-analysis of *do*-support in Modern German. ROA-837, Rutgers Optimality Archive. Retrieved on 26 May 2012 from http://roa.rutgers.edu/

Benincà, P. and Poletto, C. (2004) A case of *do*-support in Romance. *Natural Language and Linguistic Theory* 22 (1): 51–94.

Bhatt, R. and Dayal, V. (2007) Rightward scrambling as rightward remnant movement. *Linguistic Inquiry* 38 (2): 287–301.

Bobaljik, J. D. (1995) *Morphosyntax: The Syntax of Verbal Inflection*. Doctoral dissertation. Cambridge, MA: MIT Working Papers in Linguistics.

Bosković, Z. and Lasnik, H. (eds) (2006) *Minimalist Syntax: The Essential Readings*. Oxford: Wiley-Blackwell.

Bosković, Z. and Takahashi, D. (1998) Scrambling and last resort. *Linguistic Inquiry* 29 (3): 347–66.

Brasoveanu, A. and Prince, A. (2011) Ranking and necessity: the Fusional Reduction Algorithm, *Natural Language and Linguistic Theory* 29: 3–70.

Cheng, L. L.-S. (2007) Verb copying in Mandarin Chinese. In N. Corver and J. Nunes (eds) *The Copy Theory of Movement*, 151–74. Amsterdam/Philadelphia, PA: John Benjamins.

Chomsky, N. (1957) *Syntactic Structures*. Berlin: Mouton.

Chomsky, N. (1991) Some notes on economy of derivation and representation. In R. Freidin (ed.) *Principles and Parameters in Comparative Grammar*, 417–54. Cambridge, MA: MIT Press.

Chung, S. (1990) VPs and verb movement in Chamorro. *Natural Language and Linguistic Theory* 8 (4): 559–619.

Collins, C. (2001) Economy conditions in syntax. In M. Baltin and C. Collins (eds) *The Handbook of Contemporary Syntactic Theory*, 45–61. Oxford: Blackwell.

Corver, N. (1997) *Much*-support as a last resort. *Linguistic Inquiry* 28 (1): 119–64.

Culicover, P. W. (2008) The rise and fall of constructions and the history of English *do*-support. *Journal of Germanic Linguistics* 20 (1): 1–52.

Declerck, R, Reed, S. and Cappellen, B. (2006) *The Grammar of the English Verb Phrase Volume 1: The Grammar of the English Tense System*. Berlin: Mouton de Gruyter.

Dowty, D. (1979) *Word Meaning and Montague Grammar*. Dordrecht, Boston: D. Reidel.

Elías-Ulloa, J. A. (2001) Subject doubling in Capanahua. Ms., Rutgers University.

Embick, D. and Noyer, R. (2001). Movement operations after syntax. *Linguistic Inquiry* 32: 555–95.

Erb, M. C. (2001) *Finite Auxiliaries in German*. Doctoral dissertation. Katholieke Universiteit Brabant.

Grimshaw, J. (1997) Projection heads and optimality. *Linguistic Inquiry* 28 (3): 373–422.

Grimshaw, J. (2001) Economy of structure in OT. ROA-434, Rutgers Optimality Archive. Retrieved on 15 April 2011 from http://roa.rutgers.edu/

Grimshaw, J. (2002) Economy of structure in OT. *Papers in Optimality Theory* II 81–120. University of Massachusetts Occasional Papers 26.

Grimshaw, J. (2006a) Chains as unfaithful optima. In E. Bakovic, J. Ito and J. J. McCarthy (eds) *Wondering at the Natural Fecundity of Things: Essays in Honor of Alan Prince*, 97–109. Retrieved 26 May 2012 from http://escholarship.org/uc/lrc_prince. Also available as ROA 844.4, Rutgers Optimality Archive. Retrieved on 26 May 2012 from http://roa.rutgers.edu/

Grimshaw, J. (2006b) Last resorts and grammaticality. In H. Broekhuis and R. Vogel (eds) *Optimality Theory and Minimalism: A Possible Convergence?* Linguistics in Potsdam 25, 33–41. Retrieved on 26 May 2012 from http://opus.kobv.de/ubp/volltexte/2007/1190/ Also available as ROA-893, Rutgers Optimality Archive. Retrieved on 26 May 2012 from http://roa.rutgers.edu/

Grimshaw, J. (2006c) Location specific constraints in matrix and subordinate clauses. ROA-857 Rutgers Optimality Archive. Retrieved on 26 May 2012 from http://roa.rutgers.edu/

Grimshaw, J. (2008) Syntactic constraints. In Piet van Sterkenburg (ed.) *Unity and Diversity of Languages,* 43–57. Amsterdam/Philadelphia, PA: John Benjamins.

Grimshaw, J. (2011) Supplementary Material for 'Last Resorts: A Typology of do-support'. ROA-1127, Rutgers Optimality Archive. Retrieved on 26 May 2012 from http://roa.rutgers.edu/

Grimshaw, J. (in prep.) *Subordination: Complements and Complementizers.*

Grimshaw, J. and Mester, A. (1988) Light verbs and theta-marking. *Linguistic Inquiry* 19 (3): 205–32.

Haddican, B. (2007) On *egin: do*-support and VP focus in Central and Western Basque. *Natural Language and Linguistic Theory* 25 (4): 735–64.

Hagstrom, P. (1996) *Do*-support in Korean: Evidence for an interpretive morphology. In H.-D. Ahn, M.-Y. Kang, Y.-S. Kim and S. Lee (eds) *Morphosyntax in Generative Grammar: Proceedings of the 1996 Seoul International Conference on Generative Grammar,* 169–80. Seoul: Hankuk.

Haiman, J. (2010) The creation of new words. *Linguistics* 48 (3): 547–72.

Halle, M. and Marantz, A. (1993) Distributed morphology and the pieces of inflection. In K. Hale and S. J. Keyser (eds) *The View From Building 20,* 111–16. Cambridge, MA: MIT Press.

Harley, H. and Noyer, R. (1998) Mixed nominalizations, short verb movement and object shift in English. In P. N. Tamanji and K. Kusumoto (eds) *Proceedings of NELS 28,* 143–57. Amhurst, MA: University of Massachusetts.

Hinterhölzl, R. (2006) *Scrambling, Remnant Movement and Restructuring in West Germanic.* Oxford: Oxford University Press.

Hollebrandse, B. and Roeper, T. (1996) The concept of *do*-insertion and the theory of INFL in acquisition. In C. Koster and F. Wijnen (eds) *Proceedings of the Groningen Assembly on Language Acquisition,* 261–70. Groningen: Center for Language and Cognition.

Kandybowicz, J. (2010) Phono-syntactic alignment: A case study from Twi *do*-insertion. Ms. University of Texas at Arlington.

Kiss, K. (2010) An adjunction analysis of quantifiers and adverbials in the Hungarian sentence. *Lingua* 120 (3): 506–26.

Kuroda, S-Y. (1965) *Generative Grammatical Studies in the Japanese Language.* Doctoral dissertation, MIT.

Landau, I. (2006) Chain resolution in Hebrew V(P)-fronting. *Syntax* 9 (1): 32–66.

Larson, R. (1988) On the double object construction. *Linguistic Inquiry* 19 (3): 335–91.

Lasnik, H., Uriagareka, J. and Boeckx, C. (2005) *A Course in Minimalist Syntax.* Oxford: Blackwell.

Legendre, G. (2001) Masked second-position effects and the linearization of functional features. In G. Legendre, J. Grimshaw and V. Vikner (eds) *Optimality-Theoretic Syntax,* 241–77. Cambridge, MA: MIT Press.

Martins, A. M. (2007) Double realization of verbal copies in European Portuguese emphatic affirmation. In N. Corver and J. Nunes (eds) *The Copy Theory of Movement,* 77–118. Amsterdam/Philadelphia, PA: John Benjamins.

McCarthy, J. and Prince, A. (1997/1999) Faithfulness and identity in prosodic morphology. In R. Kager, H. van der Hulst and W. Zonneveld (eds) *The Morphology-Prosody Interface,* 218–309. Cambridge: Cambridge University Press.

Meinunger, A. (2001) Restrictions on verb raising. *Linguistic Inquiry* 32 (4): 732–40.

Miller, P. H. (1997) Auxiliary verbs in old and middle French: A diachronic study of substitute *faire* and a comparison with the modern English auxiliaries. In A. van Kemenade and N. Vincent (eds) *Parameters of Morphosyntactic Change,* 119–33. Cambridge: Cambridge University Press.

Miyagawa, S. (2001) The EPP, scrambling, and wh-in-situ. In M. Kenstowicz (ed.) *Ken Hale: A Life in Language,* 293–338. Cambridge, MA: MIT Press.

Müller, G. (1998) *Incomplete Category Fronting: A Derivational Approach to Remnant Movement in German.* Dordrecht/Boston, MA: Kluwer Academic Publishers.

Müller, S. (2002) Multiple frontings in German. In G. Jäger, P. Monachesi, G. Penn and S. Wintner (eds) *Proceedings of Formal Grammar 2002*, 113–24. Trento.

Newton, G. (2009) Accounting for *do*-support post-syntactically: Evidence from Old Irish. *University of Pennsylvania Working Papers in Linguistics* 15: Iss.1, Article19. Retrieved on 15 April 2011 from http://repository.upenn.edu/pwpl/vol15/iss1/19/

Pesetsky, D. and Torrego, E. (2001) T-to-C movement: Causes and consequences. In M. Kenstowicz (ed.) *Ken Hale: A Life in Language*, 355–426. Cambridge, MA: MIT Press.

Pesetsky, D. and Torrego, E. (2007) The syntax of valuation and the interpretability of features. In S. Karimi, V. Samiian and W. Wilkins (eds) *Phrasal and Clausal Architecture: Syntactic Derivation and Interpretation*, 262–94. Amsterdam: Benjamins.

Pollock, J.-Y. (1989) Verb movement, universal grammar and the structure of IP. *Linguistic Inquiry* 20 (3): 365–424.

Prince, A. (1997) Stringency and anti-Paninian hierarchies. Handout from LSA Institute. Retrieved on 26 May 2012 from http://ruccs.rutgers.edu/~prince

Prince, A. (2002a) Entailed ranking arguments. ROA-500. Retrieved on 26 May 2012 from http://ruccs.rutgers.edu/~prince

Prince, A. (2002b) Arguing optimality. In A. Coetzee, A. Carpenter and P. de Lacy (eds) *Papers in Optimality Theory II*, 269–304. GLSA, UMass. Amherst. ROA-562, Rutgers Optimality Archive. Retrieved on 26 May 2012 from http://roa.rutgers.edu/

Prince, A. (2006) Implication & impossibility in grammatical systems: What it is & how to find it. ROA-880, Rutgers Optimality Archive. Retrieved on 26 May 2012 from http://roa.rutgers.edu/

Prince, A. and Smolensky, P. (2004) *Optimality Theory: Constraint Interaction in Generative Grammar*. Malden, MA: Blackwell.

Prince, A. and Tesar, B. (2012) OTWorkplace. Retrieved on 26 May 2012 from http://ruccs.rutgers.edu/~prince/

Rizzi, L. (1997) The fine structure of the left periphery. In L. Haegeman (ed.) *Elements of Grammar*, 281–337. Dordrecht: Kluwer Academic Publishers.

Saito, M and Hoshi, H. (2000) The Japanese light verb construction and the Minimalist Program. In R. Martin, D. Michaels and J. Uriagereka (eds) *Step by Step: Essays on Minimalist Syntax in Honor of Howard Lasnik*, 261–95. Cambridge, MA: MIT Press.

Samek-Lodovici, V. (this volume, ch. 9) Optimality Theory and the Minimalist Program. Also in H. Broekhuis and R. Vogel (eds) *Optimality Theory and Minimalism: A Possible Convergence?* Linguistics in Potsdam 25, 77–97. Retrieved on 26 May 2012 from http://opus.kobv.de/ubp/volltexte/2007/1190/

Samek-Lodovici, V. and Prince, A. (2005) Fundamental properties of harmonic bounding. ROA-785, Rutgers Optimality Archive. Retrieved on 26 May 2012 from http://roa.rutgers.edu/

Schmid, T. (2005) *Infinitival Syntax: Infinitivus Pro Participio as a Repair Strategy*. Amsterdam/Philadelphia, PA: John Benjamins.

Schütze, C. (2001) Semantically empty lexical heads as last resorts. In N. Corver and H. van Riemsdijk (eds) *Semi-Lexical Categories*, 127–87. Berlin/New York: Mouton de Gruyter.

Schütze, C. (2004) Synchronic and diachronic microvariation in English *do*. *Lingua* 114 (4): 495–516.

Soh, H. L. (2007) Ellipsis, last resort, and the dummy auxiliary shi 'be' in Mandarin Chinese. *Linguistic Inquiry*, 38 (1): 178–88.

Tesar, B. and Smolensky, P. (1998) Learnability in Optimality Theory. *Linguistic Inquiry* 29 (2): 229–68.

Thrainsson, H. (2010) Predictable and unpredictable sources of variable verb and adverb placement in Scandinavian. *Lingua* 120 (5): 1062–88.

Trinh, T. (2009) A constraint on copy deletion. *Theoretical Linguistics* 35 (2–3): 183–227.

Vikner, S. (2001) V⁰-to-I⁰ and *do*-insertion in Optimality Theory. In G. Legendre, J. Grimshaw and V. Vikner (eds) *Optimality-Theoretic Syntax*, 427–64. Cambridge, MA: MIT Press.

Zepter, A. (2000) Specifiers and adjuncts. Ms. Rutgers University. ROA-413, Rutgers Optimality Archive. Retrieved on 26 May 2012 from http://roa.rutgers.edu/

IV THE ROLE OF THE INTERPRETATIVE COMPONENTS

12 Hard and soft conditions on the Faculty of Language: constituting parametric variation

Hedde Zeijlstra[*]

ABSTRACT In this chapter, I argue that both parametric variation and the alleged differences between languages in terms of their internal complexity straightforwardly follow from the Strongest Minimalist Thesis that takes the Faculty of Language to be an optimal solution to conditions that neighboring mental modules impose on it. Hard conditions like legibility at the linguistic interfaces invoke simplicity metrics that, given that they stem from different mental modules, are not harmonious. Widely attested expression strategies, such as agreement or movement, are a direct result of conflicting simplicity metrics, so that UG, perceived as a toolbox that shapes natural language, can be taken to consist of a limited number of marking strategies, all resulting from conflicting simplicity metrics. As such, the contents of UG follow from simplicity requirements, and therefore no longer necessitate linguistic principles, valued or unvalued, to be innately present. Finally, I show that the Strongest Minimalist Thesis does not require that languages themselves have to be optimal in connecting sound to meaning.

KEYWORDS parameters; Full Interpretation; hard/soft conditions; simplicity; complexity; uninterpretability; agreement; movement

1. Introduction

Following current minimalist reasoning, language is thought to be a perfect system connecting sound and meaning (cf. Chomsky 2000, 2001, 2004, 2005; Lasnik 2003). The strongest formulation of this idea is the Strong Minimalist Thesis (SMT): Language is an optimal solution to interface conditions that the Faculty of Language (FL) must satisfy (Chomsky 2005).

However, the idea that language is some kind of a perfect solution seems to be at odds with the huge amount of cross-linguistic variation that can be attested. If

---

*   Hedde Zeijlstra, University of Amsterdam, Nederlandse Taalkunde, Amsterdam, The Netherlands. E.mail: H.H.Zeijlstra@uva.nl

language is an optimal solution to interface conditions that the Faculty of Language (FL) must satisfy, why would not all languages be morpho-syntactically uniform?

Implementing this question within the Principles-and-Parameters model, initiated by Chomsky (1981), that takes cross-linguistic variation to be the result of a relatively small amount of parameters to be set during the process of language acquisition, the question arises as to why parameters should exist in the first place.

In this chapter, I argue that parametric variation is not incompatible with the SMT. Instead, I suggest that the SMT, given that it takes language to be an optimal solution to conditions that are imposed on FL by *different* mental modules, allows for multiple solutions as long as these are all optimal. If the SMT allows for multiple solutions, it would even require additional explanation why natural language would not exhibit cross-linguistic variation.

However, a question that then immediately arises is whether all languages are actually equally simple. If two languages both form an optimal solution in the task of relating sound to meaning, one language is expected not to be more complex than the other, since otherwise the simplest solution would the only optimal one.

Although the idea that languages are equally complex has been proposed by a number of scholars (see for an overview and discussion DeGraff 2001), this view is far from being uncontroversial. In a number of recent proposals, it has been argued that languages actually differ with respect to their internal complexity (e.g. Gil 2001; Kusters 2003; Ramchand and Svenonius 2006).

In this chapter, I propose that that the interplay between principles governing FL and principles governing the process of language acquisition actually allows one language to be more complex than the other.

In a nutshell, I propose that UG should be regarded as a 'toolbox' (to use Jackendoff's (2002) metaphor) that contains different strategies for expressing semantic functions (those strategies are the tools, so to speak). The existence of these tools (why exactly these, and why not any more or any fewer) follows directly from the SMT. The process of language acquisition, then, is considered as a process where language learners detect on the basis of their language input which tool(s) are used to express each semantic function. If the target language happens to use multiple tools for the expression of a single semantic function, then the language acquirer is forced to adopt both expression strategies.

This chapter is set up as follows. In section 2, I discuss the implications of the SMT and propose that hard conditions applying to FL automatically invoke soft conditions that take the shape of simplicity metrics. In section 3, I zoom in on one particular hard condition that applies at both the interface between FL and the Sensory-Motor system (SM) and the interface between FL and the Conceptual-Intentional system (C-I), namely, the requirement that the derivational outputs of FL be legible for both SM and C-I (dating back to Chomsky's (1986) formulation of Full Interpretation). I argue that Chomsky's later version of Full Interpretation, which bans uninterpretable features at LF (cf. Chomsky 1995), actually follows from simplicity metrics that are invoked by this legibility condition. In section 4, I demonstrate that the simplicity metrics that are invoked by the hard condition that the derivational output must be legible both at the level of Logical Form (LF) and Phonological Form (PF) are in conflict, and I demonstrate that this conflict calls syntactic operations such as Move and Agree into being. A side effect of these assumptions is that the existence of uninterpretable features, albeit conceived slightly different from the original notion of uninterpretable features in Chomsky (1995), receives a principled explanation. In section 5, I come back to the alleged problem that different languages may exhibit different levels of complexity and I demonstrate that, contrary to what is generally assumed, combinatorial usage of different expressing strategies of semantic functions is not banned by the SMT, but actually follows from it, given that principles that shape UG also shape the language acquisition process. Section 6 finally concludes.

2.   Hard and soft conditions imposed on the Faculty of Language

Following Chomsky (1995) and subsequent work, I will adopt the model in (1) that takes FL to be an autonomous mental module that interacts with the Sensory-Motor System (SM) and the Conceptual-Intentional System(s) C-I as well as the lexicon (LEX), an instance of memory (though in this article I remain agnostic as to whether the lexicon is another neighboring module of FL or whether it is part of it.).

(1)

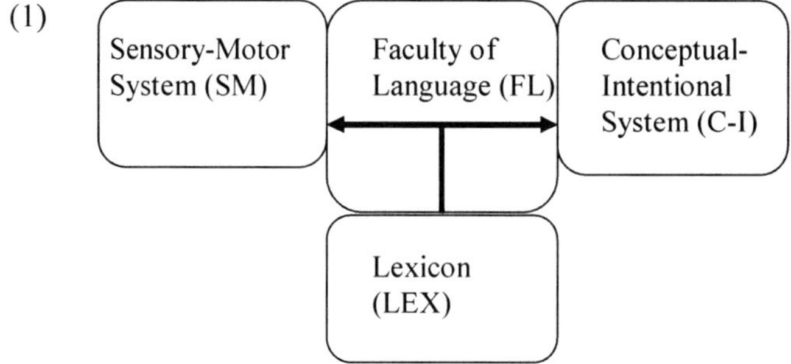

According to Chomsky – who claims that, if the SMT holds, UG would be restricted by properties imposed by interface conditions – FL must then be restricted by conditions that the SM system, the C-I system, and/or LEX induce.

Both at the level of LF (the interface between the C-I system and FL) and at the level of PF (the interface between the SM system and FL), hard conditions, such as legibility conditions, apply. Such conditions restrict the possible grammatical outcomes of the derivational process.

Although hard conditions applying to FL already severely restrict UG, the SMT not only requires that hard conditions be fulfilled, but also that they are fulfilled in an optimal way. This claim implies that different solutions to hard conditions are evaluated against simplicity metrics that evaluate possible solutions and rule out non-optimal solutions. Putting this formally:

(2) If some hard condition **C** comes along with a simplicity metric **S** and if solution S_1 to fulfill **C** is a simpler solution with respect to **S** than solution S_2, then the possible application of S_1 rules out S_2.

Hence the fact that **C** gives rise to **S** imposes another restriction on FL: $*S_2$. But it should be noted that $*S_2$ is not a hard condition by itself. On the contrary, S_2 is only ruled out by virtue of S_1 being a possible solution. If, for some reason, application of S_1 is ruled out on independent grounds, S_2 is no longer banned, and may in fact be the preferred solution.

But then the question immediately arises as to what could rule out S_1, given that it optimally satisfies **C**. Two logical possibilities arise. First, S_1 could violate another hard condition, in which case S_1 may never apply. But a second possibility arises as well. Suppose that not one but two hard conditions apply: $\mathbf{C_I}$ and $\mathbf{C_{II}}$, both with corresponding simplicity metrics $\mathbf{S_I}$ and $\mathbf{S_{II}}$, respectively. Now suppose that $\mathbf{S_I}$ and $\mathbf{S_{II}}$ have the following forms:

(3) $\mathbf{S_I}$: $S_1 > S_2 > \dots$
$\quad\ \mathbf{S_{II}}$: $S_2 > S_1 > \dots$

If the simplicity metrics in (3) both apply, they cannot be both optimally satisfied. Satisfying $\mathbf{C_I}$ in an optimal way entails that S_1 is preferred over S_2. But preferring S_1 over S_2 entails that $\mathbf{C_{II}}$ is not satisfied optimally. Alternatively, if S_2 is favored over S_1, $\mathbf{C_{II}}$ is optimally fulfilled at the expense of $\mathbf{C_I}$.

Note that in cases like (3), nothing requires that one simplicity metric is stronger than the other. Hence, if the optimal satisfaction of $\mathbf{C_I}$ over $\mathbf{C_{II}}$ is not forced on external grounds, both simplicity metrics must be equally strong. As a result, the SMT invokes two different strategies that enable FL to optimally satisfy interface conditions imposed on it.

The question then arises as to whether situations like (3), where two optimal solutions cancel each other out, are natural or expected on conceptual grounds. The answer to this is univocally yes. Since mental modules neighboring FL are (semi-) autonomous, it would in fact be surprising if all simplicity metrics induced by hard interface conditions were in harmony. Nothing guarantees that different cognitive systems like the C-I and the SM systems work in such a way that the conditions they impose on FL are identical with respect to the way that they be optimally fulfilled. Of course, nothing rules out conditions that do not face any contradictory simplicity metric, and such conditions will always be optimally satisfied but since not all conditions are in harmony, variation is already called into being.

The general and most radical hypothesis following from this line of reasoning is that the entire range of cross-linguistic variation results from conflicting simplicity metrics induced by different hard interface conditions imposed on FL. The conclusion of this chapter is that cross-linguistic variation with respect to two expressing strategies of semantic functions, morphological marking and (head) movement, is a direct result of the fact that the SMT constitutes multiple strategies for FL to fulfill hard interface conditions in an optimal way.

3.   Full Legibility and Full Interpretation

As discussed above, one hard condition that is imposed on FL is that derivational outputs must be legible for the respective interpretational systems at the levels of the interfaces. At LF the derivation must be legible for the C-I system, and at PF it must be legible for the SM system. In this section, I propose that this hard condition induces a weaker version of Chomsky's (1995) formulation of the Principle of Full Interpretation and that the current stipulative formulation of this principle is too strong.

3.1   Full Legibility and the C-I interface

Let me formalize the hard condition that derivational outputs must be legible at the level of interfaces by introducing the Principle of Full Legibility (PFL):

> (4) *Principle of Full Legibility (PFL)*:
>   The derivational output of FL must be fully legible for any interpretational system for which it forms an input.

PFL is of course reminiscent of Chomsky's Principle of Full Interpretation (PFI), but it is a weaker notion. It only requires LF representations to be legible, nothing more. In this sense it crucially differs from Chomsky's (1986) original formulation of PFI, which is also meant to rule out vacuous quantification. But, as Potts (2002) has demonstrated, the ban on vacuous quantification is not a necessary constraint on syntactic structures and therefore does not have to follow from any hard conditions applying to FL.

PFL is also weaker than Chomsky's (1995) version of PFI, which states that every element at LF must receive an interpretation:

> (5) *Principle of Full Interpretation (PFI; after Chomsky 1995)*:
>   Every element of an output representation should provide a meaningful input to the relevant other parts of the cognitive system.

The main difference between PFL and this version of PFI is that PFL states that every (part of a) syntactic object must be legible for the C-I systems, whereas PFI requires that every (part of a) syntactic object must have semantic content. However, legibility does not presuppose semantic content.

To illustrate this, take for instance the structure in (6):

(6)
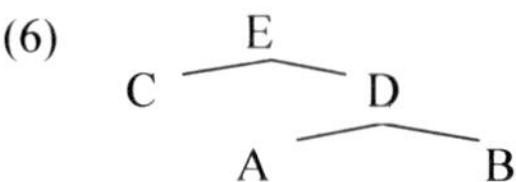

Now suppose that A is semantically empty, that is it contains only formal features at LF. In that case, the denotation of D is identical to the denotation of B. If no other grammatical condition is violated and D can be a semantic complement of C (or vice versa), nothing renders (6) illegible at LF. Following PFL, (6) is ruled in. Hence, the PFI condition that rules out semantically empty elements in syntactic representations at the level of LF does not follow from any legibility condition and therefore counts as a stipulation.

Note that in a way such a stipulation is even counterintuitive. Saying that the presence of some element blocks the interpretation of a structure that would otherwise receive a proper interpretation at LF presupposes that this element has interpretational effects and as such cannot be said to be fully uninterpretable.

But what kind of elements have such properties that they can appear at LF without adding anything to the semantic interpretation? Note that traces, if they are perceived as copies, do have semantic content. In standard semantic theory, they are considered to be variables (cf. Heim and Kratzer 1998; Sportiche 2005), whereas uninterpretable features in the sense of Chomsky (1995, 2000, 2001) are said to be free from semantic content.

Note that in its very essence, an uninterpretable formal feature (henceforth, [uF]) only drives syntactic operations and is, strictly speaking, only formal in nature: it is a formal requirement that at some point in the derivation it must stand in some particular configurational relation with an interpretable counter-feature ([iF]). [iF]'s are both formal and semantic in nature (formal in the sense that they can establish so-called agree relations with [uF]'s, semantic because they are non-vacuously interpreted at LF), but given the fact that [uF]'s are only formal, and therefore purely blind to the semantic properties of [iF]'s, it is not a semantic property of [iF]'s but a formal property that allows it to license [uF]'s.

A major advantage of this more formal perspective on (un)interpretable features is that no look-ahead problems arise, as recognition whether some element carries an [iF] or not is now taken to be part of the derivational syntactic process. Suppose that the semantically empty element A in (6) carries a feature [uF] and suppose that C carries [iF]. Then, after merger of C with D, all formal requirements of A have been met, even before the structure is transferred to LF.

Still, it remains unclear why uninterpretable features would occur at LF against the economical background of the SMT. Initially, this was the grounds on which their occurrence was banned at LF, inducing the still unsolved question as to why uninterpretable features exist in the first place. The ban on uninterpretable features at LF does not follow from PFL, the hard condition that requires that derivational outputs be legible.

But if the SMT holds, it also follows that PFL is optimally satisfied. Although legibility is not affected by the presence of uninterpretable features, their presence does not facilitate legibility either. Hence, PFL induces the following soft condition:

(7) *C-I Simplicity Metric (Zeijlstra 2009):*
     A structural representation R for a substring of input text S is simpler than an
     alternative representation R′ iff R contains less uninterpretable features than R′.

Following the line of reasoning sketched in section 2, the simplest solution to satisfy (7) is to ban all uninterpretable features. Then Chomsky's assumption that uninterpretable features be ultimately removed at the level of LF follows from the simplicity metric in (7), modulo one major difference: the C-I simplicity metric is a soft condition. If for some reason the null-option, that is absence of [uF]s, blocks another, equally strong, simplicity requirement, their presence may be motivated again.

In the following subsection, I argue that the application of PFL at the interface between FL and SM induces a simplicity metric that prefers derivational outputs at LF that contain semantically uninterpretable features over outputs that lack them.

3.2 Full legibility and the SM interface

PFL does not only apply at the level of LF, but also at the level of PF. Derivational outputs must be legible for the SM system, and this requirement must be met in an optimal way. Equivalent to the application of PFL at LF, this means that PFL induces a second simplicity metric that, being a soft condition, bans the presence of what could be metaphorically called 'phonologically uninterpretable features', that is formal features without any phonological content. Such features have the property that they are purely formal in nature but lack phonological content, i.e. phonologically null elements.

Neeleman and van der Koot (2006), who base themselves on Chomsky and Halle (1968) and McCawley (1968), take phonological outputs to be linear and prosodic categories are thought of as phonological boundaries. The prosodic/phonological structure of sentence like (8) is thus represented as (9), where U stands for Utterance boundary, I for intonational phrase boundary, Φ for prosodic phrase boundary, ω for prosodic word boundary, F for foot boundary, and σ for syllable boundary. U at the beginning and at the end of (9) means that the sentence be preceded and followed by an intonational break. Note that stronger prosodic boundaries entail weaker ones: the presence of a boundary of an intonational phrase entails the presence of a boundary of a prosodic phrase as well.

(8)   John's father suggested a two-seater but John's mother preferred a fur coat.

(9) U John's ω father Φ suggested ω a two-seater I but ω John's ω mother Φ preferred ω a fur ω coat U.

Neeleman and van der Koot claim that prosodic categories are hierarchically ordered (from weak to strong) as in (10).

(10) $\sigma < F < \omega < \Phi < I < U$

Prosodic categories, perceived as prosodic boundaries, are thus not banned from phonological representations. However, their occurrence should be as limited as possible, since their appearance cannot be motivated in terms of phonological legibility either. Hence, PFL gives rise to the following simplicity metric.

(11) *SM Simplicity Metric:*
A formal representation R for a substring of input text S is simpler than an alternative representation R' iff R contains less prosodic boundaries than R'.

Thus, both uninterpretable formal features and prosodic boundaries are dispreferred by PFL, given the C-I and SM simplicity metrics. In the next section, I demonstrate that these metrics are in conflict and that for that reason the C-I and SM simplicity metrics can never be optimally satisfied at the same time.

4. Conflicting simplicity metrics

In this section, I demonstrate that the C-I and SM simplicity metrics cannot be optimally fulfilled at the same time expressing a semantic function without using uninterpretable features must lead to the introduction of prosodic boundaries, whereas expressing such a semantic function without such prosodic boundaries will inevitably lead to the introduction of a semantically uninterpretable feature. But before I will address the question as to why expression strategies for semantic functions that lack both uninterpretable features and strong prosodic boundaries are forbidden.

The answer to this question is the following: The main effect of the SM simplicity metric is to spell out as much as possible on one and the same lexical node, but semantic functions cannot occupy any arbitrary position in the syntactic structure and require uninterpretable features to ensure possible interpretation. Let me illustrate this by discussing past tense, which is subject to cross-linguistic variation with respect to the way it is expressed. One way to express past tense is by using a single word for it. Under this strategy, which is found, for example, in Mandarin Chinese (Jing Lin, p.c.), past tense can be expressed by means of the temporal adverb *yiqian* in (12), with the result that there is a one-to-one correspondence between the word for past tense and the semantic past tense operator.

(12) Jing (yiqian) tiao-wu
Jing (past)   dance
'Jing dance(d)'

This temporal adverb then introduces a prosodic boundary, which is lacking in languages like English that use an affix to express *past*. English thus prefers a different expressing strategy.

(13) Wolfgang play–*ed* tennis.

But under this strategy semantic past tense is not directly expressed by the temporal morphological marker –*ed*, since the semantics of past tense does not allow for a direct interpretation in the position where the lexical verb *play–ed* is base-generated. Past tense is a semantic operator that must outscope the entire vP, that is the fully saturated argument structure of the predicate (see for example Klein 1994; Ogihara 1996; Abusch 1997; Kratzer 1998; von Stechow 2002). This is illustrated in (14).

(14) Wolfgang played tennis on every Sunday.   (von Stechow 2002)
   =   'For every Sunday in the past there is a time *t* at which Wolfgang plays tennis'
   ≠   'There is a past time on every Sunday at which Wolfgang plays tennis'
   ≠   'For every Sunday, there is time before it such that Wolfgang plays tennis at that time'

The only available reading is the one where past tense outscopes the distributive quantifier *every Sunday*, which in turn outscopes the lexical verb *play*. Consequently, the past tense affix *–ed* cannot be assigned the semantics of the past tense operator in the position that it occupies at surface structure. But what, then, is the contribution of *–ed*, if it cannot be interpreted at surface structure? How can *–ed* induce the semantics of past tense, if at the same time it cannot be interpreted at its base position in the sentence?

Two logical possibilities arise: either (a) *–ed* is not the semantic past tense operator itself, but merely a true marker of an abstract operator that is responsible for the semantics of past tense, or (b) *–ed* is the semantic past tense operator, but a structural transformation takes place such that both *–ed* and *play* can be interpreted in the proper position. The two strategies can be tentatively called *marking* and *displacement*, and the way they function is sketched in the LFs in (15).

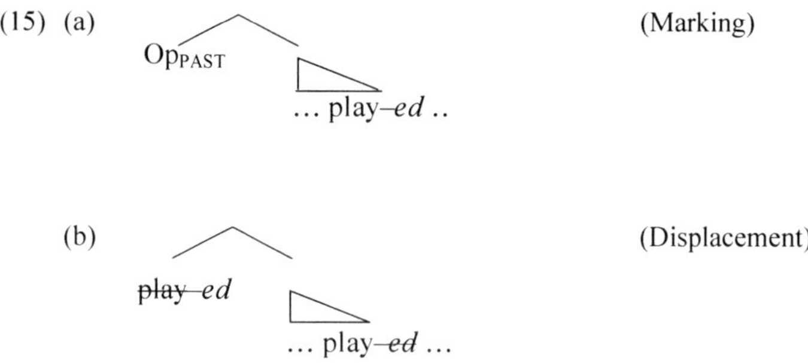

In (15a), *–ed* is a marker that signals the presence of the past tense operator in its proper position, that is above VP; in (15b), due to the transformational operation that has been applied, *–ed*, the carrier of the semantic contents of the past tense operator, is now in a position where it can be properly interpreted and as a result of the same transformational operation, be disconnected from the position where the lexical content of the verb *play* is interpreted.

In the following two subsections, I demonstrate that in both cases the presence of an uninterpretable feature is required. In a nutshell, in (15a), *–ed* must carry an uninterpretable past tense feature, marking the presence of an abstract operator carrying an interpretable past tense feature. And in (15b), we find two copies of the finite verb, whereas only one gets interpreted. For that reason, only one of the two verbs may be interpreted as carrying verbal contents; the other must be analyzed as carrying an uninterpretable verbal feature.

So both the empty operator strategy in (15a) and the movement strategy in (15b) involve uninterpretable features. If this is indeed correct, the SM simplicity metric favoring expression of as much material as possible on the same lexical node, can only be maximally satisfied at the expense of the C-I simplicity metric which bans uninterpretable features. Vice versa, the strategy in (12), which can be directly interpreted at LF without any rescue strategy that requires uninterpretable features, violates the SM simplicity metric, as it introduces new prosodic boundaries. Thus, the interplay between the SM and the C-I simplicity metrics already gives rise to two different types of strategies: one type that prefers prosodic boundaries over uninterpretable features and one type of strategies where uninterpretable features are preferred over prosodic boundaries.

Note that this does not mean that these are the only available expression strategies; other simplicity requirements assumably call other expression strategies into being (particles instead of affixes/adverbs, or reduplication, just to mention a few). Even stronger, it is not claimed either that every semantic function that is conveyed must be part of the lexical semantics of the sentence: it could be implicated or presupposed as well.

4.1 Marking, uninterpretability and agree

Now let us zoom in on the marking strategy exemplified in (16a), where a marker only indicates the presence of an abstract operator in the appropriate position. More abstractly, this means that some root X is equipped with an additional marker. Such a marker can be an affix, but it does not necessarily have to be one: vowel alternation or other instances of marking (e.g. syncretisms of multiple markers) are equally well possible. Let us call the marker F. In the case of affixation, a root plus marker is thus of the form X-F.

As discussed before, F is not the carrier of the semantic contents of the operator. The structure of a sentence containing X-F is rather like (16), where a covert operator (Op_F) is responsible for the semantic contribution, which is manifested by F.

(16)   (Marking)

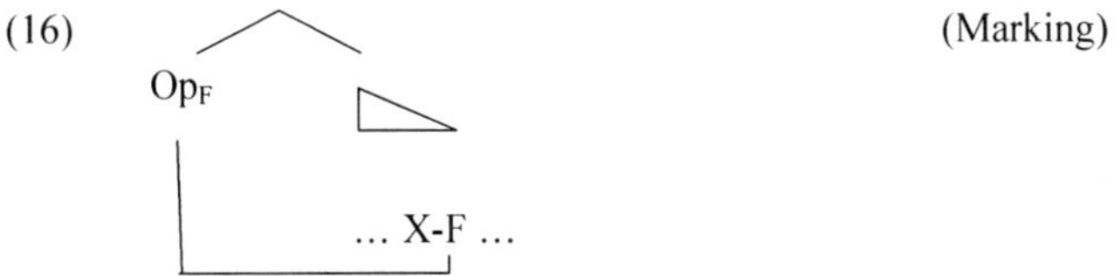

This structural relation in (16) is governed by the following three conditions:

(17) (a) $[Op_F [... \text{X-F} ...]]$
      (b) $*[... \text{X-F} ...]]$
      (c) $*[Op_F [... \text{X} ...]]$

The conditions in (17) state that F demands the presence of an operator Op_F and that abstract Op_F may only be included if F is present. The conditions in (17) are an implementation of what Ladusaw (1992) refers to as a mechanism of self-licensing. The abstract operator is licensed by the presence of Op_F and Op_F fulfils the licensing requirements of F. Since Op_F is abstract, marking strategy (16) serves the SM simplicity metric in the sense that only an affix is sufficient to express past tense and that no new morphological word needs to be included. At the same time, this marking strategy needs the formal properties that F exhibits. Hence, the question arises as to what properties does F actually exhibit, such that the conditions in (17) follow?

To recapitulate, F must be morpho-syntactically visible, F may only occur in a grammatical sentence while standing in a syntactic relation with Op_F, and F must be semantically empty. As laid out in the previous section, these are exactly the properties that define uninterpretable formal features. Thus, F must be an uninterpretable formal feature [uF]. In other words, it is only possible to mark a semantic function by means of an (affixal) marker that does not contain any semantic contribution if that (affixal) marker is the carrier of an uninterpretable feature in the Chomskyan sense.

The idea that F carries an uninterpretable formal feature directly entails the conditions in (17). Conditions (17a) and (17b) follow directly, but also (17c) is a consequence of this implementation: if a sentence is grammatical and its grammaticality is not due to any of its overt elements, then a covert element must be responsible for its grammaticality; if the grammaticality of a sentence follows directly from its overt elements, on the other hand, there is no reason for adopting abstract material, a constraint. This rules out (17c) as no grammatical constraint requires the presence of Op_F.

To sum up, the conditions under which an element F may mark the presence of an abstract matching operator, without contributing to the semantics of the sentence in which F occurs itself, follow immediately once it is assumed that F carries an uninterpretable feature [uF] that matches with the interpretable feature [iF] on the operator.

4.2 Displacement, remerge and move

Marking strategies (where elements carrying uninterpretable formal features signal the presence of matching abstract operators) are not the only ways to enable Spell-Out of semantically mismatching elements on one and the same morphological word, as favored by the SM simplicity metric. Another way would be to induce a displacement effect, such that F is semantically non-empty, and therefore does not contain any uninterpretable features, but takes scope from a different position than where X has been base-generated.

(18)  (Displacement)

This is of course reminiscent of Chomsky's (1995) copy theory of movement or chain formation is the sense of Brody (1995). Before continuing the argument that movement is motivated by the semantic content on a particular lexical item, which can only be interpreted in a higher position, let me avoid one possible misunderstanding. The existence of movement itself does not have to be motivated. As Chomsky has argued numerous times, a generative operation like Merge can apply internally and therefore the operation Remerge is pregiven by Merge (Chomsky 2005). However, movement is derivationally complex, and is therefore ruled out if it is unmotivated. Hence, what needs to be motivated is the trigger for movement, not movement itself.

Suppose a root again takes the form X-G, where X-G now means that it is the realization of two elements, X and G, that carry both semantic content, but only X can be interpreted in situ, G cannot. One solution then would be to remerge X-G and create a higher position where G is interpreted.

(19) PF: [...X-G...] → [... X-G ... [... ~~X-G~~ ...]]
      LF: [...X-G...] → [... ~~X~~-G ... [... X-~~G~~ ...]]

The representation in (19) is a direct result of the copy theory of movement, where first a lexical item has been copied, and then all doubly manifested material is deleted once, either in the highest or in the lowest position. In this case the highest copy is phonologically interpreted in the highest position (and deleted in the lowest position), but at LF X is deleted in the highest position and G in the lowest position. Note that this is the only structural representation that is legible at LF. All other combinations (X-G interpreted in the same position, or G interpreted below and X above) would be illegible at LF. This is exactly what has been observed in the case of past tense. A past tense operator must be interpreted outside the vP; the lexical content of a verb must be interpreted in situ.

However, (19) cannot be the correct derivational outcome yet, since G lacks a syntactic category. In the example, G is nothing but a purely semantic past tense operator that does not carry any formal feature at all. Therefore, if X gets deleted in the highest copy, no formal feature is left and G would not even be a syntactic object then; syntax would be completely blind to it. Even if X were interpreted in the lowest position, it would still have to be syntactically visible in the highest position. A moved noun keeps the syntactic status of a noun; a moved verb the syntactic status of a verb, etc.

Hence, the picture in (19) can not be complete. Although semantically, X is only present downstairs, X must be formally present upstairs, without receiving any interpretation. In other words, X must be an uninterpretable formal feature in the highest position, and an interpretable formal feature downstairs. The representation of semantically driven movement of X-G, due to G's semantic requirement to be interpreted in a higher position, must be as in (20).

(20) [...X-G...] → [... [uX]-G ... [... [iX]-~~G~~ ...]]

This (simplified) view on movement takes movement to be semantically motivated. As it is standardly assumed that head movement does not affect semantic interpretation, the burden of evidence is actually to demonstrate that head movement is indeed semantically motivated.

Applying these ideas to the expression of semantic tense, V-to-T movement can then be the consequence of the fact that the past tense morpheme is actually the carrier of past tense. Movement of the verb then results in interpretation of the past tense operator in the highest position and of the verbal contents in the lowest position.

(21)   [...V-PAST...] ® LF: [... [uV]-PAST ... [...[iV]-~~PAST~~ ...]]

The idea that movement is essentially triggered by semantic properties rather than by morpho-syntactic requirements is reminiscent of foot-driven movement analyses (though these analyses have never been based on semantic motivations), such as Platzack (1996), Koeneman (2000) and van Craenenbroeck (2006).

This view on movement is also supported by a recent analysis by Truckenbrodt (2006), who argues that V-to-C movement activates speech act operators and is thus semantically driven. Implemented in the proposal above, V_{fin} carries initially a purely semantic speech act feature and a formal feature V. As the feature that has the illocutionary force of a speech act cannot be interpreted on $V°$, it must move to a higher position. Given that all operators encoding illocutionary force have to precede all elements carrying propositional contents, speech act formation is easily (but not necessarily) executed by verbal fronting. V_{fin} then copies itself and the speech act is interpreted in the highest head position and the verbal contents are interpreted below. This is shown in (23) below, where the phonological, syntactic, and semantic representations are given for the imperative sentence in (22).

(22)   Kill Mary!

(23)   SEM   IMP(Kill(Mary))
       SYN   [V-fin$_{[uV][IMP]}$] ... [$_V$ ~~V-fin~~$_{[iV][IMP]}$ D]]
       PHON   /Kill Mary ... /

Move is then, similarly to Agree, a marking strategy that is imposed on FL by the SM interface condition to express as much material as possible on one and the same lexical node. This condition can only be fulfilled if natural language exhibits uninterpretable material.

Note that this view on head movement unifies head movement with other types of movement (A-movement, A'-movement) in the sense that head movement is now also an instance of pied-piping. The formal features of V constitute the vehicle that allows G to move.

4.3 Summary

In this section, I hope to have shown that both agreement and movement strategies can only be realized if uninterpretable features are involved. Uninterpretable features, on their turn, are motivated because expressing strategies involving uninterpretable features can be equally optimal as expressing strategies (such as (12)) that lack them for the very reason that reduction of prosodic boundaries can only be established by means of inclusion of uninterpretable features. Purely external merge-based strategies, internal merge-based strategies, and agreement strategies are thus all tools that are directly motivated by the SMT and thus constitute the UG toolbox.

Note that these three strategies are by no means exhaustive. I only demonstrated that, as a result of the SMT, which invokes both the C-I and the SM simplicity metric, these strategies can emerge. Other simplicity metrics, for example LEX simplicity metrics, could induce additional expressing strategies.

In any case, this line of reasoning has, I think, two major benefits. It gives a principled explanation for the existence of uninterpretable features, which has been up until now an unresolved problem in minimalist theory, and it also gives a motivated answer to the question as to why movement is triggered without appealing to notions such as EPP-features.

5. Grammatical simplicity and the parametric space

So far, the proposal explains why different types of expressions for a particular Op_F exist and are cross-linguistically attested. For instance, it provides an answer to the question why uninterpretable features exist in the first place.

However, the proposal does not say that all languages are simplest solutions, that is that all languages are maximally simple, and thus select exactly one expression strategy for each semantic function. Let me illustrate this with the following examples from Afrikaans, Italian and German.

(24) Ek sing.   Afrikaans
      I   sing
      'I sing.'

(25)   Canto.   Italian
      $pro_{[i1SG]}$ $sing_{[u1SG]}$
      'I sing.'

(26) Ich   singe.   German
      $I_{[i1SG]}$ $sing_{[u1SG]}$
      'I sing.'

Afrikaans has a C-I-based strategy to express pronominal subjecthood, Italian an SM-based strategy (Agree). Both seem to be equally simple in that respect. However, German exhibits both. It has both an Agree strategy and a C-I strategy.

As has often been observed, language seems to be suboptimal rather than optimal, which is often used as an argument against simplicity as an underlying force in grammar. So how can examples like (26) be accounted for against the background of the SMT?

As discussed before, FL, which is an optimal solution to conditions imposed on it by neighboring mental modules, constitutes UG, that is, the linguistic toolbox. This toolset consists of a number of optimal solutions to connect form and meaning.

At the same time, FL drives language acquisition. In fact, it is even the backbone of generative theory that principles that shape UG also govern language acquisition. Simplicity metrics therefore do not only constitute possible grammars, but also guide language learnability.

Simplicity metrics applying to the language acquisition process ensure that the simplest grammar consistent with the primary language data is selected during the language learning process. This explains why languages are not maximally simple, but just as simple as their target language. If for some reason the target language is not maximally simple, but takes, for instance, two marking strategies to express a single semantic function, then the language learner can do nothing but assign those two marking strategies to his or her own grammar.

The only question is why target languages should be non-optimal given the SMT. Existence of such languages is of course not expected under the SMT, but external factors may have a distorting effect. L2 acquisition in language contact situations with two maximally optimal languages may yield a new language that is less optimal. This has been the case for instance with the expression of pronominal subjecthood in German:

Weerman (2006) argues that proto-Germanic was a *pro*-drop language, just like (present-day) Italian, and that processes of language contact led to a process of deflection in the verbal paradigm: Some forms eroded and the one-to-one relation between person and verbal agreement disappeared. As a result (cf. Rizzi 1986; Neeleman and Szendrői 2006), *pro*-drop was no longer licensed. On the other hand, the language contact situation did not go so far that all morphological distinctions in the verbal paradigm were lost, as is for instance the case with Afrikaans. German is therefore somewhere in between a full *pro*-drop paradigm and the Afrikaans zero-paradigm. Consequently, it exhibits both C-I-biased and SM-biased marking strategies for pronominal subjecthood.

German language learners will adopt both strategies, since this is the simplest way to satisfy the simplicity metrics. Only if the language input undergoes total deflection will the language learner adopt the single external-merge strategy.

On the basis of this line of reasoning, a new view of cross-linguistic variation can be presented, which includes both the notion of possible and probable languages (see Newmeyer 2005 for discussion). The grammatical space is dynamic and governed by simplicity metrics that are both upward entailing (a set of expression strategies allows application of multiple strategies) and downward entailing (select the smallest number of strategies possible for each semantic function). At the same time, grammars that exhibit expressing strategies that are not part of UG are impossible. This view on the grammatical space, or as it is structured, on the parametric space can be modeled (27).

(27) The parametric space.

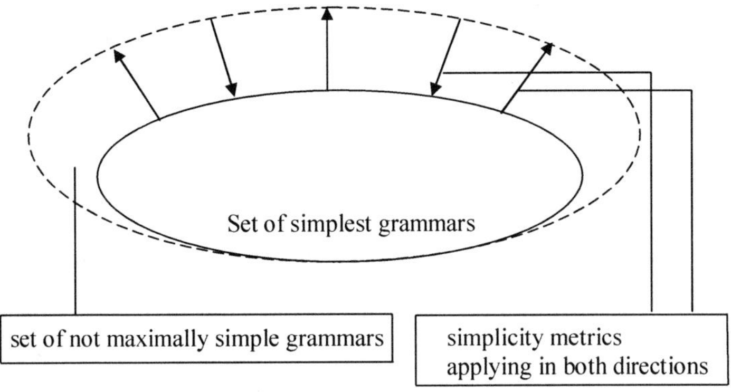

Note that this view on language allows for parametric variation following directly from the SMT. Hence, parameters do not need to be thought of as innately present, but can be taken to be derived from the idea that FL is maximally simple. Moreover, this view ensures that, even though FL is taken to be maximally simple, this does not entail that every possible grammar has to be simple as well.

6. Conclusions

In this chapter, I argued that both parametric variation and the attested differences between languages in terms of their internal complexity straightforwardly follow from the Strongest Minimalist Thesis that takes FL to be an optimal solution to conditions that neighboring mental modules impose on it.

I also suggested that hard conditions like legibility at the linguistic interfaces invoke simplicity metrics that, given that they stem from different mental modules, do not necessarily have to be harmonious. In fact, I demonstrated that legibility at the interface between FL and the SM system, and between FL and the C-I system, respectively, already invokes two simplicity metrics that cannot be maximally satisfied at the same time.

In addition, I demonstrated that maximal satisfaction of the SM simplicity metric cannot take place without alluding to the notion of uninterpretable features, and that maximal satisfaction of the C-I simplicity metric bans spelling out multiple semantic functions on one and the same word.

I proposed further that expression strategies, such as agreement or movement, are a direct result of these conflicting simplicity metrics, and that UG, perceived as a toolbox that shapes natural language, can be taken to consist of a limited number of marking strategies, all resulting from conflicting simplicity metrics. As such, the contents of UG follow from simplicity requirements, and therefore no longer necessitate linguistic principles, valued or unvalued, to be innately present.

Finally, I showed that the SMT, contrary to what has often been thought, does not require that languages have to be optimal in connecting sound to meaning. Since UG drives the process of language acquisition, language acquisition can be modeled as a selectional procedure, where it is detected for each semantic function how it is to be expressed, which does not a priori require each semantic function to be expressed by one single marking strategy only.

Acknowledgments

Many thanks to Theresa Biberauer, Hans Broekhuis, Olaf Koeneman, Ralf Vogel, Fred Weerman, an anonymous reviewer and the audience of DEAL II for their valuable comments and discussion. All errors are of course mine.

References

Abusch, D. (1997) Sequence of tense and temporal de re. *Linguistics and Philosophy* 20 (1): 1–50.
Bittner, M. (2005) Future discourse in a tenseless language. *Journal of Semantics* 22 (4): 339–87.
Brody, M. (1995) *Lexico-Logical Form: A Radically Minimalist Theory.* Cambridge, MA: MIT Press.
Chomsky, N. (1981) *Lectures on Government and Binding.* Dordrecht: Foris.
Chomsky, N. (1986) *Knowledge of Language: Its Nature, Origin, and Use.* New York: Praeger.
Chomsky, N. (1995) *The Minimalist Program.* Cambridge, MA: MIT Press.
Chomsky, N. (2000) Minimalist inquiries: The framework. In R. Martin, D. Michaels, and J. Uriagereka (eds) *Step by Step: Essays on Minimalist Syntax in Honor of Howard Lasnik.* 89–156. Cambridge, MA: MIT Press.
Chomsky, N. (2001) Derivation by phase. In M. Kenstowicz (ed.) *Ken Hale: A Life in Language,* 1–54. Cambridge, MA: MIT Press.
Chomsky, N. (2004) Beyond explanatory adequacy. In A. Belletti (ed.) *Structures and Beyond: The Cartography of Syntactic Structures*, vol. 3, 104–31. New York: Oxford University Press.
Chomsky, N. (2005) Three factors in language design. *Linguistic Inquiry* 36 (1): 1–22.
Chomsky, N. and Halle, M. (1968) *The Sound Pattern of English.* Cambridge, MA: MIT Press.
Van Craenenbroeck, J. (2006) Transitivity failures in the left periphery and foot-driven movement operations. In J. van de Weijer and B. Los (eds) *Linguistics in the Netherlands* Amsterdam: John Benjamins.
DeGraff, M. (2001) On the origin of creoles: A Cartesian critique of neo-Darwinian linguistics. *Linguistic Typology* 5 (2–3): 213–310.
Gil, D. (2001) Creoles, complexity, and Riau Indonesian. *Linguistic Typology* 5: 325–71.
Heim, I. and Kratzer, A. (1998). *Semantics in Generative Grammar.* Malden, MA: Blackwell.
Jackendoff, R. (2002) *Foundations of Language: Brain, Meaning, Grammar, Evolution.* Oxford: Oxford University Press.
Klein, W. (1994) *Time in Language.* London: Routledge.
Koeneman, O. (2000) *The Flexible Nature of Verb Movement.* Doctoral dissertation, Utrecht University.
Kratzer, A. (1998) More structural analogies between pronouns and tenses. *Proceedings of SALT VIII:* 92–109.
Kusters, W. (2003) *Linguistic Complexity: The Influence of Social Change on Verbal Inflection.* Doctoral dissertation, Utrecht University.
Ladusaw, W. A. (1992) Expressing negation. *Proceedings of SALT II:* 237–59.
Lasnik, H. (2003) *Minimalist Investigations in Linguistic Theory.* London: Routledge.
McCawley, J. D. (1968) *The Phonological Component of a Grammar of Japanese.* The Hague: Mouton.
Neeleman, A. and van der Koot, H. (2006) On syntactic and phonological representations. *Lingua* 116 (10): 1524–52.
Neeleman, A. and Szendrői, K. (2007) Radical pro drop and the morphology of pronouns. *Linguistic Inquiry* 38 (4): 671–714.

Ogihara, T. (1996) *Tense, Attitudes, and Scope*. Dordrecht: Kluwer.

Platzack, C. (1996) Germanic verb second – Attract versus Repel: On optionality, A-bar movement and the symmetrical/asymmetrical verb second hypothesis. E. Lang and G. Zifonun (eds) *Deutsch – Typologisch*. Berlin: Walter de Gruyter.

Potts, C. (2002) No vacuous quantification constraints in syntax. *Proceedings of the North East Linguistic Society* 32: 451–70.

Ramchand, G. and Svenonius, P. (2008) Mapping a parochial lexicon onto a Universal Semantics. In T. Biberauer (ed.) *The Limits of Syntactic Variation*. Amsterdam: John Benjamins.

Rizzi, L. (1986) Null objects in Italian and the theory of *pro*. *Linguistic Inquiry* 17 (3): 501–57.

Sportiche, D. (2005) Cyclic NP structure and the interpretation of traces. In H. Broekhuis, N. Corver, J. Koster, R. Huybregts, and U. Kleinhenz (eds) *Organizing Grammar: Linguistic Studies in Honor of Henk van Riemsdijk*, 599–607. Berlin: Mouton de Gruyter.

Von Stechow, A. (2002) Temporal prepositional phrases with quantifiers: Some additions to Pratt and Francez (2001) *Linguistics and Philosophy* 25: 755–800.

Von Stechow, A. (2005) Semantisches und morphologisches Tempus: Zur temporalen Orientierung von Einstellungen und Modalen. *Neue Beiträge zur Germanistik* 124: 9–54.

Truckenbrodt, H. (2006) On the semantic motivation of syntactic verb movement to C in German. *Theoretical Linguistics* 32 (3): 257–306.

Weerman, F. (2006) It's the economy, stupid! Een vergelijkende blik op *men* en *man*. In M. Hüning, U. Vogl, T. van der Wouden and A. Verhagen (ed.) *Nederlands tussen Duits en Engels*. Leiden: SNL.

Zeijlstra, H. (2009) Functional structure and parametric variation: Consequences of conflicting interface conditions. In K. K. Grohmann (ed.) *InterPhases: Phase-Theoretic Investigations of Linguistic Interfaces*, 82–113. Oxford: Oxford University Press.

13 Spell-Out rules: ranked competition of Copy Modification

Kleanthes K. Grohmann*

ABSTRACT The operation Spell-Out is typically taken to apply to syntactic objects that are transferred from the syntactic computation into the phonological component of the derivation. This contribution provides a brief synopsis of the development of Spell-Out coming into being within minimalist theorizing, coupled with relevant notions (interfaces, architecture, and so on), before putting a slightly different spin on it. This captures one of the main title's interpretations: different rules. The other interpretation follows from the proposal laid out here, that at the core of all syntactic derivations lies the need for syntactic objects assembled in the syntax to be interpreted at both interface components, PF and LF – and Spell-Out is intimately related to PF-interpretability (and realization); this is achieved through a rule-ordered 'checklist' of Copy Modification.

KEYWORDS Anti-locality; Condition of Domain Exclusivity; Copy Modification; interfaces; phases; Prolific Domain; resumption; Spell-Out; Transfer; tripartite clause structure

1. Introducing ruling and ranking

This chapter is not as much an attempt to combine ingredients of different approaches, say, (derivatives of) the Minimalist Program (MP) and Optimality Theory (OT), as it is a more general attempt to tackle one issue that used to be central to any (generative) syntactic theory of language: deletion of displaced constituents. The proposal will be couched within a larger endeavor that aims to investigate the interface systems in more detail and as such bears on the relation between the generator and filtering of the output (to use OT-terminology) and more general interface conditions imposed on the computational system (as in MP jargon); more OT-related discussion can be found in Broekhuis and Vogel (2007), which will be addressed presently, as well as in Broekhuis (2008) and Broekhuis and Vogel (2010), for example.

* Kleanthes K. Grohmann, University of Cyprus, Department of English Studies, 75 Kallipoleos, P.O. Box 20537. 1678 Nicosia, Cyprus. E-mail: kleanthi@ucy.ac.cy

The minimalist line goes as follows: Under virtually any version of the (inverted) T-model (Chomsky 1993), reflecting computations within the human faculty of language (HFL),[1] the interaction between the lexicon (LEX) and the interpretive interfaces, the conceptual-intentional (C-I) and the articulatory-perceptual or sensorimotor (SM) systems, is mediated through the computational system of human language (C_{HL}) which generates linguistic expressions and syntactic objects through successive applications of the binary operation Merge in narrow syntax (NS) and sends the information thus gathered for interpretation to the interface levels, Logical Form (LF) and Phonetic or Phonological Form (PF).

My perhaps controversial upshot will be that most of what syntacticians should really be investigating lies in the interface(s) of NS and PF. Note that, before we set out to argue for this, and before we compare MP and OT more generally in the spirit of this volume, we need to decide which MP-model we subscribe to. For more discussion, especially as it pertains to the interfaces within minimalist approaches to the grammar, see e.g. Grohmann (2007a, 2007c, 2009a, 2009b) and the contributions collected there. Part and parcel of any minimalist approach to human language has been the implicational desideratum set forth in Chomsky (1993) that levels of representation that do not follow from '(virtual) conceptual necessity' or 'bare output conditions' – now referred to as 'interface conditions' (ICs) – are to be rejected (in particular, D- and S-structure). The same can be said for any enrichment of the syntactic component in terms of operations, principles, conditions, and other filters.

For the present contribution, three questions stand out in particular (which were originally formulated in Grohmann 2007b: 176):

(1) How exactly are LF and PF accessed after (or fed by) the operation Spell-Out?

(2) Is there evidence for a more complex PF-component (or articulated PF-branch)?

(3) With an affirmative answer, what can be said about the computation towards PF?

And some related questions to be addressed, if only partially, include the following:

(4) (a) What exactly does the operation Spell-Out do?
     (b) Where, when, and how do morphology and phonology kick in?
     (c) How often does Spell-Out apply, and to what kind(s) of structure(s)?
     (d) Are the two levels of representation sufficient, too many, or not enough?
     (e) How can the interaction between syntax and prosody be formally represented?

What I will not address in any detail in what follows is the possible distinction to be made between a *level* of representation and a mere *component*. Likewise, I will not follow up on the possibility of two *types* of interfaces, what I called elsewhere 'linguistic interfaces' and 'modular interfaces' (e.g., Grohmann 2007a, 2009a). Beyond Chomsky's (2008) more recent remarks, these issues are discussed in much more detail in the collection of Ramchand and Reiss (2007), among others, but also dwell on (and in a sense stem from) what Poeppel and Embick (2005) termed the 'Granularity Mismatch Problem', which I will return to towards the end of this chapter.

However, I would like to use this opportunity and briefly address the issue of 'filters on the output' in MP versus OT, taking my cue from the *DEAL II* call for papers (Broekhuis and Vogel 2007). This will set the tone for the ensuing discussion and demarcate the notion of *filter* in the specific sense being used here (as an IC) as opposed to its more widespread use: '[M]any proponents of MP accept the idea that the generator may overgenerate and that we must assume some additional means to filter out the unwanted structures from the reference set.'

The type of filter Broekhuis and Vogel are most interested in, to select optimal candidates, can be captured by (5), which they adapted from Archangeli (1997):

(5)   The evaluator finds the candidate that *best satisfies* the ranked constraints, such that:
   (a)   violation of a lower ranked constraint is tolerated in order to satisfy a higher ranked constraint; and
   (b)   ties by violation or by satisfaction of a higher ranked constraint are resolved by a lower ranked constraint.

I will return to the relevance of (5) and a possible reformulation in terms more immediately relevant to the rest of this chapter in section 4.

Broekhuis and Vogel (2007) continue with the reasonable observation that in MP, 'there is no explicit theory of the postulated filtering device' – true as that may be (and for whatever reasons), minimalist 'filtering' must follow from ICs, as already mentioned and to be returned to throughout. Citing work by Chomsky (1995, 2001) and Sabel (2005), Broekhuis and Vogel are of course aware of this postulation when they say that 'the filtering device consists of "Effect-on-Output conditions" that may select a less economical candidate from the reference set provided that the additional operation has some effect on the output'. And again, while this view of 'filters' may pertain to the type of competition to be discussed in section 4 below, Broekhuis and Vogel's next observation, that 'the filtering component is essentially language-specific', may not. At least the mechanism to be introduced in section 4 will be argued to hold 'universally' – or rather, in the absence of a larger empirical discussion, as a desirable principle of HFL.

In the absence of a dedicated and more specialized discussion of OT, and the general filtering devices other contributions to the volume address more authoritatively, I suggest to take the next quote from Broekhuis and Vogel (2007), at least the MP-relevant parts, coupled with the set of questions in (1) through (4), as a guide for the remainder of this paper:

> OT and MP face a similar challenge, namely, determining how the filtering device can be made sensitive to the phonological and semantic properties of the optimal candidate. [...] Another aspect of this challenge for OT and MP is the nature of the interaction between the modules of the grammar [...] how do they interact, what happens in the case of conflicting requirements? [...] Furthermore, shall the interface be conceived as unidirectional or bidirectional (as in bidirectional OT)?

The roadmap of this chapter looks as follows, then. Section 2 presents two general types of approaches to the (linguistic) interfaces, what is sometimes called *static* versus the more current trend towards *dynamic* interaction between NS and LF/PF. In section 3, I sketch my own take on the latter and discuss several models of *(multiple) Spell-Out*. Possibly the (novel) core of this chapter, section 4 introduces a filtering approach towards dealing with copies of syntactic objects generated in the course of the derivation, *Copy Modification*. The conclusion in section 5 aims to place some of the ideas put forth here in a wider perspective.

2.   Interface approaches: static versus dynamic perspectives

Ultimately, this chapter is: (a) a conceptual exercise in coming to grips with the architecture of the grammar – in particular, the (inverted) T-model of MP and a (complex) view of the PF-branch; and (b) applying it to a set of syntactic structures that indicate the IC-sensitivity of copies generated in NS, to be viewed as a theory of copy modification more generally.

For starters, the type of architectural design of the grammar that MP challenged from the outset is the organization well known from the theory of Government-and-Binding (GB; Chomsky 1981), *vis-à-vis* four levels of representation and their interplay, where each is subject to a number of specific filters and constraints: D-structure (Projection Principle) feeds S-structure (Move α), which in turn branches off and leads to the semantic interpretation (LF) and the phonetic output (PF). Particular conditions (such as Subjacency or the Extended Projection Principle) apply and individual modules (such as Theta Theory, Case Filter, PRO Theorem, and so on) have to be satisfied at the respective level of representation (see also van Riemsdijk and Williams (1986); for a recent review and presentation of relevant developments since, see Hornstein *et al.* (2005), especially chapter 2).

In contrast, the classic MP architecture eliminates the levels of D- and S-structure, as in Figure 13.1.[2]

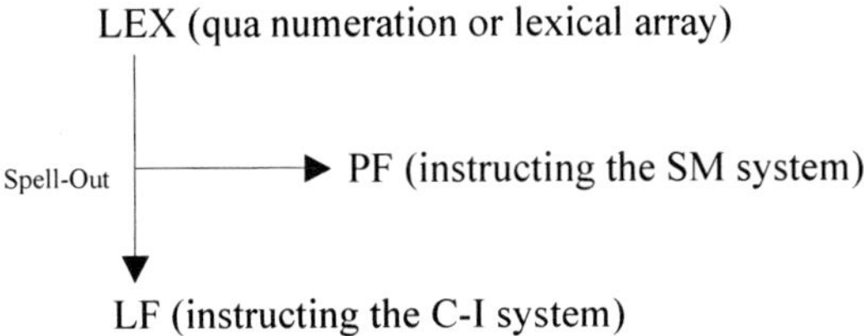

Figure 13.1 The (inverted) T-model (after Chomsky 1995: 219).

LEX feeds the syntactic derivation directly, which thus allows interspersing of the structure-building operation *Merge* and the displacement mechanism/operation *Move* rather freely (certainly not as constrained as in older models), in accordance with the licensing mechanism of grammatical properties (such as Checking Theory or Agree for formal features), and other conditions on interpretation (some of which will be addressed presently.)

Noteworthy here is the operation Spell-Out, which will be dealt with in more detail in section 3. Other than that, standard MP reasoning holds that only such entities should exist in the grammar that either follow from (virtual) conceptual necessity or fall into the category of bare output conditions (Chomsky 1995: 169–71, 219–25), that is, ICs in Phase Theory (Chomsky 2004: 2). LEX, the collection of lexical items and functional elements in the human mind/brain (specifically, HFL), is arguably conceptually necessary, whereas LF and PF are clearly motivated by or instantiated as ICs.[3] By hypothesis, these are the linguistic levels of representation which the relevant language-external systems read off. These levels, communicating with the external C-I and SM systems, are clearly '(virtually) conceptually necessary' for a faculty of language if there is anything to the characterization, in its spirit going back to Aristotle, that language is the pairing of sound and meaning. If language at some level boils down to such a pair – expressed as either $<\pi, \lambda>$, where π is the phonetic and λ the semantic output (Chomsky 1995) or the pair <Phon, Sem> (Chomsky 2000) – then sound and meaning need to be represented somehow in order to yield the two objects that make up language.

Under this conception, PF and LF are often referred to as the sole 'levels of representation' or, better perhaps, 'interface components' in the sense that they are possibly modular themselves, or at least dynamically built up, eventually feeding the C-I and SM systems.[4] Further principles and operations that are assumed to apply to the grammar, or any other additions to the grammatical system, must be motivated by what Chomsky (1995) terms '(virtual) conceptual necessity' (caused a priori) or ICs, which have a direct impact for or at the interfaces (LF and PF).

To continue this semi-historical perspective (which may indeed still be very relevant, even well into the second decade of minimalism, and perhaps useful for reflection or checks and balances), we can call the early and classic lines of MP research (say, Chomsky (1993, 1995), and much research prior to Phase Theory) *static* as regards the interaction between syntactic computation and interface interpretation. It is static in several ways, most prominently through the single feeding of the interface levels/components: Spell-Out is an operation that applies once at the end of the overt derivation. This stands in stark contrast to *dynamic* approaches to the interfaces, as encapsulated in, among other models, Phase Theory (Chomsky 2000 *et seq.*) – section 3.1 will investigate dynamic approaches in more detail. The classic lines of MP research also puts a special emphasis on Spell-Out rendering this operation quite different in character and applicability from all other computational operations, as pointed out by Uriagereka (1999); for example, it is restricted to apply only once in a given derivation (as opposed to the operations Merge and Move), and it can only take place once all strong features have been checked (or whatever the equivalent of an adequate feature-licensing mechanism other than Checking Theory would be).

The latter point may be taken further to coincide with a possible dichotomy into static and dynamic approaches. It might be argued that classic Checking Theory (Chomsky 1993) is a typical exponent in that movement must take place to license grammatical properties – 'feature-checking', be it in Spec-Head or head-adjunction configurations; 'strong' features need to be checked overtly, that is prior to Spell-Out, so once (and only when) all strong features are eliminated from the derivation, which presumably represents a single time step over a single numeration, the derivation undergoes a single Spell-Out operation, and is in this sense static. In contrast, Chomsky's (2000) Phase Theory (refined and developed further in Chomsky 2001, 2004, 2008) is a typical example of a dynamic approach. Spell-Out applies iteratively, at each relevant chunk in the course of the derivation.[5] Here formal features are eliminated from the derivation by valuation through the long-distance Agree relation (by c-command), successively, as the probes that carry an uninterpretable feature are merged into the structure and find an appropriate goal with a matching interpretable feature to agree. Whether the dichotomy can be further abstracted in terms of Move versus Agree (leaving Attract-style approaches aside) will not be further discussed here, though the implementation suggested below, based on my own work on the topic (Grohmann 2003), would cast doubt on such an attempt. In essence, I will suggest a Move-driven approach to C_{HL}, more or less within standard Checking Theory, that nevertheless allows a dynamic interface interpretation. Therefore, I will only make reference to Agree and Phase Theory in passing.

While much more can (and probably should) be said about the mechanics, this must suffice as a review summary of relatively standard assumptions of the MP architecture. In the following, I will be largely concerned with fleshing out some of these mechanics under a slightly different perspective which I will clarify as we go along.

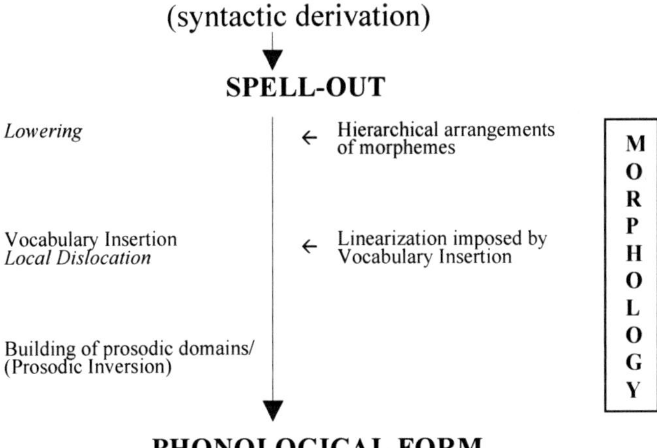

Figure 13.2 The PF-branch of the derivation (adapted from Embick and Noyer 2001: 566).

First, however, I want to briefly introduce another potential ingredient of the post-syntactic processes involved in C_{HL}. Within the framework of Distributed Morphology (Halle and Marantz 1993 and much subsequent work), Embick and Noyer (2001) explore a complex PF-branch which incorporates, or rather replaces, traditional morphology. PF-operations are ordered with respect to each other. Their architectural proposal of the resulting PF-branch is reproduced in Figure 13.2.

This kind of research explicitly explores a complex PF-branch, and I want to motivate a similar view to be taken from a minimalist syntactician's perspective (quite independently from assumptions specific to Distributed Morphology, however – that is, what follows should be implementable even without assuming that particular framework).

In general terms, the ideas pursued here follow recent 'dynamic' approaches to the computation (see also the acknowledgement note for further references and section 3.1 for more details). Relevant works of dynamic explorations include Epstein and Seely (2006) and previous work, where each application of Merge creates an interface object, Uriagereka (1999), where left branches form Spell-Out domains, and Chomsky (2000), where the Spell-Out domains are phases, which are identified (at least on the clausal level) as *v*P and CP (see also Chomsky 2001, 2004, 2005, 2008, and a host of other current research). As an additional recent dynamic approach to the computational system, I proposed that the syntactic part of the computation feeds the interface components cyclically through chunks of Prolific Domains and that consequently, some PF-like effects can be detected prior to PF proper (Grohmann 2003). This is the approach adopted here, laid out in its basics in the remainder.

3. Dynamic interfaces: [Spell-Out] [Rules]

Chomsky (1993, 1995) originally introduced Spell-Out as that kind of operation in NS that allowed the elimination of the S-structure level of representation. It was assumed to take the final product of the overt syntactic derivation and send meaning-relevant information to LF and sound-relevant information to PF for interpretation. This section summarizes the fundamental concepts relating to Spell-Out and introduces some new trends.

3.1 The operation(s) Spell-Out

The following briefly summarizes the status of Spell-Out in Chomsky's (2000 *et seq.*) more *dynamic model* of Phase Theory.[6] It should be prefaced with the observation that much of the properties hold for all recent proposals, to some degree, after the original introduction of multiple Spell-Out by Uriagereka (1999), which itself picks up on ideas expressed first in Bresnan (1971, 1972), and coinage of the term 'dynamic' (Uriagereka 2002). This includes his own explorations of multiple Spell-Out (Uriagereka 1998, 2008, 2009), the modifications found in Phase Theory (Chomsky 2000, 2001, 2004, 2005, 2007, 2008), the Spell-Out-as-you-Merge approach (e.g., Epstein *et al.* 1998; Epstein and Seely 2002, 2006), the related single-output model of Groat and O'Neil (1996) and others, as well as my own take on spelling out Prolific Domains dynamically (Grohmann 2000, 2003, 2007b).

There are at least two major issues concerning the articulatory interface theme in MP or, more specifically, some version of dynamic, multiple Spell-Out and the organization of the grammar. On the one hand, it needs to be seen empirically whether the notion of multiple Spell-Out has a practical application, and what details of such an application would look like (though, of course, all proponents mentioned put forth empirical and theoretical arguments to support their individual routes). On the other hand, the terms and conditions relating to multiple Spell-Out have to be made concrete (ditto, but differences can be observed rather easily, some of which will be addressed in the following). I take one exciting aspect of linguistic minimalism (in the sense of Boeckx 2006) to be, then, that the study of linguistic interfaces opens new doors in the large hallway of the architecture of the grammar.

According to the (inverted) T-model of the grammar in Figure 13.1, NS feeds the interpretive interface levels LF and PF directly, without assuming additional levels of representation. The operation Spell-Out was originally introduced in Chomsky (1993) to apply at one point and hand the derivation over to the interface levels (at that time restricted to PF, with subsequent operations applying at LF). With the rise of the Multiple Spell-Out Hypothesis, however, the conception of this transfer became more 'dynamic' in a way. While Uriagereka (1999) suggested to apply Spell-Out to 'command paths' with the (simplified) effect of 'freezing' left branches of assembled tree structures, Chomsky (2000) picked up the idea and developed a notion of 'cyclic Spell-Out' (eventually leading to the possible elimination of LF, as in Chomsky 2004): Spell-Out applies in a cyclic manner over specific sub-parts of the derivation, which he called phases. Phases were identified on the clausal level as introduced by *v* and C, the so-called phase heads, on the basis of a number of properties (as discussed recently by Marušič (2009); see especially Boeckx and Grohmann (2007) and literature cited for a critical overview). Phases, then, are the relevant derivational sub-parts at which Spell-Out applies cyclically.

Since the focus of the present contribution falls on spelling out to PF, this aspect will be given emphasis here as opposed to LF-syntax interface concerns (see e.g. Munakata 2009; Ott 2009; Saleemi 2009; Zeijlstra 2009, as well as references cited there).[7] More recently, Chomsky (2004) employs the 'super-operation' Transfer (Lasnik and Uriagereka with Boeckx 2005: 240), which sends the relevant information (interpretable features) to the interpretive interfaces (LF and PF). Spell-Out, under this view, is the sub-operation 'Transfer to PF' (as opposed to the alternative, 'Transfer to LF'[8]). And it is this sense that leads to the articulatory issues discussed here.

Following standard assumptions, when a phase is completed, the structure is sent simultaneously to the two interfaces where it gets interpreted. But Marušič (2005, 2009), for example, points out that certain syntactic constituents do not have phasal properties at both interfaces. This suggests that Transfer sometimes occurs to a single interface, that is, to PF but not simultaneously to LF, or vice versa – note the conceptual resemblance to Zeijlstra's (2009: 83) suggestion: 'Being a perfect solution to one interface condition may imply that another interface condition cannot be maximally solved, and vice versa'. Marušič provides a host of relevant data zooming in on both PF- and LF-relevant aspects and finds strong evidence in favor of this *non-simultaneous Spell-Out* at both the clausal and the nominal level, that is within DP.[9] He further argues that non-simultaneous Spell-Out helps deriving reconstruction effects and covert movement, two cases where place of interpretation differs from the place of pronunciation.

However, in 'standard' Phase Theory (Chomsky 2001 *et seq.*), Spell-Out (Transfer to PF) applies at the phase level on a par with Transfer to LF. The phase is thus argued to be an indispensable property of any well-designed language system that conforms to the Strong Minimalist Thesis (SMT), that language is the 'perfect' solution to the task of relating sound and meaning (Chomsky 2000 *et seq.*).[10] In essence, phases are the *only* relevant units for the mapping from NS to the external systems, the C-I system fed by LF and the SM system fed by PF. This process supposedly allows for optimal computational efficiency (though this is another term that is frequently used but rarely defined, hence difficult to assess at this point beyond conceptual rhetoric), eliminating redundant internal levels and compositional cycles in favor of the generation of a single cycle with periodic transfer to the interfaces. The units sent to Spell-Out are syntactically defined over uninterpretable features, which need to be eliminated and whose cyclic valuation ensures Full Interpretation at the interfaces.

The assumption that Spell-Out is similar to other operations in that it may apply several times in a single derivation (for book-length treatments, see Uriagereka 2002, 2008, 2009) gives rise to a multiple Spell-Out model – and what makes these 'several times' of application appropriate is somehow encoded in the dynamics of the syntactic computation. This can be illustrated as in Figure 13.3, where LF and PF are assembled cyclically in some fashion (via the purported 'mini-interface components' *lf* and *pf*; cf. Boeckx 2008) – leaving out details at this point in the introduction as to how exactly the dynamics of the system is computed. Within Phase Theory, it is the phase itself that gives rise to a dynamic computation. More specifically, it is tied to the point at which a phase head is merged into the derivation and ranges over its domain – the phase head's complement up to and excluding the next lower phase head and structures c-commanded by it, but including its edge (see below for more and subsequent sections for a reformulation in an alternative to strictly phase-based approaches).

Under such an approach, Spell-Out applies several times in the course of the derivation – and the question is to find out which units are the relevant sub-parts of the derivation at which Spell-Out applies. Chomsky's (2000 *et seq.*) answer is that phases are instrumental in that they induce spelling out of the phase head's complement, followed by freezing their contents for subsequent syntactic derivational steps; potential alternatives were briefly mentioned at the outset of this section, with one (my own) taken further throughout the remainder.

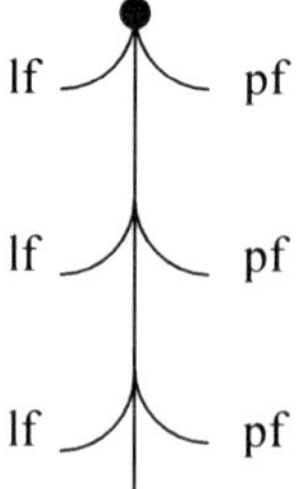

Figure 13.3 Cyclic assembly of LF and PF (Boeckx 2008: 45).

As roughly portrayed in Figure 13.3, cyclic Spell-Out allows for the dynamic linearization of syntactic structures, where each phase forms a separate linearization domain. If linearization algorithms operate on syntactic information (a reasonable but not undisputed assumption) – such as c-command relations, as under Kayne's (1994) Linear Correspondence Axiom (LCA) – dynamic linearization is not just a possibility but in fact a necessity in a phase-based system. This is because such information is lost in the course of cyclic computation, which, in accordance with the SMT, leads to minimization of computational complexity, at least by hypothesis, via a reduction in memory load (though the same point made above with respect to 'optimal computational efficiency' applies here as well). This property of a phase-based computation yields the strict cyclicity effects captured under the Phase Impenetrability Condition (PIC). The PIC originally proposed in Chomsky (2000) has received some modification, specifically in Chomsky (2001), on the basis of work by Nissenbaum (2000). The current installment of the PIC is defined as follows (Chomsky 2004: 108):

(6) Phase Impenetrability Condition: At the phase ZP containing phase HP, the domain
     of H is not accessible to operations, but only the edge of HP.

For Chomsky, then, the PIC is an inevitable consequence of any 'meaningful' system of cyclic computation. In his words, '[the phonological component] is greatly simplified if it can "forget about" what has been transferred to it at earlier phases; otherwise, the advantages of cyclic computation are lost' (Chomsky 2004: 107). Most research inspired by Chomsky in this area tends to be done by syntacticians, and thus focus on (syntacticians' conceptions of) the mapping from syntax to PF. But of course, a phonologist's perspective might be equally revealing, if not more (or at least, differently).[11]

3.2 Developments of clausal phrase structure

To illustrate the relevance of the particular dynamic implementation I sketched in previous work (see e.g. Grohmann 2003 and the summary in section 3.3 below), consider the development of clause structure over the past five decades. In and up to what has become known as (Revised) (Extended) Standard Theory (Chomsky 1965 and much work from the early 1960s to the mid-1970s), the assumed structure of the clause was roughly as in (7),

(7) $[_{S'}$ Comp $[_S$ NP (Aux/Infl) VP]]

and was later replaced in the *Barriers*-framework (Chomsky 1986) by (8):

(8) $[_{CP}$ XP C^0 $[_{IP}$ XP I^0 $[_{VP}$ (XP) V^0 ...]]]

In late GB (Chomsky (1991), especially thanks to insightful ideas put forth by Larson (1988), Pollock (1989), Belletti (1990) and many others), but also early

MP (Chomsky 1993), with X'-Theory well in place for the representation of phrase structure, functional projections gained importance (for a number of reasons, such as integrating functional material into checking configurations and thus creating the necessary Spec-Head relations). More can be said on the development and the particular proposals put forward in this period, but some consensus can be found on a clause structure like (9):

(9) $[_{CP}$ XP C^0 $[_{AgrSP}$ XP $AgrS^0$ $[_{TP}$ XP T^0 $[_{AgrOP}$ XP $AgrO^0$ $[_{vP}$ XP v^0 ... VP $]]]]]$

Here VP has been enlarged to incorporate the predicate-internal subject hypothesis through the (functional) light verb, and dedicated positions now offer room for arguments moved out of their base-generated thematic position for Case or agreement checking, for example.

At this point, mapping clause (and nominal) structure became a serious undertaking: Evidence was sought from adverbial positions, morpheme compatibility and hierarchies (Cinque (1999) and research inspired by it), verb movement, word order and reordering, and so forth. Additional work aimed at mapping out the left periphery of the clause, splitting CP into independent functional projections (Rizzi 1997 and many others).

Extending the structure in (9) considerably leads to a large array of functional projections that seems to blur the original intuition behind clause structure. I take this to be (informally) that sentences consist of a subject and a predicate, that the predicate maps thematic relations and the subject enters into close relation with the finite verb, and that this kernel sentence may be embedded under a complementizer and/ or a left-peripheral projection (hosting a moved *wh*-element or the first constituent in a V2 structure, for example). In other words, what the proliferation of functional projections hides is an intuitive tripartition of the clause – that even an extended cartography of clause structure builds on (by extending) a clear GB-result: Clauses consist of a thematic domain which is embedded under an agreement layer which, in turn, is dominated by a left periphery. This can be captured as follows (where the identification of functional projections is purely indicative):

(10)   (a) CP ≈ ForceP > TopP* > FocP > (TopP* >) FinP
      (b) IP ≈ AgrSP > TP > NegP > AgrIOP > AgrDOP > AspP
      (c) VP ≈ vP > VP (or any other implementation of VP-shells)

Most recent work in MP 'returns to basics' in the sense that C, T and v are the sole heads projecting in the clause, but it allows some flexibility on the *Barriers*-style structure – through multiple specifiers, for example, or the (re-)introduction of derivationally relevant bounding nodes of some sort (see Boeckx and Grohmann 2007 on the 're'). The phase-based framework of Chomsky (2000, 2001) assumes two strong phase heads, v and C, and the dynamics of the system derives from the interaction of these phases, the derivational computation, and the operation Spell-Out (extended in Chomsky 2004, 2005, 2007, 2008). In its most basic form, the clause structure in current MP can be represented as below (with the Kleene-star indicating potential reiteration, possibly in the form of multiple specifiers), in concordance with the structures provided above:

(11) $[_{CP}$ XP* C^0 $[_{TP}$ XP* T^0 $[_{vP}$ XP* v^0 $[_{VP}$ XP* V^0 ... $]\,]\,]\,]$
      PHASE   *PHASE*

The larger issue that arises is how to 'package' clause-structural information. Leaving aside the question of how many projections there are (in a radical way, cartography, and at the other end of the spectrum, just the bare bones in (11)[12]), could the case be made that the clausal projections relate in any meaningful way to one another, beyond extended projections in the sense of Grimshaw (1991)? Is it perhaps the case that certain projections in the clause relate to specific interpretive properties, such as information structure (topic/focus and the like)? Or is the head–phase relationship, as for C and *v* in (11), for example, the only imaginable connection between syntactic structure and computational processes? I will address this question next by suggesting that there is indeed a correlation between projections and computation, but that these relations go beyond the ones just mentioned – meaning also that the partition to be made between prominent projections must be along slightly different lines. For this purpose, I will suggest a tripartite clausal structure similar in spirit to the *Barriers*-style representation of the clause but incorporating subsequent insights from functional structure.

3.3 Anti-locality and prolific domains

With Chomsky (1995), there is one clear desideratum of a minimalist theory: the structure of the grammar is determined by (virtual) conceptual necessity. As a consequence, much of the complex and at times cumbersome GB-machinery should be reconsidered (as argued by Hornstein 2001). Regarding the ungrammaticality of expressions like (12a–c) below, we should thus be motivated to explore an alternative explanation (as discussed at length in Grohmann 2000, 2003[13]) – one that does not evoke filters of sorts or other GB-specific constructs (such as Affect Criteria which have been evoked to force a particular structural representation between a particularly marked XP and a correspondingly marked X^0). The key term to bear in mind is bare output conditions, that is the conjecture that only such conditions should be integrated into a minimalist grammar that have a direct impact on the (LF or PF) output (if they are not virtually conceptually necessary, such as the operation Merge).

(12) (a) * John likes.
     (b) * Him softly kissed her.
     (c) * What, Mary detests?

Under the copy theory of movement (Chomsky 1995; Nunes 1995), and ignoring GB-driven or other alternative explanations of the ungrammaticalities in (12), take

(13) to represent sample, appropriate structures at the relevant points ('appropriate' in the sense of technically conceivable, for example prior to interface evaluation):

(13)   (a)   # $[_{vP}$ John v^0 $[_{VP}$ likes-V^0 ~~John~~]]
     (b)   # $[_{TP}$ him T^0 $[_{AgrOP}$ ~~him~~ AgrO^0 $[_{vP}$ softly $[_{vP}$ ~~him~~ v^0 $[_{VP}$ kissed-V^0 her]]]]]
     (c)   # $[_{TopP}$ what Top^0 $[_{FocP}$ ~~what~~ Foc^0 $[_{TP}$ Mary T^0 detests ... ~~what~~]]]

The hash marks indicate derivational ill-formedness, that is signal that there is nothing wrong with the syntactic derivation sketched as such (hence no 'ungrammaticality star'), but rather that the illicitness arises at the interpretive part of the computation. Given the above introductory remarks to such data, the minimalist would then like to know why these derivations should be ruled out under MP (and non-GB) considerations.

The starting point for a purely syntactic explanation of said ungrammaticalities, from Grohmann (2003: 26), is the Anti-Locality Hypothesis:

(14)   *Anti-Locality Hypothesis*
     Movement must not be too local.

In order for this hypothesis to be interesting in any meaningful way, the evaluation metric needs to be defined within which too-local movement can be computed. Several approaches to anti-locality in grammar have been made over the past two decades (for a comprehensive overview, see Grohmann (2011)), such as excluding phrase-internal movement dependencies, but it can be argued that the relevant domain α needs to be extended further:

(15) $[_{ZP|\alpha|}$ XP $Z^0_{|\alpha|}$ ... $[_{YP|\alpha|}$ ~~XP~~ ...]]

What (15) says, as a first implementation of the Anti-Locality Hypothesis in (14), is that within some domain α, that is, phrase-structural positions that all share the same 'contextual index' $|\alpha|$ and can thus be grouped beyond a single projection, (movement) dependencies may not be formed. To handle the relevant contextual information, the notion of a Prolific Domain will be introduced, where each such Prolific Domain stands for a relevant $|\alpha|$ in (15):

(16)   *Prolific Domain* (adapted from Grohmann 2003: 75)
     A Prolific Domain is a contextually defined part of the computational system:
     (a)   which provides the interfaces with the information relevant to the context; and
     (b)   which consists of internal structure, interacting with derivational operations.

A natural implementation of contextual information would then be a clausal tripartition into three Prolific Domains: a thematic, an agreement, and a discourse domain – see also Platzack (2001) for related ideas and much current work building on this intuition, alluded to above; in addition, Ernst (2002) assumes adverbial expressions to adjoin to one of three parts of the clause, which he identifies roughly as *v*P, TP, and CP, as comes out in (17) as well.

(17) *Clausal Tripartition* (adapted from Grohmann 2003: 74)
  (a) Θ-Domain: part of the derivation where thematic relations are created.
  (b) Φ-Domain: part of the derivation where agreement properties are licensed.
  (c) Ω-Domain: part of the derivation where discourse information is established.

This understanding of clause structure is very similar to the tripartition offered in (10) above, itself expanding (8). In fact, it is one possible consequence of making sense out of the proliferation of functional projections in the clause on one hand (and, by analogy, in the nominal layer, as explored in Grohmann and Haegeman (2003); see Abney (1987), Bernstein (2001) and references cited there on the 'Clausal DP-Hypothesis'), and the fundamental intuition underlying any 'representation' of clause structure. Thus, the Θ-Domain would correspond to *v*P, the Φ-Domain to TP, and the Ω-Domain to CP. In addition, it would allow a dynamic approach to the computation *vis-à-vis* multiple Spell-Out (Uriagereka 1999) – with the concrete proposal, put forth in Grohmann (2000, 2003), that each Prolific Domain forms a part of the derivation to which the operation Spell-Out applies, shipping information to the PF- and LF-interface components (in spirit very similar to phases of Chomsky (2000) *et seq.*).

To foster such a (potential) dynamic implementation, I proposed the Condition on Domain Exclusivity (CDE), whose current formulation is given below (Grohmann 2003: 78):

(18) *Condition on Domain Exclusivity (CDE)*
  An object O in a phrase marker must have an exclusive Address Identification AI per Prolific Domain $\Pi\Delta$, unless duplicity yields a drastic effect on the output:
  (a) An AI of O in a given $\Pi\Delta$ is an occurrence of O in that $\Pi\Delta$ at LF.
  (b) A drastic effect on the output is a different realization of O at PF.

Further details and issues aside, an interesting prediction of the CDE as formulated here is the following: If a too-local, or anti-local, dependency involves two different PF-matrices, the dependency should be well formed.[14] In other words, if we understand the CDE as a PF-condition (as explicitly done in the definition), we get the following 'informal filter', where Copy Spell-Out refers to rendering a lower copy PF-distinct from a higher one (in the sense of (18b)):

(19) *CDE @ PF*
  *$[_{\Pi\Delta}$ XP … ~~XP~~], unless Copy Spell-Out applies to ~~XP~~.

However, the shorthand illustration in (19) does not make explicit reference to the 'different realization' of Copy Spell-Out, which means that Copy Spell-Out should be defined separately. (20) is a first informal approximation (from Grohmann 2011), whose parenthetical specification will be briefly returned to in section 4:

(20) *Copy Spell-Out*
In a given Prolific Domain ΠΔ, spell out the lower of two copies of some object O through the insertion of a (minimal feature-matching) grammatical formative.

A paradigmatic example supporting this prediction is so-called contrastive left dislocation (CLD) found in West Germanic varieties (illustrated with German):

(21) (a) [Seinen$_i$ Vater], den   mag jeder$_i$ Junge.
           his.ACC father RP.ACC likes every boy
           'His father, every boy likes.'
      (b) [$_{CP}$ seinen Vater C^0 [$_{TopP}$ den mag-Top^0 [$_{TP}$ jeder Junge T^0 ...]]]

Under a reasonable analysis (see work beginning, in some sense, with Vat 1981), the CLDed XP *seinen Vater* 'his father' and the resuming demonstrative *den* 'him' are in the same Prolific Domain (Ω-Domain). Moreover, (21) allows a bound-variable reading and aside from such absence of Weak Crossover effects, CLD displays other signs of reconstruction of the CLDed phrase (e.g., presence of Condition A effects, absence of Condition C effects, idiom chunks, etc., as discussed in Grohmann 2000, 2003). (As a matter of fact, so does the provided translation for English, as topicalization, in opposition to a resumptive strategy, such as *His father, every boy likes him.*) By the CDE, this difference can be understood as the result of Copy Spell-Out, represented by '➲' introducing the grammatical formative inserted, in CLD, an operation that changes the phonological form or phonetic shape (what I call the 'PF-matrix') of the lower of the two copies that are in the same Prolific Domain; this is the 'drastic effect' of (18), for which simple deletion as usual is arguably not enough, an issue yet to be addressed in more detail. The relevant part of the derivation is thus as follows:

(22) [$_{CP}$ seinen Vater C^0 [$_{TopP}$ ~~seinen V.~~ ➲ den mag-Top^0 [$_{TP}$ jeder Junge T^0...]]]

The discussions in previous and concurrent (partially co-authored) work cover a wider range of cases in support of a Copy Spell-Out analysis for a growing number of phenomena across languages, including local reflexives and reciprocals in double object constructions, ECM-structures, clitic left dislocation (all Grohmann 2003), and applications to small clauses (Grohmann 2001), prenominal possessive doubling (Grohmann 2003; Grohmann and Haegeman 2003), *shm*-reduplicated pejorative structures (Grohmann and Nevins 2005), or demonstrative doubling (Grohmann and Panagiotidis forthcoming).[15] All this might be barking up the wrong tree, but I still take it as a potentially interesting alternative to other analyses that may come to mind – predominantly because the Copy Spell-Out analysis captures a multitude of phenomena and subsumes them under one property of the grammar.

There are other properties of the model laid out in Grohmann (2003) which I will not discuss any further in this paper. For example, this approach structures the constitution of the clause quite differently from other models: (a) cyclic, multiple Spell-Out applies *at* a given sub-structure, not *after* (as in the phase-based framework; for discussion, see Boeckx and Grohmann (2007)); (b) proliferation of (functional) projections is compatible with the framework, but successive movement through them is not (such as subjects moving through [Spec,TP] to [Spec,AgrSP], for example, as argued for some languages by Bobaljik and Thráinsson 1998); (c) a 'Bare X'-Phrase Structure Theory' could be envisioned (such as that based on the notion of 'natural relations' put forth in Grohmann (2003)).

It is also clear that phonological material is inserted after the syntax (in line with a late insertion view): the PF-matrix determines the phonetic shape of syntactic material – as well as syntactically present but phonetically null material. It is this aspect that I want to zoom in on in the remainder of my contribution, although, anticipating the discussion somewhat, the very relevant 64,000 dollar question can unfortunately not be addressed here exhaustively:[16] Which language makes available which grammatical formative in which structures?[17]

At this point, the Spell-Out-per-Prolific-Domain approach faces a serious architectural question: What is spelled out when? The larger question is, of course, what exactly the operation Spell-Out itself is. In other words, in order to deal with the architectural issue, we should ask: (a) when Spell-Out applies; (b) what it does exactly; and (c) where, or to which kinds of structure exactly, it applies?

In current multiple Spell-Out models, the cyclic sub-part of the derivation that is sent to Spell-Out and subsequently to PF – be it every command unit, that is left branch (Uriagereka (1999) or the complement of a strong phase head (Chomsky 2001) – is frozen and hence not accessible for further computation. This is clearly not wanted for Prolific Domains that are vacated *after* Spell-Out in the model sketched above (and more detailed, in Grohmann 2003). The way the analysis is presented from (and explicitly understood in Grohmann 2003), Copy-Spell-Out is assumed to apply once a Prolific Domain is formed and sent to Spell-Out, but without freezing the material contained in that Prolific Domain. For example, if local reflexives are the result of Copy Spell-Out in the Θ-Domain (see also Hornstein (2001) for a new variation on this old theme whose precursors can be found in Lees and Klima (1963) as well as the more recent proposals by Lidz and Idsardi (1998) or Kayne (2002), among others), as picked up again in section 4 below, the newly created reflexive should still be able to vacate the Θ-Domain, such as in topicalization structures, for example:

(23) (a) [$_{TP}$ John T^0 [$_{vP}$ [$_{vP}$ ~~John~~ *v*^{0} [$_{VP}$ likes ~~John~~ ➲ himself]] very much]]
    (b) Himself, John likes very much.

More generally, the same goes for *any* material that is moved from one Prolific Domain to the next – any such movement step takes place *after* the Prolific Domain of origin is formed but before the next higher Prolific Domain is formed or complete (as the movement of *John* from [Spec,*v*P] to [Spec,TP] above). It looks as if some refinement of the operation Spell-Out is needed, or more specifically, of the fate of a Prolific Domain once it is formed – with respect to the further syntactic derivation on one, and the feeding of the interfaces (in particular, PF) on the other hand.

3.4   Spell-Out, transfer and the architecture of the grammar

I would thus like to suggest the beginnings of a solution to Prolific Domains 'spelling out' based on a commentary to Chomsky (2001) by Juan Uriagereka (2000: 7–8):

> Another important technical paragraph states how Spell-Out removes LF material which is uninterpretable and transfers the relevant object (WITH the uninterpretable stuff) to the phonological component. Fn. 8 of [Chomsky (1999)] discusses the technical reason pointed out in MI of why this sort of system is necessary (overt syntax eliminates uninterpretable features, but they still have to have an effect on PF, thus the distinction in the Minimalist Program between 'deletion' and 'erasure'). Technically this is somewhat curious, I think, in that you need two representations of the relevant object K: one which is sent intact to PF, and one which is sent to LF without uninterpretable stuff.

Chomsky (1999, 2001) introduces the notion of Transfer as a technical term for an operation that could be construed to be different from Spell-Out. In fact, in later work he clarifies the notion somewhat (Chomsky 2004, 2008) in that he is 'assuming one operation, Transfer, which sends material at the phase level to both interfaces. Transfer to the sensori-motor interface (some version of PF, maybe) is what is called 'Spell-Out' (Noam Chomsky, p.c.). In other words, Transfer is taken to be the super-case of Spell-Out, which is understood then as 'Transfer to PF' (as opposed to 'Transfer to LF' aka 'Interpret'; see also Lasnik and Uriagereka with Boeckx (2005: 240f.) for discussion). However, rather than working with the refined understanding of the latter, I suggest to dissociate Transfer from Spell-Out.

Under one view (as entertained by Grohmann and Putnam (2004), extending allusions in Grohmann (2003)), each Prolific Domain directly feeds the complex PF-branch. This could be interpreted similar in spirit to Zubizarreta (1998), but

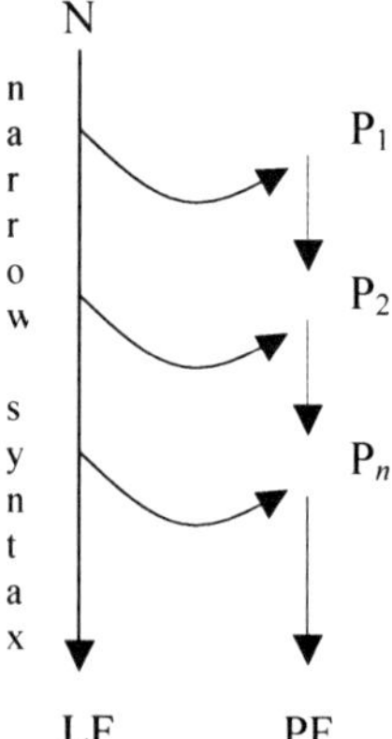

Figure 13.4 A first architecture of the grammar (from Grohmann and Putnam 2004).

it would also introduce a new level of representation, a P(rosodic)-component as shown in Figure 13.4.

We suggested Figure 13.4 as a revised architecture of the grammar (compare this with the models in Figs 1 to 3 above), where each Prolific Domain spells out to the P-component, with the P-component building up until the final piece is reached before being sent off to PF 'proper'; in other words, Prolific Domains are taken to be the relevant chunks for prosodic manipulation which are then somehow bundled to derive a final, single PF-structure of the linguistic expression. Non-prosodic phonological manipulation would presumably apply to that single PF (see Grohmann 2003: 296–301 for original discussion).

However, Figure 13.4 leaves further questions unanswered, such as the nature and justification of such an additional (interface?) interpretive component. Instead, I propose the derivational procedure, as shown in Figure 13.5, towards an improved architecture of the grammar.

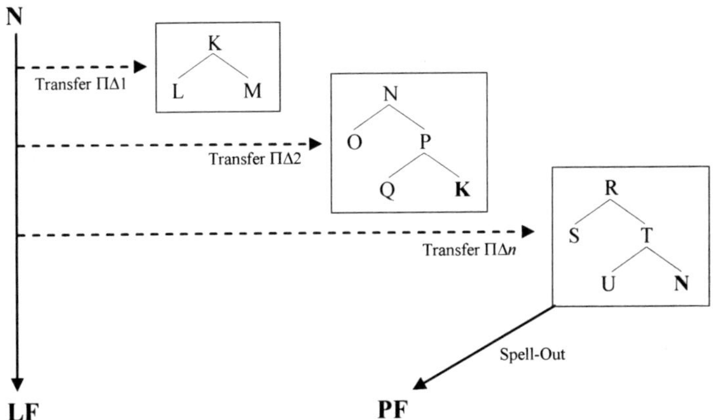

Figure 13.5 A revised architecture of the grammar (Grohmann 2007b: 189).

The labels of the syntactic objects, K, N and R in Figure 13.5, would correspond to Uriagereka's (2000: 8) remark that what is needed are 'two representations of the relevant object K: one which is sent intact to PF, and one which is sent to LF without uninterpretable stuff' (see the quote above). Indeed, K, N and R are the syntactic objects assembled in narrow syntax, each a Prolific Domain in present terminology (namely, the Q-, F- and W-Domain or the relevant CP, TP, *v*P). It is these objects that the operation Transfer applies to. Transferred N is stacked on top of K, R on N, and so on, and the resulting PF-object corresponds one-to-one to the one derived in narrow syntax. Note that the boldfaced symbols are shorthand notations corresponding to the previous 'box' (K = [$_K$ L M] and N = [$_N$ O [$_P$ Q [$_K$ L M]]]); that is to say, what is spelled out at the end is the entire phrase-marker from R to M. So, Spell-Out indeed applies only once per derivation, but Transfer is applied successively or cyclically.

I propose to dissociate the operation Transfer from the operation Spell-Out in the sense that Transfer takes a sub-part of the derivation and ships it to PF *cyclically* (where operations like building prosodic domains apply; cf. Figure 13.2 above, for example, or Grohmann and Putnam (2007)), whereas Spell-Out feeds the sensorimotor system once the PF-branch is complete, *uniquely* (i.e. once the derivation has assembled all Prolific Domains). The metric for evaluating the relevant cycle is the establishment of Prolific Domains: each Prolific Domain triggers Transfer. This proposal can be captured somewhat informally as follows:

(24)   *Transfer*
Transfer cyclically sends the structure of each Prolific Domain to PF.

(25)   *Spell-Out*
Spell-Out phonetically interprets the final PF output once.

Understood this way, (24) implies that 'transferring' a syntactic object does not eliminate it from (or make it inaccessible for) subsequent computation, as assumed in Phase Theory (Chomsky 2000 *et seq.*); by (25), PF is built up derivationally without, however, constructing an additional level of representation, as in Zubizaretta's (1998) framework, for example.

Once this idea is properly worked out, the interfacing of syntax and phonology will have to receive more attention in one aspect in particular. Beyond Embick and Noyer's (2001) ordered PF-operations, such as lowering before vocabulary insertion (as in Figure 13.2; see also Ackema and Neeleman 2004), an additional set of PF rules must be accommodated that regulates what happens to copies of syntactic objects generated in the course of the derivation – what I call Copy Modification, to be introduced presently.

Let me first add an enrichment of this idea encouraged by an anonymous reviewer's comment of the revised and reprinted version of Grohmann (2007b) that 'such a proposal actually rules out a kind of theory in which PF phenomena (phonological interactions, movement, allomorphy, etc.) are constrained by cyclic domain structure' (and supported further by the anonymous reviewer of this chapter). The answer really depends on what the 'mixed bag' called PF really is. The same reviewer also remarks that PF 'could refer (i) to a sequence of computations that "package" the output of syntax for the sensorimotor system; or (ii) to some particular late stage of this, relevant for phonological matters. Different works in the literature assume (i) versus (ii), sometimes both, leading mostly to confusion' – I could not agree more, especially with the confusion caused by unclear terminology. In fact, as I repeatedly remarked in oral presentations over the past few years (e.g., Grohmann 2009c), I concluded that, if we were honest about what we are doing, we ought to realize that much of what commonly counts as 'core syntax' is really 'PF-syntax' and, in this sense, should apply the same rigor to the phenomena at hand and architectural implications as linguists did especially in the 1980s when investigating the syntax-semantics interface. Note that what I refer to here as 'PF-syntax' might even receive the more radical description 'morphophonology' (Boeckx 2009) in the sense that this is the aspect of language where variation proper is found and that (in this sense again, quoting from Boeckx's handout), 'syntax is (featural) substance-free' and that subsequently 'there are no syntactic/structural parameters' (all linguistic variation is delegated to PF). So, rather than talking about a syntax-phonology interface, we should be looking into an articulated PF, which may ultimately differ from LF in revealing ways, and take PF-syntax as the real issue behind the interplay of syntactic derivations, phonological modifications and phonetic output. For one suggestion on the role of phonology in linguistic theorizing and coming to grips with the architecture of the grammar, with clear implications for what is often called *the* computational system of human language, see Scheer (forthcoming). It may well turn out to be the case that phonology is fundamentally different from syntax (by ways of lacking recursion, for example) in that it works on its own computational system, which raises the question what its input is – and whether it should really be 'PF'. Admittedly, at this stage this is mere stipulation, but there seems to be growing consent that syntax should be conceived of somewhat differently.

A final note to close this section. As far as I am aware, there is no consensus on – or even clear picture of – what PF looks like exactly. Bresnan (1971) argued against the EST-view (see also Adger 2007), but what kind of and/or how much structure is at PF or does PF have? It might be enough to just have some very rough phrase-marker (such as 'K "with stuff"', 'N "with stuff"', and 'R "with stuff"' from Figure 13.5) whose edges are then significant for prosodic operations (as investigated within the present model in Grohmann and Putnam (2007), for example). But just as likely, PF might contain a more precise phrase structure (where 'with stuff' for K, N and R would have to be replaced by the full phrase structure derived in the narrow syntax). This could be relevant if phrase structure and hierarchical relations play a vital role for ultimate linearization (as in Uriagereka (1999), Moro (2000) and Nunes (2004), for example, all based in more or less direct dependency on the seminal proposal of Kayne (1994) via the LCA). In other words, it is not at all clear at this point whether PF consists of little, bare structure or whether it contains a full-fledged phrase marker. Either outcome can easily be accommodated in the model sketched here. But for future investigations of syntax-phonology interactions, this question is not without charm.

4.   Copy modification: [Spell-Out rules]

In the course of the derivation, 'all NS does is to create new objects out of pre-existing morpho-lexical units' (Piattelli-Palmarini and Uriagereka 2004: 355). Does this now mean that all 'interesting' phenomena in language should be analyzed via the interfaces? Consider pronounced or spelled out copies as a case study; call this Copy Modification. As it turns out, there are several conditions under which syntactic copies are not deleted as expected, where 'expected' means that in general, movement is followed by deletion, as in the original MP definition of Move as the composite operation made up of Copy, Merge, (Form Chain) and Delete (see e.g. Chomsky (1993) and Nunes (1995) for extensive discussion) – the operation Copy-Spell-Out introduced here being only one of those.

For example, as suggested above, Copy-Spell-Out may apply to two copies within the same Prolific Domains. As such, it is a more specific operation that must be ordered before the 'default operation' Delete applies, that is regular deletion of non-top copies. As it turns out, other special applications of what is to be dubbed Copy Modification can be found as well across languages, such as pronunciation of non-top copies. This section will consider a range of options for Copy Modification in more detail and suggest an interface-driven rule ranking.

Let us start initially with a re-assessment of copy deletion, picking up from the discussion in Grohmann and Nevins (2005). One might rightly pose the question at this point: What about the standard mechanism of non-pronunciation of chains? In other words, in the copy theory of movement (Chomsky 1995), lower copies are simply not pronounced – in Nunes' (2004) formulation of the copy theory, this crucially occurs in order to avoid a violation that would be caused by a consistency requirement on the output of the LCA (Kayne 1994), while Moro (2000), for example, argues that syntactic displacement (that is, movement) occurs in order to 'break symmetry' (hence, another interpretation in which movement occurs to ensure convergence at the interface-driven mapping from dominance to precedence). Non-pronunciation (of the lower copy) and Copy Spell-Out (in the form of phonological modification) would seem to be two distinct means, with a similar effect in terms of ensuring non-identity between distinct occurrences of the same object.

In order to express the subset-of-structural-description evaluation of Kiparsky's (1973) Elsewhere Condition in a more general way, Nevins (2004) reformulates the comparison of structural descriptions in terms of Boolean predicate conjunction. In Grohmann and Nevins (2005: 155), this adaptation was stated as follows:

(26)   *Predicate-based version of the Elsewhere Condition* (adopted from Nevins 2004: 62)
Given rules R1 and R2, R1 is disjunctively ordered before R2 if
(a) the set of conjoined Boolean predicates that form the structural description of R2 are a subset of the set of conjoined Boolean predicates that form the structural description of R1 and
(b) the structural changes of the two rules are either identical or incompatible.

(26) expresses the intuition of Panini's *Astadhyayi* (and so does the original formulation of the Elsewhere Condition in Kiparsky (1973: 94)): A more specific instance of a rule will block the application of a less specific rule – the 'elsewhere' case. In particular, the structural descriptions of the two rules may fall into an Elsewhere-relation. Copy Spell-Out and Lower-Copy Deletion may be viewed in this rubric as in (27), adapted from Grohmann and Nevins (2005: 155–6), as more and less specific instances of what we may call Copy Modification:

(27)   *Copy modification as an Elsewhere-Relation*
(a) Copy Spell-Out (PF-driven viz. the CDE)
Structural Description: Given copies C_1 and C_2, where C_1 LCA-precedes C_2, and C_1 and C_2 are in the same Prolific Domain.
Structural Change: Spellout-as-Modified C_2

(b) Lower-Copy Deletion (PF-driven viz. the LCA)
     Structural Description: Given copies C_1 and C_2, where C_1 LCA-precedes C_2.
     Structural Change: Delete C_2

These formulations make evident the fact that Copy Spell-Out and Lower-Copy Deletion are in an Elsewhere-relation. Thus the empirical hypothesis is that we only observe Copy Spell-Out in the restricted range of environments in which movement is very local (as determined by the CDE through the more specific rule (27a)), and not domain-crossing (where the usual LCA-regulations hold, as per (27b)). Such cases result in a phonological modification of the lower copy.

Note that the structural change of the Copy Spell-Out rule says 'Spellout-as-Modified' – as opposed to, say, 'Copy Spell-Out' (as per (20) above). In Grohmann and Nevins (2005), we did so since our topic of investigation was so-called *shm-*reduplication in English, which we identified of a pejorative construction in which two anti-local copies underwent a form of Copy Modification akin to, but not identical with, Copy Spell-Out. In our analysis, an application of (27a) results in an echo reduplicant in the case at hand, as shown in (28):

(28) (a) Money, shmoney, who needs that stuff anyway?
      (b) $[_{PejP}$ money Pej^0 $[_{TopP}$ ~~money~~ ⊃ shmoney Top^0 $[_{FocP}$ who ...]]]

As in contrastive left dislocation (see (21)–(22) above), we assume a left-peripheral element to move from a topic position to a higher specifier – in one case, the force-marking position [Spec,CP], and in the pejorative case, the dedicated [Spec,PejP]. There are two prominent differences between the two constructions, however: first, the anti-locally moving element comes from within the clause in one but is generated in topic position in the other, and second, Copy Spell-Out comes in the shape of the pejorative morpheme *shm–* and thereby modifies the lower copy (see that article for further details). Copy Spell-Out resulting in a grammatical formative of the sort found with resumptive pronouns, for example, may be more common; the range of repairs appears to be, at present, somewhat language-specific.

The much more general case is that movement will be from a position within the Θ-Domain to a position within the Φ-Domain, for example from [Spec,vP] to [Spec,TP] with canonical subjects, or from a position within the Φ-Domain to a position within the Ω-Domain, as in argument *wh*-movement from a Case-position. In other words, (27b) refers, of course, to movement conceived of as 'business as usual': Upon displacement, Lower-Copy Deletion applies as the result of movement (Chomsky 1993 *et seq.*), arguably for linearization (Kayne (1994) and much research since; see Nunes (2004) for a recent overview):

(29) (a) Which book has John read?
      (b) *Has John which book read?
      (c) *Has John read which book?

The assumed derivation for (29) is provided in (30).

(30)   [$_{CP}$ which book has [$_{TP}$ John T [$_{AGRo}$ ~~which book~~ AGR$_O$ [$_{vP}$ ~~John~~ v [$_{VP}$ read ~~which book~~]]]]]

Holding on to a Case-position within the Φ-Domain (here, for convenience, [Spec,AgrOP]), all lower copies are deleted: the Θ-occurrence of *which book* and *John*, respectively, and the Φ-occurrence of *which book* (the argumental Case-position). In (29b), the *wh*-phrase never made it beyond its Case-position and in (29c) it stays *in situ*; alternatively, it may have moved in both instances, but the wrong copies were deleted (see the discussion of (31) right below) – 'wrong' now understood as the relevant sub-case of Copy Modification.

At this point, however, one may wonder whether Copy Modification as conceived in (27) is enough to handle all displacement. As a matter of fact, a number of 'exceptions' to Lower-Copy Deletion other than Copy Spell-Out have been floating around in the literature, some even for quite some time. Next, I will very briefly present three such cases (possibly in decreasing degree of supportive strength), concentrating on a *possible* analytical capture of the data as suggested (please refer to the cited literature for details, discussion, and debate), after which I will suggest an enrichment of Copy Modification.

Take first the pronunciation of a non-top copy in multiple *wh*-fronting structures, where the two forms in question are homophonous but for checking-theoretic purposes both should have moved syntactically (Bobaljik 1995, 2002; Franks 1998; Pesetsky 1998, 2000; Nunes 2004; Bošković and Nunes 2007). (31) illustrates with Serbo-Croatian (from Bošković 2002):

(31)   (a)   * Šta   šta   uslovljava?
                 what   what   conditions
        (b)   Šta   uslovljava   šta?
                 what   conditions   what
                 'What conditions what?'
        (c)   Šta   neprestano   šta   uslovljava?
                 what   constantly   what   conditions
        (d)   *$^?$ Šta   neprestano   uslovljava   šta?
                 what   constantly   conditions   what
                 'What constantly conditions what?'

When the *wh*-expressions are not homophonous, they all move to [Spec,CP], but, as (31a) shows, this cannot happen here; rather, one *wh*-phrase stays *in situ* (31b). Putting an adverb in between the two expressions allows multiple fronting, as in (31c), and at the same time prohibits non-movement of one, as (31d) shows.

Driven by checking-theoretic concerns, one converging view in the literature holds that the second *wh*-phrase does not stay *in situ* but is simply pronounced there. In other words, all *wh*-phrases move syntactically to [Spec,CP], but at PF, one of these copies is deleted and the lowest copy is pronounced. Leaving intermediate details aside, (32) portrays the relevant state of affairs concerning the pronunciation of a non-top copy (Bošković 2002: 369).

(32)   [$_{CP}$ šta$_i$ ~~šta$_k$~~ ... [$_{vP}$ ~~šta$_i$~~ uslovljava šta$_k$]]

I do not have anything to say on the licensing condition of such 'Higher-Copy Deletion', which is quite distinct from a CDE-driven formulation in terms of Prolific Domains; on haplology effects in the syntax, see for example Neeleman and van de Koot (2006), Richards (2006), and van Riemsdijk (2008).

As a second case that falls under neither clause of Copy Modification as formulated in (27), take so-called *wh*-copying constructions, where a moved *wh*-phrase is pronounced in apparently intermediate position (McDaniel 1986). (33) illustrates this with German:

(33) (a) Wen   glaubt Hans, wen   Jakob   gesehen hat?
         whom   *thinks* *Hans* *whom*   *Jakob*   *seen*   *has*
     (b) *Wen   glaubt Hans, wen   Jakob wen   gesehen hat?
         whom *thinks* *Hans* *whom*   *Jakob* *whom* *seen*   *has*
     (c) Wen   glaubt Hans,   hat Jakob   gesehen?
         whom   *thinks* *Hans*   *has* *Jakob*   *seen*
     (d) Wen   glaubt Hans,   daß Jakob   gesehen hat?
         whom   *thinks* *Hans*   *that* *Jakob*   *seen*   *has*
         'Who(m) does Hans think (that) Jakob saw?'

The relevant case is, of course, (33a), where the fronted *wen* is pronounced twice, in the [Spec,CP]-position of the matrix and of the embedded clause (and in fact would also be pronounced in subsequent embedding). This does not mean, however, that all copies of the *wh*-expression are pronounced, as (33b) shows, spelling out the *in-situ* phrase. ((33c) and (33d) are alternatives, with the same meaning, in which only the matrix *wh*-phrase is spelled out.)

Again, leaving aside further issues (after McDaniel's dissertation, a host of research has discussed this and similar-looking constructions for a variety of languages, some collected in Lutz *et al.* (2000)). Taking my cue again from Nunes (2004), consider the derivation sketched below (also discussed more recently in Bošković and Nunes 2007):

(34) [$_{CP}$ wen$_i$ glaubt Hans [$_{CP}$ wen$_i$ Jakob ~~wen$_i$~~ gesehen hat]]

That is, if we assume that both lexicalizations of *wen* are spelled out instances of the same movement chain, *wh*-copying suggests neither Lower-Copy Deletion nor Copy Spell-Out as understood here, and it does not involve pronunciation of non-top copies either. Rather, it looks like all Ω-domain-related copies are spelled out.

Lastly, I would like to draw attention to the copy raising construction in English, where 'some constituent appears in a non-thematic position with its thematic position occupied by a pronominal copy' (Potsdam and Runner (2001: 453), originally discussed in Postal (1974) and Rogers (1974). Consider (35):

(35) (a) It seems like this book is popular among young kids.
     (b) This book seems like it is popular among young kids.
     (c) This book seems to be popular among young kids.

While *this book* may appear in the *like*-clause embedded under raising *seems* with expletive *it* (35a), it may also be the subject of the *seem*-clause – in which case the embedded subject is *non*-expletive *it*, anaphorically related to *this book* (35b). Example (35c) shows the regular subject-raising alternative for this structure.

Although Fujii (2007) hints at the possibility, he discards an analysis according to which non-expletive *it* appears as the Copy Spell-Out of *this book*, which I nevertheless would like to illustrate in (36) in accordance with other instances of Copy Spell-Out:

(36)   [this book [seems [like [~~this book~~ ➲ it is [popular among young kids]]]]]

If such an analysis could be upheld (and there has been ample discussion suggesting that it might not, as in the sources just cited), we would be dealing with an apparent instance of Copy Spell-Out in the absence of an anti-local dependency – again, an instance of Copy Modification that is not captured in any obvious way by (27).

As suggested originally, Copy Modification expresses two conditions in an Elsewhere-relation, the more specific rule Copy Spell-Out and the less specific Lower-Copy Deletion. The relevant copy that undergoes Copy Spell-Out would be the lower of two copies within one Prolific Domain, as a repair strategy for what would otherwise count as a violation of the CDE, which the grammar may make available by inserting a grammatical formative under certain conditions. But the three cases just discussed seem to indicate that this is not all. More importantly, we are now at a point where conflicting conditions seem to apply to displaced copies. I would like to bring these cases together under a slightly revised understanding of Copy Modification.

Nunes (2004) suggests the following procedure for movement dependencies (thereby eliminating the 'operation' Move of Chomsky 1993):[18]

(37)   *Copy Theory of Movement* (Nunes 2004: 89)
    (a) Copy
    (b) Merge
    (c) Form Chain
    (d) Chain Reduction

However, irrespective of the status of '(Form) Chain', Chain Reduction as the final step is not inclusive enough – it deletes (reduces) and does not seem to allow realizing more than one copy per '(non-trivial) chain' (i.e. movement dependency). In addition, the above cases are special instances of Chain Reduction understood as deletion of copies. Roughly put, we yield three ways of how to linearize and pronounce dependencies: Chain Reduction (or regular deletion of lower copies), Copy Spell-Out (for two copies within the same Prolific Domain), and special applications, where non-top copies are pronounced (e.g., multiple *wh*-fronting of adjacent homophones, *wh*-copying, or copy raising).

Can all these operations be unified? In the present interface-driven approach, I suggest that on top of Embick and Noyer's (2001) ordered PF-operations, an additional set must be accommodated that regulates Copy Modification. The informal rule (38a) follows if Copy Spell-Out is available in the grammar, (38b) does if exceptional cases as discussed above are permitted, and (38c) reflects the 'business as usual' aspect of Copy Theory. As things stand, the formulation does indeed seem to require ordered rules in a post-syntactic PF-component.

(38) *Copy Modification (qua ordered post-syntactic rules)*
    (a) If two copies are in an anti-local relationship:
        Spell out the lower copy if possible (or else: crash).
    (b) If deletion of the lower copy would violate a constraint of the grammar:
        Pronounce it (in variation).
    (c) If two copies span across different Prolific Domains, all things being equal:
        Delete the lower copy.

Note that the real advantage of (38) over (37) does not lie in the dropping of Form Chain – that concept may well be carried over if so desired. Rather, it is the introduction of ordered rules as a 'checking list' for PF-interpretation that captures more cases of non-regular copy deletion than existing approaches. Emphasis on these approaches was put here on the idea of anti-locality in grammar; an important task for the future would be a proper marriage with 'regular', upper-limit locality approaches and a unified account for all kinds of resumptive pronouns, not only those that occur as the Copy Spell-Out within an anti-local dependency. Such a theory could be built on Boeckx (2003), for example, as attempted in Grohmann and Boeckx (2004), though it is still not encompassing enough.

5. A non-granular conclusion

In the context of architectural concerns of the organization of the grammar and computational procedures (arguably, with a heavy bias towards MP), the above discussion contained a brief recap of my previous work concerning a tripartition of the clause structure into Prolific Domains and a dynamic exploitation of such a step. The original proposal was to send each Prolific Domain to (cyclically applicable) Spell-Out, an implementation that would then give rise to the modification of identical copies within the same Prolific Domain by way of a 'drastic effect': Copy Spell-Out.

Focusing on the timing and nature of Spell-Out, I modified this picture somewhat in the present contribution. Dissociating the operation Transfer from Spell-Out, I suggest that each Prolific Domain undergoes Transfer to a cyclically composed PF, and that Spell-Out then applies to the PF output. The final outcome is a single PF-interpretation (which gets Spelled Out to the sensorimotor system), just as various operations possibly applying in covert syntax yield a single LF-interpretation of a linguistic expression – but the architecture is slightly modified over and possibly improved upon existing models.

I envision future research in this area to properly define the operations Transfer and Spell-Out as well as fix other issues left open in the anti-locality framework (see Grohmann (2011) for a discussion of a larger range of approaches to anti-locality).

A particularly interesting avenue of research, I believe, would be a unified study of Copy Modification (see below, after a roundabout train of thought): the ways PF manipulates copies left behind by syntactic operations and the order in which such manipulation proceeds. Another obvious route to take is to see whether the cyclically assembled PF argued for here can be exploited for other domains of the grammar, such as the formation of prosodic domains.

First, let me pick up Hornstein's (2009: 7) assessment of the internal modularity of the GB-model: 'It is fair to say that GB is cognitively exceptional in that its principles and operations are cognitively *sui generis* and very specific to language.' He continues in fn. 14 on the same page:

> As Embick and Poeppel [(2006)] observe, this is a serious problem for those aiming to find brain correlates for the primitives of [H]FL. They dub this the granularity problem. They propose that one aim of linguistics and neuroscience should be to solve this problem by finding a level that can serve to relate the basic conceptions of each. Their concrete proposal is that an appropriate level of abstraction is the 'circuit'. Circuits are brain structures that compute simple operations. The aim is to find those primitive operations that are at once empirically grounded and that could be embodied in neural wet-ware. Given this, *the goal for the minimalist will be to find a class of very basic primitive operations that plausibly underlie linguistic computations for consideration as candidates for possible neural circuits.*   [my emphasis – KKG]

The 'granularity [mismatch] problem' can be informally summarized as follows:

> If we had an appropriately granular analysis of what, say, syntax or word recognition actually was, we could hypothesize that certain computational subroutines are in fact localized. This is what I have called in the past 'computational organology'.
> David Poeppel on the *Talking Brains* blog (http://talkingbrains.
> blogspot.com/2007/06/jealous-of-fusiform-i-am.html)

See Poeppel and Embick (2005) for more formal discussion, including an elaboration of this:

(39)   *The Granularity Mismatch Problem* (Poeppel and Embick 2005: 104–5)
       Linguistic and neuroscientific studies of language operate with objects of different granularity. In particular, linguistic computation involves a number of fine-grained distinctions and explicit computational operations. Neuroscientific approaches to language operate in terms of broader conceptual distinctions.

One aspect of Hornstein's discussion of the Granularity Mismatch Problem was his suggestion that HFL, in fact, 'has no internal modular structure' (Hornstein 2009: 157), unlike what was assumed in GB; the other aspect concerns his proposal that much of the GB-apparatus can be captured by such a non-modular HFL assuming only three basic operations (which he calls Concatenate, Copy, and Label).[19] However, in his entire discussion, the post-syntactic components, especially PF, as well as the operation and role of Spell-Out are barely mentioned. It may well turn out to be the case that Agree, Concatenate, Copy and/or Label form the right kind of 'very basic primitive operations that plausibly underlie linguistic computations for consideration as candidates for possible neural circuits' – but, especially if the role of Copy as such does not stand on such firm footing (see Hornstein 2009: 117–125), what about Copy Modification?

The obvious answer might be that this issue does not concern the Granularity Mismatch Problem (39), at least not on the narrow-syntactic side. But since we assume post-syntactic operations to be part of linguistic computations (at least of the sort Poeppel and Embick had surely in mind), this cannot be the full answer. This issue is also partly discussed by Boeckx (2009, 2010), who actually turns the tables: '[U]ntil neurolinguists try to look for units that match what theoretical linguists hypothesize [note with references omitted – KKG], the conundrum we are in will not go away" (Boeckx 2010: 159).

In the absence of any concrete suggestions for getting a grasp on such questions, one positive outcome of the preceding discussion might be the reduction of the copy theory of movement to a true interface issue in grammar. That is, by reducing the commonly held four-step procedure (cf. (37) above from Nunes 2004), we yield the following, with the main point being that the too restrictive Chain Reduction is replaced by Copy Modification (see below):

(40)   *An interface-approach to the Copy theory of movement*
    (a) Copy
    (b) Merge
    (c) Copy Modification

(40a) and (40b) apply in the narrow syntax, (40c) in the PF-component. Moreover, for (37), the relevant metric would be a global, possibly a static system (unless or until a Nunes-style approach is extended to phases, for example), while for (40), it would be Prolific Domains within a dynamic setting (with possible extensions, such as the suggestions put forth in the context of Bantu A'-dependencies by Cheng (2006) and Schneider-Zioga (2007), for example).

What needs to be done next is to unify the ordered rules from (38) for (40c) with the Elsewhere-relation of Copy Modification formulated by Grohmann and Nevins (2005). The problem is that, while (38a) and (38c) receive a clear structural description, as in (27), this is not the case for (38b). The following is thus an unsatisfactory attempt in that (a) the structural description of (41b) is neither a superset of (41a) nor a subset of (41c) and (b) the structural change is not identical or incompatible with either, both required for establishing the desired ordering relations (as per (26)).

(41) *Copy Modification* (unsatisfactory final version)
    (a) Copy Spell-Out (PF-driven viz. the CDE)
        Structural Description: Given copies C_1 and C_2, where C_1 LCA-precedes C_2, and C_1 and C_2 are in the same Prolific Domain.
        Structural Change: Spellout-as-Modified C_2
    (b) Individual-Copy Modification (constraint-driven)
        Structural Description: Given copies C_1 and C_2, where C_1 LCA-precedes C_2, and either C_1 or C_2 violate an independent constraint of the grammar.
        Structural Change: Individually-Modify C_1 and/or C_2
    (c) Lower-Copy Deletion (PF-driven viz. the LCA)
        Structural Description: Given copies C_1 and C_2, where C_1 LCA-precedes C_2.
        Structural Change: Delete C_2

At this stage, the desired unification might be too much to ask for. Perhaps a catalogue of the sort alluded to is necessary in order to split what I tentatively call Individual-Copy Modification (41b) into several sub-conditions, each complying with (26) – arguably, a very fine-grained approach to what should be a reductionist take on the computation. This said, even (41a) entails too many variables for a clean story: not every language might allow Copy Spell-Out as a rescue operation for anti-local movement (dependencies violating the CDE), and even if they did, such applications are quite restricted and highly language-specific as concerns the domain of applicability and the grammatical formative to be inserted (not to speak of further sub-cases, such as partial reduplication involving pejorative *shm–*).

On a more positive side, what I have tried to do in this contribution is to suggest that something like (40) is superior to alternative conceptions, thereby lending further support to the interface-heavy perspective on linguistic computations assumed here: a theory of syntax that consists of the simplest operations imaginable (recursive Copy plus Merge) with a very strong interface-component (cf. the GB-related part in the above-cited Hornstein-quote).

From a more personal perspective (within the domain-driven anti-locality framework), I would like further research efforts in this area to: (a) come to grips with the notion of 'anti-locality'; and, if so warranted, (b) apply anti-locality analyses to more linguistic phenomena. In other words, for (a), we should ask whether anti-locality is a real phenomenon or a mere epiphenomenon, how we can best define the notion, what range of cases it can be applied to, what the implications are for syntactic theory/modeling, and what the implications are of syntactic anti-locality for the architecture of the grammar. Regarding (b), we would like to know whether there are any outstanding issues among grammatical phenomena and analytical approaches to them which anti-locality can be applied to, and whether there is perhaps a family of phenomena that must be analyzed this way. I have at least tried to address some of these questions (certainly for the first group; for the second group, see Grohmann (2011)), but at the same time wanted to balance things out a little and thus concentrated on more general interface issues for MP. How this can be filtered out to become less fine-grained remains a task to be carried out.

Let me close this chapter with another quote from Broekhuis and Vogel (2007):

Given the fact that OT and MP face this similar challenge, one may actually hope that the two theories may contribute to each other by highlighting ideas which are beyond the scope of research of the alternative approach, and perhaps even converge to a certain degree.

As I said already in the introduction, Broekhuis and Vogel arguably had another conception of filtering devices in mind than I pursued here, and with respect to theirs, Broekhuis (2008) is a fine example of addressing that. In contrast, I hope to have shown that even with the at first glance well understood mechanisms underlying the copy theory of movement (Chomsky 1995; Nunes 2004; Bošković and Nunes 2007; Hornstein 2009), a number of issues arise concerning the after-effects of displacement – issues that I suggest need to be filtered out somehow, and, ideally, receive a unified explanation. Whether useful towards a syntactician's response to the Granularity Mismatch Problem ('filtering' in a sense linguistic structure for possible, less fine-grained neuroscientific correlates), Copy Modification does seem to have a place in interface-driven approaches to the linguistic computation underlying the particular view of the MP-architecture of the grammar defended here.

Acknowledgments

I am indebted first and foremost to the editors of this volume, and the organizers of *DEAL II*, for inviting me to the conference and giving me the opportunity to publish these ideas further. So, a big thank-you to Hans Broekhuis and Ralf Vogel. I also appreciate all the audiences around Europe, the Eastern Mediterranean and North America as well as too large a number of colleagues, students, and friends to list here for their feedback over the past few years, but I would like to single out the anonymous reviewer of this chapter who did a great job asking me to be more precise; I'm not sure I always met up with that expectation. Work reported here has been made partially possible through the UCY research project *The Past, Present, and Future of Minimalist Investigations* (grant number 8037-61013).

Notes

1. I simply call this HFL, as opposed to the finer distinction one may want to make, in light of Hauser *et al.* (2002) and subsequent debates, between the language faculty in the broad versus the narrow sense, a distinction that does not play any further role in this paper.
2. Fortunately, there have been a lot of developments in MP mechanics since Chomsky (1993, 1995), constantly refining the minimalist enterprise. Unfortunately, this also means that subtle details may be expressed this way or that way. For expository reasons, I simplify affairs occasionally, so as not to get too side-tracked. I try to present general architectural and/or theoretical assumptions in a 'generally agreed upon' manner. For many issues not touched on here, see also recent advancements in Phase Theory (Chomsky 2000 *et seq.*).
3. Returning to question (4iv), note that Uriagereka (2008: chap. 1), originating in a 1999 manuscript co-authored by Roger Martin, makes the interesting case for a revival of D-structure (see also e.g. Uriagereka 2002: chaps. 14–15). He argues that many aspects of D-structure are essentially still packaged in MP as hidden assumptions and carefully teases apart the relevant issues: What is a 'level of representation' (as opposed to a 'component')? How can we integrate their role in a minimalist approach? The reasoning laid out in more detail in Uriagereka (2008) is quite likely going to play an important role in the near future, but not in this contribution.

4. We are possibly dealing with at most two levels of representation: Chomsky (2004) denies a separate LF-component altogether; apart from note 2, see e.g. Epstein and Seely (2006) for recent insightful discussion. Uriagereka (1998: 238), for example, addresses the level/component issue (cf. Uriagereka 1999), a subtle distinction which I will subsequently ignore (see also, Haiden 2009; Ott 2009, and the previous note).

5. This is not quite the phase, unfortunately (as criticized in Boeckx and Grohmann (2007) for example), but the complement of a phase head, as per Chomsky (2000), and, as revised in Chomsky (2001), at the time step when the next higher phase head merges to the structure.

6. Some excellent recent dissertations on Phase Theory include Richards (2004), Hiraiwa (2005) and Gallego (2007), to name but a few. For shorter textbook presentations, see for example chapter 10 of Adger (2003), Radford (2004) and Hornstein *et al.* (2005) or Lasnik and Uriagereka with Boeckx (2005: sect. 7.4), Boeckx (2008: sect. 3.2), and Radford (2009: chap. 9). See also the volumes to which the precursors of the present sections 2 and 3 served as introductions (Grohmann 2007a, 2007c, 2009a, 2009b).

7. Note that Nissenbaum (2000) – taking his cue from the single-output models of Brody (1995), Bobaljik (1995), Pesetsky (1998) and Groat and O'Neil (1996) – assumes Spell-Out to apply solely for PF purposes. This single-cycle grammar replicates the effects yielded by the Y-model (cf. Figure 13.1) without losing the dynamic character of the phase-based model.

8. On a par with *Spell-Out* as Transfer to PF, Lasnik and Uriagereka with Boeckx (2005: 240) suggest the term *Interpret* for Transfer at LF (to be revised in section 3.4, though).

9. On the phasal status of DP, see for example Svenonius (2004) and Hiraiwa (2005), a possibility acknowledged in Chomsky (2008). Note that Abels (2003) also makes the case for the phase-relevance of PP (by means of a modern twist on van Riemsdijk 1978). For a discussion of both, see especially Lee-Schoenfeld (2005). As far as I can see, these suggestions are still being tested, awaiting final judgment.

10. As formulated in Chomsky (2001: 2), 'SMT sets an appropriate standard for true explanation; anything that falls short is to that extent descriptive, introducing mechanisms that would not be found in a "more perfect" system satisfying only legibility conditions.' In other words, SMT holds that 'Universal Grammar is "perfectly" designed, that is, it contains nothing more than what follows from our best guesses regarding conceptual, biological, physical necessity' (Boeckx 2006: 4).

11. Among many others, see for example Selkirk (2006) or Kratzer and Selkirk (2007) for relevant discussion within Phase Theory. A very recent and highly stimulating piece of research is Chung's (2007) dissertation on the 'ecology' of PF. Other interesting research is carried out by Tobias Scheer and colleagues (e.g., Newell and Scheer 2007), who also provides a 'little interface library' (http://www.unice.fr/dsl/tobweb/interfacelib.htm).

   Another perspective comes from morphology, especially the framework of Distributed Morphology (Halle and Marantz 1993); see Embick and Noyer (2001) and Embick (2007) for interesting proposals concerning the 'road to PF' (Grohmann 2007b).

12. Though under a possible reading, even Chomsky himself in more recent work could be interpreted to make, at least in principle, room for the possibility of more projections, in particular within the left periphery (e.g., Chomsky 2007: 17; 2008: 143, 151).

13. The large amount of (self-)references provided in this sub-section in particular is meant to make up for the *tour de force* I'm asking the reader to engage in. Lest it be misunderstood, the emphasis of this chapter is not to provide novel (or otherwise well-documented) analyses of specific phenomena; rather, I want to tie in existing analyses with a particular perspective on interfaces (which does indeed have some novel elements).

14. Admittedly, the adjective 'anti-local' in this context (taken from the concept of 'anti-locality') might not be the best choice of terminology. However, if one considers it simply to be homonymous with the possibly more intuitive 'too local', the term might not be far off its intended coverage after all. I would think that the noun for the phenomenon in grammar, 'anti-locality', sounds better than something like 'too(y) locality'. See Grohmann (2011: 259–60: fn.1) for further information and discrimination concerning the usage of the term 'anti-locality' in the present context.

15. See also, among others, Grohmann and Putnam (2007) on prosodic stress assignment in Germanic varieties, Schneider-Zioga (2007) on anti-agreement syntax in Bantu (Kinande), and Lipták and

Vicente (2009) on VP-topicalization in Hungarian (and Spanish). Prolific Domains were employed by Ticio (2003) for empirical observations inside Spanish nominals and Putnam (2006) for Germanic clause structure and scrambling, for example; Mayr and Reitbauer (2004) analyzed emphatic topicalization in German (Bavarian) with the added flavor of Copy Spell-Out, and Cheng (2006) extended the applicability of Copy Spell-Out for Bantu relatives. Other formulations of and approaches to anti-locality include Bošković (1994), Murasugi and Saito (1995), Abels (2003) and Boeckx (2008); see Grohmann (2011) for an overview.

Another issue that cannot be discussed here concerns Copy Spell-Out with head movement, which was excluded from being relevant for anti-locality (Grohmann 2003: 80); for interesting discussion, see e.g. Beys (2006) and Quinn (2009) as well as, in the context of alternative conceptions (see section 4 below for more imminent connections), Nunes (2004), Bošković and Nunes (2007) and Kandybowicz (2007a, 2007b, 2008).

As important precursors or relevant developments in parallel, see e.g. Platzack (2001) on a tripartition of the clausal structures and some formal consequences as well as Groat and O'Neil (1996), Nissenbaum (2000), and Lasnik (2009) on other relevant contributions to the model developed here. Last but not least, of course, without the original work on stress, syntax, and the cycle by Bresnan (1971, 1972), there might not be any modern notion of multiple Spell-Out and fruitful, dynamic approaches to interface syntax to begin with – but that is mere speculation.

16. Note also (should that be a concern) that with respect to inclusiveness, nothing is inserted into the *syntactic* derivation over which inclusiveness arguably ranges (Grohmann 2003: 296 incl. n.7 on 309). In fact, as Chomsky (2004: 107) puts it: 'Optimally, mappings will satisfy the *inclusiveness condition*, introducing no new elements but only rearranging those of the domain' (original emphasis). Not only does the disclaimer here appear, to my knowledge, for the first time (that inclusiveness is satisfied 'optimally' as opposed to, say, 'always'), it also strongly suggests that on the interface/mapping side, it need not apply.

17. Granted, when a language allows Copy Spell-Out, and which grammatical formative it may employ in a given appropriate context, may sound unsatisfactorily *ad hoc*. (20) suggests a 'minimal feature-matching' element, illustrated with a demonstrative resumptive in (22) above or a local reflexive in (23a) below – but here, too, we find variation. Grohmann and Nevins (2005) suggest *shm*-reduplication to fall under Copy Spell-Out (see also section 4) and Grohmann and Panagiotidis (forthcoming) allow a null operator to be spelled out – in the absence of a more precise understanding of 'minimal', possibly less than 'minimal feature-matching' instances. As will become clear towards the end of section 4, a more complete catalogue of well-documented instances of Copy Spell-Out across languages is needed, and so is a refinement of the 'gray zone' of Copy Modification other than Lower-Copy Deletion.

18. Chain Reduction (37d) is defined as: 'Delete the minimal number of constituents of a nontrivial chain CH that suffices for CH to be mapped into a linear order in accordance with the LCA' (Nunes 2004: 27). Since I do not assume 'chains' as real (i.e. relevant) objects in syntactic derivations, I will not discuss finer aspects of this or Form Chain (37c) any further. For valuable discussion on the undesirable status of 'chains', see for example Hornstein (2001, 2009). What is relevant is that Lower-Copy Deletion – the current version of Chain Reduction and the Delete-part of Chomsky's (1993, 1995) formulation of the copy theory movement (Copy, Move, Delete) – can be motivated on grounds of linearization, such as Kayne's (1994) LCA or some version thereof.

19. Hornstein (2009: 157, fn. 7) actually alludes to the possibility of a fourth operation (Agree) and the elimination of one (Copy), but that is of little concern here.

References

Abels, K. (2003) *Successive Cyclicity, Anti-Locality, and Adposition Stranding*. Doctoral dissertation, University of Connecticut, Storrs, CT.

Abney, S. P. (1987) *The English Noun Phrase in Its Sentential Aspect*. Doctoral dissertation, Massachusetts Institute of Technology, Cambridge, MA.

Ackema, P. and Neeleman, A. (2004) *Beyond Morphology*. Oxford: Oxford University Press.

Adger, D. (2003) *Core Syntax: A Minimalist Approach*. Oxford: Oxford University Press.

Adger, D. (2007) Stress and phasal syntax. *Linguistic Analysis* 33 (3–4): 238–66.

Archangeli, D. (1997) Optimality Theory: An introduction to linguistics in the 1990s. In D. Archangeli and T. D. Langendoen (eds) *Optimality Theory: An Overview*, 1–32. Oxford: Blackwell.

Belletti, A. (1990) *Generalized Verb Movement*. Turin: Rosenberg & Sellier.

Bernstein, J. B. (2001) The DP Hypothesis: identifying clausal properties in the nominal domain. In M. R. Baltin and C. Collins (eds) *The Handbook of Contemporary Syntactic Theory*, 536–61. Malden, MA: Blackwell.

Beys, M. (2006) *The Status of Linkers in Bantu Languages: A Reply to Baker & Collins (2006)*. Manuscript, University of Cyprus, Nicosia.

Bobaljik, J. D. (1995) *Morphosyntax: The Syntax of Verbal Inflection*. Doctoral dissertation, Massachusetts Institute of Technology, Cambridge.

Bobaljik, J. D. (2002) A-chains at the PF-interface: Copies and 'covert' movement. *Natural Language and Linguistic Theory* 20 (2): 197–267.

Bobaljik, J. D. and Thráinsson, H. (1998) Two heads aren't always better than one. *Syntax* 1 (1): 37–71.

Boeckx, C. (2003) *Islands and Chains*. Amsterdam: John Benjamins.

Boeckx, C. (2006) *Linguistic Minimalism: Origins, Concepts, Methods, and Aims*. New York: Oxford University Press.

Boeckx, C. (2008) *Understanding Minimalist Syntax: Lessons from Locality in Long-Distance Dependencies*. Malden, MA: Blackwell.

Boeckx, C. (2009) What happens when syntax faces the Sensori-Motor Systems, Phylogenetically and Ontogenetically? Invited paper presented at the workshop on *Formal Approaches to the Phonology–Morphology–Syntax Interfaces*, Universitat Autònoma de Barcelona (16 December 2009).

Boeckx, C. (2010) *Language in Cognition: Uncovering Mental Structures and the Rules Behind Them*. Malden, MA: Wiley-Blackwell.

Boeckx, C. and Grohmann, K. K. (2007) Putting phases into perspective. *Syntax* 10 (2): 204–22.

Bošković, Ž. (1994) D-Structure, θ-Theory, and movement into θ-Positions. *Linguistic Analysis* 24: 247–86.

Bošković, Ž. (2002) On multiple *Wh*-Fronting. *Linguistic Inquiry* 33: 351–83.

Bošković, Ž. and Nunes, J. (2007) The Copy Theory of movement: A view from PF. In N. Corver and J. Nunes (eds) *The Copy Theory of Movement*, 13–74. Amsterdam: John Benjamins.

Bresnan, J. (1971) Sentence stress and syntactic transformations. *Language* 47 (2): 257–81.

Bresnan, J. (1972) Stress and syntax: A reply. *Language* 48 (2): 326–42.

Brody, M. (1995) *Lexico-Logical Form: A Radically Minimalist Theory*. Cambridge, MA: MIT Press.

Broekhuis, H. (2008) *Derivations and Evaluations: Object Shift in the Germanic Languages*. Berlin: Mouton de Gruyter.

Broekhuis, H. and Vogel, R. (2007) Interface theories: The filtering of the output of the generator. *DEAL II: Call for Papers*. [http://let.uvt.nl/deal08/call.html]

Broekhuis, H. and Vogel, R. (2010) Crash-Proof Syntax and Filters. In M. T. Putnam (ed.) *Exploring Crash-Proof Grammars*, 245–67. Amsterdam: John Benjamins.

Cheng, L.-S. L. (2006) Decomposing Bantu relatives. *NELS 36*: 197–215.

Chomsky, N. (1965) *Aspects of the Theory of Syntax*. Cambridge, MA: MIT Press.

Chomsky, N. (1981) *Lectures on Government and Binding: The Pisa Lectures*. Dordrecht: Foris.

Chomsky, N. (1986) *Barriers*. Cambridge, MA: MIT Press.

Chomsky, N. (1991) Some notes on economy of derivation and representation. In R. Freidin (ed.) *Principles and Parameters in Generative Grammar*, 417–54. Cambridge, MA: MIT Press. [Reprinted in Chomsky (1995), 129–166.]

Chomsky, N. (1993) A minimalist program for linguistic theory. In K. Hale and S. J. Keyser (eds) *The View from Building 20: Essays in Honor of Sylvain Bromberger*, 1–52. Cambridge, MA: MIT Press.

Chomsky, N. (1995) *The Minimalist Program*. Cambridge, MA: MIT Press.

Chomsky, N. (1999) Derivation by phase. *MIT Occasional Papers in Linguistics* 18. [Revised version published as Chomsky (2001).]

Chomsky, N. (2000) Minimalist inquiries: The framework. In R. Martin, D. Michaels and J. Uriagereka (eds) *Step by Step: Essays on Minimalist Syntax in Honor of Howard Lasnik,* 89–155. Cambridge, MA: MIT Press.

Chomsky, Noam. 2001. Derivation by phase. In M. Kenstowicz (ed.) *Ken Hale. A Life in Language,* 1–52. Cambridge, MA: MIT Press.

Chomsky, N. (2004) Beyond explanatory adequacy. In A. Belletti (ed.) *Structures and Beyond: The Cartography of Syntactic Structures* vol. 3, 104–31. Oxford: Oxford University Press.

Chomsky, N. (2005) Three factors in language design. *Linguistic Inquiry* 36 (1): 1–22.

Chomsky, N. (2007) Approaching UG from below. In U. Sauerland and H. Gärtner (eds) *Interfaces + Recursion = Language?,* 1–29. Berlin: Mouton de Gruyter.

Chomsky, N. (2008) On phases. In R. Freidin, C. P. Otero and M. Zubizarreta (eds) *Foundational Issues in Linguistic Theory: Essays in Honor of Jean-Roger Vergnaud,* 133–66. Cambridge, MA: MIT Press.

Chung, I. (2007) *Ecology at PF: A Study of Korean Phonology and Morphology in a Derivational Approach.* Doctoral dissertation, University of Connecticut, Storrs, CT.

Cinque, G. (1999) *Adverbs and Functional Heads: A Cross-linguistic Perspective.* New York: Oxford University Press.

Embick, D. (2007) Linearization and local dislocations: Derivational mechanics and interactions. *Linguistic Analysis* 33: 303–36.

Embick, D. and Noyer, R. (2001) Movement operations after Syntax. *Linguistic Inquiry* 32 (4): 555–595.

Embick, D. and Poeppel, D. (2006) Mapping syntax using imaging: Prospects and problems for the study of neurolinguistic computation. In K. Brown (ed.) *Encyclopedia of Language and Linguistics,* vol. 7, 2nd edn, 484–6. Oxford: Elsevier.

Epstein, S. D., Groat, E. M., Kawashima R. and Kitahara, H. (1998) *A Derivational Approach to Syntactic Relations.* New York: Oxford University Press.

Epstein, S. D. and Seely, T. D. (2002) Rule applications as cycles in a level-free syntax. In S. D. Epstein and T. D. Seely (eds) *Derivation and Explanation in the Minimalist Program,* 65–89. Malden, MA: Blackwell.

Epstein, S. D. and Seely, T. D. (2006) *Derivations in Minimalism.* Cambridge: Cambridge University Press.

Ernst, T. (2002) *The Syntax of Adjuncts.* Cambridge: Cambridge University Press.

Franks, S. (1998) Clitics in Slavic. Paper presented at the *Comparative Slavic Morphosyntax Workshop,* McCormick's Creek State Park, Spenser, Ind. (5–7 June 1998).

Fujii, T. (2007) Cyclic chain reduction. In N. Corver and J. Nunes (eds) *The Copy Theory of Movement,* 291–326. Amsterdam: John Benjamins.

Gallego, Á. J. (2007) *Phase Theory and Parametric Variation.* Doctoral dissertation, Universitat Autònoma de Barcelona.

Grimshaw, J. (1991) Extended projections. Manuscript, Brandeis University, Boston, Massachusetts. [Published in Grimshaw, J. (2003) *Words and Structure,* 1–73. Stanford, CA: CSLI Publications.]

Groat, E. M. and O'Neil, J. (1996) Spell-Out at the LF interface. In W. Abraham, S. D. Epstein, H. Thráinsson and C. J. Zwart (eds) *Minimal Ideas,* 189–98. Amsterdam: John Benjamins.

Grohmann, K. K. (2000) *Prolific Peripheries: A Radical View from the Left.* Doctoral dissertation, University of Maryland, College Park, MD.

Grohmann, K. K. (2001) On predication, derivation and anti-locality. *ZAS Papers in Linguistics* 26: 87–112.

Grohmann, K. K. (2003) *Prolific Domains: On the Anti-Locality of Movement Dependencies.* Amsterdam: John Benjamins.

Grohmann, K. K. (2007a) Deriving dynamic interfaces. *Linguistic Analysis* 33 (1–2): 3–19.

Grohmann, K. K. (2007b) Transfer vs. Spell-Out and the road to PF. *Linguistic Analysis* 33 (1–2): 176–94. [Revised and forthcoming in A. S. Özsoy and A. Gürel (eds) *Issues in Mediterranean Syntax.* Leiden: Brill.]

Grohmann, K.K. (2007c) Spelling out dynamic interfaces. *Linguistic Analysis* 33 (3–4): 197–208.

Grohmann, K. K. (2009a) Phases and interfaces. In K. K. Grohmann (ed.) *InterPhases: Phase-Theoretic Investigations of Linguistic Interfaces,* 1–22. Oxford: Oxford University Press.

Grohmann, K. K. (2009b) Exploring interfaces. In K. K. Grohmann (ed.) *Explorations of Phase Theory: Interpretation at the Interfaces,* 1–21. Berlin: Mouton de Gruyter.

Grohmann, K. K. (2009c) Studies on interface conditions: anti-locality in grammar. Invited paper presented at the workshop on *Formal Approaches to the Phonology–Morphology–Syntax Interfaces*, Universitat Autònoma de Barcelona (16 December 2009).

Grohmann, K. K. (2011) Anti-locality: too-close relations in grammar. In C. Boeckx (ed.), *The Oxford Handbook of Linguistic Minimalism*, 259–89. Oxford: Oxford University Press.

Grohmann, K. K. and Boeckx, C. (2004) Left dislocation in Germanic. In W. Abraham (ed.) *Focus on Germanic Typology*, 131–44. Berlin: Akademie-Verlag.

Grohmann, K. K. and Haegeman, L. (2003) Resuming reflexives. *Nordlyd* 31 (1): 46–62.

Grohmann, K. K. and Ira Nevins, A. (2005) On the expression of pejorative mood. In P. Pica with J. Rooryck and J. van Craenenbroeck (eds) *Linguistic Variation Yearbook 4 (2004)*, 143–79. Amsterdam: John Benjamins.

Grohmann, K. K. and Panagiotidis, E. P. (forthcoming) Demonstrative doubling in modern Greek. In A. S. Özsoy and A. Gürel (eds) *Issues in Mediterranean Syntax*. Leiden: Brill.

Grohmann, K. K. and Putnam, M. T. (2004) Prosodic stress assignment in dynamic computations. Paper presented at the *Michigan Linguistics Society*, University of Michigan, Flint, MI. (16 October 2004).

Grohmann, K. K. and Putnam, M. T. (2007) Dynamic stress assignment. *Linguistic Analysis* 33: 326–63.

Haiden, M. (2009) On bare prosodic structure and the Spell-Out of features. In K. K. Grohmann (ed.) *Explorations of Phase Theory: Interpretation at the Interfaces*, 67–94. Berlin: Mouton de Gruyter.

Halle, M. and Marantz, A. (1993) Distributed morphology and the pieces of inflection. In K. Hale and S. J. Keyser (eds) *The View from Building 20: Essays in Honor of Sylvain Bromberger*, 111–76. Cambridge, MA: MIT Press.

Hauser, M. D., Chomsky, N. and Fitch W. T. (2002) The faculty of language: What is it, who has it, and how did it evolve? *Science* 298 (5598): 1569–79.

Hiraiwa, K. (2005) *Dimensions of Symmetry in Syntax: Agreement and Clausal Architecture*. Doctoral dissertation, Massachusetts Institute of Technology, Cambridge, MA.

Hornstein, N. (2001) *Move! A Minimalist Theory of Construal*. Oxford: Blackwell.

Hornstein, N. (2009) *A Theory of Syntax*. Cambridge: Cambridge University Press.

Hornstein, N., Nunes, J. and Grohmann, K. K. (2005) *Understanding Minimalism*. Cambridge: Cambridge University Press.

Idsardi, W. J. (1992) *The Computation of Prosody*. Doctoral dissertation, Massachusetts Institute of Technology, Cambridge, MA.

Kandybowicz, J. (2007a) Fusion and PF architecture. *PLC 30 – University of Pennsylvania Working Papers in Linguistics* 13 (1): 85–98.

Kandybowicz, J. (2007b) On fusion and multiple copy Spell-Out: The case of verbal repetition. In N. Corver and J. Nunes (eds) *The Copy Theory of Movement*, 119–150. Amsterdam: John Benjamins.

Kandybowicz, J. (2008) *The Grammar of Repetition*. Amsterdam: John Benjamins.

Kayne, R. S. (1994) *The Antisymmetry of Syntax*. Cambridge, MA: MIT Press.

Kayne, R. S.(2002) Pronouns and their antecedents. In S. D. Epstein and T. D. Seely (eds) *Derivation and Explanation in the Minimalist Program*, 133–66. Malden, MA: Blackwell.

Kiparsky, P. (1973) 'Elsewhere' in phonology. In S. R. Anderson and P. Kiparsky (eds) *A Festschrift for Morris Halle*, 93–106. New York: Holt, Rinehart and Winston.

Kratzer, A. and Selkirk, E. (2007) Phase theory and prosodic Spellout: The case of verbs. *The Linguistic Review* 24 (8): 93–135.

Larson, R. K. (1988) On the double object construction. *Linguistic Inquiry* 19 (3): 335–91.

Lasnik, H. (2009) Island Repair, Non-Repair, and the organization of the grammar. In K. K. Grohmann (ed.) *InterPhases: Phase-Theoretic Investigations of Linguistic Interfaces*, 339–53. Oxford: Oxford University Press.

Lasnik, H. and Uriagereka, J. with Boeckx, C. (2005) *A Course in Minimalist Syntax: Foundations and Prospects*. Malden, MA: Blackwell.

Lee-Schoenfeld, V. (2005) *Beyond Coherence: The Syntax of Opacity in German*. Doctoral dissertation, University of California, Santa Cruz, CA.

Lees, R. and Klima, E. (1963) Rules for English pronominalization. *Language* 39 (1): 17–28.

Lidz, J. and Idsardi, W. J. (1998) Chains and phono-logical form. *PLC 22 – University of Pennsylvania Working Papers in Linguistics* 5 (1): 109–25.

Lipták, A. and Vicente, L. (2009) Pronominal doubling under predicate topicalization. *Lingua* 119 (4): 650–86.

Lutz, U., Müller, G. and von Stechow, A. (eds) (2000) W*h-Scope Marking* Amsterdam: John Benjamins.

Marušič, F. L. (2005) *On Non-Simultaneous Phases*. Doctoral dissertation, Stony Brook University, NY.

Marušič, F. L. (2009) Non-simultaneous Spell-Out in the clausal and nominal domain. In K. K. Grohmann (ed.) *InterPhases: Phase-Theoretic Investigations of Linguistic Interfaces,* 151–81. Oxford: Oxford University Press.

Mayr, C. and Reitbauer, M. (2004) Emphatische Topikalisierung ist Linksdislokation. Ms., University of Vienna.

McDaniel, D. (1986) *Conditions on* Wh-*Chains*. Doctoral dissertation, City University of New York.

Moro, A. (2000) *Dynamic Antisymmetry*. Cambridge, MA: MIT Press.

Munakata, T. (2009) The division of C-I and the nature of the input, multiple transfer, and phases. In K. K. Grohmann (ed.) *InterPhases: Phase-Theoretic Investigations of Linguistic Interfaces,* 48–81. Oxford: Oxford University Press.

Murasugi, K.and Saito, M. (1995) Adjunction and Cyclicity. *WCCFL* 14: 302–17.

Neeleman, A. and van de Koot, H. (2006) Syntactic haplology. In M. Everaert and H. van Riemsdijk with R. Goedemans and B. Hollebrandse (eds) *The Blackwell Companion to Syntax,* vol. IV, 685–710. Oxford: Blackwell.

Nevins, A. I. (2004) *Condition on (Dis)harmony*. Doctoral dissertation, Massachusetts Institute of Technology, Cambridge, MA.

Newell, H. and Scheer, T. (2007) Procedural First. Paper presented at the *38th Poznań Linguistic Meeting (PLM 2007),* Gniezno (13–16 September 2007).

Nissenbaum, J. W. (2000) *Investigation of Covert Phrase Movement.* Doctoral dissertation, Massachusetts Institute of Technology, Cambridge, MA.

Nunes, J. (1995) *The Copy Theory of Movement and Linearization of Chains in the Minimalist Program.* Doctoral dissertation, University of Maryland, College Park, MD.

Nunes, J. (2004) *Linearization of Chains and Sideward Movement*. Cambridge, MA: MIT Press.

Ott, D. (2009) The conceptual necessity of phases: Some remarks on the Minimalist Enterprise. In K. K. Grohmann (ed.) *Explorations of Phase Theory: Interpretation at the Interfaces,* 253–275. Berlin: Mouton de Gruyter.

Pesetsky, D. (1998) Some optimality principles of sentence pronunciation. In P. Barbosa, D. Fox, P. Hagstrom, M. McGinnis and D. Pesetsky (eds) *Is the Best Good Enough? Optimality and Competition in Syntax,* 337–83. Cambridge, MA: MIT Press.

Pesetsky, D. (2000) *Phrasal Movement and Its Kin*. Cambridge, MA: MIT Press.

Piattelli-Palmarini, M. and Uriagereka, J. (2004) The immune syntax: The evolution of the Language Virus. In L. Jenkins (ed.) *Variation and Universals in Biolinguistics,* 342–377. Oxford: Elsevier.

Platzack, C. (2001) Multiple Interfaces. In U Nikanne and E. van der Zee (eds) *Cognitive Interfaces: Constraints on Linking Cognitive Information,* 21–53. Oxford: Oxford University Press.

Poeppel, D. and Embick, D. (2005) Defining the relation between linguistics and neuroscience. In A. Cutler (ed.) *Twenty-First Century Psycholinguistics: Four Cornerstones,* 103–118. Mahwah, NJ: Lawrence Erlbaum Associates.

Pollock, J. (1989) Verb movement, universal grammar, and the structure of IP. *Linguistic Inquiry* 20 (3): 365–424.

Postal, P. M. (1974) *On Raising: One Rule of English Grammar and Its Theoretical Implications.* Cambridge, MA: MIT Press.

Potsdam, E. and Runner, J. T. (2001) Richard returns: Copy raising and its implications. *CLS* 37: 453–68.

Putnam, M. T. (2006) *Scrambling in West Germanic as XP-Adjunction: A Critical Analysis of Prolific Domains.* Doctoral dissertation, University of Kansas, Lawrence, KS.

Quinn, H. (2009) Downward reanalysis and the rise of stative HAVE *got*. In P. Crisma and G. Longobardi (eds) *Historical Syntax and Linguistic Theory,* 212–30. Oxford: Oxford University Press.

Radford, A. (2004) *Minimalist Syntax: Exploring the Structure of English*. Cambridge: Cambridge University Press.

Radford, A. (2009) *Analysing English Sentences*. Cambridge: Cambridge University Press.

Ramchand, G. and Reiss, C. (eds) (2007) *The Oxford Handbook of Linguistic Interfaces*. Oxford: Oxford University Press.

Richards, M. (2004) *Object Shift and Scrambling in North and West Germanic: A Case Study in Symmetrical Syntax*. Doctoral dissertation, University of Cambridge.

Richards, N. (2006) A distinctness condition on linearization. Manuscript, Massachusetts Institute of Technology, Cambridge, MA. [Published as chap. 2 'Distinctness' in Norvin Richards (2010) *Uttering Trees*, 3–142. Cambridge, MA: MIT Press; shorter version appeared in *WCCFL* 20: 470–83.]

van Riemsdijk, H. (1978) *A Case Study in Syntactic Markedness: The Binding Nature of Prepositional Phrases*. Lisse: Peter de Ridder.

van Riemsdijk, H. (2008) Identity avoidance. In R.Freidin, Ca. P. Otero and M. L. Zubizarreta (eds) *Foundational Issues in Linguistic Theory: Essays in Honor of Jean-Roger Vergnaud*, 227–250. Cambridge, MA: MIT Press.

van Riemsdijk, H. and Williams, E. (1986) *Introduction to the Theory of Grammar*. Cambridge, MA: MIT Press.

Rizzi, L. (1997) The fine structure of the left periphery. In L. Haegeman (ed.) *Elements of Grammar: Handbook in Generative Syntax*, 28–337. Dordrecht: Kluwer.

Rogers, A. (1974) A transderivational constraint on Richard?. *CLS* 10: 551–8.

Sabel, J. (2005) String-vacuous scrambling and the effect on output condition. In J. Sabel and M. Saito (eds) *The Free Word Order Phenomenon: Its Syntactic Sources and Diversity*, 281–333. Berlin: Mouton de Gruyter.

Saleemi, A. (2009) On the interface(s) between syntax and meaning. In K. K. Grohmann (ed.) *Explorations of Phase Theory: Interpretation at the Interfaces*, 181–210. Berlin: Mouton de Gruyter.

Scheer, T. (forthcoming) *Interface: How Morpho-Syntax Talks to Phonology. A Survey of Extra-Phonological Information in Phonology since Trubetzkoy's Grenzsignale – A Lateral Theory of Phonology*, vol. 2. Berlin: Mouton de Gruyter.

Schneider-Zioga, P. (2007) Anti-agreement, anti-locality, and minimality: The syntax of dislocated subjects. *Natural Language and Linguistic Theory* 25 (2): 403–46.

Selkirk, E. (2006) Strong minimalist Spellout of prosodic phrases. Paper presented at the *Tokyo Circle of Phonologists*, Hotel KKR Atami (9 March 2006) and the *29th GLOW (Generative Linguistics of the Old World) Colloquium 2006: Prosodic Phrasing Workshop*, Universitat Autònoma de Barcelona (5 April 2006).

Svenonius, P. (2004) On the edge. In D. Adger, C. de Cat and G. Tsoulas (eds) *Peripheries: Syntactic Edges and Their Effects*, 259–87. Dordrecht: Kluwer.

Ticio, E. (2003) *On the Structure of DPs*. Doctoral dissertation, University of Connecticut, Storrs, CT.

Uriagereka, J. (1998) *Rhyme and Reason: an Introduction to Minimalist Syntax*. Cambridge, MA: MIT Press.

Uriagereka, J. (1999) Multiple Spell-Out. In S. D. Epstein and N.Hornstein (eds) *Working Minimalism*, 251–82. Cambridge, MA: MIT Press.

Uriagereka, J. (2000) Comments on 'Derivation by Phase'. Manuscript, University of Maryland, College Park.

Uriagereka, J. (2002) *Derivations: Exploring the Dynamics of Syntax*. London: Routledge.

Uriagereka, J. (2008) *Syntactic Anchors: On Semantic Structuring*. Cambridge: Cambridge University Press.

Uriagereka, J. (2009) Spell-Out Extensions. Manuscript, University of Maryland, College Park, MD.

Vat, J. (1981) Left dislocation, connectedness and reconstruction. *Groninger Arbeiten zur germanistischen Linguistik* 20: 80–103. [Reprinted in Elena Anagnostopoulou, Henk van Riemsdijk & Frans Zwarts (eds) (1997) *Materials on Left Dislocation* 67--92. Amsterdam: John Benjamins.]

Zeijlstra, H. (2009) Dislocation effects, uninterpretable features, functional heads, and parametric variation: consequences of conflicting interface conditions. In K. K. Grohmann (ed) *InterPhases: Phase-Theoretic Investigations of Linguistic Interfaces*, 82–113. Oxford: Oxford University Press.

Zubizarreta, M. L. (1998) *Prosody, Focus and Word Order*. Cambridge, MA: MIT Press.

Index

CPSIA information can be obtained at www.ICGtesting.com
Printed in the USA
BVOW021002150113

310472BV00002B/6/P